CHILD WELFARE RESEARCH

CHILD WELFARE RESEARCH

Advances for Practice and Policy

EDITED BY
DUNCAN LINDSEY
ARON SHLONSKY

2008

OXFORD
UNIVERSITY PRESS

Oxford University Press, Inc., publishes works that further
Oxford University's objective of excellence
in research, scholarship, and education.

Oxford   New York
Auckland   Cape Town   Dar es Salaam   Hong Kong   Karachi
Kuala Lumpur   Madrid   Melbourne   Mexico City   Nairobi
New Delhi   Shanghai   Taipei   Toronto

With offices in
Argentina   Austria   Brazil   Chile   Czech Republic   France   Greece
Guatemala   Hungary   Italy   Japan   Poland   Portugal   Singapore
South Korea   Switzerland   Thailand   Turkey   Ukraine   Vietnam

Copyright © 2008 by Oxford University Press, Inc.

Published by Oxford University Press, Inc.
198 Madison Avenue, New York, New York 10016

www.oup.com

Oxford is a registered trademark of Oxford University Press

Library of Congress Cataloging-in-Publication Data
Child welfare research : advances for practice and policy/
edited by Duncan Lindsey and Aron Shlonsky. — 1st ed.
p. cm.
Includes bibliographical references and index.
ISBN 978-0-19-530496-1
1. Child welfare — Research — United States.
2. Children — Institutional care — United States.
3. Children — Institutional care — Research.
I. Lindsey, Duncan. II. Shlonsky, Aron.
HV741.C53565 2008
362.7 — dc22   2007022492

1 3 5 7 9 8 6 4 2

Printed in the United States of America
on acid-free paper

To Larry Shlonsky (1923–2006), a scientist and skeptic who always rooted for the underdog

Acknowledgments

We would like to acknowledge all of the child welfare scholars who have gone before us. This book has been built upon a foundation laid by such innovative scholars and researchers as Jane Addams, Mary Richmond, Charles Loring Brace, Julia Lathrope, Grace Abbott, Edith Abbott, Alfred Kahn, Alfred Kadushin, Henry Maas and Richard Engler, Helen Jeter, C. Henry Kempe, Douglas Besharov, Alvin Schorr, David Fanshel and Eugene Shinn, Shirley Jenkins and Elaine Norman, David Gil, Ann Shyne, Anthony Maluccio, Eli Newberger, Jeanne Giovannoni, Richard Barth, Peter Pecora, Tina Rzepnicki, Richard Gelles, Lela Costin, Kermit Wiltse, Ted Stein, Rosemary Sarri, Thomas McDonald, John Schuerman, Nigel Parton, Rosina Becerra, Alfreda Iglehart, Jill Duerr Berrick, Sara McLanahan, Greg Duncan, Neil Gilbert, Robert Goerge, Fred Wulczyn, Michael Sherraden, Brian Wharf, Susan Wells, Martin Wolins, Art Emlen, and numerous others in addition to many of the contributors to this volume. Without the groundbreaking work of these scholars, the field would still be in its infancy.

We would also like to thank all of the contributing authors for their commitment to improving the lives of children. Truly successful academics must have a passion for their work to sustain them through the long hours needed to produce such strong papers. They also graciously and patiently endured our sometimes lengthy editorial process, for which we remain eternally grateful. Putting together such a wide range of topics in a coherent fashion, even within the same substantive area of inquiry, has been rewarding and challenging. We would also like to thank the very people who will use this book: child welfare workers, supervisors, and administrators (current and future), who have an impossible job but remain committed and open to the possibility that research can help to guide the way.

This volume would not have been possible without the help of several key people. First, we would like to thank our research assistant, Alan McLuckie, for his outstanding conceptual, editorial, and structural contributions. He knows this volume as well as the editors do and has certainly given more than he has gained. We would also like to thank Oxford University Press for the opportunity to pull this text together. We are grateful for all the help provided by Mallory Jenson at OUP, including her tolerance, flexibility, and careful review of the material. We are particularly grateful to Maura Roessner, who has led the development of this volume from the outset and provided outstanding editorial guidance. In the current publishing climate, with electronic media (including peer-reviewed journals) vying with book publishers for the same limited readership, Oxford University Press has managed to maintain its high standards and continues to lead the world in academic publications.

Finally, we would like to acknowledge the many children who, throughout the last half-century, have spent time growing up in the modern child welfare system. While your personal stories and struggles are not captured here, they are not forgotten. They are the substance of child welfare. We hope to contribute, in some small way, to making everyone's childhood a time of wonder, security, and hope. To that end, let us move toward eliminating child poverty, which remains the root cause of child maltreatment.

Contents

CHILD WELFARE
RESEARCH

Child Welfare Research:
An Introduction

Duncan Lindsey

Aron Shlonsky

Alan McLuckie

The modern child welfare system represents our collective effort on behalf of needy and dependent children. In the early history of the United States, child welfare took the form of orphanages and almshouses that served poor and orphaned children. Over the years, the child welfare system has changed and evolved into a complex system designed to care for maltreated children in family-like settings. Research in child welfare, for better or worse, has both guided and been driven by this monumental shift. In 1964, Wolins and Piliavin wrote the first major review of research in the child welfare field *Institution or Foster Care: A Century of Debate*. Their extensive review of the research up to that time indicated that, for the previous century, the major focus had been on what to do with orphaned and abandoned children. Yet, by the middle of the 20th century, child welfare was primarily concerned with the development and expansion of the modern foster care system. As such, Wolins and Piliavin lamented the dearth of empirical research in child welfare with which to guide practice and policy, particularly in the area of foster care.

The emergence of empirical knowledge in the child welfare field began shortly after World War II, but the accumulation of evidence began slowly. In 1970, Alfred Kadushin wrote in the introduction of what was the first child welfare research book, "Many articles in the field make general statements of dubious validity, use words and terms imprecisely, and enumerate conclusions categorically. Many undergraduate and graduate social work students are more scholarly than is the literature in the field, and they are impatient with and irreverent toward it" (p. ii). We have come a long way in the child welfare field from this solemn assessment. Although there is still much we do not know, the quantity of research in the field has substantially advanced, as has its quality and rigor. Research in the child welfare field is now viewed by most as central to improving services and ensuring quality.

The last half-century has also seen the scope of child welfare and its composition of services fundamentally shift from assisting needy and disadvantaged families to essentially providing a child protection system (Lindsey, 1994, 2004). While there is evidence in the 21st century of a tapering of the number of children in foster care in the United States,[1] the number of children in care has rapidly and consistently increased since the mid-1980s (see the chapters by Testa and by Trocmé in this text). Between the United States (U.S. Department of Health and Human Services, 2006a) and Canada (Trocmé et al., 2005), there were an estimated 3 million child abuse investigations in 2003, and as of 2006, there were over 0.5 million children in foster care in the United States (U.S. Department of Health and Human Services, 2006b).

As the studies in this text illustrate, research has often been ahead of the field and has pointed the way to the development of new services and to new ways of conceptualizing child welfare. In this book, we embrace a broad definition of the child welfare field. The traditional definition of child welfare developed by Kadushin almost five decades ago reflected the convergence of understanding in the field during the beginning of the 20th century. This viewpoint represented the normative aspirations of child welfare professionals for most of the 20th century. Over the years, the definition achieved the character of a paradigm. This traditional view has shaped our understanding of the child welfare field and the nature of the problems to be solved. But it is a view which is no longer adequate. It is too limiting in its vision. Further, the nature of the problems confronted by child welfare agencies has changed with such trends as increased divorces and corresponding changes in family situations (see Lindsey, 1994, pp. 91–118). Consequently, the paradigm which guides our understanding of child welfare has broadened in response to the shifting ground. Kadushin's traditional definition of a system that limits itself to the neediest children no longer captures the essence of contemporary child welfare. Thus a new understanding of the limits and possibilities of child welfare which reflects the enriched knowledge base in the field and an awareness of the social conditions within which child welfare services operate has emerged.

When considering the scope of child welfare research and its influence over the last 50 years, several seminal studies come to mind that have shaped child welfare policy and knowledge development within the field. First, C. Henry Kempe and colleagues' (1962) groundbreaking investigation of young children who were severely injured by their caregivers is credited with helping to bring about the development of

mandatory reporting laws, which were codified in the Child Abuse Prevention and Treatment Act of 1974 (Pecora et al., 2000), and has been seen by some as prompting a shift from broader child welfare concerns to the protection of children from abuse (Lindsey, 1994, 2004, in press; Pelton, 1989).

Shortly before "battered child syndrome" was famously identified by Kempe et al. (1962), Henry Maas and Richard Engler (1959) released their book *Children in Need of Parents*. This representative, large-scale investigation of the child welfare system amounted to an exposé, pointing to the fact that many children "temporarily" placed in care spent years "drifting" in the foster care system, without familial contact, and often experiencing multiple placements. Another academic exposé came some 20 years later when Fanshel and Shinn (1978) released their study of New York City's foster youth. The importance of this study was not only that it confirmed many of Maas and Engler's (1959) findings with respect to parental contact and placement moves, but it also introduced the use of a more rigorous longitudinal design, a method that would later become the standard in child welfare research.

These studies, and others, influenced the development and passage of the landmark Adoption Assistance and Child Welfare Act of 1980. Responding to the identified need of children to be raised by permanent caregivers rather than in a series of temporary homes, this act codified permanency planning into law and specifically linked federal funding to the provision of placement prevention programs and adoption services (Pecora et al., 2000). In addition, it required child welfare agencies to begin monitoring the characteristics, whereabouts, and service history of children in foster care, making possible (with the later funding of statewide automated child welfare information systems) the subsequent large-scale collection of child welfare data that would drive research into the next millennium.

As individual states designed and implemented management information systems in order to meet federal standards, this information was accessed by a handful of innovative scholars who revolutionized the field. Using such administrative data to describe broad trends in child welfare, these scholars and the policy makers with whom they worked were able to use evidence to shape policy and system response. In particular, Wulczyn and Goerge (1992) began using state administrative data in New York and Illinois to model foster care caseload dynamics and introduced the use of event history analysis to correctly model time-sensitive data. These advances were quickly followed with work by Mark Courtney, Richard P. Barth, Jill Duerr Berrick, and Barbara Needell in California (see, for example, Courtney, 1994; Courtney and Needell, 1997; Berrick, Needell, Barth, & Jonson-Reid, 1998) and with the establishment of the multistate data archive at the University of Chicago's Chapin Hall. Advances in the use of administrative data have informed us about the unique trajectory of infants in the foster care system (Goerge & Wulczyn, 1998; Berrick et al., 1998) and the existence of, and potential reasons for, racial disproportionality in foster care (Courtney, Barth, Berrick, & Brooks, 1996; Ards, Meyers, Malkis, & Zhou, 2003; Needell, Brookhart, & Lee, 2003) and have facilitated the development of reliable and valid risk assessment instruments (Johnson, 2004), to name just a few.

As well, the Adoption and Foster Care Analysis and Reporting System (AFCARS) and the National Child Abuse and Neglect Data System (NCANDS) rely heavily on state administrative data to provide detailed estimates of the characteristics and number of children adopted or in foster care. Advances to come in this area include performance monitoring and integration of administrative data with detail-rich survey data.

Whereas administrative data are limited to providing fairly broad assessments of trends, experimental and detailed survey designs can provide national incidence estimates, more nuanced information about the effectiveness of interventions, and detailed information about how children and families fare within the child welfare system. The National Incidence Study (Sedlack, 2001), now in its fourth iteration, and the Canadian Incidence Study (Trocmé et al., 2005), now in its third iteration, are surveys designed to determine the prevalence and characteristics of maltreatment in the United States and Canada. Over time, trends in reporting and response can be monitored and policy adjustments made.

Though still rare in child welfare, experimental studies have also begun to inform practice and policy. Of these, Schuerman, Rzepnicki, and Littell's (1994) random controlled trial of the Homebuilders model of family preservation in Illinois stands out as exceptionally rigorous and informative. While family preservation continues to survive in many jurisdictions, its expansion has been more cautious as a result of the null findings of this study. The federal Title IV-E

Waiver Demonstration has also prompted some experimental studies, most notably the Illinois evaluation of the availability of subsidized legal guardianship as a permanency enhancement (Testa, 2002). This study reveals that a "net increase" in permanence results from allowing caregivers to assume legal guardianship of their wards while continuing to receive a stipend equivalent to the foster care board rate. Strong evidence of effectiveness lends support for the expansion of permanence to include subsidized guardianship.[2]

Still other studies using interview and survey designs have influenced, and continue to influence, practice and policy. For example, Trudy Festinger's (1983) study of 277 young adults who had left foster care between the ages of 18 and 21 documented the substantial challenges facing former foster youth, particularly those emancipating from residential group care, including limited employment opportunities and reliance on public assistance programs. Moving well beyond the limited information found in administrative data, Festinger asked youth to share their feelings about the foster care system and what could be done to make it better. This study garnered considerable attention and was instrumental in prompting the 1985 Independent Living Initiatives Program (PL 99–272) followed by the Foster Care Independence Act of 1999 (PL 106–169). Building on this earlier research, Mark Courtney and colleagues (Courtney, Piliavin, Grogan-Kaylor, & Nesmith, 2001; Courtney et al., 2005) used survey methods to track a cohort of youth aging out of foster care. This study has drawn renewed attention to this issue and substantively informs the development of emerging policy.

Increasingly, standard administrative information is being augmented with rich data sources such as surveys to escape the confines of crude explanatory factors and to shed light on what is truly happening within the child welfare system. A fine example of such work can be found in Glisson and Hemmelgarn's (1998) study of the internal and external functioning of child welfare agencies, which found that child outcomes are better explained by an agency's internal environment than its service coordination efforts with related agencies.

Large-scale representative samples of children followed over time, such as the National Survey of Child and Adolescent Well-Being (Dowd et al., 2002), have also begun to provide more detailed information about the lives of children involved with the child protection system. While child well-being may seem like an obvious consideration, it has not been adequately defined or, more accurately, it has not been adequately constrained to a set of constructs that are easily measurable and lend themselves to intervention (Shlonsky, 2006). The combination of administrative data, child well-being information, and rigorously tested service interventions (see, for example, Wulczyn, Barth, et al., 2005) offers a more nuanced and promising line of inquiry, ultimately leading to interventions that are based on evidence and are aligned with child developmental theory.

Against this backdrop of increasingly rigorous and useful research on the residual child welfare system, there are lingering questions about whether the system is serving the best interests of children and families. Specifically, the broad association of child poverty with increased rates of maltreatment (Lindsey, 1994, 2004; Pelton, 1989) and lower measures of child well-being may mean that large effects could be achieved through better prevention efforts. And there is promise in this area. The work of David Olds and colleagues (Olds, Henderson, Kitzman, et al., 1998; Olds, Henderson, Cole, et al., 1998) has shown that home visits by public health nurses to new mothers deemed to be at high risk may reduce the risk of child maltreatment. Parenting programs for high-risk families using applications derived from social learning theory have also been rigorously evaluated and show great promise for improving the lives of children and families (Barth et al., 2005).

Despite the associations among poverty, maltreatment, and child well-being, increases in income alone may not translate into broad gains in functioning for the generation of children currently involved with child protection services. For example, children exposed to poverty at a very young age appear to fare less well than children who experience poverty later in life (Brooks-Gunn, Duncan, & Maritato, 1997). Thus, the emerging research in child welfare, as a broad concept including child maltreatment and well-being, might best be understood and utilized through the multi-pronged public health approach taken by Geraldine Macdonald (2000). That is, child welfare must take a larger view by addressing the needs of both maltreating families (secondary prevention and tertiary treatment) and families at risk of entering the system (primary prevention). Such an approach, while not explicit, is evident in the chapters to follow.

The book is organized into six parts, beginning with the context of child welfare and the research in this area, and then moving to evidence-based practice, research on permanency, advances in child welfare decision making, broader policy concerns, and, finally, international perspectives on child welfare.

PART I: CHILD WELFARE RESEARCH IN CONTEXT

Part I begins with a review of the trends in child maltreatment in the United States and Canada by Nico Trocmé that demonstrates the importance of rigorous research and the use of epidemiological data in order to inform policy at the population level. Leroy Pelton then examines the nature of the child welfare system and the quality of the research conducted within it. Pelton provides a note of caution and healthy skepticism about what can be accomplished by research within the current child welfare framework.

PART II: EVIDENCE-BASED PRACTICE IN CHILD WELFARE

All evidence is not created equal. Furthermore, the techniques used to evaluate the quality of research must themselves be scrutinized. Often, what appears to be decision making that is informed by high-quality research is nothing of the sort. Here, Eileen Gambrill discusses the emergence of evidence-based or, more correctly, evidence-informed practice, and the contributions of the medical field and other professions to shaping the way in which we think about and use evidence. Specifically, she introduces the process of evidence-based practice and juxtaposes this with other forms of decision making. Next, building on her experience conducting a controversial systematic review of multisystemic therapy for the Campbell Collaboration,[3] Julia Littell articulates how evidence can be misused and offers rigorous procedures for establishing the quality of studies and their synthesis.

PART III: RESEARCH ON PERMANENCY: ADOPTION, GUARDIANSHIP, AND FAMILY TIES

During the 21st century, there has been a substantial reduction in the length of time that children linger in long-term foster care. Most important, there has been a substantial increase in the number of children adopted through public child welfare agencies. This shift is largely the result of changes in public policy brought about by advances in child welfare research, and there are other shifts taking place as well. In this part, we review recent advances in permanency.

Trudy Festinger demonstrates how high-quality research can drive child welfare policy. Festinger details a random controlled trial of an intervention designed to speed adoptions by streamlining the court process in cases where adoption is likely. One of the few experiments conducted in child welfare to date, this study is an example of how researchers and child welfare authorities can design and carry out rigorous and relevant studies to answer difficult questions lingering in the field.

Many have heralded the importance of Mark Testa's work in the area of kinship care, permanency, guardianship, and adoptions. Reacting to years of benign neglect in the child welfare and foster care fields, the judiciary in the state of Illinois placed the state's child welfare program under court supervision and mandated research-based interventions. As part of a federal Title IV-E Waiver Demonstration Project, Testa promoted and rigorously tested the use of subsidized guardianship as a permanency alternative, leading to a substantial increase in permanency for children in the state. Testa's chapter in this volume outlines the theoretical foundations of the use of kinship care as a placement resource of choice, drawing on an emerging body of evidence to support his position.

At any given time, there are more than .5 million children in the foster care system (U.S. Department of Health and Human Services Administration for Children and Families, 2007). Millions of children enter and exit the foster care system over the course of their childhood, yet little is known about what happens to children who leave foster care when they become adults. Amy Dworsky's chapter reviews the literature on youth who "age out" of the foster care system, documenting the disappointing outcomes that many foster children seem to experience. Also highlighted is the extent to which extending foster care for these youth might improve their life chances.

The last two chapters in this section focus on emerging research related to domestic violence and its impact on child welfare and, more particularly, child protection. Colleen Friend looks at efforts to intervene at the crossroads of child protection and domestic violence. She begins with the all-important task of reviewing the theories that have guided intervention in this area. Friend then describes an innovative program designed to maintain the safety of women and children in battering relationships by extensively utilizing cultural, familial, and community resources. Lynette Renner, Kristen Shook Slack, and Lawrence Berger use the Illinois Families Study to examine the intersection of domestic violence and child protection. The authors explore the issues confronting child welfare workers engaged with cases where both the mother and the children are victims of family violence. Moreover, the authors examine the multifarious problems involved in "failure to protect" cases, especially when they also include interpersonal violence directed at the mother. This area is increasingly being examined by systematic investigations and the authors set an agenda for future research.

PART IV: DECISION MAKING IN CHILD WELFARE

The linchpin of child protection and the more general field of child welfare is decision making at the individual, agency, and policy levels. In "Decision Making in Child Welfare: Constraints and Potentials," Eileen Gambrill details the individual and structural impediments to sound decision making and offers a framework for a transparent, client-involved system that learns from its own mistakes. Eileen Munro follows this broader systemic focus with an analysis of the problematic nature of individual decision-making strategies as they relate to key child welfare judgments. Munro describes the difference between probabilistic and expert decision making and provides guidance on how and when to use each.

Risk assessment is part and parcel of any decision-making process, and this is certainly true in child protection cases. Judith Rycus and Ron Hughes review the literature on risk assessment in cases of child maltreatment and explicate how standardized safety and risk assessment instruments can be used in conjunction with clinical expertise to better inform casework decisions. This chapter is followed by Ira Schwartz, Peter Jones, David Schwartz, and Zoran Obradovic's introduction of neural network programming, an innovative computational process for predicting the recurrence of child maltreatment. While still in the early stages of development, neural networks hold promise for increasing the accuracy of prediction in child protection cases.

PART V: EVIDENCE-BASED CHILD WELFARE POLICY

The contribution of research to policy and systems change in child welfare services has been considerable in the 21st century. Operating within the existing child protection framework, this section details policy and organizational innovations that have the capacity to change the way services are provided to children and families.

Jane Waldfogel begins with a follow-up to her influential 1998 book *The Future of Child Protection*, in which she describes the development and implementation of differential response, an attempt to restructure child welfare services to have agencies deliver traditional child protection services to high-risk abusive and neglectful families while delivering less coercive, voluntary support services to lower-risk families. Though still a promising course of action, Waldfogel's return visit finds mixed results in terms of systems change and child outcomes.

Building on their landmark study of the privatization of child welfare services in Michigan, William Meezan and Bowen McBeath provide an engaging report on the process component of their study. This searching and rigorous qualitative study describes how the intervention unfolded and the formidable practice, administration, and policy barriers faced by the agencies involved.

Next, Daniel Webster, Lyn Usher, Barbara Needell, and Judith Wildfire describe the process of self-evaluation, part of the Annie E. Casey Foundation's initiative aimed at reforming child welfare services. This chapter details how child welfare agencies are taught by the foundation to acquire and use administrative data (including mapping and other innovative types of analysis) to inform planning, implementation, and ongoing improvement of child welfare policies, programs, and practice.

The main service provided to families in the public child welfare system for the last half-century has been foster care. Mark Courtney, Amy Dworsky, Irving Piliavin, and Steven McMurtry compare the population of children served by the public welfare system (AFDC and TANF) with the children served by the public child welfare system and find substantial overlap. They review current policies and programs against the background of research studies. In the next chapter, Arthur Reynolds and Joshua Mersky discuss the findings from the Chicago Longitudinal Study, which began in 1985 as an internal evaluation of early childhood programs by the Chicago Board of Education. Their contribution examines the link between early intervention programs and child maltreatment. Further, Reynolds and Mersky point out that early intervention programs are most likely to be effective when they provide comprehensive family services, such as parent education, social support, vocational/educational training, home visitations, and referrals.

David Stoesz pulls back and examines the broad and historical development of social policies for children. He examines the limits of the "patchwork quilt" of the social services net and suggests that the overhaul of the child welfare system will require comprehensive reform that includes recruiting and retaining skilled workers; providing choice-based, private and public children's authorities; developing a national database that reports accurately on the current situation of children; requiring institutions to conduct research specific to child protection; and enhancing supervisory training. He argues that understanding the limits of the child welfare system can set the stage for comprehensive reform.

In the early history of child welfare research, there was considerable concern about the ineffectiveness of casework methods and other approaches used in the field. Whereas Social Security has been instrumental in reducing poverty and deprivation among seniors, there has been limited similar progress for children. One of the more promising programs to reduce poverty among children has been the effort to provide progressive child savings accounts for all children. The idea of a social savings account has been pursued and even implemented at the international level. For instance, in 2002, the United Kingdom implemented a "child trust fund" for all children. In a sense, these programs would serve the social savings function for children that Social Security provides to seniors. Reed Cramer reviews the theory and research that supports this approach.

PART VI: INTERNATIONAL ISSUES IN CHILD WELFARE RESEARCH

The international scope of child welfare programs are the main focus of this section. Sheila Kamerman and Alfred Kahn observe that the child welfare system is again shifting, in a sense moving to a renewed focus on child well-being. Their chapter reviews the changes in social policies that have affected children and their families in Western industrialized nations, including income transfers, maternity/paternity leave policies, and educational programs. The changes in and development of these policies in the United States have been paralleled by similar developments at the international level. These modifications have been largely shaped by research and policy analyses. From an international perspective, many of the limitations and concerns raised by Stoesz take on additional meaning. Although the United States is the richest developed country in the world, it reports the highest child poverty levels. Kamerman and Kahn examine many of the programs and policies that provide an explanation, pointing to important areas for transformation.

Expanding on the work of Kamerman and Kahn, Martha Ozawa and Yongwoo Lee look at the economic situation of female-headed households at an international level. The majority of children living in poverty in the United States live in female headed households. Many of the difficulties faced by such families can be addressed by social programs and policies found in the United States and in other countries, which could translate into reductions in child poverty and its attendant problems.

CLOSING REFLECTIONS

Child welfare research has come a long way in a short period of time. Since the late 20th century, there has been an ever-increasing flow of empirical studies in the child welfare field. Using both administrative data and experimental and survey research data, we have begun to build a comprehensive knowledge base for effective policies and practices in the field. As Pelton, Gambrill, Stoesz, and others indicate, child welfare research by itself will not be able to solve the problems that poor and disadvantaged children face, but it is vital for us to have the best research available to inform policy analysis and development and to improve child welfare practices.

The growing recognition of the importance of evidence-based practice has led to improved services and recognition of the limits of our current science. As several of the chapters demonstrate, child welfare practices, policies, and programs have undergone fundamental change over the years. We are now in a period of increased professionalization in the child welfare field with child welfare professionals placing more emphasis on the role and importance of evidence and research. There are many promising developments in permanency planning, differential response systems, early intervention, improved social policies, and income transfer programs. As the chapters here indicate, we are at a critical period in the development of the field. Unquestionably, child welfare research will continue to play a vital role in the development of child welfare practices and programs that will make a difference for poor and disadvantaged children and allow us to make significant progress in improving child well-being.

Notes

1. Point-in-time estimates from the U.S. Adoption and Foster Care Reporting and Analysis System (AFCARS) show a marked reduction in the number of children in care. In September 1998, there were 559,000 children in foster care, while in September 2005 there were an estimated 513,000 children in care (U.S. Department of Health and Human Services, 2007).

2. While guardianship has long been a permanency option, it is generally seen as less desirable than adoption despite findings that the two permanent plans result in similar outcomes.

3. The Campbell Collaboration is an international organization that promotes and disseminates systematic reviews in the social sciences.

References

Ards, S. D., Myers, S. L., Malkis, E. A., & Zhou, L. (2003). Racial disproportionality in reported and substantiated child abuse and neglect: An examination of systematic bias. *Children and Youth Services Review, 25*(5), 375–392.

Barth, R. P., Landsverk, J., Chamberlain, P., Reid, J. B., Rolls, J. A., Hurlburt, M. S., et al. (2005). Parent-Training Programs in Child Welfare Services: Planning for a More Evidence-Based Approach to Serving Biological Parents. *Research on Social Work Practice, 15*(5), 353–371.

Berrick, J. D., Needell, B., Barth, R. P., & Jonson-Reid, M. (1998). *The tender years: Toward developmentally sensitive child welfare services for very young children.* New York: Oxford University Press.

Brooks-Gunn, J., Duncan, G. J., & Maritato, N. (1997). Poor families, poor outcomes: The well-being of children and youth (Pp. 1–17). In G. Duncan & J. Brooks-Gunn (Eds.), *Consequences of growing up poor.* New York: Russell Sage Foundation.

Courtney, M. E. (1994). Factors associated with the reunification of foster children with their families. *Social Service Review,* 68, 81–108.

Courtney, M. E., Barth, R. P., Berrick, J. D., & Brooks, D. (1996). Race and child welfare services: Past research and future directions. *Child Welfare,* 75(2), 99–137.

Courtney, M. E., Dworsky, A., Ruth, G., Keller, T., Havlicek, J., & Bost, N. (2005). *Midwest evaluation of the adult functioning of former foster youth: Outcomes at age 19.* Chicago: Chapin Hall Center for Children.

Courtney, M. E., & Needell, B. (1997). Outcomes of kinship foster care: Lessons from California (pp. 130–149). In J. D. Berrick, R. P. Barth, & N. Gilbert (Eds.), *Child welfare research review* (Vol. 2). New York: Columbia University Press.

Courtney, M. E., Piliavin, I., Grogan-Kaylor, A., & Nesmith, A. (2001). Foster youth transitions to adulthood: A longitudinal view of youth leaving care. *Child Welfare,* 80(6), 685–717.

Courtney, M. E., & Skyles, A. (2003). Racial disproportionality in the child welfare system. *Children and Youth Services Review,* 5, 355–358.

Dowd, K., Kinsey, S., Wheeless, S., Thissen, R., Richardson, J., Mierzwa, F., et al. (2002). *National survey of child and adolescent well-being: Introduction to wave 1 general and restricted use releases.* Ithaca, NY: National Data Archive on Child Abuse and Neglect.

Fanshel, D., & Shinn, E. (1978). *Children in foster care: A longitudinal investigation.* New York: Columbia University Press.

Festinger, T. (1983). *No one ever asked us: A postscript to foster care.* New York: Columbia University Press.

Glisson, C., & Hemmelgarn, A. (1998). The effects of organizational climate and interorganizational coordination on the quality and outcomes of children's service systems. *Child Abuse and Neglect,* 22(5), 401–421.

Goerge, R., & Wulczyn, F. (1998). Placement experiences of the youngest foster care population: Findings from the multistate foster care data archive. *Zero to Three,* 19(3), 8–13.

Johnson, W. (2004). *Effectiveness of California's child welfare structured decision-making (SDM) model: A prospective study of the validity of the California Family Risk Assessment.* Oakland, CA: Alameda County Social Services Agency.

Kadushin, A. (1970). *Child welfare services.* New York: Macmillan.

Kempe, C. H., et al. (1962). *The battered child syndrome.* Chicago: University of Chicago Press.

Lindsey, D. (1994). *The welfare of children.* New York: Oxford University Press.

Lindsey, D. (2004). *The welfare of children* (2nd ed.). New York: Oxford University Press.

Lindsey, D. (2008). *The future of children.* New York: Oxford University Press.

Maas, H. S., & Engler, R. E. (1959). *Children in need of parents.* New York: Columbia University Press.

Macdonald, G. M. (2001). *Effective interventions for child abuse and neglect: An evidence-based approach to planning and evaluating interventions.* New York: Wiley.

Needell, B., Brookhart, M. A., & Lee, S. (2003). Black children and foster care placement in California. *Children and Youth Services Review,* 25(5–6), 393–408.

Olds, D., Henderson, C. R., Jr., Cole, R., Eckenrode, J., Kitzman, H., Luckey, D., et al. (1998). Long-term effects of nurse home visitation on children's criminal and antisocial behavior: 15-year follow-up of a randomized controlled trial. *Journal of the American Medical Association,* 280(14), 1238–1244.

Olds, D., Henderson, C., Jr., Kitzman, H., Eckenrode, J., Cole, R., & Tatelbaum, R. (1998). The promise of home visitation: Results of two randomized trials. *Journal of Community Psychology,* 26(1), 5–21.

Pecora, P. J., Maluccio, A., Whittaker, J., Barth, R. P., & Plotnick, R. (2000). *The child welfare challenge: Policy, practice, and research* (2nd ed.). New York: de Gruyter.

Pelton, L. (1989). *For reasons of poverty: A critical analysis of the public child welfare system in the United States.* New York: Praeger.

Schuerman, J., Rzepnicki, T., & Littell, J. (1994). *Putting families first: An experiment in family preservation.* New York: de Gruyter.

Sedlack, A. (2001). *A history of the National Incidence Study of Child Abuse and Neglect.* Rockville, MD: Westat.

Shlonsky, A. (2006). Beyond common sense: Child welfare, child well-being, and the evidence for policy reform by Fred Wulczyn, Richard P. Barth, Ying-Ying T. Yuan, Brenda Jones Harden, & John Laandsverk [Book Review]. *Social Service Review,* 80(4), 756–761.

Testa, M. (2002). Subsidized guardianship: Testing an idea whose time has finally come. *Social Work Research,* 26(3), 145–158.

Trocmé, N., Fallon, B., MacLaurin, B., Daciuk, J., Felstiner, C., Black, T., Tonmyr, L., Blackstock, C., Barter, K., Turcotte, D., & Cloutier, R. (2005). *Canadian Incidence Study of reported child abuse and neglect, 2003: Major findings.* Ottawa, Canada: Minister of Public Works and Government Services.

U.S. Department of Health and Human Services Administration for Children and Families. (2006a). *The AFCARS report: Interim FY 2003 estimates as of June 2006* [On-line]. Available: http://www.acf.hhs.gov/programs/cb/stats_research/afcars/tar/report10.htm.

U.S. Department of Health and Human Services Administration for Children and Families. (2006b). *The AFCARS report: Preliminary FY 2005 estimates as of September 2006* [On-line]. Available: http://www.acf.hhs.gov/programs/cb/stats_research/afcars/tar/report13.htm.

U.S. Department of Health and Human Services Administration for Children and Families. (2007). *The AFCARS report* [On-line]. Available: http://www.acf.hhs.gov/programs/cb/stats_research/index.htm#cw.

Waldfogel, J. (1998). *The future of child protection: How to break the cycle of abuse and neglect* Cambridge: Harvard University Press.

Wolins, M., & Piliavin, I. (1964). *Institution or foster care: A century of debate.* New York: Child Welfare League of America.

Wulczyn, F., Barth, R. P., Yuan, Y.-Y. T., Jones Harden, B., & Laandsverk, J. (2005). *Beyond common sense: Child welfare, child well-being, and the evidence for policy reform.* New Brunswick, NJ: Aldine Transaction.

Wulczyn, F. H., & Goerge, R. M. (1992). Foster care in New York and Illinois: The challenge of rapid change. *Social Service Review, 66*(2), 278–294.

Part I

Child Welfare Research
in Context

1

Epidemiology of Child Maltreatment

Nico Trocmé

INTRODUCTION

An estimated 3 million children were investigated because of alleged abuse or neglect in 2004 in the United States; 872,000 children were confirmed victims of maltreatment; and an estimated 1,490 children died from abuse or neglect (U.S. Department of Health and Human Services, 2006). Beyond the official statistics, general population surveys and surveys of health, education, and law enforcement professionals indicate that up to half to four fifths of all victims of maltreatment are not known to Child Protective Services (CPS; Bolen & Scannapieco, 1999; Sedlak & Broadhurst, 1996; Wolfe, 1999). The tip-of-the-iceberg analogy easily comes to mind when one thinks of the scope of child maltreatment.

Some combination of these or related statistics is usually included as background to many child maltreatment research, policy, and service documents; however, without more specificity such statistics are apt to create more confusion than elucidation. While the iceberg analogy is an important reminder of the scope of child maltreatment, it fails to differentiate between forms of maltreatment, which vary considerably with respect to severity, chronicity, etiology, and sequelae (English, Upadhyaya, et al., 2005; National Research Council, 1993). This chapter summarizes some of the current research on the epidemiology of child maltreatment in Canada and the United States[1] in order to provide a more specifically differentiated understanding of the scope and distribution of child maltreatment.

DEFINITIONS

Child maltreatment refers to the range of abusive and neglectful acts perpetrated by adults or older youth against children. These generally fall into the four categories of physical abuse, sexual abuse, neglect, and emotional maltreatment. *Physical abuse* ranges from severe assaults against children that can permanently injure or kill children to abusive physical punishment to shaking infants. *Sexual abuse* includes intercourse, fondling, acts of exposure, sexual soliciting, and sexual harassment. *Neglect* includes a caregiver's failure to supervise or protect a child and/or failure to meet a child's physical, medical, or educational needs. *Emotional maltreatment* includes extreme or habitual verbal abuse (threatening, belittling, etc.) and/or a systematic lack of nurturance or attention required for a child's healthy development. Children's exposure to family violence is increasingly being recognized as a form of emotional maltreatment.

In practice, there is significant variation in the classification systems used to categorize child maltreatment. In Canada and the United States, legal definitions are set by provincial or state statutes, which vary considerably with respect to the scope and severity of behaviors that are considered maltreatment (Child Welfare Information Gateway, 2005; Centre of Excellence for Child Welfare, 2005). While some efforts have been made to develop a standard set of research definitions, most notably the Barnett, Manly, and Cicchetti classification system (Barnett, Manly, & Cicchetti, 1993; Manly, 2005), the field remains far from achieving consensus on a specific set of common diagnostic categories reflecting distinct etiologic theories (National Research Council, 1993; Herrenkohl, 2005).

Definitions also vary with respect to a number of other considerations, including severity, chronicity, age of the victim, and age of the perpetrator. Some jurisdictions consider acts of maltreatment to include both situations where children have been harmed and ones where children are at significant risk of harm, whereas others limit their definitions of maltreatment to situations where harm has occurred (Child Welfare Information Gateway, 2005). The upper age boundary for childhood victimization also varies by jurisdiction, ranging from 15 to 18. The definition of a perpetrator will vary as well, with the concept of child maltreatment usually referring to maltreating acts involving adults or older youth. Peer-on-peer abuse usually falls under the concept of bullying in cases of physical abuse, or sexual play or exploration in cases of sexual relations involving children or youth within 5 years of age (Holmes & Slap, 1998).

CPS-INVESTIGATED MALTREATMENT

The most commonly reported maltreatment statistics are the annual rates of victimization identified by child protection authorities. In the United States, these statistics are reported annually by the National Child Abuse and Neglect Data System (NCANDS) which combines reports received by state authorities. An estimated 3,503,000 children received an investigation by CPS agencies in 2004, of which an estimated 872,000 children were confirmed to be victims, a rate of 11.9 victims per 1,000 children (U.S. Department of Health and Human Services, 2006). Two thirds of these cases involved child neglect or medical neglect, at a rate of 7.4 and 0.3 victims per 1,000 children, respectively (see Table 1.1). Neglect has always been the dominant form of maltreatment investigated by CPS in the United States (U.S. Department of Health and Human Services, 2006). Physical abuse was noted in less than a fifth of cases and sexual abuse in 10%. The relatively large proportion of cases labeled "other maltreatment" is a result of the significant state-level differences with respect to the forms of maltreatment covered by legislation and the classification systems used to document these.

In Canada, investigated maltreatment statistics are tracked through the Canadian Incidence Study of Reported Child Maltreatment (CIS), a periodic survey of cases investigated by provincial and territorial child protection authorities. The 2003 cycle of the CIS found that an estimated 217,319 child maltreatment investigations were conducted in Canada (excluding Quebec)[2] and that child maltreatment had been substantiated for 103,297 of these children, a rate of 21.71 victims per 1,000 children (Trocmé, MacLaurin, Fallon, Daciuk, et al., 2005). As can be seen in Table 1.2, these cases are fairly evenly distributed among neglect, exposure to domestic violence, physical abuse, and emotional maltreatment, with only 3% of cases involving sexual abuse.

Although the rate of victimization is considerably higher in Canada than in the United States, this difference reflects several important distinctions in the mandate and scope of CPS in Canada and the United States. First, the rate of case substantiation is much higher in Canada compared to the United States. Only a quarter (25.7%) of reports were substantiated in the United States in 2004, with maltreatment remaining suspected ("indicated") in another 3% of cases (U.S. Department of Health and Human Services, 2006), whereas 47% of investigations were substantiated in Canada in 2003, with maltreatment remaining suspected in another 13% of cases (Trocmé, MacLaurin, Fallon, Daciuk, et al., 2005). A second and related

TABLE 1.1 Confirmed Cases of Child Maltreatment in the United States, 2004

Form of Maltreatment	Rate per 1,000 Children	Percentage*
Physical abuse	2.1	18
Neglect	7.4	62
Medical neglect	0.3	3
Sexual abuse	1.2	10
Psychological maltreatment	0.9	8
Other maltreatment	3.2	27
Any maltreatment	11.9	

Source: U.S. Department of Health and Human Services, Administration on Children, 2006, Figure 3-3.

*Rows are not additive since a child can be the victim of more than one form of maltreatment.

point is that the rate of substantiated physical abuse is 2.5 times higher in Canada, a difference most likely associated with differences in standards with respect to the acceptability of the use of corporal punishment. Indeed, three quarters of substantiated physical abuse cases in Canada involved inappropriate use of physical punishment (Durrant et al., 2006). Third, there has been a major expansion across Canada in cases of exposure to domestic violence and, to a lesser extent, in cases of emotional maltreatment. As a result, the rate of victimization attributed to exposure to domestic violence is nearly as high as the rate of neglect, and the rate of emotional maltreatment is nearly as high as the rate of physical abuse.

Age and Sex of Victims

Rates of CPS-investigated maltreatment vary considerably by age, sex, and form of maltreatment. Rates of CPS-substantiated maltreatment are highest in the United States for younger children, ranging in 2004 from 16.1 per 1,000 for children under 3 to 9.3 per 1,000 for youth 12 to 15 (see Table 1.3). Younger children are much more likely to become involved with CPS because of neglect, which affects nearly three quarters of victims under 3 and two-thirds of children 4 to 7. While neglect remains the predominant form of maltreatment for older children, the proportion of victims who are physically or sexually abused increases substantially from 15% for children under 3 to 39% for youth 12 to 15. In 2004, just under half (48.3%) of child victims were boys, and 51.7% of the victims were girls (U.S. Department of Health and Human Services, 2006).

The pattern in Canada is somewhat different. The CIS 2003 did not show the same age-related decrease in maltreatment rates as noted in the United States. With the exception of somewhat higher rates

TABLE 1.2 Primary or Secondary Form of Substantiated Maltreatment in 2003 in Canada, Excluding Quebec

Form of Maltreatment	Rate per 1,000 Children	Percentage*
Physical abuse	5.77	27
Neglect	7.53	35
Sexual abuse	0.67	3
Emotional maltreatment	5.03	23
Exposure to domestic violence	7.38	34
Any maltreatment	21.71	

Source: Trocmé, Fallon, MacLaurin, Daciuk, et al., 2005, Tables 3-5 to 3-9.

*Rows are not additive since a child can be the victim of more than one form of maltreatment.

TABLE 1.3 Age of Victims by Form of Maltreatment, 2004

Nature of Harm	Physical Abuse	Neglect	Sexual buse	Psychological Maltreatment	Unknown	Total*	Incidence per 1,000
Age <1–3	12.8%	72.9%	2.2%	4.8%	16.2%	232,409	16.1
Age 4–7	16.8%	64%	9.15%	6.4%	14.6%	187,275	13.4
Age 8–11	19.1%	59.8%	11.4%	7.4%	14.7%	160,940	10.9
Age 12–15	22.8%	54%	16.5%	6.8%	14.1%	158,104	9.3
Age 16 and older	24.9%	52.4%	16.3%	6.2%	14.6%	45,946	6.1

Source: U.S. Department of Health and Human Services, Administration on Children, 2006, Table 3-11 and Figure 3-4.

*Row percentages are not additive since a child can be the victim of several forms of maltreatment.

of maltreatment for 8- to 11-year-olds (23.5 per 1,000), the incidence of substantiated maltreatment ranged from 20.4 to 21.9 per 1,000 (see Table 1.4). As a result, the incidence of substantiated maltreatment was over twice as high in Canada than in the United States for youth 12–15.

Older children were more often identified as victims of physical abuse and sexual abuse, whereas younger children were more often victims in cases of exposure to domestic violence. There was relatively little variation in the age distribution of children in cases of emotional maltreatment and neglect. While girls made up 49% of victims, girls made up a larger proportion of victims in cases of sexual abuse (63%) and emotional maltreatment (54%), whereas boys were more often victims in cases of physical abuse (54%), neglect (52%), and exposure to domestic violence (52%) (Trocmé, MacLaurin, Fallon, Daciuk, et al., 2005).

Comparison of rates by age and form of maltreatment between Canada and the United States further underscores the effect of variations in standards and

practices on official maltreatment rates. For example, the higher rate of reported victimization for youth 12–15 in Canada (20.4 per 1,000 compared to 9.3 per 1,000) is further compounded by the larger proportion of Canadian youth who were victims of physical abuse (35% compared to 22.8%). As a result, more than three times as many youth, 7.2 compared to 2.1 per 1,000,[3] were noted as victims of physical abuse in Canada than in the United States, indicating two very different service responses to parent-youth conflict.

Trends

Despite a steady increase in reports, rates of substantiated maltreatment have been declining since the mid-1990s across the United States. From 1990 to 2004, the rate of investigations increased from 36.1 per 1,000 children to 47.8 per 1,000, which is a 32.4% increase (Figure 1.1). During the same period, the rate of victimization decreased 11%, from 13.4 per 1,000 children in 1990 to 11.9 per 1,000 children in 2004. Furthermore, since 1993, the rate of victimization

TABLE 1.4 Age of Victims by Primary Form of Substantiated Maltreatment in 2003 in Canada, Excluding Quebec

Nature of Harm	Physical Abuse	Neglect	Sexual Abuse	Emotional Maltreatment	Exposure to Domestic Violence	Total*	Incidence per 1,000
Age <1–3	10%	33%	1%	15%	41%	22,808	21.9
Age 4–7	21%	29%	3%	14%	33%	25,052	21.3
Age 8–11	29%	28%	3%	14%	25%	29,519	23.5
Age 12–15	35%	28%	4%	16%	17%	25,916	20.4

Source: Trocmé, Fallon, MacLaurin, Daciuk, et al., 2005, Tables 6-1 and 6-3.

National annual weighted estimates based on a sample of 5,660 substantiated child maltreatment investigations with information about age and sex.

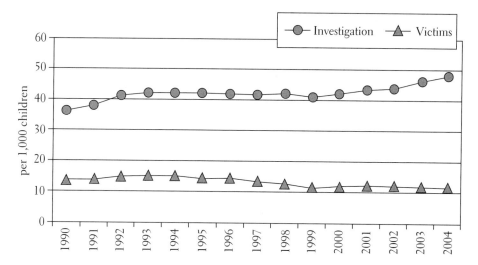

FIGURE 1.1 Rates of Reported and Substantiated Maltreatment in the United States
Source: NCANDS. From Figure 3-2, U.S. Department of Health and Human Services, Administration on Children, 2006.

decreased 22% from 15.3 per 1,000 (U.S. Department of Health and Human Services, 2006).

The decline in victimization rates has not, however, been consistent across forms of maltreatment. From 1992 to 2003, physical and sexual abuse rates declined 36% and 47%, respectively, while rates of neglect declined only 7%, and have in fact been increasing since 1999 (Jones, Finkelhor, & Halter, 2006). Jones and colleagues argue that there is compelling evidence that the decline in reports of physical and sexual abuse follow similar trends for related social indicators, such as violent crime, child poverty, teen pregnancies, and youth suicide. The fluctuation in neglect rates is more complex and may reflect a combination of a downward trend consistent with improving social conditions plus improved detection and greater sensibility to the negative effects of neglect. The continued increase in reports, however, does not lend itself well to these explanations.

In contrast, the trend in Canada has been one of unprecedented increases in rates of reported and substantiated maltreatment, with rates of substantiated maltreatment increasing at an even steeper rate than reports (Trocmé, Fallon, MacLaurin, Daciuk, et al., 2005; Trocmé, Fallon, MacLaurin, & Neves, 2005). The rate of maltreatment investigations in Canada, excluding Quebec, has increased 86%, from 24.55 investigations per 1,000 children in 1998 to 45.69 in 2003. The rate of substantiated cases increased 125%, from 9.64 substantiated cases per 1,000 children to 21.71.

The increase has been driven to a large degree by a dramatic increase in cases of exposure to domestic violence and emotional maltreatment (Figure 1.2). The rate of exposure to domestic violence increased 259%, from 1.72 substantiated cases per 1,000 to 6.17. The rate of emotional maltreatment increased 276% from 0.86 to 3.23 substantiated cases per 1,000. In 1998, these two forms of maltreatment accounted for 27% of substantiated cases. In 2003, they accounted for 43% of substantiated cases. These differences reflect a shift in awareness and, in some cases, in legislation with respect to the impact on children of emotional maltreatment and exposure to domestic violence.

Similar to the decline in sexual abuse rates documented in the United States (Finkelhor & Jones, 2004), rates of sexual abuse have been decreasing in Canada since 1993 (Trocmé, Fallon, MacLaurin, & Neves, 2005). In contrast to the United States, neglect and, even more notably, physical abuse cases have increased substantially. Part of this increase can be attributed to changes in investigation practices and standards, which have led to higher substantiation rates and the identification of more maltreated siblings. Nearly half of all investigations are substantiated in Canada, whereas less than a third are substantiated in the United States.

BEYOND CPS REPORTS

Official statistics reflect only a portion of the situations that might be considered child maltreatment. A series

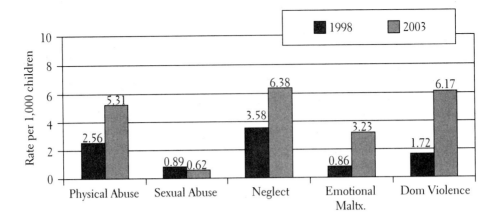

FIGURE 1.2 Changing Rates of Substantiated Maltreatment in Canada, Excluding Quebec
Source: Trocmé, MacLaurin, Fallon, Daciuk, et al., 2005

of National Incidence Studies designed to capture cases beyond official CPS reports has been conducted in the United States. While results of the 2006 wave of the NIS were not available at the time of the writing of this chapter, results from the first three NIS studies, which were conducted in 1976, 1986, and 1993, consistently pointed to a significant underdetection of cases of maltreatment known to professionals working with children. The 1993 study found that only a third of cases countable under the study's endangerment standard had been fully investigated by CPS (Sedlak & Broadhurst, 1996).

Population surveys designed to measure annual incidence also indicate that many cases are not being detected by CPS. Using the Conflict Tactic Scales (CTS) in a national sample of parents, Straus and colleagues found in 1995 that 49 per 1,000 parents reported using severe violence toward one of their children at least once in the year (Straus, Hamby, Finkelhor, Moore, & Runyan, 1998), 23 times the rate of physical abuse reported by NCANDS in 2004. Using a modified and translated version of the CTS, a 2004 survey in Quebec found that 63 per 1,000 mothers reported using "severe violence" at least once in the previous year, which is over 10 times the estimated rate of physical abuse reported to CPS in the rest of Canada for 2003 (Clement & Chamberland, 2005).

Direct comparison with reports to CPS is, however, problematic because of definitional differences and varying norms. In the case of the CTS, self-reported ratings of severe violence are not directly equivalent to ratings of abuse, since the CTS is designed to only measure parent behavior, irrespective of actual harm

or risk of harm (Straus, Hamby, Finkelhor, Moore, & Runyan, 1998). Even in examining cases where maltreatment has already been substantiated, different classification systems produce divergent results. A recent study comparing ratings by coders using NIS typologies with CPS ratings found significant differences in case classification, especially in cases of neglect and emotional maltreatment (Runyan et al., 2005).

Unlike CPS-investigated cases and surveys designed to estimate the rate of new incidents of maltreatment in a year (annual incidence), prevalence studies measure rates of victimization by asking youth or adults about abusive experiences during their childhood. Childhood maltreatment prevalence studies have been used mostly to examine the prevalence of child sexual abuse and, to a lesser extent, to examine the prevalence of physical abuse.

One of the most frequently referenced surveys of a national sample of respondents in the United Stated found that in 1985 27% of females and 16% of males disclosed a history of childhood sexual abuse (Finkelhor, Hotaling, Lewis, & Smith, 1990). The most extensive child maltreatment prevalence data available in Canada are from an adult population health survey conducted in Ontario in 1990, which found that 12.8% of females and 4.3% of males reported a history of sexual abuse (MacMillan et al., 1997). A recent meta-analysis of 22 studies using randomly sampled community respondents found that the overall prevalence of childhood sexual abuse was 30–40% for females and at least 13% for males (Bolen & Scannapieco, 1999). The study found that variations in estimates were related to the number of screening questions used to identify victims, the sizes of the samples, and the years in which the studies were conducted (Bolen & Scannapieco, 1999).

SEVERITY

Injuries

Most cases of maltreatment reported to child welfare services involve situations where children have already suffered some sort of emotional harm, or are at significant risk of being injured or of suffering some type of emotional harm. Physical harm due to maltreatment, however, is present in a relatively small proportion of cases. The CIS 2003 provides one of the more comprehensive sources of information on injury due to maltreatment (Trocmé et al., 2005). As shown in Table 1.5, physical harm was noted in only 10% of substantiated maltreatment cases (see total in Table 1.5), most of which was either bruises, cuts, or scrapes or other health conditions (such as a sexually transmitted disease or asthma aggravated by neglect). The study also tracked the severity of harm measured by the need for medical treatment: 70% of cases involving harm did not require medical intervention.

Somewhat surprisingly, no physical harm was noted in over two thirds of the cases of substantiated

physical abuse. Standards for CPS intervention across Canada have consistently stressed the importance of early intervention in situations where maltreating behaviors put children at risk of harm. The assessment of the acceptable level of risk, however, is not well defined. This may explain in part the difference between the physical abuse rates in Canada and in the United States (see Tables 1.1 and 1.2).

Fatalities

At 2.2 deaths per 100,000 (average rate 1994–1998), the United States has one of the highest rates of child maltreatment–related deaths in the developed world (based on the World Health Organisation's Mortality Database; UNICEF, 2003). Rates of child deaths due to maltreatment have been increasing in the United States. The NCANDS child maltreatment report estimates that 1,490 children died from abuse and neglect in 2004, a substantial increase from the 1,052 deaths recorded in 1998. In 2004, the ratio of child maltreatment–related deaths to child maltreatment victims was 1.71 per 1,000.[4]

The average rate of child homicides from 1995 to 1999 in Canada as reported by the UNICEF Child Maltreatment Deaths Report Card was 0.7 per 100,000, placing Canada in the middle range of developed countries. Rates of child homicides as

TABLE 1.5 Physical Harm by Primary Category of Substantiated Maltreatment in 2003 in Canada, Excluding Quebec

Nature of Harm	Physical Abuse	Neglect	Sexual Abuse	Emotional Maltreatment	Exposure to Domestic Violence	Total
No physical harm	71%	93%	95%	99%	99%	90%
Bruises, cuts, or scrapes	27%	2%	4%		1%	7%
Burns and scalds	*	1%	*	*	*	*
Broken bones	1%	*	*	*	*	*
Head trauma	1%	*	*	*	*	*
Other health conditions	2%	5%	2%	1%	*	2%
At least one type of physical harm**	29%	8%	5%	1%	1%	10%
Total substantiated investigations	25,257	30,367	2,935	15,370	29,369	103,298

Source: Trocmé, Fallon, MacLaurin, Daciuk, et al., 2005, Table 4-1(b).

Based on a sample of 5,660 substantiated child maltreatment investigations with information about physical harm.

*Too few cases to produce an estimate.

**Column percentages are not additive since a child can be harmed in several ways.

tracked through police reports have been decreasing in Canada: 55 homicides of children 0–18 were recorded in 2004, a historic 30-year low (Dauvergne, 2006). The ratio of homicides to substantiated victims in Canada was 0.48 per 1,000.[5]

While child homicide statistics are the only source of child maltreatment statistics for which we have both international comparative and historical data, the juxtaposition of statistics from Canada and the United States points to several of the challenges that emerge from such comparisons. Overall rates of maltreatment are comparable in both countries, yet rates of child maltreatment deaths appear to be three times higher in the United States. Rates of substantiated maltreatment have been decreasing in the United States, while rates of child maltreatment deaths have been increasing. In Canada, the trends are reversed.

Despite the care given to investigating, classifying, and reporting child homicides, these statistics represent a complex and heterogeneous set of phenomena that are best analyzed and interpreted in terms of more specific subpopulations. Infants and young children are at the highest risk of homicide at the hands of parents; middle childhood is a relatively safe period; whereas rates of homicides for adolescents are higher both within in the family and, most dramatically in the United States, in situations of youth-on-youth violence (Finkelhor & Ormrod, 2001). Homicides arise in a number of very different circumstances, including neonaticides, fatal child abuse, family violence, mental illness, fatal sexual assault, and teen fatal assault (Lawrence, 2004). As a result, it is misleading to interpret child homicide as the endpoint of a continuum of violence ranging from moderate neglect to homicidal physical assault. In practice, child maltreatment and child homicides are best interpreted as relatively distinct phenomena (Lawrence, 2004; Trocmé & Lindsey, 1996; UNICEF, 2003).

IMPLICATIONS FOR RESEARCH, POLICY, AND PRACTICE

For a period of 25 years, from the early 1970s to the mid-1990s, child maltreatment service statistics and epidemiological studies were consistently moving in the same direction of increasing rates driven by improved surveillance. The tip-of-the-iceberg analogy appeared to serve the field well and supported research, policies, and practices that focused predominantly on detection through the introduction of mandatory reporting laws,

the expansion of services, improved access to administrative data, and the development of finer survey tools. In many jurisdictions, rates have started to plateau or decline, a pattern that is likely to follow in others. The explosion of maltreatment reports from a few hundred cases involving battered children with multiple fractures to several million investigations conducted annually across North America has been driven both by improved detection and a broadening of our understanding of the negative impact of maltreatment by parents. The focus has moved from detection, reporting, and investigation to the more complex questions of how best to help different groups of maltreated children and youth. Closer examination of the epidemiology of child maltreatment reveals a diverse population, ranging from cases of severe physical abuse requiring urgent response, to complex cases of neglect and exposure, to domestic violence. The role of CPS is being reconceptualized (Waldfogel, 2001; Trocmé & Chamberland, 2003), and monolithic conceptualizations of child maltreatment are being challenged (English, Bangdiwala, & Runyan, 2005; Herrenkohl, 2005).

Notes

1. This chapter focuses on the epidemiology of child maltreatment in Canada and the United States because these are the jurisdictions with the comprehensive population survey and administrative maltreatment data.

2. Because of the limited amount of information available from the Quebec sample, most tables present estimates for Canada excluding Quebec. Where possible, additional tables in the original studies also present weighted estimates for all of Canada, including Quebec.

3. These incidence estimates are derived from Tables 1.3 and 1.4 by multiplying the proportion of abuse cases by the incidence rate, i.e., 0.35×20.4 and 0.249×9.3.

4. This was derived by dividing 1,490 NCANDS-reported deaths by 872,000 NCANDS-reported victims (U.S. Department of Health and Human Services, 2006).

5. This was derived by dividing the 55 CIS-reported child homicides by the 114,067 CIS-reported deaths for Canada, including Quebec (Trocmé et al., 2005).

References

Barnett, D., Manly, J., & Cicchetti, D. (1993). Defining child maltreatment: The interface between policy and research. In D. Cicchetti & S. Toth (Eds.), *Child abuse, child development, and social policy* (pp. 7–74). Norwood, NJ: Ablex.

Bolen, R., & Scannapieco, M. (1999). Prevalence of child sexual abuse: A corrective metanalysis. *Social Service Review*, 73(3), 281–313.

Centre of Excellence for Child Welfare. (2005). *Canadian child welfare legislation* [On-line]. Available: http://www.cecw-cepb.ca/Policy/PolicyLeg.shtml.

Child Welfare Information Gateway. (2005). Definitions of child abuse and neglect. *State Statutes Series 2005* [On-line]. Available: http://www.childwelfare.gov/ systemwide/laws_policies/statutes/define.cfm.

Clement, M.-E., & Chamberland, C. (2005). *La violence familiale dans la vie des enfants du Québec, 2004*. Quebec: Institut de la statistique du Quebec.

Dauvergne, M. (2006). Family related homicides against children and youth. In Canadian Centre of Justice Statistics (Ed.), *Family violence in Canada: A statistical profile* (pp. 58–60). Ottawa, ON: Statistics Canada.

Durrant, J., Trocmé, N., Fallon, B., Milne, C., Black, T., & Knoke, D. (2006). Punitive violence against children in Canada [On-line]. *CECW Information Sheet*, 1–2. http://www.cecw-cepb.ca/files/file/en/PunitiveViolence41E.pdf.

English, D. J., Bangdiwala, S. I., & Runyan, D. K. (2005). The dimensions of maltreatment: Introduction. *Child Abuse & Neglect*, 29(5), 441–460.

English, D. J., Upadhyaya, M. P., Litrownik, A. J., Marshall, J. M., Runyan, D. K., Graham, J. C., et al. (2005). Maltreatment's wake: The relationship of maltreatment dimensions to child outcomes. *Child Abuse & Neglect*, 29(5), 597–619.

Finkelhor, D., Hotaling, G., Lewis, I. A., & Smith, C. (1990). Sexual abuse in a national survey of adult men and women: Prevalence, characteristics, and risk factors. *Child Abuse & Neglect*, 14(1), 19–28.

Finkelhor, D., & Jones, L. M. (2004). *Explanations for the decline in child sexual abuse cases*. Washington, DC: Office of Juvenile Justice and Delinquency Prevention.

Finkelhor, D., & Ormrod, R. (2001). *Homicides of children and youth*. Washington, DC: Office of Juvenile Justice and Delinquency Prevention.

Herrenkohl, R. C. (2005). The definition of child maltreatment: From case study to construct. *Child Abuse & Neglect*, 29(5), 413–424.

Holmes, W. C., & Slap, G. B. (1998). Sexual abuse of boys: Definition, prevalence, correlates, sequelae, and management. *Journal of the American Medical Association*, 280(21), 1855–1862.

Jones, L. M., Finkelhor, D., & Halter, S. (2006). Child maltreatment trends in the 1990s: Why does neglect differ from sexual and physical abuse? *Child Maltreatment: Journal of the American Profes-sional Society on the Abuse of Children*, 11(2), 107–120.

Lawrence, R. (2004). Understanding fatal assault of children: A typology and explanatory theory. *Children and Youth Services Review*, 26(9), 837–852.

MacMillan, H., Fleming, J., Trocmé, N., Boyle, M., Wong., M., Racine, Y., et al. (1997). Prevalence of child physical and sexual abuse in a community sample: Results from the Ontario Health Supplement. *Journal of the American Medical Association*, 278(2), 131–135.

Manly, J. T. (2005). Advances in research definitions of child maltreatment. *Child Abuse & Neglect*, 29(5), 425–439.

National Research Council. (1993). *Understanding child abuse and neglect*. Washington, DC: National Academy Press.

Runyan, D. K., Cox, C. E., Dubowitz, H., Newton, R. R., Upadhyaya, M., Kotch, J. B., et al. (2005). Describing maltreatment: Do child protective service reports and research definitions agree? *Child Abuse & Neglect*, 29(5), 461–477.

Sedlak, A. J., & Broadhurst, D. D. (1996). *Third National Incidence Study of Child Abuse and Neglect*. Washington, DC: U.S. Department of Health and Human Services.

Straus, M. A., Hamby, S. L., Finkelhor, D., Moore, D. W., & Runyan, D. (1998). Identification of child maltreatment with the Parent-Child Conflict Tactics scales: Development and psychometric data for a national sample of American parents. *Child Abuse & Neglect*, 22(4), 249–270.

Trocmé, N., & Chamberland, C. (2003). Re-involving the community: The need for a differential response to rising child welfare caseloads in Canada. *Centre of Excellence for Child Welfare*, 32–48.

Trocmé, N., Fallon, B., MacLaurin, B., Daciuk, J., Felstiner, C., Black, T., et al. (2005). *Canadian Incidence Study of reported child abuse and neglect, 2003: Major findings*. Ottawa, ON: Minister of Public Works and Government Services.

Trocmé, N., Fallon, B., MacLaurin, B., & Neves, T. (2005). What is driving increasing child welfare caseloads in Ontario? Analysis of the 1993 and 1998 Ontario incidence studies. *Child Welfare Journal*, 84(3), 341–362.

Trocmé, N., & Lindsey, D. (1996). What can child homicide rates tell us about the effectiveness of child welfare services? *Child Abuse & Neglect*, 20(3), 171–184.

UNICEF. (2003). *A league table of child maltreatment deaths in rich nations* (No. 5). Florence, Italy: UNICEF Innocenti Research Centre.

U.S. Department of Health and Human Services, Administration on Children. (2006). *Child maltreatment*

2004: Reports from the states to the National Child Abuse and Neglect Data System. Washington, DC: U.S. Government Printing Office.

Waldfogel, J. (2001). Differential response: A new paradigm for child protective services. In J. Waldfogel (Ed.), *The future of child protection: How to break the cycle of child abuse and neglect* (pp. 137–160). Cambridge, MA: Harvard University Press.

Wolfe, D. (1999). *Child abuse* (2nd ed.). Thousand Oaks, CA: Sage.

2

Informing Child Welfare: The Promise and Limits of Empirical Research

Leroy H. Pelton

We put much faith in research to aid us in resolving our social problems. We insist that rational social policy and social interventions must be informed by social science research. Indeed, since the mid-20th century, the prospect of the use of social science research to inform social policy and services has given rise to a well-established growth industry. During that period, government funding for policy-relevant social science research projects increased enormously, while private foundations now routinely funnel hundreds of millions of dollars annually to social scientists at universities and think tanks for such enterprises. But what is the role of research in informing matters of child welfare? My objective here is to examine both the relevance and the irrelevance—and use and misuse—of research regarding public child welfare, particularly concerning such key issues as child removal, family preservation, and child protection. I will do so at four different levels of the child welfare edifice: its programs and services; the structure of the child welfare system itself; child

welfare policies; and the cognitive (and emotional) factors, including our conceptions of justice, which may determine the selection of the system, its policies, and its services. Along the way, I will explore a fundamental discrepancy between research and practice: the focus of child welfare practice is the individual child and family, while the emphasis of much social science research is on aggregate data.

PROGRAMS AND SERVICES

In the summer of 2005, a single mother and her four children found themselves homeless in Las Vegas, living out of a car. The police brought the family to Child Haven, a congregate shelter for temporary stays of "abused and neglected" children, operated by the county's child protection agency, the Department of Family Services. The children were admitted, and the mother was left to fend for herself. She complained that she was not allowed to see the children to say

25

goodbye to them, or even to instruct shelter staff as to their special needs (Pratt, 2005).

Presumably, the government authorities acted out of concern for the children's safety. But why did they separate the children from their mother? After all, their actions were clearly inconsistent with the long-standing American child welfare policy of family preservation. That policy dates at least as far back as 1909 when, at the White House Conference on the Care of Dependent Children, the nation's child welfare leaders at the time issued the proclamation that children should not be removed from their homes "for reasons of poverty" and that aid should be given to enable children to remain with their parents (in Bremner, 1971, p. 365).

We do not consider that we need research to tell us that living in the streets without shelter is harmful to children, as well as to parents. And there is little mystery in the case of the homeless family in Las Vegas as to how the children could have been protected from harm while preserving the family. Why was the family not housed together?

Concrete Services

If our aims are merely to reduce harm and the risk thereof to children, and to prevent the need to place them in foster care in order to protect them, then many possible interventions toward these ends would not require research to determine their effectiveness. Such is the case with many concrete services, which are aimed at changing the environment. If inadequate housing is causing the endangerment of children, then it could be made more adequate through the removal of peeling lead paint, the provision of heating and electricity, the placing of guard rails on windows, and the elimination of rodents and other vermin. Homeless families could be housed. Adequate food and clothing could be provided. A mother's inability to provide for child care while she is at a job that pays below-poverty-level wages could be offset by the provision of child care, which itself is seen as a preventive measure without the need for research to inform us that it is.

Concrete, or situation-changing, services often have face validity in terms of effectiveness that is acknowledged by all, because the cause-effect relationships are believed to be known (Neugeboren, 1985, pp. 253, 259–262). Because there is an apparent fit between the means and ends (i.e., homeless families

need to be housed), it suffices to simply know, in terms of evaluating program success, whether the family has been housed or not. As Handler (1973, p. 153) suggested, such concrete services can be evaluated on the basis of "mundane" measures of performance: "If they are supplied to the client, then the goal of the social service program has been accomplished."

Thus we could utilize a very basic form of research, that of needs assessment, to tell us the extent of a supply of such concrete services that we should have on hand. We could then evaluate success in terms of the *quantity* of families in need of such services that were reached. Yet despite the fact that studies in the past have shown homelessness and inadequate housing to be the precipitating reasons for placement in sizable percentages of placement cases, the federal Adoption and Foster Care Analysis and Reporting System (AFCARS) does not even report the poverty status (at the point of child removal) of the families of origin of the children in foster care, much less keep data on the numbers or percentages of children who have been placed there due to homelessness.

Nonetheless, we do know, and can say with certainty, that regardless of numbers, long-standing child welfare policy was violated when those children in the case of the homeless family in Las Vegas were placed in Child Haven. This is not a matter of numbers or even of beneficial effects found through empirical research. County officials could say that housing for the family was simply unavailable, yet only a few weeks later, in the aftermath of Hurricane Katrina, the county suddenly announced that hundreds of apartments would be made available to its victims coming to Las Vegas. What's research got to do with it?

There are many such concrete provisions that contribute in a readily apparent way to the reduction of risk of harm and, consequently, of the need for child placement, which, in any event, would not be difficult to measure through research. For example, research analyses of a statewide emergency fund developed within the New Jersey Division of Youth and Family Services in the late 1970s indicated that caseworkers made cash grants to families from the fund most frequently for the emergency purchase of food, the payment of rent, rental security deposits, rent arrears to prevent eviction (and homelessness), the payment of utility bills that were in arrears, the payment of charges involved in turning on utilities, and the purchase of furniture, such as cribs and beds. The purpose of the fund was to prevent the need for child placement, and indeed, the role of the grants in the immediate prevention of danger, and perhaps child placement, was often obvious. Most of the situations addressed by the grants, when examined on a case-by-case basis, could easily have been characterized as "deprivation of necessities" or "inadequate supervision"—and thus child neglect—if material supports had not been provided. Furthermore, although no control groups were employed, an analysis of foster care trends indicated that the initiation of the statewide fund in early 1978 coincided with the beginning of a decline in the number of children entering foster care in New Jersey, and a later increase in the monetary level of the fund coincided with an acceleration of the decline during 1980 and 1981 in the number of children *in* foster care. (See Pelton, 1994, for a longer summary.)

The Comprehensive Emergency Services Project implemented in Nashville in the 1970s included emergency caregiver and emergency homemaker services, and an around-the-clock emergency intake that enabled the swift delivery of such services to families in crisis situations. An approximately 50% reduction was reported in the number of children who entered foster care in Nashville during the first year of the program as compared with the year preceding the inception of the program (Burt & Balyeat, 1977). Since no control group was employed, a conclusive statement as to cause and effect is not possible in the aggregate. Yet the logic of individual cases is compelling. If previously, the police were called out late Saturday night to a home in which there were young children with no apparent adult supervision to be found, they would determine that an obviously dangerous situation existed. Presented with little other choice, they would remove the children to an institutional shelter. But with the advent of the project, an emergency caregiver could be called to the home, thereby allowing time for the parents to be found, and their reasons for leaving the children alone, as well as independent evidence, to be ascertained. We could expect that, in some such cases, the parents might not be found, or for other reasons government officials might determine that the children would continue to be in danger of severe harm and that the only means available for protecting them from such harm would be removal to foster care. We could expect that in some other such cases, however, government officials would have reason to conclude that (perhaps due to the unusual circumstances of the instance investigated) there is little likelihood that the children would be left alone again and decide

that placing the children might well do more harm than good.

Yet such services as enumerated above are pervasively denied to families in our public child welfare system. For example, a Nevada Division of Child and Family Services report, *Child Abuse & Neglect Statistics: 2002*, indicated that in regard to "services provided for all reports for 2002" statewide, only 0.1% of the families involved received day care, only 1.1% received homemaker service, and only 1.9% received emergency assistance. However, 43.5% received vaguely defined "casework counseling." Although this state of affairs can be documented through descriptive statistics, the answer as to why it exists, such as lack of political will, is not necessarily subject to research.

Preventive Programs

There is a wide range of situations and circumstances that may give rise to what has been called child neglect. Inadequacy of supervision, for example, may be due to any number of reasons. A single mother may face a dilemma in having no child care arrangements yet having to leave for her job. Or she may merely have poor judgment, parenting knowledge, or parenting skills. On the other hand, she may have poor skills for coping with poverty in that she is not adept at garnering from her social environment the supports that she needs, or at keeping her children safe from the hazards that abound in a poor neighborhood. Rather than blaming and accusing her, it would be reasonable to provide her with compensatory supports that could counterbalance the specific environmental and individual deficits that may be contributing to child endangerment, just as we would provide compensatory supports of both an environmentally modifying and skills-building nature in order to enable a person with physical disabilities to function more optimally.

We should, logically, strive to address as many of the contributing factors to child endangerment as we can, and so we must try to identify the personal and environmental causes in each particular case. It is futile to try to improve a parent's adequacy of supervision with parent education classes if lack of knowledge of child development or parenting skills is not present and not the reason for her inadequate supervision. Likewise, a parent's drug use may be contributing to endangerment of her child in one or several different ways, and not in others, or not at all. The probable causes must be identified as specifically as possible if the appropriate interventions are to be offered.

In any event, if the provision of rehabilitative services — by which we mean services aimed at changing the person in some way, such as those of an educative, psychotherapeutic, or treatment-oriented nature — are indicated, and since endangerment of the child is often multiply caused, then it is reasonable to offer these services together with services of a situation-changing nature. We may conclude that in order to protect endangered children from harm, the causes of the endangerment must be identified as best as possible, as specifically as possible, on a case-by-case basis, and that a full and diverse spectrum of resources must be available from which to choose the most fitting supports and services appropriate to the case at hand.

However, in recognizing the desirability of rehabilitative services, another issue arises, and that is the effectiveness of such services. While concrete services, intended to modify people's situation and environment, have a face validity, rehabilitative services, designed to change people in some way, do not, and their effectiveness is difficult to evaluate. Sophisticated research methodology is needed. Using the experimental method, we can randomly assign individuals to two or more groups, with only those in one group receiving the treatment in question. Such studies produce aggregate results in the form of statistical group-difference findings pertaining to various outcome measures. We use such group comparisons as the only procedure we have to evaluate whether or not a particular treatment, such as a particular drug treatment program, is potent enough to benefit *any* individual. It is only through the use of the experimental method that we can conclusively state whether or not a treatment (although not which aspects of the treatment, which would then require separate experiments) is effective. Moreover, we should keep in mind that people's character, personality, attitudes, beliefs, and habits are quite difficult to change, and that the most effective ways to reduce unintentional injuries are not through attempts to change individual behavior but through environmental changes and passive measures or restraints (such as guard rails on windows).

In the 1970s, the New York State Preventive Services Project provided a wide array of services to families in child welfare cases in which there was considered to be a high probability of child removal. These services included counseling, financial assistance, medical services, help with housing, family life education, education in home management and nutrition, remedial education, and recreational, vocational, and homemaker services, or in other words, a large mix of concrete and rehabilitative services. Jones, Neuman, and Shyne (1976) evaluated the project by randomly assigning cases to the experimental preventive services group and to the control group in which they would be subject to ordinary agency handling. Six months after the original 1-year intake period of the project, it was found that only 8% of the children in the experimental group had entered foster care, as compared to 23% of the children in the control group. The outcomes 5 years after the initial year were, predictably, somewhat less impressive. By that time, 34% of the children in the experimental group had entered foster care (although many did so long after their cases had been closed), compared to 46% of the children in the control group (Jones, 1985).

This project provided a high frequency of concrete services across the cases it served, such as financial assistance in 78% of the cases and help with housing in 45% of the cases (Jones, Neuman, & Shyne, 1976). We can only assume that these services were delivered, in an appropriate manner, to all cases in which they specifically fit a risk of harm to the child and the prospect of preventing the need for foster care placement. Even if they were, it should be noted that the cases in this project remained open for an average of 1.5 years, and if the need for such services arose again some time after case closure (as we might expect for families living in poverty and bouncing from crisis to crisis), such services would not have been forthcoming. We must also only assume that such rehabilitative services as family life education, education in home management and nutrition, and "counseling" (as amorphous as that term is) were fitted to particular risks in particular cases. But in regard to rehabilitative services, another question arises, and that is—even if appropriately fitted to the specific problem in a logical sense—can their efficacy be known or be established in experimental research?

The Homebuilders model, developed in 1974, was designed to prevent the need for foster care placement in high-risk families. It was not until the mid-1980s, however, after the failure of permanency planning to prevent a new rise in the nation's foster care population became apparent (see Pelton, 1991), that this model became all the rage in child welfare (at least rhetorically, if not in the quantity of families served). Designed as a short-term program (to deliver services for a period of 4 weeks to a few months), this model and its variants (together called Intensive Family Preservation Services programs) have offered a mix of services with an emphasis on rehabilitative services, including the teaching of behavioral management, communication, cognitive intervention, assertiveness, and problem-solving skills to families. Originally called "therapists," the caseworkers were largely trained in skills teaching and therapy. Although concrete services have been included in the mix of services, they have been offered at extremely meager levels, with emergency funds being limited to $100 per family in some programs and less than $20 in others, and any amount of financial assistance being limited to 16% of Homebuilders cases, with the most frequently provided concrete service being transportation (Kinney, Haapala, & Booth, 1991).

I need not recount here the history of the experimental research evaluation of the Homebuilders model and its variants which—at best—has yielded mixed findings as to the effectiveness of such programs. My purpose is to address a different but related issue. The first prerequisite for the effectiveness of a service is that it be designed to fit the specific problems to be addressed, and that it be delivered in the appropriate cases and instances. With concrete services, that is all that is necessary. If either homelessness, inadequate housing (in specific ways to be identified), lack of food, or children left alone are prompting the decision to place then, respectively, provision of housing, repair of the housing inadequacies, provision of food, or provision of child care will prevent the need for placement. Surely, more than one specific problem may have to be addressed in a particular case, but each problem requires its own solution.

Rehabilitative services, too, must be appropriately fitted to the particular conditions we seek to remedy by them, but it is not clear that programs derived from the Homebuilders model have encouraged such specificity. Program evaluations, which compare *groups* (experimental and control) of families, yield aggregate statistical outcomes that do not reveal if the services available to the experimental families were delivered to the appropriate families and to all such families. Furthermore, the effectiveness of any particular rehabilitative service must be tested by itself, not in combination with any other rehabilitative or concrete service. In the programs, and certainly in the evaluations, there has been a lack of specificity in identifying the problems and the interventions that we can say

logically fit the problems or are appropriate to them. We trust that the caseworkers, in consultation with their supervisors, have made the appropriate decisions as to which services to provide in each case, but we are not told if, for example, financial assistance was available to a particular family who needed it (perhaps the source having already run dry) or in the appropriate amount. Moreover, research evaluation in the form of statistical group comparisons on outcome measures obscures all of these issues.

We have amorphous programs addressing a vaguely defined and nebulous conceptual entity which we call "child abuse and neglect." The myriad forms of child endangerment we encompass in such terms, and the many forms of services to be considered that may fit and effectively address those forms, are obscured. We merely expect that a "shot" of the "remedy" will produce a "cure."

We may look in a similar manner at home visitor programs. These programs, too, entail mixed interventions and have been evaluated in such a manner that the independent effects of each component could not be determined. Moreover, while an early study (Olds, Henderson, Chamberlin, & Tatelbaum, 1986) showed promising results in regard to reducing harm to children, the much-vaunted Hawaii Healthy Start Program had little impact (Duggan et al., 2004). A summary of several home visitor program evaluations indicates that the results—at best—have been mixed (Gomby, Culross, & Behrman, 1999). An evaluative research study of the Healthy Families New York program throughout that state has in itself yielded mixed findings in regard to child harm (Mitchell-Herzfeld, Izzo, Greene, Lee, & Lowenfels, 2005). The home visitors in this program "emphasize parent/child interaction." The home visitors also "provide information about the importance of healthy behaviors" and "help to develop self-sufficiency skills." Although "concrete needs are not their primary focus," home visitors "help parents to access" various concrete supports (p. 13). It is impossible to sort out the potential effects of the various types of interventions, and various mixtures of these interventions, which vary across home visitor programs, without separate new experiments.

Recently, Clark County, Nevada, on behalf of its Department of Family Services, expressed the intent to request proposals from community agencies for programs they would provide to child protection cases. Such programs might include "teaching and demonstration services" and might "coordinate, connect, and/or provide" the family with "services." The agencies were asked to describe the "model or approach" to services they would use. I suggested that, on the contrary, only selected specific services, not program packages, should be procured. Recent program models in vogue, such as so-called Intensive Family Preservation Services, do not necessarily achieve their intended outcomes, perhaps owing in part to their vaguely defined hodgepodge of services.

In short, while evaluative research is useful, it has not been adequate, due to the nature of the conceptual entities that researchers have been asked to evaluate. These inadequate conceptualizations of problems and remedies, in turn, have been based on unspoken and romantic assumptions not themselves necessarily subject to research.

Risk Assessment

We need greater specificity throughout: in identifying the risk factors, in identifying the appropriate services, and in identifying the factors that should be addressed in research. Risk assessment instruments would seem to hold some promise in this regard, but the manner in which they have been developed and used has not been constructive. For example, "substance abuse" has been designated as a risk factor in risk assessment instruments without any suggestion that the level or frequency of substance use should be ascertained, that the type and level of impairment of the caretaker that the substance use might be causing be identified, that the manner in which any such impairment might be causing risk of harm to the child be specified, and that the level of harm, of which the child is at risk, be specified. The "physical condition of the home," including "dirty home," has been designated as a risk factor without any requirement that there be reason to believe that a specific condition is causing harm or risk of harm to the child in the particular case. As Mnookin (1973, p. 621) opined long ago: "Some 'dirty homes' may seriously endanger a child's growth and well-being, but most merely offend middle-class sensibilities." Yet children have been removed from "dirty homes" on the grounds that the existence of the dirty homes themselves constitute child abuse and neglect (Pelton, 1989).

Indeed, without the case specificity suggested above, the so-called risk factors identified in risk assessment instruments become mere stereotypes, and without the provision of supports and services

appropriate to specific conditions identified as causing specific types of harm or risk thereof to children, child removal decisions become discriminatory actions prejudicially taken against certain categories of families, on the basis of misapplied research.

Some years ago, the Massachusetts Department of Social Services (1990) instituted Project Protect, through which it instructed its workers to "support" child abuse and neglect in cases in which parental drug use, alcoholism, or spouse abuse was thought to be present, and even in cases in which there was a live-in boyfriend. The idea was that studies had shown that these factors were highly related to child abuse and neglect, in that they are frequently present when child abuse or neglect is present (although the higher frequency with which these factors are present when child abuse or neglect is not present was not taken into account). Thus the parent, on the inappropriate basis of grouped-data research, would be charged with child abuse or neglect not through direct confirmation of the act itself, but through "confirmation" of acts or conditions that bear some statistical relationship to such an act. A "finding" of alcoholism itself, or of spousal abuse itself, or of a live-in boyfriend itself, would be tantamount to a finding of child abuse and neglect.

By this logic, we might as well charge all impoverished parents with child abuse and neglect, because of the far stronger empirical relationship between poverty (and the material conditions to which it gives rise) and the incidence of child abuse and neglect (see Pelton, 1994). This, however, would offend even those who favor the logic, because the class bias inherent in such reasoning is too blatant. But the identification of substance abuse with child abuse and neglect for the purposes of coercive state intervention is no less discriminatory (not to mention potentially harmful to the child in the form of child removal and foster care placement), based as it is on statistical generalizations rather than upon individual findings of harmful acts toward children.

In 1999, Minnesota decided to include a child's exposure to domestic violence as part of the definition of child neglect in state law. In effect: "With the new language, the state suddenly mandated that a range of professionals report every child suspected to have witnessed adult domestic violence" (Edleson, Gassman-Pines, & Hill, 2006, p. 169). It appears that the change led to a rapid rise in child maltreatment reports across the state, resulting in a dramatic increase in child protection agency workloads. Prior to the change in legislation, "the state Senate Judiciary Committee heard testimony from academic scholars on the effects of exposure to adult domestic violence on child development" (p. 168).

In fact, all of the research on which the legislation was based is of a correlational nature. No cause-effect relations had been demonstrated in research. Even if they had, this would not mean that domestic violence could be identified as the cause of child harm in every case in which the two occurred. Yet, even if not the intent of the researchers, their research has been used to broaden the definition of child abuse and neglect, and thus the coercive net of the child welfare system as currently structured. I would not mind if such research findings, in being considered suggestive, were used to support the development of programs (for those who freely choose to participate in them) to prevent domestic violence before it arises (so long as they are effective), but this is seldom the case. And I certainly do not wish to imply that such research should be censored, or not be performed. I merely point out how research findings can be misapplied.

Stereotypes are generalizations and are no less stereotypes for being scientifically generated. What we have here are research-generated (or -supported) stereotypes that are valid in a statistical sense. They are not valid in an individual sense. Policies are made (or reinforced) that accuse individuals of abuse and neglect not because they have abused or neglected their children, but because one vaguely defined conceptual entity is correlated with another. The policies are based upon, or justified by, group assumptions about drugs, spouse abuse, live-in boyfriends, or poverty, and not on individual parents' abuse and neglect of their children. Parents are accused of abuse and neglect on the basis of their group identity as, say, drug users. Such policies are discriminatory in that they address factors on the basis of their "group relevance" that may be individually irrelevant.

One can say that spouse abuse is not child abuse; substance use (or abuse) is not child abuse; having a live-in boyfriend is not child abuse; and poverty is not child abuse (unless by a wealthy society that does not adequately address poverty). Alternatively, we could acknowledge that all definitions are arbitrary—a term means whatever we want it to mean—but then we must recognize that definitions of child abuse are rooted in ideology, not research.

Perhaps the use of research-generated group constructions to inform interventions would be less of a concern if the interventions involved targeting the offer of certain preventive services and supports to certain groupings of parents on a voluntary-acceptance basis with no coercive consequences. But they should be of great concern to us when they are used in the service of coercive policies that accuse parents and threaten the removal of children. Risk assessment instruments are often used for accusatory purposes with no fitting services offered.

For every case, information as specific as possible should be entered into a central database on the conditions causing harm or risk of harm to the child; the reasons for, or causes of, these conditions; the identification and matching of services needed to address the conditions and causes; and whether or not the services were available and provided. In this way, the agency would gain an idea of the funding levels and patterns needed for the various services it should be providing. As Gambrill and Shlonsky (2001) have suggested, risk assessment in child welfare has been narrowly focused on risks posed by parents to their children, with scant attention paid to risks posed by other factors in the environment, not least of which are the deficiencies within the child welfare system itself. Among these deficiencies (and hence risks) are not only the dearth of services provided, but the questionable effectiveness of many of those that are (often in a coerced manner, at that).

We must also attend to our ignorance in matters concerning risk of extreme harm. Early studies (in the 1960s and 1970s) indicated that in cases in which children had been killed or otherwise severely injured, there had been a series of severe injuries (see Pelton, 1989, pp. 68–73, for a summary of such studies). These findings raise the possibility that a pattern of repeated severe injuries may be the best indicant that a child will again be severely injured in the future, although I do not believe that any research to date has conclusively shown this.

Many severe injuries to children are multiply determined, i.e., are due to patterns of multiple causation. For example, a child's lead poisoning may be multiply caused by peeling lead paint on walls and the parents' ignorance of the danger. If just one partial cause in the pattern of multiple causation were to be removed (such as the lead paint), then the injury would not occur. Conversely, we must logically predict that if the same pattern of multiple determinants that resulted in severe injury to a child were to recur, severe injury would recur. We must consider the multiple causation of the event in order to determine what measures we can take to prevent the event from recurring. The uniqueness of the situation in which the severe injury occurred (what we might call a "freak accident") might convince us that nothing need be done to prevent recurrence. But if, in fact, severe injury to the child recurred, we would conclude that at least one of the partial causes of this recurring pattern must be addressed, lest the child be severely injured yet again. (See Pelton, 1999, pp. 125–163, for a more complete analysis of multiple causation and its implications, but there in regard to the criminal justice system.)

These partial causes may be both external and internal to the caretaker and the child. If we believe that we have identified one or several of these partial causes, then we can address them to prevent recurrence. For example, we might treat the caretaker's substance abuse. But this is a risky course of action to rely upon, because first, we cannot be certain that the substance abuse has contributed to the event, and second, even if it did, we cannot be certain that the treatment has been effective in eliminating it. We would not wish to take such chances with severe injury.

If there were less drastic means than foster care placement that could prevent recurrence of severe injury in the individual case, and if we could be very confident that they would work, then we should use them. Otherwise (after eliminating the possibility that the injuries are in whole or part due to some rare disease afflicting the child), the most prudent preventive step to take would be the removal of the child from the context in which he or she has been repeatedly severely injured. I do not wish to imply that we should always wait for a second severe injury (or even the first injury to a second child in the same family) before we resort to child removal. We must consider the degree of severity of the injury and the likelihood of the recurrence of such injury in the individual case (for which research of the aggregate sort is unlikely to provide an answer).

If severe injury has occurred, and the caretaker is found to be (either by commission or omission) a locus of causality of that injury, then we can conclude that the injury will occur again if that locus of causality is not modified in some way, and if the same set of causes constituting the remainder of the configuration of multiple causation arises again. Thus we are not speaking of probabilities here; we are saying that the injury *will* occur when the same set of circumstances arises again if the caretaker is not changed. Statistical probabilities are the constructions of social scientists who, in their present state of ignorance, can find no means to get closer to actuality. For it is not logical to assume that if the same exact configuration of causes arises again, there is only a likelihood that the effect will occur again. This contradicts our conception of causality. Rather, we must assume that the probabilistic form of prediction that we achieve is a reflection of our current level of ignorance. It is a reflection of the extent to which we are ignorant of the exact configuration of causation, because if that configuration is the cause, it is always the cause, and will always yield the same effect. We are not predicting dangerousness here, on the basis of empirical evidence; rather, we are concluding that the caretaker *is* dangerous, on the basis of logical analysis, and we are removing the child on that basis.

Yet if a factor is causative of a type of event in a statistical sense, it would be useful to aim preventive measures at it in the aggregate. If poverty is indeed a contributing factor in child abuse, it would be logical to conclude that a reduction of child abuse in the aggregate would follow upon a reduction of poverty in the aggregate, and that it would be wise to take steps to reduce poverty (although, of course, there are other reasons to reduce poverty). However, to take some type of coercive action, to prevent child abuse, toward people living in poverty on the grounds that poverty is a cause of child abuse would be discriminatory, just as to assume that the reduction of poverty in every particular case of child abuse in which poverty was present will prevent recurrence would be dangerous and unwise.

Finally, however, we must recognize that in matters such as harm to children, to do nothing is not a moral or just option, unless we have concluded, as we might in some instances, that to do nothing would be the least detrimental alternative. In the absence of being able to establish causation with certitude, we are still obliged to reach conclusions, make decisions, and take action. We should be guided by the weight of the evidence, reasonable hypotheses and theories, moral precepts, and precepts of justice. Policies (whether implicit or explicit) are always operative, and the task is to determine whether the weight of the evidence, reason, moral precepts, and justice favor the current operative policies and programs relative to others. We are obliged to develop plausible hypotheses as to cause and effect, consistent with the evidence, and to feed the incomplete evidence that emerges back into the process of rational discourse.

We cannot engage in sophistry divorced from the need to act in the real world. Obliged to act in the real world, we do not have the luxury of waiting until the perfect and flawless experiment has been performed, and certainty has been attained, before making decisions. For this, we would be waiting forever. But when the processes and systems that our policies set up are coercive and discriminatory, research on their "effectiveness" merely may serve to obscure the priority of ethics and the questions of justice and may be employed in the promotion of unjust policies.

THE SYSTEM

Many child welfare advocates have come to recognize that under our current child welfare system, prevention is given short shrift in comparison to investigation and foster care, and that interventions are reactive (to reports of child abuse and neglect) rather than proactive. They realize that many families who are in need of preventive and supportive services are overlooked and ignored, being provided such services, if at all, only after being accused of child abuse or neglect, and that many poor families perceive the public child welfare agency as a threat rather than as a resource. There is widespread agreement that we need to restructure the current system in a manner that reduces its coercive approach, attracts rather than drives away families in need of services, and increases its preventive efforts. Why, then, haven't we been able to transform the system, and what's research got to do with it? Why does a coercively oriented reporting law strategy still drive child welfare? And why do we allow our child welfare agencies to serve merely as investigative and foster care agencies?

A number of years ago, I proposed a fundamental restructuring of the public child welfare system (Pelton, 1989, pp. 156–177). As a first step, I suggested that the definitions of child abuse and neglect in state laws (including reporting laws) should be greatly narrowed to focus on severe harm to the child, and should specify that such severe harm, or danger thereof, must be due to clearly deliberate acts or gross abdication of responsibility. Allegations of such child abuse and neglect would be reported to and investigated by the police. Special police units would be developed for such investigation (in fact, many large police departments now have them), and they would receive special training in family crisis intervention. Such units would have the capacity

to respond immediately to serious allegations, bring the child for medical examination and emergency medical treatment, gather evidence, and refer the cases, if warranted, to civil (family) court. In rare instances, they would refer a case to the coroner and/or for criminal proceedings.

In addition, I proposed that the foster care system should be placed under the aegis of the family court system. The family court would have the responsibility of monitoring and controlling the foster care system and making all child removal and placement decisions. Special social workers would be employed by this system to serve solely as foster care workers. They would aid the court in monitoring the system and in making child removal and placement decisions.

My aim was to divest the traditional public child welfare agency (currently known as Child Protective Services, or CPS) of its investigative and child removal/foster care functions, in order to create of it a family preservation agency whose sole function would be to provide a wide array of preventive and supportive programs and services to families. My rationale was that the traditional public child welfare agency is saddled with contradictory functions in opposition to each other: An agency that investigates parents for wrongdoing cannot be supportive of families, and an agency that separates children from families cannot promote family preservation. This is evident even at the budgetary level: The agency is incapable of providing much in the way of resources for preventive and supportive services because its budget is largely devoted to investigation and foster care. Today's public child welfare agency (as it has been historically) is little more than an investigative and foster care agency. With this orientation and lack of services, children are too readily placed in foster care. A vicious circle ensues, since more money is then needed for foster care.

Moreover, due to the predilection—promoted by laws, the current system, and the child welfare literature—to see an inordinately wide swath of child welfare problems and difficulties experienced by (largely poor) families through the lens of broad and vague definitions of "child abuse and neglect," millions of reports overwhelm the public child welfare system annually, with hundreds of thousands of children entering foster care each year. In the restructuring I envisioned, the flood of reports would be reduced to a trickle, with that trickle diverted to the police, and the newly constituted public child welfare agency would devote its entire resources to offering a wide array of preventive and supportive services to all families who wanted and needed them, on a voluntary-acceptance basis.

Since the sole function of the agency would be to provide such services, its entire budget would be devoted to it, with the only question being the proportion of the budget to be allocated to each service. This question could be answered by clients "voting with their feet," so to speak, in that those services that were most in demand in the previous year could be funded most heavily for the coming year. Such an agency could be a true advocate for and friend to children and families, to which parents might come voluntarily and on their own, thus broadening the reach of preventive efforts beyond those families currently reported to the child welfare agency by others. Moreover, the separated foster care system might result in improved care with which placements are made, an improved capacity to monitor placements and placement settings, and an improved quality of care in placement. In addition, the investigation of child abuse and neglect reports, when performed by police, might be more efficient and more subject to legal safeguards of the procedural rights of individuals. Thus my concerns were of both a moral and practical nature.

The new family preservation agency would maintain state (or at least county) public agency status, for otherwise, governmental fiscal negligence would be invited. State-level status for such an agency is important to ensure that the funding of services not be left to the whims and charity of private foundations and agencies. We need to give as high a status to preventive agencies as we do to coercive agencies.

Recently, Richard Gelles and his colleagues, funded by the federal Department of Justice, evaluated a restructuring in four Florida counties that consisted of the transfer of the responsibility for investigating child abuse and neglect reports from public child welfare agencies to the sheriffs' offices. The evaluation did not find any impact of the restructuring on report recurrence, substantiation of reports, or foster care placement (Kinnevy, Huang, Dichter, & Gelles, 2005, pp. 15, 103–104). The best that can be said is that the transfer of investigative responsibility to law enforcement did not have any discernible negative impact on child welfare, either. Indeed, based on an analysis of police co-involvement in CPS investigations nationwide and a review of past literature, Cross, Finkelhor, and Ormrod (2005, pp. 241–242) conclude: "There is currently no empirical justification for concern about systematic negative effects of law enforcement involvement on CPS investigations."

The only change examined in the Florida study was the transfer of responsibility for child protective investigations from the Department of Children and Families to the sheriffs' offices in the demonstration counties. Apparently, there were no efforts in these counties to narrow the reporting-law definitions of child abuse and neglect. In fact, during the period of the Florida evaluation study, a series of much-publicized child deaths led to a dramatic increase in that state in the number of calls to the statewide hotline and in the number of reports requiring investigation. New policies were implemented to reduce the number of reports to be screened out. In response to one highly publicized child death, the Kayla McKean Act, implemented in July 1999, designated that all calls from mandatory reporters be investigated (Kinnevy et al., 2003, p. 85; Kinnevy et al., 2005, p. 5).

Furthermore, Florida, at the time of this study, had begun privatizing child welfare services throughout the state, including adoption services, foster care, in-home services, and protective services, with most counties transferring all court-ordered service cases to a lead agency, ChildNet (Kinnevy et al., 2003, p. 100; Kinnevy et al., 2005, pp. 5, 104). Apparently, it was also a series of child deaths that had prompted the state legislature to pass a bill in 1998 that called for the transfer of responsibility for child abuse and neglect investigations to the sheriffs' offices in a few counties in the first place. This same legislation "allowed individual Sheriffs to conduct the investigations themselves or to subcontract with other law enforcement or private agencies to conduct investigations related to neglect cases" (Kinnevy et al., 2005, pp. 5–6). Investigations in the demonstration counties were conducted by civilian investigators, who were hired by the sheriffs' offices and who worked collaboratively with law enforcement officers.

Contemplating this pattern of changes in retrospect, it would not be unfair to suggest that the occasion of intense media attention to child deaths in Florida merely provided the opportunity for politicians to forge ahead with a preconceived conservative ideology and agendas concerning the privatization of government services, the supposed reduction of "big" government, increased authoritarian surveillance of poor people, and the criminalization of child welfare problems. It is doubtful that any of the changes implemented will, or are meant to, pave the way for greater provision of preventive and supportive services, an increased array of such services, or concrete services for impoverished families in Florida experiencing child welfare problems or difficulties.

Some years ago, I proposed to the Edna McConnell Clark Foundation that it fund the demonstration and testing of my own restructuring plan in one county or state. I suggested that its effectiveness should be assessed by tracking and comparing, in relation to several designated comparison counties or states, such anticipated outcomes as reductions in severe physical injuries to children and child fatalities (whether attributable to child abuse and neglect or to unintentional injuries); foster care entries; the foster care population; the recidivism rate of children returned home or to relatives from foster care; adoption disruption rates; and negative perceptions of the public child welfare agency by the public and clients. In addition, we would look for the evolution of a broader array and greater quantities of services available, an increase in the number of self-referrals, and an increase in the number of families who would be provided preventive and supportive services.

I suggested to the officers of this foundation that, in order to best serve the public, they should focus on what goals they wish to achieve (such as the outcomes listed above) in regard to children's welfare, and then fund a wide array of proposals (in this case, restructuring proposals) to be compared on the basis of the outcome measures. Rather, in the past, the foundation had allowed its own preferences and prejudgments to determine its funding priorities. In the 1970s, it had latched on to "permanency planning" by funding the development of child welfare agency units that would focus on children already in foster care, to get them returned home or into adoptive homes, to the neglect of the front end of the foster care system, i.e., the issue of the prevention of the need to place children in foster care in the first instance, and the prevention of reentry. When the national foster care population began to rise steeply again in the 1980s (because of no decline in the number of children entering foster care each year; the foster care population had been reduced for a while merely by returning children home faster, but now many of these children were returning [see Pelton, 1989, pp. 81–82]), the foundation latched on to a new fad, the Homebuilders model, which it did much to promote in the funding of the Intensive Family Preservation Services (IFPS) programs, based on that model. Yet this was only one type of preventive program—

although suddenly being looked upon as a panacea for the ills of the child welfare system—in a wide array of other possible preventive programs and services.

Now, in the 1990s, when it was finally dawning upon many that a restructuring of the system itself might be desirable, it was a modest proposal, requiring minimal change, called the "differential response" paradigm (sometimes referred to as "alternative response") that was embraced by the Clark Foundation and by many other leaders in the field to the exclusion of other possibilities. In accordance with this concept, the screening of child abuse and neglect reports would still remain the starting point for child welfare services, and thus CPS as currently structured would remain as the gateway to the system. The reported family, depending upon the nature and seriousness of the allegation, might be deemed eligible for "alternative response," in which case it would be referred for "assessment" (which the family is allowed to refuse) rather than be obliged to receive the traditional investigative response (which would still be the fate of many families).

Proponents of differential response see in it the potential to reduce the adversarial nature of the relationship between the agency and parents with child welfare problems. According to the Minnesota report, to be discussed shortly, the emphasis of alternative response is on "family engagement, family participation in decision making, and voluntary participation in services" (Institute of Applied Research, 2004, p. 96). It is "positive and non-confrontational, supportive of family stability, strength-based and safety focused, holistic and, overall, more 'family friendly'" (p. 2). Yet "if new concerns arise during the initial assessment of a report, or at any later point, the response can be changed from AR [alternative response] to a traditional investigation" (p. 2). In other words, under alternative response, the families are under continuing surveillance.

In the differential response paradigm, then, the gateway to services is still the gateway to accusation, investigation, child removal, and foster care (and now, increasingly, with the advent of the Adoption and Safe Families Act of 1997, to termination of parental rights and adoption). Such a common gateway confuses coercion and control with nonjudgmental aid and prevention, deters potential clients, distorts and misdirects funding streams, and inevitably denies clients due process.

In the differential response paradigm as described by Waldfogel (1998), it seems to me that child care centers, Head Start programs, health care providers, schools, and other community-based organizations would be enlisted, more intensively than before, as CPS "partners" in the monitoring and oversight of families who potentially stand accused of "child abuse and neglect," thereby tainting such agencies with the coercive threat that CPS represents to impoverished families. This poses the prospect that parents will fear coming to health care providers, for instance, in the way they fear coming to CPS presently. With the differential response concept, we risk expanding the "poverty police," which is what current public child welfare agencies amount to, and making the tentacles of CPS even more broadly and coercively intrusive than they have been.

The most frequent variant of "restructuring" proposals, including differential response, is that preventive services be built up outside of the system, as it were, on their own more or less, with catch-as-catch-can funding. The old system would basically remain unchanged structurally, and would retain state agency status, thus perpetuating the implicit recognition that investigation and foster care are more important than preventive services.

Much is made of "public-private partnerships" these days, in child welfare and in other areas of social welfare. Not only is government encouraged to purchase services rather than to deliver them, but we are now asked to rely on private donors to help us fund what government once delivered. If government is not created to protect and enhance the security and well-being of its citizens, then I am at a loss to know why we have government altogether. While "private-sector partners" and other individuals also have responsibilities, government represents us all, and must not, in my opinion, be encouraged to shed, shift, diffuse, or obfuscate its own responsibilities. Our task is to help government to find better and more effective ways to carry out its responsibilities.

In any event, the differential response paradigm has met with quite modest or limited success, at best. For example, an alternative response demonstration project began in 20 Minnesota counties in 2001. An evaluation completed in 2004 randomly assigned families screened in for alternative response to either an experimental (alternative response) or control condition (Institute of Applied Research, 2004). While the experimental families received a family assessment, the control families received a traditional CPS investigative response. The evaluation found that alternative response families were less likely to have new child abuse and neglect reports than were control families (27.2% versus 30.3%), and fewer of them had subsequent child placements (10.9% versus 13.1%).

These differences, while statistically significant, are quite small. Moreover, the small difference in recurrence of reports may well be attributable to the greater amount of services—and specifically, concrete services—provided, in general, to the alternative response families, and not to the alternative response structuring per se. "Additional service dollars were provided to counties for AR [alternative response] cases. Counties received specially designated service dollars from the McKnight Foundation (which counties matched with one dollar for every four received) to pay costs associated with services provided to 'experimental' families" (Institute of Applied Research, 2004, p. 19).

Alternative response (experimental) families were far more likely to receive services than were control families (Institute of Applied Research, 2004, p. 42). Moreover, the alternative response families were far more likely to report that they received such concrete services as food or clothing, help paying utility bills, and other financial help (pp. 52–54). "Some McKnight dollars were specifically earmarked to pay for services that addressed very basic and practical needs" (p. 66). In fact, worker interviews suggested that the special infusion of service dollars was used, in effect, as a flexible emergency fund, largely for concrete services, reminiscent of the one developed in New Jersey many years earlier within the traditional system, but with suggestions of far better results in New Jersey. As one worker in Minnesota remarked, "some of this concrete help might have been offered before with county funds, but no one here thought of it before" (p. 57).

While the Minnesota report provides analyses indicating that the modestly lower rate of recurrence of child abuse and neglect reports among alternative response families might be associated with the provision of services, no such analyses are provided in that report in regard to the foster care placement findings. In cases in which services were not provided, there was no statistically significant difference between experimental and control families in regard to the recurrence of reports, but there was in cases in which services were provided (26.4% versus 34%; Institute of Applied Research, 2004, p. 127). Although the researchers report a statistical interaction effect between the alternative response approach and services, this difference was likely due to the greater amount and types of services available to the experimental families, and not to actual interaction.

An evaluation of an earlier, similar, alternative response approach in Missouri (Siegel & Loman, 2000), which was implemented without enhanced funding for services (stated in Loman & Siegel, 2005), found a similarly small reduction in the recurrence of reports, but no decrease in child placement rates. Indeed, an evaluation of a demonstration project in several counties in Mississippi (Siegel & Loman, 2005), in which a waiver was granted to expend Title IV-E funds on preventive services and thus to increase the amount and array of services provided, but which could hardly be said to have employed an alternative response approach, found fewer new abuse and neglect reports on experimental children (14.5%) than on control children (19.7%). Moreover, 9.1% of experimental children were removed from their homes after the start of the demonstration, compared to 14.1% of control children. These differences, while small, were statistically significant, and no smaller than in the alternative response projects. In the Mississippi project, a considerably greater percentage of experimental families than control families were provided help with housing, rent, utilities, and food. In any event, we have seen earlier in this chapter that certain approaches to expanding services within the traditional system, but without the hoopla of differential response, have yielded as good or even better results than found in this project.

A recent study found that almost two thirds of all county-level public child welfare agencies claim to employ "alternative responses" defined "as a formal response of the agency that assesses the needs of the child or family without requiring a determination that maltreatment had occurred or that the child is at risk of maltreatment" (U.S. Department of Health and Human Services, 2003). We can ask, then, if there has been any positive change in the system's outcomes, possibly attributable to this paradigm. But, although differential response has been presumably implemented in many states, the national foster care population continues to remain historically high (see Pelton, 1989, pp. 5–22, for foster care population trends from 1910 to 1985). After having more than doubled from 276,000 in 1985 to 567,000 in 1999, it declined slightly (by less than 9%) from 1999 to 2004 (Tatara, Shapiro, Portner, & Gnanasigamony, 1988; U.S. Department of Health and Human Services,

2004, 2005a). These statistics refer to 1-day counts. The number of children entering foster care each year rose from 190,000 in 1985 to 293,000 in 1999, or by 54%. In 2004, 304,000 children entered foster care. The total number of children who experienced foster care within a year increased from 460,000 in 1985, to 812,000 in 1999, or by 76%. In 2004, 800,000 children had experienced foster care within the year. And despite all of this family separation, there is no evidence that children are being better protected. Fatalities attributable to child abuse and neglect have not declined, and their number and rate (per child population) may have increased since 1985 (Lindsey, 2004, pp. 131–137; U.S. Department of Health and Human Services, 2006).

By adopting a reporting-law strategy, our nation has encouraged an informer and reactive approach to child welfare problems. This has led to an overwhelmed and dangerous foster care system. Certainly, a new infusion of funding for preventive and supportive services into the traditional child welfare system, as in the Minnesota project, is of value. But the differential response paradigm does not fundamentally change the system itself. Under it, the price of services for the family is to continue to remain under the surveillance of that system. Since even during an "assessment," the worker is on the lookout for evidence of child maltreatment, the difference between "assessment" and "investigation" is blurred. At best, the difference is reminiscent of the "good cop/bad cop" routine for interviewing criminal suspects. The dual role structure of the agency—i.e., the combination of the coercive, investigative, child removal role with the helping, preventive, supportive role—remains intact under the differential response paradigm. Under the dual role structure, the lion's share of funding and attention will continue to go for investigation and foster care, while services, and the families diverted into alternative response, will continue to receive a low priority (except perhaps in times of evaluated demonstration projects).

But let us look again at the stated procedural intent of the differential response paradigm. It is, we are told, to approach families not experiencing severe child abuse and neglect in a noncoercive manner and to offer services to them on a voluntary-acceptance basis. It is to reduce the fear that parents have that their children will be removed, thereby reducing the inherently conflictual nature of the parent-agency interaction under the current structure. It is to generate a more cooperative, nonconfrontational relation between the parents and the agency. Yet if this were the only intent, then the most logical approach would be to set up a separate governmental family preservation agency such as I described at the outset of this section. The advantages of such an agency, with respect to the stated intent of differential response, would be that it could devote its entire budget to preventive and supportive services, without having it drained by the costs of investigation and foster care. Such an agency would not be tinged with coercive threats and images. It would not have as its peculiar eligibility requirement for the receipt of preventive and supportive services that families must first be reported to the agency for alleged or suspected child abuse and neglect, as is true under the traditional structure even with the differential response paradigm. Should not *all* families experiencing child welfare problems be helped, without the need for suspicion that their difficulties are the result of parental wrongdoing? The current system, even with the differential response paradigm, oddly discriminates against parents who have not been reported for child abuse and neglect. And self-referrals are nonexistent, since the agency remains feared by rather than attractive to parents in need of help.

Why, then, is there entrenched resistance to the development and evaluation of new systems? One reason is based on the fear that unless the reporting-law strategy continues to drive the entire system, enlisting community-based agencies in the process, some cases of "child abuse and neglect" will be missed. The proponents of differential response want to have their cake and eat it too. Parents should be enticed into a voluntary, fear-free relationship with government authorities, but should be held under suspicion and surveillance at the same time. There is a fear of what poor people might do to their children if not watched. We wish to be benevolent, but in a coercive and paternalistic manner. Protective oversight must be maintained over poor families. There is a reluctance, in the end, to let go of coercive social control, or even to narrow its province. The differential response paradigm expresses an ambivalence toward poor people: The importance and decency of preventive, noncoercive approaches is acknowledged, yet surveillance and control stemming from suspicions of the poor prevail at the same time. The ethical and practical contradictions involved in this approach are not confronted.

Moreover, fears voiced by proponents of the differential response paradigm that the narrowing of reporting-law definitions of child abuse and neglect would increase tragic consequences for children are not borne out by any empirical evidence. States with narrower definitions have been found to experience no greater rates of child maltreatment fatalities than those with broader definitions (Rycraft, 1990). In addition, there was no decline in such fatalities during periods in which the quantity of reports skyrocketed, and there is no relationship between states' reporting rates and fatality rates (Lindsey, 2004, pp. 130–139). Furthermore, there is no basis in nationwide evidence on trends in child maltreatment fatalities and foster care placement rates for any connection between the two. The fatality rates neither rise nor fall with decreases or increases in child placement. This speaks to the ineffectiveness of the CPS system as a whole.

Finally, proponents of differential response might see themselves as political pragmatists. As Waldfogel (1998, p. 130) suggests: "Given the current trend to reduce federal funding for social programs and to replace entitlement programs such as welfare and child nutrition with capped block grants to the states, the political will to support an alternative system seems absent." Thus the differential response paradigm must turn to "informal helpers" and "community partner" agencies, including privately funded agencies. We must depend on charity. And if the political will to support the differential response paradigm is lacking, how much more is that the case for the development of a state family preservation agency that is attractive to poor people and solely devoted to providing preventive and supportive aid without judgment or recrimination? The proponents of modest changes in the system, which the differential response paradigm represents, are merely being pragmatic. Yet there is no conflict between tinkering with the current system through modest attempts to increase services and reduce coercive actions while simultaneously advocating for a fundamental restructuring of that system. The reluctance to even advocate for a fundamentally restructured system geared toward prevention rather than driven by a reporting-law strategy suggests a prejudicial suspicion of the motives and competencies of the poor and an unwillingness to let go of coercive social control.

POLICIES

While research is useful in comparing policy with reality, it can also be constructive in the *development* of policy. However, it is often not the primary factor in such development, nor should it be. Values and principles, implicit or explicitly stated, also inform and guide the development of policies. Yet so do prejudices. Moreover, research may be misused to support discriminatory policies.

Earlier in this chapter, I noted that the child welfare leaders at the 1909 White House Conference promoted a policy of family preservation, insisting that children should not be removed from their parents "for reasons of poverty." The leaders referred to implicit values, and not to any empirical evidence. They merely stated that "homelife is the highest and finest product of civilization" and that "children should not be deprived of it except for urgent and compelling reasons" (in Bremner, 1971, p. 365).

Many decades later, when social science had already become well established as the arbiter of social policy, permanency planning developed as a central concern of child welfare policy, based on little or shaky actual empirical evidence that continuity of care was "good" for children. Much convincing evidence (of a direct observational nature) was available that the act of separation itself caused harm to children in the form of immediate separation trauma. And wartime studies during the 1940s in England established that the institutionalization (or at least certain forms of it) of babies was associated with adverse psychological effects. In their book, *Beyond the Best Interests of the Child*, in which the idea of the child's need for "continuity of relationships" (upon which the concept of permanency planning is based) was promoted, Joseph Goldstein, Anna Freud, and Albert Solnit (1973) went little beyond such evidence and claimed to be guided by psychoanalytic theory, which itself has no credible research base. Yet they went as far as to suggest that the need for such continuity is so important that the Dutch Parliament was wrong when it decreed at the close of World War II that Jewish parents who had survived the concentration camps should be reunited with their children, whom they had entrusted to the care of non-Jewish Dutch citizens. Surely, the wishes of children should not be ignored; some of the children in question did not want to be returned to their parents. And I applaud the authors for promoting principle over intense sentiment. But is this the primary principle to be promoted—empirical evidence or no?

As I have already mentioned, when it became apparent in the 1980s that the foster care population

was rising once again despite the permanency planning movement, the new panacea was sought in the Homebuilders model. But a strange twist of rhetoric occurred. Family preservation was described as a new policy by child welfare advocates, despite eight decades' worth of policy and efforts (puny though they were) to preserve families. They defined family preservation as almost synonymous with IFPS programs based on the Homebuilders model. And they did this despite the fact that it had long been clear that the availability of a wide range of supports and services—not just a narrowly fashioned program heavily weighted toward counseling and therapy and presented as a quick fix—is needed to help struggling poor families liable to charges of abuse and neglect. Predictably, when the IFPS programs, employed in a wide range of child protection cases far beyond their potential capacities, were shown to yield only mixed results when subjected to experimental evaluation, the perception was shaped—contributed to unwittingly by child welfare advocates—that "family preservation" had now been tried and failed.

Actually, family preservation had always been, and continues to be, more myth than reality within the child welfare system, in terms of both efforts and outcomes (Pelton, 1997). Far more money had always been devoted to foster care and "child rescue" than to preventive efforts within that system, and during the 1980s and up until the present time the gap between these expenditures has continued to increase. And from 1983 on, the national foster care population continued to rise, reaching 567,000 children by 1999. Numerous studies have shown that children in foster care are overwhelmingly from poor families. Moreover, apart from the formal foster care system, an even greater number of children live apart from their parents in informally made arrangements (largely with grandparents). This is hardly "family preservation" in action.

Yet in the 1990s, a backlash against family preservation took root within the context of the prevailing politically conservative ideology and atmosphere within the United States. Newt Gingrich, while Speaker of the House of Representatives, advocated for a return to "orphanages" (Morganthau, 1994). A *Newsweek* headline proclaimed: "Why Leave Children with Bad Parents? Is It Time to Stop Patching Up Dead-End Families?" (Ingrassia & McCormick, 1994). Herrnstein and Murray (1994), in *The Bell Curve*, suggested that we should encourage single women to give up their children for adoption at birth (p. 416). And even within the child welfare professional community, the mantra of "child safety" was beginning to replace, or at least overshadow, that of family preservation.

In *The Book of David*, Gelles (1996) criticized family preservation policy largely on the basis of one case of death by child abuse in Rhode Island, and he promoted the concept of child safety, viewing it as incompatible with family preservation policy (p. 148). Such a rigid formulation of "child safety" would equate it with child removal. Yet in implicitly equating child safety with child placement, he made the same error of rigidity he attributed to family preservation policy: "The policy of family reunification and family preservation fails because it assumes that *all* biological parents can become fit and acceptable parents if only appropriate and sufficient support is provided" (pp. 149–150; italics in original). But family preservation policy has implicitly assumed, and the promoters of this policy have often explicitly stated, that families should be preserved only if it is possible to maintain the child safely within the family. The policy states a preference for family preservation, not a blind dictate. Gelles also intended, as reflected in other comments, merely that child safety should take precedence over family preservation.

It is dangerous to follow any policy blindly and rigidly. Rather, policies should serve as guidelines, with discretion in applying them left to caseworkers and supervisors who have firsthand knowledge of the individual case. If policies were meant to be followed blindly, without regard to the facts on the ground in the individual case, which are unknowable and unforeseeable by those who wrote the policies, we would not need intelligent and professionally educated workers to carry out the policies. But in drawing implications for policy change, Gelles seemed to assume that more rigidly drawn rules will fix the system, rather than make it worse. Thus he implied that deadlines should be set for terminating parental rights (Gelles, 1996, pp. 120, 160). Understanding that the foster family care system is already dangerously overloaded, he recommended "orphanages" as "plausible and cost-effective placements" (p. 163). His conclusions, though based on no research evidence, were conducive to the prevailing political ideology.

The Adoption and Safe Families Act of 1997 (PL 105-89) continues the long-standing policy of family preservation, but expresses a concern for "the safety of the child" (also long standing) through a tilt toward the favoring of adoption. It sets arbitrary time limits for the termination of parental rights for children in foster care (requiring the state, with limited exceptions, to terminate parental rights in the case of a child who has been in foster care "for 15 of the most recent 22 months"), and provides states with financial incentives to increase the number of adoptions out of foster care each year. Family reunification services under this act are time limited, and include counseling, therapy, and "treatment," but not the concrete and material aid that would address the issues often preventing reunification, such as homelessness or inadequate housing. Further, the language of the act equates adoption with permanency, even though the research evidence indicates that permanence is doubtful for many children adopted from foster care. Almost two thirds of children awaiting adoption from foster care are at least 6 years old (U.S. Department of Health and Human Services, 2005b). Yet studies have shown that adoption disruption rates rise dramatically with age at adoptive placement, with disruption rates for older children reaching well into double-digit percentages within the first 2 years of adoptive placement alone (see Pelton, 1989, pp. 92–96).

At present, it is difficult to get child welfare administrators to even say the words "family preservation," much less to ensure that their agencies will strive to provide preventive and supportive services, especially of the concrete variety. They claim to be focused on child safety, yet the safety and well-being of many children in foster care and adoption from foster care, as well as in their original homes, remain questionable. While the number and rate of children in foster care in the United States has increased considerably since the mid-1980s, there is no evidence of any subsequent reduction in the number or rate of child fatalities due to child abuse and neglect, of any other increased protection of children, or of any better outcomes for children upon entering adulthood.

Moreover, if we really intended child safety and child protection to be our goals, we would be concerned about protecting children from harm, no matter what the presumed source. But "child protection" means, more narrowly, protection of the child from harm that can be attributed to the fault of a parent. The answer to why this is so does not yield itself to research or reason, but to deeply held judgmental beliefs that have little to do with reality or harm to children. In fact, unintentional injuries (or what used to be called "accidental injuries" in the research literature) are the leading cause of child death in the United States (Grossman, 2000). In 1996, for example, more than 13,000 children and adolescents died from unintentional injuries, more than 10 times the number attributable to abuse and neglect. These deaths predominantly resulted from motor vehicle occupant and pedestrian injuries, drownings, and residential fires. Moreover, like child abuse and neglect, there is much evidence that a heightened risk of severe unintentional injury to children is strongly related to low socioeconomic status (Grossman, 2000). Indeed, most injuries due to child neglect are unintentional, and the question arises as to why the child welfare system puts more resources into parental blame and child removal than into injury prevention. The child welfare system's claimed focus on child safety amounts to hypocrisy.

The same political/ideological atmosphere that ushered in the Adoption and Safe Families Act of 1997 had also paved the way for the so-called Personal Responsibility and Work Opportunity Reconciliation Act of 1996 (PL 104-93), which replaced the Aid to Families with Dependent Children (AFDC) program with the Temporary Assistance to Needy Families (TANF) program. We may inquire, then, into the relevance of research to TANF policies. For several years now, social scientists throughout the country have been tracking and evaluating the various aspects of TANF policy by asking such research questions as: Do family caps (the disallowance of benefits, in some states, for an additional child born to a mother while she and her other children are receiving TANF) reduce the number of children born to mothers who are on TANF? Do time limits on the receipt of TANF leave families better off than they were on the old AFDC program? Do welfare-to-work programs and requirements succeed in moving mothers into jobs? Is child poverty reduced? All of these questions will be answered in an aggregate manner, in a statistical/probabilistic sense, through group data. The evidence, of course, will pertain to TANF recipients as groups, not as individuals. What if the evidence showed, for example, that family caps were successful in reducing additional births? Such births would still occur, and those children born would be denied benefits.

It would be wrong to evaluate and uphold these policies on the basis of any empirical evidence of aggregate success, because they violate the principle of nondiscrimination. The TANF "reforms" are aimed at controlling mothers' behavior, but they penalize children in a discriminatory manner. Perhaps many women who seek adequate-paying jobs will find them, but others will not. And if mothers do not comply with job-training requirements, it is their children who are denied TANF benefits. The principle of nondiscrimination, reflected in the equal protection clause of the 14th Amendment to the Constitution, requires that individuals similarly situated be treated in the same way. Even the TANF time limits on the receipt of benefits deny equal protection, in that some children similarly situated in regard to need, but for whom time limits have expired, will be denied benefits, while others will receive them. Moreover, the differential application of such policies involving sanctions and time limits (not to mention lower benefits) to one grouping of individuals, such as needy mothers and children, but not to others, such as elderly or disabled individuals in need, amounts to double discrimination.

With the advent of TANF, the arena of policy analysis has shifted away from individual need as addressed by AFDC as an entitlement, to questions of aggregate benefits to society as a whole, harm to poor children and their mothers as a group, and aggregate risks and advantages. In other words, it has shifted to the crude utilitarianism of "the greatest good to the greatest number" and the elusive "common good" that overlooks fairness to individuals. Not surprisingly, it has also shifted to the province of social science. The collection of aggregate data is consistent with, and indeed supports, a policy-debate focus on empirical outcomes as opposed to principles of justice pertaining to individuals. The special interests of social scientists in this emphasis on the greatest good to the greatest number are obvious, in that policy issues are framed in terms of empirical questions that are most suitable to their methodological tools and skills.

THE COGNITIVE ROOTS OF CHILD WELFARE PRACTICES, SYSTEMS, AND POLICIES

Research, in summary, is not necessary to confirm the effectiveness of many interventions, for situation-changing or concrete services often have face validity. Needs assessments are helpful in determining the supply of particular concrete provisions that should be developed and funded, and success can be measured in terms of the quantity of families served, although success would not be complete unless all in need have been served. The effectiveness of rehabilitative interventions, however, is difficult to evaluate, and such interventions are most appropriately evaluated through research employing the experimental method. Moreover, there has been a tendency to evaluate, and to deliver, bundled packages of a variety of concrete services, rehabilitative services, and a particular casework approach, such as in regard to IFPS or home visitor programs. Such evaluation and delivery strategies obscure the issues of specific needs and specific services that may be effective in addressing those needs. This is true whether or not an experimental evaluation indicates the effectiveness of a program in, for example, the avoidance of foster care placement.

In regard to research at the systems level, I question whether what has been evaluated to date amounts to fundamental reorganizational change, or merely tinkering with the system in its present form. In any event, the differential response paradigm has shown only modest success, if any at all, since, for example in the Minnesota project, any success was likely due to the sudden infusion of concrete services occasioned by the evaluation project, rather than to the paradigm.

Although the complete transfer of responsibility for child protective investigations to police departments, as was tested in Florida, amounts to reorganization, it did not seem to be aimed at providing a greater preventive and supportive role for the public child welfare agency or at changing traditional reporting-law approaches. Indeed, there has been an extreme reluctance to test and examine any system structuring that would differ fundamentally from the coercive "child rescue" approach to impoverished families. Although evident through much of American history, this approach became formalized in the late 1800s with the rise of the Societies for the Prevention of Cruelty to Children (SPCCs), was combined with preventive efforts by the Massachusetts SPCC in the early 1900s, and was broadened and reinforced with the advent of the reporting-law strategy developed in the 1960s in the wake of the "rediscovery" of child abuse. Although the child welfare system has gone through many administrative changes since the early days of the Massachusetts SPCC (such as being transferred to the juvenile courts, then to state public welfare agencies, and then to independent state agencies), its dual role structure—i.e., the combination of the coercive, investigative, child removal role with the helping, preventive, supportive role—has remained virtually unchanged. Research—embodying the spirit of curiosity, questioning, and uncensored exploration—is

relegated to the role of handmaiden to an entrenched system frozen in time that will define the narrow boundaries in which research will be performed.

Moreover, as we have seen, research has been misused within the existing structure of the child welfare system. It has been enlisted to support prejudicial stereotypes of impoverished families (and no less stereotypes for being statistically valid as generalizations) based upon crude correlations to be used, in turn, to rationalize discriminatory actions taken against individual families. The use of risk assessment instruments to determine coercive actions, such as child removal, rather than to offer fitting supports to families on a voluntary-acceptance basis, represents the most grievous misapplication of research in the development of policies.

Research does have a constructive role to play in the evaluation of social policies, but it is misused when enlisted to support or maintain policies, such as TANF, that are inherently discriminatory, by seemingly converting moral issues concerning the violation of individuals into empirical questions to be answered in terms of statistical generalizations. Such misapplication of research serves to make a fiction of individual realities. Moreover, while research can also play a constructive role in the development of policies, policies are often based on values not subject to empirical questioning.

We may give aid and comfort, through research yielding group outcomes, to policies that are violative of individuals, as in TANF policies or in child protection policies that violate the procedural rights of parents. Most of us endorse the concepts of family preservation, permanency, protection of the child from harm, and not removing children from their homes for reasons of poverty, because we believe them to be humane, and research has little to do with it. Policies concerning the use of foster care, for example, are not subject to merely empirical questions concerning the impact of foster care on children's development. As Stephen Magura (1989) once put it, "[B]etter prospective development in foster care is in itself no justification for removing a child from his or her own home."

There is, in fact, the matter of values, ethical priorities, conceptions of justice, and even ideology and sentiment that determine where we will place our resources. Yet the processes of the human mind in regard to these matters do not proceed without cognitive conflict, which results in confusing and contradictory manifestations in policy and action. For example, despite a long-standing policy of family preservation, foster care payments to substitute parents have always been higher than public assistance payments to the original parents. In one case of alleged "neglect" in the early 1970s, a Missouri court judge ruled that the proposition that the children would be "better off" in another home was not appropriate grounds for the termination of parental rights, concluding: "In the extreme this could lead to a redistribution of a great mass of the minor population" (*S.K.L. v. Smith*). Since the children residing in foster care in 1999 (not including the children in informally arranged placements, who were not under the aegis of the child welfare system), mostly from impoverished homes, represented almost 1 of every 20 children living below the poverty level, one can argue that it already has.

Despite the policy of family preservation, the child welfare system has always poured far more resources into foster care and family separation than into concrete assistance to the families of origin. Not to invest in concrete provisions to address the survival needs of poor families (whether done discriminatorily on a case-by-case basis for those known to the child welfare system, or more widely to all poor families) and then to declare that family preservation has failed is to beg the (research) question. It is not research, however, but the cognitive and emotional factors mentioned above that determine in what direction resources will flow, and even what questions we will ask, what theories we will develop and test, and what research we will fund. But these factors are in continual conflict, and the result is a compromise: We tinker with the system in the direction of prevention, while maintaining its fundamental structure and coercive orientation. Under these circumstances, a professed helping role serves as a façade that ironically facilitates expansion of the system's coercive, investigative, child removal apparatus (Pelton, 1997). At each level of the child welfare edifice—programs and services, system structure, and policies—there are choices to be made prior to research.

The fact that we have not been able to transform the child welfare system from its current coercive orientation toward parents, which itself harms children, is surely not a matter of lack of resources. We spend the equivalent amounts of what would be needed on the current coercive approaches, investigating impoverished parents for supposed abuse and neglect and removing children from them to be placed in foster homes. Such approaches are buttressed by current widespread attitudes among the American public and its leaders that the functions of government are to police and punish, not to help, serve, and aid—especially not poor people, who are deemed deserving of their fate. We see this in the heavily punitively weighted war on drugs, and the consequent overflowing prison system, which is populated largely by young poor people. The fact that this war is a failure does not deter its continuance, for the facts are trumped by ideology, much as with our failed child welfare system.

I used to think that to get at the roots of the dysfunction of the present system we needed to look not at the superficial level of operations (a level at which we can tinker with the system), but at the structure of the system itself. We would merely have to point out the discrepancy between the policy and the reality in terms of outcomes, and how it is driven by that structure. But I have come to realize that the system's structure is not itself at the root of the matter, for underlying the intransigence against restructuring are the unspoken beliefs about justice, fairness, and deservedness. The underlying beliefs, however, are a matter of values and ethics, not open to empirical test.

Thus, in the field of child welfare, we must move to a deeper level of explicit discussion that we rarely engage in—and often avoid by obsessing over statistics, research, and terminology—before moving upward to services, systems, and policies. The level of discussion must shift to that of underlying values and philosophical premises, political philosophy, conceptions of justice, and attitudes toward poverty and the poor. We must discuss the origins of the general lack of political will to restructure the current system. Overall, our failure to address the basic needs of all individuals and families has little to do with research, and much to do with ideology, cognitive constructs of inclusion and exclusion, and conceptions of justice.

In my book *Frames of Justice: Implications for Social Policy* (Pelton, 2005), I contended that three basic frames of justice coexist within the human mind. All three are reflected in the Hebrew Bible, as well as in the New Testament and the Koran, but can be found even earlier in history. I concluded that, in fact, they are rooted in the basic cognitive structures of the human mind. I identified these three frames as group justice, the justice of individual desert (i.e., deservedness), and what I call the principle of life affirmation. Each of the frames has its distinct implications for social policy, and all contemporary social policies reflect one or more of the three frames.

Justice as individual desert posits that individuals should get what they "deserve," in the form of either reward or punishment. This frame is deeply embedded in the human psyche, both cognitively and emotionally. The principle of life affirmation expresses a universal reverence for human life, without exception, condition, judgment, exclusion, or discrimination, and so also frames justice as an individual matter. "Group justice" might appear to be an oxymoron, yet we all succumb to it on occasion, and it is abundantly manifest in modern policies, including those of liberal democracies. This frame distinguishes among groups in social policy and applies the notion of desert to groups rather than to individuals, although it also applies itself to groups without any notion that the individuals within the group are deserving of what they will get.

Let us return to the homeless mother and her children in Las Vegas. The children were separated from their mother against their will, and were violated in the process. It made no sense for the authorities not to house or shelter them together. Or did it? If only a few weeks later they had been the victims of Hurricane Katrina, or posed as such, they would have been housed. The difference must be that when we have any reason at all to suspect parents of having contributed in any way to their circumstances, to be in any way culpable for their plight, through acts of either commission or omission, such as we do in the wide array of cases that we currently categorize as child abuse and neglect, we implicitly judge them as "undeserving" of adequate and humane provision, especially from government. Implicit suspicion, prejudgment, and blame may guide our interventions.

Perhaps, in the case of this hapless family in Las Vegas, child removal can be viewed as a misguided attempt to serve innocent children without "rewarding" their "undeserving" mother. After all, communities have always been willing to support poor children more generously in institutions or foster homes than with their own parents. But this case can also be viewed as a not uncommon example of the administration of group justice. In the famous biblical story of Job, his onlookers insisted that he must have deserved the calamities visited upon him, presumably by God, including the destruction of his children. Job is vindicated when his riches, including children, are finally restored to him. But what is often overlooked in this story is that his previous children, who were not brought back to life, did not get what *they* deserved. They were merely enlisted as instruments in the infliction of Job's earlier suffering, without regard for *their* lives. Similarly, we can make sense of the forced separation of the homeless mother from her children if we assume that her desert was read into the very fact of her homelessness, and that her children were used merely as props, without serious regard for their own well-being, in order to deepen the punishment supposedly deserved by the mother.

So too, "group justice" is meted out by the TANF program when children are denied welfare benefits in clumsy attempts to sanction and control their "undeserving" mothers. Moreover, just as only Job's circumstances were real and present, while the onlookers' inferences of desert were in the realm of idle speculation irrelevant to the actuality of Job's suffering, so also are only the homelessness and poverty real. Application of the desert and group frames of justice merely promotes condemnation and a callous disregard for human life, including child well-being.

Our notions of desert facilitate the ease with which people can be harmed with good conscience and selected for exclusion, along the lines of ostensible desert. We accuse parents of being "uncooperative" for not accepting therapeutic services, while withholding from them supports that they actually want for fear of "rewarding" people who are thought to be "undeserving" of any real benefit from government. Judgmental attitudes of desert run so deep in our psyches that we would rather take measures that are not only more costly in monetary terms but also harm many children, so long as their parents are denied benefits that we contend they do not deserve.

The deep-rooted attitudes of desert that are reflected in many social policies of the modern welfare state are based on stereotypes we have nurtured of the "child abuser" and the poor. We rationalize our attitudes based on desert by claiming that we don't want to provide the wrong incentives and disincentives for certain types of behavior. Ultimately, however, we and our society must reflect upon and reexamine our commitment to the moral value of the sanctity of human life—as an unconditional value without exception or exclusion—if we are to develop social policies and service delivery structures that incorporate more humane and effective approaches to human problems than do our current policies.

As I have said, the three frames of justice coexist in the human mind. There are competition and conflict among the frames, as is evidenced in their policy manifestations even today. Our policies and programs show manifestations of all three frames in, variously, their unconcern for the individual; their attempts to reward, punish, and control behavior; and their attempts to promote individual well-being. The prominence of one frame over another is ultimately open to human choice. We can choose the frame of justice from which we will derive our policies. The attraction that the life affirmation frame of justice has for us is that it goes to the core of what our sense of justice is, which is that life should not be violated. From the perspective of the principle of life affirmation, whenever individuals are violated, and life not supported, then justice is violated. Life cannot be violated in the name of justice, for the violation of life is injustice, and justice resides in the nonviolation of life.

If we were to be guided by the principle of life affirmation in the construction of social policies, then basic human needs would be addressed without reference to desert and without condition. Welfare benefits would be distributed to individuals in order to address dire need, and not to control the behaviors of the needy. Policies designed to address financial need would do so in a universal manner, and so there would not be separate policies, each with their own eligibility requirements, for financial aid to the elderly, women with children, disabled people, veterans, and victims of disaster. Homeless people would be provided housing, without condition. If health care insurance were to be provided to some, such as the elderly, then it would be provided to all. Government would avoid the temptations to reward, punish, provide incentives and disincentives for behaviors, and engage in social engineering through its social welfare policies.

In fact, we live in a society of unearned abundance. Wealth that accrues to individuals in a community above and beyond what they might have gained in the absence of a community is a form of common wealth, and is unearned. Such wealth is produced by community structures beyond individual efforts, and thus can be said to belong to the community as a whole. The community has benefited most of us far beyond anything we can imagine to have deserved, and most often in no way commensurate with any contributions that one has or has not made. Most of us have greatly benefited from our national community merely by having the good fortune to have been born into it. As a university professor in a near-anarchic society such as Somalia, I would obtain an exceedingly small fraction of the wealth and well-being that accrues to me by occupying the same position and putting forth the same effort in the United States. My wealth is more a function of place than of individual effort or contribution. The truth is that most of us have been getting "something for nothing." This is in the nature of a viable and successful community.

In an endless circle, it is such "excess" benefits that are taxed, and the taxes are then used to further benefit the community, through both cash and in-kind benefits. In a just community, this common wealth would be taxed in a fair and nondiscriminatory manner, and these resources, in turn, would be distributed in a manner that would benefit everyone, without discrimination. I have proposed a variant of a combined flat income tax and social dividend system, other variants of which have been proposed at least since the 1940s and in several countries, which would meet these requirements (Pelton, 2005, pp. 88–94).

I have proposed that an annual common monetary benefit be allocated to every member of the community, adjusted only for household size. There would be a flat, or strictly proportional, tax on all other income. Suppose that this benefit were to be set at $10,000 per year for an individual in a single-individual household, with combined amounts for more than one individual per household increased by $3,000 for each additional individual, and suppose that the income tax rate were to be set at 40%. Then a woman living alone who had a nonbenefit income of $25,000 for the year would pay the government nothing, since her social dividend would exactly offset her income tax. A single mother with two children who had a nonbenefit income of $25,000 would have a net income of $31,000 (because although she owed $10,000 in income tax, she would also be allocated a $16,000 benefit). Her break-even point would be $40,000. For a four-person household, perhaps consisting of a two-parent family with two children, the social dividend would be $19,000, and the break-even point would be $47,500.

The lower one's income, the more that would get added to it, in a negatively progressive manner. Yet the same tax rate applies to all. If the woman living alone did not have any nonbenefit income, the government would have paid her the full $10,000 social dividend. If this woman had $30,000 in nonbenefit income, she would owe $12,000 in tax, but because of the $10,000 allocated to her as a social dividend, she would pay only $2,000, or less than 7% of her nonbenefit income. If she had $100,000 in nonbenefit income, she would pay $30,000, or 30% of her nonbenefit income. If she had $1 million in nonbenefit income, she would pay $390,000, or 39% of her nonbenefit income. The point is that although the proposed tax system does not contain a progressive tax scheme, the tax payments are progressive with higher incomes. A person with 20 times the income of one with $50,000 would pay 39 times more in tax.

In this system, no tax breaks whatsoever would be allowed. Moreover, there would be no special categories of taxes (such as for Medicare or Social Security). All taxes would go into general funds. Additionally, the social dividend would replace Social Security, unemployment insurance, Supplemental Security Income, TANF, and other such group-specific public assistance and "insurance" programs. However, depending on the adequacy of the social dividend to be provided, in-kind programs that promote nondiscrimination would still be needed. These, addressing need and promoting reasonable opportunity in a nondiscriminatory manner, could include housing subsidies, free public education and universities, health care insurance, public day care, and public social services agencies.

Such a universal social dividend as proposed here is not radically different from what we have now. Old-age Social Security is already a "universal" benefit system, although only for those above a certain age. This proposal extends the social benefit to everyone, in the name of nondiscrimination. Such a universal social dividend and taxation system as proposed here does not fractionalize the populace into contending groups, each with their separate interests, a process that has been so detrimental to poor children. If elderly people, through their organizations, successfully lobby for a higher social dividend, then children will gain as well as the elderly. Moreover, such a system does not isolate the poor from the wealthy, but actually allies the interests of the wealthy with those of the poor. Reduction of the size of the social benefit or an increase in the tax rate would be detrimental to low-income and poor people, but would likewise not serve the interests of the wealthy. There would be no discrimination, such as against children, or in favor of the elderly, or even against the wealthy.

The sheltering of the children but not their mother in the case of the homeless family in Las Vegas seemingly reflects a "children first" attitude of an Orwellian quality, in that some citizens, namely children, are to be considered more equal than others, such as adults. Yet the children-first rhetoric, which claims children to be "innocent" and "our most precious asset," certainly has not helped poor children. Ironically, children would be better off if we were to treat all individuals, no matter what their age or class, as equals. The rhetoric of children first seems to be a cover for policies and realities that place children last along with their parents.

Of course, nowadays, when any social issue is brought to the attention of politicians and policy makers, the first question that they, along with the social science researchers, almost reflexively ask is: How many? How many homeless families are there? How many children were placed in foster care during the past year, in Las Vegas, in Nevada, in the nation, for reasons of inadequate housing or homelessness? The confidence is conveyed that we will address this problem through research and rationally proceed to the development of programs logically appropriate to that problem. But if the political will is lacking, then such research will be, at best, useless and, at worst, a stalling tactic.

It is when legislators begin to ask how many homeless people there are, what colors they are, what ages they are, that I get the queasy feeling that they don't intend to do a darned thing about housing homeless people, much less provide them any services, although they may be willing to fund research. I begin packing up to leave when they start asking how many homeless people don't want to work, enjoy their "lifestyle," like living in the streets, are "service resistant," and so on, for then they are fishing for ways to label the homeless as "undeserving," not to address their needs.

We may have our own private beliefs and emotions concerning desert, but we must come to realize that government does not operate well from this frame of justice. Needs must be addressed, consistent with our sense of justice, which recognizes the dignity of human life, and consistent with the frame of justice I call the principle of life affirmation, which recognizes the dignity of *all* human life.

References

Bremner, R. H. (ed.). (1971). *Children and youth in America: A documentary history* (vol. 2). Cambridge, MA: Harvard University Press.

Burt, M. R., & Balyeat, R. R. (1977). *A comprehensive emergency services system for neglected and abused children*. New York: Vantage.

Cross, T. P., Finkelhor, D., & Ormrod, R. (2005). Police involvement in child protective services investigations:

Literature review and secondary data analysis. *Child Maltreatment, 10*(3), 224–244.

Duggan, A. K., MacFarlane, E. C., Fuddy, L., Burrell, L., Higman, S., Windham, A., & Sia, C. (2004). Randomized trial of a statewide home visiting program to prevent child abuse: Impact in preventing child abuse and neglect. *Child Abuse & Neglect: The International Journal, 28,* 597–622.

Edleson, J. L., Gassman-Pines, J., & Hill, M. B. (2006). Defining child exposure to domestic violence as neglect: Minnesota's difficult experience. *Social Work, 51*(2), 167–174.

Gambrill, E., & Shlonsky, A. (2001). The need for comprehensive risk management systems in child welfare. *Children and Youth Services Review, 23*(1), 79–107.

Gelles, R. J. (1996). *The book of David: How preserving families can cost children's lives.* New York: Basic.

Goldstein, J., Freud, A., & Solnit, A. J. (1973). *Beyond the best interests of the child.* New York: Free Press.

Gomby, D. S., Culross, P. T., & Behrman, R. E. (1999). Home visiting: Recent program evaluations: Analysis and recommendations. *The Future of Children, 9*(1), 4–26.

Grossman, D. C. (2000) The history of injury control and the epidemiology of child and adolescent injuries. *The Future of Children, 10*(1), 23–52.

Handler, J. F. (1973). *The coercive social worker: British lessons for American social services.* Chicago: Rand McNally.

Herrnstein, R. J., & Murray, C. (1994). *The bell curve: Intelligence and class structure in American life.* New York: Free Press.

Ingrassia, M., & McCormick, J. (1994, April 25). Why leave children with bad parents? *Newsweek,* pp. 52–58.

Institute of Applied Research. (2004, November). *Minnesota alternative response evaluation: Final report.* St. Louis, MO: Author.

Jones, M. A. (1985). *A second chance for families: Five years later.* New York: Child Welfare League of America.

Jones, M. A., Neuman, R., & Shyne, A. W. (1976). *A second chance for families: Evaluation of a program to reduce foster care.* New York: Child Welfare League of America.

Kinnevy, S., Cohen, B., Huang, V., Gelles, R., Bae, H.-O., Fusco, R., & Dichter, M. (2003, June). *Evaluation of the transfer of responsibility for child protective investigations to law enforcement in Florida: An analysis of Manatee, Pasco, and Pinellas counties.* Philadelphia: Center for Research on Youth and Social Policy, School of Social Work, University of Pennsylvania.

Kinnevy, S., Huang, V., Dichter, M., & Gelles, R. (2005, February). *The transfer of responsibility for child protective investigations to law enforcement in Florida: A supplemental study: Final report.* Philadelphia: Center for Research on Youth and Social Policy, School of Social Work, University of Pennsylvania.

Kinney, J., Haapala, D., & Booth, C. (1991). *Keeping families together: The homebuilders model.* New York: Aldine de Gruyter.

Lindsey, D. (2004). *The welfare of children* (2nd ed.). New York: Oxford University Press.

Loman, L. A., & Siegel, G. L. (2005). Alternative response in Minnesota: Findings of the program evaluation. *Protecting Children, 20* (2–3), 78–92.

Magura, S. (1989). *Protecting abused and neglected children,* by M. S. Wald, J. M. Carlsmith, & P. H. Leiderman [Book Review]. *Child Welfare, 68*(5), 553–554.

Massachusetts Department of Social Services. (1990, January). *Project Protect: Guidelines for protecting children in substance abusing and violent families.* Boston: Author.

Mitchell-Herzfeld, S., Izzo, C., Greene, R., Lee, E., & Lowenfels, A. (2005, February). *Evaluation of Healthy Families New York (HFNY): First year program impacts.* Albany: New York State Office of Children and Family Services.

Mnookin, R. H. (1973). Foster care: In whose best interest? *Harvard Educational Review, 43,* 599–638.

Morganthau, T. (1994, December 12). The orphanage. *Newsweek,* pp. 28–32.

Neugeboren, B. (1985). *Organization, policy, and practice in the human services.* New York: Longman.

Olds, D. L., Henderson, C. R., Jr., Chamberlin, R., & Tatelbaum, R. (1986). Preventing child abuse and neglect: A randomized trial of nurse home visitation. *Pediatrics, 78*(1), 65–78.

Pelton, L. H. (1989). *For reasons of poverty: A critical analysis of the public child welfare system in the United States.* Westport, CT: Praeger.

Pelton, L. H. (1991). Beyond permanency planning: Restructuring the public child welfare system. *Social Work, 36*(4), 337–343.

Pelton, L. H. (1994). The role of material factors in child abuse and neglect. In G. B. Melton & F. D. Barry (Eds.), *Protecting children from abuse and neglect: Foundations for a new national strategy* (pp. 131–181). New York: Guilford.

Pelton, L. H. (1997). Child welfare policy and practice: The myth of family preservation. *American Journal of Orthopsychiatry, 67*(4), 545–553.

Pelton, L. H. (1999). *Doing justice: Liberalism, group constructs, and individual realities.* Albany: State University of New York Press.

Pelton, L. H. (2005). *Frames of justice: Implications for social policy.* New Brunswick, NJ: Transaction.

Pratt, T. (2005, August 13). Little help for families down on their luck. *Las Vegas Sun*.

Rycraft, J. R. (1990). Redefining abuse and neglect. *Public Welfare, 48*(1), 14–21.

Siegel, G. L., & Loman, L. A. (2000, January). *The Missouri family assessment and response demonstration impact evaluation: Digest of findings and conclusions*. St. Louis, MO: Institute of Applied Research.

Siegel, G. L., & Loman, L. A. (2005, June). *State of Mississippi Title IV-E child welfare waiver demonstration project: Final evaluation report: Executive summary*. St. Louis, MO: Institute of Applied Research.

S.K.L. v. Smith, 480 S.W. 2d 119.

Tatara, T., Shapiro, P., Portner, H., & Gnanasigamony, S. (1988, July). *Characteristics of children in substitute and adoptive care: A statistical summary of the VCIS National Child Welfare Data Base, based on FY 85 data*. Washington, DC: American Public Welfare Association, Voluntary Cooperative Information System (VCIS).

U.S. Department of Health and Human Services. (2003, May). *National study of child protective services systems and reform efforts: Findings on local CPS practices*. Washington, DC: Author.

U.S. Department of Health and Human Services. (2004, August). *Trends in foster care and adoption*. Washington, DC: Author.

U.S. Department of Health and Human Services. (2005a, September 15). *Trends in foster care and adoption: FY 2000–FY 2004*. Washington, DC: Author.

U.S. Department of Health and Human Services. (2005b). *The AFCARS report: Preliminary FY 2003 estimates as of April 2005* (10). Washington, DC: Author.

U.S. Department of Health and Human Services. (2006). *Child maltreatment 2004*. Washington, DC: Author.

Waldfogel, J. (1998). *The future of child protection*. Cambridge, MA: Harvard University Press.

Part II

Evidence-Based Practice
in Child Welfare

In an era of managed health care and government funding restraints, the standards for child welfare practitioners and programs have increasingly included efficiency and accountability. Within this framework of fiscal responsibility, the social work profession has witnessed an effort toward ensuring the legitimacy of interventions and programs. Beyond funding implications, the new framework for services also represents a response to historic practices and policies that relied solely on the authority of practice wisdom to substantiate claims of effectiveness.

Yet all evidence is not created equal and the techniques used to evaluate the quality of research must themselves be scrutinized. Often, what appears to be decision making that is informed by high-quality research is nothing of the sort. In her contribution, Eileen Gambrill discusses the emergence of evidence-based practice, increasingly referred to as evidence-informed practice, and the way we integrate evidence of different kinds in making decisions. Specifically, she introduces

the process and philosophy of evidence-based practice, delineates the benefits of this model for both clients and practitioners including the integration of client characteristics and circumstances with current best evidence, and suggests potential barriers to its effective implementation such as lack of attention to systemic processes (e.g., organizational cultures that promote authoritarian decision making styles). Emphasis is placed on professionals engaging in lifelong learning pursuits, the importance of attending to evidentiary, application and ethical issues, and challenging the historic divisions among researchers, practitioners, policymakers, and clients.

Julia Littell's contribution follows, providing a comprehensive overview of systematic reviews. Evidence-informed practitioners who gain a critical awareness of this methodology and its application are likely to circumvent many of the biases inherent to research searches. This chapter also invites practitioners to adopt an attitude that honors transparency and critique as essential components of effective research. To emphasize this skill, Littell provides a thorough critique of the evidence supporting multisystemic therapy, an intervention often lauded as one of the primary evidence-based interventions for working with juvenile offender populations. Littell articulates how evidence can be misused and offers rigorous procedures for establishing the quality of studies.

3

Providing More Effective, Ethical Services: The Philosophy and Process of Evidence-Based (-Informed) Practice

Eileen Gambrill

The process and philosophy of evidence-informed practice offer guidelines that can help us to make well-informed, ethical decisions and to identify obstacles to effective services. This is a process for handling the uncertainties regarding decisions that must be made in all related venues in an ethical, transparent manner (Chalmers, 2004). A willingness to acknowledge that "I don't know," combined with taking steps to see if needed information is available, increase the likelihood that important uncertainties are identified and decreased (Chalmers, 2004). This helps us to honor ethical obligations to involve clients as informed participants (Katz, 2002). Critical thinking is integral to this process. In both critical thinking and evidence-informed practice, attention is given to ethical issues and to the evidentiary status of knowledge claims. Both critical thinking and evidence-informed practice require a willingness to acknowledge the gaps between our present knowledge and skills and what is needed to make informed decisions.

WHAT IS EVIDENCE-BASED (-INFORMED) PRACTICE AND CARE?

Descriptions of evidence-based practice (EBP) differ greatly in their breadth and attention to ethical issues ranging from the broad, systemic philosophy and related evolving process envisioned by its originators, as described in original sources (e.g., Gray, 2001a; Sackett, Straus, Richardson, Rosenberg, & Haynes, 2000; Straus, Richardson, Glasziou, & Haynes, 2005), to narrow, fragmented views and total distortions. Views of EBP are promoted that ignore the ethical hallmarks of EBP, such as involving clients as informed participants. Given the many different views of EBP in the literature, it is important to review the vision of EBP and health care as described by its creators. Otherwise, potential benefits to clients and professionals may be lost (Gambrill, 2006). EBP involves the "conscientious, explicit and judicious use of current best evidence in making decisions about the care of individual [clients]." It involves "the integration of best research evidence with clinical expertise and [client] values" (Sackett et al., 2000, p. 1). Recently, more attention has been given to the gap between client actions and their stated preferences because what clients do (e.g., carry out agreed-on tasks or not) so often differs from their stated preferences, and helper estimates of participation are as likely to be inaccurate as accurate (Haynes, Devereaux, & Guyatt, 2002). (See Figure 3.1.) It is assumed that professionals often need information to make important decisions, for example, concerning risk assessment or what services are most likely to help clients attain outcomes they value.

Evidence-informed decision making arose as an alternative to authority-based decision making in which criteria such as consensus, anecdotal experience, or tradition are relied on. It describes a philosophy and an evolving process designed to forward effective use of professional judgment in integrating information regarding each client's unique characteristics, circumstances, preferences, and actions with external research findings. "It is a guide for thinking about how decisions should be made" (Haynes, Devereaux, & Guyatt, 2002, p. 2). Gray (2001a) contends that important decision-making failures occur when evidence is not used: "(1) ineffective interventions are introduced; (2) interventions that do more harm than good are introduced; (3) interventions that do more good than harm are not introduced; and (4) interventions that are ineffective or do more harm than good are not discontinued" (p. 354).

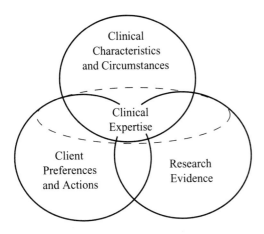

FIGURE 3.1 An Updated Model for Evidence-Based Decisions
Source: Haynes, R. B., Devereaux, P. J., & Guyatt, G. H. (2002). Clinical expertise in the era of evidence-based medicine and patient choice. *Evidence-Based Medicine*, 7, 36–38.

Clinical expertise includes the use of effective relationship skills and the experience of individual helpers to rapidly identify each client's unique circumstances, characteristics, and "their individual risks and benefits of potential interventions and their personal values and expectations" (Sackett et al., 2000, p. 1). Using clinical expertise, practitioners integrate information about a client's unique characteristics and circumstances with external research findings, clients' expectations and values, and their preferences and actions (Sackett et al., 1997; Haynes, Devereaux, & Guyatt, 2002). *Client values* refer to "the unique preferences, concerns and expectations each [client] brings to a clinical encounter and which must be integrated into clinical decisions if they are to serve the [client]" (Sackett et al., 2000, p. 1). "Evidence-Based Practice (EBP) requires that decisions about health [or social] care are based on the best available, current, valid and relevant evidence" (Dawes et al., 2005, p. 2).

EBP describes a process and a new professional education format (problem-based learning) designed to help practitioners to link evidentiary, ethical, and application issues. Professional codes of ethics call for key characteristics of evidence-informed practice, such as drawing on practice/policy-related research and involving clients as informed participants. Although its philosophical roots are old, the blooming of EBP as a process attending to evidentiary, ethical, and application issues in all professional venues (education, practice/policy, and research) is fairly recent, facilitated by the Internet revolution. It is designed to break down the divisions among research, practice, and policy—highlighting the importance of honoring ethical obligations. Although misleading because of the incorrect assumption that EBP means only that decisions are based on information regarding effectiveness, use of the term does call attention to the fact that available evidence may not be used or the current state of ignorance shared with clients. It is hoped that professionals who consider related research findings regarding decisions and who inform clients about them will provide more effective and ethical care than those relying on authority-based criteria such as anecdotal experience, tradition, or popularity. The following example illustrates reliance on authority-based criteria for selection of services:

Mr. Davis read an editorial that described the DARE program as very effective in decreasing drug use.

No related empirical literature was referred to. He suggested to his agency that it use this method.

In this example, the authority of an author of an editorial is appealed to. Evidence-informed decision making involves the use of quite different criteria; a key one is information about the accuracy of claims. Are DARE (Drug Abuse Resistance Education) programs effective? EBP draws on the results of systematic, rigorous, critical appraisals of research related to different kinds of practice questions such as: Is this assessment measure valid? Does this intervention do more good than harm? For example, review groups in the Cochrane (www.cochrane.org) and Campbell (www.campbellcollaboration.org) collaborations prepare comprehensive, rigorous reviews of all research related to a question.

Three Philosophies of Evidence-Informed Practice

Evidence-informed practice and social care involve a philosophy of ethics of professional practice and related enterprises, such as research and scholarly writing, a philosophy of science (epistemology: views about what knowledge is and how it can be gained), and a philosophy of technology. *Ethics* involves decisions regarding how and when to act; it involves standards of conduct. *Epistemology* involves views about knowledge and how to get it or if we can. The philosophy of *technology* concerns questions such as: Should we develop technology? What values should we draw on to decide what to develop? Should we examine the consequences of a given technology? Evidence-informed practice emphasizes the importance of critically appraising research and developing a technology to help clinicians to do so; "the leading figures in EBM . . . emphasized that clinicians had to use their scientific training and their judgment to interpret [guidelines] and individualize care accordingly" (Gray, 2001b, p. 26). It offers practitioners and administrators a philosophy that is compatible with the obligations described in professional codes of ethics and accreditation policies and standards (e.g., for informed consent and to draw on practice- and policy-related research findings) and an evolving technology for integrating evidentiary, ethical, and practical issues. Related literature highlights the interconnections among these concerns and suggests specific steps (a technology) to decrease gaps among them in all professional venues, including practice and policy (e.g., drawing on related research), research (e.g., preparing systematic reviews and clearly describing the limitations of studies), and professional education (e.g., exploring the value of problem-based learning in developing lifelong learners).

The uncertainty associated with decisions is acknowledged, not hidden. Evidence-informed practice requires considering research findings related to important practice/policy decisions and sharing what is found (including nothing) with clients. Transparency and honesty regarding the evidentiary status of services is a hallmark of this philosophy. For example, on the back cover of the seventh edition of *Clinical Evidence* (2002), a continually updated book distributed to physicians, it states that "it provides a concise account of the current state of knowledge, ignorance, and uncertainty about the prevention and treatment of a wide range of clinical conditions." In what books describing social work interventions do we find such a statement?

Steps in Evidence-Based Practice

Steps in evidence-based practice include the following:

1. converting information needs related to practice decisions into answerable questions;
2. tracking down, with maximum efficiency, the best evidence with which to answer them;
3. critically appraising that evidence for its validity, impact (size of effect), and applicability (usefulness in practice);
4. integrating this critical appraisal with our clinical expertise and with our (client's) unique circumstances and characteristics, including their values; and
5. evaluating our effectiveness and efficiency in carrying out steps 1–4 and seeking ways to improve them in the future. (Sackett et al., 2000, pp. 3–4)

Evidence-informed practitioners take advantage of efficient technology for conducting electronic searches to locate the current best evidence regarding a specific question; information literacy and retrievability is emphasized (Gray, 2001a). The former includes recognizing when information is needed, knowing how to get it, and developing and using lifelong learning skills. Different questions require different kinds of research methods to critically appraise proposed assumptions (e.g., Greenhalgh, 2006; Guyatt & Rennie, 2002; Sackett et al., 2000). These differences are reflected in the use of different "quality filters" to search for research findings related to a question. Thus, it is not true, as some have claimed, that only randomized controlled trials are considered of value. Kinds of questions include the following:

- *Effectiveness*: Do job training programs help clients to get and maintain jobs?
- *Prevention*: Do Head Start programs prevent school dropout?
- *Screening (risk/prognosis)*: How predictive is this risk assessment instrument?
- *Description/assessment*: Does self-report or observation of parent-child interaction provide the most accurate description of exchanges?
- *Harm*: Will community screening programs for depression do more harm than good?
- *Cost*: How much does one parent-training program cost compared to another?
- *Practice guidelines*: Are these practice guidelines for treatment of substance abuse applicable to my client?
- *Self-development*: Am I asking any well-structured questions at all? Am I keeping up-to-date with research findings related to questions that arise frequently?

Different Styles of Evidence-Based Practice

Sackett and his colleagues (2000) distinguish among three different styles of EBP, all of which require integrating evidence with the unique characteristics of a client's personal and environmental circumstances. All require step 4 (see prior list of steps in EBP), but they vary in how other steps are carried out. They suggest that for problems encountered on an everyday basis, you should invest the time and energy necessary to carry out both searching and critical appraisal of reports found. For level 2 (problems encountered less often), they suggest that you seek out critical appraisals already prepared by others who describe and use explicit criteria for deciding what research they select and how they decide whether it is valid. Here, step 3 can be omitted and step 2 restricted to sources that have already undergone critical appraisal. A third style applies to problems encountered very infrequently in which we "blindly seek, accept, and apply the recommendations we receive from authorities" (p. 5). As they note, the trouble with this mode is that it is "blind" to whether the advice received from the experts "is authoritative (evidence-based, resulting from their operating in the 'appraising' mode) or merely authoritarian (opinion-based, resulting from pride and prejudice)" (p. 5). One clue they suggest to distinguish which style is being used is uncritical reporting with a reluctance to describe what is in the documentation. Lack of time may result in using style 2 with most problems.

Origins of EBP

EBP and health care originated in medicine in part because of variations in services offered and their outcomes (Wennberg, 2002). Variations in services naturally raise questions such as: Are they of equal effectiveness? Do some cause harm? There were gaps among ethical, evidentiary, and application concerns. Consider the gaps between obligations described in the Code of Ethics of the National Association of Social Workers (1999) and everyday practice regarding informed consent, self-determination, empowerment, and drawing on practice/policy-related research. Literature in social work suggests that social workers do not draw on practice-related research findings to inform practice decisions (e.g., Rosen, Proctor, Morrow-Howell, & Staudt, 1995). Sheldon and Chilvers (2001) found that 18% of social workers surveyed had read nothing related to practice within the last 6 months (N = 2,285).

Not keeping up with new research findings related to important practice decisions renders knowledge increasingly out of date. As a result, decisions may be made that harm rather than help clients (Evans, Thornton, & Chalmers, 2006). If professionals are not familiar with the evidentiary status of alternative practices and policies, they cannot pass this information on to their clients; they cannot honor informed-consent obligations. If some alternatives are effective in attaining outcomes that clients value and practice proceeds based on ignorance of this information, clients are deprived of opportunities to achieve hoped-for outcomes. Currently, the gaps between what research suggests is effective and what services are provided are hidden. For example, rarely do we compare services offered by an agency, such as parent-training programs, and what research suggests is effective and disseminate this information to all involved parties. Clients are typically not informed that recommended services are of unknown effectiveness, or have been found to be ineffective or harmful. Yet another origin of EBP was increased attention to harming in the name of helping. The history of the helping professions shows that some common practices thought to help people were later found to harm them (e.g., see Sharpe & Faden, 1998; Valenstein, 1986).

Limitations of traditional methods of knowledge dissemination were another origin of EBP (Gray, 2001b). There are gaps between the obligations of researchers to report limitations of research, to prepare rigorous reviews, and to accurately describe well-argued alternative views and what we find in published literature. Poor-quality research continues to appear in professional journals (Altman, 2002). Programs described as effective in books like *Evidence-Based Practices for Social Workers* (O'Hare, 2005), such as family preservation, have been found not to be effective (e.g., Lindsey, Martin, & Doh, 2002). Many reasons have been suggested for this, including the special interests of those who fund research, such as pharmaceutical companies (e.g., Angell, 2004; Moynihan & Cassells, 2005). A vested interest in maintaining funding or status and a lack of critical appraisal skills may result in research projects that cannot test the questions addressed, offering clients bogus services and forwarding human service propaganda (Jacobson, Foxx, & Mulick, 2005; Lilienfeld, Lynn, & Lohr, 2003).

We often find little match between the questions addressed and the use of methods that can critically test them together with hiding limitations and inflated claims of effectiveness. In discussing the origins of EBP, Gray (2001a) notes the increasing lack of confidence in data of potential use to clinicians: peer review, which he subtitles "feet of clay," along with flaws in books, editorials, and journal articles. Examples include submission bias, publication bias, methodological bias, abstract bias, and framing bias. Conclusions based on narrative reviews are often quite misleading. In his description of hyperclaiming (telling others that proposed research is likely to achieve goals that it will not) and causism (implying a causal relationship when none has been established), Rosenthal (1994) suggests, "Bad science makes for bad ethics" (p. 128). Chalmers (1990) argues that failure to accurately describe the research methods used is a form of scientific misconduct.

As Gray (2001b) notes, "The Internet stimulated the development of a number of software tools which allowed international organizations such as the Cochrane Collaboration to function effectively" (p. 25). The Cochrane Collaboration was created to prepare, maintain, and disseminate high-quality research reviews related to a specific practice/policy question. The recognition of limitations in narrative reviews of research related to practice questions encouraged the development of the systematic review for synthesizing research findings. Such reviews "state their objectives, review as much of the evidence as possible, use explicit quality criteria for inclusion or exclusion of studies found, use explicitly stated methods for combining data, produce reports which describe the processes of achievement, inclusion and exclusion, and combining data" (Gray, 2001b, p. 25). The Internet provides rapid access to practice- and policy-related research via special Web sites and Google searches. Use of methods such as Boolean terms (i.e., and/or) facilitate searches. The limitations of traditional forms of knowledge diffusion was a key reason for the decision to make the Cochrane database of systematic reviews electronic, with routine updating by review groups.

IMPLICATIONS OF THE PHILOSOPHY OF EVIDENCE-INFORMED PRACTICE AND CARE

The philosophy and related technology of evidence-informed practice and care have implications for all individuals and institutions involved with helping clients, including professional educators, researchers, practitioners, policy makers, administrators, and those who provide funding (Gambrill, 2006). Interrelated implications include focusing on client concerns and hoped-for outcomes, increased transparency and attention to ethical obligations, consideration of populations and individuals in the distribution of scarce resources, a systemic focus attending to multiple factors that influence decisions, maximizing the flow of knowledge and minimizing the flow of ignorance and propaganda, exploring the effectiveness of problem-based learning using the process of evidence-based practice in preparing helpers who are lifelong learners, testing of claims, and preparation of systematic reviews. Research, practice, and educational issues are closely intertwined. For example, poor-quality reviews of research related to practice and policy questions may result in bogus practice guidelines, which result in poor-quality services for clients. Hallmarks and implications are interrelated. For example, the promotion of transparency contributes to both knowledge flow and honoring ethical obligations.

Move Away from Authoritarian Practices and Policies

Indicators of the authority-based nature of social work include large gaps between what is said and what is done (e.g., the NASW Code of Ethics and current practices and policies, for example basing decisions on criteria such as consensus and tradition, lack of informed consent, and the censorship of certain kinds of knowledge, such as variations in services and their outcomes).

The key contribution of evidence-informed practice and policy is encouraging social work to move from an authority-based profession to one in which ethical obligations to clients and students are honored and the critical appraisal and honest brokering of knowledge and ignorance thrive. A preference for authoritarian beliefs and actions is by no means limited to clinicians. It flourishes among researchers, agency administrators, and academics as well. Examples include misrepresenting views, hiding limitations of research studies, ignoring counterevidence to preferred views and not involving clients and clinicians as informed participants in decisions made (e.g., about whether to use a certain practice guideline).

A striking characteristic of EBP and related developments is the extent to which clients are involved in many different ways (e.g., see Entwistle, Renfrew, Yearley, Forrester, & Lamont, 1998). One is reflected in the attention given to individual differences in client characteristics, circumstances, actions, values, and preferences in making decisions. A second is helping clients to develop critical appraisal skills. A third is encouraging client involvement in the design and critique of practice/policy-related research (e.g., Hanley, Truesdale, King, Elbourne, & Chalmers, 2001). A fourth is attending to outcomes that clients value, and a fifth is involving them as informed participants. A sixth is recognizing their unique knowledge in relation to application concerns.

Honor Ethical Obligations

Evidence-informed practice has ethical implications for practitioners and policy makers as well as for researchers and educators. Hallmarks include focusing on client concerns and hoped-for outcomes, attending to individual differences in client characteristics and circumstances, considering client values and expectations, and involving clients as informed participants in decision making (see prior list of steps). There has been much greater attention to ethical issues in the helping professions in recent years, spurred in part by the philosophy of evidence-informed practice (see, e.g., Leever, DeCiani, Mulaney, & Hasslinger, 2002). Although professional codes of ethics call on practitioners to inform clients regarding the risks and benefits of recommended services and alternatives, this is typically not done. Clients are misinformed or uninformed regarding the evidentiary status of services offered and/or are offered ineffective services. This does not promote service to clients nor social justice.

A concern for involving clients in making decisions that affect their lives highlights the importance of informed (in contrast to uninformed or misinformed) consent (Edwards, Elwyn, & Mulley, 2002; Katz, 2002). Staff should be required to complete an Evidence-Informed Client Choice Form (Entwistle, Sheldon, Sowden, & Watt, 1998) for each service recommended (see Figure 3.2). This describes the evidentiary status of the services used compared to the alternatives available as well as the track record of success of the agency to which the client is referred and the staff person in the agency who will see the client. Evidence-informed practice involves sharing responsibility for decision making in a context of recognized uncertainty. Ignoring practice- and policy-related research findings and forwarding bogus claims of effectiveness violate our obligation to provide informed consent and may result in wasting money on ineffective services, harming clients in the name of helping them, and forgoing opportunities to attain hoped-for outcomes.

What are our responsibilities when we have a job but not the tools to carry it out and the results of our work affect others, especially in contexts in which we claim that our mission is to help clients? Can we simply abandon our responsibility? Such questions regarding the ethics of excuses have not received enough attention (for exceptions, see McDowell, 2000; Pope & Vasquez, 2007). If they honor their codes of ethics, professionals cannot remain silent in the face of avoidable suffering. They cannot turn a blind eye to clients' needs. They cannot become fellow travelers in a system that harms clients. They cannot succumb to becoming callous to others' suffering (e.g., see Bandura, 1999). They cannot simply say "I didn't know" (when they could have known or did know) or that "others do the same." They cannot simply say they have "compassion fatigue" and offer clients shoddy services. They cannot abandon their responsibility to honor their codes of ethics by offering unjustified excuses (McDowell, 2000). They are bound by their codes of ethics to resist such hardening of their hearts. Professionals must agitate, advocate, blow the whistle on ineffective services, and organize to protest deficient services that harm children and families. Guyatt and Rennie (2002) emphasize that evidence-based practitioners should advocate to alter conditions such as poverty that create health problems (p. 9). Professional education programs are obligated to help students avoid questionable excuses and deal ethically with the burden of "seeing." This has long been a topic of concern in medicine: how to do one's job without becoming overcome by others' suffering or becoming callous (e.g., Cassell, 1991).

Make Practices, Policies, and Their Outcomes Transparent

Evidence-informed practice encourages transparency of what is done to what effect in all venues, including practice and policy, research, administration, and professional education (see also the section on honoring ethical obligations). Ignorance and uncertainty are recognized rather than hidden. Transparency will reveal the extent to which ethical obligations are met, such as involving clients as informed participants. Consider parent-training programs. Most parents alleged to have maltreated their children are referred to parent-training programs. In how many cases is there an individualized assessment that permits tailoring of training as needed? In our exploratory work regarding parent-training pro-

---

Agency: _____   Date: _____

Client: _____

Referral agency: _____   _____

Service to be offered: _____

Staff member in this agency who will offer program: _____

A. Related External Research

____ 1. Research shows that this program will help people like me to attain hoped-for outcomes.

____ 2. This program has never been rigorously tested in relation to hoped-for outcomes.

____ 3. Research shows that other programs have been critically tested and found to help people like me attain hoped-for outcomes.

____ 4. Research shows that this program is likely to have harmful effects (e.g., decrease hoped-for outcomes).

B. Agency's Background Regarding Use of This Method

____ 1. The agency to which I have been referred has a track record of success in using this program with people like me.

____ 2. The staff member who will work with me has a track record of success in using this method with people like me.

FIGURE 3.2 Evidence-Informed Client Choice Form
Source: See, for example, Entwistle, V. A., et al. (1998). Evidence-informed patient choice. *International Journal of Technology Assessment in Health Care, 14,* 212–215.

grams (Gambrill & Goldman, 2004), there was no individualized assessment. Nor were parents given required information to make an informed decision regarding the selection of a program; they were given a list and told to choose one. They received no information regarding the evidentiary status of the programs listed. A detailed review of the offered programs showed that they did not include components likely to maximize the possibility of hoped-for outcomes. Does this kind of service honor the ethical obligations of professionals?

Evidence-informed practice will highlight the uncertainty associated with decisions as well as the opportunity costs of choices made; whenever we decide to provide one kind of service, there is less money for other services. It will reveal services that are ineffective, allowing a more judicious distribution of scarce resources (see Eddy, 1994a, 1994b). And it will not promote impossible goals such as "ensuring" that no children in protective care will be harmed. This call for transparency, so key to the process and philosophy of evidence-informed practice, is no doubt the reason that narrow views of EBP are favored—so authority-based practices and policies can continue undisturbed.

Evidence-informed practice emphasizes the importance of accurately describing the evidentiary status of assessment, intervention, and evaluation methods. If a variety of services is used to pursue a certain outcome, questions naturally arise, such as: Are they of equal cost and effectiveness? There is candor and clarity in place of secrecy and obscurity. These characteristics are at odds with authority-based practice (Chalmers, 1983). Increased transparency will highlight gaps between the resources needed to attain certain outcomes as suggested by related research and what is used. Hopefully, this will encourage advocacy on the part of clients and professionals for the resources required to offer services with a track record of success. It will reveal gaps between the causes of client problems (e.g., poverty) and the interventions used and promoted as having value. We should prepare books similar to *A Guide to Effective Care in Pregnancy and Childbirth* by Enkin, Keirse, Renfrew, and Neilson (1995), which describes the evidentiary status of each service used in child welfare settings using the following categories:

1. Beneficial forms of care. Effectiveness demonstrated by clear evidence from controlled trials (p. 391).

2. Forms of care likely to be beneficial. The evidence in favor of these forms of care is not as [firm] as for those in category 1 (p. 394).
3. Forms of care with a trade-off between beneficial and adverse effects. [Clients] should weigh these effects according to individual circumstances and priorities (p. 400).
4. Forms of care of unknown effectiveness. There are insufficient or inadequate quality data upon which to base a recommendation for practice (p. 402).
5. Forms of care unlikely to be beneficial. The evidence against these forms of care is not as [firm] as for those in category 6 (p. 406).
6. Forms of care likely to be ineffective or harmful. Ineffectiveness or harm is demonstrated by clear evidence (p. 410).

Child welfare staff should take a much more proactive stance regarding the quality of services purchased. Agencies should describe the gaps between what is needed to pursue hoped-for outcomes and what is offered. They should take a central role in revealing related information to all involved parties, including clients, in order to advocate for services to be purchased on evidentiary grounds rather than on criteria such as availability, tradition, or popularity. The use of computerized case records allows for the capture of this information. Related data could be provided to clients in waiting rooms. Child welfare agencies should keep track of the kinds of problems families confront and the services offered to address these, compare services offered with what research suggests is most effective, and distribute this information in clear language to all involved parties, including clients. Brochures should describe the evidentiary status of services offered and alternatives that have been critically tested and found to be effective. That is, clients should be accurately informed concerning the evidentiary status of services provided (see Figure 3.2).

Increased transparency discourages propagandistic ploys that hide what is done and to what effect. It also has implications for the conduct, reporting, and dissemination of research findings. It calls for candid descriptions of the limitations of research studies and the use of research methods that critically test questions asked. It calls for systematic research reviews (Oxman & Guyatt, 1993) that candidly acknowledge methodological flaws (e.g., MacCoun, 1998). A key contribution is discouraging inflated claims of knowledge that mislead involved parties. Consider terms such as "well established" and "validated," which convey a certainty that is not possible. For example, a report from the Milbank Memorial Fund (Lehman et al., 2004) and many other sources describe multisystemic therapy as an evidence-based practice. Is there evidence that it is effective? Controversies regarding this question are highlighted by a recent series of articles regarding the effectiveness of multisystemic therapy (e.g., Henggeler, Schoenwald, Borduin, & Swenson, 2006; Littell, 2006). Bogus claims hinder exploration and may result in harmful practices and policies.

Transparency requires accurate descriptions of well-argued alternative views and related evidence. The trend toward increased transparency is reflected in books such as *Controversial Therapies for Developmental Disabilities: Fad, Fashion, and Science in Professional Practice* (Jacobson, Foxx, & Mulick, 2005), *Sanctified Snake Oil* (Sarnoff, 2001), *Science and Pseudoscience in Clinical Psychology* (Lilienfeld, Lynn, & Lohr, 2003), *The Truth About Drug Companies: How They Deceive Us and What to Do About It* (Angell, 2004), and *Selling Sickness* (Moynihan & Cassells, 2005). We need such books in child welfare. Why is it usually the journalists who blow the whistle on gross missteps in child welfare? The reluctance of administrators to open their files (as in the state of New Jersey; see, for example, DePanfilis [2003]) so we can see what is going on is not acceptable.

Encourage a Systemic Approach for Integrating Practical, Ethical, and Evidentiary Issues

Evidence-informed practice describes a process designed to encourage integration of ethical, evidentiary, and application concerns. It involves a *systemic* approach to improving the quality of services, including (1) efforts to educate professionals who are lifelong learners, (2) efforts to encourage honesty (accurate reporting) on the part of researchers, (3) involving clients as informed participants in decisions made, (4) attending to management practices and policies that influence practice (e.g., evidence-based purchasing of services), and (5) attending to application challenges, including the implications of scarce resources. The literature describes a wide variety of efforts to address application concerns, including hiring knowledge inspectors whose job it is to maximize knowledge flow (Gray, 1998). Other examples include:

- the development of strategies for efficiently tracking down and appraising evidence for its validity and relevance;
- the creation of systematic reviews and concise summaries of the effects of health care (illustrated by the Cochrane and Campbell Collaboration databases);
- the creation of evidence-based journals of secondary publications (e.g., the journal *Evidence-Based Mental Health*);
- the creation of information systems for bringing the foregoing to us in seconds (e.g., electronic decision databases); and
- the identification and application of effective strategies for lifelong learning and for improving our clinical performance (e.g., see Gray, 2001a; Straus et al., 2005).

The quality of services is unlikely to improve in a fragmented approach, that is, without attending to *all* links in the system of service provision. Evidence-informed practice encourages the creation of tools and training programs designed to develop and encourage use of critical appraisal skills, such as the Critical Appraisal Skills Program (CASP).

Maximize Knowledge Flow

Evidence-informed practice and social care are designed to maximize knowledge flow. In a culture in which knowledge flow is free, claims are challenged and challenges are welcomed. Evidence-informed decision making emphasizes the importance of integrating research and practice, and its advocates have actively pursued the development of a technology and political base to encourage this, for example, involving clients in the design and interpretation of research (Hanley et al., 2002). Gray (2001a) suggests that evidence-informed organizations should include systems that are capable of providing evidence and promoting its use, including both explicit (created by researchers) and tacit (created by clinicians, clients, and managers) evidence. Clinicians and clients are involved as informed participants; there is no privileged knowledge in the sense of not sharing information about the evidentiary status of recommended methods. Benefits of a free, efficient knowledge market include:

1. increased knowledge through critical testing of knowledge claims;

2. increased staff morale because decisions will be more informed, staff will be rewarded for sharing knowledge, and staff will be free to discuss their concerns and to learn from their colleagues and others throughout the world;
3. increase in the ratio of informed to uninformed or misinformed decisions; and
4. recognition of uncertainty and ignorance (which are often swept under the rug, and staff may be blamed for not acting on knowledge that, in fact, does not, or did not, exist).

Exploration of ways to diffuse and disseminate knowledge is key to maximizing knowledge flow, and the literature on EBP is rich in the variety of efforts described (e.g., Greenhalgh et al., 2004). Identifying errors and related factors and using this information to minimize avoidable mistakes in the future contribute to knowledge flow. We learn from our mistakes and we lose valuable learning opportunities by overlooking them. There is remarkably little study of accidents and mistakes in social work (for an exception, see Munro, 1996). Research regarding errors in medicine shows that systemic causes, such as the quality of staff training and agency policy, contribute to errors made by helpers (e.g., Reason, 2001).

OBJECTIONS TO EVIDENCE-INFORMED PRACTICE

Some objections to evidence-informed practice result from misunderstandings and misrepresentations of EBP, such as claiming that only RTCs (randomized controlled trials) are of interest. Straus and McAlister (2000) suggest that some limitations of EBP are universal in helping efforts, such as lack of scientific evidence related to decisions and challenges in applying research to the care of individuals. Barriers they suggest include the need to develop new skills (e.g., consider the predictive validity of risk assessment measures) and limited funds and resources (see also Gibbs & Gambrill, 2002; Oxman & Flottorp, 1998; Regehr, Stern, & Shlonsky, 2007). Many challenges confront helpers who want to practice in an evidence-informed manner, such as gaining access to research findings related to important questions and critically appraising this knowledge in a timely manner.

CONTROVERSIES REGARDING EVIDENCE

A key way in which views of evidence-informed practice differ is in the degree of rigor in evaluating knowledge claims. Both the origins of evidence-informed practice and objections to it reflect different views of "evidence." When do we have enough to recommend a practice method? Do criteria for having "enough" differ in relation to different kinds of decisions? Such differences are illustrated by the different conclusions concerning the effectiveness of multisystemic therapy (Henggeler et al., 2006; Littell, 2006). Is it valuable to prepare reviews that encompass all community interventions? Is it misleading to mislabel unsystematic reviews as systematic? For example, a review by Ohmer and Korr (2006), referred to as "a systematic review" (p. 132), does not provide any information about effect sizes. Criteria described in widely available guidelines, such as the CONSORT (Consolidated Standards of Reporting Trials) statement (Altman et al., 2001) and the QUOROM (Quality of Reporting of Meta-analyses) statement (Moher et al., 2000), were not used. The authors state that rater reliability was calculated, but such data are not reported.

Concerns about inflated claims of effectiveness based on biased research studies were a key reason for the origin of evidence-informed practice in health care, as discussed earlier. Inflated claims obscure uncertainties that may, if shared, influence client decisions. There are many kinds of evidence. Davies (2004) suggests that a broad view of evidence is needed to review policies, including (1) experience and expertise, (2) judgment, (3) resources, (4) values, (5) habits and traditions, (6) lobbyists and pressure groups, and (7) pragmatics and contingencies. He suggests that we should consider all of these factors in making decisions about whether or not to implement a policy. He describes six kinds of research related to evidence of policy impact: (1) implementation evidence, (2) descriptive analytical evidence, (3) attitudinal evidence, (4) statistical modeling, (5) economic/econometric evidence, and (6) ethical evidence.

BARRIERS TO EVIDENCE-INFORMED PRACTICE

There are formidable barriers to encouraging evidence-informed practices and policies (see Figure 3.3). These include the characteristics of the practice environment, such as financial disincentives, organizational constraints, and client values and expectancies (Oxman & Flottorp, 1998). Obstacles such as organizational barriers may be so severe that Sackett and his colleagues (2000) refer to them as "Killer Bs." Prevailing opinion may be an obstacle, for example, influence by standards of practice, opinion leaders, professional education, and advocacy (for example, by pharmaceutical companies). Other sources suggested by Oxman and Flottorp (1998) include knowledge and attitudes about uncertainty, feelings of incompetence regarding new practices, the need to act, and information overload. Some people may be absorbed in their own lives and care little about clients. Another factor is inertia. Yet another is a reluctance to raise questions about questionable practices and policies because of fear of negative reactions.

Environmental obstacles include vested interests in current arrangements and related contingencies, limited resources, and preferred ideologies. Staff may be afraid to question authorities who are not interested in developing a culture of thoughtfulness. A residual system that pretends to be more, seems to generate a variety of ritualistic activities designed to give the illusion of benefits to children and their families, such as documentation requirements and surveillance schemes that may do more harm than good (e.g., see Lindsey, 2004; Parton, 2006). These rituals are designed to maintain the illusion that we care and are helping. They are an unacceptable substitute for revealing gaps between what is needed and what is offered to all involved parties. Some have argued that the presence of some talk shows, which air controversy, serves as a token designed to give the illusion that open debate thrives and bad practices are being rooted out. Is this the sad function of scholars such as Lindsey and Pelton: to be token whistle-blowers, to give the illusion that we care, that something is being done?

Professional education formats and content pose another obstacle. They do not help students to acquire skills in the process of evidence-informed practice. For an alternative educational format, see descriptions of problem-based learning (e.g., Straus et al., 2005). Those who provide workshops gain money or status. But do they help clients? Inflated claims of effectiveness abound in the professional literature (Kluger, Alexander, & Curtis, 2002). Those who care about clients do not promote practices and policies of dubious effectiveness. They do not proclaim that child welfare services are good when research illustrates they are

poor (Wilson & Alexandra, 2005). These tendencies emphasize the vital importance of involving clients in the quest for evidence-informed services.

ALTERNATIVES TO THE PROCESS AND PHILOSOPHY OF EVIDENCE-INFORMED PRACTICE

Given that evidence-informed practice as described here is not the norm today, it is clear that alternatives, such as relying on good intentions, are popular. The most popular view of EBP is of using evidence-based practices (e.g., using practice guidelines or "best practices"). This ignores the process and philosophy of EBP as well as constraints, such as local resources, individual characteristics, and the circumstances of clients. Critics of practice guidelines and treatment manuals argue that a particular guideline may not match the needs of multiproblem clients (for example, see Norcross, Beutler, & Levant, 2006). Yet another alternative is to make cosmetic changes, for example, simply relabel practice-as-usual as evidence-based.

As more clearinghouses and organizations are developed that include in their titles "evidence-based practice and policy," there are more opportunities to promote a narrow, top-down view of evidence-based practice and policy that is quite different than the systemic, participatory view described by its originators. For example, the recently established Clearinghouse on Evidence-Based Child Welfare Practice in California (Wilson & Alexandra, 2005) published a hierarchy of evidence that is likely to hide ineffective and harmful methods. Here, a group of researchers will decide what questions to address. This is quite different from the participatory, democratic philosophy of evidence-informed practice described in original sources. It is the clients and the practitioners at the direct-line level who know what questions arise most often and who are familiar with local obstacles. We will benefit from reading original sources describing evidence-based practice rather than secondary sources, which often distort or hide the unique process and philosophy of evidence-informed practice and policy.

CONCLUSION

Our ethical obligations to clients require us to be "conscientious, explicit and judicious" (Sackett et al.,

1. Misunderstandings and misrepresentations of EBP (deprive us of a process and related tools for making informed decisions in real time).

2. Misunderstandings of science.

3. The task environment (e.g., competing goals, uncertainties, vested interests in current practices).

4. Lack of access to needed tools and knowledge.

5. A preference for authoritarian decision-making styles (e.g., reliance on unfounded authority, reluctance to involve clients as informed participants).

6. Reluctance to criticize authorities; poor skills for doing so in a constructive manner.

7. Flawed self-assessments (inflated views of our competence).

8. Cognitive biases, such as wishful thinking, overconfidence, and confirmation biases (looking only for data that support our preferred views).

9. Underestimating our gullibility; lack of knowledge about propaganda strategies and their prevalence and consequences in the helping professions and related industries.

10. Ignoring ethical obligations of professionals (e.g., for informed consent).

11. Professional educational formats that do not provide opportunities to "educate our intuition" (Hogarth, 2001), to learn via corrective feedback.

12. Confusing good intentions with good outcomes.

13. Lack of empathy for clients.

14. Current standards of practice and opinion leaders who encourage use of untested methods (Oxman & Flottorp, 1998).

15. Appeal to questionable excuses for poor-quality services (McDowell, 2002).

16. Pressures on helpers to help and hopes of clients to be helped.

17. Invalid criteria used by professional organizations and licensing boards to evaluate competence.

18. Self-deception (fooling ourselves that we are helping when we are not).

FIGURE 3.3 Barriers to Evidence-Informed Practice

2000) in making decisions that affect clients' lives. To what extent will these hallmarks of evidence-informed practice be introduced into child welfare settings? Key choices that lie ahead include what view of evidence-informed practice and policy to forward: the broad systemic process and philosophy suggested by the originators of evidence-based practice, or a narrow view focusing on practice guidelines emphasizing a top-down approach in which administrators and researchers decide for staff and clients what is best. The choices made will reflect the different views of evidence-informed practice and policy that have been evident in the professional literature for some time (Gambrill, 2006). Our code of ethics provides direction. Honoring this would be welcome to all those who want to help clients and avoid harming them. It would not be welcomed by those who benefit from secrecy, from lack of transparency of what is done to what effect. We should clearly document the gaps and advertise these widely. We must make visible the gaps between what is needed and what is offered. Only then is change likely. Doing so would reveal that we are wasting money on services that are ineffective. For example, many parents are required to participate in parent-training programs, most of which are of questionable value (Barth, Landsverk, Chamberlain, Reid, Rolls, Hurlburt, et al., 2005; Gambrill & Goldman, 2004; for an alternative, see Budd, 2004; Hutchings, Bywater, Daley, et al., 2007).

Being a professional requires the courage to confront incompetence and quackery, fraud and corruption, which harm clients—including our own. Our code of ethics provides the grounds and, hopefully, the inspiration for taking action rather than abandoning responsibility. Professional education programs should help students to acquire the values, knowledge, and skills related to evidence-informed practice and policy. The National Association of Social Workers encourages its members to "stand up for others," even to wear a "Stand Up" wristband as a symbol of that commitment (NASW News, January 2006, p. 11). Let's make this symbol meaningful by related actions. If we do, the bleak prospect for public child welfare forecast by Alvin Schorr (2005) may turn out to be much brighter.

References

Altman, D. G. (2002). Poor-quality medical research: What can journals do? *Journal of the American Medical Association, 287,* 2765–2767.

Angell, M. (2004). *The truth about drug companies: How they deceive us and what to do about it.* New York: Random House.

Arendt, H. (1968). *The origins of totalitarianism.* San Diego, CA: Harcourt Brace Jovanovich.

Bandura, A. (1999). Moral disengagement in the perpetration of inhumanities. *Personality and Social Psychology Review, 3,* 193–209.

Barth, R. P., Landsverk, J., Chamberlain, P., Reid, J., Rolls, J., Hurlburt, M., et al. (2005). Parent-training in child welfare services: Planning for a more evidence-based approach to serving biological parents. *Research on Social Work Practice, 15,* 353–371.

Budd, K. S., Poindexter, L. M., Feliz, E. D., & Naik-Polan, A. T. (2001). Clinical assessment of parents in child protection cases: An empirical analysis. *Law and Human Behavior, 25,* 93–108.

Cassell, E. J. (1991). *The nature of suffering and the goals of medicine.* New York: Oxford University Press.

Chalmers, I. (1983). Scientific inquiry and authoritarianism in perinatal care and education. *Birth, 10,* 151–166.

Chalmers, I. (1990). Underreporting research limitations is scientific misconduct. *Journal of American Medical Association, 263,* 1405–1408.

Chalmers, I. (2003). Trying to do more good than harm in policy and practice: The role of rigorous, transparent, up-to-date evaluations. *Annals of the American Academy of Political and Social Science, 589,* 22–40.

Chalmers, I. (2004). Well informed uncertainties about the effects of treatment. *British Medical Journal, 328,* 475–476.

Clinical evidence: The international source of the best available evidence for effective health care. (2002, June). 7th issue. BMJ Publishing Group

Davies, P. (2004, Feb. 19). Is evidence-based government possible? Jerry Lee Lecture, 4th Annual Campbell Collaboration Colloquium, Washington, DC.

Dawes, M., Summerskill, W., Glasziou, P., Cartabellotta, A., Martin, J., Hopayian, K., Porzsolt, F., Burls, A., & Osborne, J. (2005). Sicily statement on evidence-based practice. *BioMed Central Medical Education, 5,* 1.

DePanfilis, D. (2003). *Review of IAIU investigations of suspected child abuse and neglect in DYFS out-of-home care settings in New Jersey.* Final Report. Baltimore School of Social Work. College Park: University of Maryland.

Eddy, D. M. (1994a). Principles for making difficult decisions in difficult times. *Journal of the American Medical Association, 271,* 1792–1798.

Eddy D. M. (1994b). Rationing resources while improving quality. *Journal of the American Medical Association, 272,* 817–824.

Edwards, A., Elwyn, G., & Mulley, A. (2002). Explaining risks: Turning numerical data into meaningful pictures. *British Medical Journal, 324,* 827–830.

Enkin, M., Keirse, M. J. N., Renfrew, M. J., & Neilson, J. P. (1995). *A guide to effective care in pregnancy and childbirth* (2nd ed.). New York: Oxford University Press.

Entwistle, V. A., Sheldon, T. A., Sowden, A. J., & Watt, I. A. (1998). Evidence-informed patient choice.

International Journal of Technology Assessment in Health Care, 14, 212–215.

Evans, I., Thornton, H., & Chalmers, I. (2006). Testing treatments: Better research for better healthcare. London: British Library, published by Athenaeum Press.

Gambrill, E. (2006). Evidence-based practice and policy: Choices ahead. *Research on Social Work Practice, 16*(3), 338–357.

Gambrill, E., & Goldman, R. (2004). *Quality of parent training programs offered to child welfare clients: An exploratory study.* Unpublished manuscript, School of Social Welfare, University of California, Berkeley.

Gibbs, L., & Gambrill, E. (2002). Evidence-based practice: Counterarguments to objections. *Research on Social Work Practice, 12,* 452–476.

Giustini, D. (2005). How Google is changing medicine. *British Medical Journal, 331,* 1487–1488.

Gray, J. A. M. (1997). *Evidence-based health care: How to make health policy and management decisions.* New York: Churchill Livingstone.

Gray, J. A. M. (1998). Where is the chief knowledge officer? *British Medical Journal, 317,* 832.

Gray, J. A. M. (2001a). *Evidence-based health care: How to make health policy and management decisions* (2nd ed.). New York: Churchill Livingstone.

Gray, J. A. M. (2001b). Evidence-based medicine for professional. In A. Edwards & G. Elwyn (Eds.), *Evidence-based patient choice: Inevitable or impossible?* (pp. 19–33). New York: Oxford University Press.

Greenhalgh, T. (2006). *How to read a paper; the basics of evidence-based medicine* (3rd ed.). Malden, MA: Blackwell.

Guyatt, G. H., & Rennie, D. (2002). *Users' guides to the medical literature: A manual for evidence-based clinical practice.* Chicago: American Medical Association.

Hanley, B., Truesdale, A., King, A., Elbourne, D., & Chalmers, I. (2001). Involving consumers in designing, conducting, and interpreting randomized control trials: Questionnaire survey. *British Medical Journal, 322,* 519–523.

Haynes, R. B., Devereaux, P. J., & Guyatt, G. H. (2002). Clinical expertise in the era of evidence-based medicine and patient choice. *Evidence-Based Medicine, 7,* 36–38.

Henggeler, S. W., Schoenwald, S. K., Borduin, C. M., & Swenson, C. C. (2006). Methodological critique and meta analysis as Trojan horse. *Children and Youth Services Review, 28,* 447–457.

Hutchings, J., Bywater, T., Daley, D., Gardner, F., Whitaker, C., Jones, K., Eames, C., & Edwards, R. T. (2007). Parenting intervention in Sure Start services for children at risk of developing conduct disorder: Pragmatic randomized controlled trial. *British Medical Journal, 334,* 678.

Jacobson, J. W., Foxx, R. M., & Mulick, J. A. (Eds.). (2005). *Controversial therapies for developmental disabilities: Fad, fashion, and science in professional practice.* Mahwah, NJ: Erlbaum.

Katz, J. (2002). *The silent world of doctor and patient.* Baltimore, MD: Johns Hopkins University Press.

Kluger, M. P., Alexander, G., & Curtis, P. A. (2002). *What works in child welfare.* Washington, DC: Child Welfare League of America Press.

Lacasse, J. R., & Gomory, T. (2003). Is graduate social work education promoting a critical approach to mental health practice? *Journal of Social Work Education, 39,* 383–408.

Leever, M., DeCiani, G., Mulaney, E., & Hasslinger, H., with Gambrill, E. (2002). *Ethical child welfare practice.* Washington, DC: Child Welfare League of America Press.

Lehman, A. F., Goldman, H. H., Dixon, L. B., & Churchill, R. (2004). *Evidence-based mental health treatments and services: Examples to inform public policy.* New York: Milbank Memorial Fund.

Lilienfeld, S. O., Lynn, S. J., & Lohr, J. M. (2003). *Science and pseudoscience in clinical psychology.* New York: Guilford.

Lindsey, D. (2004). *The welfare of children* (2nd ed.). New York: Oxford University Press.

Lindsey, D., Martin, S., & Doh, J. (2002). The failure of intensive casework services to reduce foster care placements: An examination of family preservation studies. *Children and Youth Services Review, 24,* 743–775.

Littell, J. (2006). The case for multisystemic therapy: Evidence or orthodoxy? *Children and Youth Services Review, 28,* 458–472.

MacCoun, R. J. (1998). Biases in the interpretation and use of research results. *Annual Review of Psychology, 49,* 259–287.

McDowell, B. (2000). *Ethics and excuses: The crisis in professional responsibility.* Westport, CT: Quorum.

Moher, D., Cook, D. J., Eastwood, S., Olkin, I., Rennie, D., Stroup, D. F., for the QUORUM Group. (2000). Improving the quality of reports of meta-analyses of randomized controlled trials: The QUORUM statement. *British Journal of Surgery, 87,* 1448–1454.

Moynihan, R., & Cassells, A. (2005). *Selling sickness: How the world's biggest pharmaceutical companies are turning us all into patients.* New York: Nation.

Munro, E. (1996). Avoidable and unavoidable mistakes in child protection work. *British Journal of Social Work, 26,* 793–808.

National Association of Social Workers. (1999). *Code of ethics.* Silver Spring, MD: Author.

Norcross, J. C., Beutler, L. E., & Levant R. F. (Eds). (2006). *Evidence-based practices in mental health: Debate and dialogue on the fundamental questions.* Washington DC: American Psychological Association.

O'Connor, A. M., Stacey, D., Rovner, D., Homes-Rovner, M., Tetroe, J., Llewellyn-Thomas, H., Entwistle, V., Rostom, A., Fiset, V., Barry, M., & Jones, J. (2002). Decision aids for people facing health treatment or screening decisions (Cochrane review). In *Cochrane Library,* 2. Oxford: Update Software.

O'Hare, T. (2005). *Evidence-based practices for social workers.* Chicago: Lyceum.

Ohmer, M. L., & Korr, W. S. (2006). The effectiveness of community practice interventions: A review of the literature. *Research on Social Work Practice, 16,* 132–145.

Oxman, A. D., & Flottorp, S. (1998). An overview of strategies to promote implementation of evidence based health care. In C. Silagy & A. Haines (Eds.), *Evidence based practice in primary care* (pp. 91–109). London: BMJ Books.

Oxman, A. D., & Guyatt, G. H. (1993). The science of reviewing research. In K. S. Warren & F. Mosteller (Eds.), *Doing more good than harm: The evaluation of health care interventions* (pp. 125–133). New York: New York Academy of Sciences.

Parton, N. (2006). *Safeguarding childhood: Early intervention and surveillance in a late modern society.* New York: Palgrave Macmillan.

Pope, K. S., & Vasquez, M. J. T. (2007). *Ethics in psychotherapy and counseling: A practical guide* (3rd ed.). San Francisco: John Wiley and Sons.

Reason, J. (2001). Understanding adverse events: The human factor. In C. Vincent (Ed.), *Clinical risk management: Enhancing patient safety* (2nd ed., pp. 9–30). London: BMJ Books.

Regehr, C., Stern, S., & Shlonsky, A. (2007). Operationalizing evidence-based practice: The development of an institute for evidence-based social work. *Research on Social Work Practice, 17,* 408–416.

Rosen, A., Proctor, E. K., Morrow-Howell, N., & Staudt, M. (1995). Rationales for practice decisions: Variations in knowledge use by decision task and social work service. *Research on Social Work Practice, 15,* 501–523.

Rosenthal, T. (1994). Science and ethics in conducting, analyzing, and reporting psychological research. *Psychological Science, 5,* 127–134.

Sackett, D. L., Richardson, W. S., Rosenberg, W., & Haynes, R. B. (1997). *Evidence-based medicine: How to practice and teach EBM.* New York: Churchill Livingstone.

Sackett, D. L., Straus, S. E., Richardson, W. S., Rosenberg, W., & Haynes, R. E. (2000). *Evidence-based medicine: How to practice and teach EBM* (2nd ed.). New York: Churchill Livingstone.

Sarnoff, S. K. (2001). *Sanctified snake oil: The effect of junk science on public policy.* Westport, CT: Praeger.

Schorr, A. L. (2000). The bleak prospect for public child welfare. *Social Services Review, 74,* 124–136.

Sharpe, V. A., & Faden, A. I. (1998). *Medical harm: Historical, conceptual, and ethical dimensions of iatrogenic illness.* New York: Cambridge University Press.

Sheldon, B., & Chilvers, R. (2000). *Evidence-based social care: A study of prospects and problems.* Lyme Regis: Russell House Publishing.

Straus, S. E., & McAlister, D. C. (2000). Evidence-based medicine: A commentary on common criticisms. *Canadian Medical Journal, 163,* 837–841.

Straus, S. E., Richardson, W. S., Glasziou, P., & Haynes, R. B. (2005). *Evidence-based medicine: How to practice and teach EBM* (3rd ed.). New York: Churchill Livingstone.

Valenstein, E. S. (1986). *Great and desperate cures: The rise and decline of psychosurgery and other radical treatments for mental illness.* New York: Perseus Books.

Wennberg, J. E. (2002). Unwarranted variations in health care delivery: Implications for academic medical centres. *British Medical Journal, 325,* 961–964.

Wilson, D., & Alexandra, L. (2005). *Guide for child welfare administrators on evidence-based practice.* Washington, DC: National Association of Public Child Welfare Administrators, American Public Human Services Association.

4

How Do We Know What Works?
The Quality of Published Reviews of
Evidence-Based Practices

Julia H. Littell

How do we know what works best for whom in child welfare? Rigorous evaluations of the advantages and disadvantages (relative effects) of different interventions are rarely undertaken in this field, due in part to a reluctance to "experiment" with children and families. Yet, many interventions are provided to families on an "experimental" basis, well before we know whether these interventions have their desired effects and whether they have any unintended, adverse consequences.

For example, intensive in-home family preservation services (FPS) were implemented in the United States before rigorous experiments showed that FPS did not achieve intended reductions in out-of-home placements or subsequent maltreatment (Littell & Schuerman, 1995, 1999; Westat, 2002). Despite the inability to achieve these objectives, intensive in-home services appear to be here to stay, perhaps because they provide a sensible way to assess the risk of further maltreatment and provide services to families in vivo. In wake of the FPS experiments, some

observers suggested that child welfare agencies should incorporate "evidence-based" treatments from other fields, especially mental health, juvenile justice, and substance abuse treatment.

In recent years, the emphasis on evidence-based practice has increased attention to "what works" in many fields of practice. Prominent authors have reviewed research findings and published their reviews to make this information accessible to readers who lack the time and/or technical knowledge to digest complex research reports. Now these research reviews appear in numerous books and journal articles, and concise lists of what works can be found on many government and professional organizations' Web sites.

The limitations of these reviews for child welfare practitioners and policy makers are twofold. First, the practice of research synthesis, as represented by the proliferation of published reviews and lists of evidence-based practices, has not kept up with the science of research synthesis (Littell, 2005), which has led to the publication of many haphazard and potentially misleading reviews (Petticrew & Roberts, 2006). Second, to compensate for the fact that few rigorous primary outcome studies have been conducted in child welfare settings, reviewers often turn to related fields for evidence about what works with "similar" families. It is not clear how evidence compiled in juvenile justice, mental health, substance abuse treatment, and other settings applies to families in child welfare.

In this chapter, I trace the development and dissemination of information about the efficacy and effectiveness of one of the most prominent evidence-based practices for youth and families, multisystemic therapy (MST). MST has been widely implemented with families of juvenile delinquents and was proposed as a solution to the perceived "failure" of FPS in child welfare. Below, I examine the extent to which claims about the efficacy of this program are based on scientific methods of research synthesis, and whether they are vulnerable to several sources and types of bias. First, it is necessary to consider various methods of research synthesis.

RESEARCH SYNTHESIS

The synthesis of results of multiple studies is important because single studies, no matter how rigorous, have limited utility and generalizability. Partial replications can refute, modify, support, or extend previous results. Compared to any single study, a careful synthesis of the results of multiple studies can produce better estimates of program impacts and assessments of conditions under which treatment impacts may vary (Shadish, Cook, & Campbell, 2002).

Research synthesis has a long history. Most readers are familiar with traditional literature reviews, which rely on narrative summaries of results of multiple studies. Systematic reviews and meta-analyses are becoming more common, but the traditional model prevails in the social sciences despite a growing body of evidence on the inadequacies of this approach.

Sources and Types of Bias in Research Reviews

There are several potential sources and types of bias in research reviews. These can be divided into three categories: biases that arise in the original studies, in the dissemination of study results, and in the review process itself.

Treatment outcome studies can systematically overestimate or underestimate effects due to design and implementation problems that render the studies vulnerable to threats to internal validity (e.g., selection bias, statistical regression, attrition), statistical conclusion validity (e.g., inadequate statistical power, multiple tests, and "fishing" for significance), and construct validity (e.g., experimenter expectancies, inadequate implementation of treatment, treatment diffusion; see Shadish et al., 2002). "Allegiance effects" that appear when interventions are studied by their developers (Luborsky, Diguer, Seligman, Rosenthal, Krause, Johnson, et al., 1999) may be a form of experimenter expectancy effects or may be due to high-fidelity implementation (Petrosino & Soydan, 2005).

Confirmation bias (the tendency to emphasize evidence that supports a hypothesis and ignore evidence to the contrary) can arise in the reporting, publication, and/or dissemination of results of original studies. Investigators may not report outcomes or may report outcomes selectively (Dickersin, 2005). Studies with significant, positive results are more likely to be submitted for publication and more likely to be published than studies with null or negative results (Begg, 1994; Dickersin, 2005). Mahoney (1977) found that peer reviewers were biased against manuscripts that reported results that ran counter to their expectations or theoretical perspectives. Other sources of bias in dissemination are related to issues of language, availability, familiarity, and the cost of research reports (Rothstein, Sutton, & Bornstein, 2005). Selective citation of reports with positive findings may make those results more visible and available than others (Dickersin, 2005).

These biases are likely to affect research synthesis unless reviewers take precautions to avoid them. The review process may be vulnerable to bias when reviewers sample studies selectively (e.g., only including published studies), fail to consider variations in study qualities that may affect the validity of inferences drawn from them, and report results selectively.

The synthesis of multiple results from multiple studies is a complex task that is not easily performed with "cognitive algebra." Since the conclusions of narrative reviews can be influenced by the trivial properties of research reports (e.g., Bushman & Wells, 2001), several quantitative approaches to research synthesis have been developed and tested. Perhaps the most common of these is "vote counting" (tallying the number of studies that provide evidence for and against a hypothesis), which relies on tests of significance or directions of effects in the original studies. Carlton and Strawderman (1996) showed that vote counting can lead to the wrong conclusions. Meta-analyses provide better overall estimates of treatment effects, but these techniques have limitations as well.

Systematic Reviews

Systematic reviews are designed to minimize bias at each step in the review process. Systematic approaches to reviewing research are not new, nor did they originate in the biomedical sciences (for a brief, unsystematic history, see Petticrew & Roberts, 2006). However, systematic reviews have received more attention in recent years as advances in the science of research synthesis showed that review methods matter (Cooper & Hedges, 1994), as centers for research synthesis evolved in the United Kingdom and elsewhere, and as the general public became more aware of the potential pitfalls of haphazard reviews (following, for example, the alleged suppression of negative findings on the effects of Vioxx in the United States in 2005).

Two international, interdisciplinary collaborations of scholars, practitioners, and policy makers have established principles for minimizing bias in the synthesis of research on treatment effects. The Cochrane Collaboration synthesizes results of studies on the effects of interventions in health care (see www.cochrane.org), and the Campbell Collaboration synthesizes results of interventions in the fields of social care (education, social welfare, mental health, and crime and justice; www.campbellcollaboration. org). Working together and building on advances in the science of research synthesis (e.g., Cooper & Hedges, 1994; Lipsey & Wilson, 2001; Moher, Cook, Eastwood, Olkin, Rennie, Stroup, et al., 1999), these groups have produced useful background papers and evidence-based guidelines for reviewers (e.g., Becker, Hedges, & Pigott, 2004; Higgins & Green, 2005; Rothstein, Turner, & Lavenberg, 2004; Shadish & Myers, 2004).

A systematic review follows the basic steps in the research process (Cooper & Hedges, 1994). Systematic reviews are observational studies, in which prior studies are treated as sampling units and units of analysis. The basic steps and principles in conducting a systematic review are as follows.

Transparent Intentions and Methods

A detailed plan for the review is developed in advance, specifying the central objectives and methods. Steps and decisions are carefully documented so that readers can follow and evaluate reviewers' methods (Moher et al., 1999). Conflicts of interest and sponsorship arrangements must be disclosed (Higgins & Green, 2005), because these issues can affect reviewers' conclusions (e.g., Jørgensen, Hilden, & Gøtzsche, 2006).

Explicit Inclusion/Exclusion Criteria

Systematic reviews have clear boundaries to guide the review and make it available for replication or extension by others. Reviewers specify the study designs, populations, interventions, comparisons, and outcome measures that will be included and excluded. The reasons for exclusion are documented for each excluded study. This limits reviewers' freedom to select studies on the basis of their results, or on some other basis.

Search Strategies

Reviewers use a systematic approach and a variety of sources to try to locate *all* potentially relevant studies. This involves collaboration with information retrieval specialists to generate search strings used in keyword searches of relevant electronic databases. It also involves attempts to locate the "grey literature" (unpublished and hard-to-find studies) to minimize publication bias and the "file drawer problem" (Begg, 1994; Hopewell, McDonald, Clarke, & Egger, 2006; Petticrew & Roberts, 2006; Rosenthal, 1994; Rothstein et al., 2004, 2005). This is sometimes accomplished through contacts with a snowball sample of key informants (experts on the topic) until data saturation is achieved. Hand searching of the contents of relevant journals is often needed to find eligible studies that are not properly indexed (Hopewell, Clarke, Lefebvre, & Scherer, 2006). The search process and its results are carefully documented.

Inter-Rater Agreement on All Key Decisions

Decisions on full-text retrieval, study inclusion/exclusion, and study coding are made by two independent raters, who compare notes, resolve differences, and document the reasons for their decisions (Higgins & Green, 2005).

Systematic Extraction of Data from Studies

Raters extract data from study reports onto paper or electronic coding forms. These data are then available for use in the analysis and synthesis of results. The data forms provide a bridge between the primary research studies and the research synthesis, and a historical record of reviewers' decisions (Higgins & Green, 2005).

Analysis of Study Qualities

Aspects of methodology that relate to the validity of a study's conclusions are assessed individually, rather than being summed into total study-quality scores (Shadish & Myers, 2004). Campbell's threats-to-validity approach is a useful framework in this regard (Wortman, 1994). Some reviewers focus on assessment of potential sources and types of bias.

Analysis of Study Results

Study findings are represented as effect sizes (ES) whenever possible. Reviewers document the data and formulas used for effect size calculations (Becker et al., 2004).

Synthesis of Results

Since conclusions of narrative reviews can be influenced by the trivial properties of research reports (Bushman & Wells, 2001), methods used to combine results across studies should be transparent (Becker et al., 2004). Quantitative methods (meta-analysis) lend themselves to this purpose. Meta-analysis can be used to produce pooled estimates of ES that account for variations in the precision of estimates drawn from different samples (due to variations in sample size and within-sample variance), explore potential moderators of effect size, and examine the potential effects of publication bias (Cooper & Hedges, 1994; Lipsey & Wilson, 2001; Rothstein et al., 2005). It is important to note that meta-analyses are not necessarily systematic reviews (e.g., a meta-analysis of a convenience sample of published studies is not a systematic review).

Reporting of Results

Moher and colleagues (1999) developed the Quality of Reporting of Meta-analyses (QUOROM) statement to improve reports on systematic reviews and meta-analyses. This statement includes a checklist of items that should be reported and a flow diagram for authors to use to describe how studies were identified, screened, and selected for the review.

Updating Reviews

Systematic reviews should be updated regularly so that they remain current and relevant for policy and practice.

Current Practice

What criteria and methods do reviewers actually use to find, assess, and compile evidence of intervention effects? How "systematic" are their reviews? That is, to what extent do they use explicit inclusion and exclusion criteria, well-defined search and retrieval procedures, attempts to avoid publication bias and the file drawer problem (omission of important studies), clear standards of evidence, and quantitative (or at least transparent) methods of research synthesis?

These issues have been the topic of considerable interest in medicine and meta-analysis. Several studies compared Cochrane reviews to other "systematic" reviews and meta-analyses. For example, Jadad and colleagues (Jadad, Moher, Browman, Booker, Sigouin, Fuentes, et al., 2000) analyzed 50 systematic reviews and meta-analyses of asthma treatment and found that most reviews published in peer-reviewed journals had serious methodological flaws that limited their usefulness; Cochrane reviews were more rigorous and better reported than those published in peer-reviewed journals. All industry-funded reviews were judged to have serious flaws. Shea, Moher, Graham, Pham, and Tugwell (2002) found the overall quality of systematic reviews was low, but noted that the development of evidence-based criteria for reporting systematic reviews (the QUOROM statement) may help to improve their quality.

As mentioned above, there is an extensive body of work on the biases and limitations of traditional, narrative reviews of empirical research (e.g., Bushman & Wells, 2001; Carlton & Strawderman, 1996; Cooper & Hedges, 1994). Yet narrative reviews are the norm in the social sciences. Systematic review methods have been discussed in the social sciences for decades, and systematic reviews have appeared more often in recent years (Petticrew & Roberts, 2006). However, to my knowledge, there have been no attempts to evaluate the quality of published reviews of research in the fields of social care.

A CASE STUDY: MULTISYSTEMIC THERAPY

Following standards and procedures established by the Cochrane Collaboration, the Campbell Collaboration, and the QUOROM statement, my team conducted a systematic review and meta-analysis of research on the effects of a prominent model program called multisystemic therapy (Littell, Popa, & Forsythe, 2005). Multisystemic therapy (MST) was selected as the topic for that review (and as the primary example for this chapter) because it has an unusually strong research base, including several randomized controlled trials. MST has been cited as an effective, evidence-based treatment model by the U.S. Department of Justice's Office of Juvenile Justice and Delinquency Prevention (OJJDP), the Center for Substance Abuse Prevention (2000), the National Institute on Drug Abuse (1999, 2003), National Institute of Mental Health (2001, 2003), and the surgeon general's office (U.S. Department of Health and Human Services, 1999, 2001). MST is one of the model programs identified by the Substance Abuse and Mental Health Services Administration (SAMHSA, 2004) and by the OJJDP-funded Blueprints for Violence Prevention (Henggeler, Mihalic, Rone, Thomas, & Timmons-Mitchell, 1998). Further, MST had been proposed as a solution for ailing FPS programs in child welfare.

MST is a short-term, home- and community-based intervention for families of youth with social, emotional, and behavioral problems. MST uses a family preservation service delivery model to address complex psychosocial problems and to provide alternatives to out-of-home placement. Treatment teams consist of professional therapists (mental health professionals with master's or doctoral degrees) and crisis caseworkers, who are supervised by clinical psychologists or psychiatrists. Therapists have small caseloads and are available to program participants 24 hours a day, 7 days a week. Treatment is individualized to address the specific needs of youth and families and includes work with other social systems, including schools and peer groups. "Intervention strategies are integrated from other pragmatic, problem-focused treatment models" (Henggeler & Borduin, 1995, p. 121), and MST follows nine general principles (see Henggeler, Schoenwald, Borduin, Rowland, & Cunningham, 1998; Henggeler, Schoenwald, Rowland, & Cunningham, 2002).

As of 2006, there were approximately 120 licensed MST programs in more than 30 states in the United States. At last count, there were 18 licensed MST programs in Norway, 7 in Sweden, 5 in Canada, 3 in the Netherlands, 2 in Australia, 2 in England, and single programs in Denmark, Ireland, and New Zealand (MST Services, 2006). In total, there are more than 250 licensed MST teams in North America and Europe, which treat 8,000 serious juvenile offenders each year (MST Services, 2006). Considerable attention has been paid to the dissemination of MST and the fidelity of MST replications (e.g., Henggeler, Schoenwald, Liao, Letourneau, & Edwards, 2002; Schoenwald, Henggeler, Brondino, & Rowland, 2000; Schoenwald & Hoagwood, 2001).

The results of a systematic review of research on MST (Littell et al., 2005) were not consistent with the published works of current authorities on the topic (see Henggeler, Schoenwald, Borduin, & Swenson, 2006; Littell, 2005, 2006). While most (but not all) of the primary studies showed that MST had statistically significant effects on at least one outcome measure, these effects were not consistent across studies; that is, different studies showed effects on different outcome measures. In meta-analysis, there were no significant overall effects (across studies) on any single outcome measure (Littell et al., 2005). It is possible that prior reviews focused on positive effects, not the entire pattern of positive, negative, and null results. This chapter will examine the methods used in prior reviews to identify, assess, and synthesize this body of evidence, to determine whether these reviews were vulnerable to confirmation bias.

THE QUALITY OF PUBLISHED REVIEWS

Our study sought to determine how prior, published reviews of research on the effects of MST were conducted. I expected to find few fully systematic reviews of this research, but thought published reviews might become more systematic over time (i.e., reviews published in later years might contain more of the elements of a systematic review mentioned above).

Methods

To be included in this analysis, reviews had to be published after 1996, when at least 10 reports on MST outcome studies were in print. Included reviews had to cite at least 2 original studies of the effects of MST and provide a summary of results of MST studies.

Most reviews were identified in the spring of 2003. Using keyword searches of electronic databases (including PsycINFO, MEDLINE, Dissertation Abstracts International, ERIC, CINAHL) and government Web sites (U.S. Department of Health and Human Services, Centers for Disease Control, Government Printing Office, National Institutes of Health, UK Home Office) and contacts with experts, my colleagues and I identified 86 potentially relevant, published reviews of MST outcome research. We retrieved available reviews in order to scan their reference lists to find relevant outcome studies. We read abstracts of all 86 reviews and retrieved full-text reports on 66 (77%). This purposive sample includes reviews published in scholarly books and articles, reviews that are more widely cited than those we did not attempt to retrieve.

Of the 66 reviews examined, 6 were published before 1997, 19 relied solely or primarily on other reviews, 1 did not cite its sources, and 3 reviews provided no analysis or synthesis of results for MST per se. The remaining 37 reviews met the inclusion criteria for this study and are described below.

Results

MST outcome studies have been reviewed in relation to a variety of youth and family problems. As shown in Table 4.1, reviews have focused on the effects of MST (and other interventions) on crime, delinquency, antisocial behavior, and/or conduct disorder (14 reviews); substance abuse (3 reviews); other mental health problems among children (9 reviews); and child maltreatment (2 reviews). Several reviews assessed the effects of MST across populations and problems (7 reviews) or the effects of a broader array of family-based services (2 reviews).

Purpose and Hypotheses Regarding MST

The purposes of the reviews (as stated in the abstract or introduction) were to

- describe MST (Burns, 2003; Burns, Schoenwald, Burchard, Faw, & Santos, 2000; Schoenwald, Brown, & Henggeler, 2000; Swenson & Henggeler, 2003);
- provide practitioners with information on evidence-based practices (Corcoran, 2003; Henggeler, Mihalic, et al., 1998; Schoenwald & Rowland, 2002);
- "discuss the emergent success" of MST (Borduin, 1999), provide an "empirical rationale" for MST (Borduin, Schaeffer, & Ronis, 2003), "present empirical support" for MST (Swenson, Henggeler, Schoenwald, Kaufman, & Randall, 1998);
- review treatment models that are promising (Borduin, Heiblum, Jones, & Grabe, 2000; Kazdin, 1998; Kazdin & Weisz, 1998), empirically supported (Brestan & Eyberg, 1998), effective (Chorpita, Yim, Donkervoet, Arensdorf, Amundsen, McGee, et al., 2002; Burns, Hoagwood, & Mrazek, 1999; Hoagwood, Burns, Kiser, Ringeisen, & Schoenwald, 2001; Letourneau, Cunningham, & Henggeler, 2002), or efficacious (Henggeler & Sheidow, 2003);
- review research on treatment effects (Corcoran, 2000; Farrington & Welsh, 2003; Fraser, Nelson, & Rivard, 1997; Henggeler, Schoenwald, Rowland, et al., 2002; Miller, Johnson, Sandberg, Stringer-Seibold, & Gfeller-Strouts, 2000; Smith & Stern, 1997; Sudderth, 2000; Tarolla et al., 2002; U.S. DHHS, 1999);
- review well-designed studies of treatment effects (Brosnan & Carr, 2000; Cormack & Carr, 2000; Vaughn & Howard, 2004);
- "examine effectiveness" (Curtis, Ronan, & Borduin, 2004) or "determine effects" (Woolfenden, Williams, & Peat, 2003); and
- "find programs that save more money than they cost" (Aos, Phipps, Barnoski, & Lieb, 2001).

Some reviewers acknowledged their debt to previous reviews. For example, "[g]iven the conclusions of previous authoritative reviewers of the field, this chapter is confined to a consideration of well-designed studies which evaluate the effectiveness" of selected interventions (Brosnan & Carr, 2000, p. 134; see also Henggeler & Sheidow, 2003). Some reviews began with the hypothesis that MST is "promising" (Fonagy & Kurtz, 2002), "supported" (Pushak, 2002), "well-validated" (Schoenwald & Rowland, 2002), or has "favorable outcomes" (Randall & Cunningham, 2003).

Thus, reviews varied in the clarity of their stated purpose, whether the purpose was stated in

TABLE 4.1 Summary of MST Research Reviews' Foci, Methods, and Conclusions

Author (Date)	Substantive Foci	Purpose or Hypothesis	Review Methods	Conclusions Regarding Effects of MST
Aos et al. (2001)	Programs to reduce crime	"find programs that save more money than they cost" (p. 5)	Meta-analysis, cost benefit analysis	MST reduces crime (based on 3 studies, the average effect size for recidivism is $-.31$, $SE = .1$). Net direct costs of MST = $4,743 per participant; net benefits per participant (benefits minus costs) are $131,918 for taxpayers, $131,918 when benefits to crime victims are included; the latter represents a benefit-to-cost ratio of $28.33 for every dollar spent on MST.
Borduin (1999)	Adolescent criminality & violence	"discuss the emergent success" of MST (p. 242)	Narrative	MST "can successfully reduce criminal activity and violent offending in serious juvenile offenders. Of course, extensive validation and replication are needed for even the most promising treatment approaches" (p. 248).
Borduin et al. (2000)	Serious antisocial behavior in adolescents	"review some promising models of treatment" (p. 114)	Narrative	"Considerable evidence shows that MST can decrease rates of criminal activity and incarceration for serious juvenile offenders" (p. 130).
Borduin et al. (2003)	Serious antisocial behavior in adolescents	"address the empirical rationale for . . . MST, as well as the features . . . that make it well-suited for treating serious antisocial behavior" (p. 300)	Narrative	MST "can successfully reduce criminal activity and violent offending in serious juvenile offenders. Of course, extensive validation and replication are needed for even the most promising treatment approaches" (pp. 314–315).
Brestan & Eyberg (1998)	Treatments for conduct disorder	"identify empirically supported treatments" (p. 180)	Systematic search, narrative review	MST is "probably efficacious" (p. 185).
Brosnan & Carr (2000)	Adolescent conduct problems	Consider "well-designed studies which evaluate the effectiveness" of several interventions (p. 134)	Systematic search, tables, meta-analysis	MST "was effective in reducing family-based conduct problems and halving community-based recidivism rates. [MST] also improved family functioning" (p. 151).
Burns et al. (1999)	Treatment for mental disorders in children and adolescents	Provide "an understanding of the evidence base [by reviewing] published literature for effective interventions" (p. 199)	Narrative	"Efficacy has been established in three randomized clinical trials of MST for delinquents. Each of these trials reported significant findings of behavior change, reduced contact with the justice system, and lower[ed] costs" (p. 220). "Multisystemic therapy has a well-established evidence base, including both efficacy and effectiveness studies" (p. 240).
Burns et al. (2000)	MST and wraparound services for youth with severe emotional disorders	"describe and contrast" MST and wraparound services (p. 284)	Narrative & tabular	"The evidence base for MST is characterized by considerable controlled research, but little diversity among investigators. The efficacy of MST . . . was established through three randomized clinical trials with delinquents, and effectiveness through the transfer of MST to other clinical populations . . . and to multiple organizational settings. . . . The research base meets the criteria for a 'probably efficacious' treatment, but it was not classified as 'well-established'" (pp. 309–310).

Source	Topic	Purpose	Method	Findings
Burns (2003)	Children's services	"provide a succinct summary of interventions . . . identify exemplary child initiatives . . . identify models for narrowing the gap between research and practice" (p. 956)	Narrative	MST results in "fewer arrests, fewer placements, decreased aggressive behavior" (p. 959).
Chorpita et al. (2002)	Treatments for disorders in childhood	"examine the efficacy and effectiveness of child treatments" for certain disorders (p. 165)	Narrative with some ES calculations (unspecified formulas)	"The effect size for MST was modest, suggesting that the average treated child scored better than 69% of children's scores before treatment. Also, the robustness of this treatment was rated as moderate, possibly due to the elaborate and highly orchestrated supervision network that appears to account for much of the success of the treatment. Consistent with this observation, no studies to date support MST other than those conducted by its developers. Nevertheless, the support for the effectiveness of MST is rather good, given that it has been tested with some of the most challenging youth and that it is one of the only treatments that has demonstrated superiority to realistic and commonly employed alternative treatments" (pp. 177–179).
Corcoran (2000)	Family interventions for child abuse and neglect	"critically review the research on family treatment for child physical abuse and neglect" (p. 563)	Narrative	"There has been strong empirical support for Multisystemic Therapy with juvenile offenders and their families, a population which has considerable overlap with children who have been neglected and abused" (p. 574).
Corcoran (2003)	Evidence-based family interventions	"familiarize the practitioner with evidence-based approaches for common problems for which families seek treatment" (p. 3)	Narrative & tabular	"The success of the multisystemic model seems to depend on fidelity to the treatment" (p. 181). The costs of MST "are offset by the costs saved in incarceration, institutionalization, and out-of-home placement" (p. 202).
Cormack & Carr (2000)	Treatment for drug abuse in children and adolescents	"review the outcomes of [3 groups of well-designed family-based intervention studies for adolescent drug abusers] in a rigorous manner" (p. 161)	Systematic search, narrative, & quantitative analysis	Including studies of similar interventions, "multisystemic family therapy is more effective in the short-term than individual or group-based supportive counseling and parent education in treating adolescent drug abuse. However, it was no more effective than family therapy" (p. 175).
Curtis, Ronan, & Borduin (2004)	MST	Examine "the effectiveness of MST" (p. 411)	Systematic search, meta-analysis	"As an empirically established treatment for violent and chronic juvenile offenders, MST appears to be worthy of wider implementation and continued evaluation. . . . More empirical support is required before MST can be considered an effective treatment of substance abuse in adolescents or an effective community-based alternative to the hospitalization of youths presenting psychiatric emergencies" (p. 417). Average effect size (across all outcome measures in 7 samples) $d = .55$ (not weighted by sample size or inverse variance).

(Continued)

TABLE 4.1 (*Continued*)

Author (Date)	Substantive Foci	Purpose or Hypothesis	Review Methods	Conclusions Regarding Effects of MST
Farrington & Welsh (2003)	Family-based prevention of offending	review "the effectiveness of family-based crime prevention programs" (p. 127)	Systematic search, meta-analysis	Mean ES for MST = .414 (95% CI = .281–.548). "Three MST programs reduced delinquency or behaviour problems . . . while the other three did not. . . . However, it should be noted that only two of the six MST evaluations had significant effects. . . . The large mean effect size for MST was largely driven by these two evaluations" (p. 143).
Fonagy & Kurtz (2002)	Conduct disturbance	MST "is arguably the most promising intervention for serious juvenile offenders" (p. 161)	Narrative	"MST is the most effective treatment for delinquent adolescents in reducing recidivism and ameliorating individual and family problems. It is substantially more effective than individual treatment, even for quite troubled and disorganized families" (p. 181). "Numerous other approaches have been tried but none of these are as effective as multisystemic therapy" (p. 181).
Fraser et al. (1997)	Family preservation services (including MST)	"review recent studies of family preservation and related family-strengthening programs, [and] estimate the effect sizes" (p. 138)	Narrative, tabular, & quantitative analysis	ES for MST range from .4 to .93 for prevention of rearrest, 1.01 for prevention of incarceration (p. 143).
Henggeler, Mihalic, et al. (1998)	MST	Help people to "make an informed judgment about a proven program's appropriateness for their local situation, needs, and available resources" (p. xii)	Narrative & tabular	Findings from 4 RCTs "provide strong evidence that MST can produce short- and long-term reductions in criminal behavior and out-of-home placements in serious juvenile offenders" (p. 38).
Henggeler, Schoenwald, Rowland, et al. (2002)	MST	Provide "a summary of the findings from research evaluations of MST and describe current replications of these findings and extensions of the model" (p. 205)	Narrative & tabular	"Across studies, consistent clinical- and service-level outcomes have emerged. At the clinical level, in comparison with control groups, MST improved family relations and functioning, increased school attendance, decreased adolescent psychiatric symptoms, decreased adolescent substance use, decreased long-term rates of rearrest ranging from 25–70%. At the service level and in comparison with control groups, MST has achieved 97% and 98% rates of treatment completion in recent studies, decreased long-term rates of days in out-of-home placement ranging from 47% to 64%, higher consumer satisfaction, [and] considerable cost savings" (pp. 206–208).
Henggeler & Sheidow (2003)	Conduct disorder and delinquency	"review those family-based treatments of conduct disorder and delinquency that have been identified by federal entities and leading reviewers as efficacious" (p. 505)	Narrative & tabular	In studies of juvenile offenders and delinquents, "outcomes have consistently favored MST in comparison with control conditions. For example, MST treatment effects have included improved family relations and functioning, increased school attendance, decreased adolescent psychiatric symptoms, and reduced substance use. Reductions in rates of recidivism have ranged between 25% to 70% across studies for youth treated with MST compared to treated control groups. Moreover, MST has produced decreased rates of

Hoagwood et al. (2001)	Child and adolescent mental health services	Narrative	"review the status, strength, and quality of evidence-based practice in child and adolescent mental health services" (p. 1179)	days in out-of-home placement ranging from 47% to 64% compared with usual services. Group differences have been observed as much as 5 years posttreatment" (p. 512). "Successful MST outcomes have been observed for youths presenting psychiatric emergencies . . . and for children in maltreating families" (p. 512).
Kazdin (1998)	Psychosocial treatments for conduct disorder in children	Narrative	"review research for . . . psychosocial treatments that have shown considerable promise in the treatment of conduct disorder in children and adolescents" (p. 66)	Results of MST trials "have been among the strongest found for children's services" (p. 1183). Results include lower rates of recidivism, out-of-home placements and arrest for juvenile offenders; reduced psychiatric hospitalization and improved functioning of youth and their families. Effects of MST "have been further demonstrated among juvenile sex offenders and abused or neglected children" (p. 1183).
Kazdin & Weisz (1998)	Treatments for child and adolescent internalizing, externalizing, and other disorders	Narrative	"illustrate promising treatments" (p. 19)	MST "has been shown to be superior in reducing delinquency and emotional and behavioral problems and improving family functioning in comparison to other methods of achieving these desirable goals" (p. 65). "On balance, MST is quite promising given the quality of evidence and consistency in the effects that have been produced. . . . The outcome studies have extended to youths with different types of problems (e.g., sexual offenses, drug use) and to parents who engage in physical abuse or neglect. . . . Thus, the model . . . may have broad applicability across problem domains among seriously disturbed children" (p. 79).
Letourneau et al. (2002)	MST	Narrative	(In a handbook of empirically supported interventions)	"MST is unique insofar as providing multiple replications across problems, therapists, and settings. . . . This shows that the treatment and methods of decision making can be extended and that the treatment effects are reliable. . . . Replications by others not involved with the original development of the program represent the next logical step. On balance, MST is quite promising given the quality of evidence and consistency of the outcomes" (p. 28).
Miller et al. (2000)	Marriage and family therapies	Narrative	"present a . . . complete summary of marriage and family therapy outcome research" (p. 347)	"In comparison with control groups, and at a cost of approximately $5,000 per family, MST has consistently demonstrated improved family relations and family functioning, improved school attendance, and decreased adolescent drug use . . . 25–70% decreases in long-term rates of rearrest, and 47–64% decreases in long-term rates of days in institutional placements" (p. 377).
				MST "has demonstrated its effectiveness in treating juvenile delinquency. Four outcome studies . . . show MST is more effective than standard treatments in reducing arrests, self-reported offenses, and jail time" (p. 351). Two studies "found MST to be effective in treating substance abuse" (p. 352).

(Continued)

TABLE 4.1 (Continued)

Author (Date)	Substantive Foci	Purpose or Hypothesis	Review Methods	Conclusions Regarding Effects of MST
Pushak (2002)	Mental health services for children	MST is "a model program with strong empirical support for effectiveness" (p. 174)	Narrative	"It would be safe to conclude that the total impact MST has on high-risk youth and their families and the decreased financial costs, to say nothing of the decreased psychosocial costs, of antisocial youth behavior to society is not yet matched by other psychotherapy programs" (p. 181).
Randall & Cunningham (2003)	Violence, substance abuse	Describe MST, a treatment "that has produced favorable outcomes" (p. 1731)	Narrative	"MST has been extensively validated and cited as both an effective treatment for youth with violent behavior and as a promising adolescent substance abuse treatment. . . . MST can reduce violence and substance use of chronic juvenile offenders" (p. 1736).
Schoenwald, Brown, & Henggeler (2000)	MST	Highlight key features of MST	Narrative	"MST has a strong track record in demonstrating favorable long-term outcomes for youth presenting serious clinical problems and their families" (p. 114).
Schoenwald & Rowland (2002)	MST	"to facilitate implementation of evidence-based interventions in communities" (editors, p. 13). "MST is a well-validated treatment model" (p. 113)	Narrative	"The original studies of MST documented significant benefit for multiple target populations under conditions of training and close supervision by the MST developers" (p. 116).
Smith & Stern (1997)	Delinquency and antisocial behavior	"critical review of the current research on . . . the existing treatment outcome research" (p. 382)	Narrative	"In a series of controlled group studies, [MST] has shown consistent and strong results as an effective intervention for serious antisocial behavior and juvenile delinquency in both urban and rural areas and with families of different cultural backgrounds and socioeconomic status" (p. 405).
Sudderth (2000)	Treatment for substance-abusing youth	Review of evaluations of treatment programs	Narrative	MST "has been found to be effective in reducing self-reported alcohol and marijuana use and decreasing the number of days juveniles spent incarcerated. . . . Although MST is more expensive to implement than other approaches, . . . initial results suggest that the long-term benefits of reduced residential placement and incarceration time are worth the investment" (p. 342).
Swenson & Henggeler (2003)	MST for maltreated children and their families	Description of MST	Narrative	Results from 8 RCT's "support the short- and long-term clinical effectiveness of MST as well as its potential to produce significant cost savings and capacity to retain families in treatment" (p. 75). One RCT in cases of child maltreatment showed that MST "was more effective than Parent Training for improving parent-child interactions associated with maltreatment . . . [but] Parent Training was superior to MST on in decreasing social problems" (pp. 75–76).

Source	Topic	Purpose	Review type	Findings
Swenson et al. (1998)	MST	"presents empirical support for use of an ecological approach with adolescent sexual offenders" (p. 330)	Narrative	"Findings from several randomized trials have shown that . . . [MST] . . . is an effective treatment for serious and complex problems presented by youths and their families" (p. 332).
Tarolla et al. (2002)	Juvenile offenders	"provides an overview of available evidence . . . pertaining to treatment for juvenile offenders" (p. 125)	Narrative	"MST trials have shown reductions in long-term rates of violent offending, drug-related offending, and other delinquent and criminal activities. Also recent research has documented MST's effectiveness with substance abusers, sex offenders, suicidal youth, maltreating families, and individuals with mental health problems" (p. 132).
U.S. DHHS (1999)	Mental health	Examine effectiveness of treatments	Narrative	"The efficacy of MST has been established in three randomized clinical trials for delinquents within the juvenile justice system. . . . Initial results are promising for youth receiving MST instead of psychiatric hospitalizations. . . . The efficacy of MST was demonstrated in real-world settings but only by one group of investigators" (p. 176).
Vaughn & Howard (2004)	Adolescent substance abuse treatment	"assess outcome findings and methodological characteristics of controlled evaluations" (p. 325)	Systematic search, meta-analysis	MST has "evidence of clinically meaningful effect (ES > .20) [on adolescent substance abuse] with relatively strong designs and less than 1-year follow-up and no replication" and has been "shown to be effective in other studies with reducing adolescent violence and problem behavior" (p. 334).
Woolfenden et al. (2003)	Family and parenting interventions for conduct disorder and delinquency	"determine if family and parenting interventions improve [outcomes for children, parents, and families]"	Systematic search, meta-analysis	MST (and other interventions) "have beneficial effects in reducing the length of time spent by juvenile delinquents in institutions. . . . These interventions may also reduce rates of subsequent arrest. . . . At present there is insufficient evidence that family and parenting interventions reduce the risk of [incarceration] or have a beneficial effect on parenting, parental mental health, family functioning, academic performance, future employment, and peer relations" (p. 7).

confirmatory terms (e.g., to find or show evidence of effects), and whether a priori assumptions about the state of the evidence were expressed. When assumptions or hypotheses about the direction and strength of effects were stated, reviewers usually cited previous reviews.

Review Methods

Most (22, or 60%) of the 37 reviews relied solely on narrative synthesis of the results of convenience samples of studies. One review provided a narrative synthesis based on a systematic search for published studies (Brestan & Eyberg, 1998). Five reviews described studies and their results in tables and text. Three reviews provided study-level effect sizes, 5 included quantitative synthesis (meta-analysis), and 1 included both meta-analysis and cost-benefit analysis.

More detailed information on review methods is shown in Table 4.2. In this table, reviews are organized by publication year, to see whether there have been discernible changes in review methods over time. Contrary to expectations, there were no apparent increases in the use of explicit inclusion criteria, systematic searches, unpublished reports, study assessment methods, or quantitative analysis over time.

Authors' Independence

Twenty-two (60%) of the 37 reviews were authored by people who were not affiliated with MST program developers or MST Services Inc. Hereafter, these are referred to as "independent" reviews.

Inclusion Criteria, Search Strategies, and Their Results

Eight (22%) reviews used explicit inclusion and/or exclusion criteria. With one exception (Curtis et al., 2004), the reviews that used explicit criteria were authored by independent investigators. Nine reviews (24%) used systematic keyword searches of electronic databases; 8 of these reviews also had explicit inclusion criteria. Nine reviews included references to unpublished MST research reports; only 1 (Farrington & Welsh, 2003) also had explicit inclusion criteria and/or a systematic search strategy.

As shown in Table 4.2, the number of MST research reports included in reviews ranged from 1 to 29, representing up to 25 separate studies (non-overlapping samples). Reviews that had a specific focus (e.g., substance abuse outcomes; see Cormack & Carr, 2000; Sudderth, 2000; Vaughn & Howard, 2004) cited fewer studies than those that included MST research across a range of problems and populations (e.g., Henggeler, Schoenwald, Rowland, et al., 2002).

Independent reviews were more likely than reviews coauthored by MST developers to use explicit inclusion criteria (31.8% versus 6.7%) or systematic search strategies (36.4% versus 6.7%), but were less likely to include unpublished reports (13.6% versus 40.0%). Independent reviews tended to include fewer research reports (means 4.9 versus 13.5) and fewer studies (4 versus 9.5) than those coauthored by MST developers.

Standards of Evidence

Study Design or Allocation Method   Most reviews distinguished randomized and nonrandomized studies, but variations in study quality within these two categories were rarely considered, and the results of randomized and nonrandomized studies were usually given equal weight in the analysis (a notable exception is the review by Aos et al., 2001, discussed below). Seven reviews (including Aos et al., 2001) limited the included studies to RCTs or assessed the method used to allocate participants to treatment groups.

Two reviews altered their initial methodological inclusion criteria. After a preliminary analysis showed that only 7.4% of studies met one of their initial criteria (randomization), Fonagy and Kurtz (2002) relaxed this criterion. Similarly, Carr and colleagues intended to limit their reviews to RCTs, but since this criterion "yielded a particularly small pool of studies, the criteria were relaxed and less methodologically robust studies were included" (Carr, 2000, p. 6).

Attrition   Only four reviews assessed attrition in primary outcome studies (Brosnan & Carr, 2000; Cormack & Carr, 2000; Vaughn & Howard, 2004; Woolfenden et al., 2003), but all four underestimated attrition (Littell, 2005, 2006). This is likely due to the practice (articulated by Woolfenden and colleagues) of selecting the most recent study report when there were multiple reports per study, instead of tracking attrition over time through different reports. The review by Aos and colleagues intended to address attrition and to limit

TABLE 4.2 Characteristics of Research Reviews (by Publication Year)

Pub. Year	Authors	Independent	Explicit Inclusion Criteria	Systematic Search Strategy	Include Unpublished Reports	Number of MST Study Reports Cited[a]	Unduplicated Number of MST Studies Cited	Assess Allocation Method[b]	Assess Study Attrition	Rate Study Quality	Use ITT Analysis	Report Study Level ES	Report Pooled ES
1997	Fraser et al.	✓			✓	4	2					✓	
	Smith & Stern	✓				5	4						
1998	Brestan & Eyberg	✓	✓	✓		3	3	✓		✓			
	Henggeler et al.				✓	25	21						
	Kazdin	✓				6	5						
	Kazdin & Weisz	✓				6	5						
	Swenson et al.					10	8						
1999	Borduin				✓	9	6						
	Burns et al.[c]	✓				6	6						
	U.S. DHHS	✓				5	5						
2000	Borduin et al.					8	5						
	Brosnan & Carr	✓	✓	✓	✓	7	5	✓	✓	✓		✓	
	Burns et al.[c]					16	12						
	Corcoran					7	5						
	Cormack & Carr	✓	✓	✓		1	2	✓	✓	✓		✓	
	Miller et al.	✓				5	4						
	Schoenwald et al.				✓	12	8						
	Sudderth	✓				3	3						
2001	Aos et al.	✓			✓	7	6	✓	[d]	✓	[d]	✓	✓
	Hoagwood et al.					6	5						
2002	Chorpita et al.	✓		✓		3	3						
	Fonagy & Kurtz	✓	✓	✓		9	6					✓	✓

(Continued)

79

TABLE 4.2 (Continued)

Pub. Year	Authors	Independent	Explicit Inclusion Criteria	Systematic Search Strategy	Include Unpublished Reports	Number of MST Study Reports Cited[a]	Unduplicated Number of MST Studies Cited	Assess Allocation Method[b]	Assess Study Attrition	Rate Study Quality	Use ITT Analysis	Report Study Level ES	Report Pooled ES
	Henggeler et al.				✓	29	25						
	Letourneau et al.					12	8						
	Pushak	✓				5	5						
	Schoenwald & Rowland					12	8						
	Tarolla et al.	✓				4	3						
2003	Borduin et al.				✓	13	7						
	Burns[c]	✓				2	1						
	Corcoran	✓				8	5						
	Farrington & Welsh	✓	✓	✓	✓	6	6	✓		✓			✓
	Henggeler & Sheidow					14	8						
	Randall & Cunningham					13	6						
	Swenson & Henggeler					12	8						
	Woolfenden et al.	✓	✓	✓		3	3	✓	✓	✓		✓	✓
2004	Curtis et al.		✓	✓		11	7	✓	✓			✓	✓
	Vaughn & Howard	✓	✓	✓		3	3		✓	✓		✓	
	Total (N = 37)	22	8	9	9			7	4	7	0	8	6

[a] Includes relevant unpublished reports and personal communication.

[b] Includes reviews limited to RCTs.

[c] Burns collaborated with an MST developer in a review published in 2000, but not in the reviews she published in 1999 and 2003.

[d] Contrary to reviewers' intentions, studies that did not report data on dropouts were treated as if they had no dropouts.

meta-analyses to studies that provided an intent-to-treat analysis, but did not do so. A full account of attrition was not always provided in published reports (Littell, 2005, 2006).

Study-Quality Ratings   Seven reviews rated study quality (all seven were independent). Brosnan and Carr (2000) used a 25-point scale to rate the methodological features of included studies; scores (for MST trials and other studies) ranged from 10 to 18 on this scale. Cormack and Carr (2000) used a similar, 24-item rating scale; scores ranged from 11 to 17 (MST trials were rated 11 and 12). Vaughn and Howard (2004) adapted the Methodological Quality Rating Scale (Miller, Brown, Simpson, Handmaker, Bien, Luckie, et al., 1995) for use in their review. Scores on this scale could range from 0 to 16; the actual range was 8 to 15 (MST trials were rated 10 and 13).

Brestan and Eyberg (1998) recorded information on four "minimal criteria of good designs": use of a comparison group, random assignment, use of reliable measures, and report of descriptive statistics. They also recorded information on other methodological criteria. Study-quality ratings were not reported.

The Scientific Methods Scale (SMS) was used by Farrington and Welsh (2003) to define high-quality evaluation designs. Farrington and Welsh only reviewed studies that were randomized experiments (level 5) or quasi experiments with matched control groups (level 4).

Aos and colleagues (2001) used a 5-point rating scale similar to the SMS in their analysis, and they weighted study-level effect sizes (ES) by study quality. The findings of randomized experiments (level 5) were not discounted (weighting factor = 1.0), findings of quasi experiments with controls for selection bias (level 4) were weighted .75, findings of quasi experiments with matched comparison groups (level 3) were weighted .5, and other quasi experiments (level 2) and single-group designs (level 1) were not included (weighted 0).

Synthesis of Results

Selected Outcomes   Several reviews summarized the evidence in tables of "key findings" or selected outcomes. In some reviews, this evidence was organized by outcome domains, and tables showed which studies provided evidence that MST had favorable effects on each outcome (e.g., Corcoran, 2003, p. 182). Other reviews organized the evidence by study, highlighting positive results from each study (e.g., Burns et al., 2000, pp. 291–292; Henggeler, Schoenwald, Rowland, et al., 2002, pp. 207–208). Notably, null results and negative effects were not mentioned in these summaries. A similar approach was used in some narrative syntheses (e.g., Henggeler & Sheidow, 2003; Letourneau et al., 2002). This practice of highlighting positive or favorable outcomes is an example of confirmation bias.

More complete summaries of evidence were provided by Fraser et al. (1997), who used tables to show study-level effect sizes; and by Henggeler, Mihalic, et al. (1998, p. 37), who provided a table indicating that three of four MST trials had null results on at least one outcome measure; all four trials had positive results on at least one outcome measure.

Vote Counting   Several reviews reported the number of studies that showed statistically significant differences in favor of the MST group on one or more outcome measures (e.g., Burns et al., 1999; Miller et al., 2000; U.S. Department of Health and Human Services, 1999). This vote counting method does not take sample size or precision into account; thus, it can lead reviewers to miss important effects in underpowered studies and to count trivial differences in large studies (Bushman, 1994).

The "Chambless Criteria"   Several reviews classified MST as a "probably efficacious" treatment (Brestan & Eyberg, 1998; Burns et al., 1999, 2000; Burns, 2003; Chorpita et al., 2002), according to the criteria for empirically supported treatments developed by an American Psychological Association (APA) Division 12 (Clinical Psychology) task force (Chambless, Baker, Baucom, Beutler, Calhoun, Crits-Christoph, et al., 1998).

Quantitative Synthesis (Meta-Analysis)   The first meta-analysis of results from MST trials appeared in 2000. Six reviews provided pooled ES estimates across three to six MST trials. These estimates are not comparable, since they are based on different pooling methods and some are more rigorous than others (Cooper & Hedges, 1994; Lipsey & Wilson, 2001).

Several authors used inverse variance methods to account for differences in the precision of estimates (due to differences in sample size and variability). I converted the direction of effects as needed, so that positive ES always favor MST. The results, reported as weighted standardized mean differences, for MST trials were

- .31 for recidivism (three trials, Aos et al., 2001);
- .41 for delinquency (six trials, including anti-social outcomes for studies that did not provide measures of delinquency; Farrington & Welsh, 2003); and
- .11 for family adaptability, .18 for family cohesion, .02 for peer adaptability, .02 for peer bonding, .15 for peer aggression, .03 for peer maturity, .50 for risk of incarceration, .05 for parental mental health, and .50 for child behavior (three trials, Woolfenden et al., 2003).

The pooled estimates reported by Aos and colleagues and by Farrington and Welsh were statistically significant; the pooled results for MST trials in the Woolfenden review were not significantly different from zero.

Three other reviews reported pooled ES, but these were not weighted and pooling methods were unclear. These results include:

- mean effect sizes of .8 for parent-reported improvement in conduct problems, 1.2 for self-reported improvement in these problems, .7 for improvements in family functioning, and 1.2 for recidivism rates between 2 and 4 years post-treatment (Brosnan & Carr, 2000);
- a mean effect of .5 on the Revised Behavior Problem Checklist (Chorpita et al., 2002); and
- an average effect across all outcomes of .55 (Curtis et al., 2004).

Recall that a fully systematic review showed that results for MST were not significantly better or worse than for other treatments on any (of 21) outcome measures (Littell et al., 2005).

Reviewers' Conclusions

Although there was considerable variation in the methods used and the studies included in these reviews, there was somewhat more consistency in their conclusions. As shown in Table 4.1, only 3 of 37 reviews mentioned negative or null effects in their conclusions (Farrington & Welsh, 2003; Swenson & Henggeler, 2003; Woolfenden et al., 2003). Nine reviews provided some caveats about the evidence (e.g., results were not classified as "well-established," results appeared to depend on fidelity, and findings have not yet been replicated by other research teams). However, most (25) of the reviews seemed to provide unqualified support for MST. These conclusions were not related to whether authors were independent (e.g., negative or null findings were mentioned by 9% of independent reviews and 7% of reviews authored by MST developers); hence there was no evidence of allegiance bias in the reviews.

Since all reviews included studies that had mixed results, it is not clear whether or how these results were factored into the reviewers' conclusions. How do reviewers determine whether positive results outweigh negative or null findings, especially when they do not use quantitative methods to pool results across studies? The next section takes a closer look at these issues.

FROM RESULTS TO REPORTS TO REVIEWS

In this section, I examine findings from a single published MST outcome study, and compare them to published reviews of this study. For this comparison, I selected a study that is (to my knowledge) the only completed trial of the effects of MST in cases of child maltreatment. Reported by Brunk, Henggeler, and Whelan (1987), this trial included 43 families of abused or neglected children, who were randomly assigned to MST or parent-training (PT) groups.

I categorized the direction of results on the scales and subscales used in the Brunk study, using three categories: favors MST, favors PT, and neutral (no difference between groups, unclear, or missing). I then tallied the number of items in each category. This vote counting is not an ideal method, but I will show that it is not possible to calculate accurate effect sizes from the published results of this study.

Content analysis was used to identify the number and direction (favors MST, favors PT, and neutral) of discrete phrases used by the study's authors to characterize results of the study in the original abstract. The same method was used to analyze summaries of the Brunk study that appeared in the text and summary tables of published reviews.

The Brunk Study: Findings and Reports

The sole published report on the Brunk study provided data on 33 families who completed treatment (77% of families in the experiment). Pre- and posttest means were presented for subgroups (abuse or neglect) within treatment conditions (MST or PT), but only for outcome measures with significant changes; standard deviations were not provided. Results were analyzed with a 2 × 2 × 2 (pre/post x subgroup x treatment) multivariate analysis of variance (MANOVA) of four groups of outcome measures. Three-way univariate ANOVA was used for individual outcome measures. Child age and parental age were used as covariates in the MANOVAs and ANOVAs. F values were provided in the text, but only for results that were statistically significant. No follow-up data or intent-to-treat analyses were provided.

Table 4.3 provides a summary of the results provided by Brunk et al. (1987). According to the text and

TABLE 4.3 Results of Brunk, Henggeler, and Whelan (1987)

Measure	Domain(s)	Abbreviation	Main effects MST vs. PT
Self-Reports			
Symptom Checklist-90 (Global Severity Index)	Parent psychiatric symptoms	SCL-90 GSI	NS
Behavior Problem Checklist (total score)	Parent perceptions of child behavior problems	BPC	Not reported
Family Environment Scale (90 items, 10 subscales)	Relationships, personal growth, system maintenance	FES	NS
			NS
			NS
			NS
			NS
			NS
			NS
			NS
			NS
			NS
Family Inventory of Life Events (71 items)	Parental stress	FILE	NS
Treatment Outcome Questionnaire	Parent perceptions of treatment needs and changes in needs	TOQ I-C	NS
		TOQ F-C	NS
		TOQ SS-C	PT > MST
Therapist Reports			
Treatment Outcome Questionnaire	Therapist perceptions of treatment needs and changes in needs	TOQ I-T	NS
		TOQ F-T	NS
		TOQ SS-T	NS
Observational Measures of Parent-Child Interactions			
Parental effectiveness	Attention	NO-VAT-O	NS (Ng: MST > PT, Ab: PT > MST)
		CT-NAT-O	MST > PT

(Continued)

TABLE 4.3 *(Continued)*

Measure	Domain(s)	Abbreviation	Main effects MST vs. PT
Observational Measures of Parent-Child Interactions			
		NO-NAT-O	NS
	Action	O-VAC-TC	PT > MST
		CT-VAC-TC	MST > PT
		CT-NAC-TC	MST > PT
Child passive noncompliance		O-VAC-O	MST > PT
		CT-VAC-CT	NS
			(Ab: MST > PT)
Parental unresponsiveness	O-VAT-O		MST > PT
	O-NAT-O		NS
	O-NAT-TC		NS

NS = no significant difference, > = superior, Ng = neglect group only, Ab = abuse group only.

For TOQ: I = individual, F = family, SS = social system, C = client report, T = therapist report.

For observational measures: NO = not oriented, O = oriented, VAT = verbal attention, NAT = nonverbal attention, VAC = verbal action, NAC = nonverbal action, CT = contact, TC = task completed.

tables of the original report, there were 16 client self-report measures (including 10 subscales of the Family Environment Scale, FES). PT was superior to MST on 1 measure, results for 1 measure (the Behavior Problem Checklist, BPC) were not reported (presumably because there were no significant differences between pre- and posttest scores), and there were no significant differences between treatment groups on the remaining 14 measures. There were no significant differences between MST and PT on 3 measures derived from therapist reports. On 11 observational measures, 5 favored MST, 1 favored PT, 2 showed subgroup interaction effects (MST was superior for one subgroup but not the other, with no significant main effects), and 3 showed no significant differences between MST and PT. Thus, for 30 possible tests of main effects, MST was superior to PT on 5 tests, PT was superior on 2 tests, there were no significant differences on 22 tests, and the results of 1 test were not reported.

Since the authors reported main effects of treatment and treatment effects for two subgroups plus four multivariate analyses, there were at least 94 possible tests of significance in which effects of MST could have appeared. With a total of 33 cases in three-way analyses with two covariates, these tests had little statistical power. Nevertheless, with alpha set at $p =. 05$, we would expect about 5 (4.7) of 94 tests to be statistically significant by chance.

Content analysis of the authors' summary of results in the abstract produced five codeable phrases, indicating that there were no significant between-group differences in three domains ("parental psychiatric symptomology, reduced overall stress, and . . . severity of identified problems"), MST was superior in one domain ("restructuring parent-child relations"), and PT was superior in another domain ("reducing identified social problems").

Research Reviews

Of the 37 reviews in the previous analysis, 17 cited the Brunk study, but only 13 provided specific comments on findings of that study. The bottom portion of Table 4.4 shows the results of content analyses of the text and tables in these 13 reviews.

Burns et al. (2000) summarized the results of Brunk as follows:

Parents in both groups reported decreases in psychiatric symptomatology and reduced overall stress following treatment. In addition, both groups demonstrated decreases in the severity of the identified problems. The study also included observational measures of parent-child interactions. The outcomes indicated that MST had improved such interactions, implying a decreased risk for maltreatment of children in the MST condition. (p. 293)

TABLE 4.4 Summary of Results of Brunk, Henggeler, and Whelan (1987) as Described in the Original Published Report and 13 Published Reviews

Source	Type of Information	Number of Items	Favors PT	Neutral (no significant difference between groups, unclear, or missing)	Favors MST
Original Research Report					
Brunk et al. (1987)	Data collected (subscales)	30	2	23	5
	Results reported (subscales)	29	2	22	5
	Data provided (subscales)	19	2	12	5
	Abstract (phrases)	5	1	3	1
Research Reviews					
Burns et al. (2000)	Text (phrases)	5		3	2
	Table (phrases)	1			1
Corcoran (2000)	Text (phrases)	10	3	4	3
Curtis et al. (2004)	Table (effect size)	1			1
Henggeler et al. (1998)	Text (phrases)	1			1
Henggeler et al. (2002)	Text (phrases)	3			3
	Table (phrases)	1			1
Henggeler & Sheidow (2003)	Text (phrases)	1			1
Hoagwood et al. (2001)	Text (phrases)	1			1
Kazdin (1998)	Text (phrases)	1			1
Kazdin & Weisz (1998)	Text (phrases)	1			1
Pushak (2002)	Text (phrases)	1			1
Schoenwald & Rowland (2002)	Text (phrases)	1			1
Swenson & Henggeler (2003)	Text (phrases)	5	1		4
Swenson et al. (1998)	Text (phrases)	1			1

The reviewers also provided a table describing MST studies; under the column headed "MST outcomes," the entry for the Brunk study reads, "improved parent-child relations" (p. 291). Table 4.4 shows the coding of these comments: three neutral phrases and two positive phrases in the text, and one positive phrase in the table.

Regarding the Brunk study, Corcoran (2000) said:

Both approaches acted to reduce psychiatric symptoms in parents and parental stress, as well as to alleviate individual and family problems. Each approach also offered unique advantages. Multisystemic therapy was more effective in improving parent-child interactions, helping physically abusive parents manage child behavior, and assisting neglectful parents in responding more appropriately to their child's needs. Surprisingly, parent training was more advantageous for improving parents' social lives. The hypothesis is the group setting for parent training reduced isolation and improved parents' support system. (p. 568)

As shown in Table 4.4, this passage was coded as having four neutral phrases, three phrases that favor MST, and three phrases that favor PT.

Curtis et al. (2004) computed an average effect size for the Brunk study, presumably across all outcome measures. They report a result of $d = 1.32$ ($SD = .65$, $N = 43$; p. 414). This is an enormous effect size (it indicates that, after treatment, the average family in the MST group was functioning better than 90% of cases in the PT group across all outcome measures). Given the results of the Brunk study, this appears to be a mistake. Littell and colleagues (2005) and David Wilson (an expert on effect size calculations) could not derive effect sizes from the Brunk report. Wilson, however, was able to approximate the effect size reported by Curtis et al. by (1) ignoring all nonsignificant differences, (2) assuming that all significant differences favored MST, and (3) misusing effect-size formulas (treating reported F values as if they were from one-way ANOVAs, ignoring variance extracted in the original analysis which used a mixed factorial design with covariates); even then, the d index he obtained was not statistically significant (David B. Wilson, personal communication, March 2, 2005).

Henggeler and colleagues (Henggeler, Schoenwald, Rowland, et al., 2002) cited the Brunk study as support for the following statement: "MST has consistently produced improvements in family functioning across outcome studies with juvenile offenders and maltreating families. Several of these studies used observational methods to demonstrate increased positive family interactions and decreased negative interactions" (p. 209). These authors used a single phrase to characterize results of the Brunk study in a table of MST outcomes: "improved parent-child interactions" (p. 207).

Other reviewers summarized results of the Brunk study as follows (see Table 4.4):

- "MST was significantly more effective [than PT] at restructuring problematic parent-child relations" (Henggeler, Mihalic, et al., 1998, p. 33).
- "Successful MST outcomes have been observed . . . for children in maltreating families" (Henggeler & Sheidow, 2003, p. 512).
- "The effects of [MST] have been further demonstrated among . . . abused or neglected children" (Hoagwood et al., 2001, p. 1183).
- "The [MST] outcome studies have extended to . . . parents who engage in physical abuse or neglect. . . . Thus, the model of providing treatment may have broad applicability across problem domains among seriously disturbed children" (Kazdin, 1998, p. 79).
- MST "treatment effects have been replicated . . . with parents who engage in physical abuse or neglect" (Kazdin & Weisz, 1998, p. 27).
- "MST is considered to be a promising treatment for families with children who are at risk of being abused by their parents" (Pushak, 2002, p. 181).
- "Randomized trials with . . . families in which maltreatment occurred (Brunk, Henggeler, &

Whelan, 1987) suggested the promise of MST with these populations" (Schoenwald & Rowland, 2002, p. 113).
- "MST was more effective than Parent Training for improving parent-child interactions associated with maltreatment. Abusive parents showed greater progress in controlling their child's behavior, maltreated children exhibited less passive noncompliance, and neglecting parents became more responsive to their child's behavior. Parent training was superior to MST [in] decreasing social problems (i.e., social support network)" (Swenson & Henggeler, 2003, pp. 75–76).
- "The effectiveness of MST has been supported in controlled outcome studies with . . . maltreating families" (Swenson et al., 1998, p. 332).

As shown in Table 4.4, three patterns emerged as we traced results from the original measures, through the published report, to published reviews of these findings. The first pattern is *overall data reduction*: A complex pattern of results was summarized in increasingly more succinct ways (evident in the column on "number of items"). This reduction is often essential if results are to be conveyed in ways that are meaningful and accessible to diverse audiences.

The second trend is a *reduction in uncertainty*: The proportion of neutral items or statements diminished as the data (i.e., total number of items or statements) were reduced. Put more succinctly, nonsignificant differences were minimized. This trend becomes troubling when the weight of the evidence—the balance among positive, negative, and neutral items—is not adequately represented. In the original report, the proportion of neutral items dropped from 77% (23) of 30 subscales, to 76% of 29 reported results, to 63% of 19 provided results, to 60% (3) of 5 comments in the abstract. Although the balance was not perfect, even the abstract indicated that there were more between-group similarities than differences in outcomes. However, only 2 reviews even mentioned neutral (null) results; the other 11 reviews seemed to ignore the modal pattern of nonsignificant results in the Brunk study.

Third, while the original research report retained a balance among positive, neutral, and negative results, this balance was absent in all but 1 of 13 reviews (Corcoran, 2000). Most of the reviews overemphasized the positive results of MST and minimized or ignored other findings. In fact, 11 reviews used a *single* positive number or statement to characterize the results of the Brunk study in their text or tables. Thus, there is evidence of *confirmation bias* in reviewers' summaries of the Brunk study.

LIMITATIONS

Based on a nonprobability sample of published reviews, the results reported here cannot be generalized to other reviews, to reviews of interventions other than MST, or to MST trials other than the Brunk study. However, many of the reviews in this analysis also considered evidence about other interventions and included other MST trials; there is no logical reason to believe that these reviewers would have handled the evidence for MST differently from evidence on other programs. Nor is it sensible to think that reviewers would treat the Brunk study differently from other MST studies.

DISCUSSION

Reviewers use different methods and criteria to identify, analyze, and synthesize empirical evidence. Most of the 37 reviews in this study relied on narrative summaries of convenience samples of published studies. This approach has been shown to be vulnerable to several sources and types of bias. Fewer than one quarter of the reviews used explicit inclusion criteria, systematic search strategies, unpublished studies, assessment of study allocation methods, assessment of attrition, or quantitative synthesis. Independent reviews were more likely to use some of these strategies, but less likely to include unpublished reports compared with reviews authored by program developers. Some reviews were partially systematic, but none met established criteria for systematic reviews.

Reviews tended to confirm prevailing beliefs, even when the data were equivocal. As prior conclusions were repeated, readers may have mistaken this consistency for valid evidence. (Not included in this analysis were 20 published summaries of MST trials that relied primarily or solely on previous published reviews; e.g., Kazdin, 2000, 2002; Lehman, Goldman, Dixon, & Churchill, 2004; U.S. Department of Health and Human Services, 2001; U.S. National Institutes of Health, 2004.) This confirmation bias appeared in independent reviews as well as those authored by program developers.

Understanding Confirmation Bias

Confirmation bias is the ubiquitous, often unintentional tendency to seek information that supports a hypothesis, give preferential treatment to evidence that confirms existing beliefs, and dismiss evidence to the contrary (Nickerson, 1998). Initially identified by Francis Bacon (1621/1960) and investigated by Watson (1960, 1968) and others, numerous studies show that people (including scientists) are reluctant to consider evidence that is inconsistent with their predictions (e.g., Fugelsang, Stein, Green, & Dunbar, 2004; Mahoney, 1977). This may be because confirmatory information is easier to process cognitively; that is, it is easier to see how information supports a position than it is to see how the same information might counter that position. Further, information that supports a hypothesis is more likely to be remembered than information to the contrary (Gilovich, 1993).

Confirmation bias may be the source of many myths and self-fulfilling prophecies: It gives us an illusion of consistency, leads us to misinterpret new information, and induces overconfidence in beliefs (Nickerson, 1998; Schrag, 1999). The scientific method is constructed to compensate for this human tendency, so that we must try to disprove our hypotheses. This strategy of falsifying hypotheses is not something that people do naturally (Watson, 1960, 1968; Nickerson, 1998).

Confirmation Bias in Political Context

Policy makers, practitioners, and scholars all want to know what works best in response to pressing human and social problems. Most of the reviews in this study were written by scholars and experts in the United States at a time when there was pressure to demonstrate the efficacy, effectiveness, and cost effectiveness of psychosocial interventions to ensure their continued political and financial support. This pressure may have exacerbated the natural tendency to seek information that confirms our hopes and expectations. For example, "As pressure increases for the demonstration of effective treatment for children with mental disorders, it is essential that the field has an understanding of the evidence base. To address this aim, the authors searched the published literature for *effective* interventions for children and adolescents" (Burns et al., 1999, p. 199; emphasis added). Hence, these authors cited "studies with large effect sizes" in child welfare, but did not the mention larger, more rigorous trials in that field that did not produce large effect sizes.

To their credit, the researchers and reviewers who sought to demonstrate treatment effects cared about evidence. They sought to improve fields of practice that relied (and still rely) on practices that are largely untested. However, in the search for positive, confirming examples of effective interventions, valuable information on ineffective or harmful practices was ignored. The focus on positive evidence detracted from a full understanding of the evidence base.

The pressure to find out what works *best* pits one program against others. In this competitive, market-driven context, the real message of the Brunk study—that different interventions have different partial effects—was lost. Following Brunk, the choices policy makers face may depend in part on which approaches or outcomes they *prefer*. For example, is it more important to reduce parents' social problems or to improve aspects of parent-child interactions? The Brunk study provided no guidance on which outcomes were "better" or more important than others (there were no a priori hypotheses in this regard), but other studies might.

Confirmation Bias and the High-Fidelity Hypothesis

To explain variations in outcomes across MST trials, several authors have suggested that MST may have performed better in efficacy studies than in studies of effectiveness (Henggeler, 2004; Petrosino & Soydan, 2005). In their analysis of seven MST trials, Curtis et al. (2004) classified the Brunk study as one of three efficacy studies in which MST developers exercised more control over the treatment conditions than in the remaining four studies. It is unclear why the Simpsonville, South Carolina, project (also known as the Family and Neighborhood Services study) was not included in the efficacy category, after Henggeler and colleagues described this study as one of the trials "in which the developers of MST provided ongoing clinical supervision and consultation (i.e., quality assurance was high)" (Henggeler, Schoenwald, Rowland, et al., 2002, p. 211). Since Schoenwald and colleagues observed that these original MST trials "could be considered hybrids of 'efficacy' and 'effectiveness' research" (Schoenwald, Sheidow, Letourneau, & Liao, 2003, p. 234), it appears that post hoc classifications were used in the Curtis et al. study.

Using an implausibly high effect size ($d = 1.32$) for the Brunk study (discussed above), Curtis and colleagues calculated a pooled effect size of $d = .81$ for three efficacy studies compared with an average ES of $d = .26$ for four studies of effectiveness. For unknown reasons, corrections for small sample bias were only applied to one study, and not to the Brunk study (valid $N = 33$, not 43 as reported by Curtis et al., 2004). Pooled ES were not weighted; hence, it appears that the Brunk study contributed as much to the average effect for efficacy studies as results from a much larger study ($N = 176$ cases) with a smaller ES.

These results have been used to suggest that the impact of program developers-as-evaluators on results of controlled trials has more to do with their ability to achieve high fidelity than with their allegiance bias (Henggeler, 2004; Petrosino & Soydan, 2005). However, the calculations by Curtis and colleagues do not provide a sound basis for any conclusions about the efficacy of MST or high-fidelity conditions.

From Efficacy to Effectiveness to Transportability: On What Basis?

Several states, professional organizations, private foundations, and federal agencies have taken the lead in identifying evidence-based practices and encouraging their replication. Now that lists of evidence-based practices have been compiled by experts (often with U.S. government funding), the emphasis in the health and mental health fields has begun to shift from research synthesis to the translation of results into directions for policy and practice, from questions about efficacy and effectiveness to concerns about transportability and dissemination. The movement to transport effective practices is a high priority for many government agencies (including the U.S. National Institutes of Health). This is based on the twin assumptions that (1) we already know what works in response to certain pressing social problems, and (2) this knowledge, derived largely from controlled studies, can be applied with success in other samples and settings. However, the results reported here raise important questions about the validity of current knowledge about what works for certain problems and populations.

The movement to transport effective practices may be premature if it is based on evidence of efficacy or effectiveness that has been compiled with haphazard reviews that are vulnerable to publication, selection, and confirmation biases. If knowledge about what works is tainted in these ways, we may waste valuable resources trying to transport ineffective practices (albeit ones that have produced *some* positive results in controlled trials) and fail to investigate other practices that may be equally or more effective. A closer look at the evidence is warranted.

Implications for Social Science

It is ironic that while practitioners and policy makers are urged to make better use of scientific evidence, "scientists only rarely cumulate evidence scientifically" (Chalmers, Hedges, & Cooper, 2002, p. 12). To support evidence-based practice and policy, social scientists must make better use of the science of research synthesis. "If a review purports to be an authoritative summary of what 'the evidence' says, then the reader is entitled to demand that this is a comprehensive, objective, and reliable overview, and not a partial review of a convenience sample of the author's favorite studies" (Petticrew & Roberts, 2006, p. 6).

Advanced training in systematic review methods is needed to prepare the next generation of scholars to produce valid evidence for policy and practice. Systematic methods can minimize bias in the review process. Systematic reviews can incorporate contradictory information—including much of the data that have been lost in traditional narrative or haphazard reviews—and use it to answer important questions about why intervention effects may vary. These reviews are very labor intensive, hence they are more costly than traditional literature reviews; however, systematic reviews may be more cost effective in the long run if they reduce bias (misinformation) and prevent missteps in the development and dissemination of effective practices.

Reviewers often struggle with decisions about the types of evidence to consider, sometimes lowering the bar (deviating from their original standards) in order to be able to say *something*. This is a slippery slope. Reasonable people will disagree about the qualities of evidence needed to support certain inferences. These decisions should be based on careful consideration of substantive, contextual, and methodological issues. Once the decision is made, it is worrisome when reviewers deviate from their original plan (this is not in accordance with the principles of systematic reviews). The Cochrane Collaboration has taken another approach by publishing "empty" reviews that found no credible evidence on a topic. This may not be very sat-

isfying to reviewers or policy makers, but one advantage of an empty review is that it does not lead readers to the wrong conclusions. Empty reviews identify important gaps in current knowledge and provide justification for new studies.

The peer-review process must be strengthened to counter various forms of selection bias, including confirmation bias (Mahoney, 1977). This is not an easy task, but some important inroads have been made. The American Psychological Association (APA) journals has adopted the CONSORT (Consolidated Standards of Reporting Trials) statement (Moher, Schultz, & Altman, 2001), which provides clear guidelines for reporting trials. Journals should also adopt the QUOROM statement to increase the quality of reporting on meta-analysis and other research reviews. Ultimately, social and health scientists should endorse the use of prospective registers of trials to avoid publication bias and outcome selection bias (Dickersin, 2005).

Evidence-based practice requires a long-term commitment to building valid information about and for practice, and an infrastructure that provides consumers with continued access to this information. Careful primary research and research synthesis can help to build an evidence base for the helping professions. However, there have been far too few controlled trials and too many haphazard reviews of these trials to produce enough valid evidence for practice and policy—and valuable information has been lost along the way. More scientifically sound syntheses of credible empirical studies are needed to provide a valid evidence base for practice.

Portions of this work were supported by grants from the Smith Richardson Foundation, the Swedish Centre for Evidence-Based Social Work Practice (IMS), and the Nordic Campbell Center. I thank Burneé Forsythe for her assistance with the search process and document retrieval. I thank Jim Baumohl, Dennis Gorman, Mark Lipsey, David Weissburd, and David B. Wilson for helpful comments on an earlier version of this chapter.

References

Aos, S., Phipps, P., Barnoski, R., & Lieb, R. (2001). *The comparative costs and benefits of programs to reduce crime* (Version 4.0). Document 01-05-1201. Olympia: Washington State Institute for Public Policy.

Bacon, F. (1960). *Novum organum.* New York: Bobbs-Merrill. (Original work published 1621)

Becker, B. J., Hedges, L., & Pigott, T. D. (2004). *Campbell collaboration statistical analysis policy brief.* Available: http://www.campbellcollaboration.org/MG/StatsPolicyBrief.pdf.

Begg, C. B. (1994). Publication bias. In H. Cooper & L. Hedges (Eds.), *The handbook of research synthesis* (pp. 399–409). New York: Russell Sage Foundation.

Borduin, C. M. (1999). Multisystemic treatment of criminality and violence in adolescents. *Journal of the American Academy of Child and Adolescent Psychiatry, 38,* 242–249.

Borduin, C. M., Heiblum, N., Jones, M. R., & Grabe, S. A. (2000). Community-based treatments of serious antisocial behavior in adolescents. In W. E. Martin & J. L Schwartz-Kulstad (Eds.), *Person-environment psychology and mental health: Assessment and intervention* (pp. 113–141). Mahwah, NJ: Erlbaum.

Borduin, C. M., Schaeffer, C. M., & Ronis, S. T. (2003). Multisystemic treatment of serious antisocial behavior in adolescents. In C. A. Essau (Ed.), *Conduct and oppositional defiant disorders: Epidemiology, risk factors, and treatment* (pp. 299–318). Mahwah, NJ: Erlbaum.

Brestan, E. V., & Eyberg, S. M. (1998). Effective psychosocial treatments of conduct-disordered children and adolescents: 29 years, 82 studies, and 5,272 kids. *Journal of Clinical Child Psychology, 27,* 180–189.

Brosnan, R., & Carr, A. (2000). Adolescent conduct problems. In A. Carr (Ed.), *What works with children and adolescents? A critical review of psychological interventions with children, adolescents and their families* (pp. 131–154). London: Routledge.

Brunk, M., Henggeler, S. W., & Whelan, J. P. (1987). A comparison of multisystemic therapy and parent training in the brief treatment of child abuse and neglect. *Journal of Consulting and Clinical Psychology, 55,* 311–318.

Burns, B. J. (2003). Children and evidence-based practice. *Psychiatric Clinics of North America, 26,* 955–970.

Burns, B. J., Hoagwood, K., & Mrazek, P. J. (1999). Effective treatment for mental disorders in children and adolescents. *Clinical Child and Family Psychology Review, 2,* 199–244.

Burns, B. J., Schoenwald, S. K., Burchard, J. D., Faw, L., & Santos, A. B. (2000). Comprehensive community-based interventions for youth with severe emotional disorders: Multisystemic therapy and the wraparound process. *Journal of Child and Family Studies, 9,* 283–314.

Bushman, B. J. (1994). Vote-counting procedures in meta-analysis. In H. Cooper & L. V. Hedges (Eds.), *The handbook of research synthesis* (pp. 193–213). New York: Russell Sage Foundation.

Bushman, B. J., & Wells, G. L. (2001). Narrative impressions of literature: The availability bias and the corrective properties of meta-analytic approaches. *Personal and Social Psychology Bulletin, 27,* 1123–1130.

Carlton, P. L., & Strawderman, W. E. (1996). Evaluating cumulated research I: The inadequacy of traditional methods. *Biological Psychiatry, 39,* 65–72.

Carr, A. (Ed.) (2000). *What works for children and adolescents? A critical review of psychological interventions with children, adolescents and their families.* London: Routledge.

Center for Substance Abuse Prevention. (2000). *Strengthening America's families: Model family programs for substance abuse and delinquency prevention.* Salt Lake City: Department of Health Education, University of Utah.

Chalmers, I., Hedges, L. V., & Cooper, H. (2002). A brief history of research synthesis. *Evaluation & the Health Professions, 25(1),* 12–37.

Chambless, D. L., Baker, M. J., Baucom, D. H., Beutler, L. E., Calhoun, K. S., Crits-Christoph, P., et al. (1998). Update on empirically validated therapies: II. *Clinical Psychologist, 51,* 3–16.

Chorpita, B. F., Yim, L. M., Donkervoet, J. C., Arensdorf, A., Amundsen, M. J., McGee, C., Serrano, A., Yates, A., Burns, J. A., & Morelli, P. (2002). Toward large-scale implementation of empirically supported treatments for children: A review and observations by the Hawaii empirical basis to services task force. *Clinical Psychology: Science and Practice, 9,* 165–190.

Cooper, H., & Hedges, L. V. (Eds.). (1994). *The handbook of research synthesis.* New York: Russell Sage Foundation.

Corcoran, J. (2000). Family interventions with child physical abuse and neglect: A critical review. *Children and Youth Services Review, 22,* 563–591.

Corcoran, J. (2003). *Clinical applications of evidence-based family interventions.* New York: Oxford University Press.

Cormack, C., & Carr, A. (2000). Drug abuse. In A. Carr (Ed.), *What works for children and adolescents? A critical review of psychological interventions with children, adolescents and their families* (pp. 155–178). London: Routledge.

Curtis, N. M., Ronan, K. R., & Borduin, C. M. (2004). Multisystemic treatment: A meta-analysis of outcome studies. *Journal of Family Psychology, 18,* 411–419.

Dickersin, K. (2005). Publication bias: Recognizing the problem, understanding its origins and scope, and preventing harm. In H. R. Rothstein, A. J. Sutton, & M. Borenstein (Eds.), *Publication bias in meta-analysis: Prevention, assessment, and adjustments* (pp. 11–33). Chichester, UK: Wiley.

Farrington, D. P., & Welsh, B. C. (2003). Family-based prevention of offending: A meta-analysis. *Australian and New Zealand Journal of Criminology, 36,* 127–151.

Fonagy, P., & Kurtz, A. (2002). Disturbance of conduct. In P. Fonagy, M. Target, D. Cottrell, J. Phillips, & Z. Kurtz (Eds.), *What works for whom? A critical review of treatments for children and adolescents* (pp. 106–191). New York: Guilford.

Fraser, M. W., Nelson, K. E., & Rivard, J. C. (1997). Effectiveness of family preservation services. *Social Work Research, 21,* 138–153.

Fugelsang, J., Stein, C., Green, A., & Dunbar, K. (2004). Theory and data interactions of the scientific mind: Evidence from the molecular and the cognitive laboratory. *Canadian Journal of Experimental Psychology, 58,* 132–141.

Gilovich, T. (1993). *How we know what isn't so: The fallibility of human reason in everyday life.* New York: Free Press.

Henggeler, S. W. (2004). Decreasing effect sizes for effectiveness studies: Implications for the transport of evidence-based treatments: Comment on Curtis, Ronan, and Borduin (2004). *Journal of Family Psychology, 18,* 420–423.

Henggeler, S. W., & Borduin, C. M. (1995). Multisystemic treatment of serious juvenile offenders and their families. In I. M. Schwartz & P. AuClaire (Eds.)., *Home-based services for troubled children* (pp. 113–130). Lincoln: University of Nebraska Press.

Henggeler, S. W., Mihalic, S. F., Rone, L., Thomas, C., & Timmons-Mitchell, J. (1998). *Blueprints for violence prevention: Vol. 6. Multisystemic therapy.* Boulder: Center for the Study and Prevention of Violence, Institute of Behavioral Science, University of Colorado.

Henggeler, S. W., Schoenwald, S. K., Borduin, C. M., Rowland, M. D., & Cunningham, P. B. (1998). *Multisystemic treatment of antisocial behavior in children and adolescents.* New York: Guilford.

Henggeler, S. W., Schoenwald, S. K., Borduin, C. M., & Swenson, C. C. (2006). Methodological critique and meta-analysis as Trojan horse. *Children and Youth Services Review, 28,* 447–457.

Henggeler, S. W., Schoenwald, S. K., Liao, J. G., Letourneau, E. J., & Edwards, D. L. (2002). Transporting efficacious treatments to field settings: The link between supervisory practices and therapist fidelity in MST programs. *Journal of Clinical Child and Adolescent Psychology, 31,* 155–167.

Henggeler, S. W., Schoenwald, S. K., Rowland, M. D., & Cunningham, P. B. (2002). *Serious emotional disturbances in children and adolescents: Multisystemic therapy.* New York: Guilford.

Henggeler, S. W., & Sheidow, A. J. (2003). Conduct disorder and delinquency. *Journal of Marital and Family Therapy, 29*(4), 505–522.

Higgins, J. P. T., & Green, S. (Eds.) (2005). *Cochrane handbook for systematic reviews of interventions* (Version 4.2.5). Chichester, UK: Wiley. Available: http://www.cochrane.org/resources/handbook/hbook.htm.

Hoagwood, K., Burns, B. J., Kiser, L., Ringeisen, H., & Schoenwald, S. K. (2001). Evidence-based practice in child and adolescent mental health services. *Psychiatric Services, 52,* 1179–1189.

Hopewell, S., Clarke, M., Lefebvre, C., & Scherer, R. (2006). Handsearching versus electronic searching to identify reports of randomized trials. *Cochrane Database of Systematic Reviews, 4.*

Hopewell, S., McDonald, S., Clarke, M., & Egger, M. (2006). Grey literature in meta-analyses of randomized trials of health care interventions. *Cochrane Database of Systematic Reviews, 2.*

Jadad, A. R., Moher, M., Browman, G. P., Booker, L., Sigouin, C., Fuentes, M., et al. (2000). Systematic reviews and meta-analyses on treatment of asthma: Critical evaluation. *British Medical Journal, 320,* 537–540.

Jørgensen, A. W., Hilden, J., & Gøtzsche, P. G. (2006). Cochrane reviews compared with industry supported meta-analyses and other meta-analyses of the same drugs: Systematic review. *British Medical Journal, 333,* 782–785.

Kazdin, A. E. (1998). Psychosocial treatments for conduct disorder in children. In P. E. Nathan & J. M. Gorman (Eds.), *A guide to treatments that work* (pp. 65–89). New York: Oxford University Press.

Kazdin, A. E. (2000). Treatments for aggressive and antisocial children. *Child and Adolescent Psychiatric Clinics of North America, 9,* 841–858.

Kazdin, A. E. (2002). The state of child and adolescent psychotherapy research. *Child and Adolescent Mental Health, 7,* 53–59.

Kazdin, A. E., & Weisz, J. R. (1998). Identifying and developing empirically supported child and adolescent treatments. *Journal of Consulting and Clinical Psychology, 66,* 19–36.

Lehman, A. F., Goldman, H. H., Dixon, L. B., & Churchill, R. (2004). *Evidence-based mental health treatments and services: Examples to inform public policy.* New York: Milbank Memorial Fund.

Letourneau, E. J., Cunningham, P. B., & Henggeler, S. W. (2002). Multisystemic treatment of antisocial behavior in adolescents. In S. G. Hofmann & M. C. Tompson (Eds.), *Treating chronic and severe mental* disorders: A handbook of empirically supported interventions (pp. 364–381). New York: Guilford.

Lipsey, M. W., & Wilson, D. B. (2001). Practical meta-analysis. Thousand Oaks, CA: Sage.

Littell, J. H. (2005). Lessons from a systematic review of effects of multisystemic therapy. Children and Youth Services Review, 47, 445–463.

Littell, J. H. (2006). The case for multisystemic therapy: Evidence or orthodoxy? Children and Youth Services, 28, 458–472.

Littell, J. H., Popa, M., & Forsythe, B. (2005). Multisystemic therapy for social, emotional, and behavioral problems in youth aged 10–17. Cochrane Database of Systematic Reviews, 4.

Littell, J. H., & Schuerman, J. R. (1995). A synthesis of research on family preservation and family reunification programs. Washington, DC: Office of the Assistant Secretary for Planning and Evaluation, U.S. Department of Health and Human Services. Also available: http://aspe.os.dhhs.gov/hsp/cyp/fplitrev.htm.

Littell, J. H., & Schuerman, J. R. (1999). Innovations in child welfare: Preventing out-of-home placement of abused and neglected children. In D. E. Biegel & A. Blum (Eds.), Innovations in practice and service delivery across the lifespan (pp. 102–123). Oxford: Oxford University Press.

Luborsky, L., Diguer, L., Seligman, D. A., Rosenthal, R., Krause, E. D., Johnson, S., et al. (1999). The researcher's own therapy allegiances: A "wild card" in comparisons of treatment efficacy. Clinical Psychology: Science and Practice, 6, 95–106.

Mahoney, M. J. (1977). Publication prejudices: An experimental study of confirmatory bias in the peer review system. Cognitive Therapy and Research, 1(2), 161–175.

Miller, R. B., Johnson, L. N., Sandberg, J. G., Stringer-Seibold, T. A., & Gfeller-Strouts, L. (2000). An addendum to the 1997 outcome research chart. American Journal of Family Therapy, 28(4), 347–354.

Miller, W. R., Brown, J. M., Simpson, T. L., Handmaker, N. S., Bien, T. H., Luckie, L. H., et al. (1995). What works? A methodological analysis of the alcohol treatment outcome literature. In R. K. Hester & W. R. Miller (Eds.), Handbook of alcoholism treatment approaches: Effective alternatives (2nd ed., pp. 12–44). Needham Heights, MA: Allyn & Bacon.

Moher, D., Cook, D. J., Eastwood, S., Olkin, I., Rennie, D., Stroup, D. F., et al. (1999). Improving the quality of reports of meta-analyses of randomised controlled trials: The QUOROM statement. Lancet, 354, 1896–1900.

Moher, D., Schultz, K. F., & Altman, D. G. (2001). The CONSORT statement: Revised recommendations for improving the quality of reports of parallel-group randomized trials. Lancet, 357, 1191–1194. Also published in Journal of American Medical Association, 285, 1987–1991; and Annals of Internal Medicine, 134, 657–662.

MST Services. (2006). Licensed MST programs. Available: http://www.mstservices.com/text/licensed_agencies.htm.

National Institute of Mental Health. (2001). Youth in a difficult world. NIH Publication 01-4587. Available: http://www.nimh.nih.gov/publicat/youthdif.cfm.

National Institute of Mental Health, Consortium on Child and Adolescent Research. (2003). Data trends. Available: http://www.nimh.nih.gov/childhp/datatrends.cfm.

National Institute on Drug Abuse. (1999). Principles of drug addiction treatment: A research-based guide. NIH Publication 99-4180. Bethesda, MD: Author.

National Institute on Drug Abuse. (2003). Effective drug abuse treatment approaches: Multisystemic therapy. NIDA Behavioral Therapies Development Program. Available: http://www.nida.nih.gov/BRDP/Effective/Henggeler.html.

Nickerson, R. S. (1998). Confirmation bias: A ubiquitous phenomenon in many guises. Review of General Psychology, 2, 175–220.

Petrosino, A., & Soydan, H. (2005). The impact of program developers as evaluators on criminal recidivism: Results from meta-analyses of experimental and quasi-experimental research. Journal of Experimental Criminology, 1, 435–450.

Petticrew, M., & Roberts, H. (2006). Systematic reviews in the social sciences: A practical guide. Oxford: Blackwell.

Pushak, R. E. (2002). The dearth of empirically supported mental health services for children: Multisystemic therapy as a promising alternative. Scientific Review of Mental Health Practice, 1, 174–183.

Randall, J., & Cunningham, P. B. (2003). Multisystemic therapy: A treatment for violent substance-abusing and substance-dependent juvenile offenders. Addictive Behaviors, 28, 1731–1739.

Rosenthal, M. C. (1994). The fugitive literature. In H. Cooper & L. V. Hedges (Eds.), The handbook of research synthesis (pp. 85–94). New York: Russell Sage Foundation.

Rothstein, H., Sutton, A. J., & Bornstein, M. (Eds.). (2005). Publication bias in meta-analysis: Prevention, assessment, and adjustments. Chichester, UK: Wiley.

Rothstein, H. R., Turner, H. M., & Lavenberg, J. G. (2004). The Campbell Collaboration information retrieval policy brief. Available: http://www.campbell collaboration.org/MG/IRMGPolicyBriefRevised.pdf.

Schoenwald, S. K., Brown, T. L., & Henggeler, S. W. (2000). Inside multisystemic therapy: Therapist, supervisory, and program practices. *Journal of Emotional and Behavioral Disorders, 8*, 113–127.

Schoenwald, S. K., Henggeler, S. W., Brondino, M. J., & Rowland, M. D. (2000). Multisystemic therapy: Monitoring treatment fidelity. *Family Process, 39*, 83–103.

Schoenwald, S. K., & Hoagwood, K. (2001). Effectiveness, transportability, and dissemination of interventions: What matters when? *Psychiatric Services, 52*, 1190–1197.

Schoenwald, S. K., & Rowland, M. S. (2002). Multisystemic therapy. In B. J. Burns & K. Hoagwood (Eds.), *Community treatment for youth: Evidence-based interventions for severe emotional and behavioral disorders* (pp. 91–116). New York: Oxford University Press.

Schoenwald, S. K., Sheidow, A. J., Letourneau, E. J., & Liao, J. G. (2003). Transportability of multisystemic therapy: Evidence for multilevel influences. *Mental Health Services Research, 5*, 223–239.

Schrag, J. L. (1999). First impressions matter: A model of confirmatory bias. *Quarterly Journal of Economics, 114*, 37–82.

Shadish, W. R., Cook, T. D., & Campbell, D. T. (2002). *Experimental and quasi-experimental designs for general causal inference.* Boston: Houghton Mifflin.

Shadish, W., & Myers, D. (2004). *Campbell Collaboration research design policy brief.* Available: http://www.campbellcollaboration.org/MG/ResDes Policy Brief.pdf.

Shea, B., Moher, D., Graham, I., Pham, B., & Tugwell, P. (2002). Comparison of the quality of Cochrane reviews and systematic reviews published in paper-based journals. *Evaluation & the Health Professions, 25*, 116–129.

Smith, C. A., & Stern, S. B. (1997). Delinquency and antisocial behavior: A review of family processes and intervention research. *Social Service Review, 71*, 382–420.

Substance Abuse and Mental Health Services Administration. (2004). *Multisystemic therapy: Proven results.* Available: http://modelprograms.samhsa.gov/pdfs/FactSheets/Mst.pdf.

Sudderth, L. K. (2000). What works in treatment programs for substance-abusing youth. In M. P. Kluger, G. Alexander, & P. A. Curtis (Eds.), *What works in child welfare* (pp. 337–344). Washington, DC: Child Welfare League of America.

Swenson, C. C., & Henggeler, S. W. (2003). Multisystemic therapy (MST) for maltreated children and their families. In B. E. Saunders, L. Berliner, & R.F.Hanson (Eds.), *Child physical and sexual abuse:*

Guidelines for treatment: Final report (pp. 75–78). Charleston, SC: National Crime Victims Research and Treatment Center.

Swenson, C. C., Henggeler, S. W., Schoenwald, S. K., Kaufman, K. L., & Randall, J. (1998). Changing the social ecologies of adolescent sexual offenders: Implications of the success of multisystemic therapy in treating serious anti-social behavior in adolescents. *Child Maltreatment, 3*, 330–338.

Tarolla, S. M., Wagner, E. F., Rabinowitz, J., & Tubman, J. G. (2002). Understanding and treating juvenile offenders: A review of current knowledge and future directions. *Aggression and Violent Behavior, 7*, 125–143.

U.S. Department of Health and Human Services. (1999). *Mental health: A report of the surgeon general.* Rockville, MD: Author.

U.S. Department of Health and Human Services. (2001). *Youth violence: A report of the surgeon general.* Washington, DC: Author.

U.S. National Institutes of Health. (2004). *State-of-the-science conference statement: Preventing violence and related health-risking social behaviors in adolescence.* Available: http://consensus.nih.gov/ta/023/youthviolenceDRAFTstatement101504.pdf.

Vaughn, M. G., & Howard, M. O. (2004). Adolescent substance abuse treatment: A synthesis of controlled evaluations. *Research on Social Work Practice, 14*, 325–335.

Watson, P. C. (1960). On the failure to eliminate hypotheses in a conceptual task. *Quarterly Journal of Experimental Psychology, 12*, 129–140.

Watson, P. C. (1968). Reasoning about a rule. *Quarterly Journal of Experimental Psychology, 20*, 273–281.

Westat,. (2002). *Evaluation of family preservation and reunification programs: Final report.* Washington, DC: U.S. Department of Health and Human Services' Assistant Secretary for Planning and Evaluation. Available: http://aspe.hhs.gov/hsp/evalfampres94/Final/index.htm.

Woolfenden, S. R., Williams, K., & Peat, J. K. (2002). Family and parenting interventions for conduct disorder and delinquency: A meta-analysis of randomized controlled trials. *Archives of Disease in Childhood, 86*, 251–256.

Woolfenden, S. R., Williams, K., & Peat, J. K. (2003). Family and parenting interventions in children and adolescents with conduct disorder and delinquency aged 10–17. *Cochrane Database of Systematic Reviews, 2*.

Wortman, P. M. (1994). Judging research quality. In H. Cooper & L. V. Hedges (Eds.), *The handbook of research synthesis* (pp. 97–109). New York: Russell Sage Foundation.

Part III

Research on Permanency:
Adoption, Guardianship,
and Family Ties

Since the late 1990s, we have witnessed major achievements in the child welfare field. There has been a substantial reduction in the length of time that children linger in long-term foster care. The average length of stay of children in foster care has declined approximately 25% in 5 years, from about 20.5 months in 2000 to about 15.5 months in 2005.[1] Concurrently, there has been a substantial increase in the number of children adopted through public child welfare agencies (see Figure P.1). These changes have been largely the result of public policy brought about by advances in child welfare research. In this section, we review recent research advances in permanency, adoption, and guardianship in the context of family relationships and conflict that continue these advances.

In "The Influence of an Adoption Experiment on Social Policy," Trudy Festinger demonstrates how high-quality research can drive child welfare policy. She details a randomized controlled trial of an intervention designed to speed adoptions by streamlining the court process in cases where adoption is likely. One of the most important experiments conducted in child welfare to date, this study is an example of how researchers and child welfare authorities can design and carry out rigorous and relevant studies to answer difficult questions lingering in the field.

The relevance of research to child welfare policy and practice is furthered in "New Permanency Strategies for Children in Foster Care" by Mark Testa, which stems from his work that rigorously tests the use of subsidized guardianship as a permanency alternative. Many have heralded the importance of Testa's work in the area of kinship care, permanency, guardianship, and adoptions. Reacting to years of benign neglect in the child welfare and foster care fields, the judiciary in the state of Illinois placed the state's child welfare program under court supervision and mandated research-based interventions. As part of a federal Title IV-E Waiver Demonstration Project, Testa promoted and rigorously tested the use of subsidized guardianship as a permanency alternative, leading to

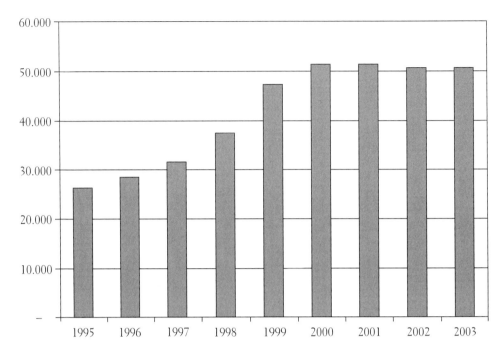

FIGURE P.1. Children Adopted Through Public Child Welfare Agencies

a substantial increase in permanency for children in the state. The chapter by Testa outlines the theoretical foundations of the use of kinship care as a placement resource of choice, drawing on an emerging body of evidence to support his position.

Child welfare researchers are also beginning to focus attention on the plight of adolescent service users within the child welfare system. With more than 0.5 million children in the foster care system at any one point in time (AFCARS, 2003, 2006), and millions entering or exiting the system over time, there is surprisingly little known about the experiences of those children once they are labeled "adults" and are no longer eligible to access child welfare services. In "The Transition to Adulthood Among Youth 'Aging Out' of Care: What Have We Learned?" Amy Dworsky reviews the literature on youth who "age out" of the foster care system, documenting the disappointing outcomes that most foster children experience. Also highlighted is the extent to which extending foster care or providing transitional programming may work to reduce this group's risk for educational deficits, mental health problems, economic insecurity, criminal justice involvement, and early child bearing.

The final two chapters of this section focus on the increasing relevance of intimate partner violence

(IPV) to child welfare. In "Moving Restorative Justice Interventions into Domestic Violence Treatment," Colleen Friend begins exploring the linkages between child protection and domestic violence by conducting a review of the theories that have guided intervention in this area. Friend then describes innovative programming with roots in Native American traditions that is designed to maintain the safety of women and children in battering relationships by extensively utilizing cultural, familial, and community resources.

Lynette Renner, Kristen Shook Slack, and Lawrence Berger conclude this section by providing a critical review of the existing theories of intimate partner violence employed within treatment protocols. In "A Descriptive Study of Intimate Partner Violence and Child Maltreatment: Implications for Child Welfare Policy" Renner, Slack, and Berger are particularly interested in preparing child welfare practitioners to view intimate partner violence as a complex multilevel dynamic that requires a strengths-based approach and total family intervention.

Note

1. According to national data from the Adoption and Foster Care Analysis and Reporting System (AFCARS), the mean length of stay in foster care was 32.6 months

in 2000 and declined to a mean of 28.6 months in 2005 (U.S. Department of Health and Human Services, 2003, 2006).

References

U.S. Department of Health and Human Services, Administration for Children and Families, Administration on Children, Youth and Families, Children's Bureau. (2003). *The AFCARS report: Final estimates for FY 1998 through FY 2002 (12)*. Available: http://www.acf.hhs.gov/programs/cb/stats_research/afcars/tar/report12.htm.

U.S. Department of Health and Human Services, Administration for Children and Families, Administration on Children, Youth and Families, Children's Bureau. (2006). *The AFCARS report: Preliminary FY 2005 estimates as of September 2006 (13)*. Available: http://www.acf.hhs.gov/programs/cb/stats_research/afcars/tar/report13.htm.

5

The Influence of an Adoption Experiment on Social Policy

Trudy Festinger

It is not often that the results of research are used as a key component of discussions leading up to the development of social legislation. It is equally rare that research results are used to provide the rationale for legislation. Yet that is what occurred with respect to legislation adopted in New York State in 2005 which, among other changes, improved the handling of adoption cases by the courts. In what follows, the research, based on two periods of data collection, will be presented. Although previously published (Festinger & Pratt, 2002; Shlonsky, Festinger, & Brookhart, 2006), the effect on legislation has to date never been reported.

The central question that propelled the study was whether keeping a case before the same judge and on the court calendar from termination of parental rights (TPR) through adoption would speed up the process of adoption for children in foster care. To answer this question, an experimental approach was used to test the effect of a little-used New York state law that permits the filing of an adoption petition while the

TPR is pending. As a result, the adoption proceeding remained on the court calendar and with the same judge who presided over the freeing.

Background

The concept of permanency was codified at the federal level through passage of the Adoption Assistance and Child Welfare Act of 1980 (PL 96-272). In the years that followed, the emphasis on permanency planning resulted in the freeing, through TPR, of a growing number of foster children and their placement in homes likely to adopt. Adoption became the preferred outcome over long-term out-of-home care for children who could not grow up in their birth families (Barth, 1997; Berry, 1998). Adoptions of foster children remained fairly flat between 1983 and 1993. Since then, the total number of such adoptions in the United States has risen (Freundlich, 2000; Maza, 2000; U.S. Department of Health and Human Services, 2005).

With the emphasis on permanency came a desire that it be reached in a timely manner. Concern about time frames led to passage of the Adoption and Safe Families Act of 1997 (ASFA), which called for the prompt establishment of permanency goals for children, emphasized the importance of reaching permanency without delay, and permitted an award of adoption incentive funds to states (Barth, Lee, Wildfire, & Guo, 2006; Courtney & Blakey, 2003; Maza, 1999). Thus ASFA focused a spotlight on accelerating permanency, including speeding the adoption process. To support permanency efforts, the Adoption and Foster Care Analysis and Reporting System (AFCARS) has routinely reported estimates of the average number of months between TPR and final adoption among children adopted from the public foster care system. State estimates for fiscal years 1999 through 2003 based on 52 jurisdictions reporting on 46,000–53,000 adoptions, over 60% of which were by unrelated foster parents, showed this average to be roughly16 months, with a median of 12 months (U.S. Department of Health and Human Services, 2005).

Various state efforts to speed adoptions have involved case reviews and hearings to determine actions needed (National Council of Juvenile and Family Court Judges, 2000b). One of the most promising methods proposed to decrease time spent in out-of-home care is a one case/one judge model. The concept of one judge remaining with a case for the entire proceeding, from entry into care through adoption, has been advocated over the years by state and city government (Duquette & Hardin, 1999) and by organizations representing judges and family courts (National Council of Juvenile and Family Court Judges, 2000a, 2005), although some concerns have been raised with respect to a possible failure to limit judicial discretion (Gaskins, 2006).

In 1997, when this project began, scenarios for courts' handling of adoption cases varied greatly across the United States. The approaches often led to discontinuity and delay. In New York and several other states, for example, TPR proceedings and adoption proceedings required separate petitions by different parties. As a result, cases frequently moved between judges, courts, and counties, and often dropped off the court calendar for a period of time between TPR and adoption. This discontinuity was compounded in New York City because the city consists of five counties, each with a family court. Cases dropped off the court calendar after the TPR, not to return until the

adopting parent filed a petition to adopt, an event that frequently occurred in a different county and with a different judge than the one who had presided over the TPR.

In 1991, New York passed a new law designated as Chapter 588 to address the discontinuity of cases and its effect on children and families. Chapter 588 allows adoption petitions to be filed in the county of freeing and prior to the freeing. The intent was for cases to remain in the same county and continuously on the court calendar between freeing and adoption.

Although the goal of these changes was to speed permanency, there were no systematic data attesting to whether or not these efforts actually decreased time frames for children awaiting adoption. Delays may occur along the path to adoption at various points. The study presented here addressed one period, the time between freeing the child for adoption and adoption finalization. Earlier data had shown that among children adopted in New York City in 1998, an average of 23 months elapsed between these two events—a lengthy duration when one considered that the majority of the children (84.5%) were already in homes that intended to adopt them at the time of the freeing (Festinger, 1998). It was hypothesized by the project team—which consisted of the original authors (Festinger & Pratt, 2002), adoption administrators, and senior legal personnel of the New York City Administration for Children's Services—that if an adoption petition were filed prior to the legal freeing, thus allowing the case to stay with the same judge and on that judge's calendar for both the freeing and the adoption, this time frame would be greatly reduced. The question posed by the study was therefore twofold: Could judicial continuity be achieved, and would this shorten the adoption process? An answer was sought to these questions by implementing Chapter 588 with respect to a service group, and comparing the results to a control group receiving the usual procedures.

METHOD

Case Selection

Cases were identified and referred to the project by the public department's attorneys who were responsible for all TPR filings in New York City. This occurred over a 9-month period. Once referred, the investigators screened each case to assure that the following inclusion criteria were met: (1) the child had a goal of adoption, (2) the foster parents lived in New York City and indicated their intent to adopt, (3) a TPR petition was either recently filed or soon to be filed, and (4) it was an abandonment case and the referring attorney had rated the case as not very or only moderately likely to be contested.

This review process resulted in a total of 175 eligible cases. Roughly 30% of these were randomly assigned to the control group, the rest to the service group, stratified by county. This was done so that most cases could be in the service group while still having sufficient cases in the control group for analytic purposes. The fidelity of the random assignment was checked by comparing the two groups on a number of descriptive characteristics. The final sample comprised 119 service cases and 56 control cases, all meeting identical criteria.

Implementing Chapter 588

Before the project could be implemented, the project team introduced all relevant parties (judges, court clerks, and attorneys) to the new procedures and solicited their suggestions and cooperation. This involved numerous meetings, the development of detailed written procedures for attorneys and caseworkers, training sessions for attorneys and staff, and planning meetings with family court judges and court clerks. There was an essential difference between the procedures used for the service and control cases. The 56 control cases received the usual procedure in that a child was legally freed, followed by a break in court calendaring until the adoption petition was filed. There was often no judicial continuity. In contrast, for the 119 service cases, the adoption petition was filed before the child was freed, with judicial continuity a goal.

Project caseworkers were assigned over time to the 119 service cases. They completed the adoption home studies, assembled all documentation required for the adoption petitions, and helped to ensure that all parts of these new and unfamiliar filing and court procedures were communicated to the relevant parties so as to assure implementation. The 56 control case home studies, following the usual procedures, were completed by adoption workers after children were freed and cases were internally transferred to the adoption department.

Data Collection

Data collection instruments were developed and staff were trained in their use. Project staff assigned to the 119 service cases completed two instruments: The first contained background descriptive information about the families and children and details of the family court proceedings, including the TPR dispositional hearing; the second captured information about the adoption finalization. Data for these instruments came from home studies, case records, court documents, the families' foster care workers, and attorneys. Other project staff completed similar instruments on the 56 control cases based on a review of case records, augmented by conversations with caseworkers and attorneys. Since these control families were not interviewed by project staff, less descriptive detail was available. The information on these instruments was cross-checked and augmented using individual child and case information in the computer files of the New York City Family Court and in New York state's child welfare tracking system.

The data collected by project staff were reviewed by supervisors in weekly meetings with investigators, and key items (for example, filing and hearing dates and dispositions) were collected from multiple sources to ensure accuracy. For consistency in the categorization of children's problems among service and control groups, the same staff member classified both groups, and these classifications were frequently double-checked for accuracy by one of the investigators.

Data collection was completed on June 30, 1999. All data were entered into the Statistical Package for the Social Sciences (SPSS). Data entry included a 10% check on inter-coder reliability. Very few errors (less than 0.5%) were noted. Even so, some variables, such as the dates of freeing and adoption, were entered twice to ensure accuracy. Data analysis was completed using SPSS. Throughout, a two-tailed .05 criterion was used.

Subsequent Data Collection

At the end of data collection for the main study in 1999, a number of children had not been adopted. Therefore, in mid-2003, the original authors received permission to return to the family court to obtain the TPR filing dates and dates of adoption for all previously censored cases.

RESULTS

The Service and Control Groups

On the whole, as can be seen in Table 5.1, the service and control groups were quite alike on a variety of descriptive characteristics. For instance, the service and control groups were similar with regard to gender, and a large majority in each group were minority children, reflecting the foster care population in New York City at the time.

Many of the children were in their adoptive homes along with their siblings. Thus, 47.1% of the service group compared to 60.7% of the control group children were placed with other siblings ($\chi^2 = 2.84$, 1 df, $p = .09$). This observed trend was subsequently examined with respect to various time frames, such as the duration from entry to legal freeing. In both the service and control groups, sibling placements took longer. The two groups differed, however, with respect to the children's medical and psychological needs. Each child had been classified with respect to eight areas, such as physical disability, mental retardation, chronic medical condition, emotional problems, and learning disability. The service group included significantly more children (64.6%) with one or more medical or psychological needs than did the control group (35.7%), suggesting that special needs do not stand in the way of adoptions, as is sometimes assumed.

The Adoptive Homes

The 119 children in the service group were living in 88 homes; the 56 control group children resided in 36 homes. Most of the adoptive parents in each group consisted of kin, primarily grandparents (41.1%) and aunts or uncles (29%). A majority of children in the service and control groups were in adoptive homes with single mothers, as can be seen in Table 5.1. The average age of adoptive mothers in the service group was 44 years, compared to age 45.1 in the control group. The 23 adoptive fathers in the service group were, on average, 47.1 years old, compared to 46.5 years for the 11 fathers in the control group.

As previously mentioned, it was possible to collect more detailed information on families in the service group than was possible with respect to control families. For instance, 53.4% of the homes contained other children, including biological children (34.1%), previously adopted children (13.6%), and custodial children (13.6%). Overall, family income consisted primarily of some form of public support, such as public assistance, Social Security, or Supplemental Security Income (56.8%), and/or wages and salaries (43.2%).

Foster Care Entry and Reentry

Following their entry into care, most of the children in the service group (97.5%) and in the control group (87.5%) remained in placement. Control group children were more likely to leave care and to reenter

TABLE 5.1 Demographic Characteristics of Children in Chapter 588 Service and Control Groups

	Total Children	
	Service Group (N = 119)	Control Group (N = 56)
Female (%)	50.4	48.2
Minority (%)	98.3	94.6
In sibling groups (%)	47.1	60.7
Medical/psych problems (%)	64.6	35.7*
	Total Homes	
	(N = 88)	(N = 36)
Kinship (%)	79.5	80.6
Adoptive mother's age at adoptive home placement (mean years)	44.0	45.1
Single adoptive mothers (%)	73.9	69.4

* p < .001

($\chi^2 = 5.3$, 1 df, $p = .02$). This difference was further examined with respect to various time frames. In both the service and control groups, reentrants showed longer durations (for instance, between entry and legal freeing).

Children's Ages at Entry, Adoptive Home Placement, and Freeing

When they entered foster care, the service group children were, on average, 1.5 years of age compared to an average age of 2.2 years for those in the control group. When placed in the home that eventually adopted them, the service group children were, on average, 1.9 years old, compared to 2.8 years for those in the control group. These differences in age were not statistically significant.

At the time they were legally freed, however, the service group children were somewhat younger (mean = 7.2 years) than the average 8.5 years for those in the control group ($t = 2.01$, df 163, $p < .05$). This age difference tended to be no longer significant when controlling for whether children were alone or part of a sibling group, using a two-way ANOVA ($F = 2.1$, df 1/161, $p > .10$).

Various Durations of Time: 1999 and 2003

The time between various adoption steps was quite alike for the two groups of children in 1999, at the end of the main study (Festinger & Pratt, 2002), as can be seen in Table 5.2. For instance, the average duration of time between foster care (FC) entry and adoptive home placement, as reported in that study, was 5.4 months for the service group compared to 7.6 months among controls. The similarities between service and control group children were also evident for the duration between adoptive home placement and court filing of petitions to free, as well as the average years between adoptive home placement and legal freeing. At the end of the project (June 30, 1999), 96.6% of the children in the service group and 89.3% of those in the control group had been legally freed.

The collection of additional TPR dates in 2003 did not change the time similarities reported in 1999. For instance, the duration between adoptive home placement and legal freeing was 5.4 and 5.9 years for service and control groups, respectively. The duration between court filing of petitions to free and the TPR dates were 11.8 and 12 months, respectively, for the service and control groups. Also, by May 2003, the vast majority of children in both the service and control groups had been legally freed.

Case Status at Project End on June 30, 1999, and 2003 Status

By the end of the main study in 1999, a much larger proportion of service group (91.6%) than control group (39.3%) children had been adopted (Table 5.2). The remaining service cases had either not yet been legally freed or had been legally freed, with an adoption petition filed, and were awaiting adoption. As for the control group, the remaining 60.7% of children were at various stages along the path toward adoption. Most were legally free and awaiting adoption, or awaiting attorney action, or awaiting home study completion. A minority had not yet been legally freed.

Not only were more service group children adopted, they were adopted more quickly than the control group children, as will shortly be shown. Therefore the 109 adopted service group children

TABLE 5.2 Adoption Steps and Age at Adoption of Children in Chapter 588 Service and Control Groups, Main Study, June 1999

Duration and Age	Service Group (N = 119)	Control Group (N = 56)
FC entry → Adoptive home placement (mean months)	5.4	7.6
Adoptive home placement → Petition to free filed (mean years)	4.4	4.9
Adoptive home placement → TPR (mean years)	5.3	5.8
Petition to free filed → TPR (mean months)	11.6	10.1
Legally free by June 30, 1999 (%)	96.6	89.3
Adopted by June 30, 1999 (%)	91.6	39.3**
Child's age at adoption (mean years)	7.6	10.4*

* p < .01; ** p < .001

were younger (mean = 7.6 years) at the time of adoption than were the 22 adopted control group children (mean = 10.4 years).

By mid-2003, following additional data collection, a large majority (96.6%) of service group children and 89.3% of control group children had been adopted. Because of the greater speed of adoption in the service group, the age difference at adoption remained, with service group children younger (mean = 7.7 years) than control group children (mean = 10.6 years).

Courts and Judges: Main Study

Past reports have shown the time between legal freeing and adoption petition filing to be lengthy, but likely to be reduced if these two legal events occur in the same court rather than moving from one county to another (Festinger, 1998). Therefore, to speed the process, one of the aims of the project was to maintain each case in the same court and, wherever possible, with the same judge throughout—from legal freeing to final adoption. This aim was achieved. As previously reported (Festinger & Pratt, 2002), most (91.7%) of the service cases, but none of the controls, remained in the same court and were heard by the same judge. As for the control group, 36.4% were legally freed in one court and the adoption proceeding occurred in a different court before a different judge. All others, 8.3% of service and 63.6% of control cases, remained in the same court but were heard by a different judge.

In addition to avoiding movement among judges and courts, a central purpose of filing adoption petitions early under Chapter 588 was to keep cases from dropping off the court calendar. In New York City, such a break in calendaring usually occurred between a TPR dispositional hearing and the adoption petition filing. Since most adoption petitions of project cases were filed before the final TPR hearing, these cases in most instances remained on the court calendar. This combination of factors—remaining on the court calendar, continuing with a judge familiar with the case, and staying in the same county—all contributed to moving cases more quickly along the adoption path. But how much more quickly?

From TPR to Adoption

To examine the length of time from legal freeing to final adoption, we used a Kaplan-Meier (1958) survival analysis.[1] This analysis permitted children who were legally free but not yet adopted by the end of data collection in the main study (June 30, 1999) and those in the augmented data set (May 2003) to be included in calculating the length of time between legal freeing and finalization. To simplify the presentation, and since the results for both data collection periods were quite similar, the focus here will be on the final May 2003 data since by that time most children had been adopted. The results for three groups can be seen in Table 5.3.

The first group of 91 children, the model group, consisted of cases where Chapter 588 was implemented as intended. The second group of 24 children, the partial group, consisted of cases where there were some problems in implementation. For instance, in 13 of these cases, the attorney present at the TPR dispositional hearing failed to inform the judge that the adoption petition had been filed under Chapter 588, and in the other 11 cases, there were adoption package or petition filing delays. Despite these problems in implementation, the partial cases were filed under Chapter 588, and every effort was made to keep them on the court calendar.

Table 5.3 shows the difference between the service and control medians and mean time in months between legal freeing and final adoption for all children who had been legally freed by May 1, 2003. As can be seen, the medians of the model and partial groups are fairly close, but the means differ by over a month because of the effect of proportionately more cases with higher durations in the partial group. These two groups differed significantly from the control group. The overall generalized Wilcoxon statistic was highly significant (2 df, p = .0000).

In sum, adoptions in the model group were faster by 18.1 months (median difference), when compared to the control group. The difference was, however, the combined result of using Chapter 588 and of having project staff specially assigned. To assess the effect of project staff alone would have required a third randomly selected group—one that assigned cases to project staff but did not use Chapter 588. Unfortunately, such an additional group was not possible. To minimize the effect of project staff, the duration of time between legal freeing and transfer to the adoption unit (Division of Child Adoption transfer) was subtracted from each control case. The usual route for cases in the public department included such a transfer before adoption workers were assigned to a case. Once adoption staff were assigned, they functioned in a similar manner as project staff. By subtracting this duration, the results come closer to isolating the effects of using Chapter 588.

TABLE 5.3 Kaplan-Meier Event History Analysis of Children Who Were Legally Free by May 1, 2003
TPR → Final Adoption

	Survival Time (months)	Standard Error	CI	N	Censored Cases
Model Group					
Median	4.64	0.29	(4.07, 5.21)	91	0
Mean	5.28	0.51	(4.28, 6.29)		
Partial Group					
Median	4.80	0.53	(3.76, 5.84)	24	0
Mean	6.94	0.71	(5.55, 8.34)		
Control Group					
Median	22.76	0.77	(21.24, 24.28)	50	5
Mean	29.86	2.45	(25.05, 34.66)		
DCA Transfer → Final Adoption					
Median	15.86	1.11	(13.67, 18.04)	50	5
Mean	22.63	2.56	(17.62, 27.64)		

The results of this more conservative DCA transfer time can be seen in the last rows of Table 5.3. These show the control group median and mean times in months between case transfer to the adoption unit and final adoption for all children who had been legally freed by May 2003. Once again, the two service groups differed significantly from the control group, and the overall test was significant (generalized Wilcoxon, 2 *df*, *p* = .0000). Even with the transfer time removed, adoptions in the model group were faster by 11.2 months (median difference), when compared to the control group.

Finally, it was important to see whether the above difference in duration was due to selection factors such as age, kinship placement, or sibling status. Cox regression analysis adjusts for these statistically (Yaffee & Austin, 1994). Thus, the possible effects of eight other variables on the observed difference between the Chapter 588 group and the control group were examined. One of the variables used, the duration of time between foster care entry and placement in the adoptive home, dropped out in the analysis because of multicollinearity. The results with respect to the remaining variables can be seen in Table 5.4.

Table 5.4 shows that, when controlling for seven time and descriptive variables, the differences between the Chapter 588 group and the control group remain highly significant. The analysis also shows that the odds of adoption by the end of final data collection were 7.7 times greater for children in the model Chapter 588 group, and 4.1 times greater for children in the partial Chapter 588 group, than for children in the control group.

CONCLUSIONS AND IMPLICATIONS FOR LEGISLATION

The study reported here set out to examine whether judicial continuity would lead to shorter time frames for children who were awaiting adoption. The findings reported show significant time saving. As a result, the conclusions of the main study stated that the findings "call for child welfare workers to support, and social work advocacy groups to urge, states and courts to expand efforts that maintain continuity of both calendar and judge" (Festinger & Pratt, 2002, p. 224). In the years that followed, the findings were indeed used as a component of discussions at the New York State Judicial Institute's Child Welfare Roundtable, presided over by the chief judge of the state of New York, and provided the rationale for the formulation of certain as-

TABLE 5.4. Cox Regression of Placement and Descriptive Variables as Predictors of Duration Between DCA Transfer and Adoption Finalization of New York City Children, as of May 1, 2003

Variable	B	SE	Sig	Exp(B)	95% CI	
Child's age at entry	−0.03	0.04	0.33	0.97	0.90	1.04
Duration of entry → legal freeing	0.06	0.07	0.41	1.06	0.93	1.21
Duration of placement in home → legal freeing	0.00	0.01	0.70	1.00	0.99	1.01
Gender	0.06	0.17	0.72	1.06	0.76	1.48
Sibling status	0.03	0.19	0.88	1.03	0.72	1.48
Kinship or non-kinship	0.23	0.25	0.36	1.26	0.77	2.04
Reentry or nonreentry	−0.21	0.45	0.65	0.81	0.33	1.98
Chapter 588, model	2.04	0.24	<0.01	7.69	4.83	12.25
Chapter 588, partial	1.42	0.30	<0.01	4.13	2.30	7.41

pects of new legislation.[2] The new Child Welfare Permanency Legislation, chapter 3 of the New York Laws of 2005, took effect on December 21, 2005. Although this bill concerns many other aspects of child welfare, there are two sections of key interest with respect to what has been reported here. The new legislation replaced the permanency hearing petition process with continuous calendaring of a case, and therefore cases will not be allowed to fall off the court's calendar. In addition, it established "court pre-scheduling, rather than agency petitioning as the mechanism for ensuring that all children have on-time permanency hearings" (Lippman, 2005, p. 1). More specifically, section 1088 indicates that if the child is freed for adoption, "the case shall remain on the court's calendar," and section 1089 states that for freed children the court shall set a specific date for a permanency hearing "no later than 30 days after the freeing" and that this be completed quickly.

In conclusion, this research provides an example of findings that were directly used in the development of social legislation—legislation that will speed the adoption process and will bring the security of a permanent home more quickly to children and families.

Notes

Much of this chapter is based on the original work found in Festinger, T., & Pratt, R. (2002). Speeding adoptions: An evaluation of the effects of judicial continuity. *Social Work Research, 26*(4). Copyright 2002, National Association of Social Workers.

1. A discussion and explication of assumptions and other methodological concerns with respect to Kaplan-Meier analysis and Cox proportional hazards regression can be found in Shlonsky, A., Festinger, T.,& Brookhart, M. A. (2006). Is survival the fittest? A post-hoc evaluation of event history estimations in an experimental design. *Children and Youth Services Review, 28*(7), 841–852.

2. Personal communication from the Division of Legal Services, New York City Administration for Children's Services, May 2006.

References

Barth, R. P. (1997). Effects of age and race on the odds of adoption versus remaining in long-term out-of-home care. *Child Welfare, 76,* 285–308.

Barth, R. P., Lee, C. K., Wildfire, J., & Guo, S. (2006). A comparison of the governmental costs of long-term foster care and adoption. *Social Service Review, 80*(1), 127–158.

Berry, M. (1998). Adoption in an era of family preservation. *Children and Youth Services Review, 20*(1–2), 1–12.

Courtney, M. E., & Blakey, J. (2003). Examination of the impact of increased court review on permanency outcomes for abused and neglected children. *Family Court Review, 41*(4), 471–479.

Duquette, D. N., & Hardin, M. (1999). *Guidelines for public policy and state legislation governing permanence for children.* Washington, DC: Children's Bureau, Department of Health and Human Services.

Festinger, T. (1998). *New York City adoptions 1998.* Unpublished manuscript, Ehrenkranz School of Social Work, New York University.

Festinger, T., & Pratt, R. (2002). Speeding adoptions: An evaluation of the effects of judicial continuity. *Social Work Research*, 26(4), 217–224.

Freundlich, M. (2000). *Adoption and ethics: The market forces in adoption*. Washington, DC: Child Welfare League of America.

Gaskins, S. (2006). Is it possible to reform a child welfare system? An evaluation of the current progress in the District of Columbia and the advocacy strategies that led to reform. *Whittier Journal of Child & Family Advocacy*. Available: http://www.perspectivesony-outh.org/Pages-Articles/Winter-2006/Whittier-Law-School-Journal/5-Shimica_Gaskins-Is_It_Possible_to_Reform_A_Child.html.

Kaplan, E. L., & Meier, P. (1958). Nonparametric estimation from incomplete observations. *Journal of the American Statistical Association*, 53, 457–481.

Lippman, J. (2005). *Implementation of new child welfare permanency legislation (Laws of 2005, ch. 3)*. [Memorandum sent to judges, judicial hearing officers, court attorney referees, and chief clerks of the family court].

Maza, P. (1999). Recent data on the number of adoptions of foster children. *Adoption Quarterly*, 3(2), 71–81.

Maza, P. (2000). Using administrative data to reward agency performance: The case of the federal adoption incentive program. *Child Welfare*, 79(5), 444–456.

National Council of Juvenile and Family Court Judges. (2000a). *Adoption and permanency guidelines: Improving court practice in child abuse & neglect cases*. Reno, NV: Author.

National Council of Juvenile and Family Court Judges. (2000b). *Child Victims Act model courts project status report 1999*. [Technical Assistance Bulletin, vol. 4, no. 1]. Reno, NV: Author.

National Council of Juvenile and Family Court Judges. (2005). *Status report 2004: A snapshot of the Child Victims Act model courts project*. [Technical Assistance Bulletin, vol. 9, no. 2]. Reno, NV: Author.

Shlonsky, A., Festinger, T., & Brookhart, M. A. (2006). Is survival the fittest? A post-hoc evaluation of event history estimations in an experimental design. *Children and Youth Services Review*, 28(7), 841–852.

U.S. Department of Health and Human Services, Administration for Children and Families, Administration on Children, Youth and Families, Children's Bureau. (2005). *The AFCARS report: Current estimates as of October 2005* (4). Available: www.acf.dhhs.gov/programs/cb.

Yaffee, R. A., & Austin, J. T. (1994). *Discrete time event history models for higher education research* [On-line]. Available: www.nyu.edu/its/socsci/Docs/dteha/dteha.htm.

6

New Permanency Strategies for Children in Foster Care

Mark Testa

Since the mid-1990s, federal and state governments in the United States have been engaged in a massive restructuring of the child welfare system from indefinite foster care to family permanence. Although permanency planning has been federal policy since the passage of the Adoption Assistance and Child Welfare Act (AACWA) of 1980, it is only in the last several years that federal and state child protective authorities have vigorously pursued new strategies to align rules and incentives with alternative permanency options for foster children who cannot safely be reunified with their birth parents.

After the authorization of federal adoption bonuses by the Adoption and Safe Families Act (ASFA) of 1997, the number of adoptions from foster care rose significantly with 33 states and the District of Columbia doubling their numbers between 1997 and 2002 (McDonald, Salyers, & Testa, 2003). The granting of IV-E waivers further boosted national permanency counts by authorizing selected states to use federal foster care dollars to subsidize caregivers who

become the legal guardians of children formerly under their foster care. Combining legal guardianships with adoptions, the nation as a whole surpassed the president's target of doubling within 5 years the number of foster children adopted or permanently placed (Administration for Children and Families, 1997). Between 1999 and 2005, the nation's 1-day count of children in foster care dipped from 567,000 to 514,000 (Administration for Children and Families, 2005). In 2002, the average number of beneficiaries of federal adoption assistance surpassed for the first time the average number of recipients of federal foster care payments. It is projected that, by 2008, the number in federally assisted permanent homes will exceed the number in federally funded foster homes by a magnitude of 2:1 (Committee on Ways and Means, 2004).

The story behind these changes, which is seldom told, is that much of the recent growth in family permanence has not come from the sources anticipated by the ASFA's backers, namely, middle-class families overcoming barriers to transracial adoption, but rather from extended family members' and nonrelatives' converting their status from temporary foster parents into permanent legal guardians and adoptive parents. The purposes of this chapter are to describe the historical and sociological forces behind these new permanency strategies and to examine the underlying tensions and questions provoked by the shifting balance from foster care to family permanence. After outlining an analytical framework for charting the broad cycle of public child welfare change in the United States, I trace the origins of the permanency planning movement and consider the latest round of debate that is being generated by the expanded public reliance on kinfolk and foster families for the permanent care and guardianship of abused and neglected children. I outline a set of questions raised by these developments and consider some coordinating mechanisms for finding a middle ground that avoids the either-or solution of restoring tradition or substituting bureaucracy.

ANALYTICAL FRAMEWORK

The key tensions and questions that characterize contemporary child welfare policy and practice may be conceived as arising from two opposing tendencies: the first concerned with the scope of public interest in child welfare and the second concerned with the appropriate form of social organization for meeting these responsibilities.

With regard to the scope of public interest, child welfare policy is pulled back and forth between two opposing conceptions of the proper relationship between the child and the state (Wolfe, 1978). Under the *narrow* scope of government's role, public intervention into autonomous family life is justified *only* if the physical safety, health, and sustenance needs of the child are jeopardized, e.g., when there are bruises, burns, malnutrition, or other bodily threats (Besharov, 1985; Wald, 1975). Under a more *diffuse* scope of interest, public intervention into the family is justified *whenever* it advances the overall well-being of the child (Kamerman & Kahn, 1990).

Since the 1960s, public child welfare has been pulling away from the narrow scope of public interest, first through the enlargement of the definition of *unsafe* from its original focus on the "battered child" to encompass, later on, malnutrition, neglect, sexual abuse, emotional maltreatment, risk of harm, and

most recently intrauterine drug exposure. Second, state involvement has been prolonged as a result of the elevation of the standards of care considered minimally necessary for family reunification above the bar set for child removal. For example, parental sobriety is a necessary condition for family reunification in many states, but lack of sobriety remains an insufficient reason, in and of itself, for initial child removal.

The expansion of the scope of public interest in child protection has brought more abused, neglected, and dependent children into an unmediated and extended relationship with the state. On the upside, this removes children from unsafe family environments; on the downside, it exposes them to the secondary harms—multiple placements, re-abuse, and emotional uncertainty—that arise from deficiencies in bureaucratic agency to safeguard child well-being. The range of potential responses to what lawyers and economists call the "principal-agent problem" falls along a continuum bounded by two contrasting perspectives on social organization: the primordial and the bureaucratic (Testa, 2001).

The *primordial perspective* holds that kinship, and its close approximations based on ethnicity, religion, and locality, ought to matter when deciding how rights in children and responsibilities for their safety, permanence, and well-being should be allocated. This perspective is reflected, for example, in the preference for kin placement that Congress attached to its 1996 welfare reform bill. It encourages states to place children with kin where such relatives meet relevant child protection standards. In the vocabulary of principal-agent theory, the assumption is that the well-being of the child-principal is best assured by placing the child under the "affine agency" (Coleman, 1990) of birth families, extended kin, and primordial agents who closely identify with the child's well-being and who can be trusted to make parenting choices and investments that will promote the best interests of the child as if they were their own interests.

In contrast, the *bureaucratic perspective* holds that rights and responsibilities should not be ascribed but instead achieved by selecting the best agent who advances the child's well-being regardless of continuity with birth family or ascribed heritage. This perspective is reflected, for example, in the Multiethnic Placement Act of 1994. It prohibits the use of race, color, or national origin to delay or deny children's placement in racially or ethnically diverse foster and adoptive homes. The assumption is that the well-being of the child-principal can be best assured by the recruitment, licensing, and training of bureaucratic agents who can be held accountable to performance standards and monitored under surveillance systems that discourage self-interested defections from responsible child caring.

CYCLES OF PUBLIC CHILD WELFARE REFORM

Cross-classifying the two dimensions of the scope of public interest by type of social organization yields an analytical framework that can be used to identify the major political tensions and organizational responses that give rise to cycles of public child welfare reform in the United States (see Figure 6.1). The four corners identify the ideological endpoints of each outcome-organization combination.

The (1) *narrow-primordial* combination emphasizes group autonomy and the insulation of the natural family and its close approximations based on kinship, race, and community from state interference into private child-rearing practices except when the child's physical safety is in jeopardy. Norms of family autonomy and community responsibility have held sway for long periods in Anglo American history and imply that all protective intervention should come from within the primordial group (Litwak, 1965). Only when the child's physical safety is jeopardized by the group's failings in the primary functions of feeding, clothing, and protecting the child does the state intervene as a last resort.

When the state intervenes for safety reasons, the action may take the form of either serving the child in his or her own family or removing the child entirely. Public authorities in late 19th-century America made child protection and care available only on the condition that the family relinquish its right of custody to the child. The laissez-faire philosophy that children's well-being should hinge primarily, if not exclusively, on their family's competitive achievement in the marketplace required that public child welfare be organized around the (2) *narrow-bureaucratic* nexus of almshouses, orphanages, and foster boarding homes in order to renounce, in the words of T. H. Marshall (1964), "any claim to trespass on the territory of wages" (p. 88).

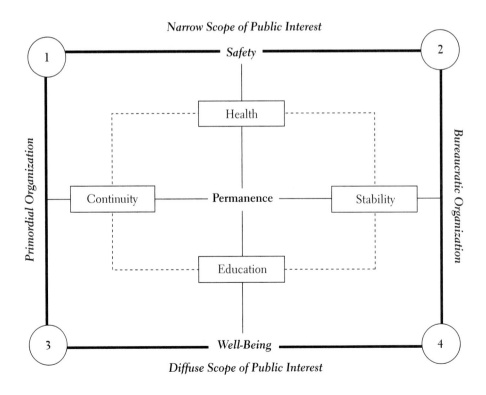

FIGURE 6.1

Reactions against the "child rescue" mentality and its encroachment on family autonomy surfaced early in the next century at the first White House Conference on the Care of Dependent Children held in 1909. Conferees declared: "Home life is the highest and finest product of civilization. . . . Children should not be deprived of it except for urgent and compelling reasons" (White House Conference on the Care of Dependent Children, 1909). These sentiments fueled the expansion of the (3) *diffuse-primordial* nexus of mothers' pensions, aid to dependent children, and Medicaid (and other programs never fully institutionalized in the United States, such as children's allowances and universal health insurance), which supported the enrichment of child-caring environments in children's own homes.

For children who, for sufficient reasons, needed to be removed or who were homeless, the 1909 conferees called for upgrading the (4) *diffuse-bureaucratic* complex of licensed foster family homes, small treatment facilities that are used as an alternative to large-scale congregate care, replete with foster care reimbursement and administrative oversight sufficient to assure the proper physical, mental, moral, and religious training and development of each child brought under public guardianship.

The growth of the diffuse-primordial nexus of in-home supports to parents and relatives accelerated with the spread of state mothers' pension programs after 1911 and was expanded nationally and to extended kin in 1935 with the enactment of the federal Aid to Dependent Children (ADC). The goal was to alleviate the financial stresses that were presumed to interfere with the biological family's natural desires to act in the best interests of their children. During this same period, the diffuse-bureaucratic complex was upgraded by emphasizing the recruitment and licensing of additional foster boarding capacity and the conversion of large congregate care facilities into smaller cottage settings, group homes, and intensive residential treatment centers in order to ensure the well-being of the remaining children who could not be cared for in their own homes.

In quantitative terms, the two-pronged reform strategy was a success: The size of the U.S. out-of-home population declined after the enactment of ADC from 5.8 per 1,000 children under 18 years old to a low of 3.7 per 1,000 children in 1961. In the 1950s, the number of children in foster families eventually surpassed the number in child-caring institutions (Lerman, 1982).

But in qualitative terms, the contribution of these changes to actual improvements in the well-being of foster children was often judged as falling short of the desired goal.

PERMANENCY PLANNING MOVEMENT

Misgivings about the capacity of bureaucratic agents to safeguard the well-being of children in public foster care first received scientific backing in the classic study by Maas and Engler (1959), *Children in Need of Parents*. They spotlighted the sizable number of children who were drifting aimlessly in indefinite foster care, which left them exposed to the secondary harms of multiple moves, uncertain identity, and psychological disturbance. These concerns were later grounded in psychodynamic theories of attachment (Bowlby, 1969) by Goldstein, Freud, and Solnit (1973), who warned of the lasting emotional damage inflicted on children who grow up without secure attachment relationships to parents or substitute caregivers.

The objections went beyond the usual criticisms of institutional care and called into question all forms of bureaucratized care whether it occurred in less restrictive, family-like settings or in more restrictive, institutional settings. Even the most family-like foster care setting was judged to be lacking in the essential home qualities that psychologists deemed indispensable for healthy child development so long as the home remained under regular agency surveillance and the child was retained in state custody.

Building on the objections to bureaucratized care, child welfare social workers in the 1970s identified four permanency qualities that they perceived to be contradicted by foster care (Pike, Down, Emlen, Downs, & Care, 1977). These included (1) an intent for the care to last permanently whereas foster care is supposed to be temporary; (2) a commitment to the continuity of family relationships whereas foster care can be terminated any time at the convenience of the agency or foster family; (3) a sense of belonging that is rooted in family norms and sanctioned by law whereas foster care lacks definitive legal status; and (4) a respected social identity whereas foster care is stigmatized.

These four qualities of intent, continuity, belongingness, and respect supplied the underlying rationale for the permanency planning framework that

Congress codified in the AACWA of 1980. What is noteworthy about the permanency planning movement was its readiness to concede the limitations of bureaucratic agents to safeguard the well-being of foster children. Instead of seeking to upgrade the diffuse-bureaucratic complex of foster care like its Progressive forerunners sought through greater funding, professionalism, and coordinated administrative control, the movement sought to reduce the child's exposure to the secondary harms of bureaucratized care by abbreviating the child's length of stay in public custody to a brief, time-limited interval between when the child could no longer be safely maintained in the home and the time when the child could either be reunified with the birth parents or become part of a new permanent family through adoption. Although permanency planning casework also allowed for judicially appointed guardianship and even "formalized long-term foster care" (Pike et al., 1977), the preference was to restore children to the natural guardianship of birth parents or to transfer them to the legally fictive "natural" guardianship of adoptive parents.

Even though the 1970s permanency planning movement pulled practice and policy back toward the narrow-primordial pole of less state involvement in autonomous family life, it did not fully embrace the claim that most dependent and neglected children would be better off left with their birth parents. Instead, it staked out an intermediate position between automatically retaining children in relationships that preserve continuity with family and cultural heritage versus bringing children under a bureaucratic structure of incentives, rules, and penalties that discourage self-interested defections of bureaucratic agents from responsible caregiving. As a method of agent selection, permanency planning bases the choice of permanency option on an individualized clinical assessment of whichever option best advances all four permanency qualities deemed crucial for healthy child development.

Similarly, as a child welfare outcome, permanence occupies an intermediate position between physical safety and overall child well-being. It is intended to secure for children a sense of family belonging and a lifelong connection that are subordinate to safety and health considerations but are accorded a higher priority than educational and employment opportunities that might require some discontinuity to achieve. In this way, permanency planning solves a major problem for liberalism (Parton, 1999), namely, how can the state intervene in the private sphere of the family in order to guarantee minimal child well-being but in a way that does not convert children into clients of an all-pervasive welfare state and undermine the role and accountability of family, kin, and community?

FROM FOSTER CARE TO FAMILY PERMANENCE

The preference for the affine agency of parents, kin, adoptive parents, and guardians over the bureaucratic agency of foster parents, caseworkers, and judges helped to moderate the growth of public foster care from 1960 to 1985. In the face of expanded child protective powers following the radiological detection of the "battered child syndrome" (Kempe, Silverman, Steele, Droegemueller, & Silver, 1962) and the infusion of federal funds into foster care with the creation of the federal foster care program in 1961, the per capita rate of U.S. foster care rose by just 14% from 3.9 per 1,000 children aged 0–18 in 1962 to 4.4 per 1,000 children in 1972. This compares to a 167% growth in child beneficiaries of Aid to Families with Dependent Children (AFDC) from 39.8 to 106.4 per 1,000 children during this same period. Figure 6.2 plots these trend lines on two different vertical scales to facilitate comparison: The foster care trends are plotted against the left vertical scale from 0 to 14 foster children per 1,000 U.S. child population aged 0–18 years old, and the AFDC/TANF trend is plotted against the right vertical scale from 0 to 140 child beneficiaries per 1,000 U.S. child population.

As shown in Figure 6.2, the time series for foster care grows murky in the 1970s after the federal government ceased its collection of state foster care statistics. Case record surveys conducted by the Children's Defense Fund (Knitzer, Allen, & McGowan, 1978) and Westat (Shyne & Schroeder, 1978) did generate "point prevalence," or 1-day estimates, that located the mid-1970s national foster care count somewhere between 450,000 and 500,000 foster children. A few observers accepted these statistical estimates as evidence of a sharp upsurge in the per capita, out-of-home care rate to 7.2 per 1,000 in 1976 (see Figure 6.2), which was followed by a rapid decline to 4.4 per 1,000 after the AACWA went into effect in 1980 (Cardenas, 1979; Pelton, 1989). Although this statistical story is still told (National Coalition for Child Protection Reform, 2006), other observers have questioned the plausibility of such a roller-coaster ascent

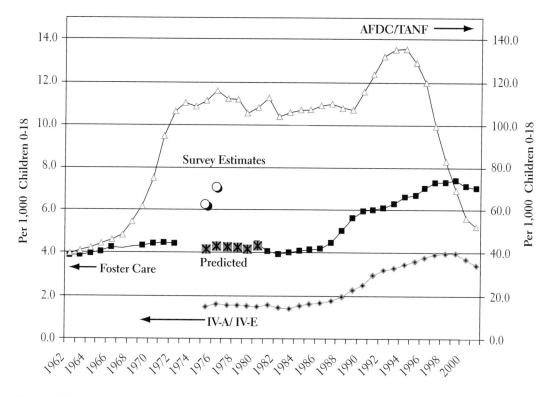

FIGURE 6.2

and decline in foster care caseloads (Steiner, 1981; Prosser, 1983). During this entire period, for example, the per capita AFDC beneficiary rate for children did not vary much from 112 per 1,000 children (see Figure 6.2).

Inspection of historical caseload trends for several large states and AFDC foster care claims indicate only a modest uptick, if any at all, in the numbers of children in public foster care during the mid-1970s. After nearly all states signed on to the AFDC foster care program in 1975, federally funded foster care caseloads flattened out. The correlation between national foster care statistics and IV-A/IV-E claims after 1980 is 0.97. The missing 1975–1979 time series predicted from the regression of foster care on IV-A/IV-E claims is asterisked in Figure 6.2. Contrary to the claim that the rediscovery of child abuse and the availability of open-ended funds for out-of-home care drove the national foster care population to unprecedented heights in the 1970s (Pelton, 1989), the best available evidence nowadays suggests that a relatively constant fraction of children was involved at any one time in the foster care system throughout the entire period from 1960 to 1985.

Hindsight is 20/20, and the best available data in hand at the time pointed to foster care conditions that were widely at variance with the idea that children's well-being depends upon first meeting their basic human needs for safety, trust, and permanence with loving and caring adults. In addition to the record numbers of children whom cross-sectional surveys estimated to be in foster care, the statistical snapshots generated from point-in-time censuses and studies slanted statistical description toward the experiences of the residual group of children left in long-term care. These statistics gave policy makers the impression that most children entered foster care only to linger in the system for years on end. The longitudinal study conducted by Fanshel and Shinn (1978), which tracked children forward in time, was appropriately based on a "length-biased" (Testa, 2001) sample of children who had been in foster care for longer than 3 months and hence missed the 20 to 25% of all children entering care who were discharged in less than this time (Wulczyn, Hislop, & Goerge, 2000).

Although packaged as a novel solution to the looming foster care crisis, the remedies embedded in the AACWA reinforced the existing preference of child welfare professionals to reduce the exposure of children to the real harms of "foster care drift." The AACWA mandated "reasonable efforts" to prevent children's unnecessary removal or to restore them expeditiously to parental custody and, when best practice recommended against reunification, to facilitate permanence by subsidizing the adoption of children with special needs. National foster care caseloads did dip after the implementation of the AACWA. However, the upward turn in foster care caseloads after 1982 (see Figure 6.2) shook people's faith in the permanency planning formula. Although subsequent statistical analyses would later indicate that most of this growth was occurring as a result of a decline in the rate of discharges from foster care (Tatara, 1992), an influential point of view came to prominence that faulted the system for failing to make adequate "reasonable efforts" to prevent children from entering public foster care in the first place (Farrow, 2001). As a result, several key states and private foundations invested in intensive family preservation models that provided short-term, crisis-oriented, in-home services, designed to maintain children safely at home in the care of their parents or other family members whenever possible.

By the time intensive family preservation became federal law in 1992, the preferences for affine over bureaucratic agency had spilled beyond the boundaries of the natural family to encompass the wider primordial solidarities of race, ethnicity, and community. This phase of reaction against bureaucratic agency added a race and class dimension to the critique. In the early 1970s, the National Association of Black Social Workers (NABSW) had startled the child welfare establishment by denouncing the emerging practice of transracial adoption as racial genocide and had demanded that Black foster children be placed within their own racial group. Historical grievances against public child welfare as an instrument of forced assimilation, especially among Native Americans, resurfaced and led to the passage of the Indian Child Welfare Act (ICWA) of 1978, which strengthened preferences for placing children within the primordial solidarities of the extended family, their own tribe, or the wider Native American community. In the mid-1980s, state governments began amending statutes to give priority to extended kin in the placement of foster children (Gleeson & Craig, 1994). The same private foundations that had spearheaded intensive family

preservation services also threw their weight behind alternative child protective response, diversion from child protective investigation, and community partnerships that buffered residents of low-income communities against child protective intervention and instead steered disadvantaged families to local community groups for voluntary family support and services (Waldfogel, 1998).

Despite the high expectations, the expanding diffuse-primordial nexus of intensive family presentation services, tribal jurisdiction over foster care and adoption, racially matched placements, kinship care preference, and community partnerships during the 1980s and early 1990s was not accompanied by the advertised contraction in foster care caseload that these practices and policies were supposed to accomplish. Instead, per capita foster care rates rose without interruption from 3.9 per 1,000 in 1982 to 6.6 per 1,000 in 1994 (see Figure 6.2), fueled in no small measure by the crack-cocaine epidemic and the consequent influx of infants into foster care. Furthermore, when shutting down the AFDC entitlement in 1996 failed to bring about the predicted inundation of new foster care cases from the families discharged or sanctioned off welfare (Sengupta, 2000), the discordance between projected outcomes and actual results planted additional doubts about the soundness and validity of the diffuse-primordial enterprise and left it further exposed to criticism and caricature.

FROM PRIMORDIAL CONTINUITY TO TRANSRACIAL ADOPTION

The first line of criticism opened up in the early 1990s along the fissures between ascription and achievement. Although the ICWA deferred to the claims of extended families and tribal communities in the placement of Native American children, efforts to extend similar prerogatives to other ethnic and racial minority groups were stopped short by a rising political backlash that fed off a more general opposition to racial preferences, quotas, and affirmative action in the late 1980s.

At the forefront of the backlash was a coalition of interest groups that included single adults and infertile couples, who wished to adopt children for both family formation and humanitarian reasons, but felt compelled to go overseas because of perceived hostility and barriers to transracial adoption in the United States. Ohio senator Howard Metzenbaum subsequently championed their cause and sponsored the Multiethnic Placement Act (MEPA) of 1994.

The initial MEPA legislation outlawed racial discrimination in foster placement and adoption but permitted a "best interests" consideration of the cultural, ethnic, or racial background of the child as one of several factors for making placement decisions. Staunch opponents to racial matching, however, believed that this exception gave states a loophole for circumventing the law and enabled workers and judges to continue deferring to primordial claims for matched-race placement and adoption. So in 1996, Congress revised the interethnic discrimination provisions (as part of the Small Business Job Protection Act) and repealed the MEPA provision that allowed consideration of a child's cultural, ethnic, or racial background. The law also imposed substantial financial penalties for violations of the law. None of these interethnic provisions, however, affected the application of the ICWA.

About the same time, a second line of attack against primordial agency opened up along the fault line between safety and family permanence. Although permanency planning clearly subordinates the goal of permanence to overriding considerations of health and safety in the home, taking the principle of reasonable efforts to scale produced agency failures that permitted the AACWA to be caricatured as requiring that every effort be made, even in high-risk circumstances, to preserve the natural family. The charge was bolstered by findings replicated in the family preservation experiments of the 1990s that showed intensive services to be no more effective than ordinary in-home casework in preventing the recurrence of maltreatment and removal of the child from the home. Even though the subsequent policy debates portrayed all family preservation efforts as misguided, these same studies found that intensive services created no increased risk of harm and that the vast majority of abused and neglected children could be safely served in their own homes. Still, for many critics, the 80% safe/20% unsafe was much too high a threshold, and the refutation of the core hypothesis of placement prevention further undercut arguments in favor of retaining children under the affine agency of birth parents and, by extension, extended family and other primordial groups (Farrow, 2001).

NEW PERMANENCY STRATEGIES FOR CHILDREN IN FOSTER CARE

The reaction against primordial agency initiated another cycle of public child welfare reform, but this time within the narrower confines of a permanency planning debate that pitted the preference for maintaining continuity with the child's family or ascribed heritage against the selection of adoptive parents for the economic advantages and stable home environment they are predicted to bring to the child's care (see box outlined with dashes in Figure 6.1). Some congressional leaders in the period leading up to the dismantling of the AFDC entitlement in 1996 did attempt to widen the parameters of the debate by conjuring up the old idea of orphanages (Welch & Phillips, 1994). This tactic was quickly consigned to the margins. Instead, the Adoption and Safe Families Act (ASFA) of 1997 helped to refocus attention on the adoption solution by requiring a permanency hearing within 12 months and instructing states to file or join a petition to terminate parental rights to any child who has been in foster care for 15 of the past 22 months. It also pulled back from the family preservation agenda by identifying circumstances of aggravated maltreatment for which reasonable efforts to maintain the child in the birth family would not be required, e.g., torture, sexual abuse, murder of another child, and prior termination of another sibling.

At the same time that the ASFA, like the MEPA, was promoting the bureaucratization of family permanence, some legislators were careful to carve out a special primordial exception from the 15-out-of-22-months' requirement for children under the foster care of extended kin. The law also explicitly recognized placement with a fit and willing relative, judicial appointment of a legal guardian, and, as a last resort, maintenance in another planned permanent living arrangement (e.g., formalized long-term foster care) as supplementary options that fulfilled federal permanency planning directives in addition to family reunification and adoption.

Some proponents of the adoption-only solution to indefinite foster care characterized the "unwelcome" appearance of these supplementary options as a "new permanency movement" (Bartholet, 1999). In actuality, federal law under the ADC since 1935 has subsidized in loco parentis placement with kin after foster care discharge, and permanency planning workers have long cited the advantages of legal guardianship over adoption for children in the custody of relatives (Taylor, 1935). The AACWA included legal guardianship as a permanency option in 1980, but Congress didn't define it in statute until the ASFA was passed in 1997.[1]

Legal guardianship permits relatives to retain their extended family identities as grandparents, aunts, and uncles rather than become mother or father. Unlike adoption, guardianship does not require the termination of parental rights, permits birth parents to retain some role, if they wish, in the upbringing of their children, and enables siblings to retain rights of association. Even though the ASFA didn't go so far as to include subsidies for relatives and foster parents who assume legal guardianship of foster children, as the AACWA had previously done for adoption, the 1997 law did expand the number of states that could offer subsidized guardianship under IV-E waiver authority.

The expectations leading up to the passage of the MEPA in 1994 and the ASFA in 1997 had been that removing the barriers to transracial adoption and speeding up termination of parental rights (TPR) proceedings would solve the foster care crisis by compelling states to tap into the presumably large pool of middle-class families who were able and willing to adopt minority children from foster care but were previously discouraged from doing so. As Richard Barth and his colleagues observe, the logic of the ASFA is that foster children are much more likely to be adopted if they can be presented to prospective parents as legally free (Barth, Wulczyn, & Crea, 2005). Because this hunch was not pretested in the same way that subsidized guardianship, drug rehabilitation services, and flexible funding options were tested under IV-E waivers, there are no solid grounds for determining whether speedier TPRs actually improve permanency results. For at least one group of hard-to-place foster children, Barth et al. (2005) find the evidentiary support exceedingly weak for the ASFA's assumption that TPRs would result in a vastly expanded pool of families ready to provide permanence for older wards. Citing Gibbs, Dalberth, Hawkins, Harris, Barth, and Wildfire (2004), they say that there is growing evidence that a substantial number of "legal orphans" will age out of care or leave by ways other than adoption after their ties to their birth families have been legally severed.

When the characteristics of the 35,900 children adopted from foster care in 1998 are compared to the 53,000 children adopted in 2002, it looks like the bulk of the increase did not come from the expected sources of speedier TPRs and transracial adoptions but mainly from the conversion of kinship and existing foster homes into adoptive homes. The latest complete data reported by the states for 2002 to the federal Adoption and Foster Care Analysis and Reporting System (AFCARS) show that 24% of all adoptive parents of children from foster care were relatives, 61% were former foster parents, and 15% were other nonrelated families. Eighty-eight percent of these adoptions were subsidized under the federal IV-E program. The comparable data for 1998 show that, at that time, 15% were relatives, 65% were former foster parents, 20% were other nonrelated families, and 86% of the adoptions were subsidized.

The decline in the percentage of adoptions by other nonrelated families from 20% to 15% between 1998 and 2002 may partially be accounted for by the fact that more states now urge prospective adoptive parents first to become licensed foster parents prior to finalization. What is more definite is the growth in kinship adoptions from 15% to 24%. In numerical terms, there was a 129% increase between 1998 and 2002, from 5,451 adoptions to 12,508 adoptions by extended kin. Added on top of this trend were a 75% increase in judicially appointed legal guardianships (most of which involve kin) from 5,836 to 10,136 and an 18% bump in the number of discharges to kin from 23,550 to 27,750 (many of which involve permanent custody or guardianship). More and more, it looks like the real revolution in permanency planning at the turn of the 21st century resulted from the conversion of safe and stable kinship foster care into legally permanent homes through adoption and guardianship (Testa & Miller, 2005).

Early research on permanency planning with kin did not anticipate this development. It assumed that cultural norms predisposed kin to disfavor formal adoption, especially among African Americans who had long-standing traditions of child sharing and informal adoption among extended family members (Burnette, 1997; Thornton, 1991). Research conducted in the mid-1990s, however, uncovered that many African American families were willing to consider formal adoption and more caseworkers were starting to ask (Gleeson, O'Donnell, & Bonecutter, 1997; Testa, Shook, Cohen, & Woods, 1996). The subsidized guardianship experiments that selected states conducted under IV-E waivers showed that families and workers were more comfortable about broaching the topic of permanence when both adoption and guardianship were put on the table than when termination of parental rights was posed as the only alternative to reunification. When offered a choice, it turned out that far more relatives were agreeable to adoption rather than guardianship because they preferred to solidify their legal claim against the competing claims of birth parents, many of whom also happened to be their daughters, sons, or siblings (Testa, 2005a).

UNCERTAINTIES OVER KINSHIP AGENCY

The spread of kinship care and subsidized guardianship has the potential for achieving a new ideological equilibrium in the long cycle of public child welfare reform in the United States. Kinship care and subsidized guardianship stand at the midpoint between ambitious efforts at intensive preservation of the birth family and the complete reconstruction of the nuclear family through TPR and adoption by non-kin. Permanence with kin also eases the tensions between the narrow scope of public child welfare, which restricts state intervention to protecting the child against physical injury, and the more diffuse scope, which expands intervention to advancing overall child well-being. Despite these equilibrating possibilities, however, kinship care still remains a contentious and highly politicized area that is vulnerable to the ideological tugs and pulls from all four corners of the scope of public interest/ social organization grid (see Figure 6.1).

Pulling toward (1) the narrow-primordial corner is the issue of whether the infusion of public subsidies and bureaucratic standards into primordial-based patterns of loyalty and mutual aid weaken traditional structures or if public assistance and government services strengthen and support people's voluntary capacity to safeguard the well-being of the child. Nathan Glazer (1988) has famously raised this issue with reference to public policies in general. He observes that every piece of social policy substitutes for some primordial arrangement a costly new bureaucratic arrangement in which public agents take over some part of the traditional role of the extended family, ethnic, or community group. Whether in doing so social policy weakens the commitments of these traditional agents and further encourages vulnerable populations to depend on the government for support rather than on the traditional structures is a question that has been asked of kinship foster care policies (Testa,

1997; Testa & Slack, 2002). It is also a caution that the U.S. Department of Health and Human Services (1999) inserted in its *Report to Congress on Kinship Foster Care.*[2]

Pulling toward (2) the narrow-bureaucratic corner is the issue of whether the habits and customs of kinship are sufficiently lasting to ensure the safety and stability of the home or if these responsibilities must be made more binding through adoption. Elizabeth Bartholet is one of the more forceful doubters of the benefits of keeping some children in permanent guardianship or kinship homes (see, for example, Bartholet, 1999). She observes that the primordial norms of kinship create no legally binding obligations on the part of the caregiver and that legal guardianship is less secure than adoption. She cautions that current methods of finding willing relative caregivers are deeply flawed and suffer from the lack of individualized, careful assessment that is necessary to ascertain whether a kin home will be as good as a non-kin home. She remarks that a great many relative foster parents are approaching old age, live on fixed incomes or on low wages, and reside in neighborhoods plagued by economic and social adversities that put children and families at higher than average risk. Bartholet also notes that child maltreatment frequently runs in families and co-occurs with drug abuse, domestic violence, and family poverty, which make the extended family a risky agent for safeguarding the best interests of the child. She hypothesizes that permanent homes will be beneficial for children only to the degree that permanent guardians and foster parents are selected not because of their continuity with the birth family or demonstrated stability as foster parents but rather on the basis of a thorough individualized look at their capacity to provide good-quality parenting.

Nearer to (3) the diffuse-primordial corner is the long-standing issue made salient once again by subsidized kinship adoption and guardianship of whether the greater financial benefits and social services that are available to relative caregivers but denied to birth parents discourages family preservation and family reunification and, if so, should the benefits and services be equalized both for fairness's sake and to conserve the integrity of the nuclear family? The general issue has been litigated going back to *Ramos v. Montgomery* (1970) in which the California Court of Appeals turned away an equal protection challenge to the usual practice of allowing more money to children in foster care than is paid to birth parents under the then-AFDC program. The rational basis given for the distinction was that foster children have greater needs and licensed foster care is more costly than care for children in the parental home. The same argument may be made for the higher benefits now paid for children in kinship foster care, but the rationale is less compelling for paying lower amounts to relative guardians under TANF than what is paid to relatives who take legal guardianship of foster children under IV-E waivers (Anderson, 2006).

Finally, tending toward (4) the diffuse-bureaucratic corner is the emerging question of whether the continuity of family, community, religion, and cultural heritage is still critically important for normal child development or if considerations of economic and social advantage ought to sometimes take precedence. Richard Barth (1999) has given thoughtful consideration to the issue of whether, after safety, it is always best to emphasize family continuity and permanence over other well-being factors, such as education and employment, that might create some discontinuity in the child's life. He makes a compelling case for the need for foster children to develop the capacity to move beyond the conventional support and boundaries of family and community in order to compete effectively in a postindustrial labor market. The assumption that these economic changes calls into question is whether family continuity and legal permanence retain much of a relationship any more to the health, longevity, or self-sufficiency of a former foster child (Barth, 1999).

VALUES AND EVIDENCE

Addressing the various questions and issues that are provoked by the new permanency strategies for children in foster care requires that we make a determination as to whether all of the questions can be answered by analyzing how well the empirical evidence stacks up in support of hypotheses of the sort that policy x increases outcome y better than counterfactual z (evidence-based argument), or if any of them ought to be answered by appealing to the inviolability of the policy as a value in its own right (value-centered argument).

James Fishkin (1983) observes that any social policy can be judged in terms of which two of three basic American values the policy upholds: (1) the *principle of merit*: the assumption that people's attainment of desired roles and rewards in society should be based

on fair competitive achievement without regard to race, sex, class, ethnic origin, or other irrelevant characteristics; (2) the *equality of life chances*: the assumption that people should be guaranteed the minimally necessary developmental conditions to give them a fair shot at leading a productive and rewarding life; and (3) the *autonomy of the family*: the assumption that parents should be guaranteed the privacy to influence substantially the development of their own children and pass along the family's cultural heritage.

Fishkin makes the argument that social policy can maximize at best only two of these three values and by doing so logically rules out the third. So, for example, pursuing the narrow-primordial (achievement–family autonomy) perspective of minimal state intervention to its logical conclusion of ending all social insurance and government aid sacrifices any credible commitment to the equality of child and family life chances. Similarly, the logical endpoint of the diffuse-primordial (equality–family autonomy) perspective is an egalitarian redistributive state that encroaches on the principle of individual meritorious achievement through massive taxation and universal transfer payments in order to even out child and family opportunities. Likewise, the endpoint of the diffuse-bureaucratic (achievement-equality) perspective is a child placement system that downplays the rights of birth parents and permits the widespread substitution of abusive and neglectful families by adoptive families or child welfare institutions in order to advance child well-being. The fact that public child welfare policy can at best maximize only two of the three desired outcomes at any one time gives rise to the recurrent cycle of public policy reform as political and cultural partisans who are aggrieved that their most cherished value is being sacrificed go on the counteroffensive.

The belief that extended families should be accorded special privileges and prerogatives as a value in its own right is a natural extension of the principle of nuclear family autonomy. It undoubtedly is the springboard for many of the kinship preferences and exceptions written into state and federal policy in recent years. But the diminishing importance of the extended family in structuring day-to-day life as it once did for the majority of folks (Giddens, 1990) strains the legitimacy of these kinship laws and opens them up to attack as antiquated and irrelevant biases (Bartholet, 1999). Even among strong defenders of kinship continuity, one finds opposing sentiments. On the one hand, there are those who consider kinship care a form of permanence in its own right without needing formalization through guardianship or adoption. On the other hand, there are those who argue for extending the richer benefits available to relative foster parents and adoptive parents to informal kinship caregivers outside of the child welfare system and even to birth parents as well.

If kinship continuity is indeed diminishing as a cherished value in its own right, the only other recourse for defending kinship care and kinship permanence is demonstrating empirically how they advance better than do other options those outcomes such as safety, stability, education, employment, and other indicators of child well-being which politicians and the wider public generally accept as important. Reliance on evidence-based solutions to policy disputes has only recently come into its own in child welfare after gaining a foothold in medicine, education, and public health. Research on the efficacy of kinship care, subsidized guardianship, and kinship adoption is growing and divides between the early scholarship that focused on safety and stability (Dubowitz, Feigelman, & Zuravin, 1993; Garnier & Poertner, 2000; Goerge, 1990) and the newer scholarship that looks at broader indices of child well-being (Carpenter & Clyman, 2004; Rosenthal & Curiel, 2006). Although much more research and rigorous evaluations are needed, the best available evidence suggests that the comparative advantage of kinship continuity may diminish as the focus shifts away from the expressive outcomes of safety, stability, and emotional security to the instrumental outcomes of education, employment, and other inputs to social mobility.

STRENGTHS AND WEAKNESSES OF KINSHIP SOCIAL CAPITAL

The hypothesized differences in expressive and instrumental outcomes by care type make sense when kinship continuity is considered within the broader theoretical framework of social capital. The concept of *social capital* has recently entered into the vocabulary of child welfare research and can be defined minimally as the resources that children and adults accrue from their social ties (Portes & Landolt, 1996). A useful distinction has been drawn between two forms of social capital—bonding and bridging (Putnam, 2000)—that has much relevance for kinship care. The former holds similar kinds of people together in groups, while the latter builds connections across social diversity.

Social capital theorists, drawing from the "strength of weak ties" argument (Granovetter, 1973), hypothesize that bonding social capital, such as permanent kinship ties, yields better expressive outcomes, such as emotional security, group solidarity, and psychological belongingness, than does bridging social capital (Lin, 2001). Vice versa, bridging social capital, such as mentoring relationships that span across diverse groups, is hypothesized to promote better instrumental outcomes, such as educational opportunities, job references, and social contacts that facilitate social advancement, than does bonding social capital. Abused and neglected children's stock of bridging social capital tends to be scarcer than other children's since their supply is heavily concentrated in fragile family ties, disadvantaged kinship networks, and socially isolated neighborhoods.

One proposed remedy for extending abused and neglected children's bridging social capital is to move foster children who cannot be safely reunited with their birth parents into "socially rich environments" (Collins & Pancoast, 1976) that afford them access to material resources and social opportunities that promote self-sufficient and productive adulthood. Richard Barth (1999) suggests that the goals of permanency planning be reoriented so that after assuring safety, placing children into socially rich permanent homes becomes the next priority even if it requires some discontinuity in order to advance their lifetime well-being. This proposal pushes child welfare policy closer toward the achievement-equality value combination and, as Fishkin argues, sacrifices any commitment to the principle of continuity of kinship, community, and ascribed heritage. This position can easily be caricatured as endorsing the wide-scale removal and transfer of children from the natural agency of disadvantaged parents to the adoptive agency of more affluent families. Barth distances himself from this nightmarish scenario of social engineering, however, by acknowledging that the preservation of existing family units still remains an intrinsic value of liberal democratic societies. Yet it is unclear by what process policy makers are able to decide that birth parents, but not the extended family, should be exempt from the social capital calculation. And what prevents future policy makers from deciding that the diminishing nuclear family of single parent and child is also no longer itself worth preserving?

COORDINATING MECHANISMS

Empirical research does not in and of itself enable policy makers to select among different intrinsic values. In order to buffer primordial solidarities against the diminishment of cultural meaning to the point that only the maximization of material well-being effectively matters, it will be important to create new coordinating mechanisms that can mediate the reciprocal flow of influence between the older primordial solidarities and the newer bureaucratic structures.

Coordination of primordial solidarities with bureaucratic structures involves creating opportunities for the impulses, desires, and values of kinship units, ethnic groups, and faith-based communities to enter into the reflexive self-steering of the bureaucracy. *Reflexivity* in this context refers to the "use of information about the conditions of activity as a means of reordering and redefining what that activity is" (Giddens, 1994, p. 86). In the primordial sphere, it assumes the form of reflecting on alternative choices and of "taking the role of the other" (Mead, 1934). The family group conference is an example of a coordinating mechanism at the level of practice; focus groups, social surveys, and participant observation are examples at the level of policy and research. It is important to make clear that the soliciting and canvassing of client wants and family desires are not intended to displace procedural regularity nor to dominate the decision-making processes of the bureaucracy, as is sometimes the risk with faith-based or affirmative action initiatives. Rather, coordination is meant to foster reciprocal understanding and sensitivity to the particular preferences of families and the universal requirements of the welfare state so that a suitable accommodation can be reached, for example, placing a child with a specific relative, having a child raised in the birth parents' faith, or accepting permanent legal responsibility for a related child under one's foster care.

Coordination of bureaucratic structures with primordial solidarities, in turn, takes the form of a results-oriented, evidence-based system of expert knowledge that is continuously updated with reliable and valid information about the efficacy of social policies and interventions in achieving the outcomes desired by children and families and valued by society at large. Better scientific knowledge about the personal and social factors that discourage self-interested defections from parental altruism and family mutualism promises to improve decision making at all organizational levels. Reliable information about the effectiveness of interventions, such as drug treatment, parenting classes, and educational programs, is necessary for the proper exercise of parental responsibilities by both affine and bureaucratic agents. Such information should be disseminated not only to caseworkers, lawyers, and judges but to kinship caregivers, foster families, and birth parents as well. Coordination of bureaucratic activities with client and community groups is an ethical obligation that goes well beyond the routine gathering of informed consent for individual treatment or engagement in research and includes involving clients as informed participants in all phases of policy management from the identification of policy questions to the selection, implementation, and evaluation of interventions to the dissemination of results (Gambrill, 2006).

The absence of effective coordinating mechanisms engenders distrust, alienates the very populations who are the intended subjects of public child welfare policies, and as a consequence undermines the capacity of bureaucratic structures to accomplish the broader social purposes for which they were constructed. For example, inattention to the special traditions of extended family care and informal adoption among African Americans blinded both researchers and policy makers to the fact that most grandparents, aunts, and uncles looking after their grandchildren, nieces, and nephews were willing to become their permanent caregivers. By building on the strengths and traditions of extended family care as expressed by clients in focus groups and service encounters, states like Illinois and California were able to embark on new permanency strategies, such as kinship adoption and subsidized guardianship, which transformed kinship from an obstacle to legal permanence into a positive asset for creating a lasting family life (Testa, 2005b). Related work also suggests that beyond a certain length of time, familiarity rather than biological relatedness per se is the crucial factor underlying bonding social capital and family stability, although kinship placement appears to thwart disruptions at the early phases of substitute care (Testa, 2001).

The new permanency strategies reflect in certain respects a break with bureaucratic universalism—the idea that well-being can be guaranteed by detaching people from their particular roles in family and local community and reattaching them instead to the universal roles of guaranteed work, lifelong marriage, and social citizenship (Marshall, 1964). Instead, they assume a model in which family identity becomes a reflexive process in which permanence is no longer accepted simply as a child's biological or legal "fate" but is actively constructed by drawing from diverse sources of bonding and bridging social capital and is enforced by a variety of permanency options that include, in addition to TPR and adoption, placement with "a fit and willing relative, legal guardian, or another planned permanent living arrangement" (Adoption and Safe Families Act, 1997). The "reflexive modernization" (Beck, 1992) of family permanence means that caregivers and caseworkers must learn to engage in dialogue about their personal and professional ambivalences, negotiate lasting commitments that best help families to manage their own agency risks, and challenge the dominant ideologies that would deny them meaningful choice while simultaneously acknowledging that their own unique accommodations will be less secure and less taken for granted (Deacon & Mann, 1999).

CONCLUSION

Changes in American public child welfare cycle among contrasting perspectives on the proper scope and organization of state intervention. For much of the early history of the United States, the care and protection of dependent and neglected children were rooted in the primordial worlds of extended kinship, ethnicity, religion, and local community. When state governments assumed a residual role in the late 19th century, public care was made available only on the condition that children were removed from the family and placed in almshouses, orphanages, and foster boarding homes. Reactions against out-of-home care spawned social movements in the early 20th century to enlarge the role of state and federal governments in advancing children's well-being in their own homes. After the invention of the juvenile court, Progressive reformers launched public child welfare along the dual tracks of expanding in-home assistance and family preservation and upgrading the bureaucratic complex of small group facilities and foster families for the residual group of homeless children.

Although the growth in out-of-home care was constrained throughout the 1960s and 1970s, misgivings about the capacity of bureaucratic agents to safeguard the well-being of foster children gave rise to the permanency planning movement, which sought to limit children's out-of-home care exposure to a brief,

time-limited interval. The AACWA aligned rules with the speedy return of foster children to the home and prevention of their removal in the first place. It created new incentives for the adoption of children who could not be safely reunified with their families. But agency failures to keep children safe at home and the inability of intensive family preservation to deliver on the promise of reducing out-of-home care fomented a backlash that stalled the expansion of the diffuse-primordial system of supported parental care and assistance. After the Personal Responsibility and Work Opportunity Reconciliation Act (PRWORA) in 1996 gutted the system of parental entitlements to minimal income assistance, the ASFA narrowed the permanency focus to adoption, legal guardianship, and long-term kinship foster care.

The new permanency strategies that federal and state governments have implemented to shift the balance from indefinite foster care to family permanence have so far yielded impressive results. Unexpectedly, most of these advances have not come as anticipated from the ranks of middle-class families interested in transracial adoption but from the conversion of kinship caregivers and foster families into permanent homes. This development has resurfaced long-simmering tensions that are threatening the future of extended-family foster care and kinship permanence.

Since 2000, the U.S. Department of Health and Human Services has sought to cut off administrative reimbursement for casework and placement services to children in nonlicensed kinship foster homes. The reason cited is that federal law demands that relatives must meet the same foster home licensing standards required of nonrelatives in order to qualify for federal foster care benefits. This proposal was softened somewhat by the budget reconciliation bill passed by Congress in 2006, which permits reimbursements for up to 1 year after placement in a nonlicensed relative home. Other provisions of the bill, however, overturn the court of appeals ruling in *Rosales v. Thompson* (2003) that declared that children who were removed from their homes and were living with relatives on an interim basis are eligible for federal foster care benefits even though they would not have been eligible in the homes from which they were taken. Other challenges to the prerogatives of kinship have surfaced in the recommendations of national judicial organizations that appear to condone the removal of children from stable kinship placements in order to place them with families more inclined to adopt (Testa, 2005a).

New policy thinking has begun to explore whether continuity with family and community should be given lesser weight than educational and other economic well-being considerations in permanency planning. As policy attention turns in this direction, research and evaluation will have an important role to play in parsing out the strengths and weaknesses of kinship social capital and legal permanence in enabling youth to acquire the cultural and human capital necessary for leading self-sufficient and productive lives in a global economy. There is research that hints at a positive association between children's educational achievement and having an affectionate relationship with their substitute caregiver, although undoubtedly the causality is bidirectional (Kang, 2004). Investment in early education programs can help abused and neglected children to obtain a leg up on academic achievement down the road (Reynolds, Ou, & Topitzes, 2004). Research is also needed to understand better whether there are alternative ways of building bridging social capital, such as mentoring programs, educational liaisons, education vouchers, and college scholarships, which can convey similar advantages as more disruptive measures, such as removing children to richer homes, better schools, and more affluent neighborhoods. Whatever the empirical findings reveal, it will always be important to coordinate permanency planning decisions with the impulses, desires, and wishes of the children and families directly involved and balance them against the morals and values of the society at large.

Notes

1. "The term 'legal guardianship' means a judicially created relationship between child and caretaker which is intended to be permanent and self-sustaining as evidenced by the transfer to the caretaker of the following parental rights with respect to the child: protection, education, care and control of the person, custody of the person, and decisionmaking. The term 'legal guardian' means the caretaker in such a relationship" 42 U.S.C. 675 (7).

2. The report noted:

[C]oncerns have also been expressed that kinship care threatens the legitimacy of the child welfare system's child protection mission. This mission would be undermined if kinship foster care causes the child welfare system to become, in fact or perception, a system of income support for families rather than a system of intervention to protect children endangered by abuse or neglect. (U.S. Department of Health and Human Services, 1999, p. 77)

References

Administration for Children and Families. (1997, February 14). *Adoption 2002: Safe and permanent homes for all children* [Fact sheet]. Washington, DC: U.S. Department of Health and Human Services. Available: http://www.hhs.gov/news/press/1997pres/970214c.html.

Administration for Children and Families. (2005). *Trends in foster care and adoption—FY2000-FY2005* Available: http://www.acf.hhs.gov/programs/cb/stats_research/afcars/trends.htm.

Adoption Assistance and Child Welfare Act. (1980). Public Law 96–272, 94 Stat. 500.

Adoption and Safe Families Act. (1997). Public Law 105–89, 111 Stat. 2115.

Anderson, S. G. (2006). The impact of state TANF policy decisions on kinship care providers. *Child Welfare*, 85(4), 715–736.

Barth, R. (1999). After safety, what is the goal of child welfare services: Permanency, family continuity, or social benefit? *International Journal of Social Welfare*, 8(4), 244–252.

Barth, R. P., Wulczyn, F., & Crea, T. (2005). From anticipation to evidence: Research on the Adoption and Safe Families Act. *Virginia Journal of Social Policy and the Law*, 12(3), 365–399.

Bartholet, E. (1999). *Nobody's children: Abuse and neglect, foster drift, and the adoption alternative*. Boston: Beacon.

Beck, U. (1992). *Risk society: Towards a new modernity*. London: Sage.

Besharov, D. J. (1985). "Doing something" about child abuse: The need to narrow the grounds for state intervention. *Harvard Journal of Law and Public Policy*, 8(3), 539–589.

Bowlby, J. (1969). *Attachment and loss: Vol. 1. Attachment*. New York: Basic.

Burnette, D. (1997). Grandparents raising grandchildren in the inner city. *Families in Society: The Journal of Contemporary Human Services*, 78, 489–501.

Cardenas, B. (1979). *Homes for all children: Our national concern*. Speech prepared by Blandina Cardenas, commissioner of the Administration for Children, Youth, and Families, cited on page 132 in Steiner, G. Y. (1981). *The futility of family policy*. Washington, DC: Brookings Institution.

Carpenter, S. C., & Clyman, R. B. (2004). The long-term emotional and physical wellbeing of women who have lived in kinship care. *Children and Youth Services Review*, 26(7), 673–686.

Coleman, J. S. (1990). *Foundations of social theory.* Cambridge, MA: Belknap Press of Harvard University Press.

Collins, A., & Pancoast, D. (1976). *Natural helping networks.* Washington, DC: National Association of Social Workers.

Committee on Ways and Means. (2004, March). *2004 green book: Background material and data on the programs within the jurisdiction of the Committee on Ways and Means.* Washington, DC: U.S. Government Printing Office. Available: http://frwebgate. access.gpo.gov/cgi-bin/getdoc.cgi?dbname=108_ green_book&docid=f:wm006_11.pdf.

Deacon, A., & Mann, K. (1999). Agency, modernity, and social policy. *Journal of Social Policy, 28*(3), 413–435.

Dubowitz, H., Feigelman, S., & Zuravin, S. (1993). A profile of kinship care. *Child Welfare, 72*(2), 153–169.

Fanshel, D., & Shinn, E. B. (1978). *Children in foster care: A longitudinal investigation.* New York: Columbia University Press.

Farrow, F. (2001). *The shifting policy impact of intensive family preservation services* (Discussion paper CS-68). Chicago: Chapin Hall Center for Children

Fishkin, J. S. (1983). *Justice, equal opportunity, and the family.* New Haven, CT: Yale University Press.

Gambrill, E. (2006). Evidence-based practice and policy: Choices ahead. *Research on Social Work Practice, 16*(3), 338–357.

Garnier, P. C., & Poertner, J. (2000). Using administrative data to assess child safety in out-of-home care. *Child Welfare, 79*(5), 597–613.

Gendell, S. J. (2001). In search of permanency: A reflection on the first 3 years of the Adoption and Safe Families Act implementation. *Family Court Review, 39,* 25–36.

Gibbs, D., Dalberth, B., Hawkins, S., Harris, S., Barth, R., & Wildfire, J. (2004). *Termination of parental rights for older foster children: Exploring practice and policy issues.* Research Triangle Park, NC: RTI International.

Giddens, A. (1990). *The consequences of modernity.* Stanford, CA: Stanford University Press.

Giddens, A. (1994). *Beyond Left and Right: The future of radical politics.* Stanford, CA: Stanford University Press.

Glazer, N. (1988). *The limits of social policy.* Cambridge, MA: Harvard University Press.

Gleeson, J. P., & Craig, L. C. (1994). Kinship care in child welfare: An analysis of states' policies. *Children and Youth Services Review, 16*(1–2), 7–31.

Gleeson, J. P., O'Donnell, J., & Bonecutter, F. J. (1997). Understanding the complexity of practice in kinship foster care. *Child Welfare, 76*(6), 801–826.

Goerge, R. (1990). The reunification process in substitute care. *Social Service Review, 64,* 422–457.

Goldstein, J., Freud, A., & Solnit, A. J. (1973). *Beyond the best interests of the child.* New York: Free Press.

Granovetter, M. (1973). The strength of weak ties. *American Journal of Sociology, 78,* 1360–1380.

Indian Child Welfare Act. (1978). Public Law 95–608, 92 Stat. 3069, codified as amended, 25 U.S.C.A. §1901 et seq.

Inter-Ethnic Adoption Provisions. (1996). Public Law 104–188 §1808, 110 Stat. 1904.

Kamerman, S., & Kahn, A. (1990). Social services for children, youth, and families in the United States. *Children and Youth Services Review, 12*(1–2), 1–184.

Kang, H.-A. (2004). *Coping with the educational disadvantages of children in public care: Substitute caregivers' educational expectations and involvement.* Unpublished doctoral dissertation, University of Illinois, Urbana-Champaign.

Kempe, C. H, Silverman, F. N., Steele, B. F., Droegemueller, W., & Silver, H. K. (1962, July 7). The battered-child syndrome. *Journal of the American Medical Association, 181,* 17–24.

Knitzer, J., Allen, M. L., & McGowan, B. (1978). *Children without homes: An examination of public responsibility to children in out-of-home care.* Washington, DC: Children's Defense Fund.

Lerman, P. (1982). *Deinstitutionalization and the welfare state.* New Brunswick, NJ: Rutgers University Press.

Lin, N. (2001). *Social capital: A theory of social structure and action.* Cambridge: Cambridge University Press.

Litwak, E. (1965). Extended kin relations in an industrial democratic society. In E. Shanas & G. F. Streib (Eds.), *Social structure and the family: Generational relations* (pp. 290–323). Englewood Cliffs, NJ: Prentice-Hall.

Maas, H., & Engler, R. (1959). *Children in need of parents.* New York: Columbia University Press.

Marshall, T. H. (1964). *Class, citizenship, and social development.* Chicago: University of Chicago Press.

McDonald, J., Salyers, N. S., & Testa, M. (2003, October). *Nation's child welfare systems double number of adoptions from foster care.* Urbana, IL: Fostering Results, Children and Family Research Center. Available: http://www.fosteringresults.org/results/reports/ pewreports_10–01–03_doubledadoptions.pdf.

Mead, G. H. (1934), *Mind, self, and society.* Chicago: University of Chicago Press.

Multiethnic Placement Act. (1994). Public Law 103–382, 108 Stat. 4056.

National Coalition for Child Protection Reform. (2006). *A child welfare timeline.* Available: http://www. nccpr.org/index_files/page0006.html.

Parton, N. (1999). Reconfiguring child welfare practices: Risk, advanced liberalism, and the government of freedom. In A. S. Chambon, A. Irving, & L. Epstein (Eds.), *Reading Foucault for social work* (pp. 101–130). New York: Columbia University Press.

Pelton, L. H. (1989). *For reasons of poverty: A critical analysis of the public child welfare system in the United States.* New York: Praeger.

Pike, V., Down, S., Emlen, A., Downs, G., & Care, D. (1977). *Permanent planning for children in foster care: A handbook for social workers* (DHEW No. OHDS 77–30124). Washington, DC: U.S. Department of Health and Human Services.

Portes, A., & Landolt, P. (1996). The downside of social capital. *American Prospect, 26,* 18–21.

Prosser, W. (1983). Number of foster care children. *Social Services Policy Staff Technical Paper.* Washington, DC: Department of Health and Human Services.

Putnam, R. D. (2000). *Bowling alone: The collapse and revival of American community.* New York: Simon and Schuster.

Ramos v. Montgomery. (1970). S.D. Cal, 313 F.Supp. 1179, 1181–1182, aff'd. 400 U.S. 1003.

Rosales v. Thompson (2003) 321 F.3d 835 (9th Cir.)

Reynolds, A. J., Ou, S., & Topitzes, J. W. (2004). Paths of effects of early childhood intervention on educational attainment and delinquency: A confirmatory analysis of the Chicago child-parent centers. *Child Development, 75*(5), 1299–1328.

Rosenthal, J. A., & Curiel, H. F. (2006). Modeling behavioral problems of children in the child welfare system: Caregiver, youth, and teacher perceptions. *Children and Youth Services Review, 28*(11), 1391–1408.

Sengupta, S. (2000, August 10). No rise in child abuse seen in welfare shift. *New York Times,* p. A1.

Shyne, A. W., & Schroeder, A. G. (1978). *National study of social services to children and their families* (DHEW No. 78–30150). Washington, DC: Children's Bureau, U.S. Department of Health and Human Services.

Steiner, G. Y. (1981). *The futility of family policy.* Washington, DC: Brookings Institution.

Tatara, T. (1992). *Characteristics of children on substitute and adoptive care: A statistical summary of the VCIS national child welfare database.* Washington, DC: American Public Welfare Association.

Taylor, H. B. (1935). *Law of guardian and ward.* Chicago: University of Chicago Press.

Testa, M. F. (1997). Kinship foster care in Illinois. In J. Duerr Berrick, R. Barth, & N. Gilbert (Eds.), *Child welfare research review* (Vol. 2, pp. 101–129). New York: Columbia University Press.

Testa, M. F. (2001). Kinship care and permanency. *Journal of Social Service Research, 28*(1), 25–43.

Testa, M. F. (2005a). The quality of permanence—lasting or binding? Subsidized guardianship and kinship foster care as alternatives to adoption. *Virginia Journal of Social Policy and the Law, 12*(3), 499–534.

Testa, M. F. (2005b). The changing significance of race and kinship for achieving permanence for foster children. In D. Derrezotes, J. Poertner, & M. F. Testa (Eds.), *Race matters in child welfare: The overrepresentation of African Americans in the system* (pp. 231–241). Washington, DC: Child Welfare League of America Press.

Testa, M. F., & Miller, J. (2005). Evolution of private guardianship as a child welfare resource. In G. R. Mallon & P. McCartt Hess (Eds.), *Child welfare in the 21st century* (pp. 405–422). New York: Columbia University Press.

Testa, M. F., Shook, K., Cohen, L., & Woods, M. (1996). Permanency planning options for children in formal kinship care. In D. Wilson & S. Chipungu (Eds.), *Kinship Care* [Special issue]. *Child Welfare, 75*(5), 451–470.

Testa, M. F., & Slack, K. S. (2002). The gift of kinship foster care. *Children and Youth Services Review, 24*(1), 79–108.

Thornton, J. L. (1991). Permanency planning for children in kinship foster homes. *Child Welfare, 70*(5), 593–601.

U.S. Department of Health and Human Services. (1999). *Report to Congress on kinship foster care.* Washington, DC: Author.

Wald, M. (1975). State intervention on behalf of "neglected" children: A search for realistic standards. *Stanford Law Review, 27*(4), 985–1040.

Waldfogel, J. (1998). *The future of child protection.* Cambridge, MA: Harvard University Press.

Welch, W. M., & Phillips, L. (1994, December 6). Orphanage idea brings an outcry: A heated debate [on] GOP idea. *USA Today,* p. 4A.

Wexler, R. (2001). Take the children and run: Tales from the age of ASFA. *New England Law Review, 26,* 129–152.

White House Conference on the Care of Dependent Children. (1909). Available: http://www.libertynet.org/edcivic/whoukids.html.

Wolfe, A. (1978). The child and the state: A second glance. *Contemporary Crises, 2,* 407–435.

Wulczyn, F., Hislop, K. B., & Goerge, R. (2000). *Foster care dynamics 1983–1998: A report from the multistate foster care data archive.* Chicago: Chapin Hall Center for Children at the University of Chicago.

7

The Transition to Adulthood Among Youth "Aging Out" of Care: What Have We Learned?

Amy Dworsky

INTRODUCTION

The Adoption Assistance and Child Welfare Act of 1980 (PL 96-272) established permanency as a fundamental goal that states should have for all children who are placed in out-of-home care. According to this landmark federal child welfare legislation, permanency can be achieved by preventing children from being placed in out-of-home care, returning children to their families if placement does occur, or finding adoptive homes for children who cannot be returned safely to their families.

For many children, permanency is a realistic goal. Reunification with their family is the discharge outcome for the majority of children who enter out-of-home care (Benedict & White, 1991; Courtney, 1994; Courtney & Wong, 1996; Goerge, 1990; Lawder, Poulin, & Andrews, 1986; Tatara, 1993), and most children who return home do so within a year (Courtney, 1994; Goerge, 1990; Lawder et al., 1986). Although adoption is a far less common discharge outcome, as many as

21% of the children who enter out-of-home care are placed in adoptive homes (Wulczyn, Hislop, & Chen, 2005).[1]

Nevertheless, for a significant number of children who experience an out-of-home care placement, permanency remains an elusive goal. As older adolescents, they exit the child welfare system through one of several routes. Some run away from the foster home or group care setting in which they are placed; others are transferred to a psychiatric hospital or correctional facility (Courtney & Barth, 1996). However, the largest percentage, by far, exit care by "aging out." That is, they are discharged from the child welfare system when they reach some statutorily defined age. Although a few states allow foster youth to remain in care until they are as old as 21 years, in most states 18 is the statutorily defined age at which they are discharged.

Approximately 20,000 foster youth are discharged by state child welfare agencies each year to live on their own (U.S. Department of Health and Human Services, 1999). Importantly, these youth are not a homogeneous group. Although some grew up in care after entering as young children, the majority did not enter until they were at least 13 years old (U.S. Department of Health and Human Services, 2002).[2]

What happens to these foster youth after they leave care is the focus of this chapter. It begins with a brief discussion of the motivation for and development of the Title IV-E Independent Living Program and its successor, the John H. Chafee Foster Care Independence Program. This is followed by a review of the literature on the outcomes of former foster youth. The review describes a number of previous studies that have examined the self-sufficiency of foster youth who aged out of care, discusses their methodological limitations, and summarizes the findings from this research. The chapter concludes with a discussion of some unanswered questions that researchers are beginning to address.

PREPARING FOSTER YOUTH TO LIVE INDEPENDENTLY

For most young people, the transition to adulthood is a gradual process. They become less dependent on their parents and more prepared to meet their own needs over time. Even then, many continue to receive financial and/or emotional support from their families. This is in stark contrast to the situation confronting foster youth aging out of care, who must make the transition to adulthood largely on their own.[3]

For many years, the needs of foster youth who would soon be making this transition were basically ignored. The federal Adoption Assistance and Child Welfare Act of 1980 (PL 96-272) did not require states to prepare their foster youth for independent living or to provide post-discharge assistance to youth after they aged out. Nor was any federal funding available to help states to pay for independent living services (DeWoody, Ceja, & Sylvester, 1993).

It was not until the mid-1980s that policy makers began to pay attention to the needs of this population. At congressional hearings held in 1984 and 1985, it was reported that these youth were at high risk of becoming homeless (Citizens' Committee for Children of New York City, 1984; New York State Council on Children and Families, 1984; Shaffer & Caton, 1984), being arrested (Shaffer & Caton, 1984), or becoming welfare dependent (Pettiford, 1981) after leaving care. In response to the testimony given at these hearings, Congress amended the Social Security Act and created

the Title IV-E Independent Living Program as part of the Consolidated Omnibus Budget Reconciliation Act of 1985 (PL 99-272).[4]

The enacting legislation authorized a total of $45 million in federal funding, which was to be allocated to the states in proportion to their share of the 1984 Title IV-E foster care caseload. States could use these federal funds to help prepare their foster youth to live on their own and were given considerable discretion with respect to how it was spent. Among other things, they could provide educational services for youth working toward a high school diploma or GED, employment services for youth who needed vocational training or career planning, and/or housing services for youth who wanted help finding a place to live. However, the legislation did impose some restrictions. Services could only be provided to Title IV-E eligible youth between the ages of 16 and 18 years old who were living in licensed family foster homes, homes run by not-for-profit organizations, and homes run by public agencies with no more than 25 beds. In addition, the funds could not be used to cover the costs of services already being funded under Title IV-E, such as room and board. Importantly, this provision prevented states from using their federal funds for independent living subsidies and transitional housing (Allen, Bonner, & Greenan, 1988; Barth, 1990).

The original legislation was amended several times before 1993, when it was granted permanent status under the Omnibus Budget Reconciliation Act (PL 103-66). Henceforth, states could be confident that funding would be available from one year to the next rather than having to rely on annual appropriations. One effect of these amendments was to expand the population of eligible foster youth. In 1988, Congress authorized states to use their Title IV-E funds to provide independent living services to all 16- to 18-year-old foster youth regardless of their Title IV-E eligibility and to former foster youth who had been discharged from care within the past 6 months. Then, in 1990, Congress gave states the option of providing independent living services to former foster youth until age 21.[5] In addition to these changes, Congress increased the program's annual appropriations from $45 million for fiscal year 1987 to $70 million in fiscal year 1992. However, under legislation passed in 1991, states were required to match whatever funds they received in excess of their share of the first $45 million at a rate of 50%.[6]

As a result of these amendments, there was a steady increase in the provision of independent living services to foster youth by both public and private child welfare agencies. A decade after the program's inception, each of the 50 states and the District of Columbia was receiving Title IV-E independent living funds. However, there was considerable variation across states in the range of services offered. Some states offered "basic" services only whereas others offered "optional" services too (DeWoody et al., 1993).[7] More important, because the increases in funding did not keep pace with the growing population of foster youth eligible for services, only some of the foster youth who might have benefited from independent living services actually received them (U.S. Department of Health and Human Services, 1999).[8]

Another problem with the program was that more than a decade after it had been established, there was little evidence that the outcomes of former foster youth had significantly improved (U.S. Department of Health and Human Services, 1999). The federal government had required very little from states beyond creation of state ILP plans and had "no established method to review the states' progress in helping youths in the transition from foster care" (U.S. General Accounting Office, 1999, p. 3). Moreover, the few studies that had been done seemed to indicate that foster youth were still not adequately prepared to live independently.[9]

Congress responded to the concerns that were again being raised about this population by passing the Foster Care Independence Act of 1999 (PL 106-169). Title I of this legislation replaced the Title IV-E Independent Living Program with the newly established John H. Chafee Foster Care Independence Program. This program doubled the maximum amount of money that states could draw down each year to $140 million, although a match of 20% was now required for all of the federal independent living funds that states received.[10] It gave states greater discretion to decide whom the recipients of independent living services would be, and allowed them to use up to 30% of their federal independent living funds to pay for the room and board of former foster youth who are at least 18 years old and not yet 21.[11] It also required states to use at least some portion of their funds to provide follow-up services to foster youth after they aged out. In the past, such services could be provided at state option.

The Foster Care Independence Act also included a number of other changes. One of the most significant was a provision granting states the option of extending Medicaid coverage to 18- to 20-year-old former foster youth. As the research discussed below will show, lack of health insurance coverage is a major problem for youth who have aged out of care. As of February 2007, however, only 17 states had exercised this option: Arizona, California, Florida, Indiana, Iowa, Kansas, Massachusetts, Mississippi, Nevada, New Jersey, Oklahoma, South Carolina, South Dakota, Texas, Utah and Wyoming (Patel & Roherty, 2007).[12]

In addition to this Medicaid provision, the Foster Care Independence Act increased the amount of assets that foster youth can accumulate and still be Title IV-E eligible from $1,000 to $10,000 and, consistent with the more general trend toward privatization of child welfare services, eliminated the prohibition against contracting with private, for-profit independent living services providers using federal funds The law was amended in 2001 when Congress created the Education and Training Voucher (ETV) Program. States can use their ETV funds to provide eligible foster youth and former foster youth with up to $5,000 per year for postsecondary education. Whether the increased funding or any of the other changes instituted by the Foster Care Independence Act will result in better outcomes for foster youth making the transition to adulthood remains to be seen.[13]

EARLY RESEARCH ON YOUNG ADULTS WHO AGED OUT OF FOSTER CARE

Research on the outcomes of youth who aged out of foster care dates back to the 1924 publication of Sophie Van Senden Theis's *How Foster Children Turn Out*. This early study examined the functioning of 797 former foster youth between the ages of 18 and 40 years. They had been placed with foster families for at least a year by the New York State Charities Aid Association between 1898 and 1922, and 562 had remained in care until they became adults.[14] Foreshadowing the findings of later studies, Van Senden Theis described 27% of these young adults as "incapable" of supporting themselves or managing their own affairs.[15]

Despite its methodological problems—most notably Van Senden Theis's reliance on other people for information about some of the former foster children—it is a respectable piece of research. Particularly striking is the richness of the data she collected about the characteristics of both biological and foster families, as well as placement histories. Nevertheless, more than

TABLE 7.1 Early Research on Young Adults Who Aged Out of Foster Care

Study	Sample Size	Response Rate	Geographic Region	Data Collection Method	Age in Years at Follow-Up	Years Since Discharge	Years in Care
Meier (1965)	66	80.5%	Minnesota	92% in-person interviews, 8% mail questionnaires	28–32	10–11	Minimum = 5 Mean = 11.8
Zimmerman (1982)	61	57%	New Orleans Parish	In-person interviews supplemented by case record data	19–29	Not reported	Minimum = 1 Median = 7.9
Festinger (1983)	277	76.1%	New York City metropolitan area	67% in-person interviews, 20% telephone interviews, 13% mail questionnaires	22–25 Mean = 23	4 to 5	Minimum = 5 Median = 15.9 for youth discharged from foster homes, 9.7 for youth discharged from group care settings
Jones & Moses (1984)	328	52.1%	West Virginia	89% in-person, 7% telephone interviews, 4% mail questionnaires	19–28 Mean = 20	Not reported	Minimum = 1 Mean not reported
Fanshel, Finch, & Grundy (1988)	106	51.4%	Seattle and Yakima, Washington	Primarily in-person interviews with some mail questionnaires	Not reported	Maximum = 15 Mean = 7.1	Minimum not reported Mean = 4.7
Barth (1990)	55	64.7%	San Francisco Bay and Sacramento areas	76% in-person interviews, 24% telephone interviews	Mean = 21	1–10 Mean = 3	Not reported
Cook et al. (1991)	Wave 1: 1,644	Wave 1: 100%	Arizona, California, Illinois, Missouri	Wave 1: Case record data	Wave 1: 16+	Wave 1: N/A	Wave 1: Minimum not reported Median = 2.5
	Wave 2: 810	Wave 2: 49.3%	Pennsylvania, New York, Tennessee, District of Columbia	Wave 2: 31% in-person interviews, 69% telephone interviews	Wave 2: 18–24 Median = 21	Wave 2: 2.5–4	Wave 2: Not reported

40 years passed before another study of this population appeared. A review uncovered only seven studies based in the United States that were published during a period of approximately 30 years: Meier (1965); Zimmerman (1982); Festinger (1983); Jones and Moses (1984); Fanshel, Finch, and Grundy (1986); Barth (1990); and Cook, Fleischman, and Grimes (1991).[16] Table 7.1 provides some basic information about these seven studies: sample size, response rate, geographic region, method of data collection, age at follow-up, years since discharge, and time in care.

All of these early studies examined the functioning of former foster youth across a variety of domains. Most commonly, researchers collected data related to education, employment, income, housing, health, social support, marriage, parenting, substance use, and criminal activity. Table 7.2 lists the specific domains that each study addressed. Although most of these studies also measured other aspects of adult functioning, a major focus of this research was on self-sufficiency.

What emerged from this research was a rather consistent but troubling pic6ture of what happened to foster youth who aged out of care:

- Many foster youth did not graduate from high-school before or after they aged out (Barth, 1990; Cook et al., 1991; Festinger, 1983; Jones & Moses, 1984).
- The earnings of those who were employed were very low (Barth, 1990; Cook et al., 1991; Festinger, 1983).
- Receipt of means-tested welfare benefits, such as AFDC/TANF, food stamps, and/or Medicaid, was not uncommon (Barth, 1990; Cook et al., 1991; Festinger, 1983; Jones & Moses, 1984).
- Former foster youth were frequently dependent on financial assistance from family and friends (Jones & Moses, 1984; Cook et al., 1991).
- They were also likely to experience housing instability or even homelessness (Barth, 1990; Cook et al., 1991; Festinger, 1983).

That foster youth were often aging out of care unprepared to live independently became even more apparent when their outcomes were compared to those of same-aged adults in the general population. For example, these comparisons indicated:

- Former foster youth were less likely to have a high school diploma (Cook et al., 1991) or had completed fewer years of schooling (Festinger, 1983).

- Former foster youth were less likely to be employed and had lower earnings (Cook et al., 1991).
- Former foster youth were more likely to be receiving welfare benefits (Cook et al., 1991; Festinger, 1983).

Although several of these studies are still cited in the literature, they are problematic in two respects. First, they were conducted over a period during which there were several major changes in child welfare policy. More than half of these studies (Meier, 1965; Zimmerman, 1982; Festinger, 1983; Jones & Moses, 1984) were based on samples of former foster youth who were discharged from care prior to the Adoption Assistance and Child Welfare Act of 1980 and before the Title IV-E Independent Living Program (ILP) was created in 1985. Even the Westat study (Cook et al., 1991), which was ostensibly a national evaluation of the Title IV-E ILP, examined the outcomes of young adults who were discharged from care shortly after implementation of the program. Given the major policy changes that have occurred since the former foster youth who comprised these were in care, it is not clear how relevant these studies are to the experiences of contemporary foster youth who are aging out in the context of the 1999 Foster Care Independence Act.

The second problem with these studies is that nearly all suffer from one or more (sometimes serious) methodological limitations (Courtney, Piliavin, Grogan-Kaylor, & Nesmith, 2001; Maluccio & Fein, 1985; McDonald, Allen, Westerfelt, & Piliavin, 1996). A brief list of the most common includes the following:

- Nonrandom sampling (e.g., Barth, 1990) and sample attrition (e.g., Cook et al., 1991) resulted in samples that were not representative of, and hence not generalizable to, the larger population of foster youth.[17]
- In some cases, former foster youth in the same sample had aged out of care at different times, and their post-discharge experiences ranged from less than 1 to many years.
- Multivariate techniques were generally not used to examine the relationship between the demographic or placement characteristics of former foster youth and the outcomes they experienced even when the sample size made this feasible.[18]
- Because most of these studies were retrospective, no data were collected while the foster youth were still in care.[19]

TABLE 7.2 Outcomes Examined by Early Studies of Former Foster Youth Who Aged Out of Care

Study	Domains
Meier (1965)	Homemaking and living arrangements, employment and economic circumstances, health, marriage, parenting, and social relationships
Zimmerman (1982)	Living arrangements, educational attainment, employment history, and income
Festinger (1983)	Education, employment, and welfare dependence; marriage, partnership, and parenthood; social support and community participation; health and perceptions of well-being; substance use and trouble with the law
Jones & Moses (1984)[1]	Education, employment, welfare dependence, living arrangements, health, family and social relationships, criminal justice involvement, and experiences in out-of-home care
Fanshel, Finch, & Grundy (1988)[2]	Housing, income, education, employment, marriage, parenting, crime, emotional health, social support, and substance use
Barth (1990)	Housing, income, employment, education, criminal activity, contact with foster and/or birth families, physical and mental health, access to health care, substance use, satisfaction with foster care, and preparation for independent living
Cook et al. (1991)	Wave 1: Demographic characteristics, family situations, placement histories, independent living skills, and services received
	Wave 2: Employment, education, income sources, housing, parenthood, social support, health care, and drug and alcohol use
	Seven indicators were used to assess self-sufficiency: ability to maintain a job for at least 1 year, graduation from high school, ability to access medical care, avoidance of early parenthood, availability of social support, overall life satisfaction, and cost to the community (e.g., welfare dependence and incarceration).

1. The author could not locate a copy of the original report, and although findings from the study have been reported in other sources, those reports often conflict. Compare, for example, Mech (1994) and McDonald et al. (1996).

2. Although reunification, emancipation, referral back to court, and running away are all possible Casey Family Program discharge outcomes, the researchers did not report separate findings for these groups.

- Because samples were generally limited to former foster youth within a particular state (Jones & Moses, 1984) or metropolitan area (Barth, 1990; Festinger, 1983), any variability across studies could reflect regional differences in unemployment or high school completion rates.

MORE RECENT RESEARCH ON YOUNG ADULTS WHO AGED OUT OF FOSTER CARE

In contrast to the handful of studies discussed above, more recent research has examined the outcomes of foster youth who aged out almost a decade or more after the Title IV-E ILP had been established. Like the earlier studies, some of this research was based on survey data collected from the youth themselves. However, other studies conducted since the mid-1990s have been based on state administrative data. Because this more recent research has generally not been included in previous reviews of the literature, and because it is relevant to current policy, several of the studies based on survey data and several based on administrative data are discussed below.[20]

RESEARCH BASED ON SURVEY DATA

The Foster Youth Transitions to Adulthood study examined the outcomes of Wisconsin foster youth who aged out of care (Courtney et al., 2001). Baseline survey data were collected from 141 foster youth, ages 17 and 18, in 1995 while they were still in care. All of the youth had been in care for a minimum of 18 months. The questions covered a variety of domains, including demographic characteristics, family background, history of maltreatment and reasons for placement, foster care experiences and preparation for independent living, receipt of mental health or other social services, current health and mental health status, education, employment, delinquency, and social support.

Two additional waves of survey data were subsequently collected. Both follow-up interviews included questions about living arrangements, income, employment, receipt of public assistance, education, health care needs, mental health, social support, trouble with the law, traumatic events such as physical or sexual assaults, and preparation for independent living. Eighty percent, or 113, of the foster youth from whom baseline data had been collected completed a second interview 12–18 months after their discharge from care. These young adults were similar to the baseline sample with respect to gender, race/ethnicity, and placement region (i.e., Milwaukee or the balance of the state).

All of the foster youth who participated in this study would have experienced the full impact of the Title IV-E Independent Living Program. However, their outcomes at wave 2 were not much different from what earlier studies had found, particularly with respect to self-sufficiency. Table 7.3 summarizes some of the major findings from the study's second wave (Courtney et al., 2001).

A third wave of survey data was collected approximately 3 years post-discharge. According to one of the principal investigators, 72%, or 102, of the foster youth from the baseline sample completed a wave 3 interview (Courtney, October 2006). To date, no findings from the third wave have been published or presented.

The Foster Youth Transitions to Adulthood study played a very important role in the passage of the Foster Care Independence Act of 1999. It was one of the studies cited at the congressional hearings leading up to its enactment. Another major study, the Midwest Evaluation of the Adult Functioning of Former Foster Youth (Courtney, Dworsky, Ruth, Keller, Havlicek, & Bost, 2005; Courtney, Terao, & Bost, 2004), has been examining the outcomes of foster youth whose transition to adulthood began after passage of the Foster Care Independence Act. This longitudinal study by researchers at the University of Chicago's Chapin Hall Center for Children is following youth as they age out of care in Iowa, Wisconsin, and Illinois—states with very different policies regarding foster youth.

Baseline survey data were collected from 732 foster youth, ages 17 and 18, between May 2002 and March 2003. These foster youth had been removed from their homes because they were neglected or abused and had entered care before their 16th birthdays. The youth were asked about their circumstances prior to being placed and their experiences while in care, including their receipt of independent living services. Other questions dealt with education and employment; physical and mental health; social support and relationships with family; delinquency and criminal justice system involvement; sexual behavior; and, in the case of females, pregnancy.[21]

TABLE 7.3 Summary of Findings from Wave 2 of Foster Youth Transitions to Adulthood Study

Employment and earnings	61% currently employed
	81% ever employed since discharge
	Mean earnings = $185 per week, range $54–613 per week
Educational attainment	60% had a high school diploma
	9% were attending college
Financial support from family or friends	35% from family, 14% from friends
Welfare dependence	32% had received welfare benefits (i.e., AFDC/TANF, general assistance, SSI, food stamps, or housing assistance) at some time since discharge
Homelessness and housing instability	12% spent at least one night in a shelter or on the streets since discharge
	22% had lived in more than three different places since discharge
Criminal justice involvement	18% had been arrested since discharge
	10% of the females and 27% of the males had been incarcerated at least once post-discharge
Victimization	25% of the males and 10% of the females reported being the victim of physical violence
	13% of the females reported being sexually assaulted or raped

Eighty-two percent, or 603, of these foster youth were reinterviewed between March and December 2004. Although most were 19 years old, nearly half (N = 282) were still state wards. This reflects the fact that, at the time the second wave of survey data was collected, Illinois was one of the few states where the courts allowed foster youth to remain under the supervision of the child welfare system until age 21. By contrast, courts in Iowa and Wisconsin generally discharged youth after they turned 18 years old. Almost three quarters of the Illinois sample (n = 280) was still in care compared to only two of the Wisconsin and Iowa youth. This second interview was similar in content to the first except that the questions focused on experiences since the baseline interview.

By age 19, these foster youth were facing a number of challenges to becoming self-sufficient young adults, including high school noncompletion, unstable employment and low wages, mental health and substance use problems, criminal justice involvement, and, for females, early child bearing. A significant number of the foster youth who were no longer in care had already received public assistance or experienced homelessness. However, the picture was not entirely bleak. Some of these foster youth were making progress toward self-sufficiency. For example, nearly one quarter were enrolled in a 2- or 4-year college. A similar percentage of those who were employed had been working at their current job for at least 1 year. Others had less tangible assets, such as a close relationship with at least one member of their biological family, especially siblings and grandparents, aspirations for postsecondary education, and a generally optimistic outlook toward the future. Some of the main findings are summarized in Table 7.4 (Courtney et al., 2005).

The researchers also compared their sample of young adults to a nationally representative group of 19-year-olds from the National Longitudinal Study

TABLE 7.4 Summary of Findings from Wave 2 of Midwest Evaluation of Former Foster Youth

Employment and earnings	67% had worked during the past year but only 41% were currently employed. They were working a mean of 32.6 hours per week for a mean wage of $7.54 per hour.
	40% of those currently employed had been working at their job for at least 6 months
	More than three quarters of those employed during the past year earned $5,000 or less.
Educational attainment	58% had a high school diploma, 5% had a GED
	48% were currently enrolled in school, including 24% who were enrolled in a 2- or 4-year college
Pregnancy and parenthood	48% of the females had been pregnant at least once
	32% of the females and 14% of the males were parents
Welfare dependence	36% of those who were no longer in care had received food stamps or cash assistance (TANF)
Post-discharge living arrangements	29% of those no longer in care were living in their own place, just over a third were living with their biological parents or other family members, 10% were living with their former foster parents
Homelessness and housing instability	14% of those no longer in care had been homeless at least once, 28% had lived in three or more different places
Criminal justice system involvement	69% of the males and 46% of the females had ever been arrested (38% and 20% since first interview)
	52% of the males and 29% of the females had ever been incarcerated (30% and 11% since first interview)
Mental health	19% had at least one mental health diagnosis, most notably depression and PTSD
	21% had an alcohol or other drug disorder
Victimization	24% had been threatened by a knife or gun, beaten up, shot, or stabbed during the past year
Disconnectedness	31% were neither working nor enrolled in school

of Adolescent Health (referred to as Add Health).[23] These comparisons indicated that the foster youth were faring worse, and in many cases much worse, than their same-age peers across a number of domains. For example, the foster youth were both less likely to have a high school diploma or GED and less likely to be enrolled in school. Despite their lower rates of school enrollment, they were also less likely to be employed. Both male and female foster youth were more likely to have engaged in a variety of delinquent behaviors and more likely to have been the victim of a violent act. Finally, compared to their Add Health counterparts, female foster youth were much more likely to have become pregnant by age 19.

Some of the most striking findings to emerge from this research were the differences related to care status at wave 2. Across a range of outcomes, the young adults who were still in care at age 19 were, on average, faring better than their peers who had already left. Those still in care were more than twice as likely to be enrolled in some type of school, and more than three times as likely to be enrolled in a 2- or 4-year college. Although some of this difference can be explained by the fact that the young adults who had left care were more likely to be employed, fewer than half were currently working. Staying in care past age 18 more than doubled the odds of being employed or in school even after statistically controlling for a variety of potential confounds, including the characteristics of the young adults and their placement histories.[24]

Some of the differences that were observed were gender specific. For example, among females, care status was related to pregnancy. Females who remained in care were less likely to have become pregnant since their baseline interview than were females who had exited. Likewise, there was a relationship between care status and criminal justice system involvement, but only among males. Compared to males who stayed in care, males who had exited were twice as likely to have been arrested and almost twice as likely to have been incarcerated since their baseline interview.

Care status was also associated with service receipt. For example, young adults who were still in care at age 19 were about as likely to have a mental health diagnosis and less likely to have a substance use disorder than their counterparts who had left. Nevertheless, they were twice as likely to have received counseling and as likely to have received treatment for a problem with alcohol or other drugs. Young adults who had exited were four times more likely to report that they

needed but did not receive medical care and three times more likely to report that they needed but did not receive dental care as those who had stayed. In part, this can be explained by differences in health insurance coverage. Less than half of those who exited had any health insurance compared to virtually all of the young adults who were still in care. Finally, although states can use their Chafee funds to provide independent living services to former foster youth until age 21, young adults who were still in care were more likely to have received independent living services since their baseline interview. Table 7.5 summarizes some of the major differences that were found.

A third wave of data collection began in March 2006 and continued through January 2007. Eighty-one percent or 591 of the young adults in the baseline sample completed a wave 3 interview. Nearly all of these young adults were 21 years old, and none was still in foster care. A report based on the wave 3 data will be released in fall 2007.

The Midwest Evaluation of the Adult Functioning of Former Foster Youth also includes a qualitative component whose purpose is to explore a number of issues that cannot be addressed using survey data, including the importance and meaning of family and the stigma associated with being in foster care. In-depth, semi-structured interviews were conducted between May and November 2005 with 44 of the foster youth from whom baseline survey data were collected. A second wave of qualitative interviews with these same youth began in June 2007.

Another recent large-scale study of former foster youth, the Northwest Foster Care Alumni Study, examined the outcomes of 659 young adults between the ages of 20 and 33 who had been placed in family foster care between 1988 and 1998 (Pecora, Kessler, Williams, O'Brien, Downs, English, White, Hiripi, White, Wiggins, & Holmes, 2005). To be included in the study, the young adults had to have (1) spent 12 or more continuous months in family foster care between the ages of 14 and 18; (2) reached their 18th birthday by September 30, 1998; and (3) had no significant physical or developmental disability. Just over three quarters of these young adults had received foster care services from the public child welfare agencies in Oregon and Washington; the others were served by Casey Family Programs, a private agency with multiple sites in those two states, although nearly all had received services from a public child welfare agency before being placed with Casey. The research-

TABLE 7.5 Summary of Differences Related to Care Status at Age 19

	Still in Care (N = 282)	No Longer in Care (N = 321)
Received any independent living services since baseline interview	75%	59%
Education and employment		
Enrolled in any type of school	67%	31%
Enrolled in a 2- or 4-year college	37%	12%
Currently employed	33%	47%
In school or employed	76%	63%
Pregnancy (females only)		
Pregnant since baseline interview	31%	44%
Pregnant more than once if ever pregnant since baseline interview	9%	25%
Access to health care		
No health insurance coverage	2%	53%
Did not received medical care	5%	21%
Did not receive dental care	7%	20%
Mental and behavioral health		
Mental health diagnosis	17%	20%
Received counseling services	29%	14%
Substance abuse or dependence	13%	28%
Received treatment for alcohol or other drug problem	7%	8%
Criminal justice involvement		
ARRESTED SINCE BASELINE INTERVIEW		
Males	25%	50%
Females	21%	20%
INCARCERATED SINCE BASELINE INTERVIEW		
Males	21%	39%
Females	11%	11%

ers reviewed case records for the entire sample and interviewed 479 of the young adults between September 2000 and January 2002. Another 26 young adults could not be interviewed because they were deceased, incarcerated, or in a psychiatric hospital.

The study focused on the outcomes of these young adults in four domains: mental health, education, employment, and economic well-being.[25] Consistent with the results of other studies, the researchers found that a majority of the Northwest foster care alumni whom they interviewed faced significant challenges. Some of their key findings are summarized in Table 7.6.

Finally, the Research Group on Homelessness and Poverty at Wayne State University completed a cross-sectional study of foster youth in three Michigan counties that comprise the Detroit metropolitan area (i.e., Wayne, Oakland, and Macomb) who aged out in 2002 or 2003 (Fowler, Toro, Tompsett, Hobden, & Miles,

TABLE 7.6 Summary of Findings from the Northwest Foster Care Alumni Study

Mental health	54% had experienced a clinically significant mental health problem during the past 12 months, 20% had experienced three or more.
	Posttraumatic stress disorder (PTSD) and depression were the two most common problems: one quarter had experienced PTSD, 20% had experienced depression
Education	56% had a high school diploma, 28.5% had a GED
	Although 43% had pursued some type of postsecondary education, only 21% had received a degree or certificate.
	This figure is likely to increase since 16% were still attending school.
Employment	Employment rate among those in the labor force was 80%*
Economic well-being	One third had incomes at or below the federal poverty threshold,
	22% had been homeless within one year post-discharge, one third had no health insurance, 52% had received AFDC or TANF since discharge, 17% were current recipients
Disconnectedness	26% were not employed nor in school

*Full-time students, homemakers, and those with severe disabilities were not counted as in the labor force.

2006). The purpose of the study was to assess how these former foster youth were functioning across a variety of domains, including housing, education, employment, emotional and behavioral well-being, substance abuse, risky sexual behavior, and victimization.

To be eligible for the study, youth had to have been at least 18 years old when their child welfare case was closed. Thirty percent, or 264, of the 867 former foster youth who were eligible to participate completed telephone interviews. These former foster youth had been in care for a mean of 3.6 years and their mean age at interview was 20.6 years old. The sample was representative of the population of youth who aged out of care in 2002 and 2003 in terms of demographic characteristics (e.g., gender, age, and ethnicity) and foster care experiences (e.g., number of placements, age at entry, reason for placement).

These young adults experienced many of the same difficulties during the transition to adulthood that the former foster youth in other studies have reported. Table 7.7 summarizes some of the major findings.

RESEARCH BASED ON ADMINISTRATIVE DATA

All of the studies discussed thus far involved the collection of survey data. Although some researchers used administrative records to identify their sample, most of the information they collected was provided by the foster youth themselves. However, this is not the only way administrative data have been used to study the transition to adulthood among foster youth. Researchers have also used administrative data to track the outcomes of foster youth after they age out.[26]

Not only is this use of administrative data part of a more general trend in child welfare research, but in addition, it can help to minimize some of the methodological problems that often plagued earlier studies.[27] For example, because administrative data are neither expensive nor time consuming to collect, sample size is typically much larger, and hence multivariate analyses are much more feasible than when survey data are used. Administrative data are also conducive to following foster youth over time without significant sample attrition and can provide details about placement histories or other experiences (e.g., receipt of welfare benefits) that might not be amenable to self-report.

Despite their methodological advantages, administrative data also come with limitations. Most notably, administrative data are collected to meet the accountability and internal monitoring needs of state agencies—not to answer questions that researchers might pose (Goerge, 1997; Courtney & Collins, 1994). This restricts both the variety of outcomes that researchers can examine and the range of covariates for which they can control in their analyses.

The first, and for many years the only, study to have relied exclusively on administrative data was Pettiford's (1981) examination of welfare receipt among 848 young adults who had been discharged to independent living from New York City's out-of-home care system between June 1979 and June 1980. Although this study suffered from a number of methodological

TABLE 7.7 Summary of Findings from the Research Group on Homelessness and Poverty Study of Michigan's Former Foster Youth

Homelessness and housing instability	17% had been literally homeless, another 33% had been precariously housed (i.e., doubled up or "couch surfed") since leaving care
Education	57% had a high school diploma or GED, 73% received some education or training since leaving care, including 25% who had attended college
Employment and earnings	Employed an average of 51% of the time since leaving care, 41% had been employed continuously, 14% had not worked at all
	When employed, their median earnings were $600 per month
Poverty and public assistance receipt	48% received some form of public assistance since leaving care (e.g., cash assistance, food stamps, WIC, SSI); 70% earned less than the 2005 federal poverty threshold
Mental health	32% scored in the clinical range for current mental health problems on the Brief Symptom Inventory (BSI)
	Approximately twice as likely to report symptoms of psychological distress as a comparison group of low-income young adults from southeast Michigan
Criminal justice system involvement	27% reported being charged with a criminal offense, 32% reported spending time in jail or prison since leaving care
Problems with alcohol or other drugs	42% reported at least one alcohol-related problem, 19% reported two or more marijuana-related problems (beyond simple use), 13% reported using harder illicit drugs such as methamphetamine, heroin, or crack-cocaine
Pregnancy and parenthood	48% reported that they or their partner had become pregnant since leaving care, 36% reported having children of their own
Victimization	16% had been sexually victimized, 55% had been physically assaulted since leaving care

problems, it was the first to illustrate how administrative data could be used to examine the outcomes of former foster youth.[28]

More recently, researchers at the University of Chicago's Chapin Hall Center for Children used administrative data to measure the employment and earnings of foster youth who aged out the year they turned 18 (Goerge, Bilaver, Lee, Needell, Brookhart, & Jackman, 2002). The study included youth from California, Illinois, and South Carolina and covered a period of 13 quarters: the 4 quarters prior to their 18th birthday, the quarter in which they turned 18, and the 8 quarters following their 18th birthday.

No more than 45% of the foster youth in any of the three states had earnings in a given quarter. In fact, 30% of the Illinois foster youth, 23% of the California foster youth, and 14% of the South Carolina foster youth had no earnings at all. Although mean quarterly earnings rose approximately $500 over the 13 quarters, they remained very low: $1,089 for Illinois foster youth, $1,097 for South Carolina foster youth, and $1,364 for the California foster youth.

The researchers compared the labor market outcomes of these foster youth to those of foster youth who had been reunified with their families at some point during the 4 years prior to their 18th birthday.[29] Although foster youth who had aged out were more likely to have been employed, they earned significantly less.[30] The researchers also examined whether there were any relationships between employment or earnings and either demographic or placement history characteristics. Although race, gender, type of placement, reason for placement, and age at first placement were related to one or more of the outcomes they measured, the effects were not consistent across states. The one exception was the relationship between earnings and race. In all three states, African Americans earned significantly less than their White counterparts.

Another study used administrative data to examine the outcomes of 6,274 former foster youth who were discharged from Wisconsin's child welfare system between 1995 and 1997 (Dworsky & Courtney, 2001) and who were at least 17 years old at the time of their discharge. It differs from the Chapin Hall analysis in two important respects. First, the sample includes former foster youth who experienced discharge outcomes other than aging out and reunification (i.e., running away, institutionalization, relative placement, or adoption). Second, it looks not only at labor market outcomes but also at public assistance receipt.

Nearly 80% of these former foster youth were employed in at least one of their first eight post-discharge quarters. However, they earned less, on average, during the first eight quarters after they were discharged from care than what an average full-time minimum wage worker would have earned over the same period of time. Although relatively few of these former foster youth received AFDC/TANF and/or food stamps during their first eight post-discharge quarters, just over a fourth had received AFDC/TANF and/or food stamps as of June 2000.

Even when public assistance benefits were added to earnings from employment, their incomes for the first eight post-discharge quarters were still very low. Mean and median income from earnings, AFDC/TANF, and food stamps for the first eight post-discharge quarters were $5,781 and $2,848, respectively—well below the poverty threshold for a one-person household in 1995.

A series of multivariate analyses revealed a number of relationships between the outcomes of these former foster youth and their demographic characteristics. Most notably, although being African American was associated with a decreased likelihood of being employed and with decreased earnings and income, it was also associated with an increased likelihood of AFDC/TANF and/or food stamp receipt. The placement history characteristics of these former foster youth were also related to some of the outcomes that were measured. For example, former foster youth who had been discharged from foster homes were more likely to have been employed, earned more, and had higher incomes than those who had been discharged from child caring institutions. Similarly, while former foster youth who were reunified, placed with relatives, or adopted earned more than those who had run away or been transferred to an institution, they earned less and had lower incomes than those who had aged out of care or been discharged to independent living.

Dworsky (2005) also examined employment, earnings, and public assistance receipt among former foster youth who had been discharged from Wisconsin's out-of-home care system using administrative data. Her sample was considerably larger ($N = 8,511$) because it included seven discharge cohorts (1992–1998) and the minimum age at discharge was 16 years old. These former foster youth were followed from the quarter in which they were discharged through the fourth quarter of 2000. Like the results of earlier studies, they provide ample reason to be concerned about the economic well-being of youth being discharged from care.

Although the vast majority of these former foster youth were employed in at least one of the first eight quarters after they were discharged from care, most experienced at least one quarter in which they did not work. Even more troubling was how low their earnings were. Quarterly earnings increased over time, but the increase was not enough to lift them out of poverty even 8 years post-discharge. Indeed, their total earnings for the first eight quarters after their discharge were below the poverty threshold for a single year.

Nearly one fifth of these former foster youth received AFDC/TANF cash assistance in at least one of the first eight quarters after their discharge, and nearly one third received food stamps. In essence, they were discharged from state care only to become dependent on the state yet again. However, chronic welfare dependency was relatively rare. Among recipients, the mean number of months of benefit receipt during the first eight post-discharge quarters was between 8 and 9.

The data also suggested that the implementation of welfare reform had a negative impact on public assistance receipt. Specifically, the percentage of former foster youth who received benefits decreased with each successive discharge cohort, and, beginning with the 1994 discharge cohort, each succeeding discharge cohort received cash assistance in fewer of the first eight quarters after their discharge.[31] Just how much of this downward trend should be attributed to welfare reform as opposed to other factors, such as a robust economy or the low unemployment rate, is not clear.

Like the other studies based on administrative data, Dworsky examined the relationship between the outcomes of these former foster youth and a number of demographic and out-of-home care history characteristics using multivariate techniques. Table 7.8 summarizes the main relationships that were found.

Two factors were related to all three outcomes. One was race/ethnicity. African Americans and Latinos experienced less favorable labor market outcomes and were more likely to be recipients of public assistance

TABLE 7.8 Results of Multivariate Analyses

	Positive Relationship	Negative Relationship
Employment	Being employed prior to discharge	Being African American or Latino
	Being reunified, placed with relatives, or adopted	Being transferred to an institutional setting
	Being female	Running away or aging out
	Age at discharge	
Earnings	Being employed prior to discharge	Being African American or Latino
	Being reunified, placed with relatives, or adopted	Being transferred to an institutional setting
	Age at discharge	Running away
Public assistance receipt	Being female	Being transferred to an institutional setting
	Being African American or Latino	Age at discharge
	Being in the care of Milwaukee County	Length of stay in care
	Being discharged from a foster or group home (rather than a child caring institution)	

than their White counterparts. The other was age at discharge. The older FFY former foster youth were when they were discharged from care, the more likely they were to experience favorable labor market outcomes and the less likely they were to receive public assistance.

UNANSWERED QUESTIONS FOR FUTURE RESEARCH

Although much has been learned from the research about what happens to youth who age out of care, a number of important questions with policy implications are only beginning to be addressed. One such question is whether the receipt of independent living services is associated with better outcomes during the transition to young adulthood. Another is whether foster youth would benefit over the long term if they were allowed to remain in care past the age of 18. Each of these questions is addressed in turn below.

Receipt of Independent Living Services

Although foster youth have been receiving federally funded independent living services since 1986 when the Title IV-E Independent Living Program began, relatively little is known about their effectiveness. Two factors have contributed to this situation. One was a lack of methodologically sound evaluations of inde-

pendent living programs (U.S. Department of Health and Human Services, 1999; U.S. General Accounting Office, 1999).[32] The other was a lack of even the most basic information about the number of youth who were receiving independent living services and the types of services they were receiving.

The Foster Care Independence Act sought to remedy this situation through a number of accountability provisions. First, states were required to develop multiyear plans describing their independent living programs and to submit annual reports explaining how their Chafee funds are being used. Second, the U.S. Department of Health and Human Services (DHHS) was required to develop outcome measures (including measures of educational attainment, high school diploma, employment, avoidance of dependency, homelessness, nonmarital childbirth, incarceration, and high-risk behaviors) that can be used to assess state performance and to collect the information needed to track the number and characteristics of the youth who receive services and the nature of the services provided.[33] Although the DHHS developed the outcome measures and submitted a plan for assessing state performance called the National Youth in Transition Database (NYTD) to Congress in September 2001, proposed regulations were not issued until July 2006 (U.S. Department of Health and Human Services, 2006), and there was still no implementation date as of August 2007 (Center for Law and Social Policy, 2005; U.S. General Accounting Office, 2004).

According to the proposed regulations, states will be required to report four types of information: the type of independent living services or financial assistance provided to foster youth, the characteristics of the youth who received those services, the outcomes of youth who are or were in foster care, and basic demographic information about each youth in the reporting population. To measure outcomes, states will be required to survey youth who are or were in foster care at three specific intervals: on or about the youth's 17th birthday while the youth is still in foster care; on or about the youth's 19th birthday; and again on or about the youth's 21st birthday. States must report on 19- and 21-year-olds who participated in data collection at age 17 even if they are no longer in the state's foster care system or receiving independent living services at ages 19 and 21. States will collect outcome information on a new cohort of 17-year-old foster youth every 3 years. Six outcomes will be tracked: financial self-sufficiency, experience with homelessness, educational attainment, positive connections with adults, high-risk behavior, and access to health insurance. States will be required to collect and report data approximately 1 year from the issuance of a final rule.

The delay in implementing the NYTD means that we still lack the information needed to determine how the Chafee funds are being used and whether the services being provided are leading to improved outcomes for foster youth. For the moment, the best source of information about whether foster youth are receiving independent living services while they are in care, whether they continue to receive those services after they leave care, and whether those services are preparing foster youth for the transition to independent living is probably the Midwest Evaluation, described above.

And third, the Department of Health and Human Services was also mandated to evaluate "innovative" programs or programs of "national significance." Toward this end, the DHHS Children's Bureau has contracted with the Urban Institute, the University of Chicago's Chapin Hall Center for Children, and the National Opinion Research Center to conduct a multisite evaluation of foster youth programs. This project involves an initial evaluability assessment as well as a 5-year impact and process evaluation of selected Chafee-funded programs (National Opinion Research Center, 2006). They include an employment services program in Bakersfield, California; a one-on-one intensive, individualized skills program in Massa-chusetts; and two programs in Los Angeles County, California: a tutoring/mentoring program and a classroom-based life skills training program.

For the impact evaluations, a total of 1,400 youth were randomly assigned to intervention and control groups. They will be interviewed three times over the course of the evaluation. Baseline interviews for both of the Los Angeles programs began in September 2003 and ended in June 2004. First-year follow-up interviews were completed in 2005. Baseline interviews in Bakersfield and Massachusetts were completed in 2006–2007. Among the outcomes being measured are educational attainment, employment, interpersonal and relationship skills, nonmarital pregnancy and births, and delinquency and crime. The process evaluation will include site visits to observe the programs; in-person interviews with program administrators, community advocates, and agency directors; and focus groups with youth and program staff. Additional program-specific data are also being collected at each site.

Benefits of Remaining in Foster Care

Results from wave 2 of the Midwest study call into doubt the wisdom of federal and state policies that encourage or require foster youth to age out at 18 years old. Foster youth who were still in care at age 19 appeared to be faring better than their peers who had left across a number of different domains. They were more likely to report a variety of positive outcomes (e.g., school enrollment, access to health care, and independent living services receipt) and less likely to report a variety of negative ones (e.g., early pregnancy, criminal justice system involvement, and problems with alcohol or other drugs). Of course, it remains an empirical question whether these differences will persist over time or, conversely, will disappear once those who were still in care are also on their own. The third wave of survey data from the Midwest study, collected from the young adults at age 21, will go a long way toward addressing this question.

This is not to say that additional research will not be needed. For one thing, the Midwest study is limited to foster youth in three states, and virtually all of those still in care were from Illinois. Although there is no reason to believe that there is something special about the foster youth in Illinois as compared to Iowa or Wisconsin, it will be important for longitudinal studies involving foster youth in other states to replicate these findings.

Moreover, even if the third wave of data from the Midwest study continues to show that foster youth experience better outcomes when they remain in care past age 18, additional research will be needed if we are to understand why this is the case. One possibility is that because foster youth have housing as long as they remain in care, they can focus more on some of the other challenges they face during the transition to adulthood. Another is that youth who remain are more connected with adults, including social workers, foster parents, and/or group home staff, who can provide support or help them to access services.

Finally, it will also be important for researchers to examine whether remaining in care past age 18 is always beneficial, and if not, to identify factors that predict who will and who will not benefit. These could include characteristics of the youth themselves as well as other factors, such as placement type, service receipt, or school enrollment.

CONCLUSION

Considerable progress has been made in the way researchers study youth aging out of foster care and transitioning to adulthood. They are increasingly using longitudinal designs that track foster youth prospectively. Researchers are also taking more advantage of state administrative data, including data on employment, earnings, and public assistance receipt. More attention is being paid to how samples are selected and to related concerns about response rate and attrition, both of which were problems for earlier studies. In addition, analysis is moving beyond simple description to incorporate multivariate techniques.

This progress notwithstanding, many questions about the transition to adulthood among this population have yet to be addressed. The potential benefits of extending care past age 18 are just beginning to be explored. Likewise, we still have much to learn about the ways in which the characteristics of foster youth and their placement histories are related to their outcomes after leaving care. There is also much we do not know about the ties that foster youth maintain with family, although recent studies suggest that they are important.

A lot has also changed since the early studies of youth aging out of foster care were conducted. Most notably, there was no federal funding specifically earmarked to help states prepare their foster youth for the transition to adulthood before the Title IV-E Independent Living Program was created. Likewise, the Chafee Foster Care Independence Act contains a number of provisions that should enable states to better address this population's needs, including housing, health care, education, and aftercare supports.

Given these significant policy changes, it is particularly striking that the findings of more recent studies are not all that different from what earlier studies reported. Regardless of whether the data were collected before the Title IV-E ILP was created or after the Foster Care Independence Act became law, foster youth continue to face many of the same challenges, including educational barriers, mental health problems, problems with alcohol and other drugs, housing instability and homelessness, criminal justice involvement, especially among males, and in the case of females, early pregnancy and child bearing. A similar trend is observed when administrative rather than survey data are used. Thus, the research continues to suggest that most foster youth are not prepared to live on their own at age 18. Whether the more recent studies will lead to additional policy changes remains to be seen.

Notes

1. The adoption figure is based on an analysis of data from the nine states included in the Multistate Foster Care Data Archive that were able to provide complete information about all of the children who first entered care between 1990 and 1999.

2. Forty-five states and the District of Columbia reported sufficient data to the Adoption and Foster Care Analysis and Reporting System (AFCARS) to determine whether foster youth who aged out of care had entered care before or after their 13th birthday (U.S. Department of Health and Human Services, 2002).

3. Recent changes in federal legislation have the potential to increase the availability of aftercare services for former foster youth. These changes are discussed below.

4. The program was strongly opposed by the Reagan administration, which marshaled an unsuccessful attempt to have the legislation repealed. Implementation was further delayed when, for 10 months, the U.S. Department of Health and Human Services failed to notify states of the availability of the funds in direct violation of the legislation (DeWoody et al., 1993).

5. These changes were enacted under PL 100-64 and PL 101-508, respectively.

6. This matching requirement was enacted under PL 101-239.

7. Title IV-E defines *basic services* as education and/or employment assistance, training in daily living skills, individual and group counseling, integration and coordination of services, outreach, and a written transitional independent living plan for each youth. *Optional services* might include training for foster parents, mentoring, teen conferences, trust funds, stipends, newsletters, and aftercare services.

8. The General Accounting Office (GAO) found that at least 42,680 youths in 40 states (only about 60% of all eligible youth) received some type of independent living services in 1998 (U.S. General Accounting Office, 1999).

9. Several of these studies are discussed below.

10. The state allocation formula was also revised.

11. States are still prohibited from using their federal funds to cover the costs of services already being funded under Title IV-E.

12. These are the only states that have exercised the expanded Medicaid option included in the Foster Care Independence Act. A number of other states provide Medicaid coverage to at least some former foster youth but limit coverage to specific subpopulations (Patel & Roherty, 2007; U.S. General Accounting Office, 2004).

13. Provisions regarding the evaluation of independent living programs are discussed below.

14. The other 235 had been adopted by their foster parents.

15. Van Senden Theis defined as "capable" those "who are law-abiding, who manage their affairs with good sense, and are living in accordance with good moral standards of their communities," and as "incapable" those "who are unable or unwilling to support themselves adequately, who are shiftless or have defied the accepted standards of morality or order of their communities" (Van Senden Theis, 1924, p. 23).

16. This list of studies is not exhaustive. It does not include studies of former foster youth in other countries, including Great Britain (e.g., Ferguson, 1966; Triseliotis, 1980), Canada (e.g., Palmer, 1976), and Australia (Kraus, 1981); Fanshel and Shinn's (1978) study, which looked at the short-term outcomes of children who had been discharged from care; Maas's (1969) study, which looked at the long-term outcomes of young adults who had been discharged from care as children; studies based on samples that were very small (e.g., Harari, 1980; Rest & Watson, 1984); or studies based on samples drawn from clinical populations (e.g., Allerhand, Weber, & Haug, 1966; Robins, 1966). For a review of these and other studies on the outcomes of former foster youth, see McDonald, Allen, Westerfelt, & Piliavin (1996).

17. Barth's "find-them-any-way-you-can" approach relied on referrals from service providers, who might have been disinclined to refer more troubled youth. Although Cook et al. (1991) selected their sample using probabilistic methods, and weighted the sample to represent the approximately 34,600 adolescents who were discharged nationally during the observation period, their response rate at wave 2 was less than 50%.

18. The study by Cook et al. (1991) is an exception in this regard.

19. In contrast, a prospective study would follow a sample of former foster youth longitudinally over the course of several years from prior to discharge through early adulthood.

20. Not included in this discussion is a study by Baker, Mincer, and Olson (2001) that examined the outcomes of 93 young men who had participated in the Children's Village Work Appreciation for Youth (WAY) program. This highly structured employment program for foster youth in residential treatment provides opportunities for postsecondary education and job training and includes a long-term aftercare component. Although the study does suggest that providing foster youth in a residential treatment setting with work experience is associated with positive educational and employment outcomes, the out-of-home care experiences of these former foster youth were quite atypical.

21. Those data were summarized in an earlier report entitled *Midwest Evaluation of the Adult Functioning of Former Foster Youth: Conditions of Youth Preparing to Leave Care* (Courtney et al., 2004).

22. In June 2006, Iowa enacted legislation that will allow foster youth to remain in care until age 21 if they are working, looking for work, or enrolled in school.

23. Add Health is a federally funded study that was intended to examine how social contexts influence the health-related behaviors of adolescents (Harris, Florey, Tabor, Bearman, Jones, & Udry, 2003). In-home interviews were completed in 1994 with a nationally representative sample of students in grades 7 through 12, who were then interviewed again in 1996 and in 2002. The data cited in this chapter are based on the sample of 19-year-olds who participated in that third wave of data collection.

24. These covariates included gender, race/ethnicity, educational aspirations (i.e., wanting to graduate from college), ever retained in school, ever received special education services, ever employed prior to baseline, number of out-of-home care placements, satisfaction with out-of-home care experience, number of independent living services received in six domains, closeness to family, having any mental health or substance disorder diagnosis, and ever incarcerated prior to baseline.

25. Mental health was assessed using the CIDI, the Composite International Diagnostic Index. This same measure was also used in the Midwest Evaluation.

26. Although McMillen and Tucker (1999) used administrative data to examine the educational attainment and employment status of foster youth at the time they were discharged from care, that study is not discussed because the researchers did not look at post-discharge outcomes.

27. For example, researchers have used administrative data to study foster care exits and reentries (e.g., Courtney, 1994, 1995; Courtney, Piliavin, & Wright, 1997; Goerge, 1990; Wulczyn, 1991); to compare kinship and nonrelative foster care (e.g., Barth, Courtney, Berrick, & Albert, 1994; Courtney & Needell, 1997; Testa, 1997); and to examine the relationship between race and length of stay in care (e.g., Goerge, 1990; McMurtry & Lie, 1992).

28. One problem was that sufficient identifying information was available for only 614 of the 848 youth. Another was that former foster youth who received public assistance outside of New York City would not have been counted as recipients.

29. Although the researchers also compared the outcomes of the foster youth who aged out of care to those of low-income youth whose families had received AFDC/TANF at any time during the 4 years prior to their 18th birthday, the results of those comparisons are not discussed here.

30. However, a multivariate analysis indicated that there was no difference in the likelihood of employment between the foster youth who aged out of care and the foster youth who were reunified in Illinois after controlling for demographic and placement history characteristics.

31. Although the state's TANF program was not implemented until September 1997, Wisconsin began reforming its welfare system almost a decade before.

32. The Westat study (Cook et al., 1991), which was ostensibly a national evaluation of the Title IV-E Independent Living Program, examined the outcomes of foster youth who had been discharged from care between January 1987 and June 1988. Given that Title IV-E allocations to the states were not made until 1987, it is unlikely that these foster youth could have experienced the full impact of federally funded independent living services.

33. These are similar to the indicators of self-sufficiency that were used in the Westat study.

References

Allen, M., Bonner, K., & Greenan, L. (1988). Federal legislative support for independent living. *Child Welfare*, 67, 19–32.

Allerhand, M., Weber, R., & Haug, M. (1966). *Adaptation and adaptability: The Bellefaire follow-up study.* New York: Child Welfare League of America.

Baker, A., Mincer, C., & Olson, D. (2001). *The WAY program: Work Appreciation for Youth, an independent living/after care program for youth leaving the foster care system and other high risk youth.* Washington, DC: Child Welfare League of America.

Barth, R. (1990). On their own: The experiences of youth after foster care. *Child and Adolescent Social Work*, 7, 419–440.

Barth, R., Courtney, M., Berrick, J., & Albert, V. (1994). *From child abuse to permanency planning: Child welfare services, pathways and placements.* New York: de Gruyter.

Benedict, M., & White, R. (1991). Factors associated with foster care length of stay. *Child Welfare*, 70(1), 45–58.

Center for Law and Social Policy. (2005). *Issue brief: National Youth in Transition Database.* Available: http://www.clasp.org/CampaignForYouth/PolicyBrief/FosterCareIssueBrief.htm.

Citizens' Committee for Children of New York. (1984). *Foster care exit: Ready or not.* New York: Author.

Cook, R., Fleischman, E., & Grimes, V. (1991). *A national evaluation of title IV-E foster care independent living programs for youth: Phase 2: Final Report* (Vol. 1). Rockville, MD: Westat.

Courtney, M. E. (1994). Factors associated with the reunification of foster children with their families. *Social Service Review*, 68, 81–108.

Courtney, M. E. (1995). Reentry to foster care of children returned to their families. *Social Service Review*, 69, 81–108, 226–241.

Courtney, M. E., & Barth, R. (1996). Pathways of older adolescents out of foster care: Implications for independent living services. *Social Work*, 41, 75–83.

Courtney, M. E., & Collins, R. (1994). New challenges and opportunities in child welfare outcomes and information technologies. *Child Welfare*, 73, 359–378.

Courtney, M., Dworsky, A., Ruth, A., Keller, T., Havlicek, J., & Bost, J. (2005). *Midwest evaluation of the adult functioning of former foster youth: Outcomes at age 19.* Chicago: Chapin Hall Center for Children

Courtney, M. E., & Needell, B. (1997). Outcomes of kinship foster care: Lessons from California. In J. Berrick, R. Barth, & N. Geilbert (Eds.), *Child welfare research review* (pp. 130–150). New York: Columbia University Press.

Courtney, M. E., Piliavin, I., Grogan-Kaylor, A., & Nesmith, A. (2001). Foster youth in transitions to adulthood: A longitudinal view of youth leaving care. *Child Welfare*, 80(6), 685–717.

Courtney, M. E., Piliavin, I., & Wright, B. (1997). Transitions from and returns to out-of-home care. *Social Service Review*, 71, 652–667.

Courtney, M., Terao, S., & Bost, N. (2004). *Midwest evaluation of the adult functioning of former foster youth: Conditions of the youth preparing to leave state care*. Chicago: Chapin Hall Center for Children, University of Chicago.

Courtney, M. E., & Wong, I. (1996). Comparing the timing of exits from substitute care. *Children and Youth Services Review, 18*(4–5), 307–334.

DeWoody, M., Ceja, K., & Sylvester, M. (1993). *Independent living services for youths in out-of-home care*. Washington, DC: Child Welfare League of America.

Dworsky, A. (2005). The economic self-sufficiency of Wisconsin's former foster youth. *Children and Youth Services Review, 27*, 1085–1118.

Dworsky, A., & Courtney, M. (2001). *Self-sufficiency of former foster youth in Wisconsin: Analysis of unemployment insurance wage data and public assistance data*. Washington, DC: U.S. Department of Health and Human Services, Office of the Assistant Secretary for Planning and Evaluation.

Fanshel, D., Finch, S., & Grundy, J. (1986). Discharge of children from foster care. *Social Work Research and Abstracts, 22*, 10–18.

Fanshel, D., & Shinn, E. (1978). *Children in foster care: A longitudinal investigation*. New York: Columbia University Press.

Ferguson, T. (1966). *Children in care—and after*. Oxford: Oxford University Press.

Festinger, T. (1983). *No one ever asked us: A postscript to foster care*. New York: Columbia University Press.

Fowler, P. J., Toro, P. A., Tompsett, C. J., Hobden, K., & Miles, B. W. (2006, April). *Youth aging out of foster care: A follow-up study*. Presentation to Michigan's Governor's Task Force on Permanency, Transition, and Youth Advocacy for Foster Care Youth.

Goerge, R. (1990). The reunification process in substitute care. *Social Service Review, 64*, 422–457.

Goerge, R. (1997). Potential and problems in developing indicators on child well-being from administrative data. In R. Hauser, B. Brown, & W. Prosser (Eds.), *Indicators of children's well-being* (pp. 457–471). New York: Russell Sage Foundation

Goerge, R.,Bilaver,L., Lee,B., Needell, B.,Brookhart,A., & Jackman, W. (2002). *Employment outcomes for youth aging out of foster care*. Washington, DC: U.S. Department of Health and Human Services, Office of the Assistant Secretary for Planning and Evaluation.

Harari, T. (1980). *Teenagers exiting from family foster care: A retrospective look*. Unpublished doctoral dissertation, University of California, Berkeley.

Harris, K., Florey, F., Tabor, J., Bearman, P., Jones, J., & Udry, J. R. (2003). *The National Longitudinal Study of Adolescent Health: Research design*. Available: http://www.cpc.unc.edu/projects/addhealth/design.

Jones, M., & Moses, B. (1984). *West Virginia's former foster children: Their experiences in care and their lives as young adults*. New York: Child Welfare League of America.

Kraus, J. (1981). Foster children grown up: Parameters of care and adult delinquency. *Children and Youth Services Review, 2*, 99–114.

Lawder, E., Poulin, J., & Andrews, R. (1986). A study of 185 foster children 5 years after placement. *Child Welfare, 65*(3), 241–251.

Maas, H. (1969). Children in long-term foster care. *Child Welfare, 48*, 321–337, 341.

Maluccio, A., & Fein, E. (1985). Growing up in foster care. *Child and Youth Services Review, 7*, 123–134.

McDonald, T., Allen, R., Westerfelt, A., & Piliavin, I. (1996). *Assessing the long-term effects of foster care: A research synthesis*. Washington, DC: Child Welfare League of America.

McMillen, C., & Tucker, J. (1999). The status of older adolescents at exit from out-of-home care. *Child Welfare, 78*, 339–350.

McMurtry, S., & Lie, G. (1992). Differential exit rates of minority children in foster care. *Social Work Research and Abstracts, 28*, 42–48.

Mech, E. (1994). Foster youths in transition: Research perspectives on preparation for independent living. *Child Welfare, 73*, 603–623.

Meier, E. (1965). Current circumstances of former foster children. *Child Welfare, 44*, 196–206.

National Opinion Research Center. (2006). *Multi-site evaluation of foster youth programs*. Available: http://www.norc.org/projects/foster_youth_update.pdf.

New York State Council on Children and Families. (1984). *Meeting needs of homeless youth*. Albany, NY: Author.

Palmer, S. (1976). *Children in long-term care: Their experience and progress*. London, Ontario: Family and Children's Services of London and Middlesex.

Patel, S., & Roherty, M. (2007). Medicaid access for youth aging out of foster care. Washington, DC: American Public Human Services Association

Pecora, P., Kessler,R., Williams,J., O'Brien,K., Downs,A., English, D., White, J., Hiripi, E., White, C., Wiggins, T., & Holmes, K. (2005). *Improving family foster care: Findings from the Northwest Foster Care Alumni Study*. Seattle, WA: Casey Family Programs.

Pettiford, P. (1981). *Foster care and welfare dependency: A research note*. New York: Human Resource Administration, Office of Policy and Program Development.

Rest, E., & Watson, K. (1984). Growing up in foster care. *Child Welfare, 63*, 291–306.

Robins, L. (1966). *Deviant children grown up: A sociological and psychiatric study of sociopathic personality.* Baltimore: Williams and Wilkins.

Shaffer, D., & Caton, C. (1984). *Runaway and homeless youth in New York City.* New York: New York State Psychiatric Institute and Columbia College of Physicians and Surgeons.

Tatara, T. (1993). *Characteristics of children in substitute and adoptive care.* Washington, DC: Voluntary Cooperative Information System, American Public Welfare Association.

Testa, M. (1997). Kinship foster care in Illinois. In J. Berrick, R. Barth, & N. Geilbert (Eds.), *Child welfare research review* (pp. 101–129). New York: Columbia University Press.

Triseliotis, J. (1980). Growing up in foster care and after. In J. Triseliotis (Ed.), *New developments in foster care and adoption.* London: Routledge and Kegan Paul.

U.S. Department of Health and Human Services. (1999). *Title IV-E independent living programs: A decade in review.* Washington, DC: U.S. Government Printing Office.

U.S. Department of Health and Human Services. (2002). *Child welfare outcomes 1999: Annual report: Safety, permanency and well being.* Washington, DC: Author. Available: http://www.acf.dhhs.gov/programs/cb/publications/cwo99/index.html.

U.S. Department of Health and Human Services. (2006). *45 CFR part 1356 Chafee National Youth in Transition Database: Proposed rule.* Washington, DC: Administration for Children and Families. Available:http://a257.g.akamaitech.net/7/257/2422/01jan20061800/edocket.access.gpo.gov/2006/pdf/06–6005.pdf.

U.S. General Accounting Office. (1999). *Foster care: Effectiveness of independent living services unknown* (HEHS-00-13). Washington, DC: Author.

U.S. General Accounting Office. (2004). *Foster youth: HHS actions could improve coordination of services and monitoring of states' independent living programs* (GAO-05-25). Washington, DC: Author.

Van Senden Theis, S. (1924). *How foster children turn out.* New York: State Charities Aid Association.

Wulczyn, F. (1991). Caseload dynamics and foster care reentry. *Social Services Review, 65,* 133–156.

Wulczyn, F., Hislop, K., & Chen, L. (2005). *Adoption dynamics: An update on the impact of the Adoption and Safe Families Act.* Chicago: Chapin Hall Center for Children, University of Chicago.

Zimmerman, R. (1982). Foster care in retrospect. *Tulane Studies in Social Welfare, 14.*

8

Moving Restorative Justice Interventions into Domestic Violence Treatment

Colleen Friend

OVERVIEW

This chapter will trace the traditional conceptualizations of domestic violence and the theories that are at the foundation of nationwide methods for addressing this issue. It will examine some key literature about what is currently known about the effectiveness of batterers' intervention programs (BIP). Principles of restorative justice practice as well as its critique will be outlined. Finally, an innovative treatment approach will be presented that draws on restorative justice principles. This experimental treatment model is currently in operation in Nogales, Arizona, and is being evaluated.

EXAMINING TRADITIONAL PERSPECTIVES

We owe a great debt to the battered women's movement, which in conjunction with the feminist movement, has helped both genders to become aware of sexist ideas and practices and the problem of intimate partner violence (IPV). To a large extent, these movements have transformed IPV from a private matter to a public issue. In so doing, IPV has been defined as mostly a woman's issue, at the root of which is patriarchal oppression, male power, and control themes, and we have learned the importance of treating the offense as a crime (Pence, 1999). This has led to an embracing of mandatory criminal justice interventions, such as arrest and prosecution. Many women are ambivalent and even avoidant of this involvement, reflected in dramatically low self-report rates for IPV and prosecutors' characterizations of the majority of IPV victims as "uncooperative" (Rebovich, 1996). Feminists have also typically eschewed couples counseling for families locked in a violent dynamic, as they have feared that the power imbalance between the male abuser and female victim would collude to make her unsafe and blamed for the violence (Barnett, Miller-Perrin, & Perrin, 1997). This chapter's contention is that this narrow characterization of the problem may be at the heart of why interventions based on these limited precepts have been unable to demonstrate effectiveness. The "Duluth model" of batterers' intervention, formally known as the Domestic Abuse Intervention Program (DAIP), is one such program that is based on feminist theory, which states that the patriarchal ideology is what drives men to control their partners and is the primary underlying cause of IPV (Pence, 1999). This model is the most common form of intervention in the United States; many states demand that BIPs conform to the Duluth model (Jackson, Feder, Forde, Davis, Maxwell, & Taylor, 2003).

Dutton and Nichols (2005) have argued forcefully that there is an established trend in outcome research that shows that models based in feminist theory are not effective. This appears to have had little impact on supporters of the feminist perspective on domestic violence (Dutton & Nichols, 2005; Augusta-Scott & Dankworth, 2002; Cavenaugh & Gelles, 2005; Babcock, Green, & Robie, 2004). One comprehensive literature review lists several possible causes of IPV, including psychopathology, alcohol abuse, skill deficits, head injuries, entitlement attitudes, low resources, feelings of powerlessness, recent stresses, and family of origin modeling (Holtzworth-Munroe, Bates, Smuztler, & Sandin, 1997). Given these multiple causal paths, the identification of risk markers and treatment issues appears to be more complex than the feminist perspective allows.

Cavanaugh and Gelles (2004) have provided another comprehensive review of the literature, concluding that not all IPV offenders escalate over time. They criticize the traditional one-size-fits-all approach of feminist theory, which locates the cause and effect in the same "control" variables. They recommend categorizing and treating offenders by type, based on level of aggression and willingness to change. A large National Institute of Justice study in 2003 (Jackson et al., 2003), reviewing the effectiveness of BIPs, concurred and recommended this as one promising approach.

The National Institute of Justice's report on two large-scale programs using the DAIP model (one located in Broward County, Florida, the other in Brooklyn, New York) showed that these treatments had no effect on changing attitudes and little to no effect on changing behavior. There are two possible explanations for these findings: The evaluations were methodologically flawed, or the design of the programs themselves, which flows from feminist theory, is flawed.

These two explanations may both be true (Jackson et al., 2003). As for methodological issues, the following were noted in the NIJ report: Batterers' treatment is marked by low response rates, high attrition rates, use of measures not designed for repeated administration, the defining of success as reduction in violence, compromises in random assignment, and attendance problems. Despite these concerns, the NIJ's closing summary report found that it was too early to abandon the BIPs. On the other hand, the report also concluded that the stakes for women's safety are too high to rely on treatment programs that do not have strong empirical evidence that they work (Jackson et al., 2003). These findings were echoed by Feder and Wilson's (2005) meta-analysis of court-mandated intervention programs; they concluded that these programs were not only ineffective, but needed to provide assurance that interventions were not inadvertently making the situation worse. In both articles, the authors argued that more research is needed so that policy makers can arrive at informed decisions on whether such treatment should be continued.

REVIEW OF RESTORATIVE JUSTICE CONCEPTS

Do restorative models hold any better promise of working to address IPV? Because restorative justice principles are widely attributed to have originated with the Maori people living in Australia (Braithwaite & Strang, 2002), an Australian conference held in 2000 was a fitting draw for the convergence of experts in criminology, courts, law, social work, and planning. Much of what follows is from the groundbreaking book that summarized this conference's findings (Brathwaite & Strang, 2002). This section provides an overview of two restorative justice practices discussed in Brathwaite and Strang (2002): family group conferencing and circles. Both of these approaches have a relationship to the model program under way in Nogales, Arizona. Other well-known restorative justice–related practices, such as victim-offender mediation and victim impact panels, have been described in other literature (Umbreit, 1998; Edwards & Sharpe, 2004; Mills, 2006). One cautionary note: Family group conferencing and circles are not the same things. Family group conferencing in the child protective service setting emphasizes the responsibility of the larger family group for its younger members

(Pennell & Burford, 2002), whereas circles aim to restore the offender to him- or herself, the victims, and the community after a harm/violence has been committed. Both honor family members' choices to remain together despite the problem or violence (although it is entirely possible that an outcome might be to decide to separate). What is important here is that both require the members to actively engage, understand, and do something to resolve the problem and halt the violence. While the model implemented in Nogales draws from both, it has been uniquely crafted to respond to that community and incorporates the thoughtful concerns of the allies and critics which follow.

Family group conferencing, as implemented by Pennell and Burford (2002) in their quasi-experimental project in Canada, used the New Zealand model of inviting extended family members and a few service providers to confer and design a solution to an identified family problem. In these cases, the identified problem was part of a referral from either public child welfare, probation, or the youth correction agency. Extensive preparation was part of a protocol to address the family's problems, which also incorporated an opportunity for private family deliberations. The subsequent emerging plan from the family group conference had to be approved by the state authorities, community organizations, and family members. The researchers reported that family privacy, women's leadership, and state control formed a web of interacting movements within the conferences (Pennell & Burford, 2002). When outcomes on the 32 participating families were compared to the 31 in the control group, three findings emerged: First, there was a reduction in the indicators of child maltreatment and domestic violence; second, there was an advancement in participating children's development; and third, participants felt an extension of social supports (Pennell & Burford, 2002).

Previous to this experiment in Canada, family group decision-making conferences were introduced in the Miami-Dade Juvenile Court in 1998. The corresponding evaluation study of the Miami program found four important outcomes. First, researchers found an increase in consumer (parent and community participant) satisfaction with the court process. Second, families felt empowered as decision makers. Third, the relationships between the public child welfare agency and its consumers were improved. Last, there was a reduction in the amount of time to permanency

for the child (Gatowski, Dobbin, & Lichfield, 2001). Speculating that the last finding was consistent with the thrust of then relatively new federal legislation driving child welfare outcomes, many states have now implemented family group decision-making models in an effort to shorten children's time to permanency and to facilitate collaborative decision making.

Restorative justice practice as conceived by Pranis (2002) and by Grauwiler and Mills (2004) describes a *circle* as a process that brings willing victims and perpetrators together to address the impact of the crime and to prevent violent behaviors in the future. Each brings to the circle a care community of friends and family to support them to address the violence. As a group and by consensus, a contract is drawn up to restore to the victim what has been lost and to make reparation to the community as a whole. The contract is preceded by two occurrences: an examination of the impact of the violence and remorse for the offender's conduct. Circles are only formed with the voluntary participation of the victim, the offender, and the community. The community also serves as the pool for the emergence of the circle co-facilitator or circle co-keeper (who serves along with a trained, master's level circle keeper) and contributes to enhancing victim safety by designating someone in the circle as the safety monitor.

A circle process has also been broadly defined by Coker (1999) in her research with Native American groups, as a gathering of disputing parties and their extended families with relevant community members to develop a resolution. Circles were endemic to the Native American cultures of the United States and Canada, the most famous being a long-standing healing circle process for family violence in Hollow Water, Manitoba (Edwards & Sharpe, 2004). When dealing with a crime or violence, the Native American circles provide a space for an encounter between a victim and offender, as well as the community. In these circles, participants typically sit in a circle as they pass a "talking piece" around to facilitate both talking and listening. A "keeper," who directs the movement of the talking piece, leads the circle. The process is voluntary and values-driven. The values often include healing, understanding, reparation, participation, transformation, accountability, reintegration, and public safety (Bazemore & Earle, 2002).

Donna Coker (1999) reports that Navajo peacemaking circles in cases of domestic violence can be very valuable in the following ways. They may (1) increase women's material resources through reparations and referrals, (2) enhance their social resources through redefined relationships, (3) disrupt financial support for battering, (4) recognize the effect of oppressive systems on men who batter, and (5) provide women with tools to change the balance of power in their relationships (see Coker, 1999; Edwards & Sharpe, 2003). Coker also identified challenges inherent in some of what she witnessed, e.g., coerced participation, poorly informed decisions on participation, and peacemaker bias against separation (Coker, 1999; Edwards & Sharpe, 2003). In a later article, she appeared to shift and indicated that she no longer had a favorable appraisal of the circle process in IPV situations (Coker, 2004).

Ruth Busch (2002) has raised additional criticism of restorative justice approaches, contending that facilitators have to be very knowledgeable about risk assessment and violence given the threat posed by bringing victim and batterer together. In addition, they must possess a willingness and the corresponding skills to confront duress in the moment. Busch is concerned that a battered woman will negotiate for what she thinks she can get, rather than what she wants, because of the power imbalance. She also takes issue with some family group conferencing outcomes in New Zealand and points out that one third of the victims felt worse after they participated in a conference (Busch, 2002). Reflecting on one child's death, Busch (2002) notes that there was no formal monitoring of this situation after the family group conference.

Unfortunately, little systematic evaluation has been conducted on the use of restorative justice for domestic violence. Indeed, the structure of these restorative justice interventions seems to be idiosyncratic to the community using them, so it is unclear if evaluation results could be generalized. We attempted to learn from these critiques in the construction and structure of the peacemaking circles in Nogales, Arizona.

ADAPTING RESTORATIVE JUSTICE FOR INTIMATE PARTNER VIOLENCE

Mills (2003) first conceptualized intimate abuse circles (IAC) in her controversial book *Insult to Injury: Rethinking Our Responses to Intimate Abuse*, which created both a challenge to the conventional feminist

paradigm and a parallel critique of the criminal justice response to domestic violence. From the beginning, Mills's (2003) approach relied on the pioneering work of Braithwaite (2001) and Braithwaite and Strong (2002), arguing that circles would seek to restore victims, offenders, families, and communities by revisiting how the violence erupted and how it could be avoided in the future. Her book found its way to Judge Mary Helen Maley in Nogales, Arizona, who resonated with its compelling argument and pitch that all that was needed was a place to test these concepts.

While agreeing that perpetrators should be held accountable, Mills proposed that any abuse "dynamic" between intimate partners should also be addressed. This departure from traditional feminism advocated for a much broader conceptualization about the roots of IPV, including the dynamics of bigendered aggression, the combination of attachment types, family of origin history, and individuals' personal reaction to the pervasiveness of violence in their own lives. The approach Mills suggested was intimate abuse circles (Mills, 2003), which drew on restorative justice principles. Dealing with a daily docket of drug and domestic violence cases, the judge felt she had the venue to test the effectiveness of such an approach. Contacting Mills, Judge Maley proposed that Mills visit the community to see if IACs might be an appropriate intervention for the cases the court was addressing.

The community of Santa Cruz County is billed as Arizona's smallest yet most fascinating county, championing its location, history, and diversity (Santa Cruz County, 2003). The 2000 Census estimated the population at 38,000 (U.S. Census Bureau, 2000). It borders the city of Nogales, Sonora, Mexico, and is Arizona's largest border town. It is home to a large immigrant Mexican population. The judge was frustrated with both repeat domestic violence case appearances and the frequent cycle of offenders disappearing by crossing the border and then becoming rearrested upon reentry. The judge believed that restorative justice approaches as outlined by Mills (2003), Braithwaite and Strang (2002), and Pranis et al. (2003) held more promise for fairness, change, and satisfaction than did the criminal justice approach in which she was currently immersed, which was a traditional BIP. (See Table 8.1.)

The new program was developed in concert with a strongly engaged group of community members in the tradition of Maori and Native American people,

TABLE 8.1 Guideines for Restorative Justice Practices in Family Violence Cases

1. *Involvement of family violence experts in the design and planning of the restorative process.*

Expertise can be both academic and experiential. It must involve those close to the issue; advocates who are former victims or offenders could work well here. Participants must be prepared to interact, and their participation has to be assessed to be voluntary.

2. *Involvement of larger community in the design and oversight of the process.*

The community members bring questions about underlying causes, prevention strategies, and what needs to happen to make the community safer.

3. *Involvement of the formal justice system in the design and oversight of the process to assure that harm is addressed.*

Although communities may have more power in influencing behavior, formal justice system members, such as police, parole officers, or child protective services workers, have a role in backing up the community in this process.

4. *Presence of persons knowledgeable about family violence.*

Subtle dynamics of power and safety have to be attended to. This means including an outside person who is well versed on safety risk, danger assessment, etc., who can raise this potential issue for participants to address.

5. *Involvement of persons outside the nuclear family who have close ties to the family, can speak the truth, and disapprove of the violence.*

There are two key components here: breaking secrecy and bringing critical disapproving gravity to the situation. This links using the power of existing relationships to influence the offender and the monitoring of safety.

6. *Establish a continual feedback loop for updates from the victims about the impact of the restorative justice process.*

Victims may use a support person or a letter written outside of the process to let the participants know if the process needs to be modified or halted.

7. *Regular self-reflection on the use of restorative justice values and principles in one's own life.*

This process moves to a model where each participant is a learner, a giver, and a taker. We learn and we are changed in the process. Much of what goes on has application to each member's personal life.

8. *Regular self-reflection by the larger community on the causes of and remedies for family violence locally.*

Family violence is a product of many forces. The aggregate experience forces community members to learn about what opportunities are lacking and what long-term prevention strategies might be put in place.

Source: Adapted from Pranis, K. (2002). Restorative values and confronting family violence. In J. Brathwaite and H. Strang (Eds.), *Restorative justice and family violence.* Cambridge: Cambridge University Press.

who embraced the concept of circles to address the domestic violence in their community. They renamed them Construyendo Circulos de Paz, or Constructing Circles of Peace (CCP). In the early development of CCP, community members remarked to this author that the principle behind the circles—bringing families and community members together to account for violence—was a good fit for this small Mexican American community, where many families have known each other for generations.

It was felt that the judge's docket of approximately 200 IPV cases yearly could accommodate the 60 cases needed for a proposed random field trial, which would be proposed as a research grant. A sample size of 60 was necessary to reach statistical significance. The initially proposed study is synopsized here, and its developmental process is described in the narrative that follows. It was designed to determine

if this intervention reduced violence (and if so, at what level) through the use of repeated quantitative measures, participant interviews, and state record reviews. The research would also attempt to qualitatively assess participants' reactions to the restorative justice intervention and their level of satisfaction. All participating study members would be followed up at 3, 6, and 12 months after the circle ended, to determine if what was found at the end of the 26-week circle process held beyond treatment.

Beyond the research conceptualization, Mills knew that parallel attention to the implementation process had to be paid. Mills developed a research group from New York University (NYU) and California State University, Los Angeles (CSULA) and engaged other experts who began a series of trainings to both sensitize the community to this new approach and assess its possible resistance. The response was mostly favorable. The judge's influence and advocacy were powerful attractions for many community members, yet some were clearly wedded to the existing approach to the problem.

To develop the program and research further, Mills (2005) and the judge decided to combine the research team with select Nogales community members into a circle to discuss ways in which Construyendo Círculos de Paz might become a reality, reflecting the uniqueness of the community. Some of the judge's earliest supporters became very engaged in this process and began volunteering to spread the word. The importance of this early preparation and foundational work cannot be underestimated in terms of community buy-in. This process led to segregating the CCP's guiding principles into three major areas: (1) restorative justice, (2) decision making by consensus, and (3) safety, integrity, and personal growth. These early theoretical underpinnings are relevant as they are not only the themes in the early training but were later paralleled in the process with local staff hired to implement the program.

IMPLEMENTATION

In March 2005, good news arrived in the form of a National Science Foundation (NSF) grant, which was awarded based on the research proposal previously described. The proposal was reworked into the treatment manual, and the circle of community members began to meet on a regular basis to help devise implementation plans. University of Arizona researchers were added to the research team to oversee local data collection. The community circle and the expanded research team devised the following plan based on CCP guiding principles, Mills's IAC approach, Pranis's guidelines (see Table 8.1), and the issues raised by critics of restorative justice approaches.

HOW PEACEMAKING CIRCLES WORK

After a restraining order, a suspended sentence, or a child welfare adjudication is issued, the judge randomly assigns a batterer participant to one of two treatment groups: batterers' intervention program (BIP; control) or Constructing Circles of Peace (CCP; treatment). Offender participants are scheduled for a screening that is essentially a psychosocial assessment that serves as both a baseline for violent history, employment, mental health status, etc., and a screen for any glaring issues that would make entry into either program unsuitable. The coordinator/intake screener is a master's level clinician who is skilled at assessing risk. After this initial intake, two separate processes occur: First, a member of the research team contacts the offender and victim independently to determine if they want to participate in the study. They can choose not to participate in the study and still remain in the program.

Second, a family and community liaison (FCL) with professional training in domestic violence completes an additional assessment for each participant (offender, victim, or family member) participating in the CCP process. This family and community liaison reassesses the offender's mental health, substance abuse, and violence history and identifies issues to be addressed in the circle. This serves as the foundation for the initial social compact; it is a preliminary list of issues the offender will address. The FCL also interviews the victim (participation is voluntary) and assesses for safety. If for any reason the liaison has a concern about the offender or if anyone needs to be excluded, a consultation is conducted with the restorative justice advisement team (RJAT). This team consists of community members and professionals with expertise in IPV who can offer important feedback. This was put in place to assure an integrated community/professional response and to provide the liaison with a sounding board. Upon acceptance into the CCP program, certain labels, such as victim and perpetrator, are modified. These changes are designed to move participants away from judgmental and hierarchical language and are integral to maintaining the spirit of a peacemaking process. Once accepted into the program, each participant identifies a care community of friends, family, and community members whom they feel will contribute to a healing process. Included in the participants is an "FCL-approved" safety monitor. The participant (who was charged with the offense) nominates the safety monitor. He or she is uniquely familiar with all of the parties, and especially familiar with the family's situation and any possible "triggers." The safety monitor is trained by the FCL on his/her responsibilities and is prepared to call in law enforcement should the person being monitored become threatening. The FCL contacts, interviews, and prepares all participants for the CCP process. At this point, the FCL can refer any participant to mental health or other community-based services as part of the commitment to change.

The CCP process is co-facilitated; the first circle keeper has advanced training in domestic violence treatment and is employed by a local mental health agency, which is contracted to deliver the CCP service. This person has extensive training in safety and IPV dynamics and is able to address these concerns as they present themselves in the circle. The circle co-keeper (the other facilitator) is recruited from interested community volunteers who have been oriented and trained in the CCP process. All CCP participants identify strengths that contribute to the healing process, including cultural and religious sensitivities, family traditions, and other relevant support structures that are integral to the change process. The CCP process also includes the use of a "transition framework," which posits that there is a neutral zone between letting go of a familiar dynamic or pattern and embracing a new beginning, i.e., a nonabusive lifestyle (Bridges, 2003). Fundamentally, Bridges (2003) says that change is external and situational, but a transition is the internal process of how we respond to the change. The Andrus Family Fund supports the CCP work in Santa Cruz County and believes that staying attuned to transition ensures a smoother change process.

Participants also address the topic of personal responsibility. Through consensus decision making, all participants further refine the social compact, focusing primarily on the behavior of the participant who was charged with the offense. All participants agree to support the family's change process by ensuring compliance with the social compact. Participants develop consequences for noncompliance with the social compact; ultimately, the judge approves it. At any time during the circle process, a circle keeper may refer the case back to court for alternative intervention. All participants, including the circle keeper, care community members, and the safety monitor, regularly assess safety during the circle process. All participants work on the social compact weekly and make adjustments as needed. The circle process generally entails 26 weeks of regularly scheduled meetings and may be followed by periodic maintenance circles for several months. Treatment and other services, such as job training or literacy classes, may continue after the circle process is no longer necessary.

CONCLUSION

The CCP intervention, which, at its core, adapts restorative justice principles for intervening in IPV was thoughtfully planned and adapted for the Nogales community. It honors the small community's strong Mexican American heritage. Table 8.2 summarizes the concerns reported here as being raised in the literature and shows how the CCP program attempted to address those concerns.

Concerns could be divided into five broad areas: Would the participating victim be safe? Would the process be voluntary? Would attention be paid to a potential power imbalance? How would the plan be enforced? How would the process be rigorously evaluated and memorialized? Addressing safety, volition, and power dynamics together, the CCP intervention utilizes advanced professional training of key staff and facilitators to bring a professional eye to these potential problems. The presence of a participant-identified, professionally prepared, and approved safety monitor melds personal familiarity with professional knowledge about risk and its management. Attention to preparation, consistent monitoring, and regular consultation with the RJAT are in the service of both safety and potential replication. Ultimately, participating offenders can be referred back to court if the social compact developed in the circle is not honored. The judge's willingness to participate in a random assignment design will enable the findings to make a strong contribution to the literature.

While we are hopeful that the quantitative aspect of this study will demonstrate that the CCP intervention reduces IPV and that its qualitative counterpart will show increased satisfaction rates for CCP participants in Nogales, Arizona, the jury is still out. As this chapter is being written, we are in the beginning phase of data collection, which means that we do not yet know the full ramifications of early recruitment issues, and whether or not we can retain those subjects we did recruit. These and other threats to validity captured from the batterers' treatment literature have demonstrated that we need to approach what we can know about the effectiveness of any intervention with considerable humbleness. However, this new model moves intimate abuse beyond the narrow parameters of mainstream feminism. It attempts to empower the couple, the family, and the community to work with the circle keeper to consider multiple causal pathways, honor their own experience/dynamic, and discover

TABLE 8.2 Raised in Literature About Circles How Concern Is Addressed in CCP as an IPV Intervention Program or Research

• General concerns about victim safety	• Intake screener (master's level clinician with risk assessmentskills) assesses for victim safety; approved safety monitorappointed, who is alert to offender's triggers; trained to involve authorities if necessary; reassessed by circle keeper (with advanced training) weekly
• Need reassurance that the circle process enhances safety and security in the family	• Weekly assessment of safety each time circle meets
• Participation by victim must be voluntary	• Family and community liaison assesses voluntary participation; reassessed by circle keeper on an ongoing basis
• Importance of extensive preparation before circle is initiated	• Family and community liaison conducts extensive preparation before circle is initiated
• Circle keeper needs to stay attuned to IPV issues and related safety dynamics	• Circle keeper has advanced training in DV/IPV treatment and is employed by a local mental health agency
• Power imbalance between partners with IPV must be neutralized in treatment	• Presence of community and family members counterbalances potential power imbalance; circle keeper with advanced training monitors dynamics to enhance safety; safety monitor provides additional insights into triggers
• Need to pay more attention to change process	• All circle participants aware of change process and use transition framework provided by Andrus Family Fund to enhance attention to transitions
• No follow-up with family group	• Circle continues for a 26-week process period with aftercare if necessary; measures for study participants administered 3, 6, and 12 months after termination
• Plan needs to be approved by	• At any time, circle keeper can refer professionals/authorities offender back to judge; social contract is approved by circle participants each week
• Reliable information on process available to decision makers and policy makers	• RJAT consulted if a particular individual should continue in a program; information is gathered for program history, for use in future studies, and to assist public policy makers
• New IPV interventions should be rigorously evaluated	• Research initiated on a small pilot study using randomization of subjects

their own solutions. It requires members to actively engage, understand, and solve the IPV. In doing so, it is hoped that families who have these problems will be less reluctant to come forward, reach longer lasting solutions, and become members of a safer community.

Note: Since the writing of this chapter, the research team has engaged in a modified data collection and analysis strategy. They are conducting a quantitative analysis of 140 defendant case records that were randomized into the study. They will measure on the following outcomes: re-arrest/recidivism, 911 complaint logs, probation violations, and warrants issued. Additionally, they will track program completion status.

Finally, they will do a content analysis of the case files to capture how re-arrests are handled differently in the circle treatment, compared to the control group. A qualitative analysis will be performed on previously gathered interview data.

References

Augusta-Scott, T., & Dankworth, J. (2002). Partner abuse group intervention: Lessons from education and narrative therapy approaches. *Journal of Interpersonal Violence, 17*(7), 783–805.

Babcock, J. C., Green, C. E., & Robie, C. (2004). Does batterers' treatment work? A meta-analytic review of domestic violence treatment. *Clinical Psychology Review, 23*, 1023–1053.

Barnett, O. W., Miller-Perrin, C. L., & Perrin, R. D. (1997). *Family violence across the lifespan: An introduction.* Thousand Oaks, CA: Sage.

Bazemore, G., & Earle, T. (2002). Challenging restorative principles. In J. Braithwaite & H. Strang (Eds.), *Restorative justice and family violence* (pp. 153–177). Cambridge: Cambridge University Press.

Braithwaite, J. (2001). *Restorative justice and responsive regulation.* New York: Oxford University Press.

Braithwaite, J., & Strang, H. (Eds.). (2002). *Restorative justice and family violence.* Cambridge: Cambridge University Press.

Bridges, W. (2003). *Making transitions: Making the most of change.* New York: Perseus.

Busch, R. (2002). Domestic violence and restorative justice initiatives: Who pays if we get it wrong? In H. Strang & J. Braithwaite (Eds.), *Restorative justice and family violence* (pp. 223–248). Cambridge: Cambridge University Press.

Cavanaugh, M., & Gelles, R. (2005). The utility of male domestic violence offender typologies. *Journal of Interpersonal Violence, 20,* 155–166.

Coker, D. (1999). Enhancing autonomy for battered women: Lessons from Navajo peacemaking. *UCLA Law Review, 47*(1), 1–111.

Coker, D. (2002). Transformative justice: Anti-subordination processes in cases of domestic violence. In H. Strang & J. Braithwaite (Eds.), *Restorative justice and family violence* (pp. 128–152). Cambridge: Cambridge University Press.

Coker, D. (2004). Race, poverty and the crime center response to domestic violence: A comment on Linda Mills' *Insult to injury: Rethinking our responses to intimate abuse. Violence Against Women, 10,* 1331–1353.

Dutton, D., & Nichols, T. (2005). The gender paradigm in domestic violence: Research and theory. *Aggression and Violent Behavior, 10,* 680–712.

Edwards, A., & Sharpe, S. (2004). *Restorative justice in the context of domestic violence: A literature review.* Alberta, Canada: Mediation and Restorative Justice Center. Available: http://www.mrjc.ca/forms/CM%20Documents/RJ-DV%20Lit%20Review%20PDF.pdf.

Feder, L., and Wilson, D. (2005). Do court-mandated domestic violence programs work? A systematic review of rigorous research on the effectiveness of courts mandating treatment. *Journal of Experimental Criminology, 1,* 239–262.

Gatowski, S., Dobbin, S., & Lichfield, M. (2001). *The Miami model court family decision making conference program: Evaluation results.* Reno, NV: National Council of Juvenile and Family Court Judges. Available: http://www.pppncjfc.org/html/TAbull_miami.html.

Grauwiler, P., & Mills, L. G. (2004). Moving beyond the criminal justice paradigm: A radical restorative justice approach to intimate abuse. *Journal of Sociology and Social Welfare, 31,* 49–69.

Holtzworth-Munroe, A., Smulzler, N., & Sandin, E. (1997). A brief review of the research on husband violence. *Aggression and Violent Behavior, 22,* 179–213.

Jackson, S., Feder, L., Forde, D., Davis, R., Maxwell, C., & Taylor, B. (2003). *Batterer intervention programs: Where do we go from here?* Washington DC: National Institute of Justice. Available: http://www.ojp.usdoj.gov.nig.

Mills, L. G. (2003). *Insult to injury: Rethinking our responses to intimate abuse.* Princeton, NJ: Princeton University Press.

Mills, L. (2005). *Peacemaking circles/construyendo circulos de paz: Program guide.* New York: NYU Center for Violence and Recovery. Unpublished manuscript.

Mills, L. M. (2006). The justice of recovery: How the state can heal the violence of crime. *Hastings Law Journal, 57,* 457.

Pence, E. (1999). Some thoughts on philosophy. In Melanie Shepard & Ellen Pence (Eds.), *Coordinating community responses to domestic violence* (pp. 25–40). Thousand Oaks, CA: Sage.

Pennell, J., & Burford, G. (2002). Feminist praxis: Making family group conferencing work. In H. Strang & J. Braithwaite (Eds.), *Restorative justice and family violence* (pp. 108–127). Cambridge: Cambridge University Press.

Pranis, K. (2002). Restorative values and confronting family violence. In J. Brathwaite & H. Strang (Eds.), *Restorative justice and family violence* (pp. 23–41). Cambridge: Cambridge University Press.

Pranis, K., Stewart, B., & Wedge, M. (2003). *Peacemaking circles: From crime to community.* St. Paul, MN: Living Justice Press.

Rebovich, D. (1996). Prosecution response to domestic violence: Results of a survey of large jurisdictions. In E. S. Buzawa & K. G. Buzawa (Eds.), *Do arrest and restraining orders work?* (pp. 176–191). Thousand Oaks, CA: Sage.

Santa Cruz County. (2003). *Official Web site.* Available: http://www.co.santa-cruz.az.us.

Umbreit, M. (1998). Restorative justice through victim offender mediation: A multisite assessment. *Western Criminology Review* [On-line]. Available: http://www.wcr.sonoma.edu/v1n1/umbreit.html.

United States Census Bureau. (2000). 2000 U.S. Census.

9

A Descriptive Study of Intimate Partner Violence and Child Maltreatment: Implications for Child Welfare Policy

Lynette M. Renner

Kristen Shook Slack

Lawrence M. Berger

BACKGROUND

Both intimate partner violence (IPV) and child maltreatment have long been recognized as critical social problems that affect the well-being of children and their caregivers. In recent years, increasing attention has been given to the association between IPV and child maltreatment, driven in part by a growing body of research on the co-occurrence of these phenomena. This association has also emerged as an important practice issue, which is complicated by insufficient knowledge about the mechanisms that link IPV and maltreatment and by tensions between child welfare professionals and battered women's advocates over the rights and protection of children and the rights and safety of victimized women (Fleck-Henderson, 2000; Magen, Conroy, & Del Tufo, 2000; Peled, 1997; Wilson, 1998).

Although both fields focus on stopping violence in the family, sources of tension arise from disagreement over whom to focus the intervention on and how to intervene. Child protection agencies are mandated to assure that children are safe, which sometimes requires removing children from a home where IPV is occurring, while battered women's advocates argue that children should not be separated from the non-abusive parent (Fleck-Henderson, 2000). Battered women's advocates adopt an adult victim-centered approach and seek to use law enforcement as a means to protect women who are abused, while child welfare professionals adopt a child-centered approach that can result in "blaming the victim" of IPV and deemphasizing the effects of IPV on the adult victim (Jones & Gross, 2000). Battered women's advocates also support a woman's decision to either remain in or leave an abusive relationship, while child welfare professionals may require a mother to leave an abusive relationship or face the legal consequences of "failing to protect" her children (Beeman, Hagemeister, & Edleson, 1999). Even if her children are removed, a woman who is abused may remain at the mercy of the perpetrator. Furthermore, the threat of child removal may deter women in abusive relationships from seeking help.

In the child welfare system, there is a need for knowledge about how to most effectively work with families reported for child maltreatment when IPV is also present. Current recommendations for improving interventions in this area include targeting practice strategies (e.g., screening for domestic violence during child protection intake or developing child safety plans in collaboration with the adult victim of domestic violence), cross-systems policies, staff training, and increased collaboration between domestic violence organizations and child welfare agencies (Child Welfare League of America, 1999; Ganley & Schechter, 1996; National Association of Public Child Welfare Administrators, 2001; National Council of Juvenile and Family Court Judges, 1999; Spears, 2000). Although professionals who provide domestic violence services and child protective services (CPS)[1] are finding common ground and working in partnership in some areas of the country (see examples of "model initiatives" in Bragg, 2003; see also Friend, chapter 8 in this volume), differences in practice philosophies, resources, and goals can give rise to counterproductive efforts and even conflicts between these service systems (Beeman, Hagemeister, & Edleson, 1999). Such incongruencies raise questions about "best practices" in interventions with families who experience IPV and child maltreatment.

In the present chapter, we contribute to the knowledge base on the intersection of IPV and child maltreatment in several ways. First, we review existing theoretical models that seek to explain the co-occurrence of IPV and child maltreatment. Second, we offer needed descriptive information about the nature of co-occurring IPV and child maltreatment in families during a relatively short time interval (i.e., approximately 1 year), as well as additional characteristics of families experiencing both IPV and child maltreatment. Third, we explore how several indicators of parenting characteristics and well-being (e.g., physical health, depressive symptoms, parenting stress, parental warmth, and discipline strategies) vary according to whether families experience IPV, child maltreatment, both, or neither. Finally, we discuss the implications of our findings for child welfare practice, particularly as it pertains to the recent trends in failure-to-protect allegations against adult caregivers who are the victims of IPV.

Although our study is descriptive in nature, it is a necessary step in building the knowledge base about families who experience both IPV and child maltreatment. Results suggest that most co-occurrence involves alleged child maltreatment by the IPV victim, and not by the perpetrator of IPV. About one third of the child maltreatment investigations in this sample name someone other than the primary caregiver as the alleged perpetrator. In our data, approximately half of the child maltreatment allegations for families also experiencing IPV are substantiated,[2] and the rates of physical abuse and neglect allegations are similar. Among families with co-occurring IPV and child maltreatment, nearly all involve psychological forms of IPV, and about 60% involve physical IPV. IPV victimization is strongly associated with differences in parenting characteristics and well-being, suggesting an indirect link between IPV and child maltreatment that requires more explicit attention in child welfare policy.

Definitions and Prevalence of IPV and Child Maltreatment

There is currently no consensus as to how broad or narrow the definition of IPV should be or how specific components (e.g., physical or emotional abuse or violence) should be defined (Gelles, 2000). The past few decades have seen an evolution in terminology, from *wife beating*, to *spouse abuse, marital violence*, or *domestic violence*, and, most recently, to *intimate partner violence*. In this study, we use the term intimate partner violence to broadly indicate the occurrence of any of a range of psychological or physical forms of maltreatment between current or former adult romantic partners. We use this term because it is generally more inclusive of a wider range of behaviors and relationships than the other terms listed above. For example, it can be used in reference to current or former spouses, cohabiting or dating partners, and opposite-sex or same-sex partners, as well as to describe the victimization of both men and women (Barnett, Miller-Perrin, & Perrin, 2005). Estimates from the National Crime Victimization Survey suggest that the majority of IPV victimization is against women; indeed, IPV accounts for 20% of all nonfatal violent crimes against women (Rennison, 2003). However, it is important to note that males and individuals involved in same-sex relationships may be less likely to report IPV victimization (Dutton & Nicholls, 2005; National Coalition of Anti-Violence Programs, 2001).

Several existing data sources have been used to estimate the incidence and prevalence of IPV. Data from the National Family Violence Survey, a nationally representative sample of about 6,000 households in 1985, indicated that just over 16% (or one out of six) of American couples experienced at least one incident of physical assault[3] in the year preceding the survey (Straus & Gelles, 1990). Straus and Gelles (1990) also found that 11.6% of husbands carried out at least one violent act toward their wife and that 12.4% of wives carried out at least one violent act toward their husband during the reference year. Data from the Commonwealth Fund, a sample of about 2,850 women and 1,500 men, suggests that 31% of women reported being physically or sexually abused (i.e., that a spouse or boyfriend had ever thrown something at them; pushed, grabbed, shoved, or slapped them; kicked, bit, or hit them with a fist or some other object; beat them up; choked them; or forced them to have sex against their will) by a husband or boyfriend at some point in their lives (Collins, Schoen, Joseph, Duchon, Simantov, & Yellowitz, 1999). Data from the National Violence Against Women computer-assisted telephone survey of 8,000 women and 8,000 men aged 18 and older revealed that 7.7% of women reported being raped, 22.1% reported being physically assaulted, and 4.8% reported being stalked by a current or former intimate partner at some time in their life (Tjaden & Thoennes, 2000).

Comparing information from national data systems and self-report surveys, estimates of the annual rates of violence against women range from 7.5 to 117 per 1,000 women (Gelles, 2000). Annual prevalence rates are often higher among low-income women. For example, reviews of several studies have found lifetime and past-year victimization rates among female recipients of welfare to exceed 23% and 74%, respectively, with most studies reporting lifetime prevalence rates in the 50–60% range and recent rates in the 20–30% range (Tolman, 1999; Tolman & Raphael, 2000).

Child maltreatment has been defined according to numerous typologies (Barnett, Miller-Perrin, & Perrin, 2005; Sedlak & Broadhurst, 1996); however, most experts agree that broad categories of child maltreatment include physical abuse, sexual abuse, neglect, and emotional abuse. In 2005, an estimated 3.6 million children received an investigation by child protective services (CPS),[4] and approximately 899,000 children were determined to be victims of child maltreatment (U.S. Department of Health and Human Services, 2007). Child victimization rates (typically approximated with the ratio of substantiated reports of maltreatment over the number of minor children in the U.S. population) have steadily declined in recent years. Between 2001 and 2004, the victimization rate dropped from 12.5 to 12.0 per 1,000 children under the age of 18. It increased to 12.1 in 2005, largely due to the addition of data from Alaska and Puerto Rico (U.S. Department of Health and Human Services, 2007).

Of substantiated cases of child maltreatment in 2005, approximately 63% involved neglect, 17% involved physical abuse, 9% involved sexual abuse, 7% involved psychological maltreatment, and 2% involved medical neglect (U.S. Department of Health and Human Services, 2007). In addition, 14% were associated with other forms of maltreatment, such as abandonment or threats of harm (U.S. Department of Health and Human Services, 2007). These categories are not mutually exclusive, since children may experience multiple forms of maltreatment. It is likely, however, that children reported to CPS represent only a fraction of those who are victimized. The general consensus among researchers in the field is that the majority of child maltreatment incidents go undetected by the child welfare system (Waldfogel, 1998).

Children's Exposure to IPV

It is estimated that 10–18 million children are annually exposed to IPV (Straus, 1992; Holden, 1998). Exposure to IPV has been shown to be associated with adverse behavioral, cognitive, and social outcomes in children. Compared to children not exposed to IPV, research has found that children exposed to IPV display increased levels of externalizing behavior problems, such as aggression (Hughes, 1988; Kernic, Wolf, Holt, McKnight, Huebner, & Rivara, 2003), increased levels of internalizing behavior problems, such as depression and anxiety (Davis & Carlson, 1987; McCloskey & Lichter, 2003; Sternberg, Lamb, Greenbaum, Cicchetti, Dawud, Cortes, Krispin, & Lorey, 1993), deficits in social competence (Davis & Carlson, 1987; Moore & Pepler, 1998), poorer physical health (Onyskiw, 2002), and poorer academic skills (Stagg, Wills, & Howell, 1989).[5] However, the evidence supporting a causal link between exposure to IPV and adverse outcomes is unclear. Furthermore, several researchers have cautioned that the lack of consistent definitions of IPV and child maltreatment is an impediment to accurately assessing forms of violence and comparing their incidence across studies (Appel & Holden, 1998; Edleson, 1999b).

Co-Occurrence of IPV and Child Maltreatment

An extensive review of studies that address the co-occurrence of IPV and child maltreatment suggests that rates of overlap are typically between 30% and 60%, although estimates range from 6.5% to 100% (Appel & Holden, 1998; Edleson, 1999b), depending on the design of the study and the scope of the measure used to assess IPV. The most common approach to collecting data on co-occurrence involves samples of battered women or child maltreatment victims, from which the percentage who simultaneously experienced another form of family violence is then estimated (Appel & Holden, 1998; Edleson, 1999b). Such studies, often described as being based on clinical samples, usually utilize case record data to access detailed information on the nature of family violence; such data are sometimes supplemented by self-report surveys. A second strategy involves the use of population-based or representative community samples (Gelles & Straus, 1988; McGuigan & Pratt, 2001; Renner & Slack, 2006), which usually collect self-reported survey data or combine self-reported survey data and child welfare administrative data. Due to variations in sampling methods, the amount of overlap between IPV and child maltreatment can differ greatly across studies. In addition, studies differ as to whether they are estimating the co-occurrence of IPV and child maltreatment in the year prior to the interview or over the course of the respondent's lifetime. This further complicates comparisons across studies (Appel & Holden, 1998).

In clinical samples of either IPV victims or maltreated children, the rate of co-occurrence has been estimated to exceed 50% (O'Leary, Slep, & O'Leary, 2000). Appel and Holden (1998), in a review of 31 studies, note an overlap ranging from 10% to 100% in studies using data from battered women and an overlap of 26–59% in studies using data based on reports of child physical abuse. Some studies have found that children are more likely to be abused when there is a history of IPV in the family (Bowker, Arbitell, & McFerron, 1988; Stark & Flitcraft, 1988). Using a 1-year cohort of cases reported to CPS in Washington state, English, Edleson, and Herrick (2005) found IPV to be indicated in one out of five CPS referrals, present in 38% of cases which were investigated, and identified in 47% of cases assigned a high standard of investigation.[6]

Data from the 1975 National Family Violence Survey and the 1986 National Family Violence Resurvey suggest the rate of co-occurring IPV and child maltreatment to be 5.6–6.9% (Hotaling, Straus, & Lincoln, 1990) among intact families with children. More recent studies involving representative samples of high-risk populations have found slightly higher rates of co-occurrence. Using data from Longitudinal Studies on Child Abuse and Neglect (LONGSCAN), Cox, Kotch, and Everson (2003) found that slightly more than one quarter of the families in a high-risk subgroup experienced both a child maltreatment report and IPV. In a study based on the CPS population of the National Survey of Child and Adolescent Well-Being (NSCAW), Hazen, Connelly, Kelleher, Landsverk, and Barth (2004) found that 44.8% of female caregivers experienced IPV in their lifetime and that 29% of female caregivers experienced IPV in the 12 months prior to the interview. The authors also report that having a history of prior substantiated reports significantly increases the likelihood of severe physical IPV.

The co-occurrence of IPV and child maltreatment is not limited to disadvantaged populations. In a study of 550 undergraduate (287 women, 263 men) students, Silvern et al. (1995) found that 61 women (21%) and 36 men (14%) reported exposure to both parental partner abuse and child physical abuse during their lifetime. IPV is also predictive of future maltreatment. For example, McGuigan and Pratt (2001) found that IPV occurring within the first few months of a child's birth was a significant predictor of subsequent substantiated reports of child maltreatment through a child's fifth year of life.

In considering the various estimates of the overlap between IPV and child maltreatment, it is important to note that studies involving families identified through either the CPS system or shelters for battered women represent only those cases of IPV or child maltreatment that have come to the attention of social services. As such, they likely represent the more severe cases of child maltreatment and potentially include a select group of women experiencing IPV (Edleson, 1999b, 2001). Furthermore, estimates of co-occurrence tend to be higher in clinical samples than in community samples.

THEORIES/FRAMEWORKS

In addition to understanding the extent to which different forms of family violence co-occur, it is important to consider how such relationships develop. IPV may co-occur with child physical abuse if the perpetrator of IPV also uses harsh physical discipline or force with the children in the home. It may also stem from the IPV victim's efforts to overdiscipline children in an attempt to avoid conflict with an abusive partner, or from the adult victim's diminished tolerance for, or ability to manage, parenting stresses (Coohey, 2004). Violence between adults may also lead to child neglect if the abused partner experiences mental health problems or stress associated with victimization that, in turn, result in neglectful parenting (Carlson, 2000; Coohey & Zhang, 2006; Hartley, 2004).

Both unidirectional and bidirectional models of co-occurrence have been proposed (Appel & Holden, 1998). In unidirectional models, both the IPV and child maltreatment are perpetrated by one parent or partner (Appel & Holden, 1998). In its simplest version, one parent (or partner) acts as the sole perpetrator of violence, while the other parent (or partner) and the child(ren) are the targets of abuse. A variation on this model involves instances where an abused adult victimizes her or his child. Such "sequential" abuse is not necessarily caused by IPV victimization, however.

Bidirectional models include a "marital" violence model (which can be easily applied to nonmarital partnerships) and a family dysfunction model (Appel & Holden, 1998). In a bidirectional model, violence within a marital model is reciprocal between the partners, and one or both adults may be abusive or neglectful toward children; however, such a model does not account for an imbalance of power between genders. The family dysfunction model captures multiple interactions and exchanges of abusive behavior between both adults and child(ren) and does not view children as passive recipients of maltreatment. Rather, IPV is viewed as a risk factor in the development of a child's behavior problems, and a child's behavior, in turn, may fuel parents' aggression toward the child, ultimately resulting in abuse or neglect (Appel & Holden, 1998).

Although many studies have identified associations between IPV and child maltreatment, few have attempted to differentiate subtypes of either IPV or child maltreatment (Edleson, 2001). A notable example of a study that distinguished maltreatment types is McGuigan and Pratt (2001), in which IPV was shown to be associated with child maltreatment reports for physical abuse, neglect, and psychological abuse. In another study involving married U.S. military families, IPV was found to be associated with subsequent physical and sexual abuse, but not with child neglect (Rumm, Cummings, Krauss, Bell, & Rivara, 2000). Other research has reported associations between severe IPV and allegations of lack of supervision, as well as between IPV and child neglect (Hartley, 2002; Shepard & Raschick, 1999). It is possible that these associations are partially driven by failure-to-protect allegations (discussed in the following section) involving IPV victims. On the whole, however, existing literature suggests that IPV is associated with multiple forms of child maltreatment, although findings are inconsistent regarding specific maltreatment types. Additionally, most studies have not identified whether alleged child maltreatment perpetrators have been the perpetrator or victim of the co-occurring IPV (Edleson, 2001).

CONFLICT AND COLLABORATION BETWEEN CHILD PROTECTION AND IPV SERVICE SYSTEMS

Since IPV and child maltreatment are often addressed by separate social service systems, the goals and strategies for intervening with families served in each system may not be congruent (Beeman, Hagemeister, & Edleson, 1999; Cowan & Schwartz, 2004; Edleson, 1999b). Family violence experts have, however, documented efforts by state and local child protective and IPV systems to comprehensively address the needs of all family members (Edleson & Beeman, n.d.; Findlater & Kelly, 1999a, 1999b; Lecklitner, Malik, Aaron, & Lederman, 1999; Whitney & Davis, 1999). For example, a study by Kohl, Barth, Hazen, and Landsverk (2005) showed that identification of IPV by a child welfare worker during the risk assessment process increased the likelihood of the caregiver receiving IPV services compared to those in families not identified by a child welfare worker. This type of finding reinforces the need to focus on the safety and well-being of all family members and to strengthen collaborations and partnerships among social service, health care, judicial, and law enforcement agencies (National Council of Juvenile and Family Court Judges, 1999).

Historically, CPS interventions have focused on the primary caregivers of alleged child victim(s), most often mothers. Yet, some evidence suggests that, although mothers are generally more likely to be involved with CPS, fathers or male partners are the perpetrators of the most severe forms of abuse (Edleson, 1999b). Thus, the focus on mothers has generated a debate about gender bias in CPS interventions, particularly with regard to women being charged with "failure to protect" in cases that involve IPV (Burke, 1999; Mills, 2000). According to Magen (1999, p. 130):

> There are two erroneous assumptions made by professionals when considering the circumstances of battered women and their children. The first is the belief that witnessing abuse is innately child maltreatment. The second is the belief that battered women should leave the batterer and the abusive situation. These two assumptions, by themselves or together, lead to poor practices on the part of child maltreatment professionals.

In addressing the first assumption, Magen (1999) goes on to state that although exposure to IPV may lead to negative outcomes for some children, such associations are not necessarily causal. He also notes that "given our knowledge about the complexities of child development, it is simplistic to engage in linear thinking that witnessing domestic violence causes these negative responses" (Magen, 1999, p. 130), particularly since exposure to IPV is often not the only negative event in the lives of the children under study. Indeed, not all studies on exposure to IPV indicate that it is associated with adjustment problems for children (Carlson, 2000).

With regard to the second assumption, Magen (1999) states that the concept of failure to protect focuses on a victim's behavior rather than the abuser's actions, such that women are often expected to leave abusive situations for the sake of their children, regardless of how this may impact their own safety. Aron and Olson (1997) further state that charging an abused mother with failure to protect her child does not acknowledge that a child's safety depends on addressing the situation endangering both the mother and the child. The formal removal of children from an abusive home can assist in keeping some members of a family safe but may not provide the woman with protection from an abusive partner and, therefore, may not adequately address the needs of all family members.

Compared to families with child maltreatment only, Beeman, Hagemeister, and Edleson (2001) find that the majority of families with co-occurring child maltreatment and IPV are assessed as having exposed children to unsafe and dangerous situations and having a disregard for safety. Such findings may be warranted. Several studies offer evidence of an interactive effect of exposure to IPV and child maltreatment on children's emotional and behavioral problems (Hughes, Parkinson, & Vargo, 1989; Wolfe, Crooks, Lee, McIntyre-Smith, & Jaffe, 2003), and the U.S. Advisory Board on Child Abuse and Neglect (1995) states that domestic violence is a significant risk factor for child abuse and neglect fatalities. However, others have documented great variability in children's responses to IPV (Edleson, 2004) and suggested that removing children from homes in domestic violence cases may be unnecessary (Bragg, 2003). While some child protection workers argue that removal from the home where IPV exists is a necessary intervention to ensure a child's safety, domestic violence advocates often view this method of child protection as unfairly penalizing or blaming battered caregivers for unsuccessful attempts at child protection (Bragg, 2003; Matthews, 1999; Shepard & Raschick, 1999). In addition, parents who are abused by their partners may be to admit to IPV in their relationship and to seek help for fear of being charged with failure to protect under such policies (Bragg, 2003).

Despite the unsettled debate between CPS and domestic violence advocates, women are increasingly being charged with failure to protect in situations where a partner is abusing both the woman and the children (Beeman, Hagemeister, & Edleson, 1999; Edleson, 1999b), and some states have considered making children's exposure to IPV a form of criminal abuse (National Council of Juvenile and Family Court Judges, 1999). Several states have also considered legislation or adopted policies mandating responses to all child welfare cases with co-occurring IPV and child maltreatment (Edleson, 2004; Kantor & Little, 2003; National Council of Juvenile and Family Court Judges, 1999; Weithorn, 2001; White, 2003). For example, in 1999, the Minnesota state legislature expanded the state's definition of child neglect to include exposure to domestic violence. However, in light of the tremendous influx of child maltreatment reports that followed this change, the statutory definition was repealed in 2000 (Edleson, Gassman-Pines, & Hill, 2006). In *Nicholson v. Scoppetta*, the New York Court of Appeals ruled in 2004 that children cannot be deemed to be "neglected" simply by virtue of exposure to domestic violence (Freedman & Kramer, 2004; Sheppard & Poris, 2005).

Such policy developments suggest that questions remain about the most effective strategies for serving families experiencing IPV and child maltreatment. The goal of the present study is to contribute to an understanding of the family dynamics associated with different and co-occurring forms of family violence, which may inform the development of more appropriate assessments and interventions.

DATA AND METHODS

The analyses presented in this chapter address the following three research questions:

1. What forms of IPV and child maltreatment most frequently co-occur?
2. To what extent are IPV victims identified as alleged perpetrators of maltreatment in families with co-occurring IPV and child maltreatment?
3. How do indicators of parenting and well-being (e.g., physical health, depressive symptoms, parenting stress, parental warmth, and discipline strategies) vary across families experiencing child maltreatment only, IPV only, and both phenomena?

Data Sources and Sample

The data for this study are drawn from combined survey and administrative sources. The primary source of survey data comes from the Illinois Families Study (IFS), a 5-year panel study of current and former Temporary Assistance for Needy Families (TANF) recipients from nine counties in Illinois, which together capture over three quarters of the state's TANF population. The IFS sample (N = 1,899) was selected from the 1998 TANF caseloads in these counties. The present study uses data from the first three waves of the IFS. The first wave of survey data collection occurred in late 1999 and early 2000. Data collection for subsequent survey waves occurred in 2001 and 2002. The response rate for the first wave was 72% (N = 1,363); retention rates for the second and third waves were 87% (N = 1,183) and 79% (N = 1,072), respectively. Analysis weights were created to adjust

for sampling stratification and survey nonresponse (see Lewis, Shook, Stevens, Kleppner, Lewis, & Riger, 2000; Slack, Holl, Lee, McDaniel, Altenbernd, & Stevens, 2003, for additional details regarding the study design).

Child protective services records were made available through the Illinois Department of Children and Family Services and have been linked to the survey data used in this study. These administrative data include investigated maltreatment allegations characterized by maltreatment type, report date, and alleged perpetrator. IFS survey respondents were asked to consent to ongoing access to child maltreatment data; 93% of IFS respondents provided this consent. The 102 respondents who did not grant permission for administrative data access were excluded from these analyses. In addition, 39 cases with male respondents were excluded from these analyses, given the low representation of male respondents in the sample.

Statistical analyses (not shown) comparing the effective sample (N = 1,011) with the 352 wave 1 survey respondents who were excluded from these analyses because they were male, did not consent to administrative data access, and/or did not participate in subsequent survey waves did not yield statistically significant differences on most key demographic factors or on indicators of IPV (although males reported lower rates of IPV than did females). However, respondents included in the final sample reported higher levels of parental stress, higher levels of depression, and poorer overall physical health compared to those excluded from the final sample. In addition, respondents included in the final sample tended to have given birth to their first child at a younger age and had more children than did excluded respondents. This may suggest that respondents retained in the analysis sample are more disadvantaged than those in the original IFS sample.

Measures

Child Maltreatment

Reports involving investigated allegations of maltreatment included allegations of physical abuse (e.g., burns/scalding; wounds; bone fractures; excessive corporal punishment; cuts, bruises, and welts; human bites; sprains/dislocations), allegations of neglect (e.g., inadequate food, clothing, shelter, medical care, or supervision), and both indicated (i.e., substantiated) and unfounded allegations. Illinois does not have a failure-to-protect allegation category. In addition, our measures of child maltreatment allegations identify whether the primary caregiver in our sample, typically the mother, is the alleged perpetrator of the child maltreatment. Due to their low incidence rates, allegations of child sexual abuse and emotional abuse were not included in the analysis.

Allegations of child maltreatment were timed according to the dates of each IFS survey and the referent period for self-reports of IPV victimization. For example, questions on IPV victimization in wave 1 referred to the 12-month period prior to the wave 1 survey interview (IPV items in waves 2 and 3 referred to the months between consecutive waves, e.g., questions on IPV victimization in wave 3 referred to the time period between wave 2 and wave 3). Child maltreatment reports that fell within each of these time periods were then identified and extracted from the state's CPS administrative data. Child maltreatment allegations were aggregated across families so that allegations involving any child in the family were included.

Intimate Partner Violence

Survey respondents' experiences with physical and psychological intimate partner violence were assessed for each IFS respondent with respect to the 12 months prior to each interview. Data on IPV are based on self-reports of the survey respondent.[7] Items addressing physical violence were adapted from the Massachusetts study of women on welfare (Allard, Albelda, Colten, & Cosenza, 1997), the Conflict Tactics Scale (Straus, 1979), and the Women's Employment Study (WES) (Danziger, Corcoran, Danziger, & Tolman, 1997). Additional items were taken from the Women's Experience of Battering (WEB) Scale (Punukollu, 2003), a 10-item scale that examines the cognitive and affective experience of battering.

An indicator of physical violence and an indicator of psychological violence were created for each survey interval. Items assessing physical IPV included questions such as: Has your current or former spouse or partner hit, slapped, or kicked you? Thrown or shoved you onto the floor, against a wall, or down stairs? Hurt you badly enough that you went to a doctor or clinic? Items assessing psychological IPV included questions such as: Has your current or former spouse or partner tried to keep you from seeing or talking with your friends or family? Told you that you were worthless or called you names? Made you feel unsafe in your own home? If the respondent provided an affirmative response to any items on the physical or psychological IPV scales, this indicated the presence of IPV.

Respondent and Family Characteristics

Several respondent (i.e., primary caregiver) and family characteristics were included in the analysis to assess which variables may be correlated with intimate partner violence and/or child maltreatment. During the wave 1 IFS interview, respondents provided information on the following: age, race and ethnicity, education level, employment and welfare histories (derived from state administrative data systems), number of biological and/or adopted children, and age at the time of their first child's birth.

All survey waves produced measures of depression, parenting stress, parental warmth, perceived social support, discipline practices, and general physical health. Depressive symptoms are measured using the 12-item Center for Epidemiological Studies Depression Scale (CES-D) (Ross, Mirowsky, & Huber, 1983). The CES-D assesses several components of depressive symptomatology, including depressed mood, feelings of worthlessness, sleep disturbance, and loss of appetite, and respondents indicate how many days (0 = less than 1 day, 3 = 5–7 days) out of the past week they experienced each symptom. A summary score is included in the analysis as a continuous variable. (Cronbach's alpha is greater than .80 in all survey waves.)

Parental stress is assessed using an eight-item modified version of the Parental Stress Index (Abidin, 1983), which was created for the Women's Employment Study (Danziger et al., 2000). Survey respondents were asked to rate their feelings over the past 12 months and to indicate how often they felt stress and pressure due to being the primary caregiver for their children. Parental warmth is measured using items adapted from the Home Observation for Measurement of the Environment and the Canadian Self-Sufficiency Project (Caldwell & Bradley, 1984; Statistics Canada, 1995). The five scale items assess the frequency with which parents played games with their children, praised their children, and did something special with them over the past 12 months. A summary scale of both parental stress and warmth are included in the analysis (Cronbach's alpha was above .70 for both measures, in all survey waves). Three items of parental discipline practices are assessed using items adapted from the Women's Employment Study (Danziger et al., 2000), which were based on the New Chance Study (Quint, Bos, & Polit, 1997). Scores range from 3 to 12, Cronbach's alpha = .73, and higher scores indicate harsher discipline practices. This measure of child discipline strategies was collected in wave 1 only.

Perceived social support is measured using items adapted from Orthner and Neenan (1996) and the Three-City Study (Winston et al., 1999). Items determine whether or not the respondent has enough people, too few, or no one to count on for material and emotional support. Overall physical health is measured using a single item, which reflects the respondent's assessment of her own health. The response options range from 1 = poor to 5 = excellent.

Table 9.1 presents the sample characteristics for the key demographic and family characteristics assessed at wave 1 of the IFS. The average age of women in the sample was approximately 32 years. About 79% of respondents were African American, and 59% had earned a high school diploma or GED. On average, earnings and incomes were quite low; the mean household income in the year preceding the wave 1 survey interview was $8,363, and the average earnings over the 4-year period 1995–1998 was less than $10,000. The average cumulative duration of TANF receipt between 1980 and 1998 was greater than 6 years. Eight percent of the sample reported both IPV and child maltreatment (with approximately 6% reporting that both occurred in the same or consecutive waves and 2% reporting that they occurred in different or nonconsecutive waves) during the three waves of data collection (an approximate 36-month interval). An additional 21% had investigated reports of child maltreatment but no IPV, and 17% reported IPV during the study period but had no CPS involvement. Over half (55%) of the sample respondents reported neither form of family violence. The scores for parenting and parental well-being (averaged across waves) are also presented.

Analysis

To address the first two research questions regarding the frequency with which various forms of IPV and child maltreatment co-occur and the extent to which IPV victims are identified as child maltreatment perpetrators in families experiencing the co-occurrence of IPV and child maltreatment, a subgroup of sample members (N = 65; 6% of the full sample) was identified who experienced both IPV and a CPS investigation within an approximately 1-year period.[8] For the 11 sample members who experienced IPV and a CPS investigation in more than one survey interval, the first episode of co-occurrence was selected. Descriptive statistics on child maltreatment allegations, IPV, and the work and relationship status of the respondents and their partners were assessed at the end point of each relevant survey interval.

To address the third research question, which aims to describe how indicators of parenting and well-being vary across families with different IPV and child maltreatment statuses, the full (N = 1,011) sample was employed. A categorical variable was created to capture each mutually exclusive combination of IPV and child maltreatment. In the analyses that follow, we utilize four IPV/child maltreatment–related indicators: no IPV or CPS reports in any survey interval; at least one CPS report, but no self-reported IPV; self-reported IPV but no CPS reports; both IPV and CPS reported at some point during the observation period. We also examined this final category separately according to whether the IPV and CPS report occurred within the same survey interval or in different survey intervals. We collapsed these categories because most (N = 25) of the 44 respondents in the latter category experienced IPV and CPS in contiguous survey waves. Furthermore, results from one-way ANOVA tests did not detect significant differences between the "across-waves" and "within-wave" co-occurrence groups. One-way ANOVAs were conducted to test for differences in key demographic variables and indicators of respondents' parenting and well-being. For measures that were repeated in each wave (i.e., parenting stress, parental warmth, depression, social support, and overall health), scores were averaged across the three survey waves, since analyses within each wave produced highly similar associations between these measures and indicators of IPV and child maltreatment.

RESULTS

Co-Occurrence of IPV and CPS Intervention

Table 9.2 shows descriptive statistics for the co-occurrence subgroup. The majority of investigated CPS reports (68%) involved the mother (the IPV

TABLE 9.1 Descriptive Statistics for Full Sample (N = 1,011)

Variable	Mean (SD) or Percentage
Demographic variables	
Respondent's age in wave 1	31.5 (8.2)
RESPONDENT'S RACE/ETHNICITY	
Non-Hispanic Black	79%
Non-Hispanic White	8%
Hispanic	12%
Respondent earned high school diploma or GED, as of wave 1	59%
Age at birth of first child	19.56 (3.8)
Sum of earnings (1995–1998)	$9,768 ($18,729)
Number of quarters with earnings 1995–1998	4.18 (4.83)
Cumulative number of months receiving TANF (since 1980)	80.5 (33.7)
Total household income in 1998[1]	$8,363 ($7,943)
IPV and child maltreatment (wave 1–wave 3)	
No IPV or CPS in any wave	55%
CPS in any wave, no IPV	21%
IPV in any wave, no CPS	17%
IPV and CPS occurring in different and nonconsecutive waves	2%
IPV and CPS occurring in the same or consecutive waves	6%
Parenting and parental well-being[2]	
Parental stress (range: 8–32)	15.2 (3.7)
Parental warmth (range: 5–20)	17.7 (1.7)
Parental depression (range: 0–36)	5.4 (5.8)
Social support (range: 6–18)	10.4 (1.7)
Harsh discipline (range: 3–12)	5.8 (1.8)
Overall physical health (range: 1 = poor, 5 = excellent)	3.6 (1.0)

1. IFS respondents reported income data in ranges on a survey item consisting of 15 categories (e.g., less than $2,500, $2,500–$4,999, etc.). We created a continuous income variable by assigning each respondent the midpoint of the range she reported. The 2 respondents reporting income in the top category ($50,000 or more) were assigned a value of $65,000.

2. These numbers represent parenting and parental well-being scores averaged across survey waves.

victim) as the alleged perpetrator of child abuse or neglect, and just over half of these reports were indicated upon investigation. This rate is notably higher than the indication rate for the sample as a whole (37% of those with a CPS allegation). Sixty-six percent of the CPS allegations associated with these families involved allegations of physical abuse; however, neglect allegations were equally prevalent

(65%). Nearly all (95%) of these respondents reported psychological IPV, and 61% reported physical IPV.

One finding that deserves mention is that the distribution of co-occurrence across the three survey waves suggests a relatively low incidence in wave 1 compared to subsequent survey waves. This may reflect the fact that in wave 1, questions about IPV

TABLE 9.2 Descriptive Statistics for Co-Occurrence Subgroup (N = 65)

Variable	Mean or Percentage
IPV/CPS variables	
CO-OCCURRENCE OF IPV AND CHILD MALTREATMENT	
In wave 1	16%
In wave 2	56%
In wave 3	40%
CPS allegation associated with respondent/caregiver	68%
CPS allegation associated with person other than respondent	32%
Status of CPS allegation was "indicated"	53%
Allegation of child neglect	65%
Allegation of child physical abuse	66%
Respondent experienced physical IPV	61%
Respondent experienced psychological IPV	95%
Demographic variables	
Respondent receiving TANF	40%
Respondent working more than 10 hours/week	45%
Respondent's partner working part or full time	50%
RESPONDENT'S RELATIONSHIP STATUS	
Married	17%
Cohabiting	12%
Dating, not cohabiting	15%
Not in intimate relationship	57%
Cohabiting relationship/marriage ended within past year	25%
Partner not biological father of any of respondent's children	48%
Number of children (<18 years) living in respondent's home	3.4

were asked by the interviewer and directly answered by the respondent, whereas in subsequent waves, respondents completed a confidential questionnaire that was sealed in an envelope and returned to the researchers. This change in measurement mode, coupled with respondents' increasing familiarity with IFS personnel over time, may suggest an underreporting of IPV in wave 1.

The bottom panel of Table 9.2 shows that approximately 40% of the respondents in this group received TANF and slightly less than half were working 10 or more hours per week at the end of the survey interval. Respondents had, on average, 3.4 minor children, 17% were married, 12% were cohabiting with an unmarried partner, and 15% were dating but not cohabiting with a partner. Forty-eight percent of those with a partner at the end of the survey interval were involved with someone who was not biologically related to any of the children in the home. Interestingly, 57% were not involved in any partnered relationship at the end of the survey interval, and 25% had ended a relationship within the past year. One possible explanation for this is that parents experiencing IPV and child maltreatment move in and out of relationships with relative frequency. Another possibility is that IPV victimization is not being perpetrated by current intimate partners, but rather by former partners who remain in the lives of respondents.

Since a significant proportion of IPV victims in this sample reported leaving a relationship within the past year, and over half reported no current relationship, we also explored whether IPV predicts the dissolution of intimate partnerships. Specifically, we used logistic regression to predict relationship dissolution among individuals who reported being in a relationship in wave 2 ($N = 454$); the outcome analyzed was the odds of *not* being in a relationship as of the wave 3 survey interview. The results for these analyses (not shown) did not suggest that IPV was associated with relationship dissolution, although other factors (such as welfare receipt, having a high school education, and being unemployed at wave 2) did predict this outcome.

Parenting and Well-Being Differences by Subgroup

Table 9.3 presents the results related to parenting and parental well-being by IPV/CPS category for the full sample ($N = 1,011$). Results from the one-way ANOVA yielded statistically significant overall differences among the four groups with respect to parental depression, physical health, stress, harsh discipline, and social support. Post hoc Scheffé comparisons indicated several differences among the groups, which are indicated in the table. For example, average parental stress scores were highest among respondents experiencing both IPV and CPS intervention and lowest among respondents with no IPV or CPS intervention. Similar results were found with respect to all other parenting and parental well-being variables. Women included in the IPV/CPS group reported the highest depression, parental stress, and harsh discipline scores, as well as the lowest scores on overall physical health. Conversely, women included in the no-IPV/no-CPS group reported the lowest scores for depression and harsh discipline and the highest physical health and social support scores. This pattern also held true with respect to the measure of parental warmth; however, the group differences were not statistically significant.

Statistically significant overall group differences were also found with respect to earnings (1995–1998) and number of children (results not shown). Respondents in the no-IPV/no-CPS group had more earned income and higher household incomes, on average. The CPS-only group had, on average, the most children in their care. Results from chi-square tests (not shown) also indicated statistically significant subgroup differences by race, with the majority (54%) of non-Hispanic White respondents present in the no-IPV/no-CPS group and lower representation in the IPV-only group. Chi-square tests showed no statistically significant ($p < .05$) subgroup differences for Hispanic or African American respondents.

DISCUSSION AND IMPLICATIONS

This study used data on current and former welfare recipients in Illinois to address three questions related to co-occurring IPV and child maltreatment (operationalized as CPS intervention). First, we described the types of IPV and maltreatment allegations that most frequently co-occur. We found that, among families experiencing both IPV and CPS, the vast majority (95%) experienced psychological IPV and nearly two thirds experienced physical IPV. These families had similar rates of child physical abuse and child neglect allegations (approximately two thirds of this group of families experienced each of these types of maltreatment). Second, we examined the extent to which IPV victims were identified as the alleged perpetrators of child maltreatment among families experiencing both IPV and CPS intervention, finding that the child maltreatment perpetrator was most often the IPV victim. Other studies have reported higher rates of child maltreatment among IPV victims compared to nonvictims (Holden, Stein, Ritchie, Harris, & Jouriles, 1998; Straus & Gelles, 1990). Such findings are suggestive of a sequential model of co-occurrence in which an abused partner (in this case, an abused woman) is abusive or neglectful toward her children, although our data do not allow us to fully test such a model.[9] Importantly, while we were able to use CPS allegations to determine whether or not the victim of IPV was the reported perpetrator of child maltreatment, for those allegations not associated with the primary caregiver (i.e., IFS respondent), we were not able to determine the relationship of the perpetrator to the child.

Another finding pertaining to the co-occurrence subgroup surrounds the rate of indicated CPS allegations. Compared to the full IFS sample, the subgroup experiencing both IPV and child maltreatment had a greater rate of indicated CPS allegations. This may suggest that child maltreatment occurs at a more extreme level in families in which IPV is also present. Conversely, it may be that CPS workers are more likely to substantiate cases in which IPV is present, perhaps in order to shield children from exposure to IPV. There is

TABLE 9.3 Frequencies and Means by IPV/CPS Subgroup (N = 1,011)

Mental Health, Physical Health, & Parenting	Group 1 IPV & CPS (N = 100)	Group 2 CPS only (N = 195)	Group 3 IPV only (N = 169)	Group 4 No IPV or CPS (N = 547)	Significance
Depression, summed score (mean) [range: 0–36]	10.08 [2, 3, 4*]	5.21 [1, 3*]	7.46 [1, 2, 4*]	4.20 [1, 3*]	.000
Overall physical health (mean) [range: 1 = poor, 5 = excellent]	3.25 [2, 4*]	3.65 [1*]	3.50	3.69 [1*]	.001
Parental stress, summed score (mean) [range: 8–32]	17.51 [2, 3, 4*]	15.66 [1, 4*]	15.81 [1, 4*]	14.45 [1, 2, 3*]	.000
Parental warmth, summed score (mean) [range: 5–20]	17.45	17.56	17.65	17.78	.249
Harsh discipline, summed score (mean) [range: 3–12]	6.40 [4*]	5.92	5.96	5.63 [1*]	.002
Social support, summed score (mean) [range: 6–18]	9.60 [2, 4*]	10.43 [1, 3*]	9.83{2, 4*}	10.64 [1, 3*]	.000

* Group mean is significantly different from mean of other group(s) at p < .05 level.

considerable debate about such practices in the child welfare field. Unfortunately, our data lack detailed information on the circumstances leading to a formal CPS investigation and whether or not an incident of IPV is intertwined with an incident of child maltreatment. As such, we are unable to determine whether or not the child maltreatment report and the IPV represent the same incident or independent events. However, Illinois does not have a failure-to-protect statute defining exposure to IPV as a reason for substantiation. Thus, if, in practice, families are being substantiated for children's exposure to IPV, this is not a result of official policy in the state.

Our data suggest that psychological IPV is extremely prevalent in families with co-occurring IPV and child maltreatment. Additionally, our results show that, in families with co-occurring IPV and CPS involvement, 61% of women experience physical IPV, 66% of families are associated with a physical abuse allegation, and 65% of families are associated with an allegation of child neglect. These findings imply that multiple forms of IPV, as well as multiple forms of child maltreatment, should be considered when assessing rates of co-occurrence.

We also described differences in caregiver characteristics (mental health, physical health, and parenting) for families with various IPV/CPS patterns. We found that families experiencing both CPS investigations and IPV tended to have worse scores than most other categories of families on nearly all of these measures, followed by those with only IPV,

those with only CPS, and those with neither IPV nor CPS (although differences between subgroups were not always statistically significant). The only exception to this is related to parental warmth, which did not yield statistically significant associations with any of the IPV/CPS categories. It is important to note that these bivariate estimates do not necessarily represent causal effects. We have no evidence as to the causal direction of these associations. It is plausible that families who score worse on mental health and parenting measures (e.g., stress) are more likely to select into violent relationships. However, it is also possible that IPV may heighten stress, which in turn increases the likelihood of child maltreatment. The presence of other stressors may also exacerbate the effects of IPV on parenting. This possibility is supported by Margolin and Gordis (2003), who found that women's child abuse potential is low when husband-to-wife aggression is isolated, but high when combined with additional financial and parental stressors. Finally, other factors for which we have not controlled may explain these associations. For example, Coohey (2004) found that battered mothers who physically abused their children were more likely to have been abused by their own mothers during childhood, had poorer quality relationships with family members, and experienced more stressful life events than battered mothers who did not physically abuse their children and than mothers who abused their children but did not experience IPV.

A considerable strength of this prospective study is that the sample is not drawn from the child welfare or domestic violence service systems, which has been a limitation of many previous studies on co-occurrence (Edleson, 1999b). Instead, the sample is drawn from a population that has been shown to be at greater risk for IPV and for CPS intervention—welfare recipients (Nagel, 1998; Slack et al., 2003; Tolman & Rosen, 2001). In addition, nearly 80% of the study respondents are African American and another 12% are Hispanic. In his review of studies assessing co-occurring family violence, Edleson (1999b) highlights the scarcity of studies of the co-occurrence of IPV and child maltreatment that include significant samples of families of color.

Twenty-nine percent of the sample had a CPS investigation over approximately 3 years, and 25% of respondents experienced IPV (see Table 9.1). Yet, only 8% of families in this sample experienced violence against women *and* alleged child maltreatment over the 3-year study period. This is similar to co-occurrence rates reported in other community-based samples.

CONCLUSION

The failure-to-protect maltreatment category is widely debated in the child welfare and legal literatures. Some argue that maltreatment allegations of this type are punitive to the IPV victim. Yet, some IPV victims will abuse or neglect their children or will be unable to effectively protect and care for their children, as our findings suggest. While we were not able to assess IPV perpetration among the women in our sample nor were we able to determine if a mother's partner was reported for child maltreatment, we found that mothers were cited as the alleged perpetrator in the majority of child maltreatment investigations. Because both men and women may be perpetrators and victims of IPV and both parents may maltreat their children, more comprehensive assessments regarding the parenting of both IPV victims and perpetrators are needed to better understand the complex nature of co-occurring victimization. In addition, the potential of child maltreatment within partnered relationships that include IPV requires more thorough assessments of family characteristics (e.g., poor health, parenting stress) which may potentially influence negative parent-child relationships or increase the likelihood of child maltreatment. Families experiencing co-occurring or single forms of family violence require interventions directed at all family members in order to determine the most effective route of intervention. The safety of family members is routinely the primary goal for child welfare workers and domestic violence advocates alike. A better understanding of the potential indirect links between IPV and child maltreatment (via the IPV victim) will aid workers and advocates from both service systems in fostering the safety of all victimized family members, while maintaining the integrity of the family unit whenever possible.

Overall, the results of this descriptive study imply that families with co-occurring forms of violence have multiple needs and require services from both the CPS and domestic violence systems. Adult victims of IPV confront the challenge of ensuring safety for their children while attempting to protect themselves from further abuse. And, IPV victims who become involved with CPS face the possibility that their children will be removed from their homes due to their perceived (or actual) inability to provide protection. Yet, requiring IPV victims to end significant partnered relationships or to seek protection orders in an attempt to lessen children's exposure to IPV and future child maltreatment may not be the most effective intervention, particularly if these relationships are likely to dissolve on their own over a relatively short time period (as our descriptive evidence suggests). In working to meet these families' needs and to ensure child safety, CPS and domestic violence workers should adopt strengths-based total-family interventions which hold abusers solely accountable for their actions while simultaneously helping all victims of IPV to secure protection and safety (National Association of Public Child Welfare Administrators, 2001; Spears, 2000). To improve safety and stability for children, CPS interventions should attempt to mitigate the adverse consequences caused by the abuser while concentrating on the ongoing needs of the child *and* adult victims (Bragg, 2003; National Association of Public Child Welfare Administrators, 2001). This strategy should lead to improved family functioning and well-being, which ultimately serve as the optimal form of child protection.

Notes

1. We use the term "child protective services" to refer to the intake and investigation end of the larger child

welfare system. Our discussion on the intersection of IPV and child maltreatment is focused on this segment of the child welfare system.

2. In Illinois, the focus of the present analysis, the term "indicated" is used, rather than substantiated, for investigated allegations of child maltreatment that are confirmed or highly probable.

3. These rates reflect "any" violence. Straus and Gelles (1990) report that most of the assaults were "minor" (e.g., pushing, slapping, shoving, throwing things) but that 6.3% of couples experienced at least one incident of "severe" violence (e.g., kicking, punching, stabbing, choking).

4. This number reflects investigations from the 50 states, the District of Columbia, and Puerto Rico (U.S. Department of Health and Human Services, 2007).

5. Comprehensive reviews on the effects of children's exposure to IPV are provided in Carlson (2000), Edleson (1999a), Fantuzzo and Lindquist (1989), Kolbo, Blakely, and Engleman (1996), and Mohr, Lutz, Fantuzzo, and Perry (2000).

6. Under the Washington CPS decision model, referrals are assigned an initial level of risk ranging from 0 (no risk) to 5 (high risk). Risk levels of 3–5 receive a high standard of investigation and risk levels of 1–2 receive a low standard. See English, Edleson, and Herrick (2005) for additional details.

7. In wave 1, self-reports of IPV were disclosed directly to the survey interviewer; in waves 2 and 3, self-reports were obtained with a confidential questionnaire that respondents completed on their own.

8. An additional 2% of the sample experienced both IPV and CPS involvement, but not within the same 1-year period.

9. It is important to note that, in some states, the victim of IPV could be considered a perpetrator of child maltreatment based solely on her decision not to (or her inability to) leave an abusive relationship and thereby her "failure to protect" her children. Although Illinois does not have a failure-to-protect category for child maltreatment, it is possible that, in practice, some IPV victims in Illinois may be labeled child maltreatment perpetrators for reasons associated with ongoing IPV in the household (which is then categorized as some other form of maltreatment rather than as failure to protect). However, our data cannot speak to this. We discuss this further below.

References

Abidin, R. R. (1983). *Parenting Stress Index: Manual (PSI)*. Charlottesville, VA: Pediatric Psychology Press.

Allard, M. A., Albelda, R., Colten, M. E., & Cosenza, C. (1997). *In harm's way? Domestic violence, AFDC receipt, and welfare reform in Massachusetts*. Boston: University of Massachusetts.

Appel, A. E., & Holden, G. W. (1998). The co-occurrence of spouse and physical child abuse: A review and appraisal. *Journal of Family Psychology, 12*(4), 578–599.

Aron, L. Y., & Olson, K. K. (1997). Efforts by child welfare agencies to address domestic violence. *Public Welfare, 55*(3), 4–13.

Barnett, O., Miller-Perrin, C. L., & Perrin, R. D. (2005). *Family violence across the lifespan: An introduction* (2nd ed.). Thousand Oaks, CA: Sage.

Beeman, S. K., Hagemeister, A. K., & Edleson, J. L. (1999). Child protection and battered women's services: From conflict to collaboration. *Child Maltreatment, 4*(2), 116–126.

Beeman, S. K., Hagemeister, A. K., & Edleson, J. L. (2001). Case assessment and service receipt in families experiencing both child maltreatment and woman battering. *Journal of Interpersonal Violence, 16*(5), 437–458.

Bowker, L. H., Arbitell, M., & McFerron, J. R. (1988). On the relationship between wife beating and child abuse. In K. Yllö & M. Bograd (Eds.), *Feminist perspectives on wife abuse* (pp. 158–174). Newbury Park, CA: Sage.

Bragg, H. L. (2003). *Child protection in families experiencing domestic violence*. Washington, DC: U.S. Department of Health and Human Services, Administration for Children and Families, Office on Child Abuse and Neglect.

Burke, C. (1999). Redressing the balance: Child protection intervention in the context of domestic violence. In J. Breckenridge & L. Laing (Eds.), *Challenging silence: Innovative responses to sexual and domestic violence* (pp. 256–268). Sydney, Australia: Allen & Unwin.

Caldwell, B. M., & Bradley, R. H. (1984). *Home observation for measurement of the environment (HOME)* (Rev. ed.). Little Rock: University of Arkansas.

Carlson, B. E. (2000). Children exposed to domestic violence: Research findings and implications for intervention. *Trauma, Violence, & Abuse, 1*(4), 321–342.

Child Welfare League of America. (1999). *CWLA standards of excellence for services for abused or neglected children and their families*. Washington, DC: Author.

Collins, K. S., Schoen, C., Joseph, S., Duchon, L., Simantov, E., & Yellowitz, M. (1999). *Health concerns across a woman's lifespan: The Commonwealth Fund 1998 Survey of Women's Health*. Available: http://www.cmwf.org/usr_doc/Healthconcerns__surveyreport.pdf.

Coohey, C. (2004). Battered mothers who physically abuse their children. *Journal of Interpersonal Violence, 19*(8), 943–952.

Coohey, C., & Zhang, Y. (2006). The role of men in chronic supervisory neglect. *Child Maltreatment*, 11(1), 27–33.

Cowan, A. B., & Schwartz, I. M. (2004). Violence in the family: Policy and practice disparities in the treatment of children. *Children and Youth Services Review*, 26, 1067–1080.

Cox, C. E., Kotch, J. B., & Everson, M. D. (2003). A longitudinal study of modifying influences in the relationship between domestic violence and child maltreatment. *Journal of Family Violence*, 18(1), 5–17.

Danziger, S. K., Corcoran, M., Danziger, S. H., Heflin, C., Kalil, A., Levine, J., Rosen, D., Seefeldt, K., Siefert, K., & Tolman, R. (2000). *Barriers to the employment of welfare recipients*. Ann Arbor: Poverty Research and Training Center, University of Michigan.

Danziger, S., Corcoran, M., Danziger, S., & Tolman, R. (1997). *Welfare reform: Barriers to employment and family functioning: Research proposal*. Ann Arbor: Poverty Research and Training Center, University of Michigan.

Davis, L. V., & Carlson, B. E. (1987). Observation of spouse abuse: What happens to the children? *Journal of Interpersonal Violence*, 2(3), 278–291.

Dutton, D. G., & Nicholls, T. L. (2005). The gender paradigm in domestic violence research and theory: Part 1. The conflict of theory and data. *Aggression and Violent Behavior*, 10(6), 680–714.

Edleson, J. L. (1999a). Children's witnessing of adult domestic violence. *Journal of Interpersonal Violence*, 14(8), 839–870.

Edleson, J. L. (1999b). The overlap between child maltreatment and woman battering. *Violence Against Women*, 5(2), 134–154.

Edleson, J. L. (2001). Studying the co-occurrence of child maltreatment and domestic violence in families. In S. A. Graham-Bermann & J. L. Edleson (Eds.), *Domestic violence in the lives of children: The future of research, intervention, and social policy* (pp. 91–110). Washington, DC: American Psychological Association.

Edleson, J. L. (2004). Should childhood exposure to adult domestic violence be defined as child maltreatment under the law? In P. G. Jaffe, L. L. Baker, & A Cunningham (Eds.), *Protecting children from domestic violence: Strategies for community intervention* (pp. 8–29). New York: Guilford.

Edleson, J. L., & Beeman, S. K. (n.d.). R sponding to the co-occurrence of child maltreatment and adult domestic violence in Hennepin County. Minnesota Center Against Violence and Abuse. Available: http://www.mincava.umn.edu/link/documents/finrport/finrport.shtml.

Edleson, J. L., Gassman-Pines, J., & Hill, M. B. (2006). Defining child exposure to domestic violence as neglect: Minnesota's difficult experience. *Social Work*, 51(2), 97–192.

English, D. J., Edleson, J. L., & Herrick, M. E. (2005). Domestic violence in one state's child protective caseload: A study of differential case dispositions and outcomes. *Children and Youth Services Review*, 27(11), 1183–1201.

Fantuzzo, J. W., & Lindquist, C. U. (1989). The effects of observing conjugal violence on children: A review and analysis of research methodology. *Journal of Family Violence*, 4(1), 77–94.

Findlater, J. E., & Kelly, S. (1999a). Child protective services and domestic violence. *Future of Children*, 9(3), 84–96.

Findlater, J. E., & Kelly, S. (1999b). Reframing child safety in Michigan: Building collaboration among domestic violence, family preservation, and child protection services. *Child Maltreatment*, 4(2), 167–174.

Fleck-Henderson, A. (2000). Domestic violence in the child protection system: Seeing double. *Children and Youth Services Review*, 22(5), 333–354.

Freedman, K., & Kramer, B. (2004, October–December). New York raises the bar for interdisciplinary practice in family violence cases. *Youth Law News*, 25(3), 1–4.

Ganley, A. L., & Schechter, S. (1996). *Domestic violence: A national curriculum for child protective services*. San Francisco, CA: Family Violence Prevention Fund.

Gelles, R. J. (2000). Estimating the incidence and prevalence of violence against women. *Violence Against Women*, 6(7), 784–804.

Gelles, R. J., & Straus, M. A. (1988). *Intimate violence: The causes and consequences of abuse in the American family*. New York: Simon & Schuster.

Hartley, C. C. (2002). The co-occurrence of child maltreatment and domestic violence: Examining both neglect and child physical abuse. *Child Maltreatment*, 7(4), 349–358.

Hartley, C. C. (2004). Severe domestic violence and child maltreatment: Considering child physical abuse, neglect and failure to protect. *Children and Youth Services Review*, 26, 373–392.

Hazen, A. L., Connelly, C. D., Kelleher, K., Landsverk, J., & Barth, R. (2004). Intimate partner violence among female caregivers of children reported for child maltreatment. *Child Abuse & Neglect*, 28(3), 301–319.

Holden, G. W. (1998). Introduction: The development of research into another consequence of family violence. In G. W. Holden, R. Geffner, & E. N. Jouriles (Eds.), *Children exposed to marital violence: Theory, research, and applied issues* (pp. 1–18). Washington, DC: American Psychological Association.

Holden,G.W., Stein,J.D., Ritchie,K.L., Harris,SD.,& Jouriles, E. N. (1998). Parenting behaviors and beliefs of battered women. In G. W. Holden, R. Geffner, & E. N. Jouriles (Eds.), *Children exposed to marital violence: Theory, research, and applied issues* (pp. 289–334). Washington, DC: American Psychological Association.

Hotaling, G. T., Straus, M. A., & Lincoln, A. J. (1990). Intrafamily violence and crime and violence outside the family. In M. A. Straus & R. J. Gelles (Eds.), *Physical violence in American families: Risk factors and adaptations to violence in 8,145 families* (pp. 431–470). New Brunswick, NJ: Transaction.

Hughes, H. M. (1988). Psychological and behavioral correlates of family violence in child witnesses and victims. *American Journal of Orthopsychiatry, 58*(1), 77–90.

Hughes, H. M., Parkinson, D., & Vargo, M. (1989). Witnessing spouse abuse and experiencing physical abuse: A "double whammy?" *Journal of Family Violence, 4*(2), 197–209.

Jones, L. P., & Gross, E. (2000). Perceptions and practice with domestic violence among child protective service workers. *Children and Youth Services Review, 22*(5), 355–371.

Kantor, G. K., & Little, L. (2003). Defining the boundaries of child neglect: When does domestic violence equate with parental failure to protect? *Journal of Interpersonal Violence, 18*(4), 338–355.

Kernic, M. A., Wolf, M. E., Holt, V. L., McKnight, B., Huebner, C. E., & Rivara, F. P. (2003). Behavioral problems among children whose mothers are abused by an intimate partner. *Child Abuse & Neglect, 27*(11), 1231–1246.

Kohl, P. L., Barth, R. P., Hazen, A. L., & Landsverk, J. A. (2005). Child welfare as a gateway to domestic violence services. *Children and Youth Services Review, 27*(11), 1203–1221.

Kolbo, J. R., Blakely, E. H., & Engleman, D. (1996). Children who witness domestic violence: A review of empirical literature. *Journal of Interpersonal Violence, 11*(2), 281–293.

Lecklitner, G. L., Malik, N. M., Aaron, S. M., & Lederman, C. S . (1999). Promoting safety for abused children and battered mothers: Miami-Dade County's model dependency court intervention program. *Child Maltreatment, 4*(2), 175–182.

Lewis, D. A., Shook, K., Stevens, A. B., Kleppner, P., Lewis, J., & Riger, S. (2000). *Work, welfare, and well-being: An independent look at welfare reform in Illinois: Project description and first-year report of the Illinois Families Study.* Evanston, IL: Institute for Policy Research.

Magen, R. H. (1999). In the best interests of battered women: Reconceptualizing allegations of failure to protect. *Child Maltreatment, 4*(2), 127–135.

Magen, R. H., Conroy, K., & Del Tufo, A. (2000). Domestic violence in child welfare preventative services: Results from an intake screening questionnaire. *Children and Youth Services Review, 22*(3–4), 251–274.

Margolin, G., & Gordis, E. B. (2003). Co-occurrence between marital aggression and parents' child abuse potential: The impact of cumulative stress. *Violence and Victims, 18*(3), 243–258.

Matthews, M. A. (1999). The impact of federal and state laws on children exposed to domestic violence. *Future of Children, 9*(3), 50–66.

McCloskey, L. A., & Lichter, E. A. (2003). The contribution of marital violence to adolescent aggression across different relationships. *Journal of Interpersonal Violence, 18*(4), 390–412.

McGuigan, W. M., & Pratt, C. C. (2001). The predictive impact of domestic violence on three types of child maltreatment. *Child Abuse & Neglect, 25*(7), 869–883.

Mills, L. G. (2000). Woman abuse and child protection: A tumultuous marriage (part I). *Children and Youth Services Review, 22*(3–4), 199–205.

Mohr, W. K., Lutz, M. J. N., Fantuzzo, J. W., & Perry, M. A. (2000). Children exposed to family violence: A review of empirical research from a developmental-ecological perspective. *Trauma, Violence, & Abuse, 1*(3), 264–283.

Moore, T. E., & Pepler, D. J. (1998). Correlates of adjustment in children at risk. In G. W. Holden, R. Geffner, & E. N. Jouriles (Eds.), *Children exposed to marital violence. Theory, research, and applied issues* (pp. 157–184). Washington, DC: American Psychological Association.

Nagel, M. V. (1998). *Domestic violence: Prevalence and implications for employment among welfare recipients* (Publication No. HEHS9912). Washington, DC: U.S. General Accounting Office.

National Association of Public Child Welfare Administrators. (2001). *Guidelines for public child welfare agencies serving children and families experiencing domestic violence.* Washington, DC: American Public Health Services Association.

National Coalition of Anti-Violence Programs. (2001, July). *Lesbian, gay, bisexual and transgender domestic violence in 2000.* New York: Author.

National Council of Juvenile and Family Court Judges. (1999). *Effective intervention in domestic violence and child maltreatment cases: Guidelines for policy and practice.* Reno, NV: Author.

O'Leary, K. D., Slep, A. M. S., & O'Leary, S. G. (2000). Co-occurrence of partner and parent aggression:

Research and treatment implications. *Behavior Therapy, 31*, 631–648.

Onyskiw, J. E. (2002). Health and use of health services of children exposed to violence in their families. *Canadian Journal of Public Health, 93*(6), 416–420.

Orthner, D. K., & Neenan, P. A. (1996). Children's impact on stress and employability of mothers in poverty. *Journal of Family Issues, 17*(5), 667–687.

Peled, E. (1997). The battered women's movement response to children of battered women: A critical analysis. *Violence Against Women, 3*(4), 424–446.

Punukollu, M. (2003). Domestic violence: Screening made practical. *Journal of Family Practice, 52*(7), 537–543.

Quint, J. C., Bos, J. M., & Polit, D. F. (1997). *New Chance: Final report on a comprehensive program for young mothers in poverty and their children.* New York: Manpower Demonstration Research Corporation.

Renner, L. M., & Slack, K. S. (2006). Intimate partner violence and child maltreatment: Understanding intra- and intergenerational connections. *Child Abuse & Neglect, 30*(6), 599–617.

Rennison, C. M. (2003). Intimate partner violence, 1993 2001 *Bureau of Justice Statistics, U.S. Department of Justice* (NCJ 197838). Available: http://www.ojp.usdoj.gov/bjs/pub/pdf/ipv01.pdf.

Ross, C. E., Mirowsky, J., & Huber, J. (1983). Dividing work, sharing work, and in-between: Marriage patterns and depression. *American Sociological Review, 48*(6), 809–823.

Rumm, P. D., Cummings, P., Krauss, M. R., Bell, M. A., & Rivara, F. P. (2000). Identified spouse abuse as a risk factor for child abuse. *Child Abuse & Neglect, 24*(11), 1375–1381.

Sedlak, A. J., & Broadhurst, D. D. (1996). *The third National Incidence Study of Child Abuse and Neglect.* Washington, DC: U.S. Department of Health and Human Services.

Shepard, M., & Raschick, M. (1999). How child welfare workers assess and intervene around issues of domestic violence. *Child Maltreatment, 4*(2), 148–156.

Sheppard, J. E., & Poris, L. K. (2005, July 21). Caring for the children: Improving the city's relationship with children exposed to domestic violence. *Office of the New York City Public Advocate.* Available: http://www.pubadvocate.nyc.gov/policy/reports.html.

Silvern, L., Karyl, J., Waelde, L., Hodges, W. F., Starek, J., Heidt, E., & Min, K. (1995). Retrospective reports of parental partner abuse: Relationships to depression, trauma symptoms and self-esteem among college students. *Journal of Family Violence, 10*(2), 177–202.

Slack, K. S., Holl, J. L., Lee, B. J., McDaniel, M., Altenbernd, L., & Stevens, A. B. (2003). Child protective intervention in the context of welfare reform: The effects of work and welfare on maltreatment reports. *Journal of Policy Analysis and Management, 22*(4), 517–536.

Spears, L. (2000). *Building bridges between domestic violence organizations and child protective services.* Harrisburg, PA: National Resource Center on Domestic Violence.

Stagg, V., Wills, G. D., & Howell, M. (1989). Psychopathology in early childhood witnesses of family violence. *Topics in Early Childhood Special Education, 9*(2), 73–87.

Stark, E., & Flitcraft, A. H. (1988). Women and children at risk: A feminist perspective on child abuse. *International Journal of Health Services, 18*(1), 97–118.

Statistics Canada. (1995). *Self-sufficiency project: Self-complete questionnaire: Parents.* Montreal: Author.

Sternberg, K. J., Lamb, M. E., Greenbaum, C., Cicchetti, D., Dawud, S., Cortes, R. M., Krispin, O., & Lorey, F. (1993). Effects of domestic violence on children's behavior problems and depression. *Developmental Psychology, 29*(1), 44–52.

Straus, M. A. (1979). Measuring intrafamily conflict and violence: The Conflict Tactics (CT) scale. *Journal of Marriage and the Family, 41*(1), 75–88.

Straus, M. A. (1992). Children as witnesses to marital violence: A risk factor for lifelong problems among a nationally representative sample of American men and women. In D. F. Schwarz (Ed.), *Children and violence: Report of the Twenty-Third Ross Roundtable on Critical Approaches to Common Pediatric Problems* (pp. 98–104). Columbus, OH: Ross Laboratories.

Straus, M. A., & Gelles, R. J. (1990). How violent are American families? Estimates from the National Family Violence Resurvey and other studies. In M. A. Straus & R. J. Gelles (Eds.), *Physical violence in American families: Risk factors and adaptations to violence in 8,145 families* (pp. 95–112). New Brunswick, NJ: Transaction.

Tjaden, P., & Thoennes, N. (2000). *Full report of the prevalence, incidence, and consequences of violence against women: Findings from the National Violence Against Women Survey.* (NCJ 183781). Washington, DC: U.S. Department of Justice.

Tolman, R. (1999). Guest editor's introduction. *Violence Against Women, 5*(4), 355–369.

Tolman, R. M., & Raphael, J. (2000). A review of research on welfare and domestic violence. *Journal of Social Issues, 56*(4), 655–682.

Tolman, R. M., & Rosen, D. (2001). Domestic violence in the lives of women receiving welfare. *Violence Against Women, 7*(2), 141–158.

U.S. Advisory Board on Child Abuse and Neglect, U.S. Department of Health and Human Services. (1995). *A nation's shame: Fatal child abuse and neglect in the United States* (5th report). Washington, DC: U.S. Government Printing Office.

U.S. Department of Health and Human Services, Administration on Children, Youth and Families. (2007). *Child maltreatment 2005*. Washington, DC: U.S. Government Printing Office.

Waldfogel, J. (1998). *The future of child protection: How to break the cycle of abuse and neglect*. Cambridge, MA: Harvard University Press.

Weithorn, L. A. (2001). Protecting children from exposure to domestic violence: The use and abuse of state statutes. *Hastings Law Journal, 53*(1), 1–156.

White, H. A. (2003). Refusing to blame the victim for the aftermath of domestic violence: Nicholson v. Williams is a step in the right direction. *Family Court Review, 41*(4), 527–532.

Whitney, P., & Davis, L. (1999). Child abuse and domestic violence in Massachusetts: Can practice be integrated in a public child welfare setting? *Child Maltreatment, 4*(2), 158–166.

Wilson, C. (1998). Are battered women responsible for protection of their children in domestic violence cases? *Journal of Interpersonal Violence, 13*(2), 289–293.

Winston, P., Angel, R. J., Burton, L. M., Chase-Lansdale, P. L., Cherlin, A. J., Moffitt, R. A., & Wilson, W. J. (1999). *Welfare, children & families: A three city study: Overview and design*. Baltimore: Johns Hopkins University Press.

Wolfe, D. A., Crooks, C. V., Lee, V., McIntyre-Smith, A., & Jaffe, P. G. (2003). The effects of children's exposure to domestic violence: A meta-analysis and critique. *Clinical Child and Family Psychology Review, 6*(3), 171–187.

Part IV

Decision Making in Child Welfare

Child welfare practitioners must make life-altering decisions on a daily basis. Within relatively short periods of time, practitioners must decide whether parents should be allowed to raise their own children, where children should live if they must be taken into care, and whether and when to return children to the care of their parents. Few professions share such a balance of power and responsibility.

Determining the risk of harm posed by a parent to a child, and what to do with that information, is a daunting task for even the most seasoned professionals. Nonetheless, such decisions at each point in the continuum of services are the linchpins of child protection and the more general field of child welfare. In the current section, the authors examine the decision-making process, the common errors made by practitioners, the role of decision-making tools, and the reception of the child welfare profession to tools designed to structure data collection and analysis. In "Decision Making in Child Welfare: Constraints and Potentials," Eileen Gambrill presents an overview of research concern-

ing judgment, problem-solving, and decision making pertinent to child welfare settings and emphasizes the need for a systemic approach. Eileen Munro follows with "Lessons from Research on Decision Making," an analysis of individual decision-making at key junctures in child welfare cases. Munro places particular emphasis on deconstructing the typical errors made by child welfare workers such as tunnel vision and shortsightedness. Munro also moves beyond these errors to provide workers with practical guidance on how and when to employ differing decision-making approaches.

Judith Rycus and Ron Hughes review the literature on risk assessment in cases of child maltreatment in "Assessing Risk Throughout the Life of a Child Welfare Case." The authors examine how standardized safety and risk assessment instruments can be used in conjunction with clinical expertise to better inform casework decisions. This chapter also highlights the ambivalence of practitioners toward the use of tools that seem impersonal but improve the quality of data gathering, decision making, and service provision.

Enhancing risk assessment is the focus of "Improving Social Work Through the Use of Technology and Advanced Research Methods" by Ira Schwartz, Peter Jones, David Schwartz, and Zoran Obradovic. The authors examine the strengths and limitations of risk determination models and highlight the many myths and misconceptions held by child welfare practitioners about decision-making tools. With the introduction of neural network programming, an advanced computational process for predicting events under complex circumstances, the authors argue that advances in technology have the potential to change the quality of service provision in child welfare.

10

Decision Making in Child Welfare: Constraints and Potentials

Eileen Gambrill

Helping clients involves making decisions about what to do and what to believe. Decisions differ in terms of how quickly they must be made, how rich the experience of the person making the decision, the kind of feedback offered, the consequences of bad decisions, and the time available to make them. One of the purposes of decision making is to reveal possibilities (Baron, 2000). As Baron (1994) points out, the whole point of good thinking is to increase the probability of good outcomes. A good outcome is one that decision makers value; it results in hoped-for goals (Baron, 2000). Klein (1998) defines a *poor decision* as one "where we regret the process we used—a person will consider a decision to be poor if the knowledge gained would lead to a different decision if a similar situation arose" (p. 16). All those who discuss problem solving and decision making highlight that the outcome should be distinguished from the process used. That is, a poor outcome may result from a sound decision-making process.

Child welfare staff make many different kinds of decisions, including classifying clients into categories, whether to use categories (and if so what kind and how many), making causal assumptions, and making predictions about the effectiveness of interventions and the future behavior of clients. They decide how to define problems. Is a client's unemployment due to lack of job skills and/or limited employment opportunities? Are these concerns related to child maltreatment? Decisions include what outcomes to seek, what data to gather, how to integrate them, what sources of assessment data to use (e.g., self-report or observation in the home), and what criteria to rely on in choosing services and evaluating progress. Other decisions concern whom to involve in pursuing outcomes (e.g., from what agencies to purchase services). Staff must weigh the relevance of different outcomes and the benefits and risks of different options. They make decisions at many different levels of complexity, requiring distinctions between causes and their effects, problems and the results of attempted solutions, personal and environmental contributors to complaints, and claims and evidence for or against them. And all these decisions are made in a context of uncertainty. "Practitioners are asked to solve problems every day that philosophers have argued about for the last 2,000 years and will probably debate for the next 2,000. Inevitably, arbitrary lines have to be drawn and hard cases decided" (Dingwall, Eekelaar, & Murray, 1983, p. 244). Sources of uncertainty include limitations in current knowledge, lack of familiarity with what knowledge is available, and difficulties in distinguishing between personal ignorance and the actual limitations of knowledge (Fox & Swazey, 1974). Uncertainties may be related to lack of information about problem-related causes, clients' ambivalence about the pursuit of certain goals, and whether needed resources are available. The degree of uncertainty in making decisions is often hidden rather than revealed. Good decision makers do the best they can with what is knowable. *Knowledge* can be defined as information that decreases (or reveals) uncertainty about how to achieve a certain outcome (Nickerson, 1986). Options and the criteria relied on to choose among them are influenced by the characteristics of clients and their circumstances (Clarkin & Levy, 2004) as well as by those of helpers and their contexts (Beutler et al., 2004; Glisson & Hemmelgarn, 1998).

A child protective services worker may have to decide whether a child's injuries resulted from parental abuse or a fall as reported by the mother. She will have to decide what type of data to gather, what criteria to rely on to evaluate their accuracy, and when she has enough material at hand. If she decides that the injuries were caused by the parent, she must estimate the probability that the parent will abuse the child again in the near future. Examples of criteria used to make choices include tradition (what is usually done in an agency), consensus (what most people believe should be done), popularity (what most people do), and scientific (what research suggests is most likely to result in hoped-for outcomes). Judgments should be based on sound criteria, such as evidence that one option is more likely than others to yield desired outcomes. Research in child welfare as well as exposures in our daily newspapers show that there is considerable room for improvement in decisions made at many levels, ranging from policy makers and legislators to direct line staff (e.g., see DePanfilis & Girvin, 2003; Munro, 1999). For instance:

- Avoidable mistakes are common.
- There are large gaps between staff knowledge, motivation, and skill levels and what is needed to address problems.

- There are large gaps between the problems confronted and the resources available, including insufficient staffing.
- Services purchased are unlikely to achieve hoped-for outcomes.
- There are large gaps between the training programs offered and what is needed to address problems.
- Supervision is scant.
- Assessment is inadequate (e.g., see Budd, Poindexter, Feliz, & Naik-Polan, 2001).
- Timely corrective feedback is absent or scant; opportunities are daily lost to identify and learn from mistakes and errors.
- A blame culture thrives in which individuals are blamed for what are typically system problems.
- Less time is spent with children and families as a result of increased documentation requirements of questionable relevance for improving services (e.g., Garrett, 1999); uninformative, time-consuming audit systems are imposed on staff.
- Bogus claims of effectiveness abound.
- Clients are uninformed regarding the evidentiary status of the services offered.

Quackery can be defined as promoting methods we either know do not work or do not know if they are effective, for a profit (Young, 1992). If this is so, many child welfare services reflect quackery. And, if we benefit financially, isn't this fraud (Chambers, 2003)? In their report based on in-depth case studies in 12 states, Karen Malm and her colleagues conclude that "most systems lack sufficient resources to protect and serve children and families adequately" (Malm, Bess, Leos-Urbel, Geen, & Markowitz, 2001, p. vii).

This chapter provides an overview of research concerning judgment, problem-solving, and decision making that can contribute to understanding the constraints and potentials for making well-informed, ethical decisions in child welfare settings. Decision making has been investigated in two quite different situations. One is the laboratory in which conditions can be tightly controlled. A second (naturalistic decision making) is one in which people make decisions under real-life time pressures, in real-life situations, such as firefighters at the scene of a fire. "Features that help define a naturalistic decision-making setting are time pressure, high stakes, experienced decision makers, inadequate information (information that is missing, ambiguous, or erroneous), ill defined goals, poorly defined procedures, cue learning, context (e.g., higher-level goals, stress), dynamic conditions, and team coordination," Klein (1998) refers to Orasanu and Connolly (1993, p. 4). There are different models of judgment and decision making. One is the *normative* model: What should we do? What decisions should we make when confronted with a certain problem? Normative models are based on probability, utility theory, and statistics. Data from these areas are used to evaluate decisions, thus the term "normative" (Baron, 2005). Another model is *descriptive*: What do we do? Research shows that there is often a lack of match between the decisions we make and whether these are optimal in terms of rules of probability. For example, our judgments do not follow the laws of probability for maximizing expected utility. Such deviations from norms are viewed as fallacies by some and as adaptive strategies by others (see later discussion). This leads to a third model, *prescriptive*, which suggests corrections based, for example, on probability theory.

The literature on judgment, problem solving, and decision making in many different fields (e.g., Baron, 2000; Gilovich, Griffin, & Kahneman, 2002; Koehler & Harvey, 2005; Salas & Klein, 2001) indicates:

- Expertise varies greatly.
- Domain-specific knowledge is important; both problem-related knowledge and self-knowledge influence success.
- Experts use different reasoning processes compared to novices, such as pattern recognition and mental simulations. Experts compared to novices organize knowledge in a different way, approach problems on a more abstract level, and can more readily identify anomalies and additional information that would be helpful.
- Problem structuring is a critical phase; some ways of structuring problems are better than others.
- Creative and critical thinking are required.
- Repeated practice providing corrective feedback is critical to the development of "informed" intuition that allows us to respond effectively; skill in learning from experience, not experience per se, is what is important, including learning from errors.
- Our goals influence our actions.
- We fall into a number of "intelligence traps," such as jumping to conclusions (deciding on one option too soon) and overlooking promising alternatives.
- Situation awareness is vital (attending to important cues).

- Local rationality must be considered (the problem context).
- The strategies we use influence our success.
- We may have the skills and knowledge required to solve problems but not use them.
- Monitoring progress is important, for example to catch false directions and to detect anomalies.
- Beliefs about what knowledge is and how to get it (our personal epistemology) influence our success.
- How we decide to allocate our resources influences our success (e.g., time spent in overall planning).
- We can learn to become better problem solvers.

Experts can be wrong, as illustrated by Sir Roy Meadow's bogus "expert testimony," which resulted in the conviction of Sally Clark, later overthrown (Hey, 2003). Successful compared to unsuccessful problem solvers think more about their thinking. They critically review their assumptions and reasoning. They are their own best critics. They pay attention to data that contradict their assumptions. They ask questions about the accuracy of data, such as: What evidence supports this claim? What evidence contradicts it? Has it been critically tested? With what results? Are there well-argued alternative views?

STRUCTURING PROBLEMS IS CRITICAL

Problem definition (clarifying and deciding how to structure a problem) is a critical step in problem solving. Consider controversies regarding behaviors associated with attention deficit hyperactivity disorder (e.g., Working Group on Psychotropic Medications for Children and Adolescents, 2006). There are different kinds of problems, and different aspects of decision making differ in their importance in relation to the kind of problem. For example, in some medical problems, if you diagnose the problem, all else falls in place. In other situations, diagnosis offers little guidance. Problems differ in their potential for resolution. Experts pay more attention to problem definition, and they structure problems at a deeper (more abstract) level compared to novices, who tend to accept problems as given. Different theories involve different problem spaces (i.e., how a problem is represented). Consider homelessness. This could be viewed as (1) the client's own fault (he is lazy); (2) a family problem (relatives are unwilling to help); (3) lack of low-cost housing due to gentrification of neighborhoods; (4) a problem with service integration; (5) due to a "mental disorder" or alcohol or other drug use; (6) a result of our basic economic structure (e.g., unskilled jobs have decreased); (7) discrimination based on racial prejudice; and (8) some mix of these possibilities. Only by clarifying and restructuring a problem may it be solved, or may we discover that there is no solution. Creative (bold guesses) and contextual thinking will often be needed to describe the "problem space" in a way that yields a solution. Only in this way may we discover interrelationships among different levels of influence (e.g., individual, family, community, service system).

Decisions concerning problem structuring at higher levels influence options at lower levels. In our current child welfare system, problems are structured as being resolvable via casework and case management. As Lindsey (2004) notes: "The core skill available to the child welfare social worker operating within the residual model has been the casework method" (p. 43). "The premise underlying casework is that the caseworker can identify the family's problem and develop a plan to fix it" (p. 44). Case management may consist of little more than referring parents to programs of unknown effectiveness and judging success by the number of sessions attended rather than by changes in behaviors that would benefit children.

In our residual child welfare system, it is assumed that the troubles of families "derive from the shortcomings in the parents (that is, a moral, psychological, physiological, or some other personal failing) that must be addressed by casework" (p. 27). The problems with this view—true in the past and still true today—have been well described: "[T]he caseworker daily encounters such obdurate, intransient, insoluble, difficult human conditions that any success the worker may count in improving them too often fails to solve the larger problems facing the client. The unfortunate reality is that many of the problems placed before child welfare agencies cannot be solved through casework" (p. 45). This has to be demoralizing as one works in such an environment year after year. It tends to breed excuses and to blame practices that work against, rather than for, improving the quality of services. Lindsey and other scholars, such as Pelton (1989), argue that social, political, and, especially, economic conditions (poverty), well outside of parents' control, create the environmental circumstances that contribute to the neglect and abuse of children:

> In many cases, the parent is actually forced to take a dangerous course of action because of impoverished living conditions and lack of child-care supports and other alternatives. A low-income mother may be forced to leave her children alone, or in the care of the oldest child, who may not be old enough or mature enough to handle such responsibility. While she is away, a small child may crawl up onto the window sill and fall out, or wander into other dangers. If a fire starts, there is no adult to rescue the child. When the impoverished mother leaves her children unsupervised, or even in the next room, the deficiencies of poor housing may lead to severe injury, and sometimes death. (Pelton, 1989, p. 148)

Exploring the costs and benefits of a psychological compared to a contextual understanding of child and family problems suggests incentives for different involved parties. Politicians and legislators do not have to spend the funds needed to address problems, such as limited educational opportunities and lack of safe, low-cost housing. They do not have to spend the money needed to ensure that staff have the skills, values, and knowledge needed to offer high-quality services. Contextual approaches to understanding behavior are inherently radical because of their broad scope, pointing to the need for changes of political and economic policies which have funding implications. These approaches do not stop at the psychological, let alone at the physiological level. We are propelled far beyond them to political, economic, and moral levels. Why is there a lack of funds to provide programs that maximize the likelihood of achieving desired outcomes, such as increasing positive parenting skills and providing high-quality day care? Altering the economic conditions that contribute to the poverty that is related to child maltreatment will require proactive policies, and some have been implemented, such as giving government the responsibility for collecting child support from biological fathers and making bank account deposits for children at birth (Lindsey, 2004; Sherraden, 2002).

GOALS—AND THE CONFLICTS AMONG THEM—INFLUENCE SUCCESS

We differ in our goals when making decisions. Some clinicians focus on helping clients. Others may be distracted from such goals because of time pressures. Meta-goals include "[m]aximizing decision accuracy, minimizing cognitive effort and negative emotions both when making a decision as well as following a decision, and maximizing how easy it is to justify a decision (Payne & Bettman, 2005, p. 126). Goal conflict is a critical concern in many areas, including child welfare. Competing goals may include providing services to parents and respecting their wishes, guarding the well-being of children who cannot protect themselves, and protecting oneself from lawsuits. As one goal is pursued, another may be forgone. "Because local rationality revolves around how people pursue their goals, understanding performance at the sharp end depends on tracing interacting multiple goals and how they produce tradeoffs, dilemmas, and double binds" (Woods & Cook, 1999, p. 160). New goals often emerge during the course of decision making (Klein, 1998). We know little about how tradeoffs are usually represented or resolved in given situations. Consider a staff member who was required to make daily visits to the home of a father of a child who was physically abused to make sure that everything was okay. He arrives at the house and is told by the father that the child is sleeping and is fine. Tradeoffs include dealing with an irate father whose assurances are questioned by the request to see the child, time pressures to get on to other visits, and trying to protect the well-being of the child. Is this child safe?

Vested interests in certain outcomes influence our decisions. We may assign exaggerated importance to some findings to protect a favored hypothesis. We are subject to wishful thinking (i.e., our preferences for an outcome increase our belief that it will occur) and to the illusion of control (simply making a prediction may increase our certainty that it may come true). Lack of interest in having a carefully thought-out position or a wish to appear decisive (e.g., a "John Wayne" style) may compromise the quality of reasoning, as may a preference for mystery over mastery and an interest in protecting excessively rosy views of our abilities and success (Dunning, Heath, & Suls, 2004). An interest in understanding and predicting our environment encourages a readiness to offer explanations for what are in fact chance occurrences and a tendency to overlook uncertainty. We may have unrealistic expectations and a desire for quick success.

SITUATIONAL AWARENESS IS VITAL

Decision makers have to make decisions about where to focus their attention. *Situational awareness* refers to the interlinking of mental models (pattern recognition) and environmental factors (Durso & Gronlund, 1999). This is an evolving process characterized by change. Situations may change from minute to minute, hour to hour, day to day, or week to week. Unless we recognize new information and rethink our initial assumptions, we may make poor decisions. "Debugging strategies" may be needed to remind ourselves to attend to important changes that may call for new approaches to break an initial mindset or framing of a situation. As Woods and Cook (1999) suggest, situational assessment and plan formulation are interlinked; that is, as we change our views of the situation, we consider what plans we may use.

Many authors highlight the role of the failure to revise our views (becoming fixated on a certain hypothesis) as a key source of poor decisions (e.g., Howitt, 1992; Farmer & Owen, 1995). Early studies of decision making by Elstein and his colleagues (1978) showed that the difference between expert diagnosticians and those who were not as accurate were that the experts held hypotheses tentatively and were open to revising them as new information, which they sought, emerged. Relevant knowledge may only be available if accurate pattern recognition occurs. If task demands are excessive, there may not be time to search our memories for patterns that facilitate success. Woods and Cook (1999) use the term *mindset* to refer to attentional control, loss of situational awareness, and framing effects. We may consider multiple interacting themes superficially and independently, losing a coherent view of a situation. Preferred practice theories may be incomplete, resulting in failure to understand a problem and its potential for resolution. We may use standardized, routinized methods when these are not what is needed; we may not attend to the unique features of a situation.

AFFECTIVE REACTIONS INFLUENCE DECISIONS

Our moods and affective reactions to different people or events influence our decisions. Slovic and his colleagues (2002) refer to the reliance on feelings of goodness and badness in guiding judgments as the *affect heuristic*. Such feelings may influence us outside of our awareness.

MEMORY IS RECONSTRUCTIVE

We rely on our memory when processing and organizing data. Research shows that memory is a "reconstructive process." "With the passage of time, with proper motivation, with the introduction of special kinds of interfering facts, the memory traces may change" (Loftus, 1980, p. 37; see also Ceci & Bruck, 1995; Loftus & Ketcham, 1994; Lynn, Lock, Loftus, Krackow, & Lilienfeld, 2003). We tend to recall our successes and overlook our failures. We are unduly influenced by vivid events (Nisbett & Ross, 1980). Memory may be imperfect because events were not accurately noted in the first place. Even if we accurately observed a sequence of events, our memory of these events may not remain accurate. We may make up events to fill in gaps in our memory, to create what seem to be "logical sequences" of actions. We then imagine that we really saw or experienced these events. Thus, we may have false memories (Roediger & Bergman, 1998).

MANY INFLUENCES LIE OUTSIDE OUR AWARENESS

We are not necessarily aware of what influences the decisions we make, such as our goals or emotional reactions. Two out of three sources of influence on our behavior (perception and associations) lie outside of our awareness. We may be unaware of contextual influences on the very goals we pursue in a situation (Gollwitzer, Bayer, & McCulloch, 2005). We are typically unaware of the heuristics we use in responding rapidly to feedback in changing environments. The downside of this is that the automatic nature of the process makes it difficult to learn that we are wrong and in what ways. Lack of recognition of our unawareness is responsible in part for biases such as the *false con-*

sensus effect—overestimating the commonness of our reactions (Pronin, Puccio, & Ross, 2002).

THERE ARE DIFFERENT DECISION-MAKING STYLES

Many different decision-making styles are used, including rational styles that involve systematic thinking and the careful consideration of assumptions and related evidence; intuitive styles that rely on inner experience; and some mix of the two. Hammond (1996) views these on a continuum. We differ in how spontaneous our styles are. Some people tend to think carefully; others are more spontaneous. Some are avoidant; that is, they try to avoid making decisions. I have had many child welfare workers tell me that they do not make decisions. Current research suggests a dual process model. What is emerging is not an either-or view of different ways of making decisions, but an integrative view in which two different processes operate: one that may often be effective in everyday decision making in which we rapidly arrive at decisions, and another which is more analytic, can override the former, and does so as needed, particularly on the part of experts (Gilovich & Griffin, 2002).

COMMON BIASES ABOUND

We are subject to a variety of confirmation biases that result in partiality in the use of evidence. That is, we tend to seek and overweigh evidence that supports our beliefs and ignore and underweigh contrary evidence (Nickerson, 1998). We try to justify (confirm) our assumptions rather than to falsify them (seek counterexamples and test them as rigorously as possible). This is an example of partiality in the use of evidence, which can result in avoidable errors. Studies of medical reasoning show that *overinterpretation* is a common error. This refers to assigning new information to a favored hypothesis rather than exploring alternative accounts that more effectively explain data or remembering this new information separately (Elstein et al., 1978). As a result of considering only one hypothesis (e.g., that a child's behavior is a result of sexual abuse) and ignoring an alternative hypothesis (e.g., that he has not been so abused), false allegations of sexual abuse have occurred (Ceci & Bruck, 1995; DeYoung,

2004). Clinicians assign labels to clients based on the *Diagnostic and Statistical Manual of Mental Disorders* (American Psychiatric Association, 2000). These labels may result in a selective search for data that confirm the label; contradictory data may be ignored. We use different standards to criticize opposing evidence than to evaluate supporting evidence.

Research regarding political judgment about real-world events within individuals' domains of expertise shows that even experts often fall prey to the following biases: (1) overconfidence, "that is, large gaps between the subjective probabilities assigned to outcomes and the objective probabilities of these outcomes occurring"; (2) cognitive conservatism: being slow to update beliefs; (3) the certainty of hindsight, that is, "mistakes may be denied: They tend to recall assigning higher subjective probabilities to those . . . outcomes that occur than they actually assign[ed] before learning what occurred"; (4) using theory-driven standards of evidence and proof: They "generally impose higher standards of evidence and proof on dissonant claims than they do on consonant ones." They use a double standard, and (5) systematic evidence of incoherence in subjective probability judgments: They "often judge the likelihood of the whole to be less, sometimes far less, common than the sum of its parts" (Tetlock, 2003, pp. 233–234).

WE USE SIMPLIFYING STRATEGIES (HEURISTICS)

Our information is typically incomplete. We can consider only so much information at one time. The consequences of this may include (1) selective perception (we do not necessarily see what is there); (2) sequential (rather than contextual) processing of information; (3) reliance on heuristics (strategies) to reduce effort (e.g., frequently occurring cues, vivid case examples); and (4) faulty memory (our memory is inaccurate). There has been great interest in inferential and judgmental errors due to the overuse of generally correct intuitive strategies and the underuse of certain formal, logical statistical strategies as suggested by Nisbett and Ross (1980) in their heuristics and biases approach. This view has been questioned by the "fast and frugal heuristics" investigators. For example, Gigerenzer (2005) argues that many events viewed as cognitive illusions are reasonable judgments given the environmental structure. A key question is: Are the decisions that

result those most likely to help clients attain valued outcomes? It seems that both intuitive thinking and pattern recognition are needed: Those two approaches are both important although perhaps in different situations, as suggested earlier (Simon, 1990).

Many errors occur because of confirmation biases, that is, searching only for data in support of a preferred view (Nickerson, 1998) and relying on questionable criteria, such as the popularity of a view, for evaluating the accuracy of claims (Gambrill, 2005). Common defaults in thinking emphasized by David Perkins (1995, p. 153) include (1) *hasty thinking*: impulsive and mindless: We don't reflect on what we think or do; (2) *narrow thinking*: tendency to think in a narrow context: We overlook the big picture (e.g., myside bias); (3) *fuzzy thinking*: imprecise, unclear: We overlook key differences and/or do not question vague terms (e.g., "support," "ego strength"); (4) *sprawling thinking*: wandering aimlessly in a disorganized manner without integrating data from diverse sources: We bounce from one view to another without ever deciding on an overview. The fundamental attribution error is common: Our tendency is to attribute causes to the psychological characteristics of individuals and to overlook environmental causes.

ERRORS ARE INEVITABLE AND PROVIDE LEARNING OPPORTUNITIES

There are many ways we could define errors. For example, Lipshitz (1997) defines *decision errors* as "[d]eviations from some standard decision process that increases the likelihood of bad outcomes" (p. 152). Woods and Cook (1999) suggest, "The label human error involves investigating how knowledge was, or could have been brought to bear in the evolving infinite" (p. 150). We may use an oversimplification that is of value in some contexts that is not of value in others. Studies of decision making in professional contexts reveal a variety of errors, such as the incorrect definitions of problems, for example, missing physical causes. Both false positives and false negatives occur, as illustrated by reports in our daily newspapers (see also Dale, Green, & Fellows, 2005). Research on error in a variety of contexts shows that it is typically due to *systemic* factors, including poor training and poor interface between technology and human factors (Reason, 1997, 2001; Woods & Cook, 1999). Often there is a *cascade effect*, in which one error, if not caught and countered, leads to another in a chain that results in an unwanted consequence (Wolf, Kuzel, Dovey, & Phillips, 2004). This highlights the value of identifying the kinds of errors that occur in relation to a decision, so that early ones in a chain can be caught, cutting off the rest of the chain from occurring. "Because there are a set of contributors, multiple opportunities arise to redirect the trajectory away from disaster. . . . an important part of safety is enhancing opportunities for people to recognize that a trajectory is heading closer to a poor outcome and to recover before negative consequences occur" (Woods & Cook, 1999, p. 144). This pattern suggests that "[t]he label 'human error' should serve as the starting point for investigating how systems fail, not as a conclusion" (p. 144).

Reason (2001) distinguishes among mistakes, violations, lapses, and slips that may occur during planning, recalling intentions, carrying out a task, or monitoring. A *violation* is defined as knowingly omitting an important step. A *lapse* involves not recalling an intention to carry out an important task at the needed time. A *slip* refers to unwittingly omitting an important task in a sequence and/or not detecting it. Studies of decision making in child welfare show the effects of *ratcheting* (persisting with a point of view in spite of evidence that it is wrong) and *templating* (inappropriately applying correlational data to individual clients; Howitt, 1992). Errors may occur both in structuring problems and in drawing inferences. Different kinds of oversimplifications include the following: (1) seeing different entities as more similar than they actually are, (2) treating dynamic phenomena as static, (3) assuming that some general principle accounts for all of the phenomena, (4) treating multidimensional phenomena as unidimensional or according to a subset of dimensions, (5) treating continuous variables as discrete, (6) treating highly interconnected concepts as separable, and (7) treating the whole as merely the sum of its parts (Feltovich, Spiro, & Coulson, 1989, cited in Woods & Cook, 1999, p. 152).

Unavoidable mistakes are those that could not have been anticipated. They occur despite taking advantage of available knowledge and critical thinking skills. Avoidable mistakes are those that could have been avoided by being better informed regarding practice-related research findings, by thinking more critically about assumptions and their possible consequences, or by arranging an agency culture that encourages staff to report errors and to work together to minimize avoidable ones. They may occur because of faulty decision-making styles, such as jumping to conclusions, and/or agency policies and procedures that interfere with sound decision making, such as an autocratic administrative style and/or a lack of staff access to relevant databases.

THE TASK ENVIRONMENT INFLUENCES SUCCESS

The setting in which decisions are made influences our decisions. Task demands are emphasized in fast and frugal models (Gigerenzer, 2002). The concept of local rationality suggested by Woods and Cook (1999) captures the idea that cognitive activity needs to be considered in view of the demands placed on us by the characteristics of the problems we confront. "The expression of expertise and error, then, is governed by the interplay of particular problem demands inherent in the field of activity and the resources available to bring knowledge to bear in pursuit of the critical goals" (Woods & Cook, 1999, p. 161). Some features of situations, such as time pressures, sources of irritability, conflicting goals, and unanticipated variations in pacing, increase problem demands (Woods & Cook, 1999). The notion of rationality favored by authors such as Gigerenzer (2002), Klein (1998), and Simon (1990) emphasizes the match between the problems we confront and the environments in which they occur. This focus is also reflected in research showing that the causes of errors are typically systemic (Reason, 1997, 2001); they are usually not due to one person or one environmental characteristic.

DOMAIN-SPECIFIC KNOWLEDGE AND SKILLS ARE IMPORTANT

As Nickerson (1998) points out, "To think effectively in any domain one must know something about the domain and, in general, the more one knows the better" (p. 13). *Content knowledge* includes facts, concepts, principles, and strategies that contribute to problem solving. *Procedural knowledge* includes the skills required to implement content knowledge. Experts compared to novices in an area possess domain-specific knowledge and can rapidly identify what information is needed to solve a problem. They have valuable "scripts" which guide decision making (Hamm, 2003). Experts seem to use a different reasoning process compared to novices based on many experiences providing corrective feedback (see also Patel & Zhang, 2007).

BARRIERS TO SOUND DECISION MAKING

The previous overview suggests the following barriers: (1) limited knowledge, (2) limited information-processing capacities, (3) the task environment, (4) perceptual and expressive blocks, and (5) personal obstacles, such as lack of perseverance, reliance on ineffective strategies, and lack of familiarity with problem-related knowledge. Problems that confront clients are often difficult ones that challenge the most skilled staff. Rarely is all relevant material available. Even if all could be known, there may not be time to know all, nor could we appropriately integrate the many sources of data without the help of special tools, such as the use of frequency rather than probability, nor may we need all relevant data to make a sound decision as emphasized by Gigerenzer (2002, 2005) in his description of fast and frugal heuristics. Even when a great deal is known, this knowledge is usually in the form of statistical associations that do not allow specific predictions about individuals (Dawes, 1988). Although we know more about behavior today than we did years ago, we know little compared to what remains unknown. We often do not know the true prevalence of behavior or its natural history. Empirical knowledge related to practice is fragmentary, and theory must be used to fill in the gaps. Predictions must be made under considerable uncertainty in terms of the relationship between predictor variables and service outcomes.

The uncertainty associated with decisions is complicated by competing values in the area of child welfare. These include protecting children from abuse, maximizing the freedom of parents, and conserving scarce resources. The probabilities of different outcomes given certain interventions may be unknown. Every source of information has a margin of error that may be small or large. We often do not know how great the range of error is. Avoidable mistakes may result from ignorance on the part of staff; that is, knowledge may be available but not used. These may occur during assessment, for example, overlooking important data or attending to irrelevant data (e.g., Budd, Poindexter, Feliz, & Naik-Polan, 2001). They may occur during intervention, such as selecting ineffective services, or during evaluation, such as selecting misleading or irrelevant measures of progress. Errors in judgment may result in misattributing problems to the psychological characteristics of clients or incorrectly predicting the reoccurrence of child abuse. They may result in (1) failing to offer help that could be provided and is desired by clients, (2) forcing clients to accept help they do not want, (3) offering help that is really not needed, or (4) relying on services that aggravate rather than alleviate concerns. Ideological explanations which are theory-driven often "trump" empirical findings (Gorman, 1998).

Gathering information about the frequency and nature of the barriers to sound decisions will be useful in planning how to decrease them (Greenhalgh, Robert, Macfarlane, Bate, & Kyriakidou, 2004). Examples reported by my students include a chaotic working space (shared phones, desks, and computers, and no private space for confidential conversations) and feeling overwhelmed by clients' problems. This may be due to a large caseload, a lack of needed resources (e.g., high-quality parent-training programs), the multitude of challenges that clients confront, and/or poor interagency communication and team collaboration. The lures of pseudoscience and propaganda capture many in the helping professions, and professional education typically does not prepare students to avoid their siren calls. Related courses designed to help students avoid such lures are offered in some medical schools (see Wilkes & Hoffman, 2001). There are inevitable uncertainties created by lack of knowledge and work demands that put pressures on limited decision-making capacities and memory. Practitioners make provisional assessments and form expectancies based on partial and uncertain data—which may not be revised as needed in response to further information.

A key barrier is the enormous gap between the problems clients confront that are directly related to the welfare of their children and their ability to protect them, and what is offered, which is due directly to how problems are structured. (See prior discussion of problem structuring.) "Individuals selected to receive casework services often confront structural and institutional barriers that the caseworker has little or no means of changing" (Lindsey, 2004, p. 53). He quotes Roberts (2002), who argues that "child welfare reflects the political choice to address dire child poverty in Black communities by punishing parents instead of confronting the structural reasons for racial and economic inequality" (p. 99). Related points have been made and documented repeatedly over the past decades and yet, the gap between what is needed and what is offered seems to widen rather than narrow. Lindsey (2004) argues that both the regulatory and administrative constraints on professional autonomy limit decision-making power and thereby the professional satisfaction that comes from exercising professional authority to achieve a desirable and effective end (p. 46). Professional autonomy is compromised by a lack of resources needed to carry out responsibilities in accord with professional judgment:

> Indeed, the caseworker with large caseloads and heavy work demands has little room to exercise professional judgment or apply professional skills and knowledge. When limited in this fashion, most casework activities require little professional training or expertise, and it is not surprising that casework tasks are often carried out by untrained employees or employees trained in disciplines other than social work. More often than not, caseworkers are viewed as little more than bureaucrats who enforce and administer programs following the rules and regulations established by the government. (Lindsey, 2004, p. 46)

How can casework and case management within a resource-impoverished residual system help families to protect their children and to move out of the very circumstances that create risks for children?

SELF-IMPOSED BARRIERS

Some barriers to problem solving are self-imposed, such as failure to revise our views when needed. Motivational barriers include a lack of interest in helping clients and acceptance of questionable excuses for poor services. Emotional barriers include a fear of making mistakes and a low tolerance for uncertainty. Focusing on justifying our beliefs rather than on critiquing them is a major obstacle. This encourages confirmation biases in which we seek only data that support our assumptions. A preoccupation with finding *the* cause of a problem can be a barrier, rather than asking *how* behaviors or events can be altered to attain desired outcomes (Feinstein, 1967). We may have ineffective interpersonal skills and make poor decisions regarding communicating information to other parties. Indeed, failure of communication was highlighted by Munro (1999) as an important contributor to avoidable mistakes. Complex interactions may occur between self-imposed and external regulations that compromise the services that clients receive, such as a personal interest in being effective in a context that demands perfection but withholds the resources needed to achieve even what is possible.

THE NEED FOR A SYSTEMIC APPROACH

The previous discussion illustrates the rich literature concerning judgment, decision making, problem solving, critical thinking, and professional education that provides guidelines for improving the quality of decision making in child welfare. This suggests that if we are to understand decisions made and to develop ways to improve their quality, a *systemic* view must be taken (Gambrill & Shlonsky, 2001). This has been recognized in many areas, including aviation, medicine, and nuclear power (Woods & Cook, 1999). We must attend to the entire system which influences decisions made by staff, including a lack of access to programs that are most likely to help clients attain hoped-for outcomes. Focusing solely on the risk of the biological parents to their children is much too narrow a view in attempts to understand the options for changes that could benefit children and families. We should consider multiple sources of risk in the service system, including use of ineffective assessment measures, poor training programs, ineffective or dysfunctional agency incentive systems (dysfunctional cultures and climates), and the external factors that influence these, such as lack of funding for high-quality parent-training programs and other needed resources, as well as ineffective professional education programs (see Figure 10.1).

A systemic view calls for minimizing risk from *all* sources that contribute to unwanted outcomes (e.g., harm to children), not only risks posed by parents to their children, but risks posed by child welfare staff and service providers to clients and all procedures put in place to decrease both, such as dysfunctional assessment systems required by the government (e.g., see Garrett, 1999). The National Patient Safety Foundation (2000)

A. Attention to Organizational Factors

1. Valid assessment measures are used, including valid risk and safety measures.
2. Effective intervention programs are used: those that have been found via critical testing to help clients attain hoped-for goals. Purchase of services from other agencies is evidence-informed, that is, they have been critically tested and found to do more good than harm.
3. Valid measures are used to assess progress.
4. Clients are involved as informed participants (see description of evidence-informed client choice here and in chapter 3).
5. A system is in place to introduce innovations that do more good than harm.
6. Case records include clear descriptions of hoped-for outcomes as well as services used and outcomes attained.
7. An accountable, accessible, user-friendly client feedback system is in place to harvest complaints and compliments. Related forms are readily available. Data gathered are used to enhance the quality of services.
8. Up-to-date, clear descriptions of outcomes sought, services offered for each, and outcomes attained, including those purchased from local agencies, such as parent-training and substance abuse programs, are readily available in waiting rooms and on user-friendly Web sites. These should include critical reviews of the evidentiary status of each service offered and descriptions of alternative, well-tested, effective programs. Staff and clients should have access to relevant databases (e.g., in waiting rooms).
9. Preparation of biannual "state of the gap" reports, which are distributed to all involved parties, including clients (for example, via brochures available in agency waiting rooms and user-friendly Web sites). These should describe:
    a. gaps between the training programs offered to staff and what is needed to maximize service effectiveness, and
    b. gaps between the services used and what related research suggests is needed to maximize success.
10. Clear performance standards for all staff and selection of standards based on what has been found, via critical appraisal, to maximize hoped-for outcomes (e.g., increase safety for children).
11. Effective supervision, including enhancing supervisees' self-learning skills and fulfilling administrative obligations.
12. Creation of a user-friendly way to identify errors and related circumstances and an agency culture that encourages their identification and the pursuit of effective ways to minimize avoidable errors.
13. A whistle-blowing policy that encourages constructive criticism of agency policies and practices.
14. Provision of user-friendly, timely, corrective feedback to staff regarding decisions made so that staff can "educate their intuition" (Hogarth, 2001); random audits of a sample of cases of each staff member and provision of individualized feedback and training as needed based on this review.
15. Hiring supervisors with evidence-informed values and knowledge and the skills required to help staff maintain desired performance levels; random audits of a random sample of related supervisory behaviors and products.
16. Hiring staff who possess values, knowledge, and skills required to fulfill expected tasks at minimal levels of competence as demonstrated by their performance on related tasks.

FIGURE 10.1   Components of a Systemic Risk Management System in Child Welfare. Based on Gambrill and Shlonsky, 2001.

(*continued*)

17. Hiring administrators who encourage evidence-informed practices and policies and who are expert in arranging positive contingencies to support related staff behaviors; routine review of policies and practices in relation to key indicators.

18. Selection of evidence-informed training programs for staff that provide values, skills, and knowledge needed to help clients, for example, programs that use instructional formats that maximize learning and that incorporate content found to help clients achieve hoped-for outcomes. Evaluation of programs offered includes review of on-the-job practices and outcomes.

19. Services from multiple agencies are well coordinated.

20. Written service agreements are prepared for each client, clearly describing agreed-on objectives and consequences that will occur depending on participation and outcomes; clients should receive a copy.

B. **Attention to Community Factors**
1. Engagement of opinion leaders who value evidence-informed practice and policies.
2. Creation of a Web site that reaches out into the community to inform people about the evidentiary status of services offered and alternatives. (See A8 above.)
3. Creation of client advocacy groups which encourage effective services.

C. **Professional Education Programs**
1. Educational content and formats are selected based on their evidentiary status and philosophy after the process.
2. Graduates are well educated in the process of evidence-informed practice.

D. **Personal Characteristics**
1. Avoid dysfunctional excuses (McDowell, 2000).
2. Commitment to continued learning.
   - Willingness to acknowledge mistakes.
   - Openness to criticism.
3. Assertiveness skills (e.g., raising questions)
4. Emotion management skills (e.g., regarding stress).

FIGURE 10.1   Components of a Systemic Risk Management System in Child Welfare

defines *patient safety* as "the avoidance, prevention, and amelioration of adverse outcomes or injuries stemming from a process of health care" (p. 1), and highlights that safety emerges from the interaction of system components (see Figure 10.2). Risks may be avoidable or unavoidable. Avoidable risks now taken in child welfare include incomplete assessment (Budd et al., 2001), referring clients to agencies that offer ineffective services, and pursuing vague outcomes (Gambrill & Goldman, 2004). Poor decisions during early phases (assessment) influence risk in later phases. For example, if assessment is fragmented and incomplete, ineffective or harmful services may be selected. We can draw on practice- and policy-related research, including content reviewed in this chapter, to identify options for increasing sound decisions which minimize risk. Some examples follow.

USE VALID ASSESSMENT FRAMEWORKS AND MEASURES

Staff should have the skills needed to conduct a contextual assessment and to use valid measures. One of the most difficult decisions that child welfare workers have to make is to assess the risk of immediate and future maltreatment given currently available information. Research in many areas shows that actuarial methods are superior to consensus-based methods in predicting future behavior (Grove & Meehl, 1996). Actuarial methods are based on empirical relationships between predictor variables and a particular outcome, such as child maltreatment. Studies comparing actuarial to consensus-based methods show that the former are more effective (Baird & Wagner, 2000). Structured decision making is now widely used. Wagner (2003)

- Organizational structures and processes
- Safety culture and the blame process
- Safety (risk) reporting (e.g., incident reporting and other mechanisms for learning about system vulnerabilities)
- Organizational learning processes and barriers
- Production pressures
- Fundamental human limitations that influence performance
- Fatigue and sleep deprivation
- Stress
- Human factors design in devices and systems
- Coordination and cooperation across people and boundaries (coordination infrastructure)
- Education and training procedures
- Resource limitations

FIGURE 10.2   Underlying Factors Related to Safety Problems
Source: National Patient Safety Foundation, 2000.

suggests that such methods may predict about 55% of the variance. Actuarial systems may classify children into categories of potential harm, for example high, medium, low. Next, a careful assessment is needed (Gambrill, 2006; Shlonsky & Wagner, 2005). In spite of the fact that actuarial methods have shown themselves superior to reliance on clinical consensus, there is considerable controversy in this area. No matter what model is used, predictive accuracy is limited (Gambrill & Shlonsky, 2000). Failure to recognize this is reflected in requirements that no child shall be harmed while in care and blaming child welfare workers for decisions that result in harm to children when indeed the consequences could not have been predicted. Challenges in this area are considerable. For example, individual risk may differ from population-derived risks. We fall into the ecological fallacy when we assume that what is a risk factor for most people is a risk factor for a particular individual. Understanding risk is easier when frequencies rather than probabilities are used (e.g., Gigerenzer, 2002; Munro, 2004). Receiver operating curve (ROC) analysis can be used to select cut points that balance false positives and false negatives.

RECOGNIZE AND LEARN FROM ERRORS

Mistakes are inevitable and provide valuable learning opportunities, *if* corrective feedback is provided. Failures and mistakes offer information that may yield better guesses next time around. They help us learn about the nature of our problems: "Only through our errors can we learn; and only he will learn who is ready to appreciate and even to cherish the errors of others as stepping stones toward truth, and who searches for his own errors: who tries to find them, since only when he has become aware of them can he free himself from them" (Popper, 1992, p. 149). The relationships among our task environments, the particular tasks we must carry out, and our personal characteristics (e.g., a tendency to jump to conclusions) influence the rate and kind of errors that occur.

There has been surprisingly little attention paid to the systemic causes of error in child welfare. Rather, there has been a "blame culture" in which one worker is singled out to take total responsibility for harm to a child (Reder, Duncan, & Gray, 1993; Stanley & Manthorpe, 2004). Certainly, there are individual lapses, such as the worker who lied about visiting a family in which two young boys were scalded to death after yet again being placed in "the hot room" (*New York Times*, December 2006). If it is true that we learn from our errors in environments in which we receive corrective feedback, then failure to identify errors and why they occur is a considerable loss. Rzepnicki and Johnson (2005) have used root cause analysis to identify decision points and related errors in the detailed death reports prepared by the inspector general's office of Illinois. Here too, there is a rich literature upon which we can draw, including the work of Reason (1997, 2001), which is incorporated, for example, in Bostock, Bairstow, Fish, and Macleod (2005).

PAY ATTENTION TO ORGANIZATIONAL VARIABLES

A systemic view of decision making requires attention to the organizational context in which decisions occur, including time pressures and conflicting goals. Do agencies provide effective, user-friendly ways to detect errors, including audit systems that provide valuable feedback to staff and avoid the negative effects of accountability (Lerner & Tetlock, 1999)? Do contingency systems facilitate effective services, including self-development opportunities for staff? The concept of local rationality (Woods & Cook, 1999) captures the idea that cognitive activity needs to be considered in view of the *demands* placed on practitioners by the characteristics of the problems that occur. "The expression of expertise and error, then, is governed by the interplay of particular problem demands [which vary in type and degree] and the resources available to use knowledge in pursuit of our goals" (Woods & Cook, 1999, p. 161). The notion of rationality favored by authors such as Gigerenzer (2002) and Klein (1998) emphasizes the match between the problems we confront and the environments in which they occur. This focus is also reflected in the systemic causes of errors (Reason, 1997, 2001); they are usually *not* caused by one person or environmental characteristic. The emphasis on the contextual nature of decision making has implications for the extent to which a given strategy is generalizable over a number of situations; it depends on the similarity and nature of the decisions and related contexts.

Child welfare agencies, especially those in urban areas, may have authoritarian, bureaucratic structures. Such cultures hinder development of a safety culture. The dual roles of helping and judging create role conflict and ambiguities that encourage high staff turnover and burnout. Reason (1997) suggests that a safety culture is comprised of four components: (1) a *reporting culture*, defined as "an organizational climate in which people are prepared to report their errors and near misses" (p. 195); (2) a *just culture*, described as "an atmosphere of trust in which people are encouraged, even rewarded, for providing essential safety-related information—but in which they are also clear about where the line must be drawn between acceptable and unacceptable behavior" (p.195); (3) a *flexible culture*, for example shifting from a hierarchical mode of taking charge "to a flatter professional structure, where control passes to the task experts on the spot and then reverts back to the traditional bu-reaucratic mode once the emergency has passed" (p. 196); and (4) a *learning culture*, which involves the "willingness and the competence to draw the right conclusions from its safety information system, and the will to implement major reforms when their need is indicated" (p. 196). Other components include not forgetting to be afraid, gathering the right kind of data, and no blame. Agencies should undertake a cultural assessment to identify opportunities to create effective procedures that minimize risk. (See Figure 10.1.)

OFFER OPPORTUNITIES FOR CORRECTIVE FEEDBACK

Some failures are avoidable as suggested by research by DePanfilis and Girvin (2003) and Munro (1999); others are not. Expectations that no child be harmed in care are impossible to achieve and can be demoralizing to staff. They can impede looking closely at outcomes since we know we will not find perfection, although bad outcomes do not necessarily reflect a faulty decision-making process. A belief that we can always succeed is likely to create dysfunctional feelings of regret that hinder decision making (see Kahneman, 1995).

PURCHASE SERVICES BASED ON THEIR EVIDENTIARY STATUS

There has been far too little critical appraisal of the services purchased by child welfare agencies. If our primary concern is to provide the services most likely to result in hoped-for outcomes (decrease risk and increase safety) as suggested by critical appraisals of related research, we must use criteria other than popularity and tradition to purchase services. Services purchased should maximize the likelihood of attaining hoped-for outcomes as demonstrated via critical appraisal. Purchasing ineffective or harmful services increases risk to children by losing opportunities to alter factors related to child maltreatment. For any service provider, we should examine the gaps among the services they provide to referred clients, what should be provided based on related research findings, and the acceptability of the services to the client. For each service, we should ask: Is anything known about its effectiveness? If so, what? Does it do more good than harm? Does it do more harm than good? Is it of unknown effect (has not been carefully evaluated)? Or is it of unknown effect but is in a high-quality research program (Gray, 2001)? (We could, for example, collate the data from evidence-informed client choice forms; see next section for more detail.) Clear written agreements between county child welfare departments and referral agencies should be prepared. Vague agreements pose an unnecessary risk to children. Payment for services purchased should be contingent on meeting agreed-on responsibilities (e.g., providing clear data regarding outcomes). Unless service agreements are clear regarding what is expected, providers cannot be held responsible for meeting hoped-for outcomes, such as timely reports.

It is the service provider's responsibility to provide information that will help child welfare staff to choose wisely among different services. It is the provider's responsibility to document the evidentiary status of services used, and staff in public child welfare agencies should request such information from agencies to which they refer clients, allowing all parties to make evidence-informed choices. Service providers should prepare clear written descriptions of services offered, the criteria used to select them (e.g., tradition or critical appraisals of related research findings), the outcomes addressed, their track record of success in relation to each outcome, and the related research describing the reliability and validity of the assessment, intervention, and evaluation methods used. Providers should be required to share this information with all interested parties, including clients, in written material available in waiting rooms and on user-friendly Web sites. Providers should be responsible for supplying clear, accurate documentation describing the fidelity of service methods used, including a description of how data were collected and the extent to which the methods used are evidence-informed. It is the responsibility of providers to select and monitor valid progress indicators related to each outcome addressed for each client and to provide data to child welfare agencies in a timely manner as described in the purchase-of-service agreement.

INVOLVE CLIENTS AS INFORMED PARTICIPANTS

Currently, clients are uninformed or misinformed regarding the evidentiary status of recommended services and alternatives. Calls for accurately informing clients are increasing (e.g., Coulter, 2002). We should require professionals to inform clients about the evidentiary status of recommended services, including the possibility that a method has never been rigorously tested in relation to hoped-for outcomes and that other methods have been so tested and found to be effective. This can be done by requiring all staff to complete an evidence-informed client choice form for each service recommended which describes the evidentiary status of the service, notes whether effective alternatives exist which are not offered, and describes the track record of success in using the method recommended with people like the client by both the agency to which the client is referred and the staff member in the agency whom the client will see (Entwistle, Sheldon, Sowden, & Watt, 1998). Clients can also be informed via brochures and Web sites, as mentioned above.

Written service agreements should be prepared for each client clearly describing agreed-on objectives as well as the consequences that will occur dependent on participation and outcome (e.g., return of a child), and copies should be given to the client. Such service agreements were recommended over a quarter of a century ago (Stein, Gambrill, & Wiltse, 1978) but are still not widely used. In service agreements I have seen, objectives are vague and there is no mention of the consequences to clients depending on outcome. This is a failure to involve clients as informed participants and, because objectives are vague, it is less likely that they can be systematically pursued.

IMPROVE INTERAGENCY COORDINATION OF SERVICES

Clients often receive multiple services from multiple agencies with little careful coordination, which results in a lack of sound decision making and the duplication of efforts. Effective coordination procedures should be established both within and between agencies.

PROTESTING DYSFUNCTIONAL GOVERNMENTAL REQUIREMENTS

Decisions made by governmental bodies may be more in the service of trying to protect politicians from blame than of helping children and families. Consider the Looking After Children system implemented across the United Kingdom in spite of no evidence that this would do more good than harm (Garrett, 1999). Consider also proposals for country-wide surveillance systems of children. Will these do more good than harm (Parton, 2006)? Those vitally interested in the welfare of children and families should take an active role in critiquing proposals that may waste money and result in harm to children. If many, including clients, act in concert, success in improving services will be greater.

CONCLUSION

Decision making is a key activity in child welfare. Research in child welfare as well as daily reports in our newspapers show that the quality of decision making is not what it should be; we can (and should) do better. We can identify and alter sources of avoidable error. There has been increased acknowledgment of gaps between what is claimed and what is done, encouraged by the process and philosophy of evidence-informed practice with its interest in transparency. Research in a variety of areas, including problem solving, decision making, and judgment, suggest valuable changes we can make, even within the current residual child welfare system. The development of processes and tools that can help staff to make well-informed decisions has been one of the advances over the past years.

Research in many fields highlights the importance of a *systemic* view in understanding both the potential for change and the obstacles. A residual approach focusing on parents as the source of the problem is greatly limited in potential to help families and children. One could argue that until we move away from such a child welfare system, little will change for the better. How can research findings regarding judgment, decision making, and problem solving be used if staff have no time to make sound judgments and/or do not have the autonomy to do so? Why train staff in effective assessment skills if they have neither the time nor the needed tools to use them? I suggest that the key route to improvement in the quality of decisions is greater attention to ethical obligations and our responsibility to take these seriously as emphasized in evidence-informed practice and policy (see chapter 3). Those with social work degrees and who belong to the National Association of Social Workers are bound by their professional code of ethics to help clients, to avoid harming them, to maximize self-determination including honoring informed-consent obligations, and to promote social justice. We can honor our ethical obligations by exposing the gaps between what is done and what is needed. We can decide that silence in the face of unmet needs is not an ethical option. Staff should join together with concerned others, including clients, and critically appraise the quality of services provided, compare this with what research suggests is effective, and widely disseminate "state-of-the-gap" reports. Agency staff and client advocacy groups could forge alliances with faculty in nearby universities who value honesty and transparency and work together to gather data to advocate for needed improvements.

This chapter is based in part on chapter 9 in E. Gambrill (2005). *Critical thinking in clinical practice* (2nd ed.). New York: Wiley.

References

American Psychiatric Association. (2000). *Diagnostic and statistical manual of mental disorders* (4th ed.). Washington, DC: American Psychiatric Association.

Baird, C., & Wagner, D. (2000). The relative validity of actuarial and consensus-based risk assessment systems. *Child and Youth Services Review, 22,* 839–871.

Baron, J. (1994). *Thinking and deciding.* New York: Cambridge University Press.

Baron, J. (2000). *Thinking and deciding* (3rd ed.). New York: Cambridge University Press.

Baron, J. (2005). Normative models of judgment and decision making. In D. J. Koehler & N. Harvey (Eds.), *The Blackwell handbook of judgment and decision making* (pp. 19–36). Oxford: Blackwell.

Beutler, L. E., Malik, M., Alimohamed, S., Harwood, T. M., Talebi, Z. H., Noble, S., & Wong, E. (2004). Therapist variables. In M. J. Lambert (Ed.), *Bergin and Garfield's handbook of psychotherapy and behavior change* (5th ed., pp. 227–306). New York: Wiley.

Bostock, L., Bairstow, S., Fish, S., & Macleod, F. (2005). *Managing risk and minimizing mistakes in services to children and families.* London: Social Care Institute for Excellence.

Budd, K. S., Poindexter, L. M., Feliz, E. D., & Naik-Polan, A. T. (2001). Clinical assessment of parents in child protection cases: An empirical analysis. *Law and Human Behavior, 25,* 93–108.

Ceci, S. J., & Bruck, M. (1995). *Jeopardy in the courtroom: A scientific analysis of children's testimony.* Washington, DC: American Psychological Association.

Chambers, D. W. (2003). Quackery and fraud: Understanding the ethical issues and responding. *Journal of the American College of Dentists, 70*(3), 9–17.

Clarkin, J. F., & Levy, K. N. (2004). The influence of client variables on psychotherapy. In M. L. Lambert (Ed.), *Bergin and Garfield's handbook of psychotherapy and behavior change* (5th ed., pp. 194–226). New York: Wiley.

Clements, R. V. (1995). Essentials of clinical risk management. In C. Vincent (Ed.), *Clinical risk management* (pp. 335–349). London: BMJ.

Coulter, A. (2002). *The autonomous patient: Ending paternalism in medical care*. London: Nuffield Trust.

Courtney, M. E., Needell, B., & Wulczyn, F. (2004). Unintended consequences of the push for accountability: The case of national child welfare performance standards. *Children and Youth Services Review, 26,* 1141–1154.

Dale, P., Green, R., & Fellows, R. (2005). *Child protection assessment following serious injuries to infants: Fine judgments*. Chichester, UK: Wiley.

Dawes, R. M. (1988). *Rational choice in an uncertain world*. Orlando, FL: Harcourt Brace Jovanovich.

DePanfilis, D., & Girvin, H. (2003). Investigating child maltreatment in out-of-home care: Barriers to effective decision-making. *Children and Youth Services Review, 27,* 353–374.

DeYoung, M. (2004). *The day care ritual abuse moral panic*. Jefferson, NC: McFarland.

Dingwall, R., Eekelaar, J., & Murray, T. (1983). *The protection of children: State intervention and family life*. Oxford: Basil Blackwell.

Dunning, D., Heath, C., & Suls, J. M. (2004). Flawed self-assessment: Implications for health, education, and the work place. *Psychological Science in the Public Interest, 5,* 69–106.

Durso, F. T., & Gronlund, S. D. (1999). Situation awareness. In F. T. Durso, R. S. Nickerson, R. W. Schvaneveldt, S. T. Dumais, D. S. Lindsay, & M. T. H. Chi (Eds.), *Handbook of applied cognition* (pp. 283–314). New York: Wiley.

Elstein, A. S., Shulman, L. S., Sprafka, S. A., Allal, L., Gordon, M., Jason, H., Kagan, N., Loupe, M. N., & Jordan, R. (1978). *Medical problem solving: An analysis of clinical reasoning*. Cambridge, MA: Harvard University Press.

Entwistle, V. A., Sheldon, T. A., Sowden, A. J., & Watt, I. A. (1998). Evidence-informed patient choice. *International Journal of Technology Assessment in Health Care, 14,* 212–215.

Farmer, E., & Owen, M. (1995). *Child protective practice: Private risks and public remedies*. London: Department of Health.

Feinstein, A. R. (1967). *Judgment*. Baltimore: Williams & Wilkins.

Feltovich, P. J., Spiro, R. J., & Coulson, R. (1989). The nature of conceptual understanding in biomedicine: The deep structure of complex ideas and the development of misconceptions. In D. A. Evans & V. L. Patel (Eds.), *Cognitive science in medicine: Biomedical modeling* (pp. 113–172). Cambridge, MA: MIT Press.

Fox, R. C., & Swazey, J. P. (1974). *The courage to fail*. Chicago: University of Chicago Press.

Gambrill, E. (2005). *Critical thinking in clinical practice* (2nd ed.). New York: Wiley.

Gambrill, E. (2006). *Social work practice: A critical thinker's guide* (2nd ed.). New York: Oxford.

Gambrill, E., & Goldman, R. (2004). *A qualitative review of parent training programs offered to parents in the child welfare system*. Unpublished manuscript, University of California, Berkeley.

Gambrill, E., & Shlonsky, A. (2000). Risk assessment in context. *Children and Youth Services Review, 22,* 813–837.

Gambrill, E., & Shlonsky, A. (2001). The need for comprehensive risk management systems in child welfare. *Children and Youth Services Review, 23*(1), 79–107.

Garrett, P. M. (1999). Mapping child-care social work in the final years of the twentieth century: A critical response to the "looking after children" system. *British Journal of Social Work, 29,* 27–47.

Gigerenzer, G. (2002). *Calculated risks: How to know when numbers deceive you*. New York: Simon & Schuster.

Gigerenzer, G. (2005). Fast and frugal heuristics: The tools of bounded rationality. In D. J. Koehler & N. Harvey (Eds.), *The Blackwell handbook of judgment and decision making* (pp. 62–88). Oxford: Blackwell.

Gilovich, T., & Griffin, D. (2002). *Introduction: Heuristics and biases: Then and now*. In T. Gilovich, D. Griffin, & D. Kahneman (Eds.), *Heuristics and biases: The psychology of intuitive judgment* (pp.1– 18). New York: Cambridge University Press.

Gilovich, T., Griffin, D., & Kahneman, D. (Eds.). (2002). *Heuristics and biases: The psychology of intuitive judgment*. New York: Cambridge University Press.

Glisson, C., & Hemmelgarn, A. (1998). The effects of organizational climate and interorganizational coordination on the quality and outcomes of children's service systems. *Child Abuse and Neglect, 22*(5), 401–421.

Gollwitzer, P. M., Bayer, U. C., & McCulloch, K. C. (2005). The control of the unwanted. In R. R. Hassin, J. S. Uleman, & J. A. Bargh (Eds.), *The new unconscious* (pp. 485–515). New York: Oxford University Press.

Gorman, D. M. (1998). The irrelevance of evidence in the development of school-based drug prevention policy, 1986–1996. *Evaluation Review, 22,* 118–146.

Gray, J. A. M. (2001). *Evidence-based health care: How to make health policy and management decisions* (2nd ed.). New York: Churchill Livingstone.

Greenhalgh, T., Robert, G., Macfarlane, F., Bate, P., & Kyriakidou, O. (2004). Diffusion of innovations in service organizations: Systematic review and recommendations. *Milbank Quarterly, 82,* 581–629.

Grove, W. M., & Meehl, P. E. (1996). Comparative efficiency of informal (subjective, impressionistic) and formal (mechanical, algorithmic) prediction procedures: The clinical-statistical controversy. *Psychology, Public Policy & Law, 2,* 293–323.

Hamm, R. M. (2003). Medical decision scripts: Combining cognitive scripts and judgment strategies to account fully for medical decision making. In D. Hardman & L. Macchi (Eds.), *Thinking: Psychological perspectives on reasoning, judgment and decision making* (pp. 315–345). New York: Wiley.

Hammond, K. R. (1996). *Human judgment and social policy: Irreducible uncertainty, inevitable error, and unavoidable injustice.* New York: Oxford University Press.

Hey, E. (2003). Suspected child abuse: The potential for justice to miscarry. *British Medical Journal, 327,* 299–300.

Hogarth, R. M. (2001). *Educating intuition.* Chicago: University of Chicago Press.

Howitt, D. (1992). *Child abuse errors: When good intentions go wrong.* New York: Harvester.

Kahneman, D. (1995). Varieties of counterfactual thinking. In N. J. Roese & J. M. Olsen (Eds.), *What might have been: Social psychology of counterfactual thinking* (pp. 375–396). Mahwah, NJ: Erlbaum.

Klein, G. A. (1998). *Sources of power: How people make decisions.* Cambridge, MA: MIT Press.

Koehler, D. J., & Harvey, N. (Eds.). (2005). *The Blackwell handbook of judgment and decision making.* Oxford: Blackwell.

Lerner, J. S., & Tetlock, P. E. (1999). Accounting for the effects of accountability. *Psychological Bulletin, 125,* 255–275.

Lindsey, D. (2004). *The welfare of children* (2nd ed.). New York: Oxford University Press.

Lipshitz, R. (1997). Naturalistic decision making perspectives on decision making. In C. Zsambok & G. Klein (Eds.), *Naturalistic decision making* (pp. 151–162). Mahwah, NJ: Erlbaum.

Loftus, E. F. (1980). *Memory: Surprising new insights into how we remember and why we forget.* Reading, MA: Addison-Wesley.

Loftus, E., & Ketcham, K. (1994). *The myth of repressed memory: False memories and allegations of abuse.* New York: St. Martin's.

Lynn, S. J., Lock, T., Loftus, E. F., Krackow, E., & Lilienfeld, S. O. (2003). The remembrance of things past: Problematic memory recovery techniques in psychotherapy. In S. Lilienfeld, S. J. Lynn, & J. M. Lohr (Eds.), *Science and pseudoscience in clinical psychology* (pp. 250–239). New York: Guilford.

Malm, K., Bess, R., Leos-Urbel, J., Geen, R., & Markowitz, T. (2001). *Running to keep in place: The continuing evolution of our nation's child welfare system.* Occasional Paper No. 54. Washington, DC: Urban Institute.

McDowell, B. (2000). *Ethics and excuses: The crisis in professional responsibility.* Westport, CT: Quorum.

Munro, E. (1999). Avoidable and unavoidable mistakes in child protection work. *British Journal of Social Work, 26,* 793–808.

Munro, E. (2004). A simpler way to understand the results of risk assessment instruments. *Children and Youth Services Review, 26,* 873–883.

National Patient Safety Foundation. 132 MASS MoCA Way, North Adams, MA, 01247: info@npsf.org

Nickerson, R. S. (1986). *Reflections on reasoning.* Hillsdale, NJ: Erlbaum.

Nickerson, R. S. (1998). Confirmation bias: A ubiquitous phenomenon in many guises. *Review of General Psychology, 2,* 175–220.

Nisbett, R., & Ross, L. (1980). *Human inference: Strategies and shortcomings of social judgment.* Englewood Cliffs, NJ: Prentice-Hall.

Orasanu, J., & Connolly, T. (1993). The reinvention of decision making. In G. Klein, J. Orasanu, R. Calderwood, & C. E. Zsambok (Eds.), *Decision making in action: Models and methods* (pp. 3–20). Norwood, NJ: Ablex.

Parton, N. (2006). *Safeguarding childhood: Early intervention and surveillance in a late modern society.* New York: Palgrave Macmillan.

Patel, V. L., & Zhang, J. (2007). Patient safety in health care. In F. T. Durso (Ed.), R. S. Nickerson, S. T. Dumais, S. Lewandowsky, & T. L. Perfect (associate eds), *Handbook of Applied Cognition* (2nd ed., pp. 307–331). New York Wiley.

Payne, J. W., & Bettman, J. R. (2005). Walking with the scarecrow: The information processing approach to decision research. In D. J. Koehler & N. Harvey (Eds.), *The Blackwell handbook of judgment and decision making* (pp. 110–132). Oxford: Blackwell.

Pelton, L. H. (1989). *For reasons of poverty: A critical analysis of the public child welfare system in the United States.* New York: Praeger.

Perkins, D. (1995). *Outsmarting IQ: The emerging science of learnable intelligence.* New York: Free Press.

Phillips, J. K., Klein, G., & Sieck, W. R. (2005). Expertise in judgment and decision making: A case for training intuitive decision skills. In D. J. Koehler & N. Harvey (Eds.), *The Blackwell handbook of judgment and decision making* (pp. 297–315). Oxford: Blackwell.

Popper, K. R. (1992). *In search of a better world: Lectures and essays from thirty years.* London: Routledge & Kegan Paul.

Popper, K. R. (1994). *The myth of the framework: In defense of science and rationality.* Edited by M. A. Notturno. New York: Routledge.

Praesidium Inc. *Abuse risk management.* 624 Six Flags Dr., Suite 110, Arlington, Texas 76011.

Pronin, E., Puccio, C., & Ross, L. (2002). Understanding misunderstanding: Social psychological perspectives. In T. Gilovich, D. Griffin, & D. Kahneman (Eds.), *Heuristics and biases: The psychology of intuitive judgment* (pp. 636–665). New York: Cambridge University Press.

Reason, J. (1997). *Managing the risks of organizational accidents.* Aldershot, England: Ashgate.

Reason, J. (2001). Understanding adverse events: The human factor. In C .Vincent (Ed.), *Clinical risk management: Enhancing patient safety* (2nd ed., pp. 9–30). London: BMJ.

Reder, P., Duncan, S., & Gray, M. (1993). *Beyond blame: Child abuse tragedies revisited.* New York: Routledge.

Roberts, D. (2002). *Shattered bonds: The color of child welfare.* New York: Basic.

Roediger, H. L., & Bergman, E. T. (1998). The controversy over recovered memories. *Psychology, Public Policy, & Law, 4,* 1091–1109.

Ross, L., & Ward, A. (1996). Naïve realism in everyday life: Implications for social conflict and misunderstanding. In T. Brown, E. Reed, & E. Turiel (Eds.), *Values and knowledge* (pp. 103–135). Hillsdale, NJ: Erlbaum.

Rzepnicki, T. L., & Johnson, P. R. (2005). Examining decision errors in child protection: A new application of root cause analysis. *Children and Youth Services Review, 27,* 393–407.

Salas, E., & Klein, G. (Eds.). (2001). *Linking expertise and naturalistic decision making.* Mahwah, NJ: Erlbaum.

Sherraden, M. (2002). *Asset-based policy and the Child Trust Fund.* St. Louis, MO: Center for Social Development, Washington University.

Shlonsky, A., & Wagner, D. (2005). The next step: Integrating actuarial risk assessment and clinical judgment into an evidence-based practice framework in CPS case management. *Children and Youth Services Review, 27,* 409–427.

Simon, H. A. (1990). Alternative visions of rationality. In P. K. Moser (Ed.), *Rationality in action: Contemporary approaches* (pp. 189–204). New York: Cambridge University Press.

Slovic, P., Finucane, M. N., Peters, E., & MacGregor, D. G. (2002). The affect heuristic. In T. Gilovich, D. Griffin, & D. Kahneman (Eds.), *Heuristics and biases: The psychology of intuitive judgment* (pp. 397–420). New York: Cambridge University Press.

Stanley, N., & Manthorpe, J. (Eds.). (2004). *The age of the inquiry: Learning and blaming in health and social care.* New York: Routledge.

Stein, T. J., Gambrill, E. D., & Wiltse, K. T. (1978). *Children in foster homes: Achieving continuity of care.* New York: Praeger Special Studies.

Tetlock, P. E. (2003). Correspondence and coherence: Indicators of good judgment in world politics. In D. Hardman & L. Macchi (Eds.), *Thinking: Psychological perspectives on reasoning, judgment and decision making* (pp. 233–250). New York: Wiley.

Wagner, D. (2003, December 3). Personal communication.

Wilkes, M. S., & Hoffman, J. R. (2001). An innovative approach to educating medical students about pharmaceutical promotion. *Academic Medicine, 76,* 1271–1277.

Wolf, S. H., Kuzel, A. J., Dovey, S. M., & Phillips, R. L. (2004). A string of mistakes: The importance of cascade analysis in describing, counting, and preventing medical errors. *Annals of Family Medicine, 2,* 317–326.

Woods, D. D., & Cook, R. I. (1999). Perspectives on human error: Hindsight biases and local rationality. In F. T. Durso, R. S. Nickerson, R. W. Schvaneveldt, S. T. Dumais, D. S. Lindsay, & M. T. Chi (Eds.), *Handbook of applied cognition* (pp. 141–171). New York: Wiley.

Working Group on Psychotropic Medications for Children and Adolescents. (2006). *Psychopharmacological, psychosocial, and combined interventions for childhood disorders: Evidence base, contextual factors, and future directions: Report of the Working Group on Psychotropic Medications for Children and Adolescents.* Washington, DC: American Psychological Association.

Young, J. H. (1992). *American health quackery.* Princeton, NJ: Princeton University Press.

11

Lessons from Research on
Decision Making

Eileen Munro

INTRODUCTION

Workers in child welfare services face many daunting decisions, whose consequences can be far-reaching. Some decisions, such as those about removing children from their parents, can literally make the difference between life and death for a child. Many have long-term implications for the safety and welfare of children and their families, including decisions, for instance, about whether to offer help and, if so, what type of help. Decisions are also daunting because they have to be made with imperfect knowledge. We have limited knowledge about how to identify dangerous families or how to assess their strengths and weaknesses; we have limited ability to help families solve their problems and function better. Decisions have to be made in conditions of uncertainty.

Research has been a valuable source of evidence about how we make decisions, and the first section of this chapter will summarize the findings on

the common errors of decision making and their implications for child welfare. Research, however, offers more than lessons about our failings; it offers ideas on how to improve decision making. In fact, it offers two contrasting models: one prescriptive and the other descriptive. The first draws on probability theory and proposes decision theory as the rational way of best computing the uncertainties faced in making a decision. The other relies on empirical studies of how people actually make decisions, in particular how experts make decisions that have a good level of accuracy, and describes how they reason critically and develop expertise.

The two approaches reflect a long-standing division in studies of human reasoning between the analytic and the intuitive, and their application in child welfare reflects a similar division between those who see progress being made through increasingly formal, analytic modes of reasoning and those who value intuition as an indispensable part of understanding and helping our fellow human beings—the classic art-science debate. In this chapter, however, they are not presented as rivals; the reader will not be asked to take sides. It will be argued that the differences between them are not, in practice, as stark as they seem at first sight and that they both offer valuable lessons for different decision-making scenarios in child welfare.

COMMON ERRORS IN DECISION MAKING

The Reluctant Decision Maker

Perhaps the research finding of most practical importance is that people are, in general, reluctant decision makers. Decisions can be intellectually and emotionally challenging to make, and people often choose the easier option of avoiding the challenge. The individual is "beset by conflict, doubts, and worry, struggling with incongruous longings, antipathies, and loyalties, and seeking relief by procrastinating, rationalizing, or denying responsibility for his own choices" (Janis & Mann, 1977, p. 15). This reluctance to be decisive has been clearly shown in studies of children who are in out-of-home care (Department of Health and Social Services, 1985; Sherman, Neuman, & Shyne, 1973; Vernon & Fruin, 1986). In this situation, the hardest decision to make is when to give up on hopes of reuniting the child with the birth family and to make alternative long-term plans, e.g., seeking adoptive parents. The decision is difficult partly for intellectual reasons: On the basis of limited evidence, workers have to estimate the likelihood of therapeutic efforts with the parents being successful enough for the child to return safely. But such decisions are also emotionally hard to make; they involve deciding to dash the hopes of birth parents for having their children returned to them. In such circumstances, it is perhaps not surprising to find that, without external pressure to decide, many workers avoid the difficult decision and allow the case to drift on with no clear long-term plans but a vague hope that the situation will improve. For the children, however, this drift is not benign but leaves many of them in settings where they have little security or permanence. In this study, their long-term outcomes were depressingly poor (Triseliotis et al., 1995).

To counter this tendency to avoid decisions, many strategies have been implemented in child welfare to encourage or compel workers to face the difficult decisions in a timely fashion. In the United States,

legislation has been created to ensure decisive action while, in the United Kingdom, clear timetables for decision making are prescribed by the central government. Although not required by statute, compliance is encouraged through the audit system that measures how well agencies have kept to the recommended time scales.

However, in implementing these strategies, it is important to remember how challenging people find it to make decisions, and the organization needs to acknowledge that making a decision is a major task requiring time and effort, not a routine administrative chore.

Tunnel Vision

Another common error is a tendency to consider only a narrow range of options when facing a decision. Sometimes this reflects a bias toward the one or two options that are familiar. Busy practitioners, for instance, can fall into fixed routines to save time and effort. These may work well enough for many families but can be a clumsy fit for some others. Some tendency to tunnel vision is almost inevitable in a busy working life, but it is beneficial for an individual or a team to be aware of the danger and set aside time for taking a broader look at the options for responding to families. Brainstorming about the services for a group of similar cases, for example, may bring to light concerns about the options currently available and the need to look for or develop new services.

Sometimes, tunnel vision results from the way the decision is initially presented. When it is framed as "we must do either A or B," the practitioner may fall in with this, forgetting to consider whether there are, in fact, other possibilities. In one child abuse tragedy in the United Kingdom, for instance, a young baby had been removed from her birth parents because of abuse and placed with a foster family. The quality of that family's level of care became problematic and the birth parents then put pressure on the social work team to agree to the baby's returning to them since the foster family was unsuitable. The records show that the practitioners' discussions focused on the choice between the birth parents and the foster family (the choice presented to them) without giving attention to the possibility of other placements, either in the extended family or in another foster family. Supervisors need to be aware of this vulnerability and pay attention to whether the way the decision is being formulated is distracting attention from other options.

Shortsightedness

People are prone to making shortsighted decisions, to thinking through the consequences only in the immediate future without considering what might happen in the longer term (Keller & Ho, 1988; Fischoff, 1996). While one can appreciate the pressures of practice that make this more likely, it is particularly problematic in children's services where we are concerned with children's long-term safety and welfare.

Taking a longer view requires practitioners to think about not only *possible* consequences but also how *probable* they are. This can challenge optimistic but vaguely thought-through hopes of providing effective help. Sometimes, for example, one finds a chronic neglect case where the parents have attended several series of parenting classes. Arranging another course of classes may solve the immediate problem of needing to take some action, but consideration of the probability of this having more success than previous courses forces practitioners to think about the possibility of failure and what they should plan to do if that happens.

Contingency plans are a major casualty of a shortsighted approach to decision making. By not thinking through what might happen, the possibility of the planned intervention not going according to plan tends to be ignored with no thought given to what might go wrong and how to deal with it.

Post Hoc and Satisficing Decision Making

Some might argue that these forms of decision making are not wrong, or at least not wrong in all circumstances. However, it is useful to include them here because they are very common ways of reaching a decision.

The first—post hoc reasoning—involves making a decision and then looking for reasons to justify it retrospectively (Klein, 2000, p. 11). This sounds as if the person decides first and thinks later but, in essence, the decision maker is relying on intuition to reach a decision and adopting a more analytic approach only when prompted to do so later. Its implications for improving decision making in child welfare are explored in more detail later in this chapter when we discuss pattern recognition.

Satisficing is a concept created by Simon (1957) after studying everyday decision makers in action. Most theorists assume that the decision maker wants to or should make the "best" decision, but Simon reports that many are not optimizers but have a lower level of aspiration. They want a decision that is "good enough," above a certain level but not necessarily the best. Therefore, they consider a list of options but, unlike the optimizer who goes through the whole list, they stop as soon as they reach one that seems good enough. Simon argues that this approach is very sensible since it is more economical of time and resources. He describes human rationality as "bounded," i.e., limited in capacity, and satisficing matches human reasoning ability better than does the ideal model.

Applying these ideas to the child welfare scenario of deciding on a suitable foster home, the optimizer would consider all of the families available while the satisficer would have some basic criteria and, as soon as a family matching these criteria was found, the search would end. This raises questions of what standard we should aim at when placing children—the best or good enough?—and whether there are some decision points in child welfare where "good enough" is too low an aspiration. But Simon's arguments about economy of time and effort also strike home in the context of the busy schedules in which most child welfare decisions have to be made. When offering advice on improving decision making, it is essential to make a realistic estimate of the demands it will make on the decision maker and tailor advice to a practical form.

THE FORMAL (ANALYTIC) MODEL OF DECISION MAKING

Turning now to the first of the two models of decision making, decision theory offers a definition of a "rational" decision and a method for computing which decision meets that criterion (Hammond et al., 1999). It aims to capture the reasoning that is implicit in intuitive decision making but makes it explicit and open to the formal application of probability theory. The rational decision to make is the one with the highest expected utility value. To explain what this means, a brief account of decision theory is necessary (see Munro, 2002, chapter 7, for a fuller account). The components of a decision are:

Options

Decision theory conceptualizes a decision as choosing between a number of possible courses of action.

In deciding on whether to remove children from their birth family, for instance, a number of options can be listed. This should not be seen simply as a choice between *either* removing them *or* leaving them at home; both categories contain a number of different options, for example, leaving them at home with close monitoring or a clear treatment plan for the father's depression, removing them and placing them with a grandparent, or removing them and placing them with a foster family, etc.

Decision theorists encourage the decision maker to spend some time on listing options, which counteracts any tendency to tunnel vision.

Consequences

Decision making is made difficult because each option can lead to a number of possible consequences, including the child left at home may be abused again or the family may respond well to therapeutic efforts so the child is safe and well.

The requirement to think through the possible consequences of each option encourages the decision maker to speculate further into the future and so counteracts the tendency to shortsightedness.

The Probability of Each Consequence

For each consequence, the decision maker needs to estimate how likely it is to happen. What is the probability of this treatment program working with this family? Although empirical evidence on the effectiveness of the treatment program can inform this estimate, the judgment is essentially an intuitive appraisal of both the empirical evidence and local knowledge—about specific factors in the family, such as their willingness to cooperate in the past, and specific factors in the treatment team, such as how experienced or busy they are, perhaps. However, by putting a number to the estimate—between 0 (impossible) and 100% (certain to happen)—the decision maker makes the intuitive judgment public and open to critical discussion by others.

I have found an exercise that helps to bring home to people the desirability of using numbers instead of words to talk about probabilities. I give an audience a list of common phrases about probability—likely to happen, almost certain, improbable, highly possible—and ask them individually to consider how they use these terms and give a number to reflect what they mean. The results have consistently shown vast discrepancies in what people mean, with probabilities varying at least 40 points for most phrases. Even a phrase like "almost certain" gets numbers ranging from 70 to 99%. This brings home the scope for misunderstanding when trying to communicate about probabilities with others in the child welfare field using the ambiguous terms of everyday speech.

The Utility Value of Each Consequence

How desirable or undesirable is each consequence? In child welfare, we rarely face a simple choice between a good and a bad consequence. All carry a mixture of pros and cons. Leaving children with their birth parents has many benefits as well as some risk of abuse; moving them to a new home carries greater safety but also many risks of broken attachments. Money also plays a part in weighing the utility value since it is a finite resource. A program of support may increase the probability of safe care for one child but make such resource demands that it limits help for other families.

The process of assigning a utility value draws on many factors but includes an element of moral judgment. There is a moral value to keeping a child safe; there is a moral value to maintaining families. Practitioners may rationally disagree on the assignment of values in a particular case and so may rationally disagree on the utility value of the consequences.

The Expected Utility Value of an Option

For each consequence, the expected utility value can be obtained by multiplying the probability and the desirability. By summing all of the consequences of an option, an overall value for that option is obtained. The rational decision maker then chooses the option with the highest expected utility value.

Decision theory offers a formal way of dealing with the problem of comparing an outcome which may be highly desirable (e.g., the child is safe at home) but also, in this case, of low probability with an alternative choice which is less desirable (the child is safe in a new setting) but more probable.

Decision theory can be taught to practitioners to use for themselves. Even without applying it in its full detail, the process of unpacking the decision process clarifies the issues raised in a particular case. Decision theory also forms the basis for a number of decision-making aids that have been developed. One feature that is common to strategies for improving decision making is that of structuring the problem so that the complex task can be broken down into smaller, simpler tasks. Some decision-making instruments also do the mathematics for the practitioner; once the relevant variables have been given values, a decision is identified as the best.

Decision theory seems to me to illustrate how analytic and intuitive reasoning should not be seen as alternatives. It clearly adopts an analytic approach in that it attempts to make every step of the reasoning public and defensible. Yet it also draws on intuitive judgment in gauging the probability and the value of a consequence. However, by encouraging the practitioner to make those intuitive judgments explicit, it makes them amenable to critical scrutiny by others, including the family in question. By asking the practitioner to assign numbers to key variables, it also makes it possible to apply probability theory formally. In view of the evidence on the frailty of people's intuitive ability to reason about probabilities (Dawes, 1994; Grove & Meehl, 1996), this is highly desirable. There is now convincing evidence that actuarial methods of risk assessment are superior to clinical judgment at predicting children's future safety (Shlonsky & Wagner, 2005), but this does not mean that clinical judgment is excluded. In general, actuarial risk assessment instruments contain variables that can only be scored by clinical judgment (Wagner, Johnson, & Johnson, 1998).

DESCRIPTIVE ACCOUNTS OF DECISION MAKING

A radically different picture of human decision making is provided by research on how people actually make decisions in professional settings. This body of literature also has much to offer child welfare as a source of ideas about improving decision making.

Studies of, for instance, firefighters and naval officers have identified a key feature as being the importance of pattern recognition (Hutchins, 1995; Klein, 2000). In contrast to the model prescribed by decision theory of a professional taking an analytic, thoughtful approach, these studies found that professionals were making swift, intuitive judgments that a case fit a certain pattern. On the basis of this categorization, they developed a plan of action: If the fire is of this sort, then we need to . . .

Although an intuitive sizing up of the situation played a major role, professionals were not relying on intuition in a blind, uncritical way. Classifying a fire as of a certain type implied what Klein calls a "story," a prediction of the way that it should behave in the future and how it should react to attempts to extinguish it. Consequently, the fire officers were able to test their intuitive judgment by seeing whether the fire behaved as expected. Unexpected features would lead them to question whether it really did fit this pattern and possibly reassign it.

Klein's account has many resemblances to studies of medical decision making (Dreyfus & Dreyfus, 1986). Dreyfus and Dreyfus studied how doctors' reasoning changed as they became more expert at making diagnoses. As novices, they tended to use checklists or a formal assessment model and work systematically through, collecting a large body of data before attempting to conjecture what was wrong with the patient. As they became more expert, they were found to be relying more on intuitive appraisals made very early in their contact with the patient. Just like the firefighters, they recognized a pattern of signs and symptoms that led them to suspect a particular diagnosis. Again, their intuitive judgment was not accepted blindly but led to testable expectations of what other signs there would be or how the patient would progress.

It is easy to see similarities between these professional groups and practitioners in children's services, and this body of literature provokes a number of questions about how best to help novices to develop expertise.

If pattern recognition is an important skill in child welfare, then how can we best develop it? In medicine, students are exposed to numerous case examples and observe their seniors interviewing a patient and making a diagnosis. Research has found that some experts are better than others in retrospectively analyzing their intuitive reasoning to help students learn (Donovan, Bransford, & Pellegrino, 1999). In social work, discussions with supervisors, colleagues, and teams are the major forums for public consideration of thinking about a case. Some use is made of videos, but if developing pattern recognition is the aim, consideration needs to be given to building up libraries of videos that will expose the student to large numbers of similar cases, helping them to hone their intuitive ability to pick out patterns.

Pattern recognition, however, needs to be used critically and students also need to be taught how to develop their hypothesis so that they can test it further and, if necessary, reject it. Klein's work showed that firefighters were using their initial decision to set priorities about what needed to be done first, to know what further information they needed, and to give them an idea about what to expect next. By recognizing a situation as of a particular type, they also knew what line of action to take. He used the concept of a story to describe how they used their imaginations to develop the pattern they had recognized and to check their decision both in the past and the future: If this is a fire of type X, then earlier signs should have been . . . and we are likely to see . . . happening soon. This concept of a story seems to resemble what can happen in casework supervision where the worker has offered her or his assessment of a family and the supervisor is helping to think through whether that assessment can take account of all the known facts and whether there is additional information that can test it.

One factor to consider in encouraging critical practice is whether services are organized in a way that enables individuals to check their decisions and learn from their successes and mistakes. In the United Kingdom, the tendency in recent years has been to divide up the process of working with a family between different teams. A family might, for example, at first referral come into contact with a duty social worker. If the concern is deemed to merit further investigation, the case will be transferred to an assessment team. If they decide that it is a significant case of abuse needing intervention, then it will again be handed on to a long-term team. While there may be good managerial reasons for this segmentation, it raises questions about whether workers are getting good enough feedback on their decisions to learn. If the importance of feedback is recognized, then it is possible to build in mechanisms for letting workers know what subsequently happens to families for whom they have made significant decisions so that they are able to know whether the case has proceeded as they expected.

The potential importance of pattern recognition as an element of expertise also raises questions about the use of assessment and decision-making instruments in child welfare designed to improve reasoning skills about what type of problem the family has, for example, or what type of service should be offered. These have mainly taken the form of assessment frameworks and structured decision-making guides. Like the checklists used by novice doctors, these un-doubtedly have their place, but what is their impact on professional development? How are practitioners, in practice, using them? Do they work systematically through the list before trying to reach a decision, as a novice does, or do they, as they become more experienced, start to develop conjectures about what type of case they are facing and let this guide their subsequent questioning and thinking? Which method leads in the long term to the best results for children?

WHICH MODEL SHOULD WE FOLLOW?

The two approaches to studying human reasoning have often, in practice, been portrayed as rivals, presenting the reader with an either-or decision. However, the above accounts have highlighted how the analytic approach of decision theory still requires clinical judgment in assigning values to some of the variables. The more intuitive pattern-recognition approach, too, can be seen on closer study to be open to use in a more analytic and critical manner. Instead of judging the two models in absolute terms, it is perhaps more constructive to assess their relative strengths and weaknesses and then ask the more complex and interesting question: What type of reasoning is best suited to which decision-making points in child welfare?

A clear merit of the formal, decision theory approach is its openness. The stages of the decision are clear to see and can be understood and challenged by others. The knowledge on which it is drawing is made explicit and can be checked. In view of the evidence on our intuitive fallibility in dealing with probabilities, its use of formal computation is also a strength.

Applying decision theory, however, takes considerable time and effort. This is clearly justified when making some of the major decisions in child welfare that are of long-term significance to a child and family. These major decisions also require public scrutiny, and decisions made with the decision theory framework are more readily explained and justified in a court setting.

However, daily child welfare practice involves countless minor decisions. In the course of an interview with a family, for example, a worker will make a number of micro-decisions—about whom to talk to, what to prioritize, how challenging to be. In these settings, the merits of intuitive decision making are more apparent. It draws on the practitioner's expertise and wisdom about human nature and is carried out with the speed that is required by the circumstances. Intuitive judgment, though, is vulnerable to a number of biases and shortcuts that can lead to significant errors in child welfare decisions (Munro, 1999). The research on pattern recognition and on how expertise is developed offers useful lessons on how to encourage practitioners to develop their intuitive skills and use them more critically.

In trying to improve decision making in child welfare, it would be a mistake to focus solely on the major decision points, such as whether to open a case for investigation or whether to remove a child from the birth family. These are important decisions that need to be held to the highest standard, and formal methods of decision making seem appropriate. But day-to-day practice is full of other, perhaps less significant, but far more common decisions. Helping practitioners to make those decisions to a higher critical standard and to develop their expertise in sizing up a situation quickly is an equally important strand in improving outcomes for children.

References

Dawes, R. (1994). *House of cards: Psychology and psychotherapy built on myth*. New York: Free Press.

Department of Health and Social Services. (1985). *Social work decisions in child care: Recent research findings and their implications*. London: HMSO.

Donovan, M., Bransford, J., & Pellegrino, J. (1999). *How people learn: Bridging research and practice*. New York: National Academies Press.

Dreyfus, H., & Dreyfus, S. (1986). *Mind over machine: The power of human intuition and expertise in the era of the computer*. New York: Free Press.

Fischoff, B. (1996). The real world: What good is it? *Organizational Behaviour and Human Decision Processes, 65*, 232–248.

Grove, E., & Meehl, P. (1996). Comparative efficiency of informal (subjective, impressionistic) and formal (mechanical, algorithmic) prediction procedures. *Psychology, Public Policy and Law, 2*(2), 293–323.

Hammond, J., Keeney, R., & Raiffa, H. (1999). *Smart choices: A practical guide to making better decisions*. Boston: Harvard Business School Press.

Hutchins, E. (1995). *Cognition in the wild*. Cambridge, MA: MIT Press.

Keller, L., & Ho, J. (1988). Decision problem structuring: Generating options. *Systems, Man and Cybernetics, 18*, 715–728.

Klein, G. (2000). *Sources of power: How people make decisions*. Cambridge, MA: MIT Press.

Janis, I., & Mann, L. (1977). *Decision making: A psychological analysis of conflict, choice and commitment*. New York: Free Press.

Munro, E. (1999). Common errors of reasoning in child protection. *Child Abuse and Neglect, 23*(8), 745–758.

Munro, E. (2002). *Effective child protection*. London: Sage.

Sherman, E., Neuman, R., & Shyne, A. (1973). *Children adrift in foster care*. New York: Child Welfare League of America.

Shlonsky, A., & Wagner, D. (2005). The next step: Integrating actuarial risk assessment and clinical judgment into an evidence-based practice framework in CPS case management. *Children and Youth Services Review, 27*, 409–427.

Simon, H. (1957). *Models of man: Social and rational*. New York: Wiley.

Triseliotis, J., Sellick, C., & Short, R. (1995). *Foster care: Theory and practice*. London: British Agencies for Adoption and Fostering.

Vernon, J., & Fruin, D. (1986). *In care: A study of social work decision-making*. London: National Children's Bureau.

Wagner, D., Johnson, K., & Johnson, W. (1998). *Using actuarial risk assessment to target service interventions in pilot California counties*. Paper presented at the 13th National Roundtable on CPS Risk Assessment, San Francisco, CA.

12

Assessing Risk Throughout the Life of a Child Welfare Case

Judith S. Rycus
Ronald C. Hughes

Child welfare practice is, first and foremost, about making effective case decisions that promote the safety of abused and neglected children. Effective child protective services intervention depends upon the accurate and timely identification of children who have been maltreated and who remain at high risk of future harm, and intervening to promote their safety. The accurate identification and assessment of risk are essential prerequisites to achieving outcomes of child safety, and the assessment of risk must be appropriately integrated throughout the continuum of child protective services assessment and decision-making strategies.

Historically, the challenge of making effective decisions for maltreated children and their families has been a source of considerable concern for the profession. Recently, these concerns have become more pronounced in response to the increasing complexity of child welfare practice. Most child welfare agencies face severely limited resources, high rates of staff turnover, burdensome work loads, and the difficulty of

responding to increasingly complex social problems, such as substance abuse and domestic violence. Many child welfare agencies are hard pressed to respond effectively because of the high volume of complex referrals of families with wide-ranging and often disparate needs (Children's Research Center, 2005).

Child welfare decisions are inherently complex because so little is certain about human behavior. This is especially evident when we consider decisions intended to protect children from future maltreatment, while concurrently promoting permanence and well-being. Assuring children's safety requires the ongoing and vigilant assessment of conditions that may place children at high risk of both imminent and future harm, and intervening to reduce these risks in a manner that also minimizes trauma, strengthens families, promotes placement stability and permanence, and provides environments that sustain children's well-being. Achieving this balance requires the identification of both the unique contributors to risk in a family and the family strengths and other mitigating conditions

201

that can be applied and enhanced to reduce risk at all stages of case involvement. While assuring children's *immediate* safety has recently been placed at the center of the national dialogue about best child welfare practices, we cannot forget the equally important goal of addressing the conditions that place children at high risk of future harm, thus enabling us to close cases with reasonable assurance that the children will remain safe in the future, even after agency involvement has been terminated.

As is true for many of life's most important and challenging decisions, accurately identifying children at risk of serious harm requires considerable skill in gathering, analyzing, weighing, and synthesizing a large body of relevant information and then applying this information to guide decision making. Some protective decisions are made more challenging because they require the capacity to estimate the likelihood of a future occurrence of child maltreatment—no easy task in even the best of circumstances. The environment in which protective services decisions are made may also be quite enigmatic and opaque. Vital case information may not be readily available, and child safety decisions must often be made in very short time frames. While the risk to children in some families may be quite apparent, in most families this is not the case. The higher the degree of uncertainty in the decision-making environment, the greater the potential for decision-making errors (Baird & Rycus, 2005).

In attempts to address these challenges and to promote reliable and valid decision making, child welfare organizations have adopted a variety of decision-making models and associated tools to help identify and respond to children at high risk of serious harm from maltreatment. Unfortunately, the utility of these models and tools has been inconsistent and their effectiveness compromised by a variety of factors (Rycus & Hughes, 2003; DePanfilis, 1994). Uniform, relevant, well-articulated criteria on which to base child welfare case decisions have not always been developed or incorporated into decision-making tools (Lyons, Doueck, & Wodarski, 1996; Cicchinelli & Keller, 1990). The tools used by many child welfare agencies to guide critical case decisions often demonstrate poor reliability and validity, or have simply never been researched and tested prior to their implementation (Gambrill & Shlonsky, 2000; Pecora, Whittaker, Maluccio, & Barth, 2000; Johnson, 1996; McDonald & Marks, 1991). There are wide variations in the decision-making criteria utilized by various tools de-

signed to achieve similar objectives. There is also a lack of consistency in decision-making methods and processes among caseworkers using the same models and tools (Gambrill & Shlonsky, 2000; Cicchinelli, 1995). Many staff using these tools have not been fully trained in their use (Hughes & Rycus, 2007; Rycus & Hughes, 2003; Pecora et al., 2000; Curran, 1995). Some child welfare systems have failed to fully and properly implement the decision-making tools they have adopted in policy (Ruscio, 1998; English & Pecora, 1994), and decision-making tools that have been implemented in practice are at times used for purposes other than those for which they were developed (Rycus & Hughes, 2003). Thus, the hoped-for improvement in outcomes for children and families from the use of standardized decision-making models and tools has often been elusive.

A more fundamental problem complicates child welfare decision making. The very concepts of *risk* and *safety* are not always defined or used logically and consistently by the child welfare field. While the meanings of *risk* and *safety* might seem self-explanatory, these terms have been used in diverse contexts with often inconsistent and idiosyncratic meanings, resulting in considerable confusion among child welfare professionals and increasing the difficulty of communicating our methods and intentions to our partner agencies, constituents, and communities (Rycus & Hughes, 2003).

In common vernacular English, the word *safety* has the opposite meaning of the word *risk*, much as *health* has the opposite meaning of *illness*. The dictionary definition of *safety* is a state of being free from injury, risk, danger, or harm, while *risk* is defined as the chance of injury, damage, or harm (Webster's, 1983). Following this logic, we would expect the child welfare field to define *risk factors* as conditions that threaten or undermine child safety, and *safety factors* to be conditions that offset or mitigate risk. However, in some widely used child safety models, *safety factors* are considered conditions that *increase* risk rather than conditions that mitigate it, and *safety assessments* typically completed at the time of intake are misconstrued as novel enterprises, not recognized as a specialized type of risk assessment concerned specifically with determining the *imminent* risk of serious harm to a child from maltreatment.

Child safety is an overarching outcome toward which all child protective services are directed. It is not possible to achieve this outcome unless we accurately identify and respond to the risk factors that undermine children's safety in all stages of case involvement. Achieving an outcome of child safety requires both an accurate understanding of the concepts of risk and safety and the mastery of those assessment and decision-making strategies which are best suited to identify and deal with risk at various stages of case involvement.

The purpose of this chapter is to outline the typical decision-making points in child protective services, to delineate how risk is assessed at each stage of case involvement, and to consider the types of strategies and tools that are best suited to promote accurate, consistent, and timely decisions that reduce risk and promote child safety. The first part of this discussion provides a brief review of some of the principles of effective decision making and how these apply to the design and structuring of decision-making tools and models to achieve our objectives. The second will review the ways in which risk is considered at each stage in the decision-making continuum.

DECISION-MAKING TECHNOLOGIES AND TOOLS

Developing relevant and effective decision-making tools to increase the accuracy and timeliness of child welfare case decisions is the first challenge in improving child welfare decisions. A field of study referred to as *decision theory* provides a framework for the development of tools and models that can achieve these objectives (Baird & Rycus, 2005).

According to Dawes (1993), the first step in developing any decision-making protocol is to break large, complex constructs, such as risk, into their component parts. Thus, while recognizing and responding to risk are essential throughout the life of a case, the manner in which risk is assessed and addressed will depend on differing degrees of urgency and the amount and type of information available at different stages of case involvement. Assessing risk to promote children's safety is an iterative process that incorporates a series of individualized assessments and decisions, performed in a prescribed order, to achieve a series of discrete case objectives (Baird & Rycus, 2005).

Consider the broad range of decisions that must be made during the life of a child welfare case, all of which require various calculations of risk and all of which directly impact children's safety. Does this referral rise to the threshold to warrant a child protective services investigation, or should the family be diverted to other community providers? How quickly should the agency respond to the referral, and is a formal child protective services investigation warranted? Do any of the children in the complaint appear to be at high risk of imminent harm and in need of immediate protection? Can a child be safely left at home while the caseworker gathers more complete information? What immediate interventions are necessary to protect the child? Is out-of-home placement the only means of assuring a child's safety? What is the likelihood that a child may be seriously harmed in the future? Should the case be opened by the agency for ongoing child protective services? What kind(s) of services and interventions will be needed to reduce risk and promote a child's long-term safety? Can a child in out-of-home care be safely reunified with his or her family? Can we close the case with reasonable assurance that the child will remain safe into the future?

One of the challenges in answering these questions is that differing amounts and quality of information will be available at each case decision point. An initial telephone referral will typically offer less essential information than what can be learned during an initial on-site assessment, and both will provide less essential information than a thorough assessment and/or investigation. The decision at each point must be as accurate as possible, given the respective urgency of each decision point and the limited availability of essential information at many decision-making points. There are obvious benefits to having decision-making tools and guidelines that prioritize the collection of information that is both essential to the decision and also likely to be available in the time frame in which the decision must be made. By structuring both the collection and analysis of this information, an effective tool can guide the decision maker to the best possible decision, given the limitations in the decision-making environment.

A related challenge is the difficulty in knowing exactly what information is most pertinent to the particular decision to be made. In child welfare, as in other human services disciplines, there is a natural tendency to gather as much information as possible about families, their historical background, their current circumstances, and the events that prompted the referral. However, especially at certain decision-making points in child welfare, too much data can create an information overload that reduces both the timeliness and the quality of decisions. Proponents of decision theory divide data into two general categories: *information* and *noise*. Information reduces uncertainty. Noise is superfluous information not directly relevant to the problem being addressed, and it can actually increase uncertainty and misjudgment. What constitutes information and what constitutes noise will change depending upon the circumstances and the nature of the decision to be made. However, whenever noise is mistaken for information, it undermines rather than enhances decisions. The most problematic noise consists of factual information that intuitively seems important and relevant, but that doesn't substantially inform the specific decision to be made. Research can help to identify and quantify the particular types of information that are most relevant at each decision point, thereby allowing the collection of this information to be formally incorporated into standardized decision-making models, essentially separating information from noise. This both enhances the quality of a decision and reduces the amount of time necessary to reach it (Baird & Rycus, 2005).

Effective decision-making tools have certain characteristics. They must be easy to understand and to use without oversimplifying either the criteria or the methods of analysis to the point that conclusions will be either ambiguous or inaccurate. Further, the criteria, items, or measures in a tool must be defined clearly enough to be recognized and understood by a wide variety of users, thereby promoting consistency among users (sometimes referred to as *inter-rater reliability*) in the use of the protocol. The criteria or items in the tool must actually measure what they are intended to measure; there must be a relationship of each measure to the specific outcome we are seeking to influence. Tools must be subjected to scientific assessment to establish their reliability and validity, thus assuring that they function in the intended manner. Finally, the type of tool must always be appropriate to the achievement of the stated objective. As the decision-making goal or objective changes, both the criteria incorporated in the tool and the methodology needed to arrive at a decision may also change.

Decision-making tools are often formalized into broader decision-making *models*. These are formal frameworks which typically include a series of individual tools that promote decisions to achieve predetermined objectives at different decision points throughout the life of a case. Decision-making models structure the decision-making process in the following manner. First, they formalize the collection, recording, and analysis of the specific information determined to be most relevant to the decision at hand. This is accomplished by incorporating predetermined and carefully defined questions, items, or measures in a protocol, thereby focusing on important information while reducing or eliminating noise. Second, the sequence in which the information should be considered is often predetermined to promote the most logical analysis and synthesis of the information. Third, each piece of information may be assigned a level of priority or a weight, based on the relative importance of the information to the desired decision. And finally, protocols often guide decision makers to arrive at the most accurate and relevant conclusions based on the answers or responses to the items in the tool (Baird & Rycus, 2005).

Two types of decision-making tools are particularly useful in structuring decisions related to assessing risk in child maltreatment. One such tool, called a *decision tree*, provides a logical framework for decision making by identifying, articulating, and prioritizing very specific criteria needed to reach a decision and then structuring the assessment into a logical series of questions, the answers to which lead to subsequent questions, until a decision is reached. In its most basic form, the criteria in a decision tree are presented as questions that can be answered either yes or no. Depending on the answer, the decision maker is directed to consider the next relevant question, until, at the end of a line of inquiry, a specific deductive decision is provided. Decision tree technology forms the framework for two common types of safety-related decision protocols widely used by child welfare agencies: establishing priorities for agency response at the time of referral and assessing the risk to a child of imminent serious harm (often called a *safety assessment*).

A second type of tool, sometimes referred to as an *additive index*, is better suited to the translation of empirical research findings into simple decision tools. Actuarial risk assessment is one application of this technology, in which a level of risk of future maltreatment in families must be assigned, based on evident family characteristics and environmental circumstances. Researchers can determine the combination of criteria that can demonstrate the highest levels of consistency and accuracy in estimating the likelihood of future recurrences of maltreatment. Actuarial tools will be discussed more fully later in this chapter.

Effective tools and models for assessing risk in child welfare must be developed to collect and utilize the most relevant and accessible information, in realistic time frames, to accomplish the objectives specific to each decision-making point throughout the life of the case. By simplifying and structuring the decision-making process, these decision-making tools and protocols can also increase effectiveness and efficiency by helping to eliminate noise and enhance the reliability and validity of the resulting decisions, thereby improving the capacity of all case decisions to promote children's safety.

STRATEGIES TO ASSESS RISK THROUGHOUT THE LIFE OF A CASE

Screening at Intake

Risk is considered for the first time during the initial child protective services referral. Intake screeners must consider the information provided by the reporter to determine whether the referral is appropriate for agency follow-up and to prioritize the urgency of initiating an agency response when one is indicated.

To determine the need for agency involvement, and to properly establish a priority for agency response, intake screeners must determine whether any of the children in the family appear to be at imminent risk of serious harm. Unfortunately, at this stage, substantial information may not be readily available and its relevance and accuracy may be difficult to determine, as reporters may lack detailed knowledge about the child or family, may not know the most relevant information to provide, may be reticent to disclose sensitive personal information, may be wrong about the facts or dynamics of maltreatment, or may have incentives to misreport. Agency screeners must be able to recognize family dynamics and environmental conditions that elevate the risk of imminent harm to children and must be able to engage, prompt, and encourage reporters to disclose as much essential information as possible in what is typically a brief telephone contact. Screeners must try to collect information that can help to determine the type and severity of the alleged maltreatment, the scope and type of apparent injuries or illness, the child's age and degree of vulnerability, the child's location, the availability and capacity of the primary caregivers, whether the alleged perpetrator is known and has unrestricted access to the child, and whether other competent adults are acting to protect the child. Referencing historical case information from agency databases can help to establish a pattern of risk in the referred family and can also help screeners to interpret the context and potential meaning of current information.

Many agencies have adopted screening protocols to guide this assessment. Because of the challenges of quickly assessing risk without a face-to-face contact, the criteria used to establish response times should be based on a few essential facts that can be reliably obtained in a brief telephone interview. The optimal screening protocol is composed of simple and straightforward questions that promote relevance and accuracy in the information collected to inform screening decisions. A decision tree is a very effective strategy for screening tools because it incorporates and prioritizes the critical and visible risk factors that should be considered in the priority decision, and it dictates the order in which these questions should be considered, leading the screener to a presumptive decision regarding the necessary speed of the response. "Yes" responses to several criteria suggest increased potential for imminent harm, warranting a more rapid agency response. Among these are significant reported injuries to a child, a need for immediate medical care, a child victim who is younger than 7 or limited by disability, the use of severe or bizarre disciplinary measures, prior allegations of maltreatment in the family, and unhindered access by the alleged perpetrator to the child (Children's Research Center, 2002).

Safety Assessment: Further Assessing Risk of Imminent Harm

The purpose of formal safety assessment is to accurately identify children who are at high risk of imminent, serious harm in order to prompt immediate protective interventions to assure their safety. Threats of imminent serious harm in child welfare cannot be ignored, and time is the enemy in such circumstances. In the time it takes to collect essential information about family circumstances to inform the development and implementation of an individualized service plan, serious harm or even death to a child may occur. By identifying children at imminent risk, we can act to assure their safety while more detailed assessment and case planning activities are being completed.

Determining the level of imminent risk to children in their own families requires the rapid and accurate identification of specific conditions that create high-risk situations for children. These conditions are widely referred to as *safety threats*. Two criteria define safety threats: their high potential for resulting in serious harm to children and the immediacy of the threat. While many risk factors in families may negatively affect children's safety and well-being over time, for a condition to qualify as a bona fide safety threat, it must have reached a sufficient threshold to place a child in *imminent danger of serious harm*. Safety assessment can best be thought of as an environmental scan for the conditions and dynamics most highly capable of inflicting serious harm to a child in the immediate future. Safety assessment is not designed to determine the potential for maltreatment in a more extended future, nor to gather thorough data regarding the complex and individualized dynamics contributing to maltreatment in each family, even though safety assessment information is generally relevant to and can enhance these assessments at a later time.

To determine the presence of safety threats, safety assessments routinely probe for information about recent or current serious child maltreatment, negligent or abusive parenting practices, out-of-control family violence, very hazardous environmental conditions, and other family circumstances with high potential for serious harm to a child. Identifying the presence of any of these conditions is sufficient to register a potential safety concern, indicating there is a high potential for imminent serious harm to a child. In these cases, the agency must act immediately to assure the child's safety.

While many conditions are serious enough to threaten the safety of all children, the degree of potential injury or harm to an individual child may vary, depending on the child's individual susceptibility. A higher degree of susceptibility is often referred to as *child vulnerability*. More-vulnerable children may include those who are very young and/or developmentally immature, children who have physical or mental disabilities or developmental delays, children who may be physically or medically fragile, children who may be temperamentally or behaviorally more challenging to parent, and children who may be less able to communicate their needs or to seek help. Because of their developmental immaturity in all domains, children under the age of 6 are categorically more vulnerable to the harmful effects of maltreatment, and infants under the age of 2 are extremely vulnerable. In very young children, both physical abuse, such as shaking or battering, and neglect, including malnutrition and lack of supervision, are more likely to result in permanent injury,

brain damage, seriously impaired development, or death. Unfortunately, the same factors that make children more vulnerable to maltreatment may also increase the likelihood that they will be maltreated, since their care may be inherently more difficult, challenging, and stressful to their caregivers. Therefore, knowing the age, condition, and developmental level of alleged child victims is essential in helping to determine the level of heightened risk of imminent serious harm in their current situations.

A significant challenge during the intake assessment is to determine whether children in unsafe environments must be removed and placed in out-of-home care in order to assure their safety. When one considers the potential detrimental consequences to both children and their families of traumatic separation and out-of-home placement, the importance of seeking strategies to maintain children's safety in their own families becomes more evident.

Historically, emergency placement decisions at intake were based primarily on the clinical judgment of investigating caseworkers, without the benefit of consistent and standardized guiding criteria or tools. A study conducted by Rossi and colleagues (1996) found little agreement among child welfare workers or child welfare experts about the specific conditions that warranted the removal of children from their homes. The researchers concluded that the likelihood of a child being taken into custody varied widely, depending largely on the individual assigned to handle the case. Wide discrepancies in placement decisions, and resulting negative consequences for many children and families, prompted the development of formal protocols to help investigators protect children from imminent harm while also promoting stability and permanence. Safety assessments were intended to provide caseworkers with information that would promote the least traumatic and least intrusive interventions, preferably applied in the child's own home, that would successfully protect them from imminent harm (DePanfilis & Scannapieco, 1994).

To protect children in their own homes, caseworkers must identify the strengths, resources, and protective capacities present in the immediate family, extended family, and community environment that can be marshaled and enhanced to mitigate and control threats to child safety, thus reducing the degree of imminent risk to the child. Safety assessment protocols generally include a series of questions intended to determine the degree to which both immediate and extended family members have the willingness and the capacity to protect the children from serious harm. Such supportive resources in the family and their broader social network may not always be immediately evident to the caseworker and may only be discerned after in-depth conversations with family members. Optimally, intake caseworkers can help family members to recognize and fully understand the nature of existing safety threats and the elevated cause for concern and can support them in devising their own solutions to keep the children safe. However, irrespective of the degree of family involvement, caseworkers must always maintain an active monitoring and supportive role to assure that family members sustain their protective functions and that the safety threats are sufficiently controlled to maintain the child safely in the home.

If effective solutions can be identified and mobilized to protect a child at home, the trauma of out-of-home care can often be prevented, sometimes without extensive or costly agency intervention. However, if sufficient protective factors do not exist within the family system, the worker must identify agency resources and interventions that can protect the child at home until the investigation and assessment can be completed. Such protective interventions might include protective or respite day care, homemaker or home management services, crisis intervention services, respite kinship care, and other in-home interventions to stabilize family situations and provide essential care to the children. If in-home agency and community-based interventions cannot protect the child, then the final option, removal and placement, is considered.

Because of the importance of asking the right questions in the right order, a modified decision tree is often used as the format for safety assessment tools and protocols. The decision tree model directs the assessor to consider essential information in a prescribed order to determine whether the children are at high risk of imminent harm, whether a family's protective capacities or agency interventions can protect the children at home, or whether out-of-home placement is the only intervention that can assure the children's safety. By structuring the assessment questions in the proper sequence, a decision to remove and place a child in out-of-home care will be made only after the child has clearly been identified as being at high risk of imminent harm, and after all other options to protect the child at home have been considered and ruled out. The internal structure of a decision tree

helps to establish safeguards that concurrently assure children's safety while helping to deter inappropriate or premature placement decisions.

The specific interventions selected to protect children at the time of intake, whether in their own homes or in out-of-home placement, should be formalized and documented in a *safety plan*. The short-term nature of safety plans promotes the effective protection of the children until further risk assessments and family assessments can be completed and longer-term service and/or placement plans can be implemented to reduce risk more permanently.

While safety assessments are most frequently conducted during initial investigations, children's safety status may change at any time because of the protean and often volatile nature of child maltreatment. Caseworkers must therefore be continually vigilant in recognizing and assessing safety threats in open child welfare cases. Continual attention to identifying children at risk of imminent serious harm must be incorporated into all family contacts and casework activities throughout the life of the case and in all placement settings.

Formal Risk Assessment: Estimating the Likelihood of Future Harm

Formal risk assessment technologies have been adopted by a majority of child welfare jurisdictions to assist caseworkers in estimating, as quickly and accurately as possible, the probability of a future occurrence of child abuse or neglect in a family.

In contrast to safety assessment, which seeks to determine the risk of imminent serious harm to children, formal risk assessment attempts to estimate the probability of serious harm to children in a more protracted future—generally calculated in weeks and months, rather than in the hours and days most relevant for safety assessments. As one component of a continuum of safety assurance strategies, formal risk assessment can help agencies to provide ongoing protective services to those families in which recurrences of maltreatment are most likely, while lower-risk families who need developmental, supportive, or preventive services can be referred to other providers, with reasonable confidence that future occurrences of maltreatment are unlikely (Hughes & Rycus, 2007; Rycus & Hughes, 2003).

Accurately estimating the probability of a future occurrence of child maltreatment is a very complicated undertaking, considering the interacting effects of multiple factors contributing to child maltreatment. Because of this complexity, it is extremely difficult to accurately estimate the likelihood of future maltreatment in a family using clinical judgment alone.

Utilizing well-tested, reliable, and valid risk assessment protocols in child welfare practice can promote assessments of risk and subsequent case decisions that are more consistent, more accurate, less biased, and therefore, more just for families and children than less structured and more informal clinical risk assessments by individual caseworkers (Hughes & Rycus, 2007; Rycus & Hughes, 2003). When properly used and uniformly implemented, reliable and valid risk assessment tools have been demonstrated to positively impact child safety by allocating services and strengthening case monitoring for those families at highest risk of future maltreatment, subsequently reducing the rates of recurrence (Children's Research Center, 2005; Baird & Wagner, 2000). Formal risk assessment should therefore be a fundamental component of any continuum of decision-making strategies to promote child safety.

Formal child welfare risk assessment protocols can generally be classified into two types: *actuarial* tools and *consensus* or *matrix* tools. Actuarial risk assessment instruments are developed using sophisticated research and statistical methods to allow more accurate estimations of the likelihood of a future event. Actuarial risk assessment tools incorporate criteria in combinations that have been found through intensive statistical analysis to have high levels of association with recurrences of maltreatment. The presence of specific groupings of conditions in families can be demonstrated to increase the likelihood that maltreatment will recur (Rycus & Hughes, 2003; Baird & Wagner, 2000). The scoring for each measure in the instrument, and the overall risk level for a family, are dictated by the previously determined statistical weighting of the variables included in the model (Children's Research Center, 2005; Shlonsky & Wagner, 2005; Macdonald, 2001; Gambrill & Shlonsky, 2000; Ruscio, 1998; Johnson, 1996). Ultimately, the stronger the statistical association between the combined variables in an instrument and the subsequent occurrence rates of future maltreatment, the greater the instrument's capacity to consistently and accurately classify families into various levels of risk.

Consensus models, by contrast, rely on professional agreement about which variables or condi-

tions are most highly associated with recurrences of child maltreatment (Hughes & Rycus, 2007; Rycus & Hughes, 2003; Pecora et al., 2000). There is a large body of professional child welfare literature that identifies and describes the individual, family, and environmental conditions found to be associated with different forms of child maltreatment. Consensus risk assessment models presume that when these factors are present, the likelihood of future maltreatment is increased. Consensus models typically rely on the clinical judgment of caseworkers to rank a risk level for each variable and to determine a level of future risk based on the presence or absence of these combined variables in a particular family.

Historically, there has been considerable confusion in the child welfare field about the appropriate use of consensus. Rather than reflecting consistent conclusions from a body of empirical data, consensus has been used to reflect the negotiated opinions of whatever group of experts or professionals is convened to develop or to modify a risk assessment tool. Ad hoc committees of practitioners are asked to consider and discuss their judgments and opinions, and try to reach agreement on the criteria, definitions, and rating methods that should be included in the tool. Referring to this process as generating consensus, further refining the model, or addressing a jurisdiction's unique circumstances gives apparent validity to a process that is notoriously subject to error and bias (Hughes & Rycus, 2007, Rycus & Hughes, 2003; Macdonald, 2001; Gambrill & Shlonsky, 2000; Ruscio, 1998; Dawes, Faust, & Meehl, 1989). A variety of factors can negatively impact the accuracy and objectivity of these judgments, including errors in information processing; personal beliefs, history, and preconceptions; selective attention; faulty memory; lack of knowledge; and organizational pressures to negotiate mutually agreeable compromises (Whitaker, Lutzker, & Shelley, 2005; Gambrill, 2003; Gambrill & Shlonsky, 2000; Munro, 1999).

There is a large body of literature describing both actuarial and consensus risk assessment models, as well as some research that compares their respective reliability and validity (Bay Area Social Services Consortium, 2005; Baird & Wagner, 2000; Baird, Wagner, Healy, & Johnson, 1999; Lyons et al., 1996). A formal risk assessment model's reliability and validity provide the litmus test of its effectiveness. The higher a model's reliability and validity, the more likely it is to promote the consistent collection of accurate information about the condition being examined, ultimately promoting more consistent and accurate conclusions regarding potential risk (Whitaker et al., 2005; Shlonsky & Wagner, 2005; Macdonald, 2001; Johnson, 1996). Conversely, risk models that lack reliability or validity formalize and sustain the collection of inconsistent and inaccurate data and promote faulty decision making using these data (Macdonald, 2001; Gambrill & Shlonsky, 2000; Ruscio, 1998).

Research has repeatedly demonstrated the superior reliability, validity, and performance of actuarial tools over consensus-based tools in estimating the likelihood of future events (Bay Area Social Services Consortium, 2005; Shlonsky & Wagner, 2005; Munro, 2004; Macdonald, 2001; Gambrill & Shlonsky, 2000; Baird & Wagner, 2000; Baird et al., 1999; Ruscio, 1998; Grove & Meehl, 1996; Dawes, Faust, & Meehl, 1993; Dawes, 1993). Further, the preponderance of the research literature continues to raise serious questions about the reliability and validity of many of the risk assessment models and instruments currently used by child welfare agencies, particularly consensus-based models (Bay Area Social Services Consortium, 2005; Shlonsky & Wagner, 2005; Macdonald, 2001; Baird & Wagner, 2000; Pecora et al., 2000; Gambrill & Shlonsky, 2000; Baird et al., 1999; Lyons et al., 1996; Camasso & Jagannathan, 1995).

It must be cautioned, however, that accurately *classifying* a particular family as high risk does not mean we can accurately *predict* whether or not an actual maltreatment event will occur (Children's Research Center, 2005; Shlonsky & Wagner, 2005; Munro, 2004; Baird & Wagner, 2000). Even though the words *prediction* and *classification* are often used interchangeably in the risk assessment literature, actuarial risk assessment instruments simply categorize or classify families into groups based upon a higher or lower probability that maltreatment will recur. Classifying a family as high risk connotes a higher probability—not a certainty—that maltreatment will recur. In fact, a large percentage of families classified as high risk do not subsequently abuse or neglect their children (Baird & Wagner, 2000). However, as indicated earlier, identifying families who are at higher risk allows child welfare agencies to allocate necessary services and resources more efficiently and to monitor these families more closely to prevent a recurrence of maltreatment.

Formal risk assessment, therefore, has a limited, albeit very important purpose in the continuum of decision-making strategies to protect children who are at high risk of serious harm. At the completion of an initial assessment or investigation, child welfare agencies must decide which families should be served and monitored by ongoing protective services, which families can be referred for alternative response or to other community providers for supportive services, and which families need no services and whose referrals can be closed. This decision, generally called the *case disposition*, is most appropriately made based on the likelihood of future serious harm to a child from maltreatment. Children who are at high risk of serious future harm are most appropriately served under the umbrella of child protective services, with ongoing monitoring and supervision in addition to more intensive and sustained services directed toward reducing risk and promoting children's safety over the long term. Other families with service needs, but for whom the probability of future maltreatment is low, are often better served in the larger human services community or by child welfare agencies under the umbrella of preventive or supportive family services rather than mandatory child protection. In many agencies, the decision to refer families to *alternative response* programs is made based on data from a reliable and valid risk assessment that indicates the family to be at relatively low risk, irrespective of its current service needs.

Comprehensive Family Assessment: Identifying Factors That Sustain Risk

Child abuse and neglect are called the *presenting problems* of child welfare. They are the visible symptoms of complex personal, family, environmental, and social conditions that, together, compromise families' ability to safely care for their children. The conditions that underlie and perpetuate child maltreatment are variously called *risk factors*, *risk contributors*, or *maltreatment contributors*. Families also have individual and collective strengths and resources, sometimes called *protective capacities*, that can be marshaled to counteract and mitigate risk factors. The ultimate goal of casework intervention is to identify, strengthen, and support the continued development of inherent or nascent family strengths and protective capacities as means of reducing or eliminating risk, thus reducing the likelihood of future recurrences of maltreatment in the family. Individualized services and supports to families can be effective means of helping them to assure their children's safety over the longer term, even after their cases have been closed by the child welfare agency.

Each family presents a unique combination of interacting problems, needs, resources, and strengths. By examining the dynamic interplay of contributing and mitigating factors in each family, caseworkers and family members can select the most appropriate services and interventions to reduce risk and to strengthen the protective capacities in a family. The most appropriate service interventions to meet a family's individual needs become formalized in the case plan, which outlines the case objectives, services to be provided, activities of each participant, and estimated time frames for completion. The case plan is the blueprint for services, and the family assessment assures that case plan activities remain focused and directed toward reducing and eliminating risk factors and strengthening family members' protective capacities, thereby promoting children's safety over the longer term.

Many agencies have adopted formal protocols to assist in collecting and evaluating the most pertinent information about each family prior to selecting service interventions and activities. The use of structured family assessment protocols can not only promote consistency in the assessment criteria, but can also assure that the most relevant criteria related to child safety are considered in the greatest scope and depth.

Differentiating Safety, Risk, and Family Assessments

There has historically been considerable confusion about the structures, criteria, and purposes of various tools used to guide decision making at different stages of case assessment and intervention. Part of the confusion is derived from the fact that the same risk factors are often reexamined and reevaluated at different decision-making points. However, the focus, emphasis, and depth of these assessments will vary depending on the objectives of the assessment, the intended use of the data, and the urgency of the decision. This point can be best illustrated using a case example.

Parental substance abuse has often been associated with several forms of child maltreatment and is widely considered to be a primary risk factor for future child maltreatment. It is thus incorporated into the majority of child welfare assessment protocols. However, the manner in which substance abuse is addressed and the impact it has on the decision-making process will change depending on the stage of the assessment and the decision that the data are intended to support.

As indicated above, the principal purpose of safety assessment is to identify children who are at high risk of imminent serious harm, allowing the agency to take immediate steps to protect them. In this context, assessment questions related to substance abuse seek to determine whether and how a parent's substance abuse poses a safety threat to the children, potentially causing them imminent serious harm. Substance abuse constitutes a safety threat if a parent is physically or psychologically unavailable or incapable of meeting a child's basic survival needs; if a parent's judgment is significantly impaired; if substance abuse results in volatile, irrational, or aggressive behavior, placing the children in potentially dangerous circumstances; or if it results in an otherwise hazardous and dangerous living or social environment. Identifying safety threats is necessary in order to properly intervene to control them and to assure children's safety in the short term. At this stage of case involvement, interventions are not intended to bring about longer-term change. In our case example, safety interventions would attempt to mitigate the negative effects of parental substance abuse on children's immediate safety, not to produce more permanent changes in parental behavior or patterns of substance abuse.

By contrast, formal risk assessment is intended to accurately estimate the probability of future serious harm from maltreatment, regardless of whether the children are at imminent risk. Because parental substance abuse has been strongly associated with recurrences of both abuse and neglect, it is included as a criterion in most formal risk assessment instruments. To complete a risk assessment, workers must identify the presence and scope of substance abuse in the family, but it is not necessary to fully understand the dynamics that underlie and support its continuance. The extent to which substance abuse increases future risk is determined by the statistical formulas inherent in the tool itself. Formal risk assessment data are used primarily to inform (not dictate) the case disposition, including whether a family's case should be opened and whether it should be served in the child protective services agency or referred to community providers.

Identifying the presence and impact of parental substance abuse, as completed during safety and risk assessments, is insufficient for case planning purposes. At this later stage of casework, the goal is to develop an individualized service plan that can directly target the particular family conditions that underlie and increase risk, to generate changes that reduce risk, and to help families sustain changes into the future. In this context, the family and environmental dynamics that underlie parental substance abuse must be fully explored and understood, as well as other potentiating problems or mitigating strengths, in order to develop a relevant case plan and to select the most appropriate service interventions. Services may vary dramatically for substance-abusing parents in different circumstances. For example, a parent who uses drugs to counteract feelings of anxiety or depression may require very different services than a parent heavily involved in a drug subculture, or one who deals drugs as a primary source of income. Still different services might be provided to treat substance abuse associated with posttraumatic stress disorder (PTSD) or bipolar disorder, or substance abuse by a teenage mother who uses drugs in an attempt to gain acceptance from her peer group. Since the intended outcome of ongoing services is long-term change, data collected during the family assessment must be broader in scope and more thorough than that needed to complete either safety or risk assessments.

Assessing Risk at Reunification and Case Closure

While the case goal for most children in out-of-home placement is reunification with their families, premature or inappropriate decisions to reunify children can potentially compromise both their immediate and future safety. Children can usually be returned home when identified safety threats have been significantly reduced or eliminated, or are being monitored and well controlled by family protective capacities or other in-home safety interventions. However, this does not suggest that cases can be closed immediately after reunification, even when the current family environment is considered to be safe for the children. Prior to closing a case, it must be determined that the risk of future harm has also been significantly reduced, thereby increasing the likelihood that the family environment is likely to remain safe over time. Prior to deciding to reunify, caseworkers and families should complete a reassessment of risk which includes reassessing the family's progress in completing case plan activities and determining whether these have effectively reduced risk and strengthened family protective capacities as they were intended.

Further, the post-reunification period is a critical time for continued monitoring to identify the reemergence of safety threats. Reunification can present a variety of challenges for families, particularly when the children have been out of their homes for more than a few days or weeks. Both children and families may have experienced significant disruptions during the time the child was in placement. These discontinuities can make the reestablishment of stable family relationships considerably more difficult, can create increased stress in the family, and can present a variety of challenges for reunifying the family (Rycus & Hughes, 1998). Because of the many complexities inherent in reunification, families may need intensive supports and services to sustain child safety and placement stability, both at the time of reunification and for extended periods after reunification. Prematurely closing cases, or closing them without an ongoing plan to assure continuing safety, can increase the risks to the children of future maltreatment.

CONCLUSION

Assessing risk throughout the life of a child welfare case is an iterative process and a key to improving child safety in the child welfare system. Although the goal of assessing risk is assuring children's safety throughout the life of a case, the objectives of each assessment change from decision point to decision point, and distinct tools have been developed to facilitate these different functions, even though they often contain similar criteria. These tools must be implemented in a logical sequence to promote ongoing attention to the factors that increase risk and the factors that mitigate it at all phases of case involvement, allowing child welfare professionals to make the most effective decisions to assure children's safety in a timely manner. Continuing research to validate and further refine these decision-making tools and models and to assure their effective and consistent implementation in practice are essential to helping us achieve safety and permanence for maltreated children.

References

Albers, M., & Roditti, M. (2004). *Management values and decision making tools: Nuts and bolts of risk assessment in California*. Berkeley, CA: Bay Area Academy.

Baird, C. (1997, August). Child abuse and neglect: Improving consistency in decision-making. *NCCD Focus*. San Francisco: National Council on Crime and Delinquency, 1–15.

Baird, C., & Rycus, J. (2005, Fall–Winter). The contribution of decision theory to promoting child safety. *APSAC Advisor, 16–17*, 2–10.

Baird, C., & Wagner, D. (2000). The relative validity of actuarial and consensus-based risk assessment systems. *Children and Youth Services Review, 22*(11–12), 839–871.

Baird, C., Wagner, D., Caskey, R., & Neuenfeld, D. (1995). *The Michigan Department of Social Services structured decision making system: An evaluation of its impact on child protection services.* Madison, WI: Children's Research Center.

Baird, C., Wagner, D., Healy, T., & Johnson, K. (1999, November–December). Risk assessment in child protective services: Consensus and actuarial model reliability. *Child Welfare, 78*(6), 723–749.

Bay Area Social Services Consortium. (2005, July). Risk and safety assessment in child welfare: Instrument comparisons. *Evidence for Practice: An Executive Summary, Issue 2.* Berkeley: University of California School of Social Welfare.

Camasso, M., & Jagannathan, R. (2000). Modeling the reliability and predictive validity of risk assessment in child protective services. *Children and Youth Services Review, 22*(11–12), 873–896.

Cash, S. (2001). Risk assessment in child welfare: The art and science. *Children and Youth Services Review, 23*(11), 811–830.

Children's Research Center. (2002). *Structured decision making (SDM) assessment profiles: Family risk and needs at investigation and case opening.* Madison, WI: Author.

Children's Research Center. (2003). *California structured decision making. Risk assessment revalidation: A prospective study.* Madison, WI: Author.

Children's Research Center. (2005). *Structured Decision Making™ in child welfare.* Madison, WI: Author.

Cicchinelli, L. (1995, Winter). Risk assessment: Expectations and realities. *Risk Assessment* [Special issue]. *APSAC Advisor, 8*(4), 3–8.

Cicchinelli, L., & Keller, R. (1990, June). *A comparative analysis of risk assessment models and systems: Final report.* Grant No. 90-CA-1302. Lakewood, CO: Applied Research Associates.

Dawes, R. (1993, June 9). Finding guidelines for tough decisions. *Chronicle of Higher Education,* A40.

Dawes, R., Faust, D., & Meehl, P. (1989). Clinical versus actuarial judgment. *Science, 243,* 1668–1674.

Dawes, R., Faust, D., & Meehl, P. (1993). Statistical prediction versus clinical prediction: Improving what works. In G. Keren & C. Lewis (Eds.), *Handbook for data analysis in the behavioral sciences: Methodological issues.* Hillsdale, NJ: Erlbaum.

DePanfilis, D., & Scannapieco, M. (1994, May–June). Assessing the safety of children at risk of maltreatment: Decision-making models. *Child Welfare, LXXIII*(3), 229–245.

DePanfilis, D., & Zuravin, S. (2001). Assessing risk to determine the need for services. *Children and Youth Services Review, 23*(1), 3–20.

Doueck, H., English, D., DePanfilis, D., & Moote, G. (1993, September–October.) Decision-making in child protective services: A comparison of selected risk-assessment systems. *Child Welfare, LXXII*(5), 441–453.

English, D., & Pecora, P. (1994, September–October). Risk assessment as a practice method in child protective services. *Child Welfare, LXXIII*(5), 451–473.

Falco, G., & Salovitz, B. (1997). *Clinical versus actuarial risk assessment in child protective services: Results from recent research in New York.* Paper presented at the 11th Annual CPS Roundtable on Risk Assessment, San Francisco, CA.

Gambrill, E. (2003). Evidence-based practice: Sea change or the emperor's new clothes? *Journal of Social Work Education, 39*(1), 3–23.

Gambrill, E., & Shlonsky, A. (2000). Risk assessment in context. *Children and Youth Services Review, 22*(11–12), 813–837.

Gambrill, E., & Shlonsky, A. (2001). The need for comprehensive risk management systems in child welfare. *Children and Youth Services Review, 23*(1), 79–107.

Grove, W., & Meehl, P. (1996). Comparative efficiency of informal (subjective, impressionistic) and formal (mechanical, algorithmic) prediction procedures: The clinical-statistical controversy. *Psychology, Public Policy, and Law, 2*(2), 293–323.

Hughes, R., & Rycus, J. (2007). Issues in risk assessment in child protective services. *Journal of Public Child Welfare, 1*(1), 85–116.

Johnson, W. (1996). Risk assessment research: Progress and future directions. *Protecting Children, 12*(2), 14–19.

Johnson, W. (2004). *Effectiveness of California's child welfare Structured Decision Making™ model: A prospective study of the validity of the California Family Risk Assessment.* Anaheim, CA: Author.

Lyons, P., Doueck, H., & Wodarski, J. (1996). Risk assessment for child protective services: A review of the empirical literature on instrument performance. *Social Work Research, 20*(3), 143–155.

Macdonald, G. (2001). Risk assessment and decision making. In *Effective interventions for child abuse and neglect: An evidence-based approach to planning and evaluating interventions,* 269–284. Chichester, UK: Wiley.

Marks, J., & McDonald, T. (1989). *Risk assessment in child protective services: Predicting recurrence of child maltreatment*. Portland: National Child Welfare Resource Center for Management and Administration, University of Southern Maine.

McDonald, T., & Marks, J. (1991). A review of risk factors assessed in child protective services. *Social Services Review*, 65, 112–132.

Meehl, P. (1954). *Clinical vs. statistical prediction: A theoretical analysis and a review of the evidence*. Minneapolis: University of Minnesota Press.

Munro, E. (1999). Common errors of reasoning in child protection work. *Child Abuse & Neglect*, 23(8), 745–758.

Munro, E. (2004). A simpler way to understand the results of risk assessment instruments. *Children and Youth Services Review*, 26, 873–883.

Munro, E. (2005). Improving practice: Child protection as a systems problem. *Children and Youth Services Review*, 27, 375–391.

Pecora, P., Whittaker, J., Maluccio, A., & Barth, R. (2000). *The child welfare challenge: Policy, practice, and research* (2nd ed.). New York: de Gruyter.

Rossi, P., Schuerman, J., & Budde, S. (1996). *Understanding child maltreatment decisions and those who make them*. Chicago: University of Chicago, Chapin Hall Center for Children.

Ruscio, J. (1998, May). Information integration in child welfare cases: An introduction to statistical decision making. *Child Maltreatment*, 3(2) 143–156.

Ryan, S., Wiles, D., Cash, S., & Siebert, C. (2005). Risk assessments: Empirically supported or values driven? *Children and Youth Services Review*, 27, 213–225.

Rycus, J., & Hughes, R. (1998). *Field guide to child welfare, I-IV*. Washington, DC: Child Welfare League of America.

Rycus, J. S., & Hughes, R. C. (2003). *Risk assessment: Policy white paper*. Columbus, OH: North American Resource Center for Child Welfare, Center for Child Welfare Policy.

Shlonsky, A., & Wagner, D. (2005). The next step: Integrating actuarial risk assessment and clinical judgment into an evidence-based practice framework in CPS case management. *Children and Youth Services Review*, 27, 409–427.

Wagner, D., Johnson, K., & Caskey, R. (1999, June). *Family Independence Agency of Michigan: Safety assessment validation report*. Madison, WI: Children's Research Center.

Wagner, D., & Meyer, B. (1998). *Using actuarial risk assessment to identify unsubstantiated cases for preventative intervention in New Mexico*. 12th National Roundtable on CPS Risk Assessment, held in San Francisco, CA. Madison, WI: Children's Research Center.

Webster's New Universal Unabridged Dictionary. (1983). 2nd ed. New York: Simon and Schuster.

Wells, S. (1995, Winter). Introduction. *Risk Assessment* [Special issue]. *APSAC Advisor*, 8(4), 1.

Whitaker, D., Lutzker, J., & Shelley, G. (2005). Child maltreatment prevention priorities at the Centers for Disease Control and Prevention. *Child Maltreatment*, 10(3), 245–259.

13

Improving Social Work Practice Through the Use of Technology and Advanced Research Methods

Ira M. Schwartz

Peter R. Jones

David R. Schwartz

Zoran Obradovic

INTRODUCTION

The social work profession and the social welfare field claim to have embraced the concept of evidence-based practice. They also claim they are quick to adopt innovative methods and practices for delivering services. Despite the rhetoric, there is mounting evidence that social work policy makers and practitioners are slow in taking advantage of breakthroughs in knowledge and in technological and research advances that are becoming commonplace in such fields as engineering, health care, and education. Unfortunately, while the social welfare field lags behind others, the consumers of social services are the ones who suffer, not the professionals.

This chapter focuses on the application of technology and advances in research to social work practice. Currently, technology in social welfare is mainly used for administrative and financial purposes. In addition, the social work profession has debated the question of whether the Internet should be used as a tool for delivering services, particularly counseling services.

The *Journal of Technology in Human Services'* three most popular articles to date address this very topic: "Offering Social Support via the Internet: A Case Study of an Online Support Group for Social Workers" (Meier, 2000), "Counseling and Technology: Some Thoughts About the Controversy" (Abney & Maddux, 2004), and "With a Little Help from My Friends: Children, the Internet and Social Support" (Tichon & Shapiro, 2003). While the use of technology for these functions is important, far greater potential lies in using robust technologies to mine and generate valuable data and information for professionals that will enhance their ability to deliver services more efficiently and effectively. Also, the use of sophisticated and advanced research protocols, which are more commonly used in such fields as engineering, epidemiology, and medicine, have the potential to lead to more-promising service interventions and programs, particularly when such protocols are integrated with the technology infrastructure that is now available to us.

TECHNOLOGY AND SOCIAL WELFARE: STATE OF THE ART AND OPPORTUNITIES

As stated above, the use of technology in social welfare has largely been confined to administrative and financial areas. For example, in the child welfare field, the federal government has invested billions in encouraging states to develop state automated child welfare information systems, more commonly referred to as SACWIS. These efforts have resulted in essentially two things. First, states have been required to collect uniform data on children in their public child welfare systems and to submit such data in aggregate form to the federal government. The states can also use the data for their own policy, administrative, and planning purposes. The data collected by the states are quite basic and consist of such things as the number of reported child maltreatment complaints, the number of complaints that are substantiated, the number of children placed in foster care, the length of time children are in placement, how often children are returned home, how often they are returned to foster care, the number of children waiting to be adopted, how long children have been waiting to be adopted, and how many children actually get adopted. The other development prompted by SACWIS is that states have invested time and effort in converting data and information from their written case records into an automated data system.

Although these developments represent improvements because of the historically poor state of child welfare data, they are of limited value. The collecting of uniform data simply allows the federal government to monitor broad general trends in child welfare nationally and in each state, provided that the data the federal government receives are accurate and timely. At the state level, states can use these data to monitor similar trends and, hopefully, use the information for policy and planning purposes. The automated case records systems that have been developed have yet to realize their potential and are proving to be difficult to keep updated.

Unfortunately, the large SACWIS information systems are of little or no use to frontline child welfare workers, foster parents, and adoptive parents. In fact, these systems are considered more of a burden to frontline social workers because they have to spend what they believe to be an excessive amount of time filling out forms or inputting data and case record information that appears to have little utility for their work with clients.

PROMISING TECHNOLOGICAL DEVELOPMENTS

As stated earlier, the social welfare field has been slow to embrace the use of technology and advanced research methods commonly used in other fields (e.g., engineering, computer sciences, and the health sciences). One of the best examples of this is in the area of risk assessment. Social scientists have long been concerned with the problem of accurately assessing and predicting the prospects or likelihood of various forms of human behavior. This is of particular concern in the field of child maltreatment, where social workers are faced with making decisions that could affect the life of a child. For example, when allegations of child maltreatment have been investigated and been proven to have taken place, social workers are often confronted with having to decide whether to let the abused or neglected children continue to live with their abusing or neglectful parent(s), or to remove the children from their home and place them in a safe environment (e.g., shelter facility, relative's home, or foster home).

Currently, the most commonly used tools upon which social workers draw to assist them in making these critical decisions are risk assessment instruments that are based on actuarial models or consensus of "professional opinion" models (Schwartz, Kaufman, & Schwartz, 2004). The best available research on such models suggests they are not much better than a flip of the coin with respect to predicting and assessing risk. Gambrill & Shlonsky (2000), for example, conclude that while actuarial models are somewhat better than consensus-based models, they are still far less than satisfactory. Yet, despite the existence of recent research suggesting that far more sophisticated, accurate, and predictive instruments can be developed utilizing neural networks, the child welfare establishment clings to the same old tools that have been in use for nearly four decades. The attraction the child welfare establishment has for these obsolete and dangerous relics is difficult to comprehend, let alone explain. However, it is an indication that the social welfare field is not as committed to evidence-based practice as many of the professionals in the field claim to be.

Risk assessment is only one area where technological advancements have been made. Another is education. Artificial intelligence–based communications software, including the use of robotics, is being used to provide diagnostic tutoring and assessment services to children, to assist in learning-disability screening, and to deliver teacher-coaching services to individuals who need to prepare for and pass state teacher certification examinations. The federal government's No Child Left Behind legislation mandates that states must have fully qualified teachers in the classroom within a certain specified period of time in order to continue receiving federal financial aid. As of 2006, none of the states had met the federal standards. The provision of artificial intelligence–based tutoring services on-line and using robotics represent promising ways for states to increase the number of qualified teachers in classrooms. In addition, the commonwealth of Pennsylvania will soon be using an artificial intelligence and robotics application to assist its citizens in using Web-based portals so they can access educational resources more easily and quickly. This same technology will also be used to get feedback on a real-time basis from consumers about the portals they used in order to learn about how helpful they were.

Health care is another area where technology is being developed to deliver services to patients. Some examples include using technology to secure informed consent from patients and to provide health education services to them. For example, Web sites already exist where individuals can access information about health care and things they need to do to develop and maintain a healthy lifestyle. However, these Web sites can become and sometimes are a significant burden for the health care practitioners and hospital staff charged with answering the numerous message postings. Also, software applications are being developed that assist in disease management with patients. For example, child and teen obesity are now recognized as very serious health issues that need to be addressed. Software applications are being developed that allow secure communication to take place between physicians and physician's assistants and young patients so that protocols can be monitored and advice given on a regular basis. This also allows for data and information to be collected on a real-time basis, data that can be used for research purposes and integrated with risk assessment technology.

stance involving increased supervision, incapacitation, and waiver to the adult criminal courts or, to a much lesser degree, adopting an improved-treatment approach focusing on effective rehabilitative and preventive strategies. With finite resources, it is evident that both approaches require the juvenile justice and child welfare systems to identify those youth who are most at risk and most at need of either type of intervention. Poor risk assessment tools with high false-positive rates will wrongfully include youth who are not at risk in the at-risk population, resulting in unnecessary and perhaps even harmful intervention in the lives of these youth. Youth incorrectly identified as being at risk may receive highly intrusive and/or incapacitative interventions that are not only unnecessary, but that damage existing bonds between the youth and his/her family, friends, and neighborhood. In contrast, assessments that produce high numbers of false negatives mean that we failed to protect adequately public safety by not intervening when we should have.

Risk assessment tools are being developed at an ever-increasing pace in a wide array of justice and child welfare settings. Whether the purpose is to predict criminal recidivism, violent behavior, or the abuse of a child, the trend to create and validate more and better risk instruments will not abate. After decades of debating the relative merits of actuarial versus clinical risk assessment, much of the contemporary effort is being put into developing and validating actuarial tools of one type or another. It is critical that clinicians and policy makers understand how such tools can add to their decision-making capability. Unfortunately, the field is fraught with many myths and misconceptions, and there remains considerable potential that policy makers will either decide not to use potentially valuable assessment tools, or that they will use poorly developed assessment tools that may well perform no better than chance. The key is being able to evaluate the quality of a risk assessment tool and to understand fully what a good risk assessment can and should be able to do within the context of contemporary technology and data analytic capabilities.

ASSESSING RISK IN SOCIAL WORK

The increasing visibility of youth violence, drug abuse, and delinquency has polarized the juvenile justice public policy response into adopting a get-tough

RISK ASSESSMENT: CONTEMPORARY ISSUES

The treatment literature shows that the most effective juvenile justice and child welfare interventions involve the ability to match the needs of the youthful client with specific services or programs selected from a comprehensive continuum of care (Palmer, 1992; Andrews, Bonta & Wormith 2006). To realize this benefit, we need to be able to accurately assess the risks and needs of young people as well as the quality and fidelity of the treatment programs themselves. Progress on the latter goal (assessing program quality and fidelity) is very limited, but it is beginning to receive attention in the literature (Jones, 2006). Progress on the issue of actuarial risk assessment is moving forward very quickly, with new developments in analysis and data collection technology pushing the field into a new phase of development.

Monahan's 1981 review of the literature showed that mental health professionals were incorrect two out of three times when they attempted to predict dangerousness. While our knowledge on violence, abuse, and delinquency has increased significantly since that time, researchers still only conclude that clinical predictions of violence have more than chance validity (Monahan, 1997). Not surprisingly, despite the improvements in clinical prediction and risk assessment, actuarial approaches have become more common in new work on the assessment of risk in juvenile justice and child welfare (Andrews, Bonta, & Hoge, 1990; Baird & Wagner, 2000; Baird, Wagner, Healy, & Johnson, 1999; Brennan, 1987; Dawes, Faust, & Meehl, 1989; Falco, 2002; S. D. Gottfredson, 1987; Hoge, 2002; Jones, 1995; Tarling & Perry, 1985; Wilkins, 1985). Most of these actuarial instruments utilize historical risk or protective factors—such as childhood behavior problems, age, gender, socioeconomic status, neighborhood, and family environment—that are stable over time. This creates the perception, voiced by Norko and Baranoski (2005, p. 24) that "actuarial methods of risk assessment are inherently insensitive to change and cannot inform clinicians' assessment of treatment progress."

Since the mid-1990s, risk prediction has started to incorporate a second broad category of risk factors, which includes dynamic factors that are more susceptible to intervention and manipulation—such as drug abuse or mental health diagnoses. Indeed, the category of dynamic factors itself can be divided into *stable* dynamic factors—those likely to remain unchanged over months or even years, such as the tendency toward aggression—and *acute* dynamic factors that can change quickly in relation to both personal and immediate environmental circumstances, such as changes to the foster home environment. The re-

search on dynamic risk factors, although increasing, is nowhere near the level of sophistication of the research on actuarial/historical/static risk factors. Actuarial instruments that rely on certain static criminal history items with a minor sampling of dynamic domains continue to function relatively well (Andrews, Bonta, & Wormith 2006). Most observers, however, believe that future improvements in the predictive-criterion validity of risk assessments will reside in continued reassessment of *dynamic* risk factors so that opportunities for effective prevention are increased.

The current state of risk assessment is problematic for a number of reasons. First, supporters of actuarial approaches to risk assessment are so convinced of their superiority over clinical risk assessment—pointing to the positive attributes of objectivity, nonarbitrariness, efficiency, and consistency—that they often fail to recognize limitations in their use and application. There is very limited understanding of what constitutes best practice in actuarial risk assessment and, consequently, risk assessment in the field is often woefully short of being acceptable. Second, the continued demonstration of the superiority of actuarial over clinical risk assessment has produced a sense that since youth cannot shed their historic stable risk factors, there is no room for treatment intervention or even hope for recovery. Together, these problems create the belief that the state of the art in risk prediction and classification is the actuarial assessment of stable historic factors, with little or no context for measuring treatment response through dynamic, changeable factors. Lindquist and Skipworth (2000) identify this problem as guilt by statistical association and call for methods that will better monitor the effect on risk of various rehabilitative strategies undertaken with youth.

REALIZING THE POTENTIAL OF ACTUARIAL RISK ASSESSMENT

A comprehensive review by Gottfredson and Gottfredson (1980) concluded that empirically driven models were superior to subjective professional decision making. However, the benefits of actuarial risk assessment are not inherent to the method, and one cannot simply assume that an actuarial approach will produce a predictive tool that is superior to clinical risk assessment. The effectiveness and validity of actuarial assessment must be demonstrated in any given setting. It is quite possible to develop ineffective and/or invalid actuarial assessment tools by using poor and inappropriate methodological and/or statistical techniques. Under such circumstances, the tool not only lacks all of the implied advantages of actuarial assessment, but also has the danger of "laundering" poor and inappropriate assessments as if they were scientific, objective results. Poorly developed or inappropriately employed actuarial risk assessment is highly damaging not only because it contributes to poor decision making, but also because it gives decision makers unwarranted optimism and faith about the validity and utility of the risk estimates that buttress their decisions.

The consequences of poor risk assessment in juvenile justice and child welfare are serious and far-reaching, leading to inappropriate and/or inequitable decisions that significantly undermine the chances of successful treatment in any given case. It can lead to abused and neglected children being kept in harm's way or prematurely removing such children from their homes. Shlonsky and Wagner found that an actuarial model with four categories of risk, ranging from low to very high, proved to be useful in child welfare. While actuarial risk assessment may have the greatest potential to predict recurrence of maltreatment, it still faces serious methodological challenges common to most empirical measurements that employ field data (Shlonsky & Wagner, 2005). As a result, they conclude that actuarial models are not sufficiently advanced to be able to develop acceptable levels of predictability. (Shlonsky & Wagner, 2005). Alternatively, inadequate risk assessment can lead to dangerous youth remaining in the community or to the placing of nondangerous youth into costly and secure youth correctional facilities. Given these potential problems, the increased use of risk assessment tools raises concern about standards of quality and appropriateness. Unfortunately, there is no clear set of minimum standards by which risk assessment tools are evaluated. As noted earlier, studies have compared clinical and empirical approaches and demonstrated the greater effectiveness and validity of the latter type (Dawes, Faust, & Meehl, 1989; Falco, 2002; Grove & Meehl, 1996; Monahan, 1997; Tarling & Perry, 1985). More-recent studies have tested the validity of existing actuarial assessment tools in different settings—sometimes finding that they work well, and occasionally showing that risk assessments fall far short of expectations (Grinberg et al., 2005; Jimerson et al., 2004; Stadtland et al., 2005. There are few studies that compare different types of actuarial risk assessment to ascertain the variability and the predictive validity of their classifications.

Until recently, the literature on the comparative performance of different actuarial approaches suggested that the type of statistical method employed in the analysis of risk made little difference (Brennan, 1987; Simon, 1971; Tarling & Perry, 1985; S. D. Gottfredson, 1987). There are several reasons that this is possible. The first is that theory in the field of juvenile justice and child welfare is still developing when compared with applications of prediction studies in fields such as medicine, econometrics, and engineering. The second is the constraint of poor data. Limitations on the range of available measures have added to problems of reliability, and the validity of the data that exist limits the ability of more sophisticated statistical approaches to achieve their potential. S. D. Gottfredson (1987) argued that without better and different data we simply cannot improve on the basic analytic approaches of the past. He warned that limited and generally poor-quality data combined with the highly random nature of delinquent behavior ensures that prediction research will rarely explain more than 15–20% of the outcome variance and may never do better than 30%. Schmidt and Witte (1988) concur and caution against overly optimistic goals for prediction studies in the field of delinquency, pointing to the fact that even in disciplines with well-developed, specific theories and relatively accurate data, prediction instruments struggle to explain more than half of the variation in the outcome measure. A third reason that researchers expect little variation across statistical approaches is that the lack of differentiation is more apparent during the validation than during the construction of a risk instrument so that apparent gains in the creation of an assessment tool will disappear upon testing. Tarling and Perry warned of this when they completed their review of seven different statistical approaches by concluding, "no method is consistently better than any other in validation samples" (Tarling & Perry, 1985, p. 264). A fourth reason is that the methods being compared are often basic regression-based techniques that share similar assumptions about the data.

Most of these comparative studies have employed traditional statistical methodologies, and it is rare to find contributions from nontraditional disciplines such as engineering or bioinformatics. More recent work by Jones et al. (2006) employed three different actuarial assessment tools that are founded upon widely different mathematical platforms and vary enormously in their range of sophistication and power.

They compared a dated but well-known and widely used risk assessment tool (the Wisconsin Delinquency Risk Assessment) with a customized risk assessment tool developed using a classification tree approach (a comparable method to that used by Monahan et al., 2000, in their MacArthur studies) and with a third assessment tool developed using state-of-the-art neural network analyses. Their results—summarized below—suggest that considerable potential for improvement exists through the use of more sophisticated analytic approaches.

COMPARING RISK CLASSIFICATIONS

Jones et al. (2006) utilized data from the ProDES database of juvenile delinquents processed by the family court in Philadelphia from 2000 to 2002 (Jones, Harris, & Fader, 1999). The ProDES database comprises data on all juveniles whose family court disposition involved more than regular probation—either probation with the condition of attending a treatment program or placement in a state juvenile correctional facility. The data set provides a wide array of measures, including official records, staff assessments, and self-reported data. For this study, the available measures included the eight variables that comprised the original Wisconsin Delinquency Risk Assessment and a wide range of additional measures pertaining to the juveniles, their families, their schools, and their peers. All cases were screened for missing data on the Wisconsin Delinquency Risk Assessment measures, and all cases missing these risk scores were removed.[1] The effective sample comprised 8,239 juveniles who were primarily male, Black, and between the ages of 14 and 17. Additional attributes show almost 40% of the sample had dispositions for personal offenses (such as robbery), 20% injured a victim, and 23% had two or more prior arrests. Approximately 30% of the juveniles had a history of chronic drug abuse and over 22% had IQ scores that classify them as "borderline intellectual functioning" or below.

The structure of the Wisconsin Delinquency Risk Assessment tool is established and required only validation. For both the configural and the neural network approaches, the respective models were developed based upon a split-sample validation method in which the model was developed using a single construction subsample (using a randomly selected 70% of all available cases) and tested on a validation subsample (the remaining 30% of cases).[2] In both cases, the models were constantly refined to minimize statistical shrinkage, the tendency for the differentiation of risk to be more apparent during construction than validation due to the statistical overfitting of potential predictors.

All juveniles in the ProDES system were monitored during their program placement (involving a variable program length of stay: sample average 32 weeks) and for 6 months following program discharge. The outcome measure for the study was juvenile re-arrests leading to new court petitions during the combined in-program and post-program periods. In total, almost 30% of the sample reoffended, though the figure varied by gender—31.9% for males and 12.7% for females.

Modeling Risk I: The Wisconsin Delinquency Risk Assessment Model

The Wisconsin Delinquency Risk Assessment model was developed in the late 1970s and remains widely used in its original form, in its revised form, or in some site-specific adaptation that reflects local needs and data availability. The assessment tool yields risk scores based on information derived from official records and interviews conducted by case management staff. The assessment should be completed within 30 days of a juvenile's assignment to a placement—and in the ProDES system, this was required of all programs.

Risk classification is based upon a total risk score, which is calculated by simple summation of the eight risk items.[3] Though the risk assessment tool has undergone revision, the one employed here comprises the following items:

- Age at first adjudication
- Prior delinquent behavior
- Prior institutional commitments of 30+ days
- Drug/chemical abuse
- Alcohol abuse
- Quality of parental control
- Evidence of school disciplinary problems
- Quality of peer relationships

The attributes of each item are weighted to reflect the magnitude of their association with recidivism. For example, "quality of parental control" involves a risk score of 0 for "generally effective," 2 for "inconsistent," and 4 for "little or none." Other risk items have different weights to reflect their specific correlation to reoffending. The procedure for determining a juvenile's risk classification involves the summation of all scores and classification into low, low-medium, medium-high, and high risk using cut-off scores of 6, 12, and 19, respectively.[4]

The Wisconsin assessment tool has been validated in different settings both in its original and various revised formats. Baird, Heinz, and Bemus (1979) reported on the validity of the original model and, using a three-level categorization based on total risk score, were able to predict rates of probation and parole revocations for a Wisconsin sample of over 4,000 cases. The overall base rate for revocations was 11%, and they identified rates of 2%, 9%, and 26% for low, medium, and high-risk cases, respectively. Clear and Gallagher (1985) reported less favorable results for a New York sample of 366 probationers for which in-program information on a variety of indices of recidivism were available. The in-program "failure" rate, as defined by the above indicators, was 30%. The New York study found no significant relationship between overall risk scores and recidivism and only 3 of the 11 components of risk individually predicted failures at levels above chance. Ashford and LeCroy (1988) used discriminate analysis to examine the extent to which the Wisconsin instrument could discriminate between recidivists and nonrecidivists. Their results showed that only 1 of the 8 variables was significantly related to recidivism and the instrument's total risk score could not discriminate between the recidivist and nonrecidivist groups.

The Wisconsin assessment–based risk classification of the juveniles in the ProDES sample is presented in Table 13.1. The cut-offs provided in the original study created four risk groups with almost 15% of the juveniles considered low risk, 32% low-medium risk, 32% medium-high risk, and 21% high risk.

TABLE 13.1 Wisconsin Risk Classification

Risk	%	N
Low	14.7	1215
Low-Medium	31.6	2603
Medium-High	32.4	2669
High	21.3	1752
Total	100	8239

Modeling Risk II: Customized Model Using Configural Analysis

The second approach to assessing risk involved the use of configural analysis on the Philadelphia sample itself. The method uses tree induction algorithms or nonparametric classification procedures to subdivide a sample into significant groupings on the basis of specific statistical and theoretical conditions (Arentze et al., 2000). The predictor variables used in the model are related to the outcome variable (reoffending) by a set of rules. The iterative technique identifies a primary predictor and, dependent on an individual's attributes on this predictor, identifies different secondary and tertiary predictors. This allows many different combinations of risk factors to classify a person as high or low risk.

The segmentation technique used here is called AnswerTree and is available within the software package Statistical Package for the Social Sciences (SPSS; Gnanadesikan, 1977). Published risk assessment research involving this technique is found in many disciplines, including the health sciences (Welte et al., 2004), marketing (Jonker, Piersma, & Van den Poel, 2004), psychology (Smith & Grawe, 2003), geography and regional planning (Casas, 2003), criminal justice (Jones, Harris, Fader, & Grubstein, 2001; Monahan, Steadman, Robbins, Silver, Appelbaum, Grisso, Mulvey, & Roth, 2000), and education (Grobler, Bisschoff, & Moloi, 2002). AnswerTree repeatedly divides the population into mutually exclusive and exhaustive subgroups, which differ with respect to the criterion measure (Magidson, 1994).

As a result, the predictors identified do not always apply to the entire sample (as would be the case with more common regression-based approaches). In the present analysis, the number of prior arrests was identified as the most significant initial predictor because it provides for a classification that maximizes the between-group discrimination on the outcome variable of reoffending (Figure 13.1). The model subsequently searches within each of the four subgroups — juveniles with no prior arrests, one prior, two priors, or more than two priors — for the next best predictor within that specific subgroup. For the first two of these subgroups, the second predictor was gender; for those with two priors, the next predictor was "injury to victim" during commission of the current offense; and for those with more than two prior arrests, the next predictor was the juvenile's age. The model adds pre-

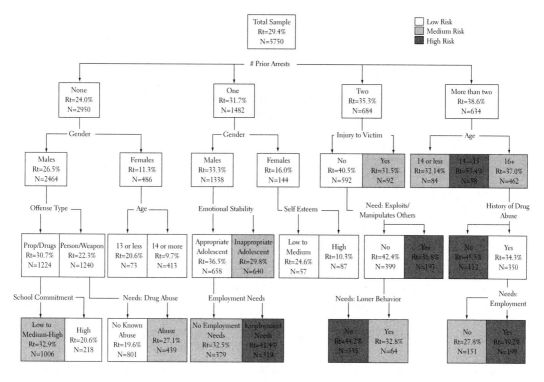

FIGURE 13.1 Dendogram of Predictors of Re-Arrest

dictors of different types to each of these subgroups, creating "branches" of different lengths, sizes, and compositions for different groupings of juveniles. The model develops until one of several stopping rules prevents further separation within a specific node or subgroup. Comparison of a model's performance within both the construction and validation samples results in a process of development and pruning of specific branches of the decision tree until a stable model with satisfactory discrimination is produced.

Each of the individual variables that comprise the Wisconsin Delinquency Risk Assessment tool was available to the configural analysis for inclusion in the model, but none was selected. Interestingly, several of the variables included in the Wisconsin needs assessment—a set of variables not considered to have predictive criminogenic value—were selected and included in the configural model. These need-based variables included staff assessments of whether or not the juvenile was manipulative of others, was a loner, had employment needs, or had a drug/alcohol abuse problem.

The resulting risk classification is presented in Table 13.2. When compared with the Wisconsin clas-

TABLE 13.2 Configural Risk Classification

Risk	%	N
Low	28.5	2349
Medium	53	4369
High	18.5	1521
Total	100	8239

sification, it is evident that the configural analysis—which has three risk groups—places far more juveniles in the low-risk group and slightly fewer in the high-risk group.

Modeling Risk III: Customized Model Using Neural Networks

The third approach uses artificial neural networks because of their ability to learn from databases and build predictive models that can evolve and update themselves using random selections of case file data. The potential of this type of statistical technique has been demonstrated in the child welfare arena by Schwartz et al. (2004), who found that the final trained network was able to successfully categorize 89.6% of the cases in the testing population.

Neural networks offer an appropriate statistical approach to risk assessment because they "are not organized around rules or programming, but learn the underlying behaviors of a model by analyzing its input and output values and adjusting the weights between neuron layers. In this respect, the behavior of a neural network is trained using supervised or unsupervised techniques" (Cox, 1995, p. 582). This type of "soft computing" methodology is widely used in research and practice by other fields because it is highly adaptive and robust. For example, neural networks have performed well as risk assessment and classification tools in the medical decision-making literature. Atienza et al. (2000) developed a network that correctly classified 123 of 132 patients, and Orr (1997) trained a network to estimate mortality following cardiac surgery to the point where he achieved 91.5% accuracy for the training set and 92.3% accuracy for the validation set. Though the prediction of health outcomes is quite different from the prediction of human behavior, the fact remains that existing actuarial models are an adaptation of health and life insurance models developed in the past. Neural networks are discussed in the child welfare literature but, with the exception of Schwartz et al. (2004), have not yet been implemented in the delinquency or child welfare field. Marshall and English (2000) compared logistic and linear multiple regression to neural networks using child protective services data from the state of Washington's risk assessment model and concluded that the neural network produced superior prediction and classification results. Caulkins, Cohen, Gorr, and Wei (1996) compared neural network models with other statistical techniques—including Burgess, multiple regression, and predictive attribute analysis—in predicting adult criminal recidivism. Their results suggested that neural networks do not offer an advantage over multiple regressions in predicting recidivism.

For the present study, the neural network analysis was run on the same ProDES database as produced the Wisconsin and configural analysis results. Though the neural network could in theory work with a wide array of potential predictor variables, it was decided, for purposes of this analysis, to restrict the model to those variables that had previously been identified as predictors in the configural analysis. The utilization of the configural model to constrain the array of

potential predictors for neural networks analysis is an unusual but appropriate application of a preliminary noise reduction strategy so that the neural network is applied only to variables that have demonstrated at least minimal levels of predictive value. Indirectly, it also enhances direct comparison with the results of the configural model. Further, although the neural network model could incorporate intermediate-level variables collected after the initial point of in-take, the present analysis restricts the model only to the data available at the point of in-take.

Classification of the data set was undertaken using a feed-forward neural network model with one hidden layer of sigmoid units trained using the back-propagation algorithm (Werbos, 1975). Such models can approximate any bounded continuous function with arbitrarily small error (Cybenko, 1989). The multilayer perceptions (MLPs) were trained with 70% of the sample and tested with a 30% validation sample that was disjoint and randomly generated. This methodology is used for predictive purposes to test the accuracy of the model on unseen instances. For the purposes of this study, the analysis was performed with a general-purpose machine learning suite with mostly default parameters. Training MLPs is a computationally expensive and complex process that requires a large number of trials to identify the optimal set of parameters, in order to produce the most accurate model. The training data are processed hundreds, thousands, or more times to obtain the final model. The model in this study was initially run on the entire sample but, because of the importance of gender differences with regard to reoffending, separate models were also run for the male and female sample subsets.

The risk classification based upon neural network analysis is presented in Table 13.3. Cases are classified as either high or low risk, and this approach identifies the largest number of at-risk cases. When compared with the Wisconsin and the configural classifications, it is evident that the neural network classification—with only two groups—places far more juveniles in

TABLE 13.3 Neural Net Risk Classification

Risk	%	N
Low	65.8	5424
High	34.2	2815
Total	100	8239

TABLE 13.4 Comparing Risk Classifications High-Risk Juveniles

Classification Agreement (No. of Tools)	N	%	% Reoffend
High (0)	4664	56.6	3
High (1)	2185	26.5	59.1
High (2)	1221	14.8	69.2
High (3)	169	2.1	91.1
Total	8239	100	29.5

either a low-risk or a high-risk group. From a clinical or practical perspective, the absence of a medium-risk category is helpful since the appropriate response or intervention for such youth is questionable. However, it remains to be seen whether the clarity of classification comes at a significant cost in terms of predictive validity.

The Risk Classifications Compared

Even though the three risk assessment tools combine different factors in different ways, it is possible that the same juveniles would be identified as high or low risk by all three methods. If one compares the Wisconsin and configural classifications, the match is generally poor: 10% of the configural classification's low-risk youth are assessed as high risk by the Wisconsin classification and, similarly, 10% of the configural high-risk youth are assessed as low risk by the Wisconsin classification. Comparing the neural network with the Wisconsin classification indicates even less agreement. Of the juveniles assessed as low risk by neural networks, only 13% were low risk in the Wisconsin classification and 21% were assessed as high risk. Similarly, of the juveniles assessed as high risk by neural networks, 20% were also assessed as high risk by the Wisconsin analysis, and 11% were assessed to be low risk. Comparing the third pair of assessments—configural and neural networks—shows greater agreement. Of the juveniles assessed as low risk by neural networks, 35% were also low risk in the configural analysis; of those assessed as high risk by neural networks, 27% were similarly assessed by the configural model.

These results provide strong evidence that type of assessment does matter. Table 13.4 focuses solely on the juveniles classified as high risk by each of the assessment tools. Almost half of the juveniles in the sample were assessed as high risk by at least one of the tools, and yet only 2% were assessed as high risk by all three tools.

Predictive Validity

The risk assessments can be tested by comparing the predicted risk classification with actual reoffending patterns. The results for the Wisconsin assessment show that 24.4% of the low-risk juveniles reoffended during the follow-up period compared with 30% of the high-risk juveniles (Table 13.5). The results for the two medium-risk categories are similar—28.6% and 32.4%, respectively. However, the fact that the medium-high risk group reoffended at a higher rate than did the high-risk juveniles suggests that the classification is not discriminating well on the basis of risk.

The results for the configural assessment represent an improvement, with 17.4% of low-risk juveniles reoffending compared with 31.2% of medium-risk juveniles and 43.3% of high-risk juveniles (Table 13.6). The configural risk tool achieves considerably better discrimination among the risk categories in terms of reoffending. Moreover, the model places a similar proportion of juveniles into the high-risk category (18.5% compared with 21.3% for the Wisconsin assessment tool) and almost twice as many juveniles into the low-risk category (28.5% compared with 14.7%).

TABLE 13.5 Wisconsin Risk Classification by Reoffending

Risk	% No	% Reoffend
Low	75.6	24.4
Low-Medium	71.4	28.6
Medium-High	67.6	32.4
High	70	30
Total %	**70.5**	**29.5**
N	**5,807**	**2,432**

TABLE 13.6 Configural Risk Classification by Reoffending

Risk	% No	% Reoffend
Low	82.6	17.4
Medium	68.8	31.2
High	56.7	43.3
Total %	70.5	29.5
N	5,807	2,432

TABLE 13.7 Neural Net Risk Classification by Reoffending

Risk	% No	% Reoffend
Low	97	3
High	19.4	80.6
Total %	70.5	29.5
N	5,807	2,432

From a decision-making perspective, the configural model is superior; it allows for the identification of a larger group of low-risk juveniles whose actual reoffending rate is lower than that for low-risk juveniles identified by the Wisconsin assessment (17.4% compared with 24.4%), and it is correct more often for the high-risk juveniles. If the configural assessment were used as part of dispositional decisions, a larger proportion of juveniles would be considered for less-intrusive interventions *and* a larger proportion of those individuals would remain delinquency-free for the period of study. Among the high-risk juveniles, we would incur a lower rate of false positives.

The results for the neural networks assessment represent a significant improvement over both the Wisconsin and the configural models (Table 13.7). Creating only two categories, it identified a group of low-risk juveniles for whom the reoffending rate was 3% and a high-risk group for which it was 81%. The predictive validity of this model far exceeds the estimated prediction capabilities forecast by S. D. Gottfredson (1987) and Schmidt and Witte (1988) 20 years ago, and it is evident that the neural networks model is far superior to either of the two other classification systems.

DISCUSSION

During the past several decades, there has been a large body of research that has established the superior predictive validity of actuarial compared with clinical risk models. The debate now focuses on such issues as the type of data used (static and or dynamic factors) and the data analytic approach employed. The results presented here indicate the significant potential for improved predictive accuracy that lies in sophisticated approaches such as neural networks. Schwartz et al. (2004) have also demonstrated that by identifying valid dynamic risk factors and utilizing state-of-the-art technology to keep collecting and updating measurements, it is possible to develop risk instruments that will provide continuous risk assessment scores rather than the fixed, single risk score that is currently employed in most settings. Such advances are critical from a treatment perspective since they will allow agencies to identify what changes (either in behavior or condition) trigger shifts in risk classification during a treatment phase. This knowledge will help to identify the most effective intervention or prevention strategy for a particular individual or group.

If continuous measurement and risk assessment represent what is possible with current analytic and technology capabilities, the fact remains that risk assessment as currently utilized in juvenile justice and child welfare settings falls far short of this level. All too often, risk assessments in the field are borrowed, adapted to fit local data conditions (by adding and/or excluding carefully identified predictors or by changing the risk scores associated with established predictors), and then utilized without validation to produce risk classifications to support potentially life-changing decisions. Such misuse and abuse of risk assessment falls well short of what might be considered best practice in the field, but the situation exists largely because of a misplaced sense that actuarial risk assessment is so robust, so superior to clinical decision making, that it can sustain these modifications without being seriously compromised.

The data presented here examine the risk classifications and predictive validity of three types of assessment—all of which could be employed in the field. The data indicate that the tools do not produce the same classifications; very few juveniles would be placed in the same risk category if assessed by all three tools. The data further indicate that the Wisconsin assessment tool performs poorly, displaying little predictive validity overall and particularly poor validity for females. The configural assessment represents an improvement, and the neural network assessment sets a new and higher standard.

The implications of the disparities among these three assessment models are not trivial. Actuarial risk instruments—even the very poor ones—have an aura of objectivity and general superiority to clinical decision making. They appear "scientific." Nevertheless, such assumptions need to be justified and the predictive validity of actuarial tools must be demonstrated. For example, if a low-risk classification produced a less-intrusive response from a juvenile justice or child welfare system, then the Wisconsin assessment tool would classify 1,215 of the current sample as low risk and it would be correct in about 75% of cases (i.e., they would not reoffend during the study period). The configural model would identify 2,349 as low risk and get 83% of them correct. The neural networks model would identify 5,424 as low risk and get 97% correct.

The appropriateness and predictive validity of risk assessment tools are clearly issues that will continue to generate considerable research activity. The degree to which these instruments shape the rights and freedoms of juveniles is less well known. This becomes particularly pertinent when it involves predictions of high risk that result in more intrusive interventions, requiring juveniles to be removed from their homes and school communities. It is also pertinent if the risk instruments contribute directly or indirectly to discriminatory decisions based upon such factors as gender and race.

The primary purpose of this study was to show that simply using off-the-shelf risk assessment instruments can be misleading and dangerous. The Wisconsin tool was used as a baseline comparison largely because it is one of, if not the, best-known instruments of its kind and because it has been used in many jurisdictions throughout the country. We have not tried to present a comparison of statistical methods nor to demonstrate that one statistical method (e.g., regression, configural, or neural networks) is superior to another. We have utilized different approaches to examine risk within a single sample of juveniles in order to identify the need for a healthy skepticism about the utilization of actuarial risk instruments. We believe that the careful and appropriate application of neural networks has great and, as yet, largely unexplored potential to advance our knowledge in risk assessment as well as in other areas. Yet even here we would urge caution. We discovered that the initial analyses using neural networks did not work nearly so well when the process was applied to the entire set of potential variables. However, the use of neural networks became quite robust when we used the results of the configural analysis—which had identified specific variables as having predictive validity—as a means of reducing the array of predictors available to the neural network model. This is similar to the experience that Schwartz and his colleagues had when they generated their remarkable results in applying neural networks to a child welfare data set (Schwartz et al., 2004). We would like to mention that it is conceivable that an actuarial model may well prove useful in developing an initial array of variables that could be subsequently used in a neural network.

As Zinger (2004) notes, most criticism of actuarial risk assessment fails to offer any reasonable alternative, and a return to clinical assessment takes us in the direction of increased and less explicit and recognizable bias. The answer is not to throw the baby out with the bathwater—it is to recognize the gap that exists between theory and practice in the field of actuarial risk assessment in the United States and to move quickly to establish minimum quality control standards. The present study has established that actuarial risk assessments can vary enormously in terms of where they place juveniles and how accurate their predictions can be. For change to occur, there needs to be explicit recognition that the potential benefits of actuarial risk assessment can be achieved only by carefully maintaining the integrity of the risk prediction process. The methodological high ground needs to be earned and not simply assumed.

POLICY CONSIDERATIONS AND NEXT STEPS

We are encouraged by the findings of our initial research with neural networks. A logical and important next step would be to launch a field test or clinical trial, using neural networks in a large jurisdiction. At the time of this writing, there are plans to conduct such a clinical trial in a jurisdiction that offers a large array of potential measures for very large samples over multiple years. This will enable the development of a neural network model on different samples through time (offering some insight into model stability over time), repeated validation testing, and performance comparison with existing actuarial models. Based upon the results of these trials, it may be possible to extend the analysis and experiment with forms of downstream data collection and model development that would allow for real-time risk classification to occur. It is hoped that subsequent papers on this topic will be derived from this clinical experiment.

Unfortunately, while other professions and fields are embracing technology and advanced research methods to improve the quality and effectiveness of services, the social work profession and, indeed, the broader social welfare field continues to lag behind. Despite the rhetoric and claims around evidence-based practice, the social welfare field tends to cling to obsolete practices and, at the same time, be quick to embrace fads and approaches that appear to be enlightened and the next panacea. Family preservation is an example of a fad that was quickly embraced by social work practitioners and administrators in child welfare, as well as by many private foundations, and that subsequently became national policy. This practice has since been largely discredited because of the absence of careful studies demonstrating its effectiveness coupled with some respected research suggesting that family preservation services do not live up to the claims of their advocates (Chaffin & Friedrich, 2004). Yet this controversial practice continues to be in vogue and is still being implemented in many jurisdictions around the country (Schwartz & Fishman, 1999). We have seen the same potential dangers in the area of risk assessment. As academicians and researchers make advances in their ability to create robust and highly predictive instruments, the social welfare field, particularly juvenile justice and child welfare, runs the risk of lagging far behind. In light of this, we urge social welfare policy makers and practitioners to consider the following:

1. Implement the latest advances in risk assessment. At the very least, test such advances against the methods and techniques that are currently being used.
2. Establish partnerships with university faculty in such disciplines as bioinformatics, engineer-

ing (particularly the decision sciences), epidemiology, and statistics to both explore and implement more advanced research methods in order to improve the quality and effectiveness of services. This should include the use of neural networks in such areas as mental health, public welfare services, employment training and job placement, criminal justice, and work with other disadvantaged populations.
3. Explore the use of technology to assist in delivering services and in conducting real-time research, as is now the case in other fields.
4. Implement carefully designed clinical trials similar to those being used in the health care and pharmaceutical fields in order to advance knowledge and improve the quality and effectiveness of service interventions.
5. Recognize that risk instruments are part of a larger decision-making process and that they must be consistent with the goals and overall philosophy of an agency. For example, risk assessment data should be readily available and in a user-friendly form so that line social workers, probation officers, and others can integrate them with other relevant information to better inform their practice. Also, agencies and not statisticians or the default settings of computer programs should decide at what level a youth stops being "low" risk and starts becoming "high" risk. Agencies should also be responsible for developing the appropriate policy responses to youth placed in either category.

There is mounting concern and debate about the apparently growing digital divide in the general population and the long-term implications this may have. The social work profession and the social welfare field need to be just as concerned about the technological divide that appears to be under way when compared to the developments in other professions. While the implications of this are somewhat unclear, they certainly cannot bode well for the future of the social work profession. Instead of waiting until this situation reaches a crisis state, social welfare policy makers and practitioners should play a leadership role and move to aggressively close the gap between the rhetoric of evidence-based practice and reality.

Notes

The authors wish to thank Chris Baird and Aron Shlonsky for their reviews of earlier drafts of this chapter and for their constructive criticisms and suggestions.

1. Removal of cases with missing data is not a problem in the present study since its function is solely to compare different methods of assessment for the same juveniles rather than to build a risk assessment tool for use in the field.

2. The split-sample approach was used because of the large sample available for analysis. In prediction studies using smaller samples, an alternative k-fold cross-validation approach would likely be more appropriate. K-fold cross-validation divides the data into k subsets of (approximately) equal size and develops the prediction model k times, each time leaving out one subset from training and using it to validate the model. The split-sample approach therefore uses a single subset (the validation set) to estimate the generalization error, instead of k different subsets, i.e., there is no "crossing."

3. Prorated total risk scores—using mean substitution for missing values—were calculated in cases involving any missing data.

4. Alternate cut-off points for the risk categories were evaluated, but none provided improvement on the overall predictive validity of the instrument.

References

Abney, P. C., & Maddux, C. D. (2004). Counseling and technology: Some thoughts about the controversy. *Journal of Technology in Human Services*, 22, 1–24.

Andrews, D. A. (2001). Principles of effective correctional programs. In L. L. Motiuk & R. C. Serin (Eds), *Compendium 2000 on effective correctional programming* (Vol. 1, chap. 2). Ottawa, ON: Correctional Service Canada.

Andrews, D. A., Bonta, J., & Hoge, R. (1990). Classification for effective rehabilitation: Rediscovering psychology. *Criminal Justice Behaviour*, 17, 19–52.

Andrews, D. A., Bonta, J., & Wormith, J. S. (2006). The recent past and near future of risk and/or need assessment. *Crime & Delinquency*, 52(1), 7–27.

Arentze, T. A., Hofman, F., Mourik, H. V., Timmermans, H. J. P., & Wets, G. (2000). Using decision tree induction systems for modeling space-time behavior. *Geographical Analysis*, 32(4), 330–350.

Ashford, J. B., & LeCroy, C. W. (1988). Predicting recidivism: An evaluation of the Wisconsin juvenile probation and aftercare risk instrument. *Criminal Justice and Behavior*, 15(2), 141–151.

Atienza, F., Martinez-Alzamora, N., De Velasco, J. A., Dreiseitl, S., & Ohno-Machado, L. (2000). Risk stratification in heart failure using artificial neural networks. In *Proceedings of the AMIA Annual Fall Symposium* (pp. 32–36). Bethesda, MD: American Medical Informatics Association. Available at http://www.amia.org/pubs/proceedings/symposia/2002/D200367.pdf.

Baird, S. C., Heinz, R. C., & Bemus, B. J. (1979). *The Wisconsin case classification/staff development project: A two-year follow-up report*. Madison: Wisconsin Bureau of Community Corrections.

Baird, S. C., Wagner, D., Healy, T., & Johnson, K. (1999). Risk assessment in child protective services: Consensus and actuarial model reliability. *Child Welfare*, 78(6), 723–748.

Baird, S. C., & Wagner, D. (2000). The relative validity of actuarial and consensus-based risk assessment systems. *Children and Youth Services Review*, 22(11–12), 839–871.

Brennan, T. (1987). Classification: An overview of selected methodological issues. In D. M. Gottfredson & M. Tonry (Eds.), *Prediction and classification: Criminal justice decision making* (pp. 201–248). Chicago: University of Chicago Press.

Casas, I. (2003). Evaluating the importance of accessibility to congestion response using a GIS-based travel simulator. *Journal of Geographical Systems*, 5, 109–127.

Caulkins, J., Cohen, J., Gorr, W., & Wei, J. (1996). Predicting criminal recidivism: A comparison of neural network models with statistical methods. *Journal of Criminal Justice*, 24(3), 227–240.

Chaffin, M., & Friedrich, B. (2004). Evidence-based treatments in child abuse and neglect. *Children & Youth Services Review*, 26(11), 1097–1113.

Clear, T. R., & Gallagher, K. W. (1985). Probation and parole supervision: A review of current classification practices. *Crime and Delinquency*, 31, 423–443.

Cole, D. P., & Angus, G. (2003). Using pre-sentence reports to evaluate and respond to risk. *Criminal Law Quarterly*, 47, 302–364.

Cox, E. D. (1995). *Fuzzy logic for business and industry*. Boston: Charles River Media.

Cybenko, G. (1989). Approximation by superpositions of sigmoidal functions. *Mathematics of Control, Signals & Systems*, 2, 303–314.

Dawes, R. M., Faust, D., & Meehl, P. (1989). Clinical versus actuarial judgment. *Science*, 243, 1668–1674.

Falco, G. (2002). *Clinical vs. actuarial risk assessment: Results from New York state*. Albany: Office of Program Evaluation for the New York State Department of Social Services.

Gambrill, E. & Shlonsky, A. (2000). Risk assessment in context. *Children & Youth Services Review*, 22(11–12), 813-837.

Gnanadesikan, R. (1977). Methods for statistical data analysis of multivariate observations 333. *Temple Law Review*, 480. #94

Gottfredson, D. M., & Tonry, M. (Eds.). (1987). *Prediction and classification: Criminal justice decision making*. Chicago: University of Chicago Press.

Gottfredson, M. R., & Gottfredson, D. M. (1980). *Decision-making in criminal justice: Toward the rational exercise of discretion*. Cambridge, MA: Ballinger.

Gottfredson, S. D. (1987). Prediction: An overview of selected methodological issues. In D. M. Gottfredson & M. Tonry (Eds.), *Prediction and classification: Criminal justice decision making*. Chicago: University of Chicago Press.

Grinberg, I., Dawkins, M., Dawkins, M. P., & Fullilove, C. (2005). Adolescents at risk for violence: An initial validation of the Life Challenges Questionnaire and Risk Assessment Index. *Adolescence*, 40(159), 573–599.

Grobler, B.R., Bisschoff, T.C. & Moloi, K.C. (2002). The Chaid-Technique and the relationship between school effectiveness and various independent variables. *International Studies in Educational Administration*, 30(3), 44–56.

Grove, W. M., & Meehl, P. E. (1996). Comparative efficiency of informal (subjective, impressionistic) and formal (mechanical, algorithmic) prediction procedure: The clinical-statistical controversy. *Psychology, Public Policy & Law*, 2, 293–323.

Hoge, R. D. (2002). Standardized instruments for assessing risk and need in youthful offenders. *Criminal Justice & Behaviour*, 29(4), 380–396.

Jimerson, S. R., Sharkey, J. D., O'Brien, K. M., & Furlong, M. J. (2004). The Santa Barbara assets and risks assessment to predict recidivism among male and female juveniles: An investigation of interrater reliability and predictive validity. *Education & Treatment of Children*, 27(4), 353–373.

Jones, P. R. (2006, August). Quality matters for program development and evaluative research. *Criminology & Public Policy*, 5(3), 571–574.

Jones, P.R., Schwartz, D.R., Schwartz, I. M., Zoran, O., & Jupin, J. (2006). Risk classificaiton and juvenile depositions: What is the state of the art? *Temple Law Review*, 79(2), 461–498.

Jones, P. R. (1995). Risk prediction in criminal justice. In A. Harland (Ed.), *Choosing correctional options that work: Defining the demand/evaluating the supply*. Thousand Oaks, CA: Sage.

Jones, P. R., Harris, P. W., & Fader, J. (1999). Evaluating services to delinquent youth in Philadelphia: The ProDES information system. *Journal of the Pennsylvania Association of Probation, Parole & Corrections*, 59(1), 10–13.

Jones, P. R., Harris, P. W., Fader, J., & Grubstein, L. (2001). Identifying chronic juvenile offenders. *Justice Quarterly*, 18(3), 479–507.

Jonker, J., Piersma, N., & Van den Poel, D. (2004). Joint optimization of customer segmentation and marketing policy to maximize long-term profitability. *Expert Systems with Applications*, 27(2), 159–168.

Lindquist, P., & Skipworth, J. (2000). Evidence-based rehabilitation in forensic psychiatry. *British Journal of Psychiatry*, 176, 320–323.

Magidson, J. (1994). The CHAID approach to segmentation modeling: Chi-squared automatic interaction detection. In R. P. Bagozzi (Ed.), *Advanced methods of marketing research* (pp. 118–160). Cambridge, MA: Blackwell.

Marshall, D. B., & English, D. J. (2000). Neural network modeling of risk assessment in child protective services. *Psychological Methods*, 5(1), 102–124.

Meier, A. (2000). Offering social support via the internet: A case study of an online support group for social workers. *Journal of Technology in Human Services*, 17(2/3), 237–266.

Monahan, J. (1981). The clinical prediction of violent behavior. Washington, DC: GPO. DHHS Publication No. ADM 81-921.

Monahan, J. (1997). Clinical and actuarial predictions of violence. In D. Faigman, D. Kaye, M. Saks, & J. Sanders (Eds.), *Modern scientific evidence: The law and science of expert testimony* (pp. 300–318). St. Paul, MN: West.

Monahan, J., Steadman, H. J., Robbins, P. C., Silver, E., Appelbaum, P. S., Grisso, T., Mulvey, E. P., & Roth, L. H. (2000). Developing a clinically useful actuarial tool for assessing violence risk. *British Journal of Psychiatry*, 176, 312–319.

Norko, M. A., & Baranoski, M. V. (2005). The state of contemporary risk assessment research. *Canadian Journal of Psychiatry*, 50(1), 18–26.

Office of Juvenile Justice and Delinquency Prevention. (1998). Comprehensive strategy for serious, violent and chronic juvenile offenders. *OJJDP Annual Report*. Washington DC: Office of Justice Programs.

Orr, R. K. (1997). Use of probabilistic neural network to estimate the risk of mortality after cardiac surgery. *Medical Decision Making*, 17, 178–185.

Palmer, T. (1992). *The re-emergence of correctional intervention*. Thousand Oaks, CA: Sage.

Schmidt, P., & Witte, A. (1988). *Predicting recidivism using survival models*. New York: Springer-Verlag.

Schwartz, D. R., Kaufman, A. B., & Schwartz, I. M. (2004). Computational intelligence techniques for risk assessment and decision support. *Children & Youth Services Review*, 26(11), 1081–1095.

Schwartz, I. M., & Fishman, G. (1999). *Kids raised by the government*. Westport, CT: Praeger.

Shlonsky, A., & Wagner, D. (2005). The next step: Integrating actuarial risk assessment and clinical judgment into an evidence-based practice framework in CPA case management. *Children and Youth Services Review, 27*, 415.

Simon, F. H. (1971). *Prediction methods in criminology*. London: Her Majesty's Stationery Office.

Smith, E. C. & Grawe, K. (2003). What makes psychotherapy sessions productive? A new approach to bridging the gap between process research and practice, *Clincial Psychology and Psychotherapy, 10*(5), 275, 278.

SPSS (Statistical Package for the Social Scientist). (2002). *AnswerTree™ 3.0 User's Guide*. Chicago: SPSS Inc.

Stadtland, C., Hollweg, M., Kleindienst, N., Dietl, J., Reich, U., & Nedopil, N. (2005). Risk assessment and prediction of violent and sexual recidivism in sex offenders: Long-term predictive validity of four risk assessment instruments. *Journal of Forensic Psychiatry & Psychology, 16*(1), 92–108.

Tarling, R., & Perry, J. A. (1985). Statistical models in criminological prediction. In D. Farrington & R. Tarling (Eds.), *Prediction in criminology* (pp. 210–231). Albany: State University of New York Press.

Tichon, J., & Shapiro, M. (2003). With a little help from my friends: Children, the internet and social service support. *Journal of Technology in Human Services, 21*(4), 73–92.

Welte, J. et al (2004). Gambling participation and pathology in the United States: A sociodemographic analysis using classification trees. *Addictive Behaviors, 29*(5), 983–989.

Werbos, P. (1975). *Beyond regression: New tools for prediction and analysis in the behavioral sciences*. Unpublished doctoral dissertation, Harvard University.

Wilkins, L. T. (1985). The politics of prediction. In D. Farrington & R. Tarling (Eds.), *Prediction in criminology* (pp. 34–53). Albany: State University of New York Press.

Zinger, I. (2004). Actuarial risk assessment and human rights: A commentary. *Canadian Journal of Criminology & Criminal Justice, 46*, 607–620.

Part V

Evidence-Based Child
Welfare Policy

In this section, the researchers examine how we translate the commitment and obligation to disadvantaged and deprived children into effective public policies. The key indicators of our society's failure in meeting this responsibility are child neglect and child poverty. In a nation as wealthy as the United States, child poverty should be eradicated. Other free market democracies in Europe and Asia have substantially reduced child poverty with effective public policies and programs that protect children and their parents from poverty, particularly poverty that families are unable to escape through paid work.

The public and its leaders share a common interest in ending child poverty. In the past, efforts to end child poverty have not met the expectations of those who have supported them. For more than a half century, the nation relied on a public welfare program to protect children from the extremes of child poverty. Welfare had built-in contradictions that may have provided money to the most needy but had the unfortunate side effect of facilitating dependence and unintentionally discouraging economic advancement.

In the mid-1990s, the most important program providing economic security to poor children in America—the federal welfare system—was essentially repealed. The rubric used was that the welfare program was reformed, but the net effect of the "reform" was to take women and children off the welfare rolls even as they remained poor (Lindsey, 2008). Other federal programs that provided for poor children—food stamps, subsidized school lunches, WIC (Women, Infants, and Children)—experienced increases in poor children seeking aid while many of these same children were being removed from the broader federal welfare program.

Welfare had provided a floor of economic protection to poor children in the United States. It was an entitlement program that expressed the nation's covenant to care and provide for the least among us. The program was ended not because the nation no longer wished to honor this covenant. Rather, the program was ended because the nation lost faith in the program's ability to serve the interests of poor children over the long term. With the end of welfare, we have now entered a new era of opportunity to find better ways to fulfill the obligation that the nation has to its children.

In this section, the authors explore child neglect and child poverty from a broad social policy perspective. The nation is at a point where programs and policies that honor the covenant can be developed, and researchers in this section examine some of the major work being done in this area.

One of the major limitations of the transformation of child welfare into child protection is that it has led to a blending of child neglect, physical abuse, and sexual abuse into a common category of child maltreatment. However, child neglect is often substantially different from physical and sexual abuse. Often, child neglect is primarily a result of poverty and unemployment. In contrast, the physical and sexual assault of a child is most often a serious crime that requires a different form of intervention than child neglect.

Jane Waldfogel has examined this situation in detail over the years. We begin this section with her chapter, "The Future of Child Protection Revisited," an examination of differential response, its effect on the current state of child protective services, and its implications for the future. Differential response, as Waldfogel explains, is the informed choice between a reactive reply to a specific case which is thought to warrant a traditional investigative response, and an alternative assessment-oriented response coupled with supportive services. With particular emphasis on developments which have occurred since the mid-1990s, this chapter examines the key elements of differential response with respect to child protection, specifically: (1) a more customized approach to families; (2) the development of a more community-based system of child protection; and (3) greater involvement on the part of informal and natural helpers.

Beginning with Missouri's experiment with differential response, one of the first (along with Florida) to be piloted and closely evaluated, Waldfogel reviews and discusses this model case and the effect it has had on the proliferation of alternative response programs in other jurisdictions. This examination poses the key question: Has differential response lived up to its promise? Waldfogel examines the evidence on this question, from the 26 states that have adopted some form of differential response to date.

Next, William Meezan and Bowen McBeath look at one state's attempt at privatization of child welfare services in "The Implementation of Market-Based Child Welfare Innovations." The Adoption and Safe Families Act of 1997 has had the net effect of increasing privatization in a number of jurisdictions. Using qualitative data from a larger pilot study of the Wayne County (Detroit), Michigan, child welfare system, Meezan and McBeath review the perceptions of staff from nine nonprofit agencies that partnered with Michigan's public welfare agency to provide foster care services. The authors provide an insightful overview of private sector involvement in the provision of child welfare services across the nation and the new organizational forms engendered by these practices. Two market-based models from the health care sector are examined: performance-based contracting and variations on managed care. They review performance-based contracting and the incentives provided for nonprofit agencies to meet contracted outcomes specified by public agencies. They also provide an in-depth look at the more complex and comprehensive responsibilities of managed care approaches. Of particular importance with regard to both issues are the scant data available for assessing effectiveness and the resultant questions that arise as to future courses of research. With respect to this matter, the authors pose a number of salient questions, which go to the very heart of public-private partnerships. Most notably, what are the effects of financially driven initiatives, and what are their effects on the ways in which personnel approach their jobs? Of particular interest is the authors' review of the research methodology used in the process evaluation of this pilot and its contextual implications for future study.

The third chapter in this section, "Self-Evaluation: Using Data to Guide Policy and Practice in Public Child Welfare Agencies," addresses the needs of child welfare agencies to assess their own achievements. Self-evaluation provides a method for child welfare agencies to structure and implement programs and practice. Today, self-evaluation is not simply a reflective exercise but a practiced methodology for assessment, planning, and operation. An outgrowth of the Annie E. Casey Foundation's Family to Family Initiative begun in 1992, self-evaluation uses data to drive the decisions and actions of organizations to better serve the particular needs of their clienteles. Defining goals and progress through the use of various technical resources, including computer technology, benefits supervisory practice, staff development, and general support.

Daniel Webster, Lynn Usher, Barbara Needell, and Judith Wildfire discuss the basic aspects of self-evaluation, including review of the organizational culture, attitude adjustment, intra-agency cooperation, and the recasting of personal opinions. On a more technical level, the authors discuss computer software that can assist in mapping and geographic study and some new possibilities for gathering and analyzing data. Also addressed is a team concept for agency organization and the consequent improvement of delivery of services by using neighborhood targeting and better assignment of caseworkers.

The major program to impact the economic situation of poor and disadvantaged children has historically been the public welfare program. However, during the last several decades, public welfare and child welfare have had almost no connection. In their chapter, "Comparing Welfare and Child Welfare Populations: An Argument for Rethinking the Safety Net," Mark Courtney, Amy Dworsky, Irving Piliavin, and Steven McMurtry examine whether the welfare reforms initiated during the 1990s have sufficiently altered the purpose of welfare programs and the populations they serve to warrant a rethinking of the relationship between economic support programs and social services for children and families. The authors use data from two ongoing studies in Milwaukee County, Wisconsin, to provide empirical evidence supporting the claim that workfare and child welfare programs serve increasingly similar populations with similar needs. In spite of the similar needs of these populations, these two systems continue to operate largely independently, if not at cross-purposes. Their findings call into question the federal welfare and child welfare policies that lead state and local policy makers to create such misaligned systems.

In the fourth chapter of this section, "Promoting Child Well-Being Through Early Intervention: Findings from the Chicago Longitudinal Study," Arthur Reynolds and Joshua Mersky examine the critical issue of early intervention. Having gained considerable attention in recent years, the practice of early intervention from birth (or before) to the formative school years would seem to be essential, with the greatest promise of success in providing educational, family, health, and social support for those at greatest risk. This is especially true for those who are likely to be facing poor

outcomes due to socioeconomic disadvantages. Contemporary research (described in the chapter) makes it clear that early intervention in the form of Head Start, preschool, and early childhood education makes a significant impact on cognitive development, school readiness, and the attendant social skills that derive from these. Of particular interest is the presentation of findings from longitudinal studies that have focused on this subject. As might be expected, the data show the substantial impact of early intervention with respect to remedial education, family support, school mobility, juvenile delinquency, and child maltreatment.

In "Heeding *Horton*: Transcending the Public Welfare Paradigm," David Stoesz asks the larger question: How much progress have we made in improving the conditions of poor and low-income children and their parents? Stoesz helps us to take our first steps toward looking beyond the public welfare paradigm to some of the other salient issues. These include mental health issues, the role of the courts, poverty, the distinction between inadequate care and abuse, institutional neglect and abuse, and "foster care drift" (the practice of moving a child from one foster home to another). Also discussed are matters relating to family preservation, the notion of supporting safe and stable families: cash assistance, waivers, single parenting, high school dropout rates, chronic health issues, employment, and eligibility issues. Of particular note in this chapter is the notion of looking beyond the child welfare paradigm to other complicating matters, such as our wholly inadequate health care system, which excludes large numbers of the general population, seniors, and, of particular concern, children. In this regard, we begin to see how a truly effective system of child welfare and protection must include and embrace a myriad of diverse but related issues affecting parents and children. Stoesz asserts that the child welfare paradigm has all but collapsed in the face of the broader problems examined in this section and that the future is vague and disconcerting.

Last, we turn our attention to one of the most promising initiatives for confronting child welfare issues: the creation of a national system of savings and asset building for children. If one can imagine Social Security in reverse—providing income for the individual beginning at birth—one can speculate as to the broad advantages and opportunities that might be afforded to that individual in many of the areas discussed in this section. With respect to having postnatal health care, access to preschool, college savings, and first- time home ownership, the concept of child savings accounts are awesome by their very nature and may well be the best course for ensuring continuous successful development of our nation's children and future stakeholders. A comprehensive plan to assist everyone in building assets—child savings accounts—represents a social investment in all children at the time of birth and throughout their formative years. For low-income families, child savings accounts would provide a means to develop a financial base and, over time, could evolve into a universal system through which all individuals would meet their lifelong financial needs. Drawing upon a large body of data to explore this issue, Reid Cramer in "Accounts at Birth: A Proposal to Improve Life Chances Through a National System of Children's Savings Accounts" looks at all sides of the question, including the tricky matter of political willingness to achieve such goals.

Beginning with an examination of the American Savings for Personal Investment, Retirement, and Education Act (ASPIRE), Cramer reviews and considers a wide variety of design choices that will ultimately shape and direct any child savings program. With the objective of assisting policy makers and advocates in implementing a universal system of child accounts, this is the most comprehensive and thoughtful examination of this subject to date.

The chapters in this section expand our awareness and comprehension of current research in the field and inform our understanding of child welfare issues and practices to the benefit of policy makers and practitioners.

References

Lindsey, D. (2008). *The future of children.* New York: Oxford University Press.

14

The Future of Child
Protection Revisited

Jane Waldfogel

Nearly 10 years ago, in *The Future of Child Protection* (Waldfogel, 1998a), I reviewed the state of child protective services (CPS) and argued that major reforms were needed to better meet the needs of children and families referred to the CPS system. In particular, my review pointed to the promise of "differential response" as a way to better engage families at the front end of CPS. Differential response, which at that time was being piloted in just a few states (e.g., Missouri and Florida), entailed the separation of reports into those that warranted a traditional, investigative response and those that could benefit from an alternative, more assessment-oriented response. Differential response offered great promise, but also posed risks and challenges, and therefore it was not clear how widely it would be adopted or what its results would be.

In this chapter, I revisit differential response and examine the evidence that has accumulated on it over the past decade. We now know a good deal more about the promise, and pitfalls, of this new approach to child protection. With the past decade's evidence

in hand, we can make a more informed judgment as to the role that differential response might play in the future of child protection.

CHILD PROTECTION AND
THE CASE FOR DIFFERENTIAL
RESPONSE

Child protection refers to a set of public policies, funding mechanisms, agencies, and services that represent society's response to child abuse and neglect. While exact legislation, funding mechanisms, and services differ across states (and even more substantially across countries), most CPS systems operate on the assumption that child maltreatment is a distinct condition that requires intervention by the state.

Child protection tends to encompass three broad areas: reporting, screening and investigation (often referred to as the intake phase), and disposition and service provision. In the area of reporting, all 50 states in the United States have laws in place that stipulate when a report of abuse or neglect should be filed and who may be required to file such a report. While all states have reporting laws that require certain individuals (e.g., doctors and teachers) to report suspected child maltreatment, voluntary reports from concerned citizens are almost always accepted. Once a report is made, there are a variety of possible responses at intake, but typically, the next stage is a screening process in which a decision is made as to whether the state has both a mandate and sufficient information to investigate the reported family. When both of these factors hold, an investigation or assessment is undertaken to determine if a child has been maltreated, whether the child and family should receive services to prevent further maltreatment, and whether the child can remain safely at home or should be removed to foster care or another out-of-home setting.

The operation of child protective services in the United States has been criticized on several counts. In particular, five major problems with CPS have been identified (Waldfogel, 1998a):

1. *Overinclusion.* Some families who are in the system should not be, and others who are low risk receive an unnecessarily adversarial response from CPS.
2. *Underinclusion.* At the same time, some families who should be involved with CPS are not (this group includes families missed by the system, families not reported, and families who ask for services voluntarily but are not provided them).
3. *Capacity.* The number of families involved with CPS at any one time far exceeds the capacity of the system to serve them.
4. *Service delivery.* Many families do not receive needed services, while for many others service delivery is fragmented and lacks coherence.
5. *Service orientation.* The dual mandate of CPS—to protect children and also to preserve families—creates tensions in the system and makes it difficult for agencies to provide services appropriately tailored to individual families' needs. Instead, agencies tend to adopt a one-size-fits-all response which, depending on the case, may be too oriented toward child protection and insufficiently oriented toward family preservation, or vice versa.

To address these fundamental problems and tensions within CPS, a new approach to child protection is needed, one that I have called "differential response." The key elements of a differential response to child protection are (1) a more customized approach to families; (2) the development of a more community-based system of child protection; and (3) greater involvement on the part of informal and natural helpers. Each of these is essential if CPS agencies are to move away from a one-size-fits-all approach and toward one that better meets the needs of the diverse range of children and families coming to the attention of CPS.

If differential response can achieve these aims, it offers great promise. Writing in 2000, I predicted optimistically:

> The CPS of the future, and its partners, will provide a differential response, tailored to the specific needs of each family with a child at risk of abuse or neglect. CPS will retain primary, but not sole, responsibility for the most serious cases of abuse or neglect, because other community partners, formal and informal, will also play a role. For less serious cases, non-CPS partners will exercise primary responsibility, but they too will draw upon other partners, formal and informal, on a case by case basis. From a family's perspective, the system will look and feel quite different. Services will be provided by a team, rather than a CPS social worker and other workers acting independently. Critically important from the family's perspective, services will be provided on a voluntary basis unless the severity of the abuse or neglect makes authoritative intervention necessary. (Waldfogel, 2000, pp. 54–55)

WHAT DOES DIFFERENTIAL RESPONSE ENTAIL?

For CPS agencies wishing to move toward a more customized approach to families, the starting point is to implement differential response at the point of screening and intake. Typically, CPS agencies have had a narrowly prescribed response to reports of abuse or neglect, and reports that are screened in must be investigated in a way that satisfies strict rules and regulations that specify who must be seen and in what time frame. The focus of a traditional investigation is to determine whether a child has been abused or neglected and by whom, and also whether services, including removal, are needed on an emergency basis in order to guarantee the child's safety. The investigation concludes with a determination as to whether a child was abused or neglected and a recording of the identity of the likely perpetrator. In this respect, a CPS investigation bears some similarity to a police investigation, and in some jurisdictions, police investigators actually carry out CPS investigations, or accompany CPS investigators on at least some cases.

There are good reasons for the investigative orientation of the traditional CPS response. In the highest-risk cases, where a child is at risk of serious injury or harm by a caregiver, a quick and authoritative response is necessary. And, contacts with the alleged perpetrator necessarily will be adversarial. Many of these cases, after all, will result in court involvement, involuntary removal of the child, and possibly criminal charges against the perpetrator.

But what about the less serious cases? A large share of the cases referred to CPS do not involve serious or criminal abuse or neglect but rather involve less serious forms of maltreatment or the risk of maltreatment. A typical low-risk case might involve a 7-year-old child who is missing school a lot, perhaps because she is being kept home to help care for her 4-year-old brother when her mother is not feeling well. Such cases are typically screened in by CPS but arguably do not need a heavy-handed and adversarial response, which might only serve to alienate the family. Rather, they could benefit from a more assessment-oriented response that asks families how they are doing and what services might help them to meet their children's needs.

In a low-risk case like this, the challenge is not so much to determine whether the child is missing school, but rather why it is happening and what might be done to remedy the situation. In such a case, removal of the child, or long-term involvement with CPS, is unlikely. Rather, the most that is likely to be offered is short-term services by CPS or a referral for services from another provider in the community. For this reason, engaging with the family in a constructive way and enlisting the help and services of community partners or informal helping networks are crucial. Not to engage in this way is to miss an opportunity. Cases such as this may deteriorate and return with more serious problems if initial referrals are not responded to appropriately. At the same time, if approached in a low-key and non-threatening way, many low-risk families may be willing to accept help on a voluntary basis.

The alert reader will have spotted already the challenges that moving to a differential response system pose. Most obviously, there is the challenge of distinguishing which cases need a traditional investigation versus which ones could safely benefit from a more assessment-oriented response. Perhaps a case which appears at the time of the report to involve serious and criminal abuse is not so serious after all, while a case that looked to be just a benign instance of a child missing school from time to time actually involves serious abuse at home. Agencies that use a differential response approach, therefore, must have a very good system for distinguishing high-risk and low-risk cases and a fail-safe system for transferring cases between the two tracks should the need arise (if a low-risk case is inappropriately placed in the investigation track, or a high-risk case inappropriately referred to the assessment track).

A differential response system must have the capacity to effectively deliver both types of response: a police-oriented investigation that determines whether a child has been abused or neglected and by whom and that can take immediate steps to assure his or her protection, and a service-oriented assessment that engages families and identifies service needs and that has the capacity to meet those needs. Thus, a differential response system must have, in addition to trained investigators, workers who know how to engage families. It must also have links with community-based partners and with informal helping networks, links that traditional CPS agencies have not typically had. With limited resources and the need to always give priority to investigative and protective activities, CPS agencies cannot provide long-term services to low-risk families. The involvement of other partners, not traditionally involved with CPS, is crucial. So too is the capacity to engage families and to work with them to make lasting changes.

THE EVIDENCE: HOW WIDELY HAS DIFFERENTIAL RESPONSE BEEN ADOPTED AND WITH WHAT RESULTS?

When differential response was first proposed, it was clear that the challenges, and risks, involved in implementing differential response would make it unlikely that it would be adopted in all jurisdictions overnight. Rather, CPS agencies would understandably be cautious and might hesitate to adopt the new approach, or might wish to pilot it in selected areas first (as one of the early pioneering states, Missouri, did). It was also not clear that differential response would succeed in meeting all of its objectives: providing better protection to children and better meeting children's and families' needs. Perhaps children referred to the assessment track would not receive adequate protection, or would not receive additional services. What does the evidence from the past decade show? How widely has differential response been adopted and with what results?

As noted earlier, Florida and Missouri were the first states to experiment with differential response, starting in 1993 and 1994, respectively (Waldfogel, 1998a, 1998b). Florida's experiment was relatively short-lived, as subsequent reforms moved that state's system in a different direction; but Missouri's reforms (discussed in further detail below), after being piloted and closely evaluated, were subsequently extended statewide, serving as a model for other states to follow.

By 2001, a literature review conducted by Walter A. McDonald Associates found a total of 10 states that had differential response systems at intake (Iowa, Louisiana, Minnesota, New Jersey, North Dakota, Texas, Virginia, and Washington, in addition to Florida and Missouri; U.S. Department of Health and Human Services, 2001). Of these, 5 (Florida, Iowa, Missouri, Virginia, and Washington) had some form of evaluation or review (for reports on Florida, see Hernandez & Barrett, 1996; Wakeling, 1995, 1996; for Iowa, see Center for the Study of Social Policy, 1996; for Missouri, see Siegel & Loman, 2000; for Virginia, see Virginia Department of Social Services, 1999; and for Washington, see English, Wingard, Marshall, Orme, & Orme, 2000).

These initial reports were fairly positive, finding that a substantial share of families referred to CPS could be safely handled on the assessment rather than the investigative track (in Missouri and Virginia, for example, two thirds or more of families referred were seen on the assessment track). Families seen on the assessment track were open for services with CPS for less time and were more likely to receive community-based services (Florida and Missouri). And, the Missouri evaluation found that fewer children were re-referred in the pilot counties. The report from Washington state was less positive (for instance, although fewer children were re-referred in the alternative response track than in the CPS track, the difference was not statistically significant). However, Washington state's reform was not really comparable, as it involved the referral of screened-out cases to a community-based agency (rather than the referral of screened-in cases for an alternative response).

Following its literature review, Walter A. McDonald Associates conducted a national study of child protective services systems and reform efforts for the federal Department of Health and Human Services. Completed in 2003, the national study identified 20 states that were offering an alternative response at intake in at least some jurisdictions, with an alternative response defined as "a formal response of your agency that assesses the needs of the child or family without requiring a determination that maltreatment has occurred or that the child is at risk of maltreatment" (U.S. Department of Health and Human Services, 2003a, p. 5.1). Of these, 11 had alternative response systems in place statewide (Georgia, Kansas, Kentucky, Maine, Missouri, Oklahoma, Pennsylvania, South Dakota, Vermont, Virginia, Wyoming), while 9 had pilot or local programs only (Alaska, Arizona, Indiana, Louisiana, Minnesota, Nevada, Utah, Washington, West Virginia). Subsequent to the review, several other states began experimenting with differential response systems. North Carolina began a pilot in 2002, which was implemented statewide in 2005. As of 2006, California, Connecticut, Maryland, and Wisconsin also had at least some counties experimenting with differential response. In addition, New Jersey had (since 2000) an alternative response system (although it was not included in the 2003 Walter A. MacDonald study).

The alternative responses in the 20 states included in the national study had in common that they were intended for lower-risk families and designed to be more assessment- and service-oriented and less threatening and intimidating to families (U.S. Department of Health and Human Services, 2003b). However, in practice, it was not always clear just how different the assessment and investigation tracks were (U.S. Department of Health and Human Services, 2003b, 2003c). In many jurisdictions, the same workers carried out both assessments and investigations, and some reported that many of their activities were similar regardless of the track. The main difference seemed to be that workers had more discretion when carrying out an assessment; that is, the list of activities that they had to carry out was shorter, consisting mainly of reviewing prior CPS records, interviewing or observing the children, interviewing the caregivers, and consulting with involved professionals as needed. In addition, as noted above, the overall goal of the alternative response was different, focused less on whether maltreatment had occurred and who had committed it, and more on what services might be necessary. In line with this, families receiving an alternative response were less likely to be listed on a central registry tracking victims and perpetrators of child abuse and neglect than were families who had been investigated.

Agencies that had implemented differential response also commented on the challenges they faced and the needs they saw to improve their systems (U.S. Department of Health and Human Services, 2003b). Several of the challenges they mentioned resonate with those identified earlier: to establish mechanisms to move cases from one track to another if needed, to better integrate CPS services with community-based services, and to train workers in how to engage families. Other challenges were unexpected: the need to review workloads and to establish specific and limited goals for intervention. Agencies also pointed to the specific challenge posed by domestic violence cases, which needed attention to both family needs and safety and thus did not fit neatly into either the standard investigative or assessment model.

A subsequent in-depth study of six states with differential response systems (Kentucky, Minnesota, Missouri, New Jersey, Oklahoma, and Wyoming) sheds further light on how alternative responses differ from traditional investigative responses and how families offered alternative responses are faring (Shusterman, Hollinshead, Fluke, & Yuan, 2005). Using data from the National Child Abuse and Neglect Data System (NCANDS), the report examined outcomes for 313,838 children who were reported to CPS agencies in 2002, of whom 140,072 received an alternative response. The six states studied represent all of the states with differential response systems for which case-level data were available in 2002 and which had more than 1% of their caseload receiving an alternative response. Within these six states, there was considerable variation in the share of reported families receiving an alternative (rather than investigative) response, ranging from 20% in both Oklahoma and Minnesota, 27% in Kentucky, to 58% in Wyoming, 64% in Missouri, and 71% in New Jersey (Shusterman et al., 2005, Figure 1). Nevertheless, the six states were consistent in that each used the alternative response for lower-risk cases (cases involving older children, children reported by schools or nonprofessionals, and children at risk of less serious forms of maltreatment, in particular, not sexual abuse).

In terms of outcomes, families seen on the assessment track were more likely to receive in-home services and less likely to have their children placed than were families seen on the investigation track. Children who were assessed were no more likely to have repeat reports of maltreatment within the next 6 months than children who were investigated (and in one state, Oklahoma, were less likely to be re-reported). This finding is consistent with individual state studies (such as Missouri's) that also found that differential response systems did not lead to higher recurrence rates among those provided with an alternative response. However, given that children who are referred to the assessment track are lower-risk cases to begin with, it is not clear how much weight should be placed on the recurrence results when differences in case characteristics or risk levels are not controlled.

For this reason, evidence from a random assignment evaluation in Minnesota is particularly relevant. Minnesota began its experiment with differential response in 2001 by randomly assigning families who had been determined to be eligible for an alternative response to receive either an alternative response or a traditional investigative response. Because of the random assignment, families who were assessed were comparable to those who were investigated in terms of their level of risk at referral and presumably also their risk of recurrence. The results as of 2004 indicated that families randomly assigned to the alternative response received more services and were less likely to have a repeat report than similar families randomly assigned to the investigative track (Loman & Siegel, 2004, 2005). Both families and workers liked the assessment approach better, and families were more likely to say they had been involved in decision making and had benefited from their involvement with CPS. In addition, although handling a case on the assessment track cost more money in the short run (due to increased worker time and services costs), it saved money in the long run, due to the reduction in subsequent costs associated with the lower recurrence rates.

Non-experimental evaluations conducted in several states provide further information about differential response (see, for example, Center for Child and Family Policy, 2004; Loman & Siegel, 2004; Siegel & Loman, 2000; Virginia Department of Social Services, 2004; Texas Department of Social Services, 1999). Missouri is a particularly informative case, having been one of the earliest states to experiment with differential response and one of the most extensively evaluated. The initial stage of Missouri's reform, begun in 1994, had a quasi-experimental design. The reform was implemented in 14 small and medium-sized counties across the state and in selected zip codes from St. Louis County and the city of St. Louis. It was then evaluated against a control group drawn from similar areas (from around the state, St. Louis County, and the city of St. Louis). The evaluation of this initial pilot (Siegel & Loman, 2000) found that child safety was as good or better in the reform areas and that recurrence of abuse/neglect reports was lower, while families received services sooner, were more cooperative, and were more satisfied. The findings on child safety—in particular, the lower recurrence rate for reports—were echoed in the findings of an evaluation of community partnerships for child protection, which also found reductions in repeat reports in its Missouri site (St. Louis) (Daro, Budde, Baker, Nesmith, & Harden, 2005). Nevertheless, the magnitude of the effects was relatively modest, a finding that the evaluators attributed to high caseloads and limited resources to fund services for low-risk families. The Missouri legislature had stipulated that the reform had to be cost-neutral and had not allocated any new funding for additional caseworkers, nor had it funded additional services for families on the assessment track, instead counting on community-based agencies to provide these.

A 5-year follow up (Loman & Siegel, 2004) found that re-report rates for families in the reform areas continued to be lower 5 years post-referral. However, the 5-year follow-up also found that out-of-home placement rates were slightly higher for families from the reform areas, a finding that seemed to be linked to a lack of services for low-risk families, in particular, those with teenagers.

In 1998, differential response in Missouri was converted from a pilot into a statewide policy, and by 1999 had been implemented in every county in the state. An evaluation using data up to 2002 (Loman & Siegel, 2004) found varied opinions among staff about the new approach, with some endorsing the underlying philosophy and feeling that families were better served, while others did not agree with or understand the rationale or saw other challenges to implementing the new approach. The evaluation also compared the status of a sample of cases reported to CPS pre-reform and post-reform (in counties that had not been part of the initial pilot). The pre-reform families all received an investigative response, whereas the post-reform families received either an investigation or an assessment, depending on the nature of the case. Two years after referral, few differences were apparent when comparing the pre-reform and post-reform cases, although

placement rates were slightly higher post-reform for the highest-risk families. However, given the simple pre-versus-post design, it is not clear if the results were due to the reform or to other changes over time.

CONCLUSIONS

A decade ago, differential response was a new approach that had been implemented in just two pilot states, Florida and Missouri. Today, it is becoming a more widely accepted form of CPS practice. At least 26 states (the 20 identified as of 2003 plus at least 6 others—California, Connecticut, Maryland, New Jersey, North Carolina, and Wisconsin) have some kind of alternative response in place alongside the more traditional investigative response, and national reports such as the *Child Maltreatment* series (U.S. Department of Health and Human Services, 2006) routinely collect and report data on families receiving an alternative response as well as those being investigated.

Has differential response lived up to its promise? Are families who are offered an alternative response faring better than they would have under a more investigation-oriented system, that is, are children better protected and are children and families more likely to receive services they need? The evidence thus far suggests that the answer may well be yes. To the extent that child safety and repeat maltreatment can be measured, children seem to be as well, or better, off on these indicators under differential response. And, families seem to be receiving more services and to be more satisfied with them, although long-run outcomes for children and families have yet to be evaluated.

But the evidence also points to challenges. Differential response is not a panacea. Even with a more assessment-oriented response for the lower-risk cases, the challenges of working with families referred to CPS remain: assessing risk, engaging families, and walking that fine line between protecting children and preserving families. Differential response requires well-trained staff, good relations with community-based agencies, and funding for services for low-risk as well as higher-risk families. But, even with these challenges, the evidence suggests that differential response may offer an improved response for lower-risk families, without jeopardizing children's safety in either low- or higher-risk cases. In a system as beleaguered as CPS, that surely is good news.

References

Center for Child and Family Policy, Duke University. (2004). *Multiple response system (MRS) evaluation report to the North Carolina Division of Social Services (NCDSS).* Durham, NC: Author.

Center for the Study of Social Policy. (1996). *A review of the impact of Iowa's assessment legislation.* Washington, DC: Author.

Daro, D., Budde, S., Baker, S., Nesmith, A., & Harden, A. (2005). *Community partnerships for protecting children: Phase II outcome evaluation: Final report.* Chicago: Chapin Hall Center for Children.

English, D., Wingard, T., Marshall, D., Orme, M., & Orme, A. (2000). Alternative responses to child protective services. *Child Abuse and Neglect, 24*(3), 375–388.

Hernandez, M., & Barrett, B. (1996). *Evaluation of Florida's family services response system.* Tampa: Florida Mental Health Institute.

Loman, L. A., & Siegel, G. L. (2004). *Minnesota alternative response evaluation: Final report.* St. Louis, MO: Institute of Applied Research. Available: http://www.iarstl.org.

Loman, L. A., & Siegel, G. L. (2005). Alternative response in Minnesota: Findings of the program evaluation. *Protecting Children, 20*(2–3), 79–92.

Siegel, G. L., & Loman, L. A. (2000). *The Missouri family assessment and response demonstration impact evaluation: Digest of findings and conclusions.* St. Louis, MO: Institute of Applied Research. Available: http://www.iarstl.org.

Shusterman, G.R., Hollinshead, D., Fluke, J.D., & Yuan, Y.T. (2005). *Alternative responses to child maltreatment: Findings from NCANDS.* Washington, DC: U.S. Department of Health and Human Services, ASPE. Available: http://aspe.hhs.gov/hsp/05/child-maltreat-resp/report.pdf

Texas Department of Social Services. (1999). *Flexible response evaluation.* Austin: Author.

U.S. Department of Health and Human Services. (2001). *National study of child protective services systems and reform efforts: Literature review.* Available: http://aspe.hhs.gov/hsp/cps-status03.

U.S. Department of Health and Human Services. (2003a). *National study of child protective services systems and reform efforts: Review of state CPS policy.* Available: http://aspe.hhs.gov/hsp/cps-status03.

U.S. Department of Health and Human Services. (2003b). *National study of child protective services systems and reform efforts: A summary report.* Available: http://aspe.hhs.gov/hsp/cps-status03.

U.S. Department of Health and Human Services. (2003c). *National study of child protective services systems and reform efforts: Findings on local CPS practices.* Available: http://aspe.hhs.gov/hsp/cps-sta tus03.

U.S. Department of Health and Human Services. (2006). *Child maltreatment 2004.* Available: www. acfhhs.gov/programs/cb/stats_research/index. htm#can.

Virginia Department of Social Services. (1999). *Final report on the multiple response system for child protective services in Virginia.* Richmond: Author.

Virginia Department of Social Services. (2004). *Evaluation of the differential response system.* Available: http://www.dss.state.va.us/files/division/dfs/cps/reports/eval_drs.pdf.

Wakeling, S. (1995). *Child protective services reform in Florida.* Cambridge, MA: Kennedy School of Government.

Wakeling, S. (1996). *Child protective services reform in Florida: A brief update.* Cambridge, MA: Kennedy School of Government.

Waldfogel, J. (1998a). *The future of child protection: How to break the cycle of abuse and neglect.* Cambridge, MA: Harvard University Press.

Waldfogel, J. (1998b). Rethinking the paradigm for child protection. *Future of Children, 8*(1), 104–120.

Waldfogel, J. (2000). Reforming child protective services. *Child Welfare, 79*(1), 43–58.

15

The Implementation of Market-Based Child Welfare Innovations

William Meezan

Bowen McBeath

INTRODUCTION

In response to escalating foster care caseloads and costs, and reports of state child welfare system failures, Congress passed the Adoption and Safe Families Act in 1997 (PL 105-89). Placing child safety, permanency, and well-being as the paramount concerns of the child welfare system, PL 105-89 changed previous law in ways that legislators believed would move children through the child welfare system more efficiently without compromising their safety. Many of the precepts undergirding this federal legislation had been articulated and translated into law in a number of states prior to the passage of the federal statute. For example, in Michigan, the "Binsfield legislation" (Craig, Kulik, James, & Nielsen, 1998) had codified many of the principles that were eventually articulated in PL 105-89.

With its strong focus on improving the performance of child welfare systems, PL 105-89 encouraged states to develop and implement child welfare innovations, and since its passage, many states have received federal Title IV-E waivers to reorganize the ways in which they deliver child welfare services (Wulczyn, 2000a, 2000b; U.S. General Accounting Office, 1995). Some child welfare systems have embraced privatization through expanded purchase-of-service contracting arrangements and have thus developed new ways to shift the responsibility for portions of their public child welfare system to private agencies (U.S. General Accounting Office, 1998; Craig et al., 1998).

While many child welfare services have traditionally been provided through purchase-of-service contracts between the public sector and private nonprofit agencies (a service arrangement particularly prevalent in large eastern cities), private sector involvement in the provision of child welfare services has expanded nationally.[1] In many states, this public-private partnership has taken on a number of new organizational forms, as public child welfare agencies have borrowed market-based models from the health care sector and applied them to their contractual relationships with nonprofit child welfare agencies. Two market-based models that have been embraced by public child welfare systems are performance-based contracting and variations on a number of managed care models. In *performance-based contracting* approaches, public agencies provide incentives for nonprofit agencies to meet contractually specified outcomes. *Managed care* models are usually more comprehensive in that they usually involve some combination of performance-based contracting, prospective payments, capitation, and/or the transfer of case management responsibilities (Geen & Tumlin, 1999; Malm, Bess, Leos-Urbel, Geen, & Markowitz, 2001). As of 1998, the most recent year for which data are available, 29 state child welfare systems had initiated a total of 47 performance-based or managed care initiatives (McCullough & Schmitt, 1999, 2000; U.S. General Accounting Office, 1998).

The growing incidence of contracting out and experimentation with financially driven models, such as performance-based contracting and managed care, is symptomatic of a broader trend of marketization in social services, through which public agencies have sought to incorporate various organizational models and practices from the private sector. For example, managed care and other market-based contracting mechanisms have become increasingly common in other sectors that impact child welfare-involved children and families, including the physical health, mental health, and substance abuse sectors (Mechanic, 1999; S. R. Smith, 2002). It is assumed that the incorporation of these approaches into child welfare will result in demonstrable cost savings and improved performance.

Some is known about the impact of these market models on services provision in non-child welfare sectors. It has been demonstrated that special needs populations, including low-income, minority, chronically ill, and disabled groups, may receive fewer important services under these models. Studies have also suggested that considerable variation may exist in how service providers respond to managed care environments and in how such service arrangements impact the well-being of clients. (For reviews of this literature, see Glied, 1999; Hutchinson & Foster, 2003; McBeath, 2006; Miller & Luft, 1994, 1997; Simpson & Fraser, 1999; Szilagyi, 1998.)

Unfortunately, the diffusion of managed care and other financially driven models into child welfare has not been accompanied by research exploring the impact of these initiatives on those involved with services provision. How these innovations are being imple-

mented, and whether the implementation of these market-based models is proceeding as intended by policy makers, are questions that have attracted little empirical research in child welfare (Embry, Buddenhagen, & Bolles, 2000; Snyder & Allen, 2003). Thus, the organizational changes and managerial adaptations that child welfare agencies make as they transition to these market-based contracting environments are unclear.

As a result, child welfare researchers have little systematic information about how managed care and/or performance-based contracting impact core organizational functions and frontline child welfare practices. It is consequently unclear whether child welfare agencies (be they public or private) are able to adapt to market-based environments in a manner that promotes quality service provision and positive child and family outcomes.

Data on some of these topics should become available in the near future, as evaluations are part of roughly half of the 47 state market-based innovations identified by McCullough and Schmitt (2000). However, McCullough and Schmitt (2000) note that these evaluations are likely to emphasize the collection of benefit-cost data (e.g., the average cost of service per case, the percentage of performance indicators met). It is less likely that these evaluations will examine the process by which service providers respond to their financially driven environments, or whether and how these organizational responses alter the manner in which agencies and their workers interact with clients. This neglect of process questions will undermine knowledge development: Without understanding how state initiatives are implemented, and whether they are implemented with fidelity, knowledge of their impact will be limited.

Process evaluations of these market-based initiatives might illuminate at least three currently neglected areas of child welfare research. First, what are market-based child welfare innovations? Given the diversity of managed care and performance-based arrangements within and across various states, it cannot be presumed that these initiatives have similar goals, underlying incentives, target populations, and operational mechanics. Conceptual and operational clarity concerning these initiatives might help to link the various parts of each innovation with their impacts on service providers and clients. Second, what types of agencies "buy in" or provide services under market-based approaches (Shortell, 1997; Goerge, Wulczyn, &Fanshel, 1994)? When given the option, do only certain types of child welfare agencies adopt managed care or other market-driven arrangements? Are differences in organizational structure and processes related to how well or poorly agencies perform in market-based situations (Wulczyn, Orlebeke, & Martin, 2001; Courtney, 2000a, 2000b; Fraser, 1997)? Do nonprofit service providers respond uniformly to managed care and/or performance-based mechanisms, or is there diversity in service provision, networking with other service providers, and/or relations with public child welfare agencies? Finally, do market-based initiatives impact the child welfare agencies and employees who implement them? What changes do child welfare agencies make as they adapt to market-based approaches? How do these market-based approaches impact the ways in which personnel perform their job functions, and the work pressures they feel? As these innovations are implemented, it seems reasonable to assume that the "work" of child welfare will be transformed, and that this transformation will have to be implemented by frontline child welfare workers.

This argument has not yet been empirically tested. Yet the street-level bureaucracy model (Lipsky, 1980; Smith & Donovan, 2003) suggests that researchers should explore the possible differences in how frontline workers, supervisors, and executive staff respond to financially driven work arrangements. Do market-based approaches require child welfare employees to reconceptualize and reorder their roles and tasks? Is worker retention, already low in child welfare (Pecora, Whittaker, Maluccio, & Barth, 2003; Schorr, 2000; U.S. General Accounting Office, 1995), affected by managed care and/or performance-based contracting, and if so, how and why?

This chapter concerns this last set of questions. It examines these questions with data from a qualitative process evaluation of a performance-based, managed care contracting initiative in the Wayne County (Detroit), Michigan, foster care system. In particular, this chapter reviews the perceptions of staff from nine nonprofit child welfare agencies that contracted with Michigan's public welfare agency to provide foster care services under one of two payment mechanisms: a traditional fee-for-service reimbursement system and a performance-based, managed care reimbursement system that contained bonuses for the movement of foster children into permanent placements and the sustainment of those placements.

Data from a structured telephone survey of agency employees allowed for the assessment of market-related changes across various types of staff and on a range of topics, including service delivery, interdepartmental and interorganizational relations, staffing patterns and staff training, staff roles and responsibilities, and financial management and information technology. Additionally, interviews with staff from foster care agencies that were not operating under performance-based, managed care contracts at the time (but that expected to operate under this system in the near future) provided a comparative perspective of the changes that agencies expected they would have to make if they were to implement the market-based contracting initiative.

The first section of this chapter provides an overview of the performance-based, managed care contracting initiative (the pilot). The second section reviews the research methodology used in this part of the process evaluation of the pilot. The third section describes the impact of the pilot on child welfare agencies and their staffs. The chapter then moves to a discussion of the study's principal results, their implications for child welfare researchers and practitioners, and issues that merit further study. It concludes by placing these results in the context of the larger evaluation that was completed of this performance-based, managed care initiative.

THE WAYNE COUNTY FOSTER CARE PERMANENCY PILOT INITIATIVE

Nonprofit agencies currently serve roughly 85% of the foster children and families in Wayne County; in addition to handling all CPS responsibilities, the county public welfare agency cares for the remaining foster children and families. This percentage has not changed significantly since the mid-1980s, which suggests that in recent history nonprofit social service agencies have provided most of the services received by foster children and their families, as well as foster families, in Wayne County. Since the 1960s, nonprofit agencies in Wayne County have entered into purchase-of-service contracts with the state public welfare agency (called the Family Independence Agency [FIA] at the time of the study). In return for public funding, nonprofit agencies in Wayne County accept the responsibility for shepherding children and their families through the foster care system and providing the services deemed necessary to move foster children toward permanent placements, including reunification with birth families, kin placements, and adoption.

Until 1997, all nonprofit foster care agencies in Wayne County operated under purchase-of-service contracts in which they were reimbursed for their service-related expenses on a per- child, per-diem basis. The per-child reimbursement rate ranged from $17 to $34 per day, depending on the severity of the needs of the foster child and his or her family; an agency would be reimbursed at a higher per-diem rate if it cared for a child deemed by FIA to need specialized services.

In 1997, FIA implemented, on a limited basis, a performance-based, managed care contracting initiative in the Wayne County foster care system that came to be known as the "pilot." Three factors led FIA to design and implement this initiative. First, state legislators wanted FIA to design a reimbursement system that might shorten the length of time that children spent in foster care. Second, Orchards Children's Services, a nonprofit agency that cared for about 20% of the Wayne County foster care caseload, asked FIA to add to its standard foster care contract elements of performance-based contracting and an up-front lump sum payment that its caseworkers could use to provide flexible services to foster children and their families. Third, under the Binsfield legislation, FIA and its contracting nonprofit agencies faced shorter time frames for making decisions in cases of child maltreatment, including a shorter period between the date of entry and the date when a permanency hearing must be held by the court, and shorter timelines and stricter guidelines around the termination of parental rights (Craig et al., 1998).

The pilot had two primary objectives: to reduce the number of days that children spent in foster care and to increase the number of foster children who reach a permanent placement, defined as the reunification of a foster child with his or her biological parent(s), the placement of the child with a relative, the establishment of legal guardianship for the child, independent living, or adoption. A secondary objective of the pilot was to allow nonprofit agencies to provide services to foster children and families in a more flexible manner, thereby better meeting clients' needs (Family Independence Agency, 2000).

In order to encourage agencies to meet these objectives, FIA altered the provisions for agency reimbursement in its standard purchase-of-service contract. Rather than being reimbursed for service costs on a per-child, per-diem basis, agencies with pilot contracts provided services on a reduced per-diem basis. The new contracts did not contain a graduated per-diem rate for foster children and their families that was determined by the child or family's needs; instead, agencies were reimbursed at a flat rate of $13.20 per day. Agencies' revenues, however, were supplemented by an initial payment of $2,210 per child, as well as additional per-child bonus payments that ranged from $1,290 to $1,900 if performance milestones were met. These milestones included the achievement of permanent placements for children within specified time frames, the timely termination of parental rights, and the sustainment of children within permanent placements. Agencies were allowed to use their bonuses and per-diem payments as they saw fit. Table 15.1 illustrates the way in which pilot contracts differed from FIA's fee-for-service contracts.

The pilot contracts thus contained two financial mechanisms that are characteristic of managed care models: risk shifting and cost containment (Embry, Buddenhagen, & Bolles, 2000; Wernet, 1999; Wulczyn, 2000b).[2] The fiscal logic undergirding the pilot suggested that nonprofit agencies would benefit financially if they reached the performance milestones within preset guidelines; if agencies were unable to achieve these benchmarks, they would incur a monetary loss. Moreover, where agencies were unable to meet pilot milestones, FIA would not bear further financial burden since agencies would have to continue to serve children and families at the lower per-diem rates until the child was discharged from the foster care system.

Between 1997 and 2002, the implementation of the pilot proceeded in three phases. In the first phase, 4 out of 19 nonprofit foster care providers in Wayne County voluntarily contracted with FIA to provide services under this new purchase-of-service arrangement. The second phase began in January 2000, when FIA expanded the number of nonprofit organizations voluntarily operating under the pilot to 6. At this point, 49% of all foster children and families in Wayne County were being served by pilot agencies. In October 2002, FIA expanded the initiative countywide. In this third phase, which lasted until 2004, all 19 nonprofit foster care providers' contracts were altered to reflect the pilot guidelines, and as a result all new foster care entries fell under the pilot reimbursement rules.

TABLE 15.1 Per-Child Reimbursement Structure of the Wayne County Foster Care Permanency Pilot Initiative

	Traditional	Pilot System
Per-diem rate	$18–$34	$13.20
Payment upon intake into pilot	0	$2,210
Performance Incentives		
Achievement of performance standard (either child's return home or to a relative, or achievement of legal guardianship, or independent living in 290 days; or achievement of termination of parental rights in 515 days)	0	$1,900
Child at home 6 months post–initial discharge	0	$1,290
Child at home 12 months post–initial discharge	0	$1,600
Adoption placement made within 7 months of termination of parental rights	0	$1,290

THE QUALITATIVE PROCESS EVALUATION OF THE PILOT INITIATIVE

In 2001, the authors began an evaluation of the Wayne County pilot that involved the six pilot agencies operating at that time and a comparison group of three nonpilot agencies, to examine the effects of this initiative on service providers and the foster children and families served by these nonprofit agencies.[3] In total, the agencies that participated in the evaluation served nearly two thirds of all foster children and families in Wayne County.

The qualitative process evaluation reported in this chapter was part of a larger study that contained both process and outcome components. The qualitative process evaluation examined child welfare agencies' organizational adaptations to the pilot initiative. In addition, using the equivalent of a true experimental design, a quantitative process evaluation tracked service delivery patterns for a sample of 243 foster children and their families (McBeath, 2006; McBeath & Meezan, 2008). And a quantitative outcome evaluation examined placement outcomes for this same sample of 243 children and their families in order to determine how and at what rates children moved through the foster care system under the different contracting conditions (Meezan & McBeath, 2003, 2005).

In order to understand how nonprofit agencies adapted or expected to adapt to the performance-based, managed care contracting environment, telephone interviews were conducted between August and December 2001 with administrators ($N = 45$) and foster care supervisors ($N = 19$) from the nine pilot and nonpilot

agencies. The respondents in the sample were purposefully chosen for their knowledge of foster care and the pilot. This purposive sampling strategy allowed interviewers to cover a broad set of topics, including service delivery, interdepartmental and interorganizational relations, staffing patterns and staff training, staff roles and responsibilities, and financial management and technology use. These qualitative data allowed for an assessment of pilot-related changes across various levels of agency employees and with employees who performed different tasks within each agency. Thus, the possible impact of the pilot on various organizational dimensions could be examined. Table 15.2 presents summary statistics on the respondents, organized by agency type and the respondent's position within the agency.

Interviews were structured and contained mostly open-ended questions. Personnel in pilot agencies were asked how moving to the pilot had impacted their agencies and their roles within them; nonpilot respondents were asked to consider how they thought moving to the pilot might impact their job functions and their agency. Thus, for example, on questions concerning the effects of the pilot on foster care departments, comparisons between pilot and nonpilot respondents refer to comparisons between *perceived* changes due to the move to a performance-based, managed care contracting system compared to *anticipated* or *expected* changes that might have to be made if nonpilot agencies transitioned to this new market-based environment.

Interview respondents were asked to respond to two types of questions regarding how their agencies adapted—or, in the case of nonpilot respondents, planned to adapt—to the pilot initiative. Respondents were first asked what barriers had existed (or might

TABLE 15.2 Characteristics of Administrators and Supervisors Interviewed

	Administrators				Supervisors			
	Full Sample	Pilot	Nonpilot	p	Full Sample	Pilot	Nonpilot	p
	(N = 45)	(N = 30)	(N = 15)		(N = 19)	(N = 12)	(N = 7)	
Work experience								
Years in social services	18.2	19.1	16.5	NS	14.2	14.5	13.5	NS
Years in child welfare	16.5	16.9	15.7	NS	12.2	12.8	11.2	NS
Years within the agency	10.8	12.5	7.5	*	6.9	8.8	3.6	NS
Years in present position	6.6	7.4	4.9	NS	4.3	5.1	2.9	NS
Employment status (full time)	96%	97%	93%	NS	100%	100%	100%	NS
Education			NS					NS
M.S.W. or other advanced degree	67%	76%	47%		58%	58%	57%	
B.A. or B.S.	29%	20%	47%		42%	42%	43%	
Less than B.A. or B.S.	4%	3%	7%		0	0	0	
Race/ethnic origin				NS				NS
Caucasian	69%	73%	60%		53%	50%	57%	
African American	27%	20%	40%		47%	50%	43%	
Other	4%	7%	0		0	0	0	
Gender (female)	53%	53%	53%	NS	95%	92%	100%	NS
Age	48.7	48.5	49.1	NS	40.1	41.2	38.1	NS
Supervisory load	NA	NA	NA	NA	5.2	5.5	4.6	NS

Notes: NS = not significant   * = p <.05   NA = not applicable.

exist) in organizational practice (e.g., the process by which staff training was carried out) or organizational structure (e.g., staffing patterns) as their agency moved to the pilot initiative; they were then asked to describe how the agency actually changed (or expected to change) its organizational practices or structures in response to moving to the pilot contracting environment.

AGENCY RESPONSES TO THE PILOT INITIATIVE

Analyses of the interviews with pilot and nonpilot agency staff point to three areas that are of particular interest to child welfare researchers and practitioners: (1) key departments within agencies experienced deep operational changes in response to the pilot initiative; (2) agencies were required to overcome significant barriers to change as they transitioned to the pilot contracting environment; and (3) a respondent's role and organizational affiliation led to perceptual differences about what was important in moving toward an incentive-based payment system.

The Depth of Organizational Change Involved in the Transition to the Pilot Initiative

While the pilot affected agencies' major departments either directly or tangentially, foster care departments were particularly transformed by the pilot initiative. Key changes were made in order to assess clients' needs more quickly, to focus additional resources on collecting client and service information, and to pool funds to address the multiple needs of clients systematically and simultaneously. Nearly all agencies created (or expected to create) foster care–specific databases to help staff track client status, services rendered, impending performance payment deadlines, and the expenditure of flexible funds. Some agencies undertook processes that would allow them to identify relative placements during the initial client assessment process.

Many pilot agencies created new types of positions within their foster care departments—case aides, family engagement workers, and relative assessors—whose jobs were specifically aimed to move clients more efficiently through the system and thus meet performance milestones. One pilot administrator noted:

The relative assessor is probably the most important position that you can have in foster care. You're dealing with a multi-problem family. To be able to get out there and start assessing relatives, you can't have your foster care worker do that. There are just too many crises that the worker has to deal with. So you need a worker dedicated to nothing but [assessing relatives]. You need somebody who lives and breathes the idea that the relative is going to provide a safe environment for the kids, and is willing to meet with the relatives at any time.

For some pilot agencies, staffing these new positions with paraprofessionals came at the expense of retaining more expensive clinical staff.

We added more case aides and behavior specialists. The latter were supposed to do more of the hands-on case management with birth parents—helping them find housing, helping to supervise visits, transportation. The former were to do case management functions that we could take away from the case managers. We reduced the number of clinicians to hire case aides and behavior specialists. (Pilot administrator)

The responsibilities of many existing staff changed in response to the pilot. Some agency administrators paid (or expected to pay) increased attention to case-specific issues that might impact their ability to meet performance timelines. One pilot administrator mentioned, "[The pilot] definitely brought me closer to our foster care services. I bet you that I know every name of the kids we have now. Now I can tell you their service plan—where each one is going." Many supervisory-level respondents also mentioned that they paid (or expected to pay) greater attention to pilot-related timelines and to helping frontline staff move foster children and families toward permanency more quickly. One pilot supervisor noted, "The deadlines—the purpose of the pilot is to do faster, better business—so you have to do more assessment, more visiting, you basically need to know what the kid's about."

Interdepartmental communication between foster care and other departments increased as many pilot agencies transitioned to the new contracting environment. In some pilot agencies, cross-departmental interactions rose in response to administrative mandates establishing pilot-focused task forces and interdepartmental work groups involving departments that were historically familiar with one another (e.g., case review teams involving foster care, licensing, and clinical staff). In other cases, staff from departments that had previously been ignorant of one another were required to collaborate on specific tasks. For example, a number of pilot respondents suggested that, before the pilot, it was unusual for staff from foster care, accounting, and information technology to meet, but that they now did so to plan and implement pilot-specific tracking systems. These respondents suggested that regular communication between departments reduced payment complications and maintained accurate agency information on client status (e.g., days in care, days until next performance deadline) and service plans.

Many agencies responded to the pilot by networking aggressively with other service providers. Respondents noted that the pilot necessitated increased communication and cooperation with other agencies, FIA, and the courts to obtain needed information, secure collateral services, settle financial issues, resolve case-related concerns, and move children through the system expeditiously. Some agencies engaged in (or expected to engage in) pilot-related interorganizational activities such as multi-agency task forces to inform FIA workers and court officials of policy changes that occurred because of the pilot.

> We participated in every opportunity that came down the pike. There were a number of times where we were engaged in dialogue with the courts and FIA to try to make sure they knew what [the pilot] was about and what we hoped to accomplish. We sat at the table, talked to FIA and the court, and knocked on doors. We also had off-the-cuff conversations between [this agency's] management and direct staff with the court system and FIA, to educate them. (Pilot administrator)

Finally, many agencies made substantial changes in their financial management and accounting procedures. As mentioned, some respondents noted the need to create new pilot-specific payment tracking systems, cost centers, and accounting systems. Many respondents noted that they had experienced difficulties in budgeting and forecasting due to insufficient information, hidden costs, and other unexpected barriers such as late reimbursements from FIA. Nearly uniformly, agencies sought to better forecast the expected costs of providing foster care under the pilot program. These increased demands for foster care–specific information made many finance and accounting departments increase the pace of their work:

> We had to generate as many as eight new management reports, because . . . we wanted to be sure we weren't missing anything we shouldn't be. But it changed the amount of information and the speed of transmittal of information. We used to obtain information [about foster care] on a quarterly basis. We're now getting that information weekly, which is helpful to us. I'd attribute that change 100 percent to the pilot. There was just a real fear that we were going to screw the pilot up. It was such a sea change in where we'd been. (Pilot administrator)

Responding to Barriers to Organizational Change

Agencies experienced numerous internal and external barriers as they sought to enact these organizational changes. Some agencies were able to quickly dispatch obstacles as they adapted to the pilot contracting environment. Other agencies struggled to move past certain issues.

A significant internal barrier was staff resistance to the pilot itself. Most agencies experienced (or expected to experience) conflict between the goals of the pilot and employees' conceptions of the appropriate goals of foster care. Many respondents associated with the pilot were concerned that the initiative might lead to unjustifiably short lengths of stay for children in foster care and less service to children and their families, a prospect that was antithetical to what they considered to be best practice. Other respondents noted that staff feared that the pilot would allow agencies to profit at the expense of child safety, thereby compromising staff members' professional values. Underlying this perspective was a concern that managed care results in agencies returning children to biological families at the expense of their safety and well-being, or terminating parental rights before parents are given an adequate chance of rehabilitation through the provision of appropriate, long-term services. One pilot administrator said:

> The reason that [staff] generally go into foster care is that it's perceived as being [a place] where we can keep kids safe. So we had to focus staff on birth parents not as bad guys, but as people who need

help. . . . I think one of the reasons why [the pilot] was a barrier was just that whole philosophy with foster care that we were going to create safe places for kids, and the parents were secondary.

Internal staff resistance to the pilot was particularly present among clinicians and therapists. Some pilot respondents suggested that the aversion that clinical staff felt toward foster care workers was due to their belief that delivering services according to pilot time frames would hurt foster children. One pilot administrator noted, "Our counseling unit was very opposed to entering into the pilot, because they felt that the time frames were artificial and did not protect the child and could compromise service delivery to the child."

Agencies depended (or expected to depend) on their human resources departments to allay employees' concerns through staff trainings that presented what some respondents termed the "managed care mindset"—a focus on immediate, targeted service provision with the intent to reduce the number of days children spend in foster care.

> We had a lot of meetings and did a lot of training and talking. What felt weird was talking with line staff about what amounts to politics and money— that people in child welfare across the nation were moving to a managed care model, that there were good parts of managed care and bad parts of managed care, and that at least FIA was letting us sit in the driver's seat, so we were lucky to be there. That we had to deliver service differently in order to survive fiscally. (Pilot administrator)

Agencies had (or expected to have) an increased number of staff trainings, workshops, and retreats to discuss the pilot. These meetings commonly provided information on pilot timelines, reviewed staff responsibilities concerning pilot cases, and described how flexible funds were to be used. Finally, all pilot agencies attended FIA-led pilot training sessions, and a few pilot agencies hired organizational consultants to facilitate the process of transitioning to the pilot environment.

For many agencies, understaffing and turnover were (or were expected to be) internal obstacles to successful implementation of the pilot. Many respondents noted that even had the pilot not come into being, staff turnover levels would be high among frontline caseworkers, but that the pressure of the pilot compounded this problem. One pilot supervisor said: "We can't keep staff. We used to expect them to stay for two years, but

if we can get them to stay for a year now, we're lucky. The turnover is horrible. When my staff come to me and say they're leaving, you hate it, but you understand, because it's burnout." In this light, pilot agencies' increasing use of paraprofessionals allowed some foster care departments to continue to provide core services to clients even in the face of high caseworker turnover.

Other barriers that agencies experienced were external in nature. Most pilot agencies experienced difficulties in being reimbursed by FIA in a timely manner for their services rendered. Some pilot respondents noted that their agencies were still waiting for payment for services they had provided years before. While there was no clear explanation for why foster care payments were not made to agencies more efficiently, some pilot respondents suggested that the delay stemmed from FIA workers' lack of understanding of the pilot and what services were reimbursable under the new guidelines. These late reimbursements led many agency accounting departments to more carefully monitor whether they had been paid for the achievement of pilot milestones.

A considerable concern was the prospect that the court would reduce agencies' ability to reach pilot milestones. Most agencies experienced (or expected to experience) court-related delays as they served pilot cases. Various explanations were proposed as to the cause of these delays, including full court dockets that prevented timely permanency hearings, judges who were generally reluctant to terminate parental rights, and judges who were attempting to protect their case-related authority and who viewed the pilot as FIA's attempt to impose its guidelines on them. Numerous respondents also suggested that court officials had little knowledge of or training on the pilot initiative:

> Well, with the court, from what I'm hearing, even though [the pilot] has been going on for four years, they're just finding out about it. So that's a barrier, because even if we're doing whatever we can to get these kids out, if the court doesn't adopt our recommendation, the kids don't return home. And that's a major barrier. (Nonpilot administrator)

Perceptual Similarities and Differences Based on Roles and Agency Status

While there were some similarities in perspective in terms of what it takes to move to a performance-based, managed care system of foster care, the findings from the interviews with agency employees suggest that the respondent's role and agency affiliation impacted what the respondent saw as being important in this process.

Perceptions of Administrators and Supervisors

On a number of issues, administrators and supervisors agreed on the changes that were necessary to implement the pilot. There was considerable agreement across different types of respondents that agencies would need to alter how they delivered foster care services if they were to succeed in the pilot contracting environment. Respondents at all levels of the agencies suggested that increased communication, cooperation, and/or meetings with FIA, the court, and other private agencies were (or would be necessary) if they were to succeed in this new environment. Thus, there was agreement that interagency interactions would increase as a result of entering the pilot process.

There was also agreement that these increased interactions would not be easy. Both administrators and supervisors saw the court as a significant obstacle to progress. Respondents suggested that some of the difficulty that agency staff had (or expected to have) in interacting with the court was due to factors outside of the court's ability to control, such as full court dockets. The large proportion of court-related responses, however, noted that judges and referees chose not to (or would choose not to) help move pilot cases through legal proceedings, or to learn about the goals and purposes of the pilot program itself. Problems with interactions with FIA were seen as being generally less severe and less difficult to overcome.

Yet the perceptions of respondents at varying organizational levels were often different, and these differences seemed to be based on the nature of their jobs, their responsibilities, and the roles they occupied in the agency. Administrators tended to emphasize the organizational and structural changes their agencies made (or were planning to make) in order to move to the pilot, while supervisors tended to note the changes that they and their coworkers made (or expected to make) in how they served children and families in order to successfully implement the pilot. A number of examples will demonstrate this difference in perspective.

Administrators were more concerned than supervisors with how the pilot required (or would require) fundamental transformations in agencies' foster care departments and in how staff viewed foster care, particularly in terms of the appropriate goals of foster care, the primary target of foster care services (families versus children), and the speed with which foster care activities were completed. Mentioned more often by administrators than supervisors were issues regarding intake and assessment, the use of flexible funds, the need to change staffing patterns, and the need to track foster care cases more closely. Administrators also mentioned the need for increased interactions with FIA, the court, and/or other agencies more often than did supervisors. Finally, administrators were more likely than supervisors to recognize the need to train frontline workers differently.

Supervisors, on the other hand, were more likely than administrators to state that accessing community resources and services was (or would be) a barrier to achieving pilot milestones. They were also more likely to conceive barriers to service delivery as being a product of systemic or community-level, rather than within-agency, difficulties. And they were more likely than administrators to mention that they had to be more focused on timelines; concern about issues of efficiency and speed in assessment and service delivery was more likely to be mentioned by this group.

Perceptions of Pilot and Nonpilot Respondents

Pilot and nonpilot respondents agreed on some general areas of change that needed to take place in order for agencies to move successfully to the pilot contracting environment. For example, service delivery–related barriers were of serious concern to both pilot and nonpilot respondents. Both types of respondents were apt to mention that understaffing and/or staff turnover was (or would be) a barrier to moving to the pilot model. There was also general agreement that there would need to be changes in the area of budgeting and financial management if the pilot were to be successfully implemented; many pilot and nonpilot administrators mentioned that their agencies changed or would change tracking- and billing-related forms, software, and/or systems; and all agencies either redesigned (or expected to redesign) their management information systems (MIS) and the way they tracked children in care. Finally, many pilot and nonpilot administrators mentioned that their accounting departments created (or would have to create) new cost centers and/or accounting mechanisms.

Nonpilot respondents, however, rarely mentioned three key operational changes that nearly all pilot agencies made in transitioning to the pilot initiative. First, no nonpilot respondent mentioned that conflict might occur between the agency's foster care and clinical departments, and some nonpilot respondents mentioned that these units would have improved relationships as a result of the pilot program. In contrast, few pilot respondents mentioned that the foster care–clinical relationship improved as their agency adopted the pilot model, and many pilot respondents noted the antipathy with which foster care and clinical staff viewed each other. In general, it appears that nonpilot agencies expected interdepartmental conflicts to occur primarily around technical and fiscal issues related to tracking children and the payments attached to them rather than around "turf" and philosophical issues between foster care case managers and clinicians.

Second, nonpilot respondents appeared to underestimate the depth of changes that pilot agencies made within their foster care departments. Pilot respondents stated more often than nonpilot respondents that foster care units altered in-take and assessment procedures, how they tracked open foster care cases, and the way they accessed and managed flexible funds. While nonpilot respondents mentioned more frequently than pilot respondents that there would be changes in foster care job foci and/or expectations, and mentioned focusing on making alterations within existing staffing patterns, few nonpilot respondents mentioned that moving to the pilot might necessitate creating new foster care staff positions.

Third, pilot respondents noted more frequently than did nonpilot respondents that there were more meetings, trainings, and communication involving different departments within the agency as a result of the pilot initiative. Pilot administrators were much more likely than nonpilot administrators to suggest that the pilot process required (or would require) more communication and operational changes in the areas of financial management, information systems, and accounting. For example, pilot administrators noted more often than did nonpilot administrators that there was (or would be) great uncertainty in forecasting costs; insufficient information with which to craft foster care budgets; and difficulties involved in designing and implementing new foster care case- and payment-tracking databases. In sum, agencies that were beginning to transition to the pilot appeared to underestimate the breadth and depth of necessary changes that pilot agencies had made or were making.

Little Evidence of Knowledge Sharing Between Organizations

Finally, few themes were mentioned by most or all respondents, and it thus appears that there were few common organizational adaptations to this performance-based, managed care initiative. Nor do interagency knowledge sharing, resource sharing, or common problem solving seem to be suggested by these data. Because FIA provided little technical assistance to agencies during this phase of the implementation of the pilot, these agencies appeared to be at great risk for "reinventing the wheel." In short, agencies adapted to this market-based initiative largely independently and idiosyncratically; and the overall implementation of this initiative appears to have been non-uniform.

DISCUSSION

This chapter has examined nonprofit child welfare agencies' adaptations in shifting to a performance-based, managed care reimbursement system, and compared the nature of these adaptations to changes that other agencies anticipated having to make in order to adjust to this specific contracting environment. These results contribute to the small but growing literature concerned with the impact of market-based models on child welfare agencies. In many ways, these results are similar to those from other studies. They also, however, call some previous empirical findings into question and add knowledge to areas that have not been previously explored.

The Effects of Market-Based Models on Foster Care Departments and Personnel

Child welfare agencies in market-based environments have strong incentives to improve their service departments' efficiency and performance. This study found that, in response to the pilot contracting initiative, agencies reorganized their foster care units by streamlining in-take and assessment procedures and by constructing databases to track services provision, client status, and the utilization of flexible funds. This conclusion is consistent with prior research suggesting that managed care requires service providers to assess clients efficiently (Emenheiser, Barker, & DeWoody, 1995; Simms, Freundlich, Battistelli, & Kaufman, 1999), collect client and service information longitudinally (Simpson & Fraser, 1999; Wernet, 1999), and craft service treatment plans that respond quickly to clients' major needs (Stroul, Pires, & Armstrong, 1998).

Child welfare researchers have not yet examined the effects of market-based initiatives on new and existing agency personnel. A strong theme of the interviews with those in the pilot agencies, but not with nonpilot staff, was the creation of new foster care positions designed to help move children and families toward permanent placements. Additionally, supervisors generally felt that they were required to increase the speed with which foster care cases were assessed and served. This focus on specificity and speed of services provision implies that new and existing positions in market-driven organizations may be shaped by increased demands for performance. It will be important for future research to assess how these heightened expectations for performance and accountability impact the child welfare workforce, given the considerable worker turnover, caseloads, inexperience, and insufficient training and supervision that characterize the child welfare workforce (Hasenfeld, 2005; Pecora, Whittaker, Maluccio, & Barth, 2003; U.S. General Accounting Office, 2003).

Another issue for empirical examination concerns how child welfare workers navigate potential goal conflicts in market-based environments. This study found that nonpilot respondents underemphasized the degree of conflict between the objectives of the pilot and employees' conceptions of the appropriate goals of foster care. Many pilot agency staff expressed concern that it would push agencies to move foster children into permanent placements too quickly for frontline staff to provide necessary services to biological parents and to ensure that children would be safe.

The conflict between managed care and child welfare principles has been noted previously. Wells and Johnson (2001) suggest that managed care distorts child welfare agencies' notion of performance, which has traditionally been specified as encompassing child safety, permanency, and well-being (Altshuler & Gleeson, 1999; Ben-Arieh, Kaufman, Andrews, Goerge, Lee, & Aber, 2001; Poertner, McDonald, & Murray, 2000; Whittaker & Maluccio, 2002). Managed care objectives, which were developed in the behavioral and mental health sectors, may have poor analogues in child welfare. In foster care, for example, clients come into care involuntarily and must be served, the state has a legal responsibility to ensure child safety, and permanency is desirable. In contrast, managed care systems were initially designed in the private sector to provide short-term interventions to voluntary, fee-for-service patients. Additionally, the managed health care focus on decreasing systemwide cost savings may translate poorly to the resource-poor child welfare sector. Kahn and Kamerman (1999, p. 50) quote an individual as stating, "Managed care made sense in the medical field because there was excessive expenditure to be squeezed out. But why child welfare, a field with problems because it is badly underresourced?"

At the agency level, researchers have suggested that managed care may result in "mission collision" (Stroul, Pires, & Armstrong, 1998, p. 142), where service providers find it impossible to transition to managed care environments in a way that is consistent with strongly held agency values and operational norms, and where agencies' client advocacy functions are diminished in the new managed care environment (Koloroutis & Thorstenson, 1999; Mechanic, 2000). Yet it is also possible that agencies in these environments may renew their commitment to children and families while seeking to improve service efficiency and client outcomes. Therefore, research is needed to assess how child welfare agencies in market-based environments create the conditions for caseworkers and supervisors to serve clients appropriately while reaching performance milestones.

Managing Financial Risk in Market-Based Environments

Child welfare agencies may redesign their financial management and accounting practices in order to manage the heightened financial risk in performance-based, managed care contracting environments. Similar proportions of pilot and nonpilot respondents mentioned the need to design new foster care–specific tracking- and billing-related forms, software, and/or systems. Pilot respondents made these changes despite (and in some cases, because of) the difficulties they experienced in budgeting and forecasting due to insufficient information, hidden costs, and other unexpected barriers, such as late reimbursements from FIA. These results are quite compatible with empirical evidence from managed health and behavioral health care settings concerning the importance of designing systems that are capable of forecasting per-case revenues and expenditures in addition to automating billing processes (Rycraft, 1999; Wernet, 1999; Wulczyn, Orlebeke, & Martin, 2001; U.S. General Accounting Office, 1998).

It remains to be seen whether and how child welfare agencies' day-to-day operations are affected by the level of financial risk they must bear in these market-based environments. Only two respondents (from the same agency) mentioned that their agency experienced no pilot-related barriers in either budgeting or accounting, which suggests that nearly all study agencies experienced difficulties in adapting their fiscal functions to suit the pilot initiative. These findings suggest that future research should examine how financial constraints affect organizational behavior and clients. Do some child welfare agencies experience more difficulty than others in managing their finances in managed care systems, and if so, which ones? What are the long-term effects of such fiscal difficulties on agencies and their clients? How does the loss of revenue due to reimbursement problems, which many pilot administrators reported, affect the availability of services to clients in foster care and other agency programs?

These findings also suggest that researchers work to identify how agencies make service decisions in market-based environments, and in particular whether budgetary difficulties legitimize less costly service packages over others (Gitterman & Miller, 1989; Hasenfeld, 2000; S. R. Smith, 2002). For example, do agencies allocate services based on each client's expected income stream, such that necessary services are provided up to some critical point where net expected case revenue minus agency costs is either rapidly declining or negative, at which point services are discontinued? Or do organizations pool their financial resources for use across an agency's entire caseload, to be used regardless of the percentage of revenue or cost a case generates? If the answer to the first question is affirmative, one is choosing to capitate funds to certain clients, and this sort of financial management might lead to disproportionately negative outcomes for the most difficult-to-serve cases. While no study agency appeared to be operating under either of these conditions, it was clear that respondents realized that, in the performance-based, managed care contracting environment, service and child placement decisions had significant financial consequences.

The Influence of Market Pressures on Interdepartmental and Interorganizational Network Development

This study found that key agency departments (particularly foster care and accounting) collaborated with each other in order to adapt to the market-based environment. These interdepartmental interactions may not be without conflict, however. Future research might examine why conflict and/or cooperation arises between agency departments in market-based settings. Given the deprofessionalization of clinical departments that has been identified as an effect of managed care in other research (Buescher & Wernet, 1999; Drissel, 1997; Emenheiser, Barker, & DeWoody, 1995), the fear of being replaced by paraprofessionals might well be a reason that conflict arises. More generally, this result suggests that we should pay greater attention to how departments within child welfare agencies interact under differing policy and fiscal conditions.

The pilot also appeared to spur the development of fragile interorganizational relationships among child welfare agencies, FIA, and the courts. Study agencies had considerable financial incentives to solidify their network stature, since case-related service authorization and permanency decisions were affected by FIA and the court. This result recalls empirical studies from the health and mental health sectors that concluded that managed care positively influences provider network development (Beinecke, Goodman, & Lockhard, 1997; Emenheiser, Walgree, Joffe, & Penkert, 1998; Kohn, 2000; Mordock, 1996; Provan, Milward, & Isett, 2002; Scott, Ruef, Mendel, & Caronna, 2000).

But there is a difference between models in which voluntary associations are seen as mutually beneficial and somewhat egalitarian and models of association where power structures are unequal and roles between agencies are dictated by law. One empirical result that is not anticipated by the literature on managed care network development that was found in this study is the high percentage of all respondents noting that the courts and FIA were barriers to implementing the pilot successfully. This study demonstrates that, at least to some extent, comparisons between interorganizational activity in the pilot and the institutional development of provider networks in the behavioral and mental health sectors are specious. In the latter case, agencies may have clear financial and reputational inducements to collaborate, and there may be factors that result in peer agencies being comparable in size and authority. In foster care systems, however, the relationship between child welfare agencies and the courts is characterized by imbalances of power and authority: Courts have no obvious financial incentives to cooperate with child welfare agencies despite having substantial authority over the children and families for whom they care. The development and consequences of interorganizational relationships among private child welfare agencies, public fiduciaries, and the courts thus merit further empirical attention.

Innovation and Independence Among Child Welfare Agencies

Finally, the considerable variation in how agencies adapted to the performance-based, managed care initiative is noteworthy. While there were some common organizational changes, agencies generally responded to the pilot contracting environment in varied and individualistic ways. This result suggests that researchers should explore the potentially different ways that child welfare agencies respond to institutional changes and implement new policies and programs. Child welfare agencies (and the caseworkers within them) are commonly understood to be constrained by state and federal laws (Hasenfeld & Powell, 2004; Maynard-Moody, 2003; Meyers, 2003; Smith & Donovan, 2003), fiscal concerns, and workforce issues. This predominant view emphasizes isomorphism and conformity and deemphasizes issues of agency, entrepreneurship, and innovation. In contrast, however, this study found that some but not all pilot agencies adopted easier-to-use assessment tools, developed interdepartmental teams that built upon existing worker expertise, streamlined information systems to reduce caseworkers' paperwork burdens, and/or developed interorganizational networks of care. Faced with considerable financial risk and substantial staff turnover, agencies found new ways to serve children and families.

This result redirects attention to the agency as a unit of analysis in child welfare research. The child welfare agency is an uncommon subject of study (Ezell, Casey, Pecora, Grossman, Friend, Vernon, & Godfrey, 2002). As researchers seek to understand the impact of market-based models and other child welfare innovations on children and families, it will remain important to chart how child welfare agencies

respond to changing external environments and whether agencies' managerial, programmatic, and staffing adaptations have demonstrable effects on clients (Poertner, 2006; Smith & Donovan, 2003; Yoo, 2002). As evidenced by this study, a systemwide child welfare innovation may be responded to in a variety of ways by the nonprofit agencies responsible for its implementation. Thus, some child welfare systems may resemble mosaics rather than paintings, in that they may rely on a patchwork of independent agencies that operate autonomously but within guidelines. It may therefore be reasonable to expect heterogeneous organizational behavior within privatized child welfare systems. Researchers would therefore do well to consider the different strategies that child welfare agencies use to balance their existing obligations as they move into new market environments.

Limitations

While this study drew on a sample of 64 agency employees across nine agencies, it was nevertheless an evaluation of one county-based initiative. In this sense, this process evaluation is comparable to a multisite case study of how a few nonprofit child welfare agencies adapted to changing fiscal conditions. The generalizability of this study's results therefore depends on the extent to which the Wayne County performance-based, managed care contracting experience is similar to other states' market-based initiatives and the ways in which the Detroit-based agencies studied here are similar to agencies studied in other areas.

Additionally, because participation in the pilot was voluntary, selection bias may have existed at the level of study agencies. Given the possible financial and structural risks involved in entering the pilot environment, it is possible that only those agencies that were prepared to adapt to the new contracting environment volunteered to move to it. This bias may have affected respondents' discussions of the barriers that agencies faced and the changes they made in moving to the pilot initiative; other agencies may experience more and different barriers in adapting to the pilot initiative.

Finally, the purposive sampling strategy used to identify interview respondents may have biased results. Individuals who had left agencies prior to sample selection (e.g., those who were not able or did not want to adapt to the new fiscal system) were not eligible for inclusion in the study. Potentially, "leavers" might have been more pessimistic concerning the presence and magnitude of barriers to implementation of the pilot than were the study respondents. In addition, the validity of the findings are also dependent on how reflective the perceptions of this purposively chosen sample are of the realities of those involved in this initiative.

Despite these limitations, these data provide a systematic understanding of how different child welfare staff perceived the transition their agencies were making (or were seeking to make) to the performance-based, managed care contracting environment. Because interviews were conducted with different types of respondents and agencies, varying perspectives could be incorporated, thus increasing the comprehensiveness and validity of the study results.

CONTEXTUALIZING THE QUALITATIVE STUDY

It will be recalled that many pilot agency staff expressed concern that adaptation to this market-based environment would diminish service provision to children and families and would push agencies to move foster children into permanent placements too quickly. Others noted that service providers in market-based environments may emphasize efficiency over effectiveness and that these models may be less appropriate for the child welfare sector than for the health and behavioral health sectors from which they originated. These concerns are predicated upon the possible negative impacts of market-based models on children and families.

Given its focus on documenting organizational, managerial, and staff-related changes, the qualitative process evaluation did not directly assess the effects of the performance-based, managed care contracting initiative on clients. As state child welfare systems adopt market-based models, researchers should seek to identify how these models impact the services that foster children and families receive and outcomes for foster children. Multivariate statistical models explaining changes in levels of service provision and in the achievement of permanent placements should drive the empirical assessment of how well or poorly child welfare agencies adapt to market-based environments.

As noted earlier, the authors have conducted a number of studies on these issues using data from the quantitative process and outcome evaluation of the pilot initiative (McBeath, 2006; McBeath & Meezan, 2008; Meezan & McBeath, 2003, 2005). While a detailed discussion is beyond the scope of this chapter, the results of these studies validate the concerns voiced by many of the participants in this study, and thus add some contextual depth to the results presented in this chapter.

In terms of service provision, we have identified a significant, negative relationship between being in a performance-based, managed care contracting environment and service provision in the foster care system. Controlling for time in care, various types of allegations of maltreatment, and child, primary caregiver, and caseworker characteristics, children and families served by pilot agencies received 43% fewer nontherapeutic services, 83% fewer therapeutic services, and 20% fewer completed referrals for out-of-agency services than did nonpilot children and families (McBeath, 2006; McBeath & Meezan, 2008). Considered in conjunction with comparable findings from the only other study of managed care service provision using a foster care sample (Cuellar, Libby, & Snowden, 2001; Snowden, Cuellar, & Libby, 2003), these results imply that performance-based, managed care models negatively impact the provision of important services to foster children and their families.

In terms of outcomes for children, we have found significant differences in the rates of achievement of various permanent placements between children served through pilot as compared to nonpilot agencies. At the end of 930 days of data collection, all but about 8% of the children served under either reimbursement system had achieved or were on their way to achieving a permanent plan as defined in this initiative, and few children in either group who had left care had returned. However, significantly more children served by pilot agencies were returned to relatives, whereas significantly more children served by nonpilot agencies were returned to their biological parents. And while significantly more children served by pilot agencies had already been adopted (many by kin), more children from the nonpilot agencies were on their way to adoption (many by foster parents).

It thus appears that one effect of the pilot was to create and use a different pathway to permanency for which agencies received monetary compensation: Pilot agencies viewed kin as a permanency resource and used them in that way much more often than did their nonpilot counterparts. In contrast, nonpilot agencies appear to have continued to emphasize reunification with biological parents as their primary goal of service before they turned to the adoption alternative (Meezan & McBeath, 2005).

Thus, what the market-based environment seems to have done is to shift child welfare agencies' attention from biological parents to kin. Whether this occurred because it was in the child's best interest, because it was usually easier to work with kin than with biological parents, or because mission drift was encouraged by the payment system is unknown. What is clear is that this unintended consequence of the performance-based, managed care contracting system raises value questions concerning the purpose(s) of the child welfare system. Do reimbursement mechanisms such as the pilot (as well as the current direction of child and family policies) lead child welfare agencies to place less emphasis on "saving families for children" and more emphasis on "saving children from families"? What consequences arise for children, biological parents, and kin as these relatives are increasingly viewed as permanent, as opposed to temporary, resources? It is possible that these new incentive-driven approaches to financing child welfare services may be altering the underlying philosophy of child welfare systems (and thus child welfare service planning and frontline decision making) in important ways—a pendulum that has shifted numerous times in the past in response to economic, political, social, and service delivery changes.

Unfortunately, it is not possible to explore these questions using the data that were collected for the pilot evaluation. Nor will it be possible to collect new data from the participating agencies that might be able to answer these questions. In October 2004, after the pilot had been implemented countywide, FIA terminated the initiative. Publicly, FIA based its decision upon two factors: an internal benefit-cost study (that was never made public) that showed that FIA was authorizing more outlays to nonprofit agencies for foster care services under the pilot than it had under the per-diem reimbursement system; and the preliminary results from this evaluation (Meezan & McBeath, 2003). Political considerations may have also played a large part in this decision.

After the pilot ended, our hard-won and once superb relationships with the agencies that participated in this study deteriorated (for a full description of how the evaluation was conducted and its demise, see Meezan & McBeath, 2006), and access to new data became impossible. Thus, the findings from the studies that were conducted will inform some students, researchers, and practitioners and will add to a growing body of litera-

ture on the impact of market-based models on child welfare agencies and clients. Unfortunately, as is too often the case, they will have less influence than they might have had on future design and implementation considerations that could have occurred within this initiative, as well as on future child welfare innovations with which the field will undoubtedly experiment.

Notes

1. Currently, over half of all publicly funded child welfare services in the United States are provided by private nonprofit agencies (Kahn & Kamerman, 1999; Salamon, 2002).

2. While the pilot did not contain some common managed care characteristics, such as capitation or uniform case management services, it was considered by both FIA and the nonprofit agencies to be a managed care initiative. Official FIA documents described the pilot as a managed care system (Family Independence Agency, 2000), and administrators from agencies with pilot contracts made public presentations in which they referred to the pilot as a managed care system. Additionally, during the telephone interviews conducted as part of the process evaluation of the pilot, agency respondents noted repeatedly that they believed the pilot to be a managed care system.

3. The nine participating agencies were (alphabetically): Catholic Social Services of Wayne County (pilot); Evergreen Children's Services (nonpilot); Homes for Black Children (pilot); Judson Center (pilot); Lutheran Child and Family Services of Michigan (pilot); Lutheran Social Services of Michigan (nonpilot); Orchards Children's Services (pilot); Spectrum Human Services (pilot); and St. Francis Children's Services (nonpilot).

References

Adoption and Safe Families Act. (1997). PL 105-89, §111 Stat. 2115.

Altshuler, S. J., & Gleeson, J. P. (1999). Completing the evaluation triangle for the next century: Measuring child "well-being" in family foster care. *Child Welfare, 78*, 125–147.

Beinecke, R. H., Goodman, M., & Lockhard, A. (1997). The impact of managed care on Massachusetts mental health and substance abuse providers. *Administration in Social Work, 21*(2), 41–53.

Ben-Arieh, A., Kaufman, N. H., Andrews, A. B., Goerge, R. M., Lee, B. J., & Aber, J. L. (2001). *Measuring and monitoring children's well-being*. Dordrecht: Kluwer Academic.

Buescher, K. E., & Wernet, S. P. (1999). Managed psychcare. In S. Wernet (Ed.), *Managed care in human services* (pp. 121–142). Chicago: Lyceum.

Courtney, M. E. (2000a). Managed care and child welfare services: What are the issues? *Children & Youth Services Review, 22*, 87–91.

Courtney, M. E. (2000b). Research needed to improve the prospects for children in out-of-home placements. *Children & Youth Services Review, 22*, 743–761.

Craig, C., Kulik, T., James, T., & Nielsen, S. (1998, December). *Blueprint for the privatization of child welfare*. (Reason Public Policy Institute, Policy Study No. 248). Boston: Author.

Cuellar, A. E., Libby, A. M., & Snowden, L. R. (2001). How capitated mental health care affects utilization by youth in the juvenile justice and child welfare systems. *Mental Health Services Research, 3*, 61–72.

Drissel, A. B. (1997). *Managed care and children and family services*. Baltimore: Annie E. Casey Foundation.

Embry, R. A, Buddenhagen, P., & Bolles, S. (2000). Managed care and child welfare: Challenges to implementation. *Children & Youth Services Review, 22*, 93–116.

Emenheiser, D., Barker, R., & DeWoody, M. (1995). *Managed care: An agency guide to surviving and thriving*. Washington, DC: Child Welfare League of America Press.

Emenheiser, D. L., Walgree, D., Joffe, V., & Penkert, V. (1998). *Networks, mergers, and partnerships in a managed care environment*. Washington, DC: Child Welfare League of America Press.

Ezell, M., Casey, E., Pecora, P. J., Grossman, C., Friend, R., Vernon, L., & Godfrey, D. J. (2002). The results of a management redesign: A case study of a private child welfare agency. *Administration in Social Work, 26*(4), 61–79.

Family Independence Agency. (2000). *Guidelines for the permanency pilot*. Unpublished document. State of Michigan Family Independence Agency.

Fraser, I. (1997). Research on health care organizations and markets: The best and worst of times. *Health Services Research, 32*, 669–677.

Geen, R., & Tumlin, V. (1999). *State efforts to remake child welfare: Responses to new challenges and increased scrutiny*. (Occasional Paper 29). Washington, DC: Urban Institute

Gitterman, A., & Miller, I. (1989). The influence of the organization on clinical practice. *Clinical Social Work Journal, 17*, 151–164.

Glied, S. (1999). *Managed care*. NBER Working Paper Series, National Bureau of Economic Research, Cambridge, MA.

Goerge, R., Wulczyn, F., & Fanshel, D. (1994). A foster care research agenda for the '90s. *Child Welfare, 73*, 525–549.

Hasenfeld, Y. (2000). Organizational forms as moral practices: The case of welfare departments. *Social Service Review, 74*, 329–350.

Hasenfeld, Y. (2005). *Worker-client relations: Social policy in practice*. Paper presented at the workshop on New Directions for Research on Social Policy and Organizational Practices, National Poverty Center, University of Michigan, Ann Arbor.

Hasenfeld, Y., & Powell, L. (2004). The role of non-profit agencies in the provision of welfare-to-work services. *Administration in Social Work, 28*(3), 91–110.

Hutchinson, A. B., & Foster, E. M. (2003). The effect of Medicaid managed care on mental health care for children: A review of the literature. *Mental Health Services Research, 5*(1), 39–54.

Kahn, A. J., & Kamerman, S. B. (1999). *Contracting for child and family services: A mission sensitive guide*. Baltimore: Annie E. Casey Foundation.

Kohn, L. T. (2000). Organizing and managing care in a changing health system. *Health Services Research, 35*, 37–51.

Kolouroutis, M., & Thorstenson, T. (1999). An ethics framework for organizational change. *Nursing Administration Quarterly, 23*(2), 9–18.

Lipsky, M. (1980). *Street-level bureaucracy*. New York: Russell Sage Foundation.

Malm, K., Bess, R., Leos-Urbel, J., Geen, R., & Markowitz, T. (2001). *Running to keep in place: The continuing evolution of our nation's child welfare system* (Occasional Paper 54). Washington, DC: Urban Institute.

Maynard-Moody, S. (2003). *Beyond implementation: A sketch of a theory of policy enactment*. Paper presented at the Annual Research Conference of the Association for Public Policy Analysis and Management, Washington, DC.

McBeath, B. (2006). *Shifting principles in a sacred market: Nonprofit service provision to foster children and families in a performance-based, managed care contracting environment*. Unpublished doctoral dissertation, University of Michigan.

McBeath, B., & Meezan, W. (2008). Market-based disparities in foster care service provision. *Research on Social Work Practice, 18*, 27–41.

McCullough, C., & Schmitt, B. J. (1999). *Child Welfare League of America managed care and privatization child welfare tracking project: 1998 state and county results*. Washington, DC: Child Welfare League of America Press.

McCullough, C., & Schmitt, B. J. (2000). Managed care and privatization: Results of a national survey. *Children & Youth Services Review, 22*, 117–130.

Mechanic, D. (1999). *Mental health and social policy: The emergence of managed care*. Needham Heights, MA: Allyn & Bacon.

Mechanic, D. (2000). Managed care and the imperative for a new professional ethic. *Health Affairs, 19*(5), 100–111.

Meezan, W., & McBeath, B. (2003). *Moving toward managed care in child welfare: First results from the evaluation of the Wayne County foster care pilot initiative.* Ann Arbor: University of Michigan School of Social Work.

Meezan, W., & McBeath, B. (2005). *Placement outcomes of foster children and families in an incentive-based, managed care setting: New findings from the Wayne County pilot evaluation.* Paper presented at the Ninth Annual Conference of the Society for Social Work and Research, Miami, FL.

Meezan, W., & McBeath, B. (2006). When the results disappoint, the process matters little. *Reflections: Narratives of Professional Helping, 12*(1), 66–85.

Meyers, M. K., & Lurie, I. (2003). *Organizational processes as policy instruments: The welfare application process.* Paper presented at the Annual Research Conference of the Association for Public Policy Analysis and Management, Washington, DC.

Miller, R. H., & Luft, H. S. (1994). Managed care plan performance since 1980. *Journal of the American Medical Association, 271,* 1512–1520.

Miller, R. H., & Luft, H. S. (1997). Does managed care lead to better or worse quality of care? *Health Affairs, 16*(5), 7–26.

Mordock, J. B. (1996). The road to survival revisited: Organizational adaptation to the managed care environment. *Child Welfare, 75,* 195–218.

Pecora, P. J., Whittaker, J. K., Maluccio, A. N., & Barth, R. P. (2003). *The child welfare challenge: Policy, practice, and research* (3rd ed.). New York: de Gruyter.

Poertner, J. (2006). Social administration and outcomes for consumers. *Administration in Social Work, 30*(2), 11–22.

Poertner, J., McDonald, T. P., & Murray, C. (2000). Child welfare outcomes revisited. *Children & Youth Services Review, 22,* 789–810.

Provan, K. G., Milward, H. B. & Isett, K. R. (2002). Collaboration and integration of community-based health and human services in a nonprofit managed care system. *Health Care Management Review, 27*(1), 21–32.

Rycraft, J. R. (1999). Challenges and opportunities for public child welfare. In S. Wernet (Ed.), *Managed care in human services* (pp. 27–52). Chicago: Lyceum.

Salamon, L. M. (2002). The resilient sector: The state of nonprofit America. In L. M. Salamon (Ed.), *The state of nonprofit America* (pp. 1–25). Washington, DC: Brookings Institution Press.

Schorr, A. L. (2000). The bleak prospect for public child welfare. *Social Service Review, 74,* 124–136.

Scott, R. W., Ruef, M., Mendel, P. J., & Caronna, C. C. (2000). *Institutional change and health-care organizations: From professional dominance to managed care.* Chicago: University of Chicago Press.

Shortell, S. M. (1997). Managed care: Achieving the benefits, negating the harm. *Health Services Research, 32,* 557–560.

Simms, M. D., Freundlich, M., Battistelli, E. S., & Kaufman, N. D. (1999). Delivering health and mental health care services to children in family foster care after welfare and health care reform. *Child Welfare, 78,* 166–183.

Simpson, L., & Fraser, I. (1999). Children and managed care: What research can, can't, and should tell us about its impact. *Medical Care Research and Review, 56,* 13–36.

Smith, B. D., & Donovan, S. E. F. (2003). Child welfare practice in organizational and institutional context. *Social Service Review, 77,* 541–563.

Smith, S. R. (2002). Social services. In L. M. Salamon (Ed.), *The state of nonprofit America* (pp. 151–188). Washington, DC: Brookings Institution Press.

Snowden, L. R., Cuellar, A. E., & Libby, A. M. (2003). Minority youth in foster care: Managed care and access to mental health treatment. *Medical Care, 41,* 264–274.

Snyder, N. M., & Allen, M. (2003). *Managing the un easy partnership between government and nonprofits: Lessons from the Kansas child welfare privatization initiative.* Paper presented at the Annual Research Conference of the Association of Public Policy and Management, Washington, DC.

Stroul, B. A., Pires, S. A., & Armstrong, M. I. (1998). *Health care reform tracking project: Tracking state managed care reforms as they affect children and adolescents with behavioral health disorders and their families: 1997 impact analysis.* Tampa: Louis de la Parte Florida Mental Health Institute, University of South Florida.

Szilagyi, P. G. (1998). Managed care for children: Effect on access to care and utilization of health services. *Future of Children, 8*(2), 39–59.

U.S. General Accounting Office. (1995). *Child welfare: Complex needs strain capacity to provide services* (GAO/HEHS-95-208). Washington, DC: Author.

U.S. General Accounting Office. (1998). *Child welfare: Early experiences implementing a managed care approach* (GAO/HEHS-99-8). Washington, DC: Author.

U.S. General Accounting Office. (2003). *Child welfare: HHS could play a greater role in helping child welfare agencies recruit and retain staff* (GAO-03-357). Washington, DC: Author.

Wells, S. J., & Johnson, M. A. (2001). Selecting outcome measures for child welfare settings: Lessons for use in performance management. *Children & Youth Services Review, 23,* 169–199.

Wernet, S. P. (1999). An introduction to managed care in human services. In S. Wernet (Ed.), *Managed care in human services* (pp. 1–22). Chicago: Lyceum.

Whittaker, J. K., & Maluccio, A. N. (2002). Rethinking "child placement": A reflective essay. *Social Service Review, 76,* 108–134.

Wulczyn, F. W. (2000a). Federal fiscal reform in child welfare services. *Children & Youth Services Review, 22,* 131–159.

Wulczyn, F. W. (2000b). Fiscal reform and managed care in child welfare services. *Policy and Practice of Public Human Services, 58*(3), 26–31.

Wulczyn, F., Orlebeke, B., & Martin, N. (2001). *Linking permanency and finance in child welfare: ACS Safe and Timely Adoptions and Reunifications (STAR) program.* Paper presented at a meeting of the National Association of Welfare Research and Statistics, Baltimore, MD.

Yoo, J. (2002). The relationship between organizational variables and client outcomes: A case study in child welfare. *Administration in Social Work, 26*(2), 39–61.

16

Self-Evaluation:
Using Data to Guide Policy
and Practice in Public Child
Welfare Agencies

Daniel Webster

Charles L. Usher

Barbara Needell

Judith Wildfire

Public child welfare agencies have contended since the mid-1990s with chronic problems, poor systemic performance, and swelling caseloads — leading to what has been termed a "foster care crisis" (Ainsworth & Maluccio, 2003; Curtis, 1999). Among the problems are reliance on congregate care rather than family foster care, placement instability, poor permanency outcomes, and disparities in outcomes for African American and other minority families and children. The Annie E. Casey Foundation launched the Family to Family initiative in 1992 in response to this urgent situation as an effort to reform the child welfare system. The foundation's goal is to support child welfare agencies and the communities they serve in building neighborhood-centered responses to vulnerable children and families who are at risk of maltreatment (Annie E. Casey Foundation, 2001). The project has been implemented in over 60 sites in 13 states across the country and continues to grow.

Among the four core reform strategies of Family to Family is self-evaluation: Establishing structures and processes for using data to guide the planning, implementation, and evaluation of policies, programs, and practice. Researchers and practitioners have long understood the need for such an approach to improve practice in child welfare and other domains of social work (Jamieson & Bodonyi, 1999; Moore, Rapp, & Roberts, 2000; Shahar, Auslander, & Cohen, 1995; Shyne, 1976; Usher, 1995). Lack of clarity in defining program goals and poor measurement of progress (Gardner, 2000; Shyne, 1976), inherent biases of human judgments that result when decision making is not informed by data (Ruscio, 1998), and the benefits of utilizing data and computer-based technology to aid in policy formation (Shahar et al., 1995), improved supervisory practice (Moore et al., 2000), staff training (Leung, Cheung, & Stevenson, 1994), and standardizing large-scale outcomes (Courtney, 1993) are all examples that support the notion of using data to improve child welfare outcomes.

A core precept of Family to Family is that child welfare agencies must coordinate their efforts with all persons concerned with the well-being of a child: birth families, foster and adoptive families, neighborhoods, communities, public and private organizations, and agencies from other service systems. It is therefore crucial that child welfare agency staff forge partnerships with these other stakeholders and that all involved develop a strategy to articulate important outcomes and ensure that progress toward those goals can be measured and understood by everyone involved. This ongoing process recognizes the benefits of decisions and practice reforms that are data-driven in child welfare (Jamieson & Bodonyi, 1999) and is fundamental to self-evaluation.

Since the inception of Family to Family, much has been accomplished in sites across the country through the work of technical assistants headed by researchers from the University of North Carolina at Chapel Hill and the University of California at Berkeley. A tool that documents the self-evaluation process and provides guidance on how to become self-evaluating has been produced and is available on-line and in hard copy from the foundation (Annie E. Casey Foundation, 2001). This chapter discusses some of the challenges and successes encountered by the university technical assistants, the child welfare agency administrators, frontline workers, and community partners as they have worked together toward using data to improve their social work practices.

WHAT IS SELF-EVALUATION?

A key strategy of the Family to Family initiative is an effort to build a capacity for self-evaluation among social service agencies and their community partners. This idea is based on the premises that the planning, implementation, and evaluation of child welfare policy and practices have to be guided by clear and specific goals and that progress toward those goals requires good performance data (Usher, 1995). A number of child welfare researchers have argued in favor of the concept of better child welfare practice guided by performance measures (Barth, 1997; Jamieson & Bodonyi, 1999; Moore, Rapp, & Roberts, 2000), and significant examples exist of large-scale performance indicators (Needell et al., 2006; Wulczyn, Brunner-Hislop, & Goerge, 2000). Nonetheless, in spite of the large quantity of information available about children in out-of-home care, child welfare agencies are often unable to provide quick and reliable responses to

questions posed by policy makers, senior administrators, and the public.

Overcoming Skepticism

The inability to respond to basic questions concerning child welfare trends even when there is pertinent information available stems largely from preconceived notions that data are not useful, inadequate data systems, and poor understanding of the information that is available. Further, a lack of cooperation, mistrust, and even animosity can exist between different units within agencies, which are the legacy of a fragmented child welfare system (Brooks & Webster, 1999).

Overcoming skepticism regarding the usefulness of data and the fragmented nature of child welfare agencies is a critical initial challenge in the implementation of Family to Family. After this initial challenge, several crucial pieces comprise the process of fostering agency self-evaluation: attitude adjustment, creating self-evaluation teams, measuring performance with longitudinal data, and understanding the interrelated nature of outcomes. By putting these pieces together, participants move beyond the dubious notion that data are useless or "something someone else does"—that is, the traditional evaluation approach based on independent appraisals from a detached third party (Usher, Wildfire, & Gibbs, 1999)—to understand that data actually exist that can be helpful for their immediate planning and practice concerns.

Attitude Adjustment

Attitude adjustment is an important aim in the early stages of implementing self-evaluation. It is necessary that upper management, supervisors, line staff, and community partners are won over to the idea that numbers and other data are not solely useful for information technology (IT) staff or other "data geeks." This change in perspective is crucial in order for all stakeholders to become data-driven and outcome-focused (Jamieson & Bodonyi, 1999; Moore et al., 2000).

A common sentiment among many agency managers is that, while they are inundated by data from the Child and Family Services Review (CFSR) process and other sources, this information is not useful for planning, evaluation, or other decisions. Invariably, their experience has been one in which existing data systems used by the agency were designed for other purposes and do not have the capacity to provide answers to pressing current questions. For example, one meeting with regional managers of a prospective Family to Family grantee site revealed that the Department of Social Services routinely produced over 200 data reports for managers—but these decision makers had no idea of the contents of the reports or whether the information was even pertinent to current agency operations.

The shared values and behaviors of any agency—its organizational culture—shape staff attitudes toward data (Moore et al., 2000). A useful way, therefore, to promote attitude adjustment is by a day-long "Data Are Your Friends" workshop where clear examples are presented of ways that data can be informative and helpful. To begin the process of cooperation among agency units, members of the IT department can present and explain examples of data reports they currently produce and invite input on tailoring the information to better meet other staff's needs. Workshop attendees can be encouraged to brainstorm about what they would really like to know to aid them in their practice and how using data can help them to answer these questions. By influencing organizational culture such that the uses and merits of data are supported rather than maligned, staff opinions can begin to be recast (Moore et al., 2000).

Using geo-maps as "data treats" is another way to spark interest and change attitudes toward data. Though relatively new to the field of social work, desktop geographic information software (GIS) has become increasingly available and more easily accessible to use; and researchers have begun to demonstrate its beneficial application in child welfare (Ernst, 2000; Queralt & Witte, 1998; Robertson & Wier, 1998). The evidence that presently exists indicates that GIS might be better suited for policy and research issues, and more limited in terms of its application to direct practice (Coulton, Korbin, Su, & Chow, 1995); however, this technology has undoubtedly created new possibilities to analyze information that is usually part of any data system (e.g., county, zip code, census tract information) but was formerly difficult to analyze by other means (Queralt & Witte, 1998).

Desktop mapping enables workers to manipulate and present geographical information. By analyzing and displaying information geographically, mapping can reveal trends that might otherwise not be as apparent when using different means, such as frequencies or contingency tables. For example, by mapping the home addresses of children in foster care, maps can be used to reveal neighborhoods that have large numbers of children investigated and removed for maltreatment (Coulton et al., 1995; Ernst, 2000). For example, Figure 16.1 displays, by zip code, the rate of children first entering foster care per thousand children in the population. Such a map highlights geographic target areas where needs are greatest and can be crucial for helping an agency focus its staff and other resources. Equally as important, the strong visual appeal of geo-maps makes them useful as an early step in the path toward attitude adjustment. Maps can attract workers' attention and generate interest in using this tool to display trends pertaining to ongoing performance and outcomes (Queralt & Witte, 1998).

Creating Self-Evaluation Teams

After staff have overcome their initial aversion to data and have shifted their attitude toward a recognition of the potential usefulness of data, the next step involves creating self-evaluation teams (Annie E. Casey Foundation, 2001; Meier & Usher, 1998). This group is composed of staff representing different parts of the agency (administrators and program staff, information technology staff, and analysts) in an effort to draw upon the experience and knowledge of their respective areas of expertise, promote dialogue and cooperation between units, and link data to program and policy decisions. Other evaluation research examining the integration of data, policy, and practice has demonstrated positive results (Gardner, 2000; Jamieson & Bodonyi, 1999; Moore et al., 2000).

Knowledgeable data analysts who can query the system to get information concerning pressing policy issues are often a scarcity, and it is not uncommon for there to be a lack of positive interactions between information specialists and line workers. Sharing information and perspectives among team members creates an opportunity to promote cooperation among agency units and helps staff to realize their individual potential for using data and to increase their understanding of their interconnected roles. The objective is to create a framework in which all members of self-evaluation teams, including those with limited data analysis experience, are able to use data. This is an iterative procedure as consultation and feedback occur at different points in the process. Thus it is critical to establish regular and frequent meetings that include line staff, supervisors, IT staff, and analysts. These

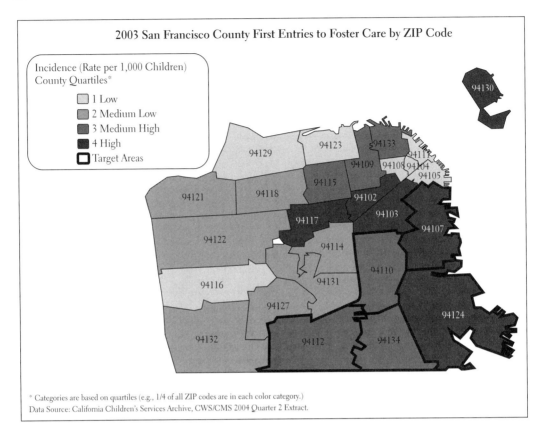

FIGURE 16.1 Map of Foster Care Incidence Rates per 1,000 Children in the Population by Home Zip Code for San Francisco County

meetings provide a venue for the presentation and discussion of analysis results and their implications and encourage staff to keep work moving forward between meetings. Community partners should also be team members whenever possible. This approach creates a progressive refinement in practice and concomitant improvements in the delivery of services to clients (Gardner, 2000; Jamieson & Bodonyi, 1999).

Drawing on input from among agency units, the self-evaluation team is crucial for promoting coordination and disseminating useful data to inform decision making and to monitor practice. In Los Angeles County, for example, IT staff, analysts, and Casey Foundation technical assistants worked to develop tables that indicated, at the zip code level, the number of children in care and the number of available foster beds. The "capacity-to-need ratio" was a clear indication of where targeted foster care recruitment was required if children were to be placed in their neighborhoods (a Family to Family goal). When recruitment staff received

funding to put signs encouraging foster parenting on bus benches throughout the county, they used these tables to decide where the bench signs would be most useful. Realizing that the data were actually useful for something concrete like bus bench signs won over many skeptics in the department. As another example, analysis of data shared at team meetings made it clear that the Family to Family strategy of geographic assignment of workers (having a worker's entire caseload in the same neighborhood or area) was not at all business as usual prior to implementation. In one zip code in another site, there were 300 children in care and 200 workers assigned to them.

Tracking Outcomes with Longitudinal Data and GIS Technology

Readjusting attitudes and fostering intra-agency shared perspective through self-evaluation teams are necessary, but not sufficient, means to successfully realize the self-evaluation process. Another important piece that must be implemented involves using longitudinal data and GIS technology to track agency performance. This process entails tapping into information that is often already collected in routine program operations, configuring these data into a longitudinal format, and utilizing new tools such as desktop mapping software to understand current caseload and resource characteristics at the neighborhood level. Because of the earlier use of maps as incentives, or data treats, staff are generally quite motivated to employ GIS technology.

Data systems used by child welfare agencies are often inadequate and suffer from a number of shortcomings (Courtney & Collins, 1994). A principal limitation is that much of these data are composed of periodic snapshots of the caseload of children in care at given points in time. While this information is important for providing basic management accountability, it does not accurately capture the experience of all children who come in contact with the child welfare system and can actually be misleading when examining issues such as length of stay or placement moves in care (Courtney & Collins, 1994; Courtney et al., 2004; Goerge, 1990; Usher, Gibbs, & Wildfire, 1995; Wulczyn, Kogan, & Dilts, 2001).

There is an inherent bias in snapshot estimates in that they tend to overrepresent the children who have the worst experiences in care—that is, those entering at different times who stay in care for long periods (Goerge, 1990; Wulczyn, 1996). Figure 16.2 illustrates this phenomenon: The horizontal axis represents a timeline from January 1, 2004, to January 1, 2006, and the six numbered horizontal lines represent the duration in care of six children in foster care. A point-in-time snapshot taken of the caseload on January 1, 2005, will only observe four of the six children (lines 1, 2, 4, and 6). The other two children (lines 3 and 5) will not be detected by this snapshot. As such, any mean or median measure of length of time spent in care will be biased by the children observed in the snapshot who have longer lengths of stay. Therefore, by relying exclusively on caseload data, staff may not recognize the opportunity to effectively focus resources because of the assumption that most children in the system are poorly served.

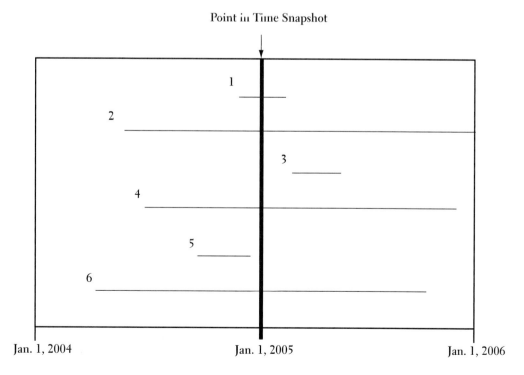

FIGURE 16.2 Bias in Estimation of Length of Stay in Foster Care Created by Using Point in Time Snapshot

Longitudinal data on a cohort of children as they move through out-of-home care do not suffer from this bias since children are not systematically excluded from the study population if they leave care (Goerge, 1990; Wulczyn, 1996; Wulczyn et al., 2001). Reliable information on children's child welfare experiences requires following an entry cohort over time for the duration of its stay in out-of-home care. An important part of the self-evaluation process thus involves constructing data tracking systems that follow children from first entry to care through placements within and exits from the system and, for some children, subsequent reentries to care (Usher et al., 1998). Unlike snapshot counts that only contain information on children who are still in care at a given point in time, longitudinal data systems enable inquiries that capture information on all children who enter foster care and follow them across their entire tenure in care (Goerge, 1990).

Many states have already developed these longitudinal tracking systems, and the Family to Family initiative strives to help county-level child welfare agencies tap into these resources and begin using the information to guide their practices (Usher et al., 1998). The University of California, Berkeley, has developed a longitudinal database that contains information on all children who have been in foster care since 1988 (Barth et al., 1994; Needell et al., 2006). For the sites that have not built this capacity themselves, Casey Foundation technical assistants have worked for years to assist in the construction of data systems and to train agency staff in analyzing and using longitudinal information for evaluation and planning. All sites are required to measure outcomes, such as the length of stay in foster care, the rate of planned reunifications, and the rate of placement disruptions. By periodically reviewing these and other outcomes, agencies can use the information to inform and modify practice during the reform process and beyond.

GIS mapping technology and the use of longitudinal cohort data play important roles in ongoing assessment and evaluation. Other research has begun to demonstrate the usefulness of GIS for informing child welfare policy and practice (Ernst, 2000; Queralt & Witte, 1998; Robertson & Wier, 1998). Similarly, we have observed in Los Angeles that maps can be produced at regular intervals to indicate, for example, where children who come into foster care from specific neighborhoods are placed. Since one goal of the Family to Family initiative is to keep children who cannot remain at home close to their families whenever possible, these maps can be used to plot the progress toward community-based placement over time. Complementing this work, the use of longitudinal data to track entry cohorts of children provides evaluation teams with an inclusive and accurate picture of child welfare outcomes, such as length of stay or placement moves in out-of-home care (Goerge, 1990; Wulczyn, 1996; Wulczyn et al., 2001).

Understanding the Cycle of Experiences in Outcome Data

Data tell a story, and the relationship between outcomes must be taken into account when evaluating agency performance. For example, while we may seek to reduce the number of children entering care, when we succeed in doing so, we must be aware of how the smaller population entering care will likely be more difficult to work with (i.e., we have prevented more families from oversight by the agency—but those families who do require intervention have more challenging circumstances). Thus a reduction in entries may affect other measures, such as time to permanency or placement stability (Usher, Wildfire, & Gibbs, 1999).

Appreciating and anticipating the interrelated nature of outcome data are crucial tenets of self-evaluation. Any particular measure, viewed in isolation, tells you nothing useful about an agency's performance. Outcome "standards" based on point-in-time comparisons of states or localities are inherently misleading because they ignore two factors: (1) the historical evolution of a given level of performance and whether performance is improving or declining across time; and (2) the overall pattern of outcomes that collectively depicts safety and permanency outcomes. The classic illustration is an ill-advised emphasis on reducing length of stay and making hasty reunifications, which merely result in an increased rate of reentries to care. A positive illustration is an agency shift to greater use of kinship care with a resulting reduction in placement moves (Usher, Randolph, & Gogan, 1999). In each case, the apparent "success" in improving outcomes must be interpreted in the broader context of its effect on other outcomes.

The perspective on outcomes depicted in Figure 16.3 attempts to convey the dynamic nature of outcomes for families and children coming in contact with the child welfare system. It emphasizes that decisions early

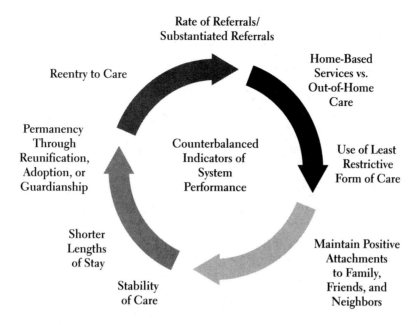

FIGURE 16.3 The Cycle of Experiences in Child Welfare

in the placement process impinge on outcomes later in the process. It also highlights the fact that viewing the cumulative experiences of families and children reveals important facts about the performance of the system in which those experiences occur. Most particularly, by comparing changes in the pattern of experiences across successive cohorts of children, it is possible to see how policy and practice changes (Usher, Gibbs, & Wildfire, 1995).

Staff can make a more realistic assessment of the impact their work is having on their clients through awareness of the interrelated nature of outcomes. Workers and administrators will not be overly pessimistic, for example, when the number of children reunified during a period of time drops—if they are also monitoring entries to care and note that it is the case that a smaller number of children with greater needs is coming into care. By the same token, they will not prematurely think that they do not need to continue efforts to improve reunification services just because an increasing number of children are going home from the agency. They will know to also track the proportion of those reunifying who later return to care to ensure that the apparently successful reunification efforts are not being followed by unintended negative outcomes (e.g., increased rates of reentry).

Finally, understanding the relationships between outcomes through self-evaluation enables staff—working

at all levels of the agency—to more clearly, forcefully, and accurately "tell the story" of how well children and families are being helped and where change is needed most. Better understanding of the cycle of experiences in child welfare manifests in practice, then, whenever a supervisor is motivating staff in a unit meeting, a management team is assessing the need for program and policy change, or an agency director is demonstrating accountability to relevant members of the community (e.g., judges, child advocates, legislators, boards of supervisors).

STAYING THE COURSE FOR SYSTEM REFORM

Participants in the initial phase of the Family to Family initiative found that self-evaluation was a worthwhile effort and recommended that it be identified as one of four core strategies in subsequent phases of the initiative. It bears noting, however, that implementing agency self-evaluation is neither a simple nor uniform process, and the necessary reforms do not occur overnight. The process varies from one agency to the next due to differences in organizational structure, culture, and resources, such as staff and data systems. Both support and resistance have been encountered and can be expected from agency managers, line workers, and community partners, as well as birth and foster families. Part of the ongoing challenge is the need to make self-evaluation a routine feature of planning, management, and practice. Regular meetings of intra-agency self-evaluation teams with representatives from different units are one way to reinforce the notion of needed reform and keep this process moving forward.

An important next step for Family to Family concerns the implementation of self-evaluation in the community context. That is, while community partners are integral members of self-evaluation teams, instituting the self-evaluation process in community-based organizations is not a simple task. Like child welfare agencies, these organizations would benefit from using data to inform their work, but in most cases their resources are not sufficient to support infrastructure such as technical staff or data systems. Thus, in addition to the barriers faced by child welfare agencies, there are additional needs to be addressed in helping community-based organizations to build their own capacity for self-evaluation. The foundation is currently exploring the use of an easily modified Web browser–based data collection tool developed, maintained, and technically supported by a private vendor. This Efforts to Outcomes software would enable community partners with little to no data infrastructure to track the impact of their service delivery and work with the child welfare agency. While these issues are an ongoing challenge, clearly, helping to expand self-evaluation beyond the child welfare agency into organizations in the community will only enhance the success of reform initiatives like Family to Family.

In spite of these challenges, many sites have reported that the initiative has been effective in improving child welfare program operations and outcomes for children and families (Usher et al., 1998). This is similar to results seen in other research on efforts to use data to inform child welfare policy and practice (Gardner, 2000; Jamieson & Bodonyi, 1999; Moore et al., 2000), and agencies from across the Family to Family grantee states now routinely use outcome data that they previously did not (Omang & Bonk, 1999). In some sites, foundation-funded technical assistants have worked to introduce additional aids to self-evaluation, such as population profiles (descriptions of children in out-of-home placements across all systems and agencies) and statistical forecasting procedures for outcomes of interest (Annie E. Casey Foundation, 2001).

TAKING STOCK AND MOVING THE PROCESS FORWARD

Beginning in 2006 and continuing through 2009, a nationwide evaluation of Family to Family is being conducted to track changes in policy and practice and to assess the effects of those changes on safety and permanency outcomes in 15 anchor sites. The first phase of the evaluation seeks to identify and describe the challenges of fully implementing the organizational and practice changes associated with Family to Family. The implementation analysis will focus, first, on the changes in structure and process that agencies have undertaken in their efforts to create child welfare systems that reflect the values and operating principles on which the initiative is based. This includes the identification of factors and circumstances that led to decisions *not* to make certain changes. The second broad area of focus is an analysis of the efforts to implement each of the four core strategies, including self-evaluation. The objective is to learn about the challenges of implementation and the strategies for overcoming barriers to implementation in participating agencies, their community partners, and the families they serve. The information learned from this analysis will have implications for the continuing development of Family to Family and for evaluating how it has affected outcomes for families and children.

CONCLUSION

Using data to inform and direct child welfare policy and practice has been called for by a number of researchers and practitioners (Barth, 1997; Jamieson & Bodonyi, 1999; Moore et al., 2000), has been demonstrated to produce positive results (Gardner, 2000; Jamieson & Bodonyi, 1999; Moore et al., 2000), and is a core strategy of the Family to Family initiative. By changing staff attitudes about data, encouraging collaboration among agency and community partners, employing longitudinal data and GIS technology to monitor change, and understanding the interrelated nature of outcomes, self-evaluation can become a powerful force in child welfare system reform. Access to timely data and the capacity to analyze this information can help agency staff and community partners to identify and quickly respond to changing population needs.

Finally, the child welfare system does not exist in a static environment. A significant change in the landscape in which Family to Family will be operating is the second round of the Child and Family Services Review, which began in 2007. New federal outcome standards based on composites, components, and measures pose a new challenge with respect to self-evaluation efforts in Family to Family sites and in other state and local child welfare agencies. Considerable effort will be needed to inform and educate public agency staff about the strengths and limitations of the new measures and how they can be used to guide practice reform. Developing staff expertise to use data is an ongoing challenge as self-evaluation efforts seek to use data to improve practice and, in turn, to achieve further improvements in outcomes.

References

Ainsworth, F., & Maluccio, A. (2003). Towards new models of professional foster care. *Adoption & Fostering*, 27, 4, 46–50.

Annie E. Casey Foundation. (2001). The need for self-evaluation: Using data to guide policy and practice. *Family to Family: Tools for rebuilding foster care*. Baltimore: Author.

Barth, R. P. (1997). Permanent placements for young children placed in foster care: A proposal for a child welfare services performance standard. *Children and Youth Services Review*, 19, 615–631.

Barth, R. P., Courtney, M., Berrick, J., & Albert, V. (1994). *From child abuse to permanency planning: Child welfare services pathways and placements*. New York: de Gruyter.

Brooks, D., & Webster, D. (1999). Child welfare in the United States: Policy, practice and innovations in service delivery. *International Journal of Social Welfare*, 8, 296–306.

Coulton, C., Korbin, J., Su, M., & Chow, J. (1995). Community level factors and child maltreatment rates, *Child Development*, 66, 1262–1276.

Courtney, M. (1993). Standardized outcome evaluation of child welfare services in out-of-home care: Problems and possibilities. *Children and Youth Services Review*, 15(5), 349–369.

Courtney, M., & Collins, R. (1994). New challenges and opportunities in child welfare outcomes and information technologies. *Child Welfare*, 73, 359–378.

Courtney, M., Needell, B., & Wulczyn, F. (2004). Unintended consequences of the push for accountability: The case of national child welfare performance standards. *Children and Youth Services Review*, 26, 1141–1154.

Curtis, P. (1999). Introduction: The chronic nature of the foster care crisis. In P. Curtis, G. Dale, & J. Kendall (Eds.), *The foster care crisis: Translating research into policy and practice* (pp. 1–14). Lincoln: University of Nebraska Press.

Ernst, J. (2000). Mapping child maltreatment: Looking at neighborhoods in a suburban county. *Child Welfare*, 79(5), 555–572.

Gardner, F. (2000). Design evaluation: Illuminating social work practice for better outcomes. *Social Work*, 45(2), 176–181.

Goerge, R. (1990). The reunification process in substitute care. *Social Service Review*, 64(3), 422–457.

Jamieson, M., & Bodonyi, J. (1999). Data-driven child welfare policy and practice in the next century. *Child Welfare*, 78(1), 15–30.

Leung, P., Cheung, K., & Stevenson, K. (1994). Advancing competent social work practice: A computer-based approach to child protective service training. *Computers in Human Services*, 11(3–4), 317–332.

Meier, A., & Usher, C. L. (1998). New approaches to program evaluation. In R. Edwards et al. (Eds.), *Skills for effective management of nonprofit organizations* (pp. 371–405). Washington, DC: National Association of Social Workers Press.

Moore, T., Rapp, C., & Roberts, B. (2000). Improving child welfare performance through supervisory use of client outcome data. *Child Welfare*, 79(5), 475–497.

Needell, B., Webster, D., Armijo, M., Lee, S., Cuccaro-Alamin, S., & Shaw, T. (2006). *Performance indicators for child welfare services in California project*. Available: http://cssr.berkeley.edu/CWSCMSreports.

Omang, J., & Bonk, K. (1999). Family to family: Building bridges for child welfare with families, neighborhoods, and communities. *Policy and Practice of Public Human Services*, 57, 15–21.

Queralt, M., & Witte, A. (1998). A map for you? Geographic information systems in the social services. *Social Work*, 43, 455–469.

Robertson, J., & Wier, K. (1998). Using geographic information systems to enhance community-based child welfare practice. *Child Maltreatment*, 3, 224–234.

Ruscio, J. (1998). Information integration in child welfare cases: An introduction to statistical decision making. *Child Maltreatment*, 3(2), 143–156.

Shahar, I., Auslander, G., & Cohen, M. (1995). Utilizing data to improve practice in hospital social work: A case study. *Social Work in Health Care*, 20(3), 99–111.

Shyne, A. (1976). Evaluation in child welfare. *Child Welfare*, 55(1), 5–18.

Usher, C. L. (1995). Improving evaluability through self-evaluation, *Evaluation Practice*, 16, 59–68.

Usher, C. L., Gibbs, D., & Wildfire, J. B. (1995). A framework for planning, implementing, and evaluating child welfare reforms. *Child Welfare, 74*, 859–875.

Usher, C. L., Gibbs, D., & Wildfire, J. (1998). *Evaluation of family to family.* Research Triangle Park, NC: Research Triangle Institute.

Usher, C. L., Randolph, K. A., & Gogan, H. C. (1999). Placement patterns in foster care. *Social Service Review, 73*, 22–36.

Usher, C. L., Wildfire, J., & Gibbs, D. (1999). Measuring performance in child welfare: Secondary effects of success. *Child Welfare, 78*, 1, 31–51.

Wulczyn, F. (1996). A statistical and methodological framework for analyzing the foster care experiences of children. *Social Service Review, 70*, 318–329.

Wulczyn, F., Brunner-Hislop, K., & Goerge, R. (2000). *An update from the multistate foster care data archive: Foster care dynamics 1983–1998.* Chicago: Chapin Hall Center for Children, University of Chicago.

Wulczyn, F., Kogan, J., & Dilts, J. (2001). The effect of population dynamics on performance measurement. *Social Service Review, 75*(2), 292–317.

17

Comparing Welfare and Child Welfare Populations: An Argument for Rethinking the Safety Net

Mark E. Courtney

Amy Dworsky

Irving Piliavin

Steven McMurtry

INTRODUCTION

Before 1972, the income maintenance and social service functions of public welfare agencies were integrated; one worker was responsible not only for eligibility determination and grant supervision but also for service provision. In June of that year, the Department of Health, Education and Welfare (HEW) issued a mandate requiring states to have two separate and autonomous organizational units in their public welfare agencies, each with its own staff and administration; one unit would be responsible for income maintenance, the other for social services.[1] In practice, this meant that a family's income maintenance needs would be addressed by one worker, its social service needs by another.

Although the mandate for separation was eventually rescinded in 1976 as part of the Nixon administration's New Federalism, most states continued to operate as if it were still in effect (Benton, 1980; Hagen, 1987; Wyers, 1981). Now, however, with the evolution of welfare reform, the pendulum seems to be swinging back toward integration, with consequent implications for public welfare agencies and the clients whom they serve. In many ways, the Personal Responsibility and Work Opportunity Reconciliation Act of 1996 (PRWORA) represented a reintegration of economic assistance with social services, albeit with an emphasis on moving parents into the workforce rather than helping them maintain a basic income or better care for their dependent children. Notwithstanding recent efforts to amend the legislation to emphasize poverty reduction or its impact on children, nothing in the current federal law speaks effectively to the well-being of children in low-income families, the assumption being that parental success in the workforce will lead to better outcomes for children.

At the time the law passed, concern was expressed about how this shift of emphasis might affect the well-being of children. Research findings are mixed and for the most part not very conclusive regarding welfare reform's impact on children in poor families, though benefits appear most likely for younger school-age children and harm most likely for adolescents (Morris, Knox, & Gennetian, 2002). There is no convincing evidence of large positive or negative effects, but this may be a function of the difficulty of teasing out such effects given the heterogeneity of welfare reform efforts around the country, significant policy changes in other areas of child policy (e.g., the Adoption and Safe Families Act, 1997), and changes in the overall economy.

One question that has seldom been asked by researchers or policy makers is whether welfare reform has sufficiently altered the purpose of welfare programs and the populations they serve to warrant a rethinking of the relationship between economic support programs and social services for children and families. At first glance, one might assert that this has already taken place, since TANF (Temporary Assistance for Needy Families) agencies now provide a range of services to parents not typically provided by AFDC (Aid to Families with Dependent Children) programs. However, this perspective ignores the fact that much has changed since the time that income maintenance and social services were separated in 1972. Federal social services funding went from being an entitlement to a block grant and thereafter declined significantly in real terms. In contrast, child welfare services evolved from being sideline tasks of social services departments in the 1960s to comprising a major service system that now operates virtually independently of public welfare programs and consumes billions of federal dollars. Moreover, in the mid-1960s, the family welfare and child welfare functions of government were largely integrated: Services to rehabilitate parents so as to help them become self-sufficient were not seen as radically distinct from those that might help them become better parents. This is no longer the case. In fact, income maintenance per se is no longer the focus of federal welfare policy; work is. Services provided to parents by TANF agencies are largely if not exclusively targeted at moving them into the paid workforce, whereas services intended to support parenting are now largely provided by or paid for by child welfare agencies.

It is time to rethink the radical separation between workfare and child welfare policies and services. In this chapter, we use data from two ongoing studies in Milwaukee County, Wisconsin, to provide empirical evidence supporting the claim that workfare and child welfare programs serve increasingly similar populations with similar needs. In spite of the similar needs of these populations, indeed, even a large overlap between the populations, these two systems continue to operate largely independently, if not at cross-purposes. We believe that our findings call into question both the structure of service systems in jurisdictions like Milwaukee and the federal welfare and child welfare policies that lead state and local policy makers to create such misaligned systems.

To provide a context for our findings and policy analysis, we start with a history of the separation of income maintenance from social services. We then briefly describe the current situation. We describe the two studies that we are conducting in Milwaukee and compare selected findings across studies to show the common needs of the respective service populations. We conclude with a discussion of what we believe our findings suggest for federal and state policies.

A BRIEF HISTORY OF SEPARATION

Title IV of the 1935 Social Security Act, more commonly known as Aid to Dependent Children (and later, Aid to Families with Dependent Children), granted federal aid to states on a matching basis to help offset the costs of providing economic support to children in mother-only families. Although some AFDC families received social services in addition to cash payments (Hoshino, 1963, 1971a; Wickenden, 1976), those social services were not funded under Title IV and, as a result, tended to be "fragmentary and incidental" (Greenleigh Associates, 1960, p. 50, cited in Wickenden & Bell, 1961).

More than 20 years passed before Congress officially recognized the important role that social services could play in dependency reduction with the 1956 Social Security Amendments (Schottland, 1956). According to that legislation, states were supposed to "furnish financial assistance and other services as far as practicable . . . to needy dependent children and their parents . . . to help maintain or strengthen family life and . . . attain the maximum self support and personal independence" (Social Security Amendments, 1956, 42 U.S.C. § 601). Yet, even in the wake of the 1956 amendments, states had little incentive to augment the service component of their public assistance programs because federal funding for social services was not appropriated by Congress (McEntire & Haworth, 1967).

It was not until the early 1960s that the necessary funding was forthcoming. The Kennedy administration introduced a new strategy to reduce dependency in response to concerns about growth in AFDC caseloads. Henceforth, public assistance would cease to be a "straight cash handout operation" (1961 quote from Abraham Ribicoff, secretary of HEW, cited in Handler, 1972; Handler & Hollingsworth, 1971). Instead, the emphasis would be on, in President John F. Kennedy's words, "services in addition to support, rehabilitation instead of relief and training for useful work instead of prolonged dependency" (Kennedy at the signing of the 1962 Public Welfare Amendments as cited in Woolley & Peters, n.d.).

Central to this new strategy were the Public Welfare Amendments of 1962. Among other things, that legislation raised the federal government's share of social service costs from 50% to 75%, thereby giving states a financial incentive to provide more, and presumably better, services (Cohen & Ball, 1962). The amendments also stipulated that states could be reimbursed not only for services provided to current AFDC recipients, but also for services provided to families "at risk" of welfare receipt, that is, both former and potential recipients.[2] Like Kennedy, President Lyndon B. Johnson and his administration favored an antipoverty strategy based on rehabilitation and so continued to implement the strategy the previous administration had begun.

However, by 1967, there were indications that another major change was on the horizon. Following the Social Security Amendments of 1967, there was a discernible shift from "soft" services, such as social casework or counseling, to "hard" services along the lines of job training and child care (Bell, 1983; Trattner, 1994).[3] It was also in that year that then–Secretary of Health, Education and Welfare John Gardner first voiced official support for the concept of separation. Although this support was subsequently reaffirmed by Secretaries Wilbur J. Cohen, Robert H. Finch, and Elliot Lee Richardson (Wickenden, 1976), it was not until 1972 that HEW finally issued its mandate along with a set of guidelines for states to carry it out (U.S. Department of Health, Education and Welfare, 1972).

The fundamental shift in social service provision represented by separation was largely motivated by policy makers' disillusionment with rehabilitation as a way to reduce dependency on welfare. Given an increase of more than 300% in the number of families receiving AFDC between 1960 and 1972, many policy makers reached the conclusion that providing social services would not reduce welfare dependence (Derthick, 1975; Sanger, 1990).[4] However, what really convinced policy makers that this rehabilitative strategy was ineffective was that AFDC caseloads had continued to grow despite unprecedented levels of federal spending on social services.[5] Social services expenditures by the federal government doubled between 1967 and 1972 (Derthick, 1975), yet the number of families receiving AFDC in 1972 had more than doubled, and the cost of AFDC payments to those families had almost tripled since 1967 (U.S. Bureau of the Census, 1968, 1973).[6]

Although AFDC families could still receive services under separation, provision of those services would no longer be routine; only if families requested services would they be provided. The notable exception to this was child protective services. Policy makers assumed (or were led to believe) that most AFDC families had never wanted services in the first place and, hence, that the number of requests would be relatively low.[7] Because this meant that federal funding for social services for the poor could be substantially reduced, if not phased out altogether, separation found strong support among Republicans in Congress (and little opposition among Democrats) during the Nixon administration.

Separation was also expected to reduce federal social services expenditures by increasing accountability. As critics of the 1962 amendments rightly pointed out, nowhere in the legislation was the term "social services" clearly defined. Whether intentional or not, this "loophole" was not lost on state policy makers, who recognized that federal reimbursement could be maximized by adopting a broad definition of social services, one that would encompass "anything done for, with, or about a client by a social worker" (President's Commission on Income Maintenance, 1970, p. 307; see also Derthick, 1975; Hoshino, 1971b, 1972). Capitalizing on the argument that states were claiming reimbursement for costs that Congress had never intended, proponents of separation contended that if income maintenance and social services were administratively as well as organizationally separate, there would be greater accountability (Dattalo, 1992; Hoshino, 1972).

It should be noted that although the Nixon administration sought to reduce spending on services for the poor, this did not translate into an across-the-board cut in social services spending. In particular, the 1974 amendments to the Social Security Act

(Title XX) expanded eligibility for free or subsidized social services to the non-poor and shifted the focus from social services aimed at reducing dependency to those aimed at enhancing the quality of life (Gilbert, 1977; Katz, 1996). The 1974 amendments did however impose a spending cap of $2.5 billion. Federal spending on social services was significantly curtailed during the Reagan administration (Trattner, 1994).

Even if complete separation was never fully achieved (Fisher, 1971; Schubert, 1974; Wyers, 1983), a distinction between social services and income maintenance was retained. One important consequence of this separation was that social services increasingly came to mean services for families whose children had been or were at risk of being neglected or abused. Indeed, whereas in the past, AFDC families might have been offered services by their caseworker, involvement with the child welfare system currently is the only way that many vulnerable families receive needed services. Several authors (Hutchinson, Datta, & Rodwell, 1994; Kamerman & Kahn, 1990; Waldfogel, 1998) have speculated that if the child welfare system were not the only route through which families could obtain the services they need, perhaps fewer families would require protective intervention. What is particularly ironic about this development is that when families receive services through the child welfare system, their participation in those services is typically mandated by the courts—arguably, a highly coercive situation. Even if the service participation of some clients before separation had been coerced in the sense that failure to participate might mean loss of cash assistance, it was generally not the case that service participation was court ordered.

Although there is some evidence that AFDC eligibility technicians did, over the years, provide AFDC clients with access to services such as referrals, information, and advocacy, any social services role they may have played was highly circumscribed and minor in comparison to eligibility determination (Hagen, 1987; Hagen & Wang, 1993; Kahn, 1978). Eligibility technicians did not provide either therapeutic or rehabilitative services. This reflects not only the lack of time they had to provide services given the size of their caseloads, but also their lack of training in assessment and service provision.

Throughout the 1970s and much of the 1980s, public assistance programs were primarily dispensers of financial aid; social services were peripheral to most programs, if they were provided at all. However, since the late 1980s, the focus of public assistance programs has undergone a fundamental change: from supporting families with cash assistance to making families self-sufficient.[8] This trend began with the Family Support Act of 1988, under which the Job Opportunities and Basic Skills (JOBS) Training Program was created.[9] It culminated with PRWORA, which replaced AFDC, an entitlement, with TANF, a time-limited program without entitlement status.

Since the late 1990s, individual states have implemented their own versions of welfare reform within the broad parameters laid out by the PRWORA.[10] Although the specifics of these programs vary greatly from state to state, in general, the social service function of public assistance programs has become increasingly important. To help family heads become and remain employed, these programs offer not only child care and transportation assistance, but job readiness training, life skills training, and, in some cases, counseling or rehabilitation services.

One consequence of this trend toward programs that emphasize self-sufficiency has been a change in the role of the agency worker. Whereas income maintenance had been the primary, if not exclusive, concern of eligibility technicians, agency workers today are performing both income maintenance and social service functions. Although their responsibilities may still include eligibility determination, they are also functioning as case managers, brokering and coordinating the various services that clients need to make the often difficult transition from welfare to work.

In some respects, it would appear that these agency workers are doing essentially what caseworkers had done before separation: handling both financial and nonfinancial needs. However, this similarity belies important differences. In the heyday of social service provision by AFDC workers, the prevailing assumption was that dependency was caused by some pathological condition and that it was the caseworker's role to "treat" it through counseling and social casework. Although concrete services like child care and training might also have been provided, the caseworker's role was primarily seen as one of changing individuals. In contrast, agency workers today are expected to play a much more facilitative role and one that is more narrowly focused on work than on parental functioning more generally. Agency workers help parents to cope with all of the stresses and strains associated with the work requirements and time limits that the parents now face.

This is not to say that changing clients is not an important program goal. On the contrary, the goal of welfare-to-work programs is largely to change parents' behavior so that parents will become, and remain, employed. However, the agency worker is not so much the agent of change as a facilitator of that goal. Moreover, the role of helping parents to better care for their dependent children, one that was central to practice under the older form of integration, is now beyond the purview of the welfare worker. In any case, in their efforts to help parents enter and remain in the workforce, welfare agency workers today are clearly performing both income maintenance and social service functions. We believe that this development has implications for public welfare and child welfare agencies alike.

MILWAUKEE: A LABORATORY FOR WELFARE AND CHILD WELFARE REFORM

The number of Wisconsin families receiving cash assistance has significantly declined under the state's TANF program, Wisconsin Works (W-2). In August 1997, the month before implementation of W-2 began, 34,491 Wisconsin families were receiving AFDC.[11] By September 2000, the state's W-2 cash assistance caseload was 6,772 families (Wisconsin Department of Workforce Development 2001, 2002). Other states too experienced caseload reductions in the wake of PRWORA, though they have generally been smaller than the Wisconsin declines. Numerous so-called leavers studies have sought to examine the experiences of families who have left the welfare rolls since 1997. In addition, interest has grown in the characteristics, needs, and well-being of the residual TANF caseload, since the rapid caseload reductions may have resulted in changes in the nature of the help-seeking population.

Wisconsin's welfare program is of particular interest for several reasons and not only because it was created by U.S. Health and Human Services secretary and former governor Tommy Thompson. First, Wisconsin's TANF program is considered to be one of the more radically work-driven of the state welfare reform programs that were initiated following implementation of PRWORA. W-2 participants receive cash payments only when they are actively participating in activities intended to prepare them for unsubsidized

employment. Second, Wisconsin's caseload decline preceded that of most states. Wisconsin experienced a significant reduction in its AFDC caseloads prior to the implementation of W-2. Wisconsin's caseload declined by 44% between January 1993, when 81,291 families received AFDC, and January 1997, when 45,586 families received AFDC (U.S. Department of Health and Human Services, 2007). Therefore, examining W-2 and the population it serves may help to illustrate the issues that arise for a "post–caseload decline" welfare program and population. Third, Wisconsin chose to regionalize and privatize TANF services in Milwaukee, contracting out responsibility for service provision in six geographically defined regions of Milwaukee County to for-profit and not-for-profit agencies. Many other states and localities have chosen to privatize public welfare functions in recent years. Finally, as the only major urban center in Wisconsin and the jurisdiction that accounts for most of Wisconsin's remaining TANF caseload, Milwaukee is an excellent place to study welfare reform.

Milwaukee is also an important place to study child welfare programs. Like most other urban child welfare jurisdictions, Milwaukee saw its out-of-home care caseload rise consistently, and often rapidly, during the 1990s. The Milwaukee caseload grew by 86% from 3,065 at the end of 1990 to 5,712 at the end of 1999 (Courtney & Dworsky, 2001). In 1997, the state of Wisconsin created the Bureau of Milwaukee Child Welfare (BMCW) within the Wisconsin Department of Health and Social Services, Division of Child and Family Services. The BMCW was formed in response to court challenges to the previously county-run child welfare program in Milwaukee. Counties still operate their own child welfare programs in the remainder of the state.

The state takeover of child welfare programs in Milwaukee is an attempt to correct the problems that plagued the county-run system. The state has significantly increased child welfare funding and has privatized most child welfare services through dividing Milwaukee County into five regions and contracting with private agencies for provision of services to children and families, including out-of-home care, in each region.[12] State workers handle calls to the child maltreatment phone in-take unit for the county and screen calls to determine whether they are appropriate for investigation. When deemed appropriate, investigations are then conducted by state workers who, in consultation with their supervisors, then decide on a course of action. They can conclude that the report does not require immediate intervention by the BMCW and close the case, sometimes referring the family to voluntary services in the community. Alternatively, they can conclude that the report is valid but that the child victim is not in immediate danger. In these cases, the child remains in the home while the family is referred for in-home voluntary services (called "safety services"), which are provided by contract agencies in the regions.[13] Last, they can conclude that the victim would face an unacceptable risk by staying in the home, in which case court consent is sought by the state bureau to place the child in out-of-home care. Ongoing case management services for these latter cases are also provided by contract agencies. Thus, in many ways, Milwaukee is a laboratory for Wisconsin's efforts to reform both its child welfare and welfare programs. Privatization is a central element of both reforms. Yet, welfare reform was from the beginning a high-priority initiative of Governor Tommy Thompson's administration, while the takeover of the Milwaukee child welfare system was undertaken, at least initially, with considerable reluctance.

OUR RESEARCH IN MILWAUKEE

Milwaukee presents a unique opportunity to compare the characteristics of welfare and child welfare populations due to the presence there of two ongoing longitudinal studies. The Milwaukee TANF Applicants Study (referred to here as the "W-2 study") is following the progress of 1,075 families in which a parent applied for W-2 assistance in Milwaukee County in 1999. The study involves in-person interviews with parents at three points in time over a 3-to-4-year period and linking of the resulting survey data to administrative data pertaining to public assistance receipt, earnings from covered employment, and child welfare services involvement. The Bureau of Milwaukee Child Welfare Evaluation (BMCWE) is following approximately 1,500 children whose families have received voluntary in-home safety services or who were in out-of-home care. Data are collected through in-person and telephone surveys with parents, Web-based surveys of case managers, interviews with older children and youth, paper-and-pencil surveys of out-of-home care providers, and the state's child welfare administrative data system. For the purposes of this

chapter, we focus primarily on the part of the BMCWE study that is examining the population referred for safety services. Before comparing the parents and children served by the W-2 and safety services agencies in Milwaukee, we briefly describe each of the studies.[14]

The sample for the W-2 study was selected from among parents with at least one dependent child applying for assistance at any of the six sites administered by the five private agencies operating the W-2 program in Milwaukee County between March 1999 and August 1999.[15,16] Potential W-2 applicants met with a "resource specialist," who decided whether applicants should be referred to a "Financial and Employment Planner" (FEP) for final eligibility determination. Applicants referred to a FEP were informed about the study by the resource specialist and were directed to a survey interviewer stationed at the agency. Less than 2% of the applicants informed about the study declined to participate.[17] We employed a stratified sampling strategy in order to obtain approximately 200 sample members per site. A total of 1,207 interviews were originally conducted, but after review of the integrity of the procedures used in identifying sample members and comparison of survey responses to administrative data on program participation, we ended up with a final sample of 1,075 W-2 applicants.

Computer-assisted personal interviewing was used to conduct the wave 1 interviews, from which the data used for this chapter were derived, with interviews averaging about an hour. Part of the interview asked parents about a randomly selected focal child in their family. Interviews covered household composition, nonresident children, employment histories of family members, child care use and problems, education and vocational training of parents, housing history and problems, government program participation, household income, respondent parenting practices and problems, child health and development, child school performance, child behavior problems, and respondent health and well-being.

As noted above, families are referred to safety services in Milwaukee County pursuant to a child maltreatment report, when a state investigator determines that there are safety risks to a child, but not enough to warrant immediate placement in out-of-home care. In practice and in the child welfare literature, these services are referred to as "family preservation services." A total of 480 families were included in the BMCWE study of safety services, representing the first 100 cases that opened at each of the bureau's five safety services sites between November 2000 and November 2001. We accepted new cases into the sample until each site reached 100, though later we dropped 20 cases that were determined to be invalid for various reasons. Data on each case come from two potential sources: assessments by case managers collected via a Web-based survey and telephone or in-person interviews with the child's primary caregiver (usually a parent). Surveys were administered within 30 days of case opening (Time 1) and again within 30 days of case closing (Time 2). We selected one child at random from each family as the "target child" for the surveys. Case manager surveys focused on perceived child and family needs and provision of services. Caregiver surveys focused on most of the same domains covered in the W-2 study, with a greater focus on more in-depth assessment of caregiver and child problems and less attention to work history and welfare program participation. Information on some cases was lost due to nonresponse by case managers or caregivers or focusing survey questions on the incorrect child. Complete case manager results were thus available for 433 children (90.2%), and caregiver results were available for 324 children (67.5%).

Our studies provide an unusual opportunity to compare two groups of low-income, help-seeking parents/caregivers in one urban area.[18] These parents were studied at the time they either sought (in the case of W-2) or were referred to (in the case of safety services) government-supported family support services, albeit services with distinctly different foci. We assessed the characteristics of the two populations at roughly the same time. Importantly, in both cases, the service systems in which they were involved were well along in terms of implementation, though incremental changes continue in both programs.

COMPARISON OF THE W-2 AND SAFETY SERVICES POPULATIONS

Before comparing the characteristics of the two study samples, some caveats are in order. First, both studies employed stratified sampling strategies in order to allow for comparison of outcomes of interest across the six W-2 and five child welfare service sites. In principle, this should not cause much of a problem for making inferences to the overall populations of interest since the boundaries of the program regions were designed to ensure equal demand for services across sites. Nevertheless, to the extent that our stratification process caused an oversampling of some sites relative to their contribution to the total service population in Milwaukee, this may have resulted in total samples that are not representative of the overall W-2 and child welfare services populations in Milwaukee. Although in this chapter we have not weighted our samples to try to compensate for this potential problem, prior comparison of our samples to aggregate data on program applicants suggests that our samples are comparable to the overall service populations of interest.

Second, although our survey response rates are very respectable for the W-2 survey (98% at baseline) and safety services case manager survey (90.2%), the response rate for parents in the safety services study is less than ideal (67.5%). The lower parent response rate in the child welfare study is not surprising given that we did not have the luxury of interviewing them at the agency site as we did in the W-2 study. Moreover, some of these parents may have been uncomfortable discussing their interactions with child protective services. Of the potential safety services survey respondents who did not complete the interview, about two thirds could not be located and about one third refused to be interviewed.

Third, the two studies did not always employ identical measures for a given construct, making clear comparisons across samples difficult in some cases. In particular, we have more detailed data on earnings and government program participation for the W-2 sample than for the child welfare services sample. In contrast, measures of parental health, mental health, and parenting behavior are more detailed in the BMCWE study than in the W-2 study.

In spite of these limitations, we believe that the comparison of findings across the samples is instructive. As we noted above, the samples we obtained are generally representative of the relevant service populations in Milwaukee at the time we collected the data. At any rate, there is no compelling reason to believe that our samples differ in substantively important ways from the overall service populations on our variables of interest. Furthermore, the lack of strictly comparable measures across samples for some domains of interest does not significantly detract from the overall impression given by the data presented below. Our data provide for the most robust comparison of welfare and child welfare populations of which we are aware.

We make comparisons between the characteristics of the households in the two samples, with particular emphasis on the characteristics of primary caregivers and randomly selected focal children. Unless otherwise noted, the findings reported here come from the baseline surveys in both studies (i.e., at the time of application for W-2 or referral to safety services). Table 17.1 provides some basic demographic data on the two samples of caregivers. The table shows that the overwhelming majority of the caregivers in both groups are women and that few of them are married. They are primarily women of color, though the safety services

group is somewhat more likely to be White and less likely to be African American than the W-2 applicant group. The parents who received safety services are somewhat older than the W-2 applicants. The parents in the safety services sample have more children than do the parents in the W-2 applicant sample, though a substantial proportion of both groups has three or more children. This distinction may be largely a function of the age difference between the two samples (i.e., the women in the safety services sample have had more time to have children). Both groups have relatively little human capital to work with, which is reflected in their low labor market participation. Of course, the W-2 applicants might be expected to be

TABLE 17.1 Demographic Characteristics of Parents in W-2 and Safety Services Study Samples

Attribute	% Safety Services Parents (N = 324)*	% W-2 Parents (N = 1,075)
Female	90.3	95.9
Race/Ethnicity		
White	25.9	10.6
African American	60.8	75.3
Hispanic	9.8	11.4
Native American	1.2	1.6
Other/Missing	2.3	1.2
Currently married**	16.7	5.0
Median age	33.1	27
Number of Resident Family Children		
1	19.4	41.1
2	26.8	26.0
3	23.8	16.3
4 or more	30	16.7
Less than high school diploma/GED	43.8	56.5
Currently employed full or part time	40.6	12.4
Median annual household income***	$11,750	$9,430

* Figures in this table on safety services sample members come from the parent surveys, with the exception of age, which comes from administrative data.

** The difference in marriage figures should be interpreted with caution because the safety services sample participants were asked whether they lived with their spouse, whereas the W-2 sample participants were asked if they were currently married.

*** The income figures are not strictly comparable across groups. Median income for the safety services sample is self-reported household income for the year before the interview. In contrast, income for the W-2 sample is a combination of administrative data on the respondent's unemployment insurance wage records, W-2 cash assistance and food stamps, and self-reported data on other sources of income (e.g., spouse/partner earnings, Supplemental Security Income, Earned Income Tax Credit, child support) for the year before the first follow up interview and is based on an N of 856, the number of study participants from whom wave two data were collected. We used this income measure because it was not possible to construct a measure of total income for the year before the baseline interview that would have included all of these potential sources.

jobless because employment status affects program eligibility. Although the respective measures of income in the two studies are not strictly comparable, it is clear that the vast majority of both groups of parents and their families live in poverty.

Not surprisingly, given the income reported by our study participants, both samples reported experiencing a wide array of economic hardships in the year before they were first interviewed (see Table 17.2). For example, between two fifths and one half of both samples report not having enough money to afford one or more basic necessities at some point in the past year. Significant percentages of both samples report varying levels of food insecurity over the course of the year. Over one in seven households in each sample had lost utility service at some point and over one third had lost telephone service. More than one in ten families in each sample had been evicted at least once, and a similar number had been homeless at some point in the past year. The only notable difference in the level of economic hardship experienced between the two groups is in the percentage that reported financial debt, with W-2 applicants less often reporting debt than did members of the safety services sample.

We also compared the two groups of parents on several indicators of psychosocial and health problems that might affect their ability both to work and to parent effectively (see Table 17.3). Significant percentages of both samples report relatively poor health and/or a disability, though these potential challenges are more common among the safety services sample. These parents exhibit high levels of depression, and over one fifth of the W-2 sample and over two fifths of the safety services sample reported wanting professional help for a mental health problem. About one seventh of each group reported being involved in an unsafe relationship, and one tenth of each group reported being in a physically abusive relationship. Over one quarter of the safety services sample and one tenth of the W-2 group reported being physically abused as children.

Table 17.4 compares the two samples of focal children. The characteristics listed are potential indicators of a child's difficulty of care (e.g., disability) and/or behavior problems (e.g., school problems, early pregnancy, delinquency). Questions pertaining to school, pregnancy, and delinquency were restricted to parents with children in the appropriate age ranges. Children in the safety services sample generally experienced more problems than those in the W-2 sample. These differences should be regarded with caution, however, since the children in the W-2 sample are much younger (median age = 5 years) than those in the safety services sample (median age = 10 years). Thus, the differences, even for the age-restricted outcomes, may reflect the fact that the safety services group has simply been around longer to experience a given out-

TABLE 17.2 Economic Hardships Experienced by Parents in W-2 and Safety Services Study Samples

Hardship Experienced in Previous Year	% Safety Services Parents* (N = 324)	% W-2 Parents (N = 1,075)
Any debt	42.3	26.2
Not enough money for clothing or shoes	48.5	42.2
Not enough money to pay rent or mortgage	40.4	45.5
Not enough money to pay important bill	50.3	48.0
Furniture, car, or belongings repossessed	5.2	2.7
Sometimes or often not enough food to eat	14.5	16.5
Visited food pantry or community meal program	32.7	30.4
Utilities shut off	16.4	15.2
Phone service shut off	36.4	33.8
Evicted	13.9	10.8
Homeless	10.8	12.8

* Figures in this table on safety services sample members come from the parent surveys.

TABLE 17.3 Psychosocial and Health Problems Reported by Parents in W-2 and Safety Services Study Samples

Problem	% Safety Services Parents* (N = 324)	% W-2 Parents (N = 1,075)
Described health as fair or poor	38.1	25.0
Reported having a disability	32.1	20.9
Depression**	29.3 (clinically depressed)	47.4 (score of 16 or higher on CES-D)
Wanted help for a mental health problem	42	22.0
Involved in unsafe relationship	16	14.6
Involved in physically abusive relationship	9.6	10.1
Physically abused as child	27.5	11.5***

* Figures in this table on safety services sample members come from the parent surveys.

** For the safety services study, we used the World Health Organization's Composite International Diagnostic Interview, Short Form (CIDI-SF). One of the CIDI modules we used produces a self-report diagnosis of major depression. In contrast, for the W-2 study, we used the Center for Epidemiological Studies Depression Scale (CES-D). Scores of 16 and above are generally considered indicative of depression (Radloff & Locke, 1986). The measures cannot be directly compared, but the CIDI estimate of depression for our safety services sample likely understates the level of depression that would have been found had we used the CES-D.

*** The question about childhood physical abuse was only asked of W-2 study participants during our first follow-up interview (N = 856).

TABLE 17.4 Selected Characteristics of Focal Children in W-2 and Safety Services Study Samples

Child Attribute	% Safety Services Focal Children* (N = 324)	% W-2 Focal Children (N = 1,075)
Has a disability	27.2	13.7
Placed in special education**	22.8	16.4
Suspended from school	66	36.9
Expelled from school	14	4.8
Dropped out of school***	14.7	4.9
Repeated grade	32.5	26.8
Became pregnant or parent***	12.8	4.4
Involved in juvenile delinquency****	—	13.9
Arrested	—	10.4
Convicted of crime against a person	9.3	—
Convicted of crime against property	8.2	—
Placed in juvenile detention	7.7	—

* Figures in this table on safety services sample members come from the parent surveys.

** In both studies, questions about the school outcomes for children were only asked of parents with a school-age focal child.

*** In both studies, questions about school dropout, pregnancy, and parenting were only asked of parents with a focal child 12 or older.

**** In both studies, questions about delinquency were only asked of parents with a focal child 10 or older.

come. At any rate, even the W-2 child sample faced a number of significant challenges.

In both studies, we asked parents a set of questions about how often they experienced various stresses asso-ciated with parenting the focal child. Response options for each question ranged from "almost never" to "almost always." Table 17.5 shows the percentage of parents in each group who answered that they experienced a particular stress "more than half the time" or "almost always." Although the safety services sample generally reports more stress than the W-2 applicant sample, nevertheless about one fifth to one third of the W-2 applicant sample reports frequently feeling unhappy when asked about specific experiences of parenting ("giving up own life," "trapped by responsibilities," and "more work than pleasure"). Interestingly, two of the largest differences between the groups are on items that pertain to the perceived characteristics of the child (i.e., "great deal of trouble to raise" and "harder to care for"), perhaps reflecting differences between the groups, suggested in Table 17.4, in the frequency of child problems.

The comparative data provide powerful evidence that the populations served by the W-2 and safety services programs in Milwaukee have much in common. Both sets of caregivers must try to find employment to support their families in the face of significant human capital deficits. The level of poverty experienced by these families and the economic hardships that go along with it attest to the difficulty the parents in both groups are having succeeding in the labor market. Many parents in both groups experience psychosocial and health problems that might affect their ability to hold down a job or to parent effectively. Many of their children are having problems in school and exhibit other behavioral problems. Not surprising, given the challenges they face, many of these parents report significant stress associated with parenting.

To be sure, there are also differences between the two groups. Some psychosocial problems appear to be more common among recipients of safety services than among applicants for TANF. Children in the families receiving safety services may be somewhat more troubled than those in the W-2 applicant families. Yet, the similarities loom larger than these differences. Moreover, given the age difference between the two groups, it may be the case that many of the W-2 applicants are on their way to later becoming safety services clients.

Indeed, when we examined the child welfare services involvement of our W-2 sample, we came up with some rather startling results (Courtney, Piliavin, Dworsky, & Zinn, 2005). Between 1989 and September 2001, 47.2% of our sample had been investigated by child welfare authorities in Milwaukee subsequent to a child maltreatment report. Nearly one quarter (23.2%) had been investigated since they had applied for W-2 and participated in our first wave of interviews.[19] Moreover, 11.6% had one or more children placed in out-of-home care between their interview in 1999 and September 2001. These rates of maltreatment investigation and foster care placement among public assistance populations are not only much higher than pre-TANF rates reported in other states, they are also much higher than the rates experienced by AFDC applicants in Milwaukee in 1996, before PRWORA (Courtney et al., 2005). Based on earlier work, we believe that the increased risk for child welfare services involvement among TANF

Table 17.5 Parenting Stress Reported by Parents in W-2 and Safety Services Study Samples

Parenting Concern*	% Safety Services Parents** (N = 324)	% W-2 Parents (N = 1,075)
Feel they are giving up own life to meet child's needs	26.2	36.8
Feel trapped by their responsibilities as parent	23.8	20.0
Feel taking care of their child is more work than pleasure	24.4	19.1
Are really bothered by things their child does	29.9	19.9
Lose patience with their child	13.3	9.0
Feel angry with their child	10.8	5.8
Feel their child has been quite a bit or a great deal of trouble to raise	22.6	8.7
Feel child is harder to care for than most other children	22.2	11.9

* Participants in both studies were asked how often they experienced a range of different feelings about the focal child. This table shows the percentage that reported feeling a particular way about their child "more than half of the time" or "almost always."

** Figures in this table on safety services sample members come from the parent surveys.

entry cohorts compared to AFDC entry cohorts in Milwaukee results from changes in the characteristics of the entering population.[20] Specifically, as the caseload has decreased in size and the number of people applying for assistance has decreased, those families left applying face more challenges than prior entry cohorts. For example, 1999 W-2 applicants were less likely to be married, less likely to have a high school diploma, and more likely to have three or more children than the 1996 AFDC applicants (Piliavin et al., 2001).

It is reasonable to assume that involvement with child welfare services programs is a crude but important indicator of the need for parenting support among a population. Given this assumption, our data suggest that a significant percentage of TANF applicants in Milwaukee need such support. Moreover, this need has risen significantly over time as the AFDC and TANF caseloads shrunk. One could of course argue that a nontrivial proportion of applicants for public assistance have always been in need of social services, including parenting supports, regardless of the level of involvement of public assistance populations with the child welfare system. We would not dispute this claim. Our data simply suggest that this need has become much more acute as the welfare cash assistance population has evolved into a much smaller residual population, made up of families headed by parents that on average have many more challenges than did their predecessors.

If many TANF applicants need parenting support, what about the needs of those families that come into contact with child welfare authorities? Interestingly, when we asked the parents in our safety services study what kind of help they needed, their answers looked more like the types of support associated with public assistance programs than those associated with child welfare services. Table 17.6 shows the service needs identified by parents in our safety services sample. Note that "counseling," a typical service provided by child welfare agencies, is fifth on the list after several basic needs (i.e., transport, income, food and clothing, housing). Parents cited the need for help in finding and maintaining employment, the central function of TANF agencies, about as often as the need for parenting classes and more often than day care, home management skills, or various forms of behavioral and mental health interventions.

In summary, at least in Milwaukee, it appears that welfare reform has led to a decline in the welfare caseload associated with increased need for social services, including parenting support. Our data on the historical involvement of TANF applicants with the child welfare program in Milwaukee suggest that *most* recent applicants for TANF have been or will be involved with the child welfare system at some point in time.[21] In addition, our data on the circumstances of families receiving in-home services from the Milwaukee child welfare system show this population to face severe economic hardships, to have limited

TABLE 17.6 Service Needs Identified by Safety Services Recipients at In-Take (N = 324)

Need	Number	Percentage
Help with transportation	177	54.6
Help applying for financial assistance or income support	163	50.3
Help with basic food or clothing needs	157	48.5
Housing services, such as home repair/maintenance	154	47.5
Counseling (any reason)	152	46.9
Help finding a place to live	149	46
Parenting classes	144	44.4
Help with finding and maintaining employment	142	43.8
Day care services	116	35.8
Home management skills	109	33.6
Medications for emotional/mental health reasons	81	25
Respite care	80	24.7
Substance abuse treatment	27	8.3
Psychiatric hospitalization	18	5.6

prospects for rapid and successful integration into the workforce, and to perceive a high level of need for the kinds of help that workfare programs are designed to provide.

TIME FOR RETHINKING THE ORGANIZATION OF WELFARE AND CHILD WELFARE SERVICES

It is time to reconsider the radical separation in federal policy between financial assistance to poor families and social services intended to help poor parents cope with the variety of challenges they often face. This separation began in an era when poor families were entitled to financial assistance and social services. The federal government provided financial assistance to help keep poor children in single-parent families from suffering the effects of poverty. The main goal of social services were to rehabilitate parents so that they could both gain financial self-sufficiency and take adequate care of their children. Put simply, financial assistance and social services were two parts of an *integrated* strategy to help poor parents.

The separation that began in the 1970s continues today, albeit in a very different policy context. Poor families are no longer entitled to financial assistance or social services. Cash assistance is now a stopgap (i.e., time-limited) measure to help parents while they do whatever is necessary to enter and remain connected to the job market. To be sure, child care funding has increased significantly under federal welfare reform, but even this was justified on the basis that poor parents cannot work if they have no one to supervise their children, not as an effort to improve child care for poor children. Likewise, when TANF agencies provide social services, they do so almost exclusively to help parents work, not to help them parent. In contrast to the 1970s, when public welfare agencies carried much of the public responsibility for social services to parents, state and local child welfare agencies now support the lion's share of social services intended to help adults do a better job of parenting.

Our research in Milwaukee helps to illustrate how this separation has continued to develop in a state with a model approach to welfare reform. On the one hand, our data indicate that the "voluntary" workfare and child welfare populations served by the two systems share many characteristics.[22] Many of these shared characteristics are challenges to both work and parenting. Indeed, there is even a fair degree of overlap between the two populations over time. On the other hand, the organization of the two service systems does not reflect a shared understanding of the families they serve nor the inextricable relationship between the goals.

The most obvious example of this in Milwaukee is the fact that the state created six geographic regions to provide TANF assistance in the county but five regions to provide child welfare services. This is at least partly a result of largely uncoordinated planning efforts by the state workforce development and child welfare agencies. There is little relationship between the boundaries of the TANF and child welfare regions. Thus, even if the private agencies that provide TANF and child welfare services in Milwaukee were inclined to collaborate, geographic distinctions in service areas makes this more difficult than it would have been had the state agencies chosen to better coordinate their planning.

Unfortunately, there is little reason for the W-2 agencies to collaborate with safety services agencies, given the incentives that drive the two systems. Although their contracts with the state have evolved over time, the primary goal of W-2 agencies has been to move eligible TANF applicants into unsubsidized employment, and the contracts have provided fiscal incentives to achieve various indicators of this goal. How the children in these families were faring did not enter into the performance equation at all. One might expect safety services agencies to frequently refer their clients to W-2 agencies for assistance, given the nature of the difficulties these families often face (e.g., poverty, unemployment, housing instability, etc.). However, W-2 agencies have no incentive to give priority to child welfare services clients since such families typically have multiple barriers to employment and are therefore less likely to contribute favorably to the agency's measurable contract outcomes. Ironically, a family participating in W-2 who had all of the children placed in foster care might contribute to the "success" of that W-2 agency by removing from the agency's responsibility a particularly difficult case.

Perhaps it should not be surprising, given this context, that safety services agencies tend to focus their efforts on providing "soft" services, such as parenting classes and counseling, though they do provide some short-term help with families' basic needs (Courtney et al., 2003). Interestingly, our surveys of safety services case managers and parents receiving safety services show a significant disconnect between what parents perceive their families need and what case managers perceive that the families need. Although parents are about as likely as case managers to report that they need parenting assistance and mental health services, case managers are much less likely than parents to report that families need help with income, housing, transportation, and other basic necessities (Courtney et al., 2003). One possible explanation for this discrepancy is the fact that safety services workers would be unable to provide families with significant help regarding basic needs even if the workers wanted to do so.

Our argument up to this point has relied on data from Milwaukee, thus begging the question of whether Milwaukee is a good example upon which to base a critique of federal welfare and child welfare policy. In Milwaukee, reduction of the welfare caseload to a small fraction of its former size has clearly contributed to a situation in which new applicants have more barriers to employment than did earlier AFDC applicants. We believe that Milwaukee is a good example of what the residual welfare caseload might look like when states experience the kind of caseload reduction that Wisconsin has seen, but this is an unanswered empirical question. Answering this question will require more TANF applicant studies. So-called welfare-leavers studies tell us almost nothing about new applicants, and the few cross-sectional samples of the welfare caseload being followed over-represent welfare recipients with long histories of welfare receipt. Similarly, the privatization of welfare and child welfare functions that has taken place in Milwaukee is happening elsewhere as well, but only time will tell if this becomes the norm. Moreover, it is possible that states will use privatization to integrate their welfare and child welfare service functions, though we are unaware of any examples of this.

Milwaukee is certainly not at the forefront of efforts to get TANF and child welfare agencies to work together, but it does not appear to be too far behind the curve either. To be sure, some state and local administrators have tried to pay attention to the overlap of TANF and child welfare services populations. A survey of TANF directors in September 2001 by the Urban Institute found a variety of efforts under way to improve collaboration between TANF and child welfare agencies (Andrews, Bess, Jantz, & Russell, 2002). Most states provide guidance to local TANF adminis-

trators concerning the need to coordinate TANF case plans with the case plans of child welfare agencies for so-called dual-system families and otherwise to share information with child welfare agencies. Fewer than half of the states have engaged in co-location of TANF and child welfare services. Most states have also clarified their policies concerning the use of TANF to provide child-only payments to relative caregivers, whether or not the child welfare agency supervises the care. The common element in all of these efforts is the focus on trying to avoid the confusion that can arise when families are involved with both child welfare services and TANF. These are commendable efforts. Indeed, had the Wisconsin TANF and child welfare agencies taken the issue of dual-system families more seriously in their planning, they might have at least come up with common service regions in Milwaukee.

Nevertheless, we believe that these collaborative efforts at the state level will inevitably fail to adequately address the problems caused by the fundamental disconnect in federal policy between the provision of economic assistance and support for troubled families. Current federal policy sends the message to administrators and parents alike that parents need not seek the help of TANF programs unless they have already failed at maintaining stable employment. In other words, those parents who are reasonably well equipped to find employment on their own are doing so. Most who show up at the door of the TANF office nowadays probably need more help than a job referral. Still, they can expect that the help TANF agencies offer will focus almost exclusively on improving their prospects for employment, regardless of what else may be going on in their lives. If their own limitations or circumstances make parenting difficult, they should not expect that TANF workers will pay much attention to this, or know how to help. Instead, in all likelihood, they will need to "fail" some way in their parenting responsibilities and come to the attention of child welfare authorities before they will receive any social services to help them address their problems. At best, they can then only hope that the two systems that now have significant control over their lives will "coordinate" efforts to help them.[23]

The problem with current welfare policy is not its emphasis on work. Rather, we believe that the policy shift to work-based public assistance failed to take adequate account of the social services needs of the population likely to require continuing support in balancing the demands of work *and* parenting. It also failed to take into account the role that public assistance programs had played in supporting the work of child welfare services. After the separation of income maintenance from social services in the 1970s, few members of the AFDC caseload needed social services to meet the demands of the AFDC program, since for the most part there were few demands.[24] In contrast, much of the residual TANF population in Milwaukee, and perhaps elsewhere, arguably need parenting support if they are to succeed in the labor market. These parents do not have the luxury of allowing their health and psychosocial needs or those of their children to go unmet, since failure to address these challenges can ultimately leave them without work or public assistance. Yet, PRWORA privileges work over all other outcomes, and TANF agency practices have followed suit.

At the same time, most families who come to the attention of child welfare agencies live in marginal economic circumstances that contribute to the risks faced by their children. Moreover, our findings suggest that the parents in these families freely admit their need for concrete assistance, including help in acquiring and maintaining employment. Yet, welfare reform has if anything reduced the access that child welfare agencies once had to basic economic support for troubled families. Child welfare programs have never been designed or funded to provide employment, housing, and other basic necessities. They have always relied primarily on public welfare agencies for those kinds of resources, though admittedly the resources may have often been inadequate to the task.

CONCLUSION

We believe that a natural consequence of welfare reform is that access to financial assistance will increasingly mean involvement with social services. As the shrinking residual TANF population exhibits more barriers to work, TANF agencies will increasingly augment services intended to improve parents' human capital with social and behavioral health services intended to stabilize the circumstances of troubled families and help them with problems of mental illness, substance abuse, and domestic violence.[25] TANF agencies would be well served by acquiring the expertise to assess the health and psychosocial needs of parents and their children before they send parents into a labor market that they may be poorly equipped to enter. Of course, provision of services that are appropriate to the needs of families should follow a thorough up-front assessment of need.

Why not take this process to its logical conclusion and turn TANF into the nation's primary family support program? Ongoing success in implementing welfare reform calls for the integration of work-based financial assistance with the supports (e.g., child care and health care) and social services that working-poor parents need to successfully balance the demands of work and parenting. Many TANF applicants need social services, and our research suggests that many will at some point become involved with child welfare services. Child welfare advocates have long lamented the fact that families must be reported for child maltreatment before they can obtain help from child welfare agencies for problems in parenting. This does not make child welfare agencies a likely source to which parents in need will readily turn for help. TANF agencies, in contrast, are often the first place that families turn when economic circumstances put family well-being at risk. Broadening the purpose of TANF to encompass family and child welfare along with parental employment could serve as a catalyst for the creation of a more comprehensive and integrated system of supports for low-income families with children.

The old arguments for the separation of financial assistance from social services are no longer valid, if they ever were.[26] Cash assistance and social services are no longer entitlements, undermining the original concern of fiscal conservatives about the apparently bottomless pit of social services spending. Although one can still reasonably question the effectiveness of social services in rehabilitating parents, research on welfare populations has clearly shown that many of these families do have needs that income alone does not address. TANF agencies cannot afford to abandon social services; they simply need to learn which services best serve whom.

Many liberals originally encouraged separation because they believed that family poverty was a function of the labor market and that requiring families to accept social services in return for public assistance was demeaning. Liberals may have underestimated both the service needs of welfare recipients in the 1960s and '70s and their willingness to take advantage of social services. Indeed, the work of Piliavin and Gross (1977) suggests that welfare recipients generally appreciated the help that they received and asked for more of it when it was combined with help meeting basic needs. At any rate, the political consensus has shifted, and poor parents must work, or at least make serious efforts in that direction, in order to obtain financial assistance. Most liberals no longer argue that welfare recipients do not need help; if anything, they are at the forefront of those who say that welfare recipients need more help to move into the labor force, including more assistance with their health and psychosocial problems in addition to education and training.

What policy changes are necessary to facilitate a better integration of programs intended to support low-income families in parenting and work? First, TANF must be broadened to include a much stronger focus on family and child welfare. Although the language of the current law pays lip service to providing assistance to needy families so that children can be cared for in their own homes, states are only held accountable for achieving the law's employment goals. How the TANF mandate should expand is beyond the scope of this chapter, but areas for consideration include family poverty and the basic health and safety of family members (e.g., prevention and reduction of child maltreatment, particularly neglect; improved physical and mental health of poor parents; reduction of domestic violence in poor families). Leaving employment as the sole measured outcome of TANF sends the wrong message to states, and the private entities with which some states now contract to run their TANF programs, about how to maximize the welfare of working-poor families.

Second, federal financing of welfare, social services, and child welfare programs must be restructured to better recognize the interrelatedness of the goals of federal social welfare programs directed at poor children and their families. In State Fiscal Year (SFY) 2000, total federal, state, and local spending on child welfare programs exceeded $20 billion, with nearly half ($9.9 billion) coming from the federal government (Bess, Andrews, Jantz, Russell, & Geen, 2002). Altogether, TANF, the Social Services Block Grant (SSBG), and Medicaid accounted for 42% of total federal spending on child welfare programs (Bess et al., 2002). Of the federal total, nearly a quarter, or $2.3 billion, came from TANF alone.[27] In contrast, Title IV-E foster care and adoption assistance and Title IV-B child welfare services, the funding streams normally associated with child welfare programs, now account for just over half (53%) of federal child welfare spending. The other side of this equation is the fact that child welfare programs consume a significant percentage of federal funding sources not specifically dedicated to such purposes. For example, states spent over half of their SSBG funds and about 14% of their TANF funds on child welfare programs in SFY 2000 (Bess et al., 2002).[28]

We make these comparisons to point out the futility of trying to reform child welfare financing by focusing solely on Title IV-E and Title IV-B, particularly if the purpose of reform is to free up resources to provide preventive services and supports to low-income families at risk of involvement with the child welfare system. Once again, a detailed discussion of alternative funding strategies is beyond the scope of this chapter but, at a minimum, federal child welfare fiscal reform efforts must take into account the billions in child welfare spending that now come from TANF and the SSBG. Better yet would be an approach that integrated the TANF and SSBG funding streams to create a flexible source of economic and social services support for low-income families struggling with the demands of work and parenting. Historically, the vast majority of parents who came to the attention of child welfare authorities were receiving public assistance (U.S. Department of Health and Human Services, 2000). Therefore, a reasonable place to locate family-based child maltreatment prevention services is in the programs that first have contact with at-risk families, not those programs that only become involved *after* harm has been done.

Notes

1. States had to be in compliance with this mandate by January 1, 1973.

2. Families were considered potential recipients if it were likely that they would become AFDC eligible within the next year (and after the 1967 amendments, within the next 5 years).

3. In part, this may reflect the reorganization of the Department of Health, Education and Welfare in 1967, which shifted control of service funding from the Bureau of Family Services, which was dominated by social workers under social work advocate Ellen Winston, to the Social and Rehabilitation Service headed by Mary Switzer (Derthick, 1975; Wickenden, 1976).

4. Some policy makers also began to question the assumptions on which this strategy was based, namely, that people were poor because they were deficient in some way and, hence, what they needed was rehabilitation. For example, a report issued by President Johnson's Council of Economic Advisors emphasized the structural causes of poverty, like unemployment and inadequate

wages, that social services could not address. Nevertheless, government job creation was not among the council's recommendations for reducing dependency (Katz, 1989). As Austin observed, "[T]he issue is really why a service strategy when you have a structural diagnosis" (Austin, 1973, p. 184, cited in Katz, 1989).

5. In 1960, approximately 780,000 families were receiving AFDC; by 1972, this number had risen to nearly 3 million (U.S. Department of Health and Human Services, 2007). This increase was attributed to a variety of factors, including a series of Supreme Court decisions that struck down exclusionary rules in a number of states, which had made many families ineligible for assistance (Katz, 1989).

6. There were approximately 1.3 million families on AFDC in 1967. AFDC payments to those families totaled $2.28 billion and total expenditures for the program, including administrative costs were $2.71 billion. By 1972, the number of families had risen to 3.12 million, total payments had risen to $6.71 billion and total expenditures had risen to $6.91 billion (U.S. Census Bureau, 1968, 1973).

7. In fact, what little is known about the impact of separation on clients' requests for and perceptions of social services comes from a single experimental investigation (McDonald & Piliavin, 1980, 1981; Piliavin & Gross, 1977). The investigators found that separation may have had a negative effect not only on service requests, but also on clients' perceptions of the helpfulness of services. In particular, "under the circumstances of separation, recipients tend[ed] to reduce requests for services and to perceive services as less helpful" (Piliavin & Gross, 1977, p. 403).

8. This is not to say that there were no efforts to add a service component to public assistance programs prior to 1988. However, previous welfare-to-work initiatives, most notably WIN (Work Incentive Program), were poorly funded and relatively small in scale (Blank & Blum, 1997; Wickenden, 1976).

9. JOBS provided public assistance recipients with an array of education, training, and employment services as well as supportive services, like child care and transportation (Blank & Blum, 1997; U.S. General Accounting Office, 1995). However, the real importance of the Family Support Act may have been largely symbolic. A 1995 report by the General Accounting Office estimated that in a given month approximately 13% of single mothers on AFDC were participating in the JOBS program. Another 60% were exempt from participation, primarily because their youngest children were under 3. The report also noted that because most states did not provide sufficient matching funds to draw down all of the federal funding for which they were entitled, JOBS programs were not able to provide services to all of those in need (U.S. General Accounting Office, 1995).

10. Some of these state welfare reforms had already begun to take shape under federal waivers issued prior to the PRWORA.

11. The 1997 figure includes not only regular AFDC cases, but also the 3,593 NLRR (non–legally responsible relative) and 5,600 SSI "child-only" cases that were not eligible for conversion to W-2 (Mary Jo Larson, Wisconsin Department of Workforce Development, February 23, 2001, personal communication). The NLRR cases were converted to W-2 kinship care cases, and SSI cases were converted to caretaker supplement cases.

12. The state of Wisconsin has since restructured the Milwaukee County child welfare system into three regions instead of five.

13. In 1998, when the state takeover first went into effect, the County of Milwaukee still operated some in-home and ongoing case management services under contract to the state. However, since then, the state has canceled these contracts due to perceived poor performance by the county agency.

14. For a more complete description of these studies, please refer to Piliavin, Courtney, and Dworsky (2001) and Courtney, McMurtry, Maldre, Power, and Zinn (2003).

15. One of the Milwaukee County W-2 regions was subsequently eliminated and only four private agencies are currently administering the program (Wisconsin, Department of Workforce Development, 2006).

16. Applicants who were pregnant but did not have any children were excluded from the sample since a major focus of the study was child well-being.

17. Several factors likely contributed to the high rate of survey participation. First, nearly all of the interviews (95%) were conducted at the agencies at the time of application. Second, agencies provided child care at no charge while the applicants were being interviewed. Third, we provided a $25 honorarium to survey participants.

18. The vast majority of the caregiver respondents in both studies were the biological or adoptive parents of one or more of the children in their household. Therefore, we have generally chosen to use the term "parent" throughout the remaining discussion.

19. The period of observation during which participants could have been reported to child welfare authorities averaged 28 months between our interview with the study participants and the final date of the administrative data on child welfare services involvement.

20. Alternative explanations for the increased risk of child welfare services involvement include (1) the possibility that welfare reform in Milwaukee increased the overall risk of maltreatment among the low-income population and (2) that changes in the functioning of the Milwaukee

child welfare system led to an overall increase in reports. In an earlier paper, we argued that W-2 may have increased the risk of maltreatment to children, and hence the risk of child welfare services involvement, but there are no empirical data yet to support such a claim (Courtney et al., 2005). The second explanation seems to us implausible given that the overall number of child maltreatment investigations in Milwaukee County actually declined over the period of our study (Courtney & McMurtry, 2001).

21. Although our data show 47.2% of our applicants to have been investigated by child welfare authorities, this no doubt significantly underestimates the true rate. First, many sample members lived outside of Milwaukee for some period before or after our interview, making it possible that they were involved in other state or county child welfare systems from which we have no data. Second, our strategy of linking TANF and child welfare services data in Milwaukee was conservative and almost certainly missed some parents who have been involved in both systems.

22. One could reasonably argue that safety services are not strictly voluntary since they are only provided to families who have been the subject of a child maltreatment report. Moreover, failure to collaborate with a safety services worker might affect the worker's perception of the safety of a given home and thereby increase the likelihood of a subsequent maltreatment report by the worker. Likewise, since W-2 agencies are the only avenue for obtaining cash assistance in Milwaukee, one could argue that destitute families are not entirely free to decide whether to participate in W-2. Nevertheless, the important point for our purposes is that these parents are seeking help from services in their communities and still have custody of their children. In contrast, families involved with the child welfare system whose children are in out-of-home care have no choice but to submit to court-ordered services lest they permanently lose their parental rights.

23. We are aware of some exceptional efforts to use TANF funds to reorient the entire range of services and supports to poor children and families (Berns & Drake, 1999). Nevertheless, we believe that these examples will remain the exception rather than the rule in the current federal policy environment.

24. This is not to say that AFDC recipients did not need any social services, only that very few needed such help to retain access to AFDC cash assistance.

25. Of course, welfare caseloads will rise and fall with the economy, but our argument primarily concerns that part of the caseload who have significant barriers to employment, which are amenable to change through family supports and services.

26. The positions for and against separation are more complex than we are able to describe here. For a more detailed description of these arguments and an analysis of why they are no longer valid, see Dworsky (1998).

27. States spent approximately $1.7 billion in TANF funds directly on child welfare programs while they spent an additional $631 million on child welfare programs that were transferred from TANF to the Social Services Block Grant.

28. We recognize that states have always used SSBG funds to support child welfare programs. Nevertheless, states can use SSBG funds for a wide array of social services for all age ranges. The heavy state use of SSBG funds for child welfare programs simply illustrates the great need that states have to find funding for these services.

References

Andrews, C., Bess, R., Jantz, A., & Russell, V. (2002). *Collaboration between state welfare and child welfare agencies*. Washington, DC: Urban Institute.

Austin, D. (1973). *Poverty and urban policy*. Conference transcript of 1973 group discussions of the Kennedy administration urban poverty programs and policies. Boston, MA: John F. Kennedy Presidential Library and Museum Archives.

Bell, W. (1983). *Contemporary social welfare*. New York: Macmillan.

Benton, B. (1980). Separation revisited. *Public Welfare*, 38, 15–21.

Berns, D. A., & Drake, B. J. (1999). Combining child welfare and welfare reform at the local level. *Policy and Practice*, 57, 26–34.

Bess, R., Andrews, C., Jantz, A., Russell, V., & Geen, R. (2002). *The costs of protecting vulnerable children III: What factors affect states' fiscal decisions?* Washington, DC: Urban Institute.

Blank, S., & Blum, B. (1997). A brief history of work expectations for welfare mothers. *Future of Children*, 7, 28–38.

Cohen, W., & Ball, R. (1962). Public Welfare Amendments of 1962 and proposal for health insurance for the aged. *Social Security Bulletin*, 25, 3–22.

Courtney, M. E., & Dworsky, A. (2001). *Children in out-of-home care in Wisconsin: 1990–1999*. Madison, WI: Department of Health and Family Services.

Courtney, M. E., & McMurtry, S. (2001). *Trends in child maltreatment investigations in Milwaukee County: 1996–1999*. Madison, WI: Institute for Research on Poverty.

Courtney, M. E., McMurtry, S., Maldre, K., Power, P., & Zinn, A. (2003). *Evaluation of safety services provided by the Bureau of Milwaukee Child Welfare*. Chicago: Chapin Hall Center for Children, University of Chicago.

Courtney, M. E., Piliavin, I., Dworsky, A., & Zinn, A. (2005). Involvement of TANF applicants with child welfare services. *Social Service Review, 79,* 119–157.

Dattalo, P. (1992). The gentrification of public welfare. *Social Work, 37,* 446–453.

Derthick, M. (1975). *Uncontrollable spending for social services.* Washington, DC: Brookings Institution.

Dworsky, A. (1998). *Separation, social work and welfare reform.* Unpublished manuscript.

Fisher, G. (1971). What to do until GAI and universal services arrive: Early lessons of separation. *Public Welfare, 29,* 468–474.

Gilbert, N. (1977). The transformation of social services. *Social Services Review, 53,* 75–91.

Greenleigh Associates. (1960). *Facts, fallacies and the future.* New York: Author.

Hagen, J. (1987). Income maintenance workers: Technicians or service providers? *Social Service Review, 61,* 261–271.

Hagen, J., & Wang, L. (1993). Roles and functions of public welfare workers. *Administration in Social Work, 17,* 81–103.

Handler, J. (1972). *Reforming the poor: Welfare policy, federalism, and morality.* New York: Basic.

Handler, J., & Hollingsworth, E. (1971). *The "deserving poor": A study of welfare administration.* Chicago: Markham

Hoshino, G. (1963). Will the services provisions of the 1962 public welfare amendments reduce costs? *Social Casework, 44,* 439–444.

Hoshino, G. (1971a). Money and morality: Income security and personal social services. *Social Work, 16,* 16–24.

Hoshino, G. (1971b). The public welfare worker: Advocate or adversary? *Public Welfare, 29,* 35–41.

Hoshino, G. (1972). Separating income maintenance from social service. *Public Welfare, 30,* 54–61.

Hutchinson, E., Datta, P., & Rodwell, M. (1994). Reorganizing child protective services: Protecting children and providing family support. *Children and Youth Services Review, 16,* 319–338.

Kahn, A. (1978). *Social policy and social services.* New York: Random House.

Kamerman, S., & Kahn, A. (1990). If CPS is driving child welfare—where do we go from here? *Public Welfare, 48,* 9–13.

Katz, M. (1989). *The undeserving poor: From the war on poverty to the war on welfare.* New York: Pantheon.

Katz, M. (1996). *In the shadow of the poor house: A social history of welfare in America.* New York: Basic.

McDonald, T., & Piliavin, I. (1980). Separation of services and income maintenance: The workers' perspective. *Social Work, 25,* 264–267.

McDonald, T., & Piliavin, I. (1981). Impact of separation on community service utilization. *Social Service Review, 55,* 628–635.

McEntire, D., & Haworth, J. (1967). The two functions of public welfare: Income maintenance and social service. *Social Work, 12,* 22–30.

Morris, P., Knox, V., & Gennetian, L. A. (2002). *Welfare policies matter for children and youth: Lessons for TANF reauthorization.* New York: Manpower Demonstration Research.

Piliavin, I., Courtney, M., & Dworsky, A. (2001). *What happens to families under W-2 in Milwaukee County: Report from wave one: Information collected from parents at the time of application for TANF assistance: March–August 1999.* Madison, WI: Institute for Research on Poverty.

Piliavin, I., & Gross, A. (1977). The effects of separation of services and income maintenance on AFDC recipients. *Social Services Review, 51,* 389–406.

President's Commission on Income Maintenance. (1970). *Background papers.* Washington, DC: Government Printing Office.

Public Welfare Amendments. (1962). PL 87-543.

Radloff, L. S., & Locke, B. Z. (1986). The community mental health survey and the CES-D scale. In M. M. Weissman, J. K. Myers, & C. E. Ross (Eds.), *Community surveys of psychiatric disorders* (pp. 177–189). New Brunswick, NJ: Rutgers University Press.

Sanger, M. (1990). The inherent contradiction of welfare reform. *Policy Studies Journal, 18,* 663–680.

Schottland, C. (1956). Social Security Amendments of 1956: A summary and legislative history. *Social Security Bulletin, 19,* 3–15.

Schubert, M. (1974). The eligibility technician in public assistance. *Social Service Review, 48,* 51–59.

Social Security Amendments. (1956). PL 84-880.

Social Security Amendments. (1967). PL 90-248.

Social Security Amendments. (1974). PL 93-647 (Title XX).

Trattner, W. (1994). *From poor law to the welfare state: A history of social welfare in America.* New York: Free Press.

U.S. Census Bureau. (1968). *Statistical abstracts of the United States: 1968, 89th edition.* Washington, DC: Author.

U.S. Census Bureau. (1973). *Statistical abstracts of the United States: 1973, 94th edition.* Washington, DC: Author.

U.S. Department of Health, Education and Welfare. (1972). *The separation of services: A guide for state agencies.* Publication No. 73–23015. Washington, DC: Author.

U.S. Department of Health and Human Services, Office of the Assistant Secretary for Planning and Evaluation. (2000). *Dynamics of children's movement among the AFDC, Medicaid, and foster care programs prior to welfare reform: 1995–1996.* Washington, DC: Author.

U.S. Department of Health and Human Services. (2007). *Temporary Assistance for Needy Families Separate State Program-Maintenance of Effort Aid to Families with Dependent Children Caseload Data.* Washington, DC: Administration for Children and Families, Office of Family Assistance. Available: http://www.acf.hhs.gov//programs/ofa/caseload/caseloadindex.htm#afdc.

U.S. General Accounting Office. (1995, May). *Welfare to work: Participants' characteristics and services provided in JOBS* (GAO/HEHS-95-93). Washington, DC: Author.

Waldfogel, J. (1998). *The future of child protection: How to break the cycle of abuse and neglect.* Cambridge, MA: Harvard University Press.

Wickenden, E. (1976). A perspective on social services: An essay review. *Social Service Review, 50,* 570–585.

Wickenden, E., & Bell, W. (1961). *Public welfare: Time for change.* Mount Vernon, NY: Golden Eagle.

Wisconsin Department of Workforce Development. (2002). *Wisconsin Works and related program data.* Available: http://www.dwd.state.wi.us/dws/rsdata/w2data.htm.

Wisconsin Department of Workforce Development. (2006). Wisconsin state plan, FFY 2006–FFY 2007. Retrieved September 13, 2007, from http://www.dwd.state.wi.us/tanf/pdf/tanf_plan06_07.pdf.

Woolley, J., & Peters, G, (n.d.). Statement by the President upon approving the Public Welfare Amendments bill. *The American Presidency Project* [online]. Santa Barbara, CA: University of California, Retrieved September 13, 2007 from http://www.presidency.ucsb.edu/ws/?pid=8788.

Wyers, N. (1981). Income maintenance revisited: Functions, skills and boundaries. *Administration in Social Work, 5,* 15–28.

Wyers, N. (1983). Income maintenance and social work: A broken tie. *Social Work, 28,* 261–268.

18

Promoting Child Well-Being Through Early Intervention: Findings from the Chicago Longitudinal Study

Arthur J. Reynolds

Joshua Mersky

Early childhood interventions from birth to the formative school years have earned considerable attention for their effectiveness in promoting positive development across a range of domains. As defined in this chapter, *early childhood interventions* are programs that provide educational, family, social, and/or health services during any of the first 5 years of life, especially to children at risk of poor outcomes due to socioeconomic disadvantages or developmental disabilities. Among these programs, school-based initiatives for young children have shown particular promise. It is well known that early school-based interventions can improve short-term outcomes, including cognitive skills and school readiness. Contemporary research has also demonstrated that early interventions have long-term impacts on educational and social competencies, including increased achievement, attainment, and economic well-being as well as reduced grade retention, remedial education, and delinquency (Barnett, 1995; Currie, 2001; Karoly et al., 1998; Reynolds, 2000; Yoshikawa, 1995).

Since the inception of Project Head Start in 1965, early childhood interventions have been a focal point of scholastic and social reform nationwide. In the 21st century, expenditures at the federal, state, and local levels for preschool programs exceed $20 billion annually (U.S. General Accounting Office, 2000; Office of Management and Budget, 2003). Support for early childhood interventions continues to be strong, in part because of their documented cost effectiveness, especially when compared to the well-known limits of remediation and treatment (Barnett, 1995; Karoly et al., 1998; Reynolds, Temple, Robertson, & Mann, 2002; Schweinhart et al., 2005). Despite the social and economic justification for greater investments in preventive measures, most services to children and families continue to be corrective. The untapped potential of primary prevention is particularly evident in child welfare services, which are almost exclusively designed to treat children and families after problems have occurred.

Few early childhood programs have been structured specifically to prevent initial events of child maltreatment. Thus, most evidence in this area is derived from studies that have estimated the effects of known risk and protective factors that, in turn, impact maltreatment. Taken together, findings from these evaluations show modest impacts, at best, and many suffer from substantial methodological shortcomings (e.g., Erickson, 1998; Owens & Fercello, 1999). However, some early childhood interventions, such as the Nurturing Parent Program (Bavolek, 2000), Hampton Healthy Families (Galano et al., 2001), and Project STEEP (Steps Toward Effective, Enjoyable Parenting) (Erickson, 1998), have demonstrated effects on proximal risks associated with maltreatment.

There is growing evidence that early childhood programs also have the potential to directly impact child maltreatment. Home visiting programs, such as Hampton Healthy Start, Hawaii Healthy Start, the Nurse Home Visitation Program, and Project 12-Ways, have been shown to reduce official reports of substantiated maltreatment (Bugental et al., 2002; Earle, 1995; Galano & Huntington, 2002; Olds et al., 1997). Other types of interventions have also been shown to reduce substantiated reports of maltreatment, including parent education (Britner & Reppucci, 1997) and community-based social service programs (DePanfilis, 2002). In addition, one school-based early intervention, the Chicago Child-Parent Center (CPC) program, had a sizable impact on reducing maltreatment prevalence between the ages of 4 and 17.

In this chapter, we present evidence from the Chicago Longitudinal Study (CLS) on the impacts of the CPC program, which provides educational and family support services to economically disadvantaged children and their parents from preschool through third grade. After describing its basic philosophy and service model, we highlight some of the salient effects attributed to the CPCs, including impacts on child maltreatment and child welfare services. We then link program theory to the estimated effects by detailing the hypothesized mechanisms of change through which the intervention operates. Finally, we discuss the implications of our findings for tailoring effective prevention programs and child welfare policy.

THE CHICAGO LONGITUDINAL STUDY

The CLS is a prospective longitudinal investigation of a single cohort of 1,539 minority children (93% African American) who were born in 1979 or 1980 and were raised in high-poverty neighborhoods across Chicago, Illinois. In this matched-group, quasi-experimental study, approximately two thirds of the sample ($N = 989$) attended one of the 20 CPC preschool centers located throughout the city beginning in 1983 or 1984. The remaining participants ($N = 550$) attended alternative full-day kindergarten programs from randomly selected schools in the Chicago public school system. The major goals of the CLS are to (a) evaluate the effects of the CPC program over time, (b) identify which subgroups of children and families benefit most from program participation, (c) identify the mechanisms through which the effects of participation are achieved, (d) determine the economic benefits of participation, and (e) investigate the contribution of a variety of individual, family, and school factors, especially those that are alterable, on children's well-being.

The study began in 1985 as an internal evaluation of the effects of government-funded early childhood programs in the Department of Research and Evaluation at the Chicago Board of Education. This led to a university-community collaborative study funded primarily by the National Institutes of Health and the U.S. Department of Education with extensive involvement of teachers, managers, and principals. Collaborative activities included developing survey instruments, assisting in data collection and ensuring high response rates, communicating with schools and families, identifying primary outcome measures, and disseminating study findings. Chicago school personnel were invaluable in helping the study investigators to access data from school records and standardized test scores; the Departments of Child and Family Services (DCFS), Human Services, and Public Health; county juvenile courts and departments of corrections; and colleges and universities. These data offer a unique opportunity to investigate how program participation, environmental conditions, and personal experiences contribute to later well-being.

As shown in Table 18.1, the program and comparison groups are similar on a number of sociodemographic characteristics. An overall summary is represented by the Family Risk Index, a sum of eight factors (e.g., low parent education, single-parent family status) associated with poor child outcomes. Unadjusted comparisons of the follow-up sample show that the intervention group had a higher proportion of females, a higher proportion of parents who had completed high school, and fewer siblings. The intervention group was also more

TABLE 18.1 Sample Sizes and Characteristics for Program and Comparison Groups in the CLS

	Child Parent Center Intervention Group	Comparison Group
Sample Characteristics		
Female child	51.8	47.2
African American child	92.7	93.5
Family child welfare service receipt <age 4	3.4	5.4
Family Risk Index (0–8, mean)	4.45	4.35
Neighborhood poverty > 40%	51.7*	35.5
Eligible for subsidized lunch	83.3	81.5
AFDC (TANF) receipt	62.7	61.2
Primary guardian did not complete h.s.	50.8*	59.7
Primary guardian not employed	64.4	60
Single-parent status	76	74.8
Four or more children in household	16.5	18.7
Mother ever a teen parent (<age 18)	35.1	36.2
Sample Sizes for Major Outcomes		
Original sample	989	550
Child abuse and neglect, age 0–17	914	497
Juvenile arrest by age 18	911	495
Adult crime by age 24	918	500
School remedial services, age 6–18	841	445
Educational attainment by age 24	888	480

Notes: All sample characteristics are measured between the child's birth and age 3, except for AFDC (TANF) receipt, which was measured by age 9. Unadjusted statistics are expressed as percentages unless otherwise specified as mean values.

* Denotes significant group difference at the .05 level.

likely than the comparison group to live in high-poverty neighborhoods. The latter difference is the result of the centers being located in the most disadvantaged neighborhoods and school personnel enrolling children with the most educational disadvantages.

CPC PROGRAM

The CPC program (Sullivan, 1971) is a center-based early intervention that provides comprehensive educational and family-support services to economically disadvantaged children and their parents from preschool to early elementary school. It began in 1967 with funding from the Elementary and Secondary Education Act of 1965. Title I of the act provided grants to local public school districts serving high concentrations of children from low-income families. As shown in Figure 18.1, the centers provide comprehensive educational and family services under the direction of the head teacher in collaboration with the elementary school principal. Each center integrates services from several primary staff members, including parent-resource teachers, school-community representatives, bachelor's-level classroom teachers, aides, nurses, speech therapists, and school psychologists.

The mission of the CPC program is congruent with four major assumptions that guide early childhood interventions (Reynolds, 2000). First, the environmental conditions of poverty impede healthy development. Second, educational enrichment can help to compensate for these disadvantages. Third, early childhood educational programs promote later educational success, which is strongly linked to other positive social

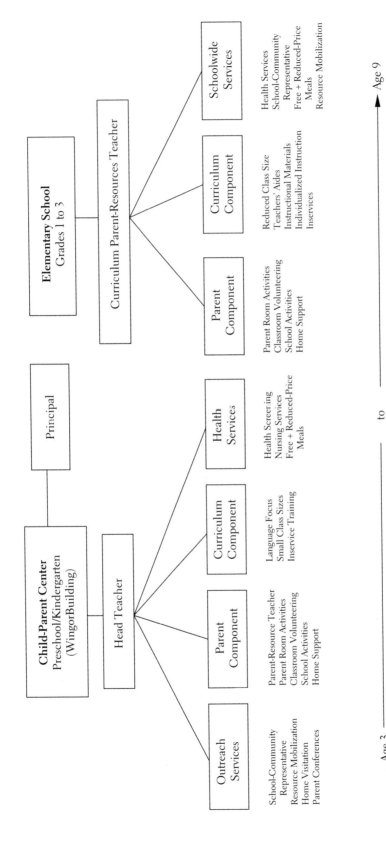

FIGURE 18.1 Child-Parent Center Program

outcomes. The fourth assumption of early childhood intervention is that program effects are likely to be more stable over time if interventions are extended beyond the preschool years into the primary grades. Thus, the CPC program's major rationale is that a stable, enriched learning environment throughout early childhood (ages 3–9), supported by parents who participate actively in their children's education, facilitates academic and social success.

The CPC program emphasizes five core components: early intervention, parent involvement, a structured language/basic skills approach, health and social services, and program continuity between the preschool and early school-age years. Program theory suggests that children's readiness for school entry and beyond can be enriched with systematic language-learning activities and opportunities for family-support experiences through direct parental involvement in the centers. Parental involvement in the program is expected to enhance parent-child interactions, parent and child attachment to school, and social support among parents, and it consequently promotes children's school readiness and social adjustment. Each center is equipped with a parent-resource room adjacent to the classrooms, where a parent-resource teacher facilitates parent educational activities, connections among parents, and parent-child interactions. Specific areas of training include consumer education, nutrition, personal development, health and safety, and home-making arts. Parents may also attend general equivalency diploma (GED) classes at the centers. Staff also assess the service needs of parents and children and provide referrals to health, mental health, vocational, and social services.

KEY FINDINGS FROM THE CLS

We will describe the major findings of program group differences in the study in several domains, including school readiness and achievement, remedial education, family support, school mobility and school quality, educational attainment, juvenile delinquency and crime, and child maltreatment (see Table 18.2).

School Readiness and Achievement

Relative to the comparison group and adjusted for family demographics, CPC preschool participation was associated with significantly higher levels of school readiness at kindergarten entry. About twice as many program participants (46.7%) as comparison group participants (25.1%) scored at or above the national norms on the cognitive composite of the Iowa Tests of Basic Skills, which includes vocabulary, word analysis, math, and listening subscales. A similar pattern occurred for reading achievement over the school-age years, although group differences were somewhat reduced (Reynolds, 2000). CPC program participants also had higher passing rates on a consumer skills test, which was required for high school graduation.

Remedial Education

Consistent with previous findings (Barnett, 1995; Reynolds, 2000), program participation was associated with lower rates of grade retention and special education placement. Preschool participation was associated with a 40% reduction in grade retention and a 41% lower rate of special education placement from ages 6 through 18. Intervention that continued in the primary grades also was associated with lower rates of remedial education.

Family Support

Family outcomes of early intervention have received less attention than school success. Preschool participation was associated with higher levels of parent involvement in school from ages 8 through 12, higher parent expectations for children's educational attainment, and increased parent satisfaction with children's education (Reynolds, 2000).

School Mobility and School Quality

CPC participation was associated with reduced school mobility, measured as the number of times children changed schools from third through seventh grades. Findings also indicate that the program is linked with higher rates of attendance in magnet schools for 1 or more years between the ages of 10 and 14 (Reynolds, Ou, & Topitzes, 2004; Reynolds & Robertson, 2003).

Educational Attainment

Preschool participation was linked to greater educational attainment by age 21. CPC participants had a 20% higher rate of high school completion (including GED; 61.99% versus 51.4%). They also had a higher mean number of years of completed education (11.2

TABLE 18.2 Proportion of CPC Preschool and Comparison-Group Children Achieving School and Social Competence

Child Outcome	Age	Program Group	Comparison Group	Group Difference	% Change over Comparison Group
School Readiness and Achievement					
At/above national norm on scholastic readiness	5	46.7	25.1	21.6	+86
At/above national norm in reading achievement	14–15	35	22	13	+59
Consumer skills	14–15	62.5	52.3	10.2	+20
Family Support Behavior					
Three or more positive ratings of parent involvement	8–12	30.9	21	9.9	+47
Parent expects child to graduate from college	8–12	52	44	8	+18
Remedial Education					
Repeated a grade	6–15	23	38.4	15.4	–40
Special education	6–18	14.4	24.6	10.2	–41
Juvenile Delinquency					
Juvenile arrest	10–18	16.9	25.1	8.2	–33
Arrest for violent offense	10–18	9	15.3	6.3	–41
Two or more arrests	10–18	9.5	12.8	3.3	–26
Educational Attainment by Age 21					
Completed high school	18–21	61.9	51.4	10.5	+20
Highest grade completed (mean number of years)	13–21	11.23	10.87	0.36	—

Notes: All differences were statistically significant. Rates adjusted for group differences in sex of child, race/ethnicity, participation in school-age intervention, and family risk status. % change = percentage change over the comparison group. Sample sizes range from 1,102 (school readiness) to 1,404 (juvenile delinquency).

versus 10.9). A recent follow-up of the sample to age 24 revealed that preschool participation was also associated with increased attendance in a 4-year college (14.7% versus 10%; Reynolds et al., 2005).

Juvenile Delinquency and Crime

Preschool participants had a significantly lower rate of petitions to the juvenile court by age 18 than the comparison cohort (16.9% versus 25.1%). They also had significantly lower rates of multiple arrests and arrests for violent offenses. Analysis of criminal offending by age 24 indicated that preschool participants had lower rates of arrest convictions and incarceration than the comparison group (Mersky, Topitzes, & Reynolds, 2006; Ou, Mersky, Reynolds, & Kohlet, 2007).

Child Maltreatment and Child Welfare Services

One area of program evaluation that has received scant attention in the literature is the impact of early childhood programs on child maltreatment and other child welfare outcomes. This is a significant gap in the literature considering the deleterious impacts associated with maltreatment and the potential for early childhood programs to prevent abuse and neglect. The CLS has collected data on official records of child abuse and neglect from two administrative sources maintained at the Chapin Hall Center for Children: petitions to Cook County Juvenile Court and referrals to the Child Protection Division of DCFS.

Table 18.3 presents unadjusted rates of indicated (substantiated) maltreatment reports from both court and DCFS records. Overall, 13.5% of the sample had an indicated report from birth through age 17 in at least one of the two administrative sources. As shown in Table 18.3, this base rate, while alarming, roughly approximates other estimates obtained for highly disadvantaged populations (Aos, Lieb, Mayfield, Miller, & Pennucci, 2004; Smithgall, Gladden, Howard, Goerge, & Courtney, 2004).[1]

Table 18.3 also shows that the CPC and comparison group differed significantly at the zero-order level on any indicated reports of maltreatment from ages 4 through 17, a measure which corresponds to the beginning of preschool until participants reached majority. Findings from adjusted probit regressions also indicate that the groups differ significantly. After controlling for relevant background characteristics, such as sex, race/ethnicity, and family risk, preschool participation was associated with a 52% reduction in substantiated maltreatment (Reynolds & Robertson, 2003). Results were robust across a number of different model specifications. Notably, most of the group differences were detected between the ages of 10 and 17 (3.5% versus 6.6%); the rate of maltreatment between the ages of 4 and 9 marginally favored the program group (4.2% versus 7.8%).

The CLS has also obtained child welfare service data from three unique sources maintained by Chapin Hall. First, a child protective services history file provides information on abuse and neglect events linked to the child. The second and third data sets both originate from the Child and Youth Centered Information System (CYCIS). A child history file details the out-of-home placement history of the child. A family history file provides information about the family experience of linked children, such as whether the child was living at home at the start of the case records and if the family is "intact" or not. From birth through age 17, approximately 116 children were placed out of home.[2]

As shown in Table 18.3, CPC preschool services were associated with lower unadjusted rates of out-of-home placement from age 4 to 17 (6.1% versus 11.3%).

The effects of maltreatment are expected to be profound and diverse. A long line of research has shown that abuse and neglect are associated with adverse effects on the socioemotional, behavioral, cognitive, mental, and physical well-being of children (National Research Council, 1993). Preliminary findings from the CLS generally comport with previous scholarship. For example, controlling for relevant sociodemographic variables, participants with a substantiated report of maltreatment by age 12 had significantly higher rates of any official delinquency petition, any official or self-reported delinquency, and total number of official petitions (Mersky, 2006). Results indicate that the negative behavioral impacts of maltreatment extend into adulthood, as maltreated children were at an increased risk of arrest and incarceration by age 24 (Topitzes, 2006). Reynolds et al. (2004) also discovered that children who were maltreated between ages 4 and 12 had significantly lower rates of high school completion.

While empirical studies of child maltreatment date back several decades, research on child welfare services has only begun to take shape since the mid-1990s. Several studies bearing less-sophisticated research designs have shown that most children who received foster care services became competent, productive adults (see Maluccio & Fein, 1985, for review), but few rigorous investigations have explored outcomes into adolescence and adulthood. Interestingly, CLS participants who were maltreated and subsequently placed in out-of-home care had significantly lower rates of delinquency, early child bearing, substance use/abuse, and public aid receipt (TANF) than maltreated children who were not removed from the home (Mersky, 2006; Robertson, Mersky, Topitzes, & Reynolds, 2005). This supports previous evidence indicating that out-of-home placement may offer some compensatory benefits for certain populations of minority children (Jonson-Reid & Barth, 2000; McMurtry & Lie, 1992).

MECHANISMS OF CHANGE

One of the key attractions of early childhood interventions is their capacity to prevent problem behaviors and to promote well-being long after program participation. Reynolds and Temple (1998) have emphasized the

TABLE 18.3 Rates of Substantiated Maltreatment and Out-of-Home Placement during Selected Child Age Points

Indicated Abuse and Neglect	Total Sample N = 1411	Gender		CPC Preschool		Follow On		CPC Extended Intervention		
		Boys	Girls	Any	None	Any	None	4 to 6	1 to 4	0
Any indicated report of neglect, %										
Ages 4–9	5.5	4.6	6.3	4.2	7.8	5.0	6.0	3.1	6.8	7.1
Ages 10–17	4.6	4.4	4.8	3.5	6.6	4.1	5.4	3.1	4.9	6.5
Ages 4–17	8.6	7.9	9.4	6.2	13.1	7.6	10.1	5.1	9.8	12.5
Any indicated report of physical abuse, %										
Ages 4–9	1.3	1.6	1.0	1.2	1.4	0.9	1.8	0.7	1.5	1.8
Ages 10–17	2.3	2.4	2.3	1.9	3.2	2.2	2.5	2.2	1.9	3.3
Ages 4–17	3.3	3.6	3.1	2.7	4.4	2.8	4.0	2.6	3.2	4.7
Any indicated report of sexual abuse, %										
Ages 4–9	1.1	0.4	1.7	0.9	1.4	0.9	1.3	0.6	1.1	1.8
Ages 10–17	0.6	0.1	1.1	0.5	0.8	0.7	0.5	0.6	0.6	0.9
Ages 4–17	1.7	0.6	2.8	1.4	2.2	1.6	1.8	1.1	1.7	2.7
Any indicated substantial risk of physical injury, %										
Ages 4–9	3.1	3.1	3.1	3.0	3.4	2.9	2.9	2.4	3.6	3.6
Ages 10–17	3.9	3.4	4.4	3.3	5.0	3.9	3.9	2.8	5.1	3.9
Ages 4–17	6.6	6.3	6.9	5.6	8.5	6.5	6.7	4.8	7.9	7.4
More than 1 category of maltreatment, %										
Ages 4–9	3.1	2.7	3.5	2.8	3.6	2.9	3.4	2.0	3.8	3.9
Ages 10–17	3.4	3.0	3.8	2.7	4.6	3.6	3.2	2.6	4.0	3.9
Ages 4–17	6.3	5.7	6.9	5.1	8.5	6.4	6.2	4.2	7.6	7.7
Any indicated report of maltreatment, %										
Ages 0–3	1.8	1.9	1.7	1.4	2.4	1.5	2.2	1.1	1.9	2.7
Ages 4– 9	6.9	6.3	7.6	5.8	9.1	6.1	8.0	4.2	8.7	8.6
Ages 10–17	7.5	7.0	8.0	6.1	10.1	6.9	8.4	5.7	7.9	9.8
Ages 4–17	12.5	11.4	13.6	10.2	16.9	10.9	14.7	8.3	14.6	16.3
Ages 0–17	13.5	12.6	14.5	11.3	17.7	12.0	15.6	9.4	15.5	17.2
Any out-of-home placement, %										
Ages 0–3	1.1	1.3	1.0	1.2	1.0	1.1	1.2	1.1	1.1	1.2
Ages 4–9	3.0	2.8	3.1	2.2	4.4	3.2	2.7	1.7	4.0	3.5
Ages 10–17	6.4	6.3	6.6	5.3	8.7	5.9	7.2	4.6	7.0	8.5
Ages 4–17	7.2	7.0	7.5	5.7	10.1	6.9	7.7	5.0	8.1	9.4
Ages 0–17	8.2	8.2	8.2	6.8	10.9	7.9	8.7	5.9	9.2	10.3

Note: Children may be in more than one age and maltreatment category.

importance of moving toward a causal explanation for estimated effects through confirmatory program evaluation (CPE). This approach suggests that main-effects findings are strengthened to the extent that plausible mechanisms associated with effectiveness are theoretically linked to the program (Bunge, 1997; Rosenbaum, 1995). In order to meet the challenging task of determining the precise sources of program effects, it is useful to investigate the extent to which the main effects of participation are mediated by intervening factors after participation ends. Doing so in a systematic fashion can help to direct additional intervention services to maintain or enhance the effects of early intervention.

Reynolds (2000) has hypothesized five pathways through which the CPC program confers benefits to participants. These are summarized in Figure 18.2. The *cognitive advantage* hypothesis suggests that the long-term program impacts are promoted by boosting children's developed abilities (e.g., language and literacy skills, school readiness). The *family support* hypothesis indicates that long-term benefits are initiated by increasing parents' participation in their children's education and by enhancing parenting practices, attitudes, and expectations. A third mechanism through which program impacts may be achieved is by augmenting children's *social adjustment*, as evidenced by the internalization of social rules, self-regulation skills, and the ability to get along with others. A fourth pathway, the *motivational advantage* hypothesis, posits that distal outcomes are improved when children's task persistence, perceived competence, self-efficacy, or other self-system attributes are enhanced. Finally, the *school support* hypothesis suggests that CPC effects are partly derived and maintained by increasing the likelihood of attendance in high-quality schools and decreasing the likelihood of school mobility.

Research that has specifically tested any one of these hypotheses is limited, and comprehensive investigations of multiple mechanisms are particularly scarce. Studies that explore a single pathway from program participation to selected outcomes are informative, yet prone to model misspecification (Reynolds et al., 2004). Analyses integrating several hypotheses are needed to help distill direct and indirect program effects, particularly given that the pathways interrelate and model effects that are nested and complex. We will provide a cursory overview of two hypotheses—family support and school support—and their role in explaining the impacts of CPC participation on reducing maltreatment.

Family Support Hypothesis

A central theory of the CPC program is that parents' participation in children's schooling, through a variety of activities with or on behalf of their children, will reduce stress, enhance parents' personal and educational development, and thus promote children's social competence. Early intervention programs often include a parental involvement component, assuming that family processes are integral to fostering longer-term effects on child outcomes (Reynolds, Mavrogenes, Bezruczko, & Hagemann, 1996). With few exceptions (White, Taylor, & Moss, 1992), reviews of the literature have shown that early childhood interventions are more successful in promoting positive parent-child interactions and lasting impacts on child well-being if they involve parents (Benasich, Brooks-Gunn, & Clewell, 1992; Bronfenbrenner, 1975; Olds et al., 1997; Schweinhart et al., 2005; Seitz, 1990).

Reynolds and Robertson (2003) tested the mediating influence of family support in explaining the main-effect association between CPC participation and significantly lower rates of substantiated maltreatment. Family support was operationalized as the total number of years that teachers rated parents as average or better on parental involvement in school from first through sixth grade. Previous CLS investigations have shown that this parental involvement measure acts as a mediator between program effects and a variety of child and family outcomes (Reynolds, 2000; Reynolds et al., 1996). Exploratory analysis using hierarchical regression revealed that parental involvement partially mediated the effect of CPC preschool participation (20% reduction) and substantially mediated the effect of extended program participation (52% reduction).

As an alternative test of the family support hypothesis, the CLS has also investigated whether the documented program effects on maltreatment mediate the long-term impacts on educational attainment and crime. Using a dichotomous measure indicating whether a participant experienced a substantiated report of abuse or neglect between ages 4 and 12 according to official petitions to the juvenile court, findings indicated that maltreatment acted as a direct mediator on high school graduation and completion (plus GED) and on total number of official juvenile arrest petitions (Reynolds, Ou, & Topitzes, 2004). There was no evidence, however, that maltreatment mediated program effects on a dichotomous indicator of any delinquency petition.

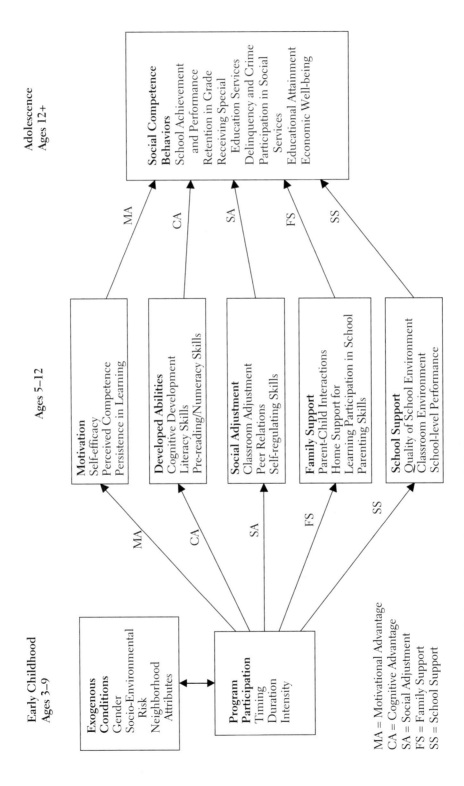

Early Childhood
Ages 3–9

Ages 5–12

Adolescence
Ages 12+

Exogenous Conditions
Gender
Socio-Environmental Risk
Neighborhood Attributes

Program Participation
Timing
Duration
Intensity

Motivation
Self-efficacy
Perceived Competence
Persistence in Learning

Developed Abilities
Cognitive Development
Literacy Skills
Pre-reading/Numeracy Skills

Social Adjustment
Classroom Adjustment
Peer Relations
Self-regulating Skills

Family Support
Parent-Child Interactions
Home Support for Learning Participation in School
Parenting Skills

School Support
Quality of School Environment
Classroom Environment
School-level Performance

Social Competence Behaviors
School Achievement and Performance
Retention in Grade
Receiving Special Education Services
Delinquency and Crime
Participation in Social Services
Educational Attainment
Economic Well-being

MA = Motivational Advantage
CA = Cognitive Advantage
SA = Social Adjustment
FS = Family Support
SS = School Support

FIGURE 18.2 Alternative Paths Leading to Competence Behaviors

300

These findings should be interpreted in light of two important caveats. First, the dichotomous measure of maltreatment only includes cases reported to the juvenile court. The CLS has subsequently collected official reports of abuse and neglect from DCFS that, when combined with indicated reports from the juvenile court, provide a more comprehensive estimate of official rates of maltreatment in the sample. Furthermore, official records of maltreatment are subject to reporting biases that undermine reliability and likely underestimate the true prevalence of abuse and neglect in a population (Cicchetti & Carlson, 1989; Miller-Perrin & Perrin, 1999). Second, truncating the abuse and neglect indicator prior to age 12, while methodologically prudent to maintain causal ordering with the delinquency criterion, is also likely to produce a downward bias in the estimated effects of maltreatment. Subsequent analyses (Mersky et al., 2006) have shown that maltreatment, defined as any indicated report from ages 4 to 18, acts as a direct mediator between program participation and adult crime (e.g., any incarceration, any arrest conviction).

School Support Hypothesis

Less is known about the degree to which early childhood program benefits are conferred by increasing later school support. This hypothesis suggests that program participation is linked to increased social competence and reduced child and family problem behaviors, including child maltreatment, by enhancing the quality of children's later school experiences (Currie & Thomas, 2000; Reynolds, 2000). In particular, Reynolds (2000) postulates that CPC effects are transmitted by promoting post-program enrollment in quality schools and by increasing child and family commitment to and satisfaction with school, which leads to reduced school mobility. While there are a number of possible causes for school transitions, it is well established that mobility is associated with poor academic and social outcomes, above and beyond the impact of various socioeconomic conditions (Astone & McLanahan, 1994; Haveman, Wolfe, & Spaulding, 1991; Reynolds, Ou, & Topitzes, 2004).[3] It has also been established that economically disadvantaged children, ethnic and racial minority children, and children who change schools during the primary grades are especially vulnerable to school mobility (Mehana & Reynolds, 2004).

Reynolds and Robertson (2003) used a measure of school mobility, constructed from Chicago public school records, indicating the number of times that children changed schools between the third and seventh grades. Findings indicated that preschool and extended participation in the CPCs was negatively associated with school mobility and that, in turn, school mobility was positively associated with child maltreatment. The indicator for school mobility was associated with an 18% reduction in the direct preschool effects and a 24% reduction in the extended program effects.

Although the family and school support hypotheses represent unique pathways and have generally been investigated separately, they are not incompatible and may well be interrelated. In combination, the two hypotheses explained roughly one third of the CPC preschool main effects and two thirds of the extended program effect on child maltreatment. It should be noted that the cognitive advantage hypothesis contributed negligible mediating impacts (Reynolds & Robertson, 2003). This makes intuitive sense given the limited degree to which cognitive improvements are likely to act as a causal mechanism in reducing child maltreatment.

A follow-up confirmatory investigation of the program's effects on child maltreatment has also been conducted, and findings generally comport with previous estimates (Mersky et al., 2006). In this investigation, we tested all five hypotheses as plausible mechanisms of change in an SEM model in LISREL (Jöreskog & Sörbom, 1996). The results largely support previous findings, in that the family and school support hypotheses continued to act as the central mediators between program participation and lower rates of child maltreatment. There was also evidence that the social adjustment hypothesis, operationalized by measures of socioemotional maturity from first through third grade and troublemaking behaviors from third through sixth grade, partially mediated child maltreatment, albeit indirectly. The cognitive and motivational advantage hypotheses contributed minimally to mediation and overall model fit.

LIMITATIONS

The evidence presented here should be interpreted in the context of three limitations. First, the generalizability of the findings is limited to children and families with similar socioeconomic characteristics, primarily low-income children in large urban areas. The CPC's long history of successful implementation also restricts generalizability to programs that are relatively established. Second, the internal validity of the estimated program effects hinges on the quasi-experimental design of the CLS. Naturally, it is more difficult to rule out threats to validity in a quasi-experimental study than in one based on an experimental design. However, confidence in the findings is strengthened by the use of contemporary techniques of bias reduction (e.g., econometric and latent-variable structural modeling). Moreover, previous studies have demonstrated that there is no indication of selection bias attributable to group assignment or attrition (Reynolds, 2000; Reynolds & Temple, 1998; Reynolds, Temple, Robertson, & Mann, 2002). Third, some of the hypothesized mechanisms of change are narrowly defined by their respective indicators. For example, parental involvement in school and child maltreatment are only two dimensions of family support that may help to explain program effects. Future work will explore a wider array of measurement specifications to continue specifying linkages between the program and long-term impacts.

IMPLICATIONS AND RECOMMENDATIONS

There is widespread consensus that child maltreatment is a major social problem associated with harmful impacts on children. In response, the federal government devotes more than $7 billion annually to child welfare services, such as foster care and adoption assistance (U.S. Department of Health and Human Services, 2002). Yet, research indicates that traditional treatment responses from the child welfare system have not produced large or enduring positive impacts on child outcomes (Heckman, 2000). Certainly, there will always be a need for programs designed to intervene with indicated populations, yet it is also evident that too little is being invested in primary prevention efforts. Toward this end, the evidence suggests that early childhood programs have the potential to promote children's long-term well-being by preventing child maltreatment.

Among the many promising investments in children, early childhood education programs have demonstrated the largest, most enduring benefits. Compare the evidence from early childhood interventions to that from other social programs that take up the larger shares of government expenditures. Reduced class sizes are associated with increased school achievement, but effects are not large or persistent. Likewise, the benefits of remedial education, such as tutoring and summer school, are inconsistent and short-lived. Findings from this study and others indicate that society needs greater investments in high-quality programs that provide child education and intensive resources for parental involvement.

In a review of childhood programs, Temple and Reynolds (2007) found that the most effective preschool programs for low-income children provided an economic return of $9–10 for every dollar invested. Programs for infants and toddlers had economic returns of $3–5. Other childhood programs subjected to cost-benefit analysis had lower economic returns. Reduced class sizes in the elementary grades is linked to about a $2 return per dollar invested, and Job Corps is linked to a return of $1.32 per dollar invested whereas the remedial practice of grade retention is associated with an economic loss of $3.32 per dollar invested as a consequence of higher rates of school dropout among retained children. Most other social programs, from child welfare treatment to delinquency prevention, have even weaker records of effectiveness, let alone cost effectiveness (Durlak, 1997; Guterman, 1999). Certainly, many of these programs have an important role to play, but preventive investments in early education have demonstrated the most enduring benefits. They deserve a greater share of public investments. Indeed, the percentage of the total expenditures spent on social programs that goes to prevention services is less than 1% (National Science and Technology Council, 1997).

As a child development program, the CPC's comprehensive family services provide many opportunities for positive learning experiences in school and at home (Zigler & Styfco, 1993). Because each center has a staffed parent-resource room and provides school-community outreach, parental involvement is more intensive than in other programs. Those with special needs or those most at risk benefit from intensive, comprehensive services. Parents also profit from opportunities to enhance their own educational and personal development. Thus, the centers show that literacy education and comprehensive family services can be integrated successfully.

Findings indicating that CPC participation was associated with a significant reduction in child maltreatment reports may be attributed, in part, to the parental involvement component of the program. These effects were somewhat serendipitous, in that the program was not specifically designed to prevent child maltreatment. However, a strong case can be made that the program's effects on maltreatment are congruent with the program's theory, particularly to the extent that it was designed to enhance family and school support. The findings are also bolstered by confirmatory evaluations detailing the pathways leading from program participation to reduced maltreatment (Mersky et al., 2006; Reynolds & Robertson, 2003).

Further support for the preventive potential of early childhood programs has been documented at length in the literature, although less so for maltreatment outcomes. Emerging evidence does suggest, however, that there are opportunities to successfully intervene in the school (Reynolds & Robertson, 2003), home (e.g., Olds et al., 1997), and community (DePanfilis, 2002). Findings indicate that early childhood interventions are more likely to be effective if they provide comprehensive family services, such as parent education; social support; home visitation; referral to health, mental health, and child welfare services; and opportunities for vocational and educational development. Alternatively, child welfare services can be more effective if they are better integrated with early intervention services and school, address children's educational and social needs comprehensively, and provide a larger constellation of preventive services to promote child well-being.

The CPCs represent a unique nexus between school-based services and child welfare services. Young children in the child welfare system may benefit from referral to intensive and comprehensive early childhood programs like the CPCs. As communities increase access to early education, public schools appear to be a location of choice for organizing educational, social, and family services. Based in part on the findings from the CLS, Chicago and other cities have made greater investments in early childhood programs. Yet, nearly half of all eligible children do not enroll in center-based early care and education programs, and the quality of services that many receive is not high. Sensible public policy should increase investments in programs, such as the CPCs, with demonstrated effectiveness in preventing child maltreatment and other unwanted outcomes.

Based on the accumulated knowledge base, a main principle of effective intervention is that a coordinated system of early education should be in place beginning at age 3 and continuing through the early grades. Program implementation within a single administrative system within schools and partnerships with communities can promote stability in children's learning environments, which can provide smooth transitions from preschool to kindergarten and from kindergarten to the early grades. The most effective and enduring programs have this organizational framework. This intervention approach is a "first decade" strategy for promoting children's learning (Reynolds, Wang, & Walberg, 2003). Today, most preschool programs are not integrated within public schools, and children usually change schools more than once by the early grades. In the movement to universal access to early education, schools could take a leadership role in partnership with community agencies. More generally, programs that provide coordinated or "wrap-around" services may be more effective under a centralized leadership structure rather than under a case-management framework. The CPC program, for example, is an established program in the third largest school system in the nation. Findings from a cost-benefit analysis of a complete cohort of CPC participants gives a good indication of the size of the effects that could be possible in public schools, the largest administrative system of any universal access program. The Schools of the 21st Century, which provide education from preschool to grade 12, are a more comprehensive exemplar of this approach (Finn-Stevenson & Zigler, 1999).

Recommendations that are consistent with this principle of system coordination are (a) to increase the amount of Title I funds that go to preschools (less than 5% of over $12 billion allocated to schools under Title I went to preschool programs; see U.S. General Accounting Office, 2000); (b) to increase the number of Head Start programs administered by public schools (only about one third of Head Start grantees are schools); (c) to expand the availability of full-day programs in both preschools and kindergartens; and (d) to develop systems of shared financing among schools, child welfare, and social services to increase access to high-quality prevention programs.

Notes

1. The National Child Abuse and Neglect Data System (NCANDS) records national incidence rates of substantiated maltreatment from official reports. However, because children can be reported for abuse and

neglect multiple times, it is challenging to extrapolate the cumulative incidence of substantiated maltreatment. Thus, estimates from previous studies are used for comparison.

2. This number does not include children who were placed out of home for less than 2 weeks or children who received a code for being placed temporarily with DCFS guardianship.

3. The incidence of school mobility in any given year tops 30% in many urban settings (U.S. General Accounting Office, 1994). According to Mehana and Reynolds (2004, n.p.):

> [T]he link between school mobility and lower achievement may be a byproduct of economic hardships in the lives of children and families. In this regard, mobility is an indicator of broader economic hardships such as low socioeconomic status, family residential mobility, transitions in employment as well as dissatisfaction with the children's school.

References

Aos, S., Lieb, R., Mayfield, J., Miller, M., & Pennucci, A. (2004). *Benefits and costs of prevention and early intervention programs for youth*. Olympia: Washington State Institute for Public Policy.

Astone, N. M., & McLanahan, S. S. (1994). Family structure, residential mobility, and school dropout: A research note. *Demography, 31*(4), 575–584.

Barnett, W. S. (1995). Long-term benefits of early childhood programs on cognitive and school outcomes. *Future of Children, 5*(3), 25–50.

Bavolek, S. J. (2000). *The nurturing parenting programs*. Washington, DC: Department of Justice, Office of Juvenile Justice and Delinquency Prevention.

Benasich, A. A., Brooks-Gunn, J., & Clewell, B. C. (1992). How do mothers benefit from early intervention programs? *Journal of Applied Developmental Psychology, 13,* 311–362.

Britner, P. A., & Reppucci, N. D. (1997). Prevention of child maltreatment: Evaluation of a parent education program for teen mothers. *Journal of Child and Family Studies, 6*(2), 165–175.

Bronfenbrenner, U. (1975). Is early intervention effective? In M. Guttentag & E. Struening (Eds.), *Handbook of evaluation research* (Vol. 2, pp. 519–603). Beverly Hills, CA: Sage.

Bugental, D. B., Ellerson, P. C., Lin, E. K., Rainey, B., Kokotovic, A., & O'Hara, N. (2002). A cognitive approach to child abuse prevention. *Journal of Family Psychology, 16,* 243–258.

Bunge, M. (1997). Mechanism and explanation. *Philosophy of the Social Sciences, 27,* 410–465.

Cicchetti, D., & Carlson, V. (Eds.). (1989). *Child maltreatment: Theory and research on the consequences of child abuse and neglect*. New York: Cambridge University Press.

Currie, J. (2001). Early childhood education programs. *Journal of Economic Perspectives, 15*(2), 213–238.

Currie, J., & Thomas, D. (2000). School quality and the longer-term effects of Head Start. *Journal of Human Resources, 35,* 755–774.

DePanfilis, D. (2002). *Final report: Helping families prevent neglect* (No. 18). Baltimore: University of Maryland.

Durlak, J. A. (1997). *Successful prevention programs for children and adolescents*. New York: Plenum.

Earle, R. B. (1995). *Helping to prevent child abuse—and future criminal consequences: Hawai'i Healthy Start*. Washington, DC: U.S. Department of Justice, Office of Justice Programs.

Erickson, M. F. (1998). *Strong beginnings: Promoting resiliency through secure parent-infant relationships* (No. 10). Madison: University of Wisconsin, Center for Excellence in Family Studies.

Finn-Stevenson, M., & Zigler, E. (1999). *Schools of the 21st Century: Linking child care and education*. Englewood, CO: Westview.

Galano, J., Credle, W., Perry, D., Berg, S. W., Huntington, L., & Stief, E. (2001). Developing and sustaining a successful community prevention initiative: The Hampton Healthy Families Partnership. *Journal of Primary Prevention, 21*(4), 495–509.

Galano, J., & Huntington, L. (2002). *Healthy Families Partnership benchmark study: Measuring community-wide impact*. Hampton, VA: Applied Social Psychological Research Institute, College of William and Mary, & Huntington Associates.

Guterman, N. B. (1997). Early prevention of physical child abuse and neglect: Existing evidence and future directions. *Child Maltreatment, 2,* 12–34.

Haveman, R., Wolfe, B., & Spaulding, J. (1991). Educational achievement and childhood events and circumstances. *Demography, 28,* 133–158.

Heckman, J. J. (2000). Policies to foster human capital. *Research in Economics, 54,* 3–56.

Jonson-Reid, M., & Barth, R. P. (2000). From maltreatment report to juvenile incarceration: The role of child welfare services. *Child Abuse and Neglect, 24*(4), 505–520.

Jöreskog, K., & Sörbom, D. (1996). *LISREL 8: User's reference guide*. Chicago: Scientific Software.

Karoly, L. A., Greenwood, P. W., Everingham, S., Hoube, J., Kilburn, M. R., Rydell, C. P., Sanders, M., & Chiesa, J. (1998). *Investing in our children: What we know and don't know about the costs and benefits of early childhood education.* Santa Monica, CA: RAND.

Maluccio, A. N., & Fein, E. (1985). Growing up in foster care. *Children and Youth Services Review, 7,* 123–136.

McMurtry, S. L., & Lie, G. Y. (1992). Differential exit rates of minority children in foster care. *Social Work Research Abstracts, 28,* 42–48.

Mehana, M., & Reynolds, A. J. (2004). School mobility and achievement: A meta-analysis. *Children and Youth Services Review, 26*(1), 93–119.

Mersky, J. P. (2006). *Disentangling the connections between child maltreatment and juvenile delinquency: Main effects, moderators, and subgroups.* Unpublished doctoral dissertation, University of Wisconsin, Madison.

Mersky, J. P., Topitzes, J. W., & Reynolds, A. J. (2006, January). *Mediating paths from early childhood intervention to child maltreatment and adult crime.* Paper presented at the 10th Annual Conference for the Society for Social Work Research, San Antonio, TX.

Miller-Perrin, C. L., & Perrin, R. D. (1999). *Child maltreatment: An introduction.* Thousand Oaks, CA: Sage.

National Research Council. (1993). Understanding child abuse and neglect. In *Panel on research on child abuse and neglect: Commission on behavioral and social sciences and education* (pp. 161–207). Washington, DC: National Academy Press.

National Science and Technology Council. (1997, April). *Investing in our future: A national research initiative for America's children for the 21st century.* Washington, DC: Executive Office of the President, Office of Science and Technology Policy, Committee on Fundamental Science, & Committee on Health, Safety, and Food.

Office of Management and Budget. (2003). Funding of early education programs. White House Conference on Early Childhood Development. Washington, DC.

Olds, D. E. J., Henderson, C. R., Kitzman, H., Powers, J., Cole, R., Sidora, K., Morris, P., Pettit, L. M., & Luckey, D. (1997). Long-term effects of home visitation on maternal life course and child abuse and neglect: Fifteen-year follow-up of randomized trial. *Journal of the American Medical Association, 278*(8), 637–643.

Ou, S., Mersky, J. P., Reynolds, A. J., & Kohler, K. M. (2007). Alterable predictors of educational attainment, income, and crime: Findings from an inner-city cohort. *Social Service Review, 81* (1): 85–128.

Owens, G., & Fercello, C. (1999). *The Family Support Project evaluation: Final report.* St. Paul: McKnight Foundation & Minnesota Department of Human Services.

Reynolds, A. J. (2000). *Success in early intervention: The Chicago child-parent centers.* Lincoln: University of Nebraska Press.

Reynolds, A. J., Mavrogenes, N. A., Bezruczko, N., & Hagemann, M. (1996). Cognitive and family-support mediators of preschool intervention: A confirmatory analysis. *Child Development, 67,* 1119–1140.

Reynolds, A. J., Ou, S., & Topitzes, J. W. (2004). Paths of effects of early childhood intervention on educational attainment and delinquency: A confirmatory analysis of the Chicago child-parent centers. *Child Development, 75*(5), 1299–1328.

Reynolds, A. J., & Robertson, D. L. (2003). School-based early intervention and later child maltreatment in the Chicago Longitudinal Study. *Child Development, 74,* 3–26.

Reynolds, A. J., & Temple, J. A. (1998). Extended early childhood intervention and school achievement: Age 13 findings from the Chicago Longitudinal Study. *Child Development, 69,* 231–246.

Reynolds, A. J., Temple, J., Ou, S., Robertson, D. L., Mersky, J. P., & Topitzes, J. W. (2005, May). *Effects of a school-based early childhood intervention on adult health and well-being: A 20-year follow-up of low-income children and families.* Paper presented at the 13th Annual Conference for the Society for Prevention Research, Washington, DC.

Reynolds, A. J., Temple, J. A., Robertson, D. L., & Mann, E. A. (2001). Long-term effects of an early childhood intervention on educational achievement and juvenile arrest: A 15-year follow-up of low-income children in public schools. *Journal of the American Medical Association, 285*(18), 2339–2347.

Reynolds, A. J., Temple J. A., Robertson, D. L., & Mann, E. A. (2002). Age 21 cost-benefit analysis of the Title 1 Chicago Child-Parent Centers. *Educational Evaluation and Policy Analysis, 24,* 267–303.

Reynolds, A. J., Wang, M. C., & Walberg, H. J. (Eds.). (2003). *Early childhood programs for a new century.* Washington, DC: Child Welfare League of America Press.

Robertson, D. L., Mersky, J. P., Topitzes, J. W., & Reynolds, A. J. (2005, May). *Child maltreatment and foster care: Examining the influence of different child welfare service indicators on young adult outcomes.* Paper presented at the 13th Annual Conference for the Society for Prevention Research, Washington, DC.

Rosenbaum, P. R. (1995). *Observational studies.* New York: Springer-Verlag.

Schweinhart, L. J., Montie, J., Xiang, Z., Barnett, W. S., Belfield, C. R., & Nores, M. (2005). *Lifetime effects: The High/Scope Perry Preschool Study through age 40.* Ypsilanti, MI: High/Scope.

Seitz, V. (1990). Intervention programs for impoverished children: A comparison of educational and family support models. *Annals of Child Development*, 7, 73–103.

Smithgall, C., Gladden, R., Howard, E., Goerge, R., & Courtney, M. (2004). *Educational experiences of children in out-of-home care.* Chicago: Chapin Hall Center for Children, University of Chicago. Available: http://www.chapinhall.org/article_abstract. aspx?ar=1372.

Sullivan, L. M. (1971). *Let us not underestimate the children.* Glenview, IL: Scott, Foresman.

Temple, J. A. & Reynolds, A. J. (2007). Benefits and costs of investments in preschool education: Evidence from the Child-Parent Centers and related programs. *Economics of Education Review*, 26, 126–144.

Topitzes, J. W. (2006). *Maltreatment effects on adult crime: An examination of a long-term developmental model.* Unpublished doctoral dissertation, University of Wisconsin, Madison.

U.S. Department of Health and Human Services. (2002). *Administration for children and families: All-purpose table: Fiscal years 2001–2002.* Office of Legislative Affairs and Budget. Available: http://www.acf.dhhs.gov/programs/olab/budget/apt02.htm.

U.S. General Accounting Office. (1994). Elementary school children: Many change schools frequently, harming their education. (GAO/HEHS-94-95). Washington, DC: Author.

U.S. General Accounting Office. (2000). *Title I preschool education: More children served but gauging effect on school readiness unclear* (GAO/HEHS-00-171). Washington, DC: Author.

White, K. R., Taylor, M. J., & Moss, V. D. (1992). Does research support claims about the benefits of involving parents in early intervention programs? *Review of Educational Research*, 62(1), 91–125.

Yoshikawa, H. (1995). Long-term effects of early childhood programs on social outcomes and delinquency. *Future of Children*, 5, 51–75.

Zigler, E., & Styfco, S. J. (1993). *Head Start and beyond: A national plan for extended childhood intervention.* New Haven, CT: Yale University Press.

19

Heeding *Horton*: Transcending the Public Welfare Paradigm

David Stoesz

Only a few years after the child welfare provisions were included under Title IV of the 1935 Social Security Act, Theodore Geisel, more commonly known as Dr. Seuss, published *Horton Hatches the Egg* (1940), the tale of a compassionate elephant who is manipulated by a ne'er-do-well mother into caring for her egg. Through mounting adversity—miserable weather, the disrespect of friends, assaults by hunters, and the ignominy of a sideshow—Horton remains adamant about keeping his promise, sitting on the egg until it hatches. Defying insults to his good intentions, Horton restates his commitment:

> I meant what I said
> And I said what I meant . . .
> An elephant's faithful
> One hundred percent!

In the 21st century, Horton's struggle can be seen as a prophetic allegory for American public welfare: Social programs that benefit troubled children and their families are disorganized, rigid, understaffed, and unaccountable. Like the story, public welfare is sustained largely as an article of faith.

THE PUBLIC WELFARE PARADIGM

The public welfare infrastructure put in place through Title IV of the Social Security Act institutionalized how the nation would care for at-risk children and poor families in the coming decades. Aspiring to replicate the fully evolved welfare states of Northern Europe, the public welfare paradigm promised to assure basic benefits and services—primarily income, child welfare services, employment, and health—as a right of citizenship. As a programmatic paradigm, however, public welfare was anything but elegant. Foremost, the determination of eligibility of children and families for services was assigned to the states, with the federal government subsidizing care (Stoesz, 2000).

The inception of a means test on income and assets in order to determine eligibility effectively restricted public welfare to the poor. Yet, states contrived ways to deny benefits to children and families by restricting eligibility, as they often did with cash payments for Aid to Families with Dependent Children (AFDC; Quadagno, 1994). Public welfare services were to be provided by trained social workers, professionals being credentialed by the graduate schools of social work that not only staffed the caseloads of the burgeoning welfare state, but also oversaw its administration (Lubove, 1969). Thus, the public welfare paradigm was organized around three themes: federalism, means testing, and professionalization.

As initially conceived, public welfare promised, under public auspices, to provide professional services to troubled families. Yet, more than a generation after its introduction, Leontine Young (1964) questioned the effectiveness of public welfare:

> Because over the years social services have grown like a patchwork quilt to answer specific behaviors and problems, they are divided into pieces not easily integrated. The neglecting mother supervised by the child welfare worker may also be the patient known to the social service department of the mental hospital, the parent known to the court probation officer who works with her child, the client who receives some form of financial assistance from public welfare. She is four different people to four different agencies. Each carries a part of the responsibility, and each tends to perceive her and her children within the confines of that responsibility. The consequence is to obscure both the nature and the extent of the problems. (p. 112)

Programmatically, Young's concern was about the increasing categorization of services, a feature that would further encumber the public welfare paradigm.

A maternalist assumption was implicit in public welfare: Needy children should be cared for by their mothers unless the mothers were determined to be unfit, in which event the children were provided with surrogate mothers through foster care (Gordon, 1994). Maternalism was augmented in the 1960s with a medical model. In 1962, C. Henry Kempe and his associates published research substantiating the "battered child syndrome." Subsequent studies indicated that the prevalence of child abuse and neglect was much more extensive than had earlier been suspected, eventually resulting in the Child Abuse Prevention and Treatment Act (CAPTA) of 1974. CAPTA established a definition of child abuse and neglect, suggested standards for reporting maltreatment, granted immunity to those who reported maltreatment, funded prevention services, and authorized the first studies to determine the prevalence of child abuse and neglect (Costin, Karger, & Stoesz, 1996).

The medical evidence that drove the passage of CAPTA eclipsed the fuzzy social factors with which child welfare workers had dealt earlier. Soon, the number of children who were removed from their homes as a result of maltreatment rose, and, because institutional care often meant care by surrogate families who had trouble managing traumatized children, many abused and neglected children bounced from foster home to institutional care and back again, some spending years in surrogate-family limbo. During the 1970s, of the 500,000 children in foster care, many had been in substitute family care for years; in some instances, states were simply unable to locate children under state supervision. The 1980 Adoption Assistance and Child Welfare Act (AACWA) established permanency planning for all children in out-of-home care in order to prevent "foster care drift." As state child welfare agencies developed permanency plans for children, the number of children in foster care dropped to 276,000 in the mid-1980s, even as the number of foster children per 1,000 children was steadily rising (from 4.5 in 1980 to 7.6 in 1996) (Waldfogel, 1998, pp. 73, 70).

By the early 1990s, the number of foster children approached 500,000 again, and attention turned to avoiding out-of-home placement. The Homebuilders Project had demonstrated that intensive in-home services by child welfare workers could prevent more expensive alternatives, such as institutionalization or foster care. Keeping children with a biological parent also dovetailed with an ascendant conservatism that valued the privacy of the home while portraying professional intervention as intrusive. These circumstances provided the rationale for the Family Preservation and Support Program (FPSP), a provision of the 1993 Omnibus Budget Reconciliation Act. Funded at $930 million over 5 years, FPSP established family preservation as the focus of services to children and families, further complicating the public welfare paradigm (Costin, Karger, & Stoesz, 1996, pp. 126–129).

Despite supportive, largely anecdotal evidence, the promise of family preservation foundered. A flurry of exposés graphically documented the failure of many families to care for their children, some of whom died after their families had been accepted for services by public child welfare agencies. Apprehension about family preservation on the part of child welfare workers contributed to increasing numbers of children languishing in foster care, an outcome contrary to the intentions of the 1980 AACWA. In 1997, the Adoption and Safe Families Act (ASFA) attempted to expedite the disposition of children by requiring a permanency hearing within 12 months of a child's removal from home and requiring states "to terminate parental rights for children who had been in foster care for 15 of the most recent 22 months" (Committee on Ways and Means, 2004, p. 11-138). Essentially, ASFA was designed to correct for the insecurities experienced by children due to family preservation.

Increasing numbers of children in foster care meant that many would eventually reach the age of emancipation. Prospects for those youth were problematic, many evincing "low rates of education or job experience, and high rates of emotional disturbance, drug abuse, health problems, and pregnancy" (Committee on Ways and Means, 2004, p. 11-50). In recognition of this, the Chafee Foster Care Independence Program was introduced in 1999, providing $140 million in transitional supports to 19,000 children who aged out of foster care in 2001 (Stoltzfus, 2004). Transitional services targeted to young adults in foster care thus further encumbered the public welfare paradigm.

In 2001, FPSP was renamed Promoting Safe and Stable Families (PSSF). In addition, states were further encouraged to seek waivers to demonstrate alternatives to traditional child welfare services, and state reporting requirements were enhanced. Despite increased programming, PSSF's $305 million in mandatory funding, augmented by an additional $200 million in discretionary funds, has never been realized. Total mandatory and discretionary funding totaled $403 million in 2005 and $434 million in 2006 (Child Welfare League of America, 2006). After a series of initiatives designed to help children and troubled families—foster care, child protection, permanency planning, family preservation, independent living— federal funding for at-risk children through the public welfare paradigm stagnated.

WELFARE REFORM

Since its inception, child welfare has been inextricably bound to cash assistance to poor families (Waldfogel, 1998). Indeed, this connection is so enduring that, even though AFDC was replaced by Temporary Assistance for Needy Families in 1996, federal funding for foster care is still predicated on eligibility under the defunct AFDC program. As had been the case with foster care, family cash assistance was predicated on the assumption that children were best cared for at home; government aid served as a substitute for the breadwinner's income, hence its initial justification as a widow's pension program. In the decades following the Social Security Act, the percentage of families receiving cash assistance due to the death of a breadwinner declined, however. By the 1980s, widows represented only 2% of AFDC recipients, while the proportion of those who were unwed mothers skyrocketed. Critics of unconditional family welfare highlighted the association between receipt of AFDC and several negative social factors: teen pregnancy, dropping out of high school, unemployment, crime, and drug abuse. Subsequently, conservatives exploited the notion of "behavioral poverty" to reform family welfare. Adherents of behavioral poverty incriminated liberal social programs on the grounds that, in subsidizing counterproductive behavior, welfare actually exacerbated the poverty of recipients (Stoesz, 2000).

The behavioral approach to antipoverty policy was most clearly expressed by Lawrence Mead, whose ideas were first introduced in the 1988 Family Support Act, but with little obvious effect. The Reagan administration had, however, encouraged states to seek waivers from AFDC, and as an increasing number did, the number of experiments to reverse behavioral poverty proliferated. By the time President Bill Clinton signed the 1996 welfare reform act, some 40 states were operating under waivers; traditional AFDC was provided by a distinct minority of states. Focusing on employment, welfare reform often encouraged mothers to take the first available job, while the state provided some transitional benefits, such as Medicaid and child care. The results of welfare reform were as striking as they were disputed. Conservatives hailed the work mandate, noting that a third of welfare recipients were working, that when coupled with the Earned Income Tax Credit, their earnings brought many of them over the federal poverty level, and that caseloads had plummeted by 50%. Liberals countered that most welfare recipients struggled against significant barriers to employment, that working welfare families had only joined the ranks of the working poor, and that a significant number of families with children had simply vanished from the welfare radar screen (Stoesz, 2005).

A decade after welfare reform, its consequences for children were just becoming clear. Paxson and Waldfogel (2003) pointed out that two outcomes were possible: "If single mothers who work become more organized and are in better mental health, then conceivably their parenting might improve. If, in contrast, single mothers who work become more stressed and have poorer mental health, their parenting might deteriorate" (p. 87). Analyzing data from 1990 to 1998, Paxson and Waldfogel observed that the more-rigorous provisions of welfare reform, sanctions of aid to an entire family, and denying additional benefits to another child born to a family were all associated with increases in substantiated child maltreatment. Moreover, the immediate imposition of a work mandate was associated with an increase in foster care placement (p. 103). An examination of Illinois welfare families receiving assistance in 1998 revealed that recipients who were able to combine welfare benefits and employment had lower reports to child protective services (CPS). "For those combining work and welfare, this may reflect an enhanced ability to manage the demands of work and parenting when cash welfare benefits continue" (Slack, Holl, Lee, McDaniel, Altenbernd, & Stevens, 2003, p. 531). The few studies on the interaction between welfare reform and child welfare suggest, then, that employment is associated with a demand for less child welfare, but that more punitive provisions of welfare reform have the reverse effect.

Since welfare families are not uniform, then some probably present more risk to children than do others. Since the research on welfare reform has favored those who are better candidates for work, more is known about them than about those who are unemployable. What are the circumstances of the most troubled welfare families and their children? Pavetti and Kauff (2006) examined welfare families confronting time limits in St. Paul, Minnesota, in 2003 and 2005, and documented an alarming degree of dysfunction. Families received extensions from time limits on receipt of benefits for specific reasons, several suggesting the compromised care of children. Most prominent among these were that 33.7% had an IQ lower than 80; 9.6% were ill or incapacitated for 30 days or more; and 9.2% were mentally ill (p. 9). That over half of welfare families were facing the end of benefits due to time limits is quite troubling, considering that all

of the families included children. The implications of this are ominous, since the optimal disposition of the most troubled families in the study was a transfer from TANF to Supplemental Security Income (SSI), a disability program with no specific provisions for children:

> [S]taff concluded that low cognitive functioning, serious mental health issues, and chronic health problems affect not only TANF recipients' ability to find and sustain paid employment but also their ability to be good parents. In some homes, staff saw a need for immediate assistance if parents were to learn how to provide a safe environment for their children. It was more common, however, to find parents who could provide a safe environment but not necessarily the stimulation important to early childhood development. This is especially true in the homes of TANF recipients with low cognitive functioning and serious mental health problems, where very young children were often left to fend for themselves and to act as a caretaker for their mother. While participation in a structured early learning environment may be ideal for these children, the same issues that keep parents from participating in welfare employment programs keep them from enrolling their children in appropriate programs. In addition, child care assistance is available to families on the basis of the parents' work activity, not the children's needs or status. Therefore, a mother who ends up on SSI has very little chance of getting child care assistance, and her children have very little chance of ending up in a formal early childhood program. (Pavetti and Kauff, 2006, p. 19)

In a study that charted more directly the relationship between welfare reform and child welfare, Courtney and Dworsky (2006) examined the experience of 1,075 Milwaukee families in 1999. The researchers noted that more than half, 54.3%, of families had been investigated by CPS prior to the study. Although the researchers were unable to state a significant relationship between low earnings and the need for child welfare, they did find that having a child placed in foster care and having a prior CPS investigation were strongly related to having a child placed in foster care. Regardless, the authors of the study suspected that the rigors of Wisconsin's welfare reform contributed to higher demand for child welfare services.

Despite cautionary evidence about the implications of welfare reform for child welfare, behavioral strategies continue to shape antipoverty efforts. In this vein, Haskins and Sawhill (2003) evaluated the effects of four behavioral factors on the federal poverty level: working full time, marrying, completing high school, and limiting family size. "The combined effect of these four tests is a 9.3 percentage-point drop in the poverty rate among families with children, from 13 percent to 3.7 percent. Thus, the poverty rate among families with children could be lowered 71 percent if the poor completed high school, worked full-time, married, and had no more than two children" (p. 4). Ultimately, the behavioral strategy, such as that advanced by Haskins and Sawhill, influenced the 2005 reauthorization of the welfare reform act, reinforcing the goal of employment, although not so far as the Brookings scholars had proposed: Welfare recipients "would be expected to stay in school at least through high school, delay child-bearing until marriage, work full-time to support any children they chose to bear outside marriage, and limit the size of their families to what they could afford to support" (p. 6). The implications of this strategy for the children of parents who are less compliant with this behavioral regimen were not addressed.

HEALTH CARE

Omitted from the 1935 Social Security Act, health care policy would become an intractable problem for American social policy. Wage controls imposed during World War II encouraged employers to include benefits, among them health insurance, as a way to attract employees. The determination that such benefits were tax deductible furthered their evolution, creating a system of "private social benefits" (Hacker, 2002, p. 65), paralleling public welfare benefits. With the introduction of Medicare and Medicaid in 1965, Congress decided to avoid establishing a national public health infrastructure, opting to reimburse private providers instead. Within two decades, burgeoning markets in nursing home care and hospital management were being actively exploited by health care corporations, leading to subsequent markets in home health, assisted living, child care, corrections, and welfare (Karger & Stoesz, 2005). Even though the commercialization of health care had been factored into the Health Security Act of 1993, it failed, furthering the suggestion that a "medical-industrial complex" was actively shaping health policy. The suspicions of

many analysts were confirmed with the Medicare Modernization Act of 2003, which included provisions favorable to the managed care and pharmaceutical industries.

Initially intended to provide health assistance to the poor, Medicaid paralleled AFDC as a state-operated program, the federal government subsidizing the states, which determined people's eligibility for benefits. Because Medicare limited benefits for the elderly requiring long-term care, many became dependent on Medicaid to pay for extended nursing home care. As the number of elderly ballooned, states began to limit benefits to those whose eligibility was not assured by law. Subsequently, Medicaid benefits for the elderly were ten times those for children, $11,928 versus $1,237 in 2000. In the 1990s, Medicaid eligibility was expanded to assure benefits to pregnant women and children in families below the federal poverty line (Committee on Ways and Means, 2004, pp. 15–58, 15–33, 15–34). As Medicaid costs continued to rise, the federal government granted states waivers to experiment with alternative care arrangements, including behavioral contracts with recipients, customizing care for groups of beneficiaries, and encouraging recipients to sign up with managed-care companies (Goldstein, 2006). Thus, reform in welfare appears to presage that in health care.

After Medicaid, the most significant public health program for children is the State Children's Health Insurance Program (SCHIP), which was included in the 1997 Balanced Budget Act. SCHIP encourages states to provide health insurance to low-income children who are not covered by Medicaid, offering states the opportunity to add the children to their extant Medicaid program or to establish a separate initiative. By 2004, over 6 million children were enrolled in SCHIP at a cost of $4.6 billion; yet 8 million children went without health insurance (Census Bureau, 2006, pp. 107–108).

PARADIGM COLLAPSE

The grab bag of programs that evolved as public welfare would have been justifiable perhaps if it were associated with enhanced care of at-risk children or, in the absence of such evidence, if related policies, such as welfare reform, did so. But this has not been the case. Child welfare, arguably the most urgent program since it is mandated to address the needs of abused and neglected children, is a debacle. The child welfare system "has faced confusion about its purposes and methods, declining professionalism, and progressive disorganization," wrote Alvin Schorr (2000). "The immediate future of public child welfare is relatively clear—child welfare around the country is in a parlous state. . . . In many places the debasement of services, the decline of staff, and the absence of sustained citizen engagement are so advanced that it is difficult to see how these may be reversed" (pp. 124, 131). Despite the caseload implosion, welfare reform has not documented obvious improvements in the circumstances of the nation's poorest children. Billions of dollars are expended in an incoherent arrangement of health programs, yet millions of children and their families remain uninsured. One thing that is remarkable about the failure of public welfare is that welfare scholars have conceded as much (Epstein, 1997, 1999; Stoesz, 2000, 2005; Gilbert, 2002).

Systematic data from governmental agencies and private foundations as well as anecdotal information indicate that child welfare is failing its mandate to serve children from troubled families. In 2003, an Annie E. Casey Foundation report portrayed the human services workforce in less than flattering terms: "Millions of taxpayer dollars are being poured into a compromised system that not only achieves little in the way of real results, but its interventions often do more harm than good" (2003, p. 2). A review of the child welfare literature by the Child Welfare Workforce Task Group, which meets at the Children's Defense Fund, documented the serious personnel problems of the field: 90% of states experience difficulty recruiting and retaining child welfare workers; only 28% of child welfare staff hold a social work degree; fewer than 15% of child welfare agencies require professional credentials; and the average tenure of a child welfare worker is less than 2 years (Child Welfare Workforce Task Group, 2006).

The Child and Family Services Reviews (CFSRs) released in 2005 by the Department of Health and Human Services determined that of the 50 states and the District of Columbia, which were evaluated on seven standards of child welfare, not one state was able to assure that maltreated children had a permanent and stable living arrangement; not one state was in compliance with regard to families having improved their ability to care for their children; and only one state demonstrated that it adequately met a child's physical and mental health needs (Department of Health and Human Services, 2005). In December 2005, the Office of the Inspector General of the Department of Health and Human Services reported that "only twenty states demonstrated their ability to produce statewide reports detailing the extent to which [foster care] visits occurred during FY 2003; seven of the twenty statewide reports indicated that fewer than half of children in foster care were visited monthly in FY 2003" (Department of Health and Human Services, 2005).

Management data indicate that child welfare is compromised, and this is borne out by data on foster children. Children who are placed with surrogate families have special needs: 40% are premature or low birth weight, 80% were prenatally exposed to substances, 25% have three or more chronic health problems, and 20% are fully handicapped (Children's Rights, 2006, p. 5). A study of children who have aged out of foster care in the Northwest revealed that, within the 12 months prior to being interviewed, 20% had a major depressive episode, 12% suffered from alcohol and drug dependence, and 25% were diagnosed with posttraumatic stress disorder (Pecora et al., 2005, p 34).

The shoddy state of child welfare has resulted in critical reviews such as *The Book of David* by Richard Gelles (1996) and *Children Who Could Have Been* by William Epstein (1999). Prominent among these is *The Lost Children of Wilder* by Nina Bernstein (2001), the account of Marcia Robinson Lowry's valiant attempt to obtain a measure of justice for foster children in New York City. Lowry founded Children's Rights, a legal advocacy organization that by 2006 had secured consent decrees from ten public child welfare agencies. Two teams of journalists have won Pulitzer Prizes for their exposés of child welfare: Marjie Lundstrom and Rochelle Sharpe for *Getting Away with Murder* in 1990 and Sari Horwitz, Scott Higham, and Sarah Cohen a decade later for their coverage of child welfare in the District of Columbia. Another journalist, Richard Wexler, directs the National Center for Child Protection Reform, electronically transmitting weekly stories of the ineptitude of child welfare workers across the country. "Foster care has swollen into a colossally inflexible, $8.0 billion IV-E bureaucracy that stifles reform, strait-jackets innovation, and discourages spending on options other than long-term foster care," concluded Mark Testa, director of the Children and Family Research Center at the University of Illinois, Urbana-Champaign (2005, p. 4).

The systemic failure of child welfare should not be attributed to caseworkers alone. With a handful of exceptions, social work and the applied social sciences have been negligent in pursuing field experiments to identify optimal interventions. The rarity of field experiments in child welfare led the authors of *Beyond Common Sense* (Wulczyn, Barth, Yuan, Harden, & Landsverk, 2005) to state somewhat inaccurately that "there is not a single intervention that has generated a published peer-review article based on a study in which they accepted referrals from a child welfare agency, randomly assigned them to a treatment condition, and evaluated the outcome" (p. 155). The paucity of field experiments in child welfare is striking in two respects: First, many field experiments on welfare reform have been conducted and evaluated since the 1980s by private research organizations. Thus, their absence in child welfare is, in a word, inexcusable. Second, for years, the nation's schools of social work have received millions of dollars ($280 million in 2006) to train students, agency staff, and parents to better care for at-risk children, yet there has never been an accounting for the use of these funds.

What data are available on public welfare document a nonsystem that has failed those it is mandated to protect. Since it was inaugurated as federal policy in the 1930s, child welfare has become a convoluted bureaucracy which fails to attract sufficient staff, episodically reports on essential program activities, and is unable to document how it has enhanced the well-being of children. Rather than attracting the allegiance of a public whose sympathies would normally align with the needs of young victims, the public welfare paradigm has alienated many citizens. A disillusioned public has come to conclude that cash assistance often induces generational dependence, that child welfare is implicated in the unnecessary deaths of neglected and abused children, and that many benefits are irrelevant to the circumstances of deserving families. The absence of public support for social programs is fatal in a democracy; the extensive failure of the public welfare paradigm justifies its replacement.

HUMAN SERVICES

The origin of public welfare in the Progressive era explains the primary values upon which it was based: Recipients were to be provided with adequate services and benefits; provisions were to be distributed equally throughout the population; and governmental regulation would assure high-quality programming. Seven decades after passage of the Social Security Act, the American institution of public welfare has made a mockery of these principles. By itself, TANF provides families with subpoverty benefits, assuring that the vast majority of recipients remains poor. Program provisions vary strikingly from wealthier to poorer states; some regions of the nation boast social indicators that resemble those of the Third World. Inferior public services are not only perceived by many recipients as loathsome, but the field has become a career of last resort for human services professionals (Green, Baskind, Mustian, Reed, & Taylor, 2007). In a postindustrial economy with an expanding service sector which provides individualized services for the majority of Americans, the government maintains a public monopoly of services and benefits for the poor, assuring second-rate provisions for second-class citizens. A cynic would observe that the United States maintains public welfare in the same manner that the Soviet Union manufactured tractors—only there isn't a Soviet Union any more.

In place of public welfare, a new human services paradigm should be crafted premised upon mainstream values. Program provisions should accelerate the upward mobility of recipients; citizens should be empowered by having choices among service and benefit options; and social program provisions should be local, customized, and responsive to recipients' preferences (Stoesz, 2005). Instead of compounding the failed public welfare paradigm with incremental additions, advocates of social and economic justice should jettison it for one built around human services.

Children's Authorities

A network of children's authorities—public-private entities that would assure families an array of high-quality services from which to choose—should replace the existing child welfare bureaucracy. The experience of the Chatham/Savannah (Georgia) Youth Futures Authority is illustrative. Two decades after its inception, the Youth Futures Authority publishes an impressive array of data on program performance. For example, the number of out-of-home placements decreased from 400 in 2003–2004 to 266 the following year, even though the number of CPS investigations had increased from 1,506 to 1,824 (Youth Futures Authority, 2006). In New York City, Dennis Smith and William Grinker (2005) have proposed applying the dynamic data model used to reduce crime to the city's Administration for Children's Services.

Drawing on such innovations, child welfare should be reformed according to the following precepts:

1. Reorganize child welfare through a local children's authority which would be held accountable for the provision of a range of services for children and their families.
2. Require the children's authority to institute a validated risk assessment instrument integrated with a management information system which allows aggregating data and following families longitudinally.
3. Construct a national database that follows abusers and children who are under the supervision of a children's authority across jurisdictions.
4. Enable public access to records of cases where children have been seriously injured or died after being placed under agency care.
5. Require the children's authority to report accurate data on the disposition of cases on a monthly basis in exchange for public funding.
6. Publish annually a report on child welfare comparing children's authorities with respect to specific variables relating to child abuse and neglect.
7. Consolidate funding for categorical programs into a block grant which is open-ended so long as children's authorities meet specific performance standards.
8. Establish national certification of child protection supervisors, which includes training in forensics, investigation techniques, family and juvenile law, management information systems, research, and ethics.
9. Require educational institutions in receipt of child welfare training funds to conduct state-of-the-art research in child protection, especially field experiments designed to demonstrate the effectiveness of various interventions.
10. Reassign all data relating to child morbidity and mortality to the Centers for Disease Control and Prevention.

In these ways, children's authorities could restore the credibility that has eroded in child welfare programs.

Community Credit Unions

Capitalizing on the latent interest of welfare mothers to participate in the labor market, welfare reform ended the cash entitlement to poor families. Yet, the momentum of welfare reform has stalled due to the protracted poverty of current and former welfare recipients. Policy reform that provides the welfare poor with the opportunity to join the ranks of the working poor will be perceived as a hollow promise if it is not complemented by an ambitious effort to accelerate their upward mobility. In the 21st century, the promise of welfare reform has been compromised by the very welfare bureaucracy entrusted to its administration. The Earned Income Tax Credit now provides twice as much cash benefit to poor families as does TANF, yet welfare departments often fail to inform recipients about transitional benefits: "[F]ewer [welfare] offices have created effective mechanisms for informing diverted applicants and recipients leaving welfare about the availability of food stamps, Medicaid, and other benefits" (Lurie, 2002, p. 41). Worse, welfare workers "rarely mention the federal Earned Income Tax Credit, a program that pays up to $4,000 per year to low income working families with children" (p. 44). Thus, even though virtually all TANF recipients who are engaged in employment are eligible for the EITC, welfare departments fail to notify them of this essential benefit. Moreover, employer-oriented tax credits, such as the Welfare-to-Work Tax Credit and the Work Opportunity Tax Credit, which could significantly augment the wages of welfare recipients, remain underutilized.

The upward mobility of the welfare poor and working poor could be accelerated by replacing public welfare departments with community credit unions (CCUs), which would be contracted to not only provide eligibility determinations for public benefits but also provide an array of financial products relevant to low-income families. CCU members would have account managers to assist them in financial management, coordinating access to traditional products, such as checking and savings accounts, and innovative services, such as tax preparation, establishing individual development accounts (tax-exempt matching accounts for buying a first home, finishing vocational school or college, or establishing a business), and financial literacy education. Using electronic benefit transfer of public benefits as well as paychecks, CCUs would be depositories; hence, their accrued capital could be used to leverage community development projects. Self-Help in Durham, North Carolina, and the Alternatives Credit Union of Ithaca, New York, have demonstrated how financial services can be oriented to the poor while capitalizing community development (Stoesz, 2000).

Upward mobility for poor families will always be subverted so long as public assistance benefits are predicated on a means test. The EITC avoids the pitfall of restricting refunds to those with low assets; however, current tax expenditures targeted to the poor are fragmented. Consequently, Sawicky and Cherry (2001) have proposed replacing the dependent exemption, the EITC, and the Child Tax Credit with a refundable Simplified Family Credit calibrated according to family size, with the credit ranging from a minimum of $1,500 for a family with one child to $9,000 for families with six children (p. 4).

CCUs will not evolve as true alternatives to public welfare departments unless recipients have a choice in where they receive their financial services. Accordingly, public assistance recipients would be able to designate the CCU to which they would assign their electronically deposited benefits. Logically, CCUs that offer a pleasant ambience, prompt service, and a relevant array of products and that are integrated into the economic life of the community will prosper while those whose staff are hostile to consumers, require recipients to sit for hours in the waiting room, and are indifferent to the long-term success of beneficiaries will lose clientele. That the latter descriptors are frequently employed to describe the culture of the public welfare department is reason enough to trade it in for an organization that is more responsive to consumer preferences.

Vouchers for Health Insurance

The United States spends 15% of its Gross Domestic Product for health care, yet 42 million Americans go without health insurance, one fifth of them children. For many families who qualify for Medicaid and for children enrolled in SCHIP, health care is compromised since providers often refuse to participate. Despite these shortcomings, the prospect of unified health reform, either under a British national health system or a Canadian single-payer arrangement, is remote. Regarding the future of health care, reformers would be advised to recall the words of the late Daniel Patrick Moynihan: "The issues of social policy the United States faces today have no European counterpart nor any European model of a viable solution. They are American problems and we Americans are going to have to think them through by ourselves"

(Moynihan, 1988, p. 291). In the case of health care, that means conceding the importance of markets, the significance of employers, and the role of the states.

In 2006, Massachusetts enacted a four-point strategy to assure health care to every state resident: (1) a "connector" allowing individuals and workers to purchase portable health insurance, (2) converting state subsidies for charitable care into health insurance premiums assistance, (3) a surcharge assessed on employers who do not offer insurance to employees, and (4) mandating that individuals obtain health insurance (Haislmaier, 2006). "States are taking the lead in health care reform, and Massachusetts' new system includes important innovations," concluded analysts from the Heritage Foundation. "Much can and should be learned from states' efforts. Successful health care reform in the United States is much more likely to come from such experimentation and its lessons than from imposing solutions from Washington" (Moffit & Owcharenko, 2006, pp. 2–3).

State health reform can be expedited by exploiting information technology and tax policy. Generic insurance forms and electronic patient records could reduce unnecessary administrative costs. Comparative evaluations of providers and procedures could optimize medical decision making (Nichols, 2006). The federal government could support state health reform by creating a refundable tax credit for individuals and employers through which they could purchase health insurance (Butler, 2004), effectively instituting a health insurance voucher. A logical site for the poor and for small employers to obtain information on vouchers for health insurance would be CCUs, discussed above. As state health reforms proliferate, the case for a federal regulatory function in health care also builds, similar to the role played by the Federal Reserve in national banking (Barlett & Steele, 2004).

DENOUEMENT

The 2006 midterm election effectively halted conservative approaches to social entitlements, yet the prospect of reviving the public welfare paradigm remained remote. Liberal relief was palpable as Democratic majorities in Congress were soon moving on legislation more favorable to middle-income Americans. Noticeably absent from this agenda were public welfare programs, however. Having unseated Republican officeholders, victorious Democrats were disinclined to revert to a discredited liberalism in social policy. The 110th Congress thus reflected the deep reservations the public still held about liberal social programs for poor families.

Conservative reversals at the polls did not equate to a resurgence of liberalism. Among the casualties in November 2006 was a proposal to make preschool universal in California, a ballot proposition that failed. "Progressives can find plenty of excuses" for the loss, observed E. J. Dionne, Jr. "Instead they need to deal with the sources of voter skepticism about public spending" (2006, p. A23). At best, the 2006 midterm election offered a window of opportunity for progressives to rethink their traditional assumptions vis-à-vis social programs for poor, vulnerable children. If liberal advocates of child welfare are to avoid reverting to a discredited orientation to social programs and to seize the opportunity of crafting an array of services for families congruent with the 21st century, they will find in *Horton* a serviceable benchmark, the elephant that chose to be responsible even under the most adverse of circumstances.

References

Barlett, D. L., & Steele, J. B. (2004). *Critical condition: How health care in America became big business and bad medicine.* Garden City, NY: Doubleday.

Bernstein, N. (2001). *The lost children of Wilder: The epic struggle to change foster care.* New York: Vintage.

Casey Foundation. (2003). *The unsolved challenge of system reform.* Baltimore: Author.

Census Bureau. (2006). *Statistical abstract of the United States.* Washington, DC: U.S. Government Printing Office.

Children's Rights. (2006). *Legal cases.* New York: Author.

Child Welfare League of America. (2006). *Promoting safe and stable families program.* Washington, DC: Author.

Child Welfare Workforce Task Group. (2006). *The research is clear: Child welfare workforce issues must be addressed.* Washington, DC: Children's Defense Fund.

Committee on Ways and Means. (2004). *Overview of entitlement programs.* Washington, DC: Author.

Costin, L., Karger, H., & Stoesz, D. (1996). *The politics of child abuse in America.* New York: Oxford University Press.

Courtney, M., & Dworsky, A. (2006). *Child welfare services involvement: Findings from the Milwaukee TANF applicant study.* Chicago: Chapin Hall Center for Children.

Department of Health and Human Services, Administration for Children and Families. (2006). *Summary of the child and family services reviews.* Washington, DC: Author.

Department of Health and Human Services, Office of the Inspector General. (2005). *State standards and capacity to track frequency of caseworker visits with children in foster care.* Washington, DC: Author.

Dionne, E. J. (2006, June 9). Lessons for liberals from California. *Washington Post.*

Epstein, W. (1997). *Welfare in America: How social science fails the poor.* Madison: University of Wisconsin Press.

Epstein, W. (1999). *Children who could have been.* Madison: University of Wisconsin Press.

Geisel, T. (1940). *Horton hatches the egg.* New York: Random House.

Gelles, R. (1996). *The book of David.* New York: Basic.

Gilbert, N. (2002). *Transformation of the welfare state: The silent surrender of public responsibility.* New York: Oxford University Press.

Goldstein, A. (2006, June 12). States' changes reshape Medicaid. *Washington Post.*

Gordon, L. (1994). *Pitied but not entitled.* Cambridge, MA: Harvard University Press.

Green, R., Baskind, F., Mustian, B., Reed, L., & Taylor, H. (2007). *Professional education and private practice: Is there a disconnect?* Richmond: Virginia Commonwealth University Press.

Hacker, J. (2002). *The divided welfare state.* Cambridge: Cambridge University Press.

Haskins, R., & Sawhill, I. (2003). *Work and marriage: The way to end poverty and welfare.* Washington, DC: Brookings Institution Press.

Horwitz, S., Higham, S., & Cohen, S. (2001, September 9). "Protected" children died as government did little. *Washington Post.*

Karger, H., & Stoesz, D. (2005). *American social welfare policy.* New York: Allyn & Bacon.

Kempe, C. H., Silverman, F. N., Steele, B. F., Droegemueller, W., & Silver, H. K. (1962). The battered child syndrome. *JAMA, 181,* 17–24.

Lubove, R. (1969). *The professional altruist.* New York: Atheneum.

Lundstrom, M., & Sharpe, R. (1990). Getting away with murder. *Gannett News Service.*

Lurie, I. (2002). Changing welfare offices. In I. Sawhill et al. (Eds.), *Welfare reform and beyond: The future of the safety net* (pp. 41–48). Washington, DC: Brookings Institution Press.

Moffit, R., & Owcharenko, N. (2006). *Understanding key parts of the Massachusetts health plan.* Washington, DC: Heritage Foundation.

Moynihan, D. P. (1988). *Came the revolution*. San Diego, CA: Harcourt Brace Jovanovich.

Nichols, L. (2006). Health reform Massachusetts style. Washington, DC: New America Foundation.

Pavetti, L., & Kauff, J. (2006). *When five years is not enough: Identifying and addressing the needs of families nearing the TANF time limit in Ramsey County, Minnesota.* Washington, DC: Mathematica Policy Research.

Paxson, C., & Waldfogel, J. (2003). Welfare reform, family resources, and child maltreatment. *Journal of Policy Analysis and Management, 22*(1), 85–113.

Pecora, P., Kessler, R., Williams, J., O'Brien, K., Downs, A. C., English, D., et al. (2005). *Improving Foster Care: Findings from the Northwest Foster Care Alumni Study.* Seattle, WA: Casey Family Programs.

Quadagno, J. (1994). *The color of welfare*. New York: Oxford University Press.

Schorr, A. (2000, March). The bleak prospect for public child welfare. *Social Service Review, 74*, 124–136.

Slack, K., Holl, J., Lee, B., McDaniel, M., Altenbernd, L., & Stevens, A. (2003). Child protective intervention in the context of welfare reform: The effects of work and welfare on treatment reports. *Journal of Policy Analysis and Management, 22*(4), 517–536.

Smith, D., & Grinker, W. (2005). *The transformation of social services management in New York City: "CompStating" welfare.* New York: Seedco.

Stoesz, D. (2000). *A poverty of imagination: Bootstrap capitalism, sequel to welfare reform.* Madison: University of Wisconsin Press.

Stoesz, D. (2005). *Quixote's ghost: The Right, the liberati, and the future of social policy.* New York: Oxford University Press.

Stoltzfus, E. (2004). *Child welfare: The Chafee foster care independence program.* Washington, DC: Congressional Research Service.

Waldfogel, J. (1998). *The future of child protection.* Cambridge, MA: Harvard University Press.

Wulczyn, F., Barth, R. P., Yuan, Y-Y. T., Harden, B. J., Landsverk, J. (2005). *Beyond common sense: Child welfare, child well-being, and evidence for policy reform.* New Brunswick, NJ: Aldine.

Young, L. (1964). *Wednesday's children: A study of child neglect and abuse.* New York: McGraw-Hill.

Youth Futures Authority. (2006). *Community profile fast facts.* Savannah, GA: Author.

20

Accounts at Birth:
A Proposal to Improve Life Chances Through a National System of Children's Savings Accounts

Reid Cramer

Beyond a focus on protection, child welfare policy should rightfully be asked to provide the support systems necessary to maximize life chances. To do so may require a consideration of the social conditions that children will confront as adults and the skill sets and resources they will need to successfully navigate their world. This perspective builds on an expanded definition of child welfare and necessarily encompasses a wide range of policy issues that extend beyond the current confines of the child welfare system.

In the 21st century, a number of innovative proposals have emerged that focus on developing strategies that encourage savings and asset development as a means of promoting economic security and maximizing life chances. These proposals are based on the general notion that achieving security in today's economy requires not just a job and growing income, but increasingly the ability to accumulate a wide range of assets. Yet many Americans have low asset holding, and many children are disadvantaged from the start of their lives relative to those children

born into affluence. Regrettably, the asset-building system already in place that facilitates wealth creation disproportionately benefits those households with higher incomes, better job benefits, and larger income tax liabilities. Lower-income families are offered fewer—and less attractive—ways to build wealth. Enabling all Americans the opportunity to take full advantage of our prosperous society will require the development of more-inclusive asset-building policies.

One promising idea is to begin promoting savings and asset-building activities with children, particularly with children's savings accounts (CSAs).[1] Endowing every child with a savings account, opened at birth, represents a social investment in every child at the same time as it gives children a stake in the broader society throughout their lives. For low-income Americans, CSAs will provide a means to develop savings and assets—an opportunity not offered by existing public policy. Over time, these accounts could evolve into a universal system through which all Americans would meet their lifelong asset needs, helping them to accumulate the resources necessary to make productive investments.

In July 2004, a bipartisan coalition of legislators offered a bill in both houses of Congress to create a national system of children's savings accounts. The America Saving for Personal Investment, Retirement, and Education Act (ASPIRE) would provide each newborn child with a KIDS account and an initial endowment of $500.[2] While this piece of legislation was the most detailed proposal to date, there are many different ways in which to structure a CSA proposal. In fact, the introduction of the ASPIRE Act generated increased interest in the general concept of children's accounts, which in turn led to additional proposals from across the political spectrum. In the summer of 2006, Senator Hillary Clinton (D-NY) came out in support of a universal accounts-at-birth system, which she initially called "baby bonds," and later that year Senator Jeff Sessions (R-AL) announced a proposal for universal retirement accounts, called Portable, Lifelong Universal Savings Accounts (PLUS Accounts), which would be opened automatically for workers and newborn children.

This chapter seeks to consider the broad array of policy design choices that will give any CSA proposal its ultimate shape and direction. To do so, the chapter begins by outlining the main elements of a prototypical children's savings account proposal, modeled on the ASPIRE Act, and then presents a discussion of the broader policy context, which includes a review of past proposals, current public sector programs, and private sector initiatives that build the case for some type of children's account system. New research and recent developments in the field, both in the United States and abroad, have added to the knowledge base from which these proposals can draw, including the expanding track record of Individual Development Account (IDA) programs, which continue to provide insights into the impact of incentives and financial education on the savings patterns of lower-income families, and the experience of the United Kingdom in implementing a national, universal system of children's savings accounts, the Child Trust Fund. Recognizing that there are many forms such a system could take, the chapter proceeds to examine the range of policy design, program implementation, and fiscal policy choices that have to be made in constructing a system of children's savings accounts. The chapter concludes with an examination of the broader issues of an account-based approach to asset building and considers the benefits and challenges of constructing such a system, particularly with respect to child welfare policy.

A PROTOTYPE PROPOSAL FOR CHILDREN'S SAVINGS ACCOUNTS

There are multiple ways to design children's savings accounts, depending upon the public resources available and the ultimate ranking of strategic goals. For the sake of clarity, a prototype proposal is described here modeled on the ASPIRE Act, which creates a network of KIDS accounts, while a more in-depth discussion of potential program features is presented later in the chapter. The prototype proposal is intended to distill the most current analytical thinking about how to create a large-scale system of accounts while keeping the implementation as simple and transparent as possible.

At its core, the prototype proposal depends on the creation of an account for every newborn. Participation would be mandatory, and eligibility would be universal. Any child with a Social Security number would have an account opened automatically when the number was issued. Each account would be endowed with an initial contribution provided by the federal government with the opportunity for additional contributions. The system would be run by a newly created entity called the KIDS Account Fund. Parents and legal guardians would serve as account custodians and make investment decisions until the account holder reaches the age of 18. The account holder custodian would decide how money in the KIDS account is invested, choosing among a small set of investment options.

Contributions

Each account would be endowed with a one-time $500 contribution. Children living in households earning below the national median income would be eligible for both a supplemental contribution of up to $500 at birth and the opportunity to earn $500 per year in matching funds for amounts saved in the account. Voluntary, private contributions of up to $1,000 a year could be made to the account to facilitate asset accumulation. These contributions could come from any source, including the account holder, family members, friends, employers, or nonprofit organizations.

Withdrawals

Rather than facilitate consumption, CSAs are designed to promote asset accumulation. Therefore, account holders can only use the resources that accrue in the accounts for specific purposes. When children enter adulthood, they would gain access to their account resources to use for asset-building investments, such as paying for postsecondary education, buying a home, or saving for retirement. Rules governing distributions would be similar to existing Roth IRA rules, where account holders' withdrawals are tax free, but they are reported to the IRS and subject to audit.

THE POLICY RATIONALE

By almost any standard, the United States has been particularly successful at generating wealth. The interaction between the country's political and economic systems has created a foundation for wealth creation on a massive scale, producing some of the world's largest corporations and richest families.[3] Beyond the fortunes of the rich, the rise of a broad middle class is one of the major social achievements of the United States as the sharing of wealth has ensured that a majority of citizens have a stake in the functioning of the economy and in society as a whole. Through an array of policies and programs, the public sector has played a significant role in both the expansion of wealth and its distribution. American history is marked by a series of major policy initiatives that have successfully expanded the ownership of capital and promoted stakeholdership.

Historic initiatives, such as the Homestead Act of 1862, the GI Bill of 1944, and the creation of the Federal Housing Administration (FHA) in 1934, have expanded access to important elements of wealth creation and produced tangible results. By providing land to those who would go west, stake a claim, and work it for 5 years, the Homestead Act provided an opportunity to build wealth by developing property. For the million and a half people who successfully took the government up on its offer, passing this wealth and property on to the next generation proved to be one of the most enduring legacies of the act.[4] The GI Bill offered veterans grants to pay for training and higher education, loans for setting up new businesses, and mortgages to purchase homes. Through this law, some $14.5 billion was spent by the federal government between 1944 and 1956, benefiting almost 8 million veterans.[5] A congressional report has estimated that the GI Bill generated returns of up to $7 for every dollar invested, an impressive perfor-

mance by any standard.[6] In addition to the economic multiplier effects, the influx of veterans permanently transformed the American university system, creating "an avenue for mass mobility rather than gentlemanly certification."[7] The FHA was created to help many Americans purchase a home. Through its mortgage insurance and other financing products, the FHA has played a role in the country's rising home-ownership rate, which reached an all-time high of 68% in 2002.[8]

Each of these efforts was grounded in the twin objectives of ownership and opportunity. The underlying assumptions were that ownership creates stakeholders, and expanding opportunities for people to accumulate productive assets has broad social and economic benefits. The role of public policy in encouraging asset building continues to this day; it is a hallmark of the prevailing policy framework which identifies wealth creation as a central policy objective.

Many of the policy levers used to achieve these ends are promoted through the tax code. Tax expenditure programs in the guise of tax deductions, tax credits, preferential tax rates, tax deferrals, and income exclusions are a primary vehicle for achieving these policy objectives. Collectively, they subsidize a broad range of activities, including many asset-building investments, such as mortgage payments, business investments, retirement savings, and educational expenditures. The value of these asset-building tax expenditure programs exceeds $300 billion on an annual basis.[9] Although these tax expenditures may subsidize worthy activities and generate sizable social and economic returns, they are not accessible to a large number of citizens who would benefit from them the most. Many lower-income households do not have large enough tax liabilities to take advantage of these tax expenditure programs. Not surprisingly, 90% of the benefits in the two largest tax expenditure categories (home ownership and retirement) reach households with incomes above $50,000 a year.[10]

Federal policy has historically discouraged asset building among households with fewer resources. Not only has the structure of tax expenditure programs denied benefits to poorer households but antipoverty policy efforts have been, and remain, focused on facilitating income maintenance and short-term consumption. In this spirit, many federal programs impose asset limits as an element of means-testing program eligibility. An unintended consequence of this approach is that it creates a disincentive to engage in the types of activities which can help a family to move up and out of poverty, namely, savings and asset building.

Consequently, the benefits of stakeholding, which have made a difference for many American families, have not been experienced by all. Millions of Americans live in households with few or no assets. One quarter of White children and half of non-White children grow up in households without any significant levels of savings or resources available for investment.[11] This represents an important dimension to the problem of inequality, which is usually discussed in terms of income. Wealth inequality is more severe than income inequality. According to the 2001 Survey of Consumer Finances, conducted by the Federal Reserve, the top 10% of households in the United States ranked by income earn 44% of the nation's income but own 57% of total family net worth.[12] In contrast, the bottom 60% earn 22% of the nation's income and own less than 17% of the nation's wealth.[13]

The pattern of wealth distribution is instructive because it reflects inequalities which have formed over an extended period of time. In the 21st century, two thirds of U.S. wealth is held by households with incomes in the top 20%.[14] Yet the more pressing issue from a policy perspective is the plight of those households that are asset poor, possessing insufficient resources to sustain a household through any extended period of economic disruption.[15] Research on asset poverty has focused on developing measures of economic vulnerability that can provide an accounting of households without a stock of resources to survive a loss of income.[16] Haveman and Wolff have estimated that the number of asset-poor households with precarious resource shortages substantially exceeds the official poverty rate and that the disparity has grown since the mid-1980s. In 1998, one out of eight Americans was officially classified as poor, 34.3 million people or 12.7% of households, but the ranks of the asset poor included one of every four, 69.1 million people or 25.5% of households.[17] And that disparity has grown. Between 1983 and 1998, income poverty declined about 16%, while asset poverty rose 14%.[18]

While there are many indicators which reflect the relatively high concentration of wealth in the United States, measures of asset poverty are instructive because they identify a clear challenge. Rather than penalize those with wealth, policies need to identify ways

to create opportunities for those without resources to save and accumulate assets.

The value of assets is based not only on the economic security they provide but in how they enable people to make investments in their future and to exert a stake in the broader society that income alone cannot provide. Michael Sherraden, author of *Assets and the Poor*, observes, "Few people have ever spent their way out of poverty. Those who escape do so through saving and investing for long-term goals."[19] Oliver and Shapiro write, "Wealth is a particularly important indicator of individual and family access to life chances. . . . It is used to create opportunities, secure a desired stature and standard of living, or pass class status along to one's children."[20] Recent research efforts have increasingly supported these claims with a growing body of evidence.[21] In a review of the literature on the effects of asset holding, Scanlon and Page-Adams found that much of the research focused on the impacts of home ownership, but a number of other studies focused on assets in the form of savings, net worth, or small business ownership. Despite the variety of asset measures used in this literature, they concluded that, together, financial and property assets appear to have positive effects on economic security, household stability, physical health, educational attainment, and civic involvement.[22] This conclusion has also been supported by work in the United Kingdom which examined the effects of assets on life chances and found a "persistent effect of assets on a number of outcomes, which were impervious to a wide range of controls," and "the assets effect was sustained, with employment, psychological health, belief in the political system and values, all appearing to be enhanced by assets."[23]

Thus, the body of evidence that links asset holding with positive outcomes is significant and growing, and has been shown to work for both the poor and non-poor alike. Recent findings from a national demonstration project of matched savings accounts for low-income individuals found that program participants responded positively to savings incentives, overcoming doubts among policy makers as to whether the poor could save.[24] The research results do not in and of themselves justify a rejection of income maintenance programs, but they provide support for building on approaches that combine income and assets perspectives.

In many ways, asset-building policies can be conceptualized as an investment strategy, with large multiplier effects for the entire economy. Modest investments in children can grow and, with responsible stewardship, can provide a means of ensuring that every citizen is afforded opportunities to succeed. As such, CSAs are intended to play a role in supporting the achievement of diverse national policy objectives, including the promotion of child welfare, an increase in the national savings rate, the enhancement of financial literacy, the incorporation of the unbanked into the financial mainstream, and the support of educational achievement. These are broad and worthy objectives; fulfilling any of these goals would represent a major societal achievement. Yet the success of this effort will be found at the household and community level. All children will grow up knowing there is an account with their name on it that can be used as they mature to help them make productive investments. These accounts will provide a vehicle to promote civic engagement, social participation, and economic security, which are vital outcomes for every child but are particularly relevant for children interacting with the child welfare system.

The policy rationale for implementing the CSA proposal in a universal manner is that it would provide a foundation for a broad account-based asset-building system. Governed by a uniform set of rules and administrative structures that would serve as the "plumbing" to support a national system of accounts, universally accessible to each and every child, these accounts would help to integrate the currently disparate account-based vehicles at the same time as they guarantee that everybody is included in the system. Since the late 1970s, there has been a profusion of asset-building accounts, including 401(k)s, individual retirement accounts (IRAs), Roth IRAs, Coverdell educational savings accounts, Section 529 plan accounts, medical savings accounts, and proposed individual accounts in Social Security. While this has represented a shift toward asset-based policy, the implementation of these efforts has been considerably more regressive than the social insurance and means-tested transfer programs developed since the New Deal.[25] As a universal program, the accounts-at-birth approach offers each child an economic opportunity to participate in asset building, and also provides an opportunity to construct an integrated system for managing account-based asset building on a large scale. The importance of this achievement may be profound as it would provide a unifying structure to integrate the asset-building policies currently spread throughout the tax code.

THE POLICY CONTEXT: HISTORIC AND CONTEMPORARY

The CSA proposal is innovative in many respects, but it has historic precedents both here and abroad. There are several policy traditions within which this proposal should be considered: stakeholder proposals, savings incentives, and aid to children.

Internationally, the United Kingdom has recently embarked on an effort to unite all three with the implementation of a national system of child trust fund accounts. All children born in the United Kingdom after September 2002 are eligible to receive a voucher of £250 and an additional £250 if they live in lower-income families, which will be invested to ensure that all children have financial assets when they reach adulthood.[26] Similarly, Singapore has begun to assist children with savings and financial incentives in the form of a "baby bonus" deposit at birth and a matched-savings children's development account program.[27] Although these incentives are part of a pronatal policy where benefits apply only to the second and third children, they represent use of an account-based system to provide support for families with children and to create a foundation for a national system of stakeholding and asset building. While the United States has successfully employed a range of stakeholding policies, the universal nature of these two efforts sets them apart from what has been achieved here. Despite the absence of such a universal children's savings account program in the United States, there has been a range of proposals, both historic and contemporary, that have signaled the promise and potential of this idea. As a sign of political success, the last 10 years has produced an increasing number of account-based proposals. The fate of these proposals should be examined closely in order to understand the current policy terrain and to provide insights into how to potentially structure a children's savings account system.

A Founding Precedent

Even before many of the stakeholder policies that encouraged home ownership, investment, and savings took shape in the 20th century, one of the most influential founding fathers expounded a universal stakeholder proposal. In one of his last great pamphlets, *Agrarian Justice*, Thomas Paine argued for the creation of a national fund from which each citizen would be given an asset pool upon entering adulthood in order to formalize equal citizenship.[28]

Paine believed that individuals should be offered opportunities to participate in the creation of economic wealth, and he was concerned with the effects of pervasive poverty on social cohesion. The £15 sterling he proposed every adult receive upon reaching the age of 21 would be enough to get them started in an occupation or economic endeavor. He thought that rather than allowing people to suffer deprivation and then asking society to intervene, it would be more logical to intervene beforehand. Paine wrote, "Would it not, even as a matter of economy, be far better to adopt means to prevent their becoming poor?"[29] Given society's role in creating affluence, Paine funded his proposal by proposing a 10% tax on inherited property, so that the wealth of one generation could endow the next. A key element of the proposal is its universality, where the grant would be provided as a right of citizenship for all, regardless of wealth or poverty. Paine's concept is distinct from other forms of universal social insurance because the plan enforces a particular social message; each endowment functions as an investment and an opportunity. He argued:

A plan upon this principle would benefit the revolution by the energy that springs from the consciousness of justice. It would multiply also the national resources; for property, like vegetation, increases by offsets. When a young couple begin the world, the difference is exceedingly great whether they begin with nothing or with fifteen pounds apiece. With this aid they could buy a cow, and implements to cultivate a few acres of land; and instead of becoming burdens upon society . . . would be put in the way of becoming useful and profitable citizens.[30]

The provision of resources to buy a cow is not all that different from other, more-modern stakeholding policies that encourage business investment, home purchase, or land development.

Public Sector Efforts

Beyond stakeholding and citizenship, CSAs should be compared with government policies that provide financial resources to families with children. Historically, grants to children are intended to provide income security, and thus have taken the for m of ongoing children's allowances. Following the Sec-

ond World War, child allowance programs began to expand worldwide. Most of these focused on social policy with the primary objective of ensuring the welfare of children. A few programs were focused on profamily or pronatal objectives. In the United States, Aid to Families with Dependent Children (AFDC) began as a small, emergency program during the New Deal in 1935 and was greatly expanded in the 1960s through court intervention, establishing an entitlement to assistance for low-income families who qualified. The purpose of this program was to provide financial assistance to needy dependent children. While this type of effort is basically an income transfer program, receiving benefits is contingent upon the characteristics or behavior of the family. AFDC regulations included provisions regarding work requirements and eligibility standards. This program was replaced in 1996 by Temporary Assistance for Needy Families (TANF), a block grant to states to provide time-limited cash assistance for very low-income families as they prepare to enter the workforce. Assistance remains linked to recipient behavior, and the statutory goals have been expanded to encompass broader social goals, such as reducing out-of-wedlock pregnancies and encouraging two-parent families.

AFDC and TANF are not universal programs that provide consistent, direct support to families with children. Among the developed world, the United States is the only country without such a program.[31] In the United Kingdom, for example, every family is eligible for the child benefit, which is a per-child family allowance paid directly to each family.[32] Single-parent households receive a slightly higher allowance, but each child in every family is eligible for this universal benefit. This is in addition to a Child Tax Credit and a Working Family Tax Credit, which are available to lower-income households. In the United Kingdom, the tax credits and child benefit are paid throughout the year as income supports rather than as a lump-sum asset payment.

The idea of providing a child allowance in the United States has been considered and has received bipartisan support. In 1989, the National Commission on Children was convened by President Ronald Reagan and Congress to explore policy proposals to improve the welfare of children. Its final report, issued 2 years later, declared, "Investing in children is no longer a luxury, but a national imperative."[33] One of the commission's central recommendations was a $1,000 refundable child tax credit for families in need. This proposal is distinguished from the child allowance programs of Europe because it was not intended to be universal and it uses the tax code to deliver its benefits. A smaller version of this proposal was later implemented by President Bill Clinton in 1997 with a $300 per-child tax credit for dependent children below the age of 13 for families with incomes under $75,000.

Since this child credit was not refundable, families only benefited if they had sufficient tax liabilities to take advantage of the deduction. Today, the Child Tax Credit is more generous, having been expanded as part of changes to the tax code in 2001 and 2003, and is scheduled to increase to $1,000 per child by 2010. The current structure of the Child Tax Credit makes it refundable for some, but not all, lower-income families; millions of low-income working families with children continue to receive no benefit from the policy.[34] Refundable tax credits are a valuable tool for providing benefits to lower-income families because they allow the amount in excess of a household's tax liability to be received in a refund check from the U.S. Treasury. If a family has no federal tax liability, as is the case with many working low-income families, increasing the size of a nonrefundable tax credit provides zero benefit.[35]

Prior to the expansion of the Child Tax Credit, low-income families with children received tax benefits from three primary sources: the dependent exemption, the Child and Dependent Care Tax Credit, and the Earned Income Tax Credit (EITC).[36] While all three of these sources benefit families with children, the first two are not refundable and thus have the greatest usefulness for middle- and upper-income families with tax liabilities.

The dependent exemption allows taxpayers to lower their taxable income for each dependent child, which lowers the overall tax bill.[37] The Child and Dependent Care Tax Credit, created in 1986, does the same for employment-related child care expenses.[38] The EITC is a refundable credit, so families with tax liabilities less than the value of their eligible credit receive the difference as a government payment in the form of a tax refund.[39] Created in the 1980s, it was greatly expanded in the mid-1990s and has received bipartisan support as an alternative to welfare assistance programs that promotes workforce participation. The EITC provides over $36 billion annually to lower-income workers and represents a significant financial resource for beneficiaries, most of whom receive EITC benefits in a lump sum after filing their tax returns. Research on the EITC program has confirmed its effectiveness as a work incentive, and the participation of eligible households, estimated at over 80%, is relatively high when compared with other assistance programs in the United States.[40] However, even an impressive take-up rate should be compared with other universal benefit programs in other countries. For example, the United Kingdom's child benefit has a take-up rate of over 98%.

The main distinction between the set of child benefit and child allowance programs described above and the CSA approach is the focus on long-term savings rather than immediate consumption. Several legislative proposals have been made in recent years which also would support children through savings vehicles tied to specific uses, including retirement, education, and first home purchase. These proposals were often presented in the context of debates over reforming Social Security, but collectively they reflect a degree of bipartisan support for the concept of children's savings accounts. Although these proposals differ in their details, each makes the connection between the welfare of children and lifelong security.

The most widely recognized scheme was KidSave, initially advocated by Senator Bob Kerrey (D-NE) in 1995; the concept of KidSave was to create individual retirement savings accounts to supplement Social Security. Various funding mechanisms were considered, including direct deposits of federal money, a tax credit for parents, and family contributions, but in each scenario, resources were placed in an Individual Retirement Account (IRA) for children. Similar to the conventional IRA, taxes on the principal and interest would be deferred until they were withdrawn. Withdrawals before the age of 59 would be subject to a penalty similar to those governing the traditional IRA. One version of the proposal permitted a child to borrow from his or her account temporarily in the form of a 10-year loan in order to pay for postsecondary educational expenses without incurring a tax penalty. There were several innovative features of the KidSave proposals, but the most historic might have been the requirement that the Social Security Administration open and endow an account for every newborn. By 2000, the KidSave proposal had an impressive array of bipartisan cosponsors.

Another, and in some ways more comprehensive, proposal was made in 1997 by Representative Amo Houghton (R-NY), who proposed to establish a child retirement account for every citizen under the age of 6. The retirement account allowed borrowing

TABLE 20.1 Value of Select Child Benefit Tax Expenditures: Fiscal Year 2008 (in millions of dollars)

	Effect on Receipts	Effect on Outlays (Refundable)
Earned Income Tax Credit (EITC)	5,340	36,461
Child Credit	32,341	14,931
Child and Dependent Care Credit	1.740	NA
Total	39,421	51,392

Source: Office of Management and Budget, Executive Office of the President. (2007). *Budget of the U.S. government, fiscal year 2008: Analytical perspectives.* Washington, DC: Office of Management and Budget. Table 19-1.

to support higher education and first-time home purchase, but it also called for the U.S. Treasury to contribute $1,000 to each child's account every year until the age of 6. The program would be universal in the sense that it would be open to all and provide access to an asset-building mechanism regardless of family status or behavior. Two years later, Senator Bill Frist (R-TN) introduced a version of this bill which allowed parents to open and contribute to child savings accounts within the Roth IRA structure; these accounts could be used for the broad purchases outlined in Houghton's bill without the direct federal cash contributions.

While none of these efforts resulted in enacted legislation, the profusion of congressional activity since the mid-1990s reflects a large degree of interest in the potential of child savings accounts and the search for viable mechanisms to deliver savings opportunities for children.[41] For a coalition of bipartisan members of Congress, this search led to the introduction of the ASPIRE Act in July 2004. Sponsored by Senators Rick Santorum (R-PA) and Jon Corzine (D-NJ), along with Representatives Harold Ford, Jr. (D-TN), Patrick Kennedy (D-RI), Phil English (R-PA), and Thomas Petri (R-WI), the ASPIRE Act would create a universal system of children's savings accounts in order to encourage savings, promote financial literacy, and expand opportunities for young adults. It is the fullest statement of an account-at-birth approach focused on asset-building objectives. Account uses would not be restricted to retirement security but could also be used on human capital investments or home purchase. In addition to the initial contribution, it has several progressive features, most notably a one-time supplemental contribution and annual matching contributions for children in families earning under the national median income.

The litany of these legislative proposals corresponded with a period of time when Congress was also actively creating new savings vehicles tied to specific purchases, particularly saving for education and retirement. These proposals were often account-based and employed tax preferences, such as the Coverdell education savings accounts and Section 529 college savings plans, created in 1997 and 1996, respectively.[42] While a few states have sought to create incentives to encourage lower-income households to open accounts, the structure of these policies will confer most benefits on middle- and upper-income families.

Since the introduction of the ASPIRE Act, additional legislative proposals have been made which build on the concept of children's savings accounts. For example, Senator Max Baucus (D-MT) reintroduced a proposal to create a Roth IRA for children, called young savings accounts, in his Savings Competitiveness Act (2006). Representative Clay Shaw, Jr., offered the 401Kids Family Savings Act (2006), which would allow Coverdell education savings accounts to be converted into accounts that would have expanded uses beyond education. Furthermore, Senator Jeff Sessions (R-AL) developed legislation to establish savings accounts for children at birth as well as for those currently in the workforce in order to promote retirement security, and Senator Hillary Clinton (D-NY) announced support for the concept of offering each newborn child a savings account, which they could use as a platform to promote savings and asset building.

Private Sector Initiatives

While the public sector has explored the possibilities of child savings accounts through legislative proposals and enacted account-based savings vehicles, the private sector has taken the lead in pioneering some of the concepts central to the CSA approach. Two initiatives are worth highlighting.

The first is a privately funded demonstration project of child accounts, called the Saving for Education, Entrepreneurship, and Downpayment

(SEED) initiative, which is a 6-year effort to develop, administer, and test matched savings accounts and financial education for children and youth.[43] SEED accounts are long-term savings and investment accounts established at birth and allowed to grow over the course of a lifetime. Seeded with an initial deposit of $200 to $1,000 and built by deposits from family, friends, and account holders themselves, as well as augmented by other public and private sources, SEED savings are restricted for the primary purposes of financing education and training, starting a small business, buying a home, or financing retirement. Participation in the program will include financial education. Launched in 2003 in partnership with community organizations at 10 sites across the country, each community partner will work with different age cohorts and offer a range of savings incentives and financial education approaches. It is expected that 1,100 accounts will be created across the country.

Another facet of the SEED initiative is the Universal Model Experiment, which is offering 1,000 randomly selected newborns in the state of Oklahoma access to a 529 college savings plan. Participants will receive incentives to contribute to these accounts, and their experience will be compared to a control group. This portion of the initiative was launched in 2006 and is expected over time to add to the understanding of specific program features and institutional characteristics that lead to higher savings outcomes.

This combined effort is designed to set the stage for a universal, progressive policy for asset building among children, youth, and families. A long-term evaluation strategy has been developed which will assess each community partnership through ongoing monitoring and periodic outcomes surveys. Analysis is intended to help answer a range of questions regarding the psychological, social, behavioral, and economic effects of holding an account; effective means of engaging participation; the potential roles of the public, private, and nonprofit sectors; and the delivery systems capable of being scaled up in a national accounts system.

The second initiative is the work of the I Have a Dream Foundation (IHAD), which runs a series of tuition guarantee programs for students in low-income communities across the country. Initially inspired by philanthropist Eugene Lang, IHAD provides long-term educational support programs that work with entire grades in specific elementary schools or entire same-age cohorts in public housing developments. The objective of the program is to ensure that every participant graduates from high school and has the option of attending college or obtaining rewarding employment. Once participants graduate from high school, the foundation provides tuition assistance to assure that they have the opportunity to receive postsecondary education. Begun in 1981 in East Harlem, New York, there are now 180 projects nationwide with 13,500 participants since inception; 6,000 are in active projects. The program combines personal financial commitment with individual support services.

Evaluations of the initiative have shown positive results when outcomes are compared to control groups in particular project cities.[44] Measurable effects include high rates of high school graduation, college attendance, academic performance, and school attendance. Studies commissioned by the IHAD Foundation and by other private funders, such as the MacArthur Foundation, have also examined the attitudinal and behavioral effects of program participation and found that participation in the program has produced tangible benefits. IHAD programs vary by project site, and the interaction with project coordinators and other support services has moved the program beyond tuition assistance, yet the high expectations and tuition rewards appear to have an enduring impact on program participants.

The proposals, initiatives, and enacted policies described in this section reflect the policy context within which any children's savings account proposal should be considered. Collectively, they demonstrate a historic interest in stakeholding policies which, up until now, have neither been universal in scope nor focused on children. The profusion of these proposals also reflects a widespread and growing interest in account-based solutions to achieving national policy objectives. The savings incentives that accompany these accounts are increasingly offered through the tax code, which limits their value for lower-income families. People in lower-income households have, in fact, been shown to respond to other savings and achievement incentives, such as matched savings accounts and tuition guarantees, creating an opportunity to craft more effective policies. What is needed is a unifying proposal capable of promoting stakeholding, opportunity, and ownership through an accounts-based asset-building system open to all.

PRIMARY POLICY DESIGN ISSUES

From a design and implementation perspective, three fundamental questions must be addressed when considering how to construct a national system of children's savings accounts: (1) How are the accounts to be administered? (2) What rules will govern distributions? (3) How are the accounts to be funded?[45] While many of the concerns embedded in these questions overlap, there is a benefit to trying to untangle them by distinguishing among issues of policy design, program implementation, and fiscal matters. Each issue represents a series of decision points, usually with multiple options of how to proceed.

Large-scale initiatives intended to address broad policy objectives are often critiqued in terms of how they handle the tradeoff between equity and efficiency. Economists assert quite confidently that equity and efficiency cannot be achieved in consort. The classic formulation of this tradeoff by Arthur Okun asserts that any dollar transferred from a wealthier individual to a poorer one results in less than a dollar's increase in income for the recipient.[46] Okun offers several basic explanations for this "leaky bucket" phenomenon. There are costs to administer the transfer as well as changes in effort, savings, investment, and attitude induced by the transfer. Furthermore, the imposition of equity cannot be achieved with perfect precision. Programs that redistribute public resources to people in need are likely to benefit some without need. Consequently, government efforts to achieve greater equity necessarily create a smaller level of total income and a less efficient use of resources. The prevailing policy question then becomes: How much leakage is society willing to accept in order to achieve a desirable level of equity?[47]

While there are plenty of examples that support the thesis that government transfers designed to create greater equity produce inefficiencies, in some cases the effect created is quite small. Economist Rebecca Blank suggests that there are three policy situations in which equity-increasing transfers can occur without seriously reducing efficiency: when public assistance is directed to particular populations that cannot change their behavior; when public assistance is provided through programs that include behavioral mandates; and when public assistance functions as a long-term investment that may accrue benefits down the road.[48]

The leaky bucket thesis is undoubtedly more applicable to the classic welfare formulation, where a wealth transfer reduces labor supply through cash supports to the poor, but may be less relevant to populations that do not exert individual agency, such as children and the elderly.[49] While the equity and efficiency tradeoff has been used as a cautionary tale to dissuade policy makers from crafting redistributive interventions, for several reasons this tale is less applicable to the children's savings accounts approach. First, the beneficiaries of the accounts are initially children, who have no behavioral response to participation. Second, as children mature, there is a link between program benefits and behavior incentives; participants can access additional contributions if they continue their education through high school. Third, the overall effect of the transfer subsidizes future investments that will create opportunities for participants to increase their welfare in subsequent years. This may be particularly true when benefits are restricted to asset investments, such as human capital expenditures, rather than cash accruals, which can be used to support less-restricted consumption. Yet the most effective response to concerns about the equity/efficiency tradeoff is to establish a set of rules for participation that will provide universal eligibility, guaranteeing all participants equal access to program benefits under identical conditions.

Participation and Eligibility

The manner in which the twin issues of participation and eligibility are addressed will impact the equity and efficiency tradeoff and determine the ultimate scale and scope of the initiative. Restricting program eligibility will increase the potential that program benefits will flow inefficiently because it is difficult to create a set of thresholds that perfectly defines a population in need. Conversely, if participation is universal and benefits are not means tested, greater efficiency can be achieved because no one will fall through the cracks. Such an approach imposes a high degree of equity because everyone is subject to the same rules; no one is treated differently.

Universal eligibility minimizes the equity/efficiency tradeoff and gives every family an interest in how the program operates. The account offers each child a stake in the society as a whole and becomes a feature of citizenship, eventually giving everyone the right to share in the nation's wealth by virtue of being a member of the national community. To achieve the full benefits of universal eligibility, it is likely that program participation will have to be made mandatory. This approach mirrors that of the Social Security program, which offers a successful model of how to compel participation.[50] Universal eligibility ensures a level playing field, and mandatory participation ensures that everyone gets in the game. Denying the option to opt out of the program affords each participant a degree of protection from decisions made by their guardians which are beyond their control.

There are alternatives to a universal eligibility and mandatory participation approach. One alternative is to restrict eligibility to families and children who would achieve greater benefit from the program and prevent the subsidizing of families who already have sufficient means. This targeting approach could be achieved by creating a means test designed to create a threshold that distinguishes worthy beneficiaries or that crafts a phase-out that offers fewer benefits to children in wealthier families. Advocates of a means test with phase-outs argue that families with higher incomes can fund savings accounts for their children on their own and thus should not be subsidized by the federal government. Conversely, some families with means will not necessarily use them to establish savings accounts for their children, and family income is subject to fluctuation; it may be high during the initial funding period but decline at another point in a child's life.

There are two primary challenges to a means test. The first is the difficulty in crafting such a test without unwittingly denying access to some who could benefit or including some with comparatively less need. The second is the additional costs incurred by administering a targeted and restricted system. These costs are associated with workload issues involved in processing applications, providing case management and technical assistance, and verifying income and monitoring fraud. A means-tested program is susceptible to fraud and noncompliance because it conveys benefits to those who claim eligibility even if they are not entitled.[51] The Earned Income Tax Credit offers benefits through a means-tested criterion, and even though it is widely regarded as an effective work incentive that lifts many families out of poverty, it has been criticized for providing benefits to ineligible recipients. Congress has responded by subjecting the EITC program to compliance testing beyond what the rest of the tax system receives.[52] Restricting eligibility to children's

savings accounts adds complexity and administrative costs that a universal system avoids. Regardless of cost and complexity, a restricted program curtails the impact of the effort, denying some people the potential to build assets and leaving key policy objectives unmet.

Another alternative is to create a program where participation is voluntary. This would allow families uninterested in receiving public support the option of refusing benefits. Since a universal program is unlikely to have a social stigma attached to participation, the voluntary approach would more likely be used to require families to opt in. Moving away from a mandatory, universal system increases the likelihood that children eligible to participate in the program will fail to do so, lowering the take-up rate. This assertion is based on the historic take-up rates of public assistance programs, defined as the portion of the population eligible for assistance that participates in the program. For example, it has been estimated that only one third of elderly persons eligible for food stamps participate in the program, while the take-up rate is only approximately two thirds for families with children.[53] A variety of reasons have been used to explain low take-up rates. Families may not be interested in receiving public support because of the stigma associated with welfare programs, or they may not believe they have a need that the program will meet. More troubling would be cases where families do not participate because they have incomplete or inaccurate information about program requirements. Research has revealed that many people who are eligible for the food stamp program do not believe they meet the requirements to receive benefits.[54]

While it may be assumed that targeting eligibility and relaxing participation rules would reduce the overall cost of the effort, since fewer families would be enrolled, this approach introduces a number of administration issues that create complexities and add to the program costs. For an initiative that focuses on children, there is a virtue in crafting a universal program that is open to all, regardless of income. The universal eligibility and mandatory participation approach may work best to establish the basic foundation of a children's accounts system, and it does not necessarily preclude the introduction of more progressive features tied to the crafting of means-tested savings incentives.

Funding Mechanism

Answering the question of how child accounts will be funded is one of the most fundamental issues to confront in designing a children's savings account system. The choice of funding mechanism, whether accounts are funded through direct government expenditures or through some form of tax expenditure, creates the basis for the support structures required to administer the program.

The prototype proposal calls for a system of direct government deposits into each child's account. This approach is preferable because it has the virtue of simplicity, where every transaction is transparent to the recipient and the budgetary process. Contributions to accounts can be made via transfers from the U.S. Treasury in a manner similar to the issuing of tax refunds. The Financial Management Service (FMS), a bureau of the U.S. Treasury, is already engaged in the activities of issuing checks and transferring cash and has the demonstrated capacity to disburse payments to a large number of beneficiaries; all that is needed is an address or bank account routing number.[55] This is already one of the core competencies of the government.

Funding these accounts through a direct expenditure on the discretionary side of the budget would subject the effort to the annual appropriations process. Alternatively, as a universal program, Congress could classify it as mandatory spending, which refers to expenditures controlled by laws other than appropriations acts. This is the designation given to spending for entitlement programs, such as Social Security and the food stamp program. Regardless of whether the accounts-at-birth program were placed on the discretionary or mandatory side of the budget, the magnitude of the commitment would be relatively easy to track compared to the accounting of tax expenditure programs. For some, this would pose a problem because both of these budgeting scenarios would create a level of political scrutiny that might hinder its long-term political viability.[56]

The alternative is to structure the program through the tax system and administer it with the assistance of the Internal Revenue Service. This can be done, but designing and implementing a tax credit creates a plethora of administrative issues, including the consideration of tax rules, tax enforcement strategies, and tax filing requirements.[57]

If this path is pursued and a tax credit mechanism is used, the first question is whether it should be a refundable credit or available only to offset income or payroll tax liability. The refundable credit would provide a means to benefit children regardless of their family's tax liability. Goldberg has proposed funding child saving accounts with such a refundable tax credit system. Currently, there are only two refundable tax credits that provide benefits this way, the EITC and, to some extent, the Child Tax Credit. The vast majority of tax credits are nonrefundable, providing deductions in the calculation of income or tax liability. Nonrefundable credits only provide benefits to the extent that there is a tax liability. Structuring a children's account system in this manner would limit the program's ability to benefit children in lower-income households because the amount of any credit would be limited to the lesser of the value of the credit or the taxpayers' tax liability. For example, given current tax rates and tax rules, a nonrefundable $1,000 credit would exclude almost 50% of children.[58]

Goldberg's other reason for supporting a refundable tax credit system is its ability to facilitate a means-tested approach. Tax benefits can be phased out for taxpayers who report higher incomes. This approach has some value, especially in capping the overall price tag of the effort, but it creates the need for additional rules. If taxpayers with incomes over a certain threshold begin to lose some tax benefits, there would need to be rulings on whether they would be permitted to fund these accounts on an after-tax basis and how the credit would be apportioned if the taxpayer had more than one eligible child.

A mixed system is also plausible, where direct deposits are made initially but additional deposits are encouraged through tax incentives. Another approach is a dual system for contributions, which can be funded directly or through reimbursement credits after taxpayers report contributions on their tax returns.

In the spirit of simplicity and transparency, the United Kingdom has opted to use the direct approach rather than create a new tax credit to support its child trust fund effort. The funding mechanism of this effort is a version of the direct deposit approach, but employs a voucher system. This general approach is direct but is specifically designed to work in an accounts system with a range of financial providers and account managers. Vouchers function as a special kind of check, which can only be redeemed by account providers participating in the program. It is an approach that could work in the United States if a similar system of accounts management were employed.

Contributions and Incentives

Children's savings accounts are designed to help build a modest asset pool that can help all individuals invest in their future, but these accounts are also intended to provide a signal that the broader community has invested in them. In this spirit, the depositing of public sector funds directly into the account of every child sends a powerful message, and the timing of these deposits has the potential to provide positive reinforcements. These deposits can be triggered by the opening of the account and by subsequent savings deposits. Beyond the government contributions, the accounts will build more resources, the more they are stocked with savings. Voluntary contributions by family and friends, as well as the child, should be encouraged through financial education and other incentives. The tax treatment of the account and of contributions to the account offers an opportunity to incorporate incentives into the policy design.

There is a strong case to be made for making the initial deposit soon after birth once eligibility and a Social Security number have been established. Linking the account to the Social Security system ensures that everyone is included in the system, and endowing the account as close to the birth of the child as possible will enable the child's fund to begin to grow as soon as possible. The contribution rules also afford an opportunity to create a more progressive scheme. Families with incomes at or below the national median could receive a pro-rated bonus and be eligible to have their private contributions matched up to a certain amount on an annual basis. For example, the first $500 that is contributed to an account each year could be matched by the government on a dollar-for-dollar basis if the account holder's family has a qualified income. The matching incentives create the ability to channel program benefits to those families with less income and fewer opportunities to save. While there is a tradeoff between simplicity and progressivity, tax returns provide a source of verification, and the possibility for information sharing between the Internal Revenue Service and the federal entity in charge of the system could keep administrative costs down.

To achieve the goal of asset building through a national system of accounts, additional voluntary contributions to each account would be allowed and encouraged. Parents, family members, and friends, as well as the account holders, once they are old enough, would be allowed to contribute to children's accounts; there would be no restrictions on who invests in the account. To facilitate contributions, a system would have to be created to allow irregular and smaller-value cash payments. Allowing such contributions, along the lines of how investors purchase shares of mutual funds, would help to build a child's account balance.

The question then becomes whether or not there should be incentives to promote these voluntary contributions. The choice of whether or not to provide incentives, and to whom to provide them, will then affect whether or not there is a limit on these types of contributions. In accordance with the simplicity principle, the ASPIRE Act proposes that contributions be made on an after-tax-basis and that all gains be exempt from taxes as long as they are withdrawn according to the prevailing rules that govern distributions. For some, this tax exemption is an effective incentive. However, the initiative may be expanded to include additional incentives that are more powerful and attractive to diverse types of households.

Two types of incentives should be considered. The first type of incentive is designed to encourage contributions by lower-income persons and could take the form of an expansion of a refundable credit. For example, lower-income taxpayers could receive a larger EITC and/or Child Tax Credit, perhaps limited to $500 per person per year, provided that the additional amount is saved directly in their CSA. This could be achieved by allowing tax refunds to be saved into a CSA directly on a federal tax return. Another approach is to use progressive matches for resource-deficient households. The second type of incentive is a tax benefit that would accrue to taxpayers who contributed to their children's accounts.

These incentives could also be made stronger for lower-income taxpayers if they were in the form of refundable credits. In both of these cases, the incentives would be directed at the parents of the account holder, who would qualify for the incentive based on the information provided on their tax return. The benefits of this approach are that it has the potential to create some additional sources of incentives. Alternatively, tying incentives to the tax-filing process complicates the administration, creating additional oversight responsibilities to guard against fraud and abuse.

As with any investment strategy, there are many factors that affect returns; however, the degree to which contributions are made to an account creates large differences in asset accumulation over the life of an account. Modeled on the provisions of the ASPIRE Act, Table 20.2 illustrates how different contribution schemes, investment strategies, and rates of return

TABLE 20.2 Potential Account Accumulation for Varying Contribution Amounts

		Age			
		18	25	35	65
Contribution at birth	$500				
Supplemental contribution	$500				
Annual private contribution	$250				
Annual match contribution	$250				
Accrued balance 7%		**21,480**	34,492	67,851	516,496
Accrued balance 5%		17,409	24,496	39,901	172,452
Minimum Private Contribution Scenario					
Contribution at birth	$500				
Supplemental contribution	0				
Annual private contribution	0				
Annual match contribution	0				
Accrued balance 7%		**1,690**	2,714	5,338	40,636
Accrued balance 5%		1,203	1,693	2,758	11,920

KIDS Account Provisions

• Every child receives an automatic $500 contribution at birth.

• Children living in households that earn under $21,000 receive a one-time supplemental contribution of $500.

• Children living in households that earn up to $42,000 receive a dollar-for-dollar match on annual contributions up to $500 for 17 years.

Note: Accrued balances are calculated as a net rate of return (earnings minus fees), no withdrawals.

influence the asset pool these accounts can generate. Although there are many alternative ways to structure incentives to trigger additional deposits, the examples displayed in Table 20.2 reinforce the impact of contributions beyond the initial seed deposit.

Withdrawals and Use Restrictions

Another fundamental issue for the policy design of a children's account system is how account funds are distributed to beneficiaries. This raises the related questions of: What restrictions should be placed on the use of account funds? How long can these accounts be held? At what age can participants gain access to their funds? In many ways, the rules surrounding this issue will have the greatest influence on the public's perception of the effort because they will specify most clearly the overall purpose of the policy.

The assets which accumulate in the accounts are designed to facilitate opportunities for all children to invest in their future. There is a broad range of assets that can make a difference in people's lives, includ-

ing investing in their own human capital, buying a home, and developing some financial security. The nature of these investments will necessarily depend on the unique circumstances of each individual, so the policy design should allow for flexibility, but at issue is how much. A policy that restricts fund uses to a set of popular choices, aligned with asset-building strategies, may have a better chance of achieving stated policy goals. Alternatively, the prescribed uses may not be appropriate for every participant, some of whom might be able to make a better investment for themselves if given the chance. The rules which govern the distribution and use restrictions of account funds will make the difference in determining whether the CSAs are linked specifically to asset-building activities or can be vehicles to promote long-term savings.

The prototype proposal enables participants to have restricted access to their accounts when they reach the age of 18. At this age, they can use account resources to pay for qualified uses, such as home ownership, retirement savings, and business investment in addition to educational expenses. Indeed, many IDA programs throughout the country focus only on these asset-building activities. Before the implementation issues that must be addressed to ensure that funds are only used for these purposes, the philosophical issues should be considered first.

Given the primary role that education plays in the ability of each individual to achieve self-sufficiency and security, it appears logical to connect resources accrued in CSAs to postsecondary education. A quality education is often a precondition for other forms of wealth and asset building. The economic benefits of a college education have been reinforced repeatedly in the research literature, and the difference in earnings among workers with different levels of educational attainment has grown in recent decades. Over the course of a working life, individuals with bachelor's degrees earn on average nearly twice that of individuals with only high school degrees.[59] Furthermore, the costs of obtaining a degree continue to rise. According to the College Board, the cost of tuition and fees rose in 2003 by 14.1% at 4-year public institutions and 6% at 4-year private institutions, and it appears this trend has continued.[60]

An array of other public benefit programs exist that are focused specifically on postsecondary education, most notably Pell grants, Section 529 plans, and Coverdell education accounts, but if any children's ability to pay for college falls short, they should be able to access the resources that have been set aside for them in their CSAs. In this spirit, it will be important for these funds to be made available when participants are considering the pursuit of postsecondary education.

Beyond education, there is an array of potential investments for young adults that can make a material difference in their lives. Unfortunately, there is no standard template or standard age. Excellent choices for some may be poor choices for others. For many, the choice to become a home owner creates an opportunity to achieve a level of security, and it has documented social and economic benefits.[61] Yet even the decision to become a home owner is not advisable for all, and there is certainly no predictable age when the next generation will decide to take an interest in buying a home. But because home ownership has worked for so many Americans, there have been proposals to tie child savings accounts to home ownership as a designated eligible use. Others have focused on small business capitalization, because starting and growing these enterprises has been a successful strategy for many households to achieve security and success. Retirement savings is another common objective that has been linked to increased security and peace of mind. In 20 years' time, there may be other types of investment that will be available to children being born today that will greatly enhance their opportunity to thrive; we just don't know what they are at this time.

Because of the broad investment choices that may be beneficial to individuals, the system of children's savings accounts being introduced in the United Kingdom will impose no use restrictions on accumulated funds once account holders reach the age of 18. This approach was decided upon after a series of public consultations. While recognizing that there is benefit in trying to ensure that some funds are not "wasted" on undesirable spending, the policy makers felt that restricting uses would create additional implementation costs and run counter to the policy objectives: "to help make young adults more aware of the financial opportunities and responsibilities that they will face."[62] This choice was also made with the expectation that the child trust fund initiative would be augmented by a national campaign to increase financial literacy. The main concern of the architects of the UK effort was the policing of restrictions, and although the experience of restricted IDA programs in the United States was cited, it was noted that these programs were small scale and locally delivered.

Establishing an age threshold when account holders may access their accounts does not imply that there should be a requirement to spend down account resources. It could be that the account functions as a lifetime savings account, where the account can be kept open and funds used when needed. The key would be to have account rules that govern distributions in a manner that combines some flexibility with maintaining asset-building use restrictions.

PROGRAM IMPLEMENTATION

The universal provision of children's savings accounts will require that a centrally administered account management system be created. The most logical manager of such a system is the federal government. Yet there are many roles to play, including account manager, rule maker, and compliance enforcer. Some of these functions can be contracted out to private sector entities or assigned to the states.

The prototype proposal calls for the creation of an administrative entity similar to the one that currently operates the retirement savings plan which the federal government provides to its employees. The Thrift Savings Plan (TSP) is a government-sponsored retirement savings and investment plan, which offers the same type of savings and tax benefits that many private corporations offer to their employees. The TSP was established by Congress in 1986 to provide retirement income; it is a defined contribution plan that accrues assets based on participant contributions and the financial performance of invested contributions.

One of the central features of the TSP that should be replicated in a CSA system is a choice of investments. Participants may choose between five index funds designed to track the performance of different market segments, such as government securities, international markets, small cap firms, and the broad U.S. stock market. Index funds provide a relatively prudent way to invest, and participants are allowed to distribute their assets among these funds, so they may increase or decrease their diversification and manage their own risk. The experience of the TSP is an appropriate reference model because it currently manages accounts for over 3 million active and retired federal employees and has a similar set of services as would be required by a CSA system, which would serve the 4 million children born each year.[63] The economies of scale that the TSP has achieved help to keep its administrative costs low.[64] The size of the overall investment pool has enabled the TSP to negotiate a low investment management fee with its private sector investment manager compared to other types of accounts.[65]

The two central distinctions between the TSP and the CSA proposal is funding and the use of the funds. As a traditional, employer-sponsored retirement plan, contributions to the TSP are administered by the employer, and the distribution rules are designed to meet the needs of retirement. The CSA system would not be employer based, and there could be more complex distribution rules if uses are restricted. Still, the experience of the TSP identifies the necessary components of an implementation system; they include an oversight board, an account manager, an investment manager, and account servicing.

As with the TSP, CSAs will require federal oversight, but other functions may be performed by governmental or nongovernmental entities. From an investment and management standpoint, the TSP provides a good model because a private sector fund manager can oversee investments and offer a limited set of investment options, enough to provide for a range of risk aversion and market opportunity. Account servicing can, likewise, be contracted out.

However, it may be practical to have other functions administered directly by the federal government. Having a federal entity fund the CSA system and hold the accounts may help to solve one of the more cumbersome implementation issues: how to identify and provide account benefits to children in families who have no experience with the financial sector. This will be particularly true if the program is one of universal eligibility and mandatory participation. Since many households have no connection to the financial services sector and more than 30% of all families have no financial assets, creating a federal system is an effective way to introduce many to the "world of assets."[66]

An additional implementation model to consider for CSAs would replicate the structure of the Section 529 plans for college savings, which have taken shape in the unique context of American federalism. While the federal government has established a broad set of rules to govern these savings accounts, it has allowed each of the 50 states to craft its own system. Section 529 rules require each state to run a centralized program, so all participants are in the same system, but this franchise can be awarded to a single provider in the private sector. Offering the provider the chance to develop economies of scale, each state is in a strong position to negotiate among competing providers for a competitive fee structure. Federal policies ensure full portability so Section 529 plan investors can keep an account in one state even if they move to another, but individual states can take the initiative and introduce additional incentives to promote progressivity and savings.[67]

The development of appropriate oversight measures to ensure that account holders are complying with program rules will depend on the program's ultimate policy design and implementation structure. Whatever system is created, there will be an interest in minimizing and deterring fraud. The imposition of use restrictions will require a more-extensive strategy to oversee the distribution of funds than if funds can be withdrawn without restrictions. Likewise, additional mechanisms to monitor accounts may be needed if these accounts are held by a range of financial institutions rather than the public sector. Regardless of what approach is pursued, it is envisioned that each account will have a unique reference number tied to a child's Social Security number. This will make it possible for the compliance agent to certify that only one account has been opened for each eligible child.

The system most amenable to monitoring compliance is one with universal eligibility, unrestricted use of funds, and central administration. This mirrors the path taken by the United Kingdom in the child trust fund initiative, although a range of financial institutions will provide accounts. If account holders are permitted to use their accumulated resources for any purpose they choose, then many administrative compliance issues are minimized. But if account holders are allowed to withdraw funds only for a restricted set of uses, then a series of implementation mechanisms will be required to ensure that funds are used properly.

Establishing a policy to provide every child with an account will be a significant undertaking, representing a large national commitment. From a policy perspective, there are associated costs and benefits which must be untangled before policy makers should be expected to confirm this commitment. Developing precise budget costs is beyond the scope of this chapter, but it is possible to distinguish the key cost components of the ASPIRE Act proposal and evaluate the factors which would influence any CSA proposal. The program costs are primarily composed of the costs of the public contribution to the accounts. A universal system will require an account for each of the approximately 4 million children born each year. If every one of these children were given an account at birth endowed with $500, the size of the government's commitment would be $2 billion a year. Additional public contributions would eventually raise the cost of the effort as the initial cohort matures. Some of these costs may eventually be offset if this cohort is required to repay the value of the initial seed contribution once they enter the workforce. Given the unique nature of the policy, the overall costs (and many of the benefits) will not be realized for decades to come.

Another component of program costs would be the augmentation of the initial contribution with annual savings incentives. The cost of this feature depends on how households respond to the savings incentive and how the incentive is structured over time. Key

questions to answer in order to estimate the cost of the match contributions include:

- What is the match rate? ($1:1, $.50:1)
- What is the annual cap of the voluntary contributions that can be matched? ($500, $1,000)
- When is the incentive available? (every year, tied to specific ages)
- What are the limits placed on the incentives? (limited number of years, a lifetime cap)
- Should voluntary contributions be after-tax or eligible for a tax deduction?
- Who is eligible to receive a match? (80%, 100%, 120% of national median income)

The number of issues that these questions raise makes it difficult to estimate the program costs of different incentive schemes. Initial cost estimates for the ASPIRE Act is $37.5 billion over 10 years. The cost in the first year when accounts are opened is $3.25 billion. Annual costs will rise as each year as a new cohort becomes eligible for account benefits. Over 20 years, the total estimated cost is $85.6 billion. These estimates assume that only children born after the program's commencement date will be eligible.

Another component of the costs which should be taken into account over the long term is the cost of tax-free withdrawals. Normally, the government would be in line to collect taxes on accrued savings, but if these accounts are created as tax-preferred vehicles, the earnings are sheltered from future taxation. However, given that these are accounts created at birth, the impact of this cost does not appear for several decades. It will become a significant cost component of the proposal, but one that depends on predicting tax rates in the distant future.

Program costs can be lowered if the contributions and match rates are less generous. The UK's child trust fund proposal is being launched without matching incentives and with a more modest initial contribution (equivalent to $400 for each newborn, and $800 for each child born to a low-income family). Replicating this approach for the 4 million Americans born each year would have a 10-year program cost of $15.7 billion, or only $2.13 billion on an annual basis. While more parsimonious, the universal provision of an account for every child has the potential to serve as a powerful savings vehicle for all citizens. The major contribution of this approach from a policy

TABLE 20.3 Estimates of Program Cost for Prototype Children's Savings Accounts: Net Present Value

First Year	10 Years	20 Years
$3.25 billion	$37.5 billion	$85.6 billion

Assumptions: 4 million children born each year; $500 endowment at birth; $500 supplemental contribution prorated for children in families earning up to the national median income; dollar-for-dollar matching contribution up to first $500 for children in families earning up to the national median income; contributions indexed to inflation rate of 3%; and 6% discount rate.

standpoint is that it establishes the infrastructure to promote subsequent savings and asset-building strategies rather than committing to investment in these accounts upfront.

AN ACCOUNTS-BASED APPROACH TO ASSET BUILDING FOR CHILDREN

Program Benefits and Challenges

The growing body of theoretical and empirical research that links asset holding to a range of positive outcomes has strengthened the rationale for incorporating an assets perspective into the formulation of social policy.[68] This is because many of the observed asset effects are linked to greater economic and social well-being, such as increased household and residential stability and a greater sense of security and control over one's life. Furthermore, the presence of assets in a household appears to influence behavior and leads individuals to plan and think about the future.

Understanding the dynamics of these asset effects is particularly relevant when thinking about child well-being. For children nested within families, the presence of assets is associated with a range of positive outcomes. For example, home ownership appears to improve child well-being through higher educational attainment, academic performance, and emotional and cognitive development as well as lower teenage pregnancy and behavioral problems.[69] Beyond home ownership, other types of assets, such as savings and net worth, have been shown to have a positive effect on child well-being. The very presence of savings in a household is associated with higher expectations of high school graduation.[70] Also, household income and wealth are positively associated with children's cognitive development, health, and behavioral development.[71] These empirical findings provide sup-

port for asset-based policy interventions that focus on children.

Creating a universal system of accounts for children is a powerful approach to social policy because it has the potential to contribute to both economic growth and social development. It does so by investing on an individual basis in a manner that creates widespread opportunities. While investment returns are not guaranteed, they are likely to offer all participants access to a modest stock of financial assets when they begin their adult lives. For some, this asset pool can be used to seed profitable and productive investments; for others, it may provide a sense of security that many now lack. The public investment signals that society has an interest in the success of all children, and they, in turn, will be responsible to make appropriate choices throughout their lives.

In addition to the individual benefits, investing in children can have large multiplier effects, especially when it is linked to increasing social engagement and expanding opportunity. In the long run, building wealth through children's accounts and other means has the potential to help break the vicious cycle of intergenerational poverty by equipping children with valuable skills and resources they need to maximize their life chances. These include access to some of the most basic aspects of financial literacy—a vital skill set which will be needed to navigate throughout the life course—and a modest pool of resources at their disposal to help them succeed. Furthermore, for several reasons, it makes the most sense to focus an asset-building policy on children. The very nature of asset building is long term; investing when children are born provides the most time for assets to grow, and the dynamics of accumulation will provide their own lessons. Also, the experience of asset holding may itself be transformative, changing attitudes for the better. It is precisely the extended time horizon which accompanies asset and account ownership which should be incorporated into the current thinking about child welfare policy.

A policy of children's saving accounts should be designed to reinforce a message that combines rights with responsibilities. For many, the public contributions into their accounts will be an important incentive for savings. For others, it will signal the importance of planning for the future. And there will be rules governing account withdrawals that will send vital social messages about what types of purchases are productive investments. The repayment of the initial deposit, once steady employment has been secured, will facilitate the seeding of the next generation's growth. The sharing of prosperity may have social benefits that cannot be predicted, and the ultimate impact of giving every child a stake is, of course, unknown, yet broad inclusion is itself a worthy public investment that will increase society's collective capacity to participate in the economy and society as a whole.

An additional benefit to implementing a system of children's accounts is that it is consistent with contemporary approaches to social policy, which have moved away from guaranteed entitlements and toward more account-based support mechanisms. In contrast to traditional income supports, the investments in the account are no substitute for social protection. Rather, they are intended to promote social and economic development at the household level, at the same time as they advance fiscal stability, savings, and investment at the macroeconomic level. This account-based approach to social policy has been emerging for decades and is linked to the rise of policies designed specifically to promote asset holdings. The state creates the accounts (401(k)s, IRAs, Section 529s, etc.), defines the policies, provides the regulations, and offers the tax benefits. The collective intent is to subsidize asset building through a system of asset accounts. The proliferation of asset accounts as a main instrument of social policy is a historic development, described by Sherraden as a transition from a social welfare state to a social investment state.[72] Whether asset-based policy should replace social insurance is open for debate, but the emerging transition is grounded in the broad policy consensus that asset holdings make a material difference in people's lives and open the door to economic and social opportunity.

Yet the tools are incomplete. The reliance on tax benefits to promote asset building has until now been problematic because the poor, who do not qualify for the tax benefits, are unable to benefit. The current structure of the tax code has made asset-based tax benefits highly regressive. There is no universal, progressive, asset-based policy, and the state has become an instrument of reinforcing the prevailing inequality of asset holdings among the population.

A major benefit of the CSA initiative would be its ability to reach all citizens, especially those currently excluded from receiving asset-building incentives, and provide access to asset-building activities that could last a lifetime. The universal extension of this opportunity will reduce social inequality and increase economic activity. Encouraging and subsidizing asset holding by all citizens can contribute to growth in the long term. American history is full of examples where small initial investments were remade into substantial fortunes, but more profoundly, small investments have been shown to make significant differences in people's lives when they are used to provide security or an investment in the future. Still, devising any system of child accounts faces a series of challenges that policy makers will have to overcome.

Reaching out to households that currently have no connection to mainstream financial services will be a major achievement of any CSA initiative, but it also represents one of its greatest challenges. Creating a system that is truly inclusive will be no small task given that roughly 10% of the general population, and 30% of low-income households, have no connection to mainstream financial institutions.[73] Ensuring that everyone has access to an account would be a major achievement, which would, in turn, facilitate additional public and private investments. The tax return, which is used to facilitate other asset-building objectives, is not an ideal vehicle for a universal account because many low-income families are not required to file. A refundable credit may provide an incentive to file if that is the chosen funding mechanism, but this incentive may not be available every year, creating some confusion.

It may not be possible to implement a universal, inclusive system all in one blow; there may be a period of transition during which the initiative is ramped up to scale. The transition period creates its own challenges, including how to keep costs down and how to avoid the arbitrary awarding of benefits. A full phase-in of an accounts-at-birth program will eventually leave no child behind, but initially a threshold eligibility date will necessarily create arbitrary distinctions which may be troubling.

Assessment of the Current Terrain

The challenges in building a universal account-based system are significant, but they certainly can be addressed through the process of program design and implementation. Constructing a system of accounts that is workable and effective is achievable. The greater challenge is gaining political support for the proposal, sufficient to shepherd it through the legislative process. This may ultimately depend on policy makers accepting the premise that inclusive asset-building policies are a means to promote social and economic development. These policy goals should be distinguished from other antipoverty objectives because, at the core, asset-based policy is intended to enable individuals to exert greater control over their lives and to expand their capacity to take advantage of the diverse opportunities offered by American society. Any large-scale asset-based policy effort should complement, rather than replace, existing policies that provide social insurance.

The central problem with the current array of asset policies is that they are regressive and, for the most part, exclude the poor. A targeted effort may address this deficiency, but it creates a new problem of how to craft an effective targeting mechanism. More significantly, it loses much of its political appeal. For better or worse, policy makers are likely to be more responsive if program benefits are distributed broadly. In order to make the effort progressive, it should be made universal. Beyond the political calculation this strategy entails, there are sound justifications for pursuing universal children's accounts. Asset building and savings are sound objectives for every citizen, and universal access to an account offers all citizens the opportunity to participate, regardless of the income status of their family.

The fiscal impact of a children's account system depends on the manner in which the policy is crafted. The issues laid out in this chapter have identified the major cost variables of a children's account system and signaled how the budgetary costs can be minimized. A voluntary system with no public contribution would replicate existing policies that exclude many of the people who would benefit from the policy the most. A universal system is able to reach those currently excluded while providing every participant the opportunity to benefit. Given the preceding analysis, the most promising approach would be a universal system, with progressive public contributions and incentives to encourage voluntary contributions, deposited in a range of no-frills investment funds. Unfortunately, the most promising approach may be the one that requires the most political leadership to enact.

Notes

1. Boshara's (2003c) formulation of this proposal was called "American stakeholder accounts." Also see Curley and Sherraden (2000); and Goldberg (2005).

2. The ASPIRE Act, introduced in the 108th congressional session (S. 2751 and H.R. 4939), was initially sponsored by Senators Rick Santorum (R-PA) and Jon Corzine (D-NJ) and Representatives Harold Ford, Jr. (D-TN), Phil English (R-PA), Thomas Petri (R-WI), and Patrick Kennedy (D-RI).

3. Phillips (2002).

4. Williams (2003b) estimates that up to one quarter of the adults in the United States may have ancestors who can trace their legacy of asset ownership to the Homestead Act.

5. Skocpol (1996).

6. Subcommittee on Education and Health of the Joint Economic Committee (1988).

7. Skocpol (1996, p. 63) cites the statistics that only 9 out of 100 young people attended college in 1939, but the rate doubled by 1947.

8. U.S. Department of Housing and Urban Development (2003).

9. Cramer, Parrish, and Boshara (2006).

10. U.S. Congress, Joint Committee on Taxation (2002).

11. Shapiro (2004).

12. Aizcorbe, Kennickell, and Moore (2003).

13. Aizcorbe, Kennickell, and Moore (2003).

14. Aizcorbe, Kennickell, and Moore (2003).

15. Oliver and Shapiro (1995) first proposed a definition for asset poverty in their 1995 book, *Black Wealth/White Wealth*. They defined "resource deficient" households as those without enough net financial worth reserves to survive 3 months at the poverty line.

16. Haveman and Wolff (2000) have built upon this approach and used existing data sources to estimate a series of asset poverty measures.

17. Haveman and Wolff (2000).

18. Haveman and Wolff (2000).

19. Sherraden (1991), p. 7.

20. Oliver and Shapiro (1995), p. 2.

21. Scanlon and Page-Adams (2001).

22. Scanlon and Page-Adams (2001).

23. Bynner and Despotidou (2001), p. 3.

24. Key findings from *Saving and performance in the American dream demonstration: A national demonstration of individual development accounts* (Schreiner, Clancy, & Sherraden, 2001) include the observation that the majority of people who participated in the demonstration were savers; and program characteristics, such as match rate, financial education, and use of direct deposit, are linked to savings performance.

25. Sherraden (2003).

26. HM Treasury (2003).

27. Sherraden (2001).

28. Thomas Paine's essay on *Agrarian Justice* was written in 1795–1796 and introduced the broad themes of rights and reciprocity, security and humanity, and poverty and social justice. He proposed "to create a national fund, out of which there shall be paid to every person, when arrived at the age of twenty-one years, the sum of fifteen pounds sterling, as a compensation, in part for the loss of his or her natural inheritance, by the introduction of the system of landed property" (p. 476).

29. Paine (1795), p. 484.

30. Paine (1795), p. 483.

31. Curley and Sherraden (2000).

32. According to the Inland Revenue, the child benefit in the United Kingdom for 2007 is £18.10 per week for the eldest child and £12.10 per week for each other child, worth approximately $1,800 and $1,200, respectively, each year.

33. National Commission on Children (1991), p. 12.

34. Lee and Greenstein (2003).

35. According to Lee and Greenstein (2003), the 2003 legislation that accelerated the schedule to increase the Child Tax Credit provided fewer benefits to lower-income households because it did not accelerate the increase in the credit's refundability.

36. Haveman (2003).

37. For 2006 returns, for example, each dependent exemption allowed a filer to cut taxable income by $3,400.

38. In 2003, the Child and Dependent Care Tax Credit provided a maximum credit of $3,000 for one dependent and $6,000 for two or more dependents for employment-related child care.

39. The EITC functions as a work incentive because it adds 40 cents to every dollar of earnings up to about $10,000 for families with two or more children. It has a maximum benefit of $4,000. The credit is phased out beginning when the taxpayer's income exceeds $13,520 at a rate of 21.06% in families with two or more children. It is completely phased out when this family's modified adjusted gross income reaches $33,178.

40. Scholz (1994).

41. Another set of proposals focused on introducing refundable tax credits linked to educational objectives. The Education for the Twenty-First Century Act was introduced by Senator Tom Daschle (D-SD) to create a refundable tax credit of up to $1,500 per academic year. The act would have provided additional tax deductions of up to $10,000 per student for higher education costs and tax deductions for interest paid on student loans. A similar approach was proposed in the House of Representatives by Representative Joseph Pitts (R-PA) to create an annual refundable credit of up to $450 per child to pay for educational expenses.

42. Coverdell education savings accounts initially allowed taxpayers to contribute up to $500 annually (since expanded to $2,000 annually) to an account for each child under the age of 18. Section 529 college savings plans allow earnings on after-tax contributions to be withdrawn tax-free for educational purposes.

43. The SEED Policy and Practice Initiative is a partnership among funders, Corporation for Enterprise Development (CFED), Center for Social Development (CSD), University of Kansas School of Social Welfare, New America Foundation, and a number of community and experimental partners across the country. See http://seed.cfed.org.

44. Coons and Petrick (1992); Higgins et al. (1991).

45. These questions were first raised and considered by Fred Goldberg, a former IRS commissioner, in an article that provides a valuable discussion of implementing children's savings accounts using a tax credit approach (Goldberg 2005).

46. Okun (1975).

47. Okun (1975).

48. Blank (2002), p. 25.

49. Blank writes, "It is possible that the general distaste for redistributive transfers that characterize the opinion of many economists may be the result of a highly selective set of research studies, which have focused on populations where the costs of redistributive transfers are likely to be highest" (Blank, 2002, p. 25).

50. The Social Security program should be considered as a universal system, but it only applies to covered workers.

51. There is an important distinction between fraud and noncompliance. Noncompliant applicants may unwittingly claim benefits to which they are not entitled if they do not understand program requirements.

52. Congress has appropriated funds to increase EITC compliance after receiving reports that the noncompliance rate was between 27% and 32%.

53. Haider et al. (2003).

54. Brauner and Zedlewski (1999).

55. FMS annually disburses more than $1.7 trillion to over 100 million individuals via Social Security, veterans' benefits, income tax refunds, and other federal payments.

56. Goldberg (2005).

57. These issues were addressed by Goldberg (2005) in some detail.

58. Goldberg (2005), p. 23.

59. Day and Newburger (2002).

60. According to the College Board (2003a), tuition and fees at a 4-year public institution averaged $579 more than the previous year ($4,694 versus $4,115, a 14.1% increase). At 4-year private institutions, tuition and fees averaged $1,114 more than the previous year ($19,710 versus $18,596, a 6% increase).

61. Scanlon and Page-Adams (2001).

62. HM Treasury (2001), p. 16: "To restrict use of assets at maturity would undermine the sense of being a responsible stakeholder that the Child Trust Fund and its associated education would be intended to provide to young adults."

63. In 2002, the TSP had $101 billion in assets under management, paid out $2.5 billion in benefits, and cost $70.6 million to operate.

64. According to the Thrift Savings Plan (2003) financial statement, administrative overhead costs per participant were $23. Additional factors in minimizing administrative costs include providing relatively restricted access to the account and account information, limiting investment options, and restricting the ability to change investment choices compared to private sector mutual fund companies.

65. TSP has an expenses management ratio that ranges between .06% and .07%, or 6–7 cents for every $1,000 invested.

66. Barr (2003).

67. Rhode Island and Maine, for example, use fees generated from their Section 529 account holders to fund a savings match for low- to moderate-income state residents, and Michigan and Louisiana provide a savings match through state appropriations. See Clancy (2003).

68. Sherraden (1991); Scanlon and Page-Adams (2001); Bynner and Despotidou (2001).

69. Scanlon and Page-Adams (2001).

70. Zhan and Sherraden (2003).

71. Williams (2003a).

72. Sherraden (2003).

73. Aizcorbe, Kennickell, and Moore (2003). According to the Survey of Consumer Finances, of households in the bottom 20% of income, only 70.9% have transaction bank accounts. Overall, 90.9% of households have such accounts.

References

Aizcorbe, A., Kennickell, A., & Moore, K. (2003). *Recent changes in U.S. family finances: Evidence from the 1998 and 2001 Survey of Consumer Finances.* Washington, DC: Federal Reserve Board.

Barr, M. (2003). *Banking the poor.* A working paper prepared for the Center on Urban and Metropolitan Policy. Washington, DC: Brookings Institution.

Blank, R. (2002). *Can equity and efficiency complement each other?* Cambridge, MA: National Bureau of Economic Research.

Boshara, R. (2001). The rationale for assets, asset building policies, and IDAs for the poor. In R. Boshara (Ed.), *Building assets* (5–23). Washington, DC: Corporation for Enterprise Development.

Boshara, R. (2003a). *American stakeholder accounts.* Issue Brief No. 2. Washington, DC: New America Foundation.

Boshara, R. (2003b). *Federal policy and asset building.* Issue Brief No. 1. Washington, DC: New America Foundation.

Boshara, R. (2003c, January–February). The $6,000 solution. *Atlantic Monthly.*

Brauner, S., & Zedlewski, S. (1999). *Declines in food stamp and welfare participation: Is there a connection?* Washington, DC: Urban Institute.

Bynner, J., & Despotidou, S. (2001). *Effect of assets on life chances.* London: Centre for Longitudinal Studies, Institute of Education.

Cavanaugh, F. (2002). *Feasibility of Social Security individual accounts.* Washington, DC: AARP.

Clancy, M. (2001). *College savings plans: Implications for policy and for a children and youth savings account policy demonstration.* Research background paper CYSAPD 01-6. St. Louis, MO: Center for Social Development, Washington University.

Clancy, M. (2003). *College savings plans and individual development accounts: Potential for partnership.* St. Louis, MO: Center for Social Development, Washington University.

College Board. (2003a). *Trends in college pricing 2003.* Washington, DC: Author. Available: http://www.collegeboard.com

College Board. (2003b). *Trends in student aid 2003.* Washington, DC: Author. Available: http://www.collegeboard.com.

Coons, C., & Petrick, E. (1992). A decade of making dreams into reality: Lessons from the I Have a Dream Program. *Yale Law and Policy Review, 10*(1), 1–10.

Cramer, R., Parrish, L., & Boshara, R. (2006). *The asset report 2006: A review, assessment, and forecast of federal assets policy.* Washington, DC: New America Foundation.

Curley, J., & Sherraden, M. (2000). *Policy lessons from children's allowances for children's accounts.* Arlington, VA: Child Welfare League of America.

Day, J., & Newburger, E. (2002). *The big payoff: Educational attainment and synthetic estimates of work-life earnings.* Washington, DC: U.S. Census Bureau.

Employee Benefit Research Institute. (2001). *Individual Social Security accounts: Administrative issues.* Issue Brief 236. Washington, DC: Employee Benefit Research Institute.

Fitzgerald, P. (2004, March 1). *Statement to Senate Committee on Governmental Affairs: Oversight of the thrift savings plan: Ensuring the integrity of federal employee retirement savings.* Washington, DC: The Federal Retirement Thrift Investment Board.

General Accounting Office. (1999). *Social Security reform: Information on using a voluntary approach to individual accounts.* (GAO 03-309). Washington, DC: General Accounting Office.

Goldberg, F., Jr., (2005). The universal piggy bank: Designing and implementing a system of savings accounts for children. In M. Sherraden (Ed.), *Inclusion in the American dream: Assets, poverty, and public policy* (303–322). New York: Oxford University Press.

Haider, S., Jacknowitz, A., & Schoeni, R. (2003). Food stamps and the elderly: Why is participation so low? *Journal of Human Resources,* 38(Spring), 1080–1111.

Haveman, R. (2003). When work alone is not enough. In I. Sawhill (Ed.), *One percent for kids* (40–55). Washington DC: Brookings Institution Press.

Haveman, R., & Bershadker, A. (2001). The "inability to be self-reliant" as an indicator of poverty: Trends for the U.S., 1975–97. *Review of Income and Wealth,* 47(3), 335–360.

Haveman, R., & Wolff, E. (2000). *Who are the asset poor: Levels, trends and composition, 1983–1998?* St. Louis, MO: Center for Social Development, Washington University.

Higgins, C., Furano, K., Toso, C., & Branch, A. (1991). *I Have a Dream in Washington DC: Initial report.* Philadelphia: Public/Private Ventures.

HM Treasury. (2001). *Delivering saving and assets for all, and delivering savings and assets—consultation responses.* London: Author.

HM Treasury. (2003). *Detailed proposals for the child trust fund.* London: Author.

Howard, C. (1997). *The hidden welfare state: Tax expenditures and social policy in the United States.* Princeton, NJ: Princeton University Press.

Kelly, G., & Lissauer, R. (2000). *Ownership for all.* London: IPPR.

Lee, A., & Greenstein, R. (2003). *How the new tax law alters the child tax credit and how low-income families are affected.* Washington, DC: Center on Budget and Policy Priorities.

LeGrand, J., & Nissan, D. (2000). *A capital idea: Helping the young to help themselves.* London: Fabian Society.

National Commission on Children. (1991). *Beyond rhetoric: A new American agenda for children and families.* Washington, DC: Author.

Office of Management and Budget, Executive Office of the President. (2007). *Fiscal year 2008 federal budget: Analytical perspectives.* Washington, DC: Office of Management and Budget.

Okun, A. (1975). *Equity and efficiency: The big tradeoff.* Washington, DC: Brookings Institution.

Oliver, M., & Shapiro, T. (1995). *Black wealth/white wealth: A new perspective on racial inequality.* New York: Routledge.

Paine, T. (1795). Agrarian justice. In M. Foot and I. Kramnick (Eds.), *Thomas Paine reader* (1987). New York: Penguin Books.

Phillips, K. (2002). *Wealth and democracy.* New York: Broadway.

Scanlon, E., & Page-Adams, D. (2001). Effects of asset holding on neighborhoods, families, and children: A review of research. In R. Boshara (Ed.), *Building assets.* Washington, DC: Corporation for Enterprise Development.

Scholz, J. K. (1994). The earned income tax credit: Participation, compliance, and antipoverty effectiveness. *National Tax Journal,* 47(1), 63–87.

Shapiro, T. (2004). *The hidden cost of being African American.* New York: Oxford University Press.

Sherraden, M. (1991). *Assets and the poor.* New York: Sharp.

Sherraden, M. (2001). *Singapore announces "baby bonus" and children's development accounts.* St. Louis, MO: Center for Social Development, Washington University.

Sherraden, M. (2003). From the social welfare state to the social investment state. *Shelterforce, 128,* 10–15.

Sherraden, M., Schreiner, M., & Beverly, S. (2003). Income, institutions, and saving performance in individual development accounts. *Economic Development Quarterly,* 17(1), 95–112.

Schreiner, M., Clancy, M., & Sherraden, M. (2001). *Savings and performance in the American Dream demonstration: A national demonstration of individual development accounts.* St. Louis, MO: Center for Social Development, Washington University.

Skocpol, T. (1996). Delivering for young families. *American Prospect,* 7(28), 66–72.

Subcommittee on Education and Health, Joint Economic Committee. (1988, December 14). *A cost-benefit analysis of government investment in post-secondary education under the World War II GI Bill.* Washington, DC: Author

Thrift Savings Plan. (2003, March 19). *Financial statements of the Thrift Savings Plan.* Washington, DC: The Federal Retirement Thrift Investment Board.

U.S. Congress, Joint Committee on Taxation. (2002). *Estimates of federal tax expenditures for fiscal years 2002–2006.* Washington, DC: U.S. Government Printing Office.

U.S. Department of Housing and Urban Development. (2003). *Housing market conditions 2003.* Washington, DC: Author

Williams, T. (2003a). *The impact of household wealth and poverty on child development outcomes: Examining asset effects.* Unpublished doctoral dissertation, Washington University, St. Louis, MO.

Williams, T. (2003b). *Asset building policy as a response to wealth inequality: Drawing implications from the Homestead Act.* St. Louis, MO: Center for Social Development, Washington University.

Wolff, E. (2001). Recent trends in wealth ownership, 1983–1998. In T. Shapiro & E. Wolff (Eds.), *Assets for the poor* (34–73). New York: Russell Sage Foundation.

Zhan, M., & Sherraden, M. (2003). Assets, expectations, and educational achievement. *Social Service Review, 77*(2), 191–211.

Part VI

International Issues in Child Welfare Research

In this final section, we examine the broader program design and policy issues in child welfare from an international perspective. What responsibility do societies have to provide for the common good of all their children? What is the collective responsibility societies have to make sure that all children have the basic rights of a decent childhood, adequate health care, a good education, and reasonable opportunity? How do societies ensure the safety and security of all children? Clearly, the basic foundation for a good childhood experience is in place for most children in the United States and other developed democracies. Most children have parents who deeply love them, are committed to their success in life, and have resources to provide them with ample opportunity. But there are also many children for whom the basic foundation is not assured, and this shortcoming is often related to insufficient resources at the family and community levels. The central assumption of this section is that a good society, a wealthy society, a civilized society has an obligation to ensure that all children have the

basic foundation required to fully participate in a free-market democratic society. The measure of a society is how well it is able to meet this obligation.

In the first chapter of this section, "Beyond Child Welfare: International Perspectives on Child and Family Policies," Sheila Kamerman and Alfred Kahn look beyond child welfare to child well-being. With a growing awareness that investment in children is increasingly urgent, Kamerman and Kahn propound holistic development as the means to better meet the needs of vulnerable populations. This approach is propelled by a growing attention to children's rights as the basis for intervention. Relying on a review of a UNICEF study of the UN Convention on the Rights of the Child (of which the United States is, tellingly, not a signatory), the authors discuss the progress that has been made by families and children in response to advancing the right of a child to be raised in a healthy family environment with government support and assistance. According to the authors, "This focus on children's rights as the framework for new child and family policy initiatives points to a significantly broader focus than that of protection—or a deficit policy model, targeted on problems." Highlighting the growing awareness of these rights among industrialized nations, the authors engage in a review and analysis of child welfare in the European Union. While they find declines in mortality rates and teen suicide, they emphasize the continued exclusion of children and their families from mainstream society.

As common sense would dictate and studies have corroborated, a major factor predicting the welfare of children is whether children are raised in a female-headed household. At this writing, the United States is one of a small number of industrialized countries that pay little or no attention to the gap between wages and family need, thus creating a "penalty" for many families who choose to have children. In "The Effect of Children on the Income Status of Female-Headed Households: An Intercountry Comparison," Martha Ozawa and Yongwoo Lee present findings from studies detailing the financial challenges faced by women raising children on their own. This is a particularly important area because female-headed households are the fastest growing group of families living in poverty, and this fact underscores the tendency in the United States to blame such poverty, disadvantage, social exclusion, and lack of opportunity on the very people who find themselves experiencing such problems.

Beginning with a historical perspective that examines the effect of changing economies on the ability of families to survive and prosper—from agriculture to manufacturing, industrialization to service industries, open trade to rapid globalization—the authors examine the deficit between individual earnings and the financial needs of families. At a time when the middle class is shrinking and real wages are falling, this economic conundrum is a significant factor in the child welfare debate. Looking at other countries—Great Britain, France, Denmark, and Sweden—the authors are able to confirm that a significant proportion of those living in poverty do so as a result of a system that fails to help families earn enough income to keep pace with the addition of dependents and their ever-increasing needs. Since World War II, several European countries, particularly Nordic countries, have made progress in this regard. With policies developed to meet the particular needs of workers with children, these countries have narrowed the gap between worker income and disposable family income. Most significant among their conclusions is that the United States is ambivalent at best with regard to this issue. A country that blames its downtrodden for their state is slow to act on matters of public policy. Most significant in this regard is the persistent failure of the government to address the effect of the shortcomings of the current economic system on female-headed households.

It is important to note that the studies, data, ideas, suggestions, and speculations contained in this section are cast in a less than fertile environment for the protection and welfare of children. Since the mid-1990s, there has been little progress toward a cohesive and comprehensive approach to dealing with the structural causes and consequences of poverty. At the core of this dilemma is a lack of meaningful public discourse, a failure to acknowledge the severity of the problem, and a persistent apathy or, worse, an unwillingness to confront "someone else's" problem. While discussion of the value of the social safety net has been on the table since 1935, the United States continues to lag behind the rest of the developed world in the attention it pays to the needy.

21

Beyond Child Welfare: International Perspectives on Child and Family Policies

Sheila B. Kamerman

Alfred J. Kahn

INTRODUCTION: FROM CHILD WELFARE TO CHILD WELL-BEING

The history of child welfare is a story of a constantly growing base or an expanding view of scope: from undifferentiated institutional care to more specialized institutional care; from "child saving" and protection to group care, to foster family care; from selective and specialized foster care, to community-based interventions stressing family preservation and support—and so forth. This was inevitable as child welfare agencies sought to be responsive to demographic and social changes and to be effective in reducing child and family problems. It was a major milestone and a building on experience when conviction spread that a prevention mandate must be added, although since the "problem" was variously conceptualized, there were always diverse concepts of prevention. Now, in the 21st century, we may be entering a new phase.

In 1989, findings from our research on the state of social services for troubled children, youth, and families in the United States emphasized that child welfare in the narrow sense, and social service reforms in the broader sense, albeit important, were not sufficient, alone, to solve the serious problems confronting children and their families (Kamerman & Kahn, 1990a, 1990b). Even if all of the recommendations for the reform of child welfare and social services are implemented and prove successful, troubled children and families will remain. We stated then:

> Only the naïve or the irresponsible would blame major social problems on social service failures or claim that social services reform will eliminate poverty or social pathology. Social service reform is urgent but it cannot be successful unless the society attends to much else as well. (Kamerman & Kahn, 1990a, p. 167)

Social services hold no mystical power to wipe away human suffering. At best, we can hope to sustain, rehabilitate, and perhaps enrich people's lives. . . . We also need to do more. Social service reforms should be but one facet of a comprehensive crusade against the root causes of pain and misery: poverty, substance abuse, homelessness, hunger, and disease. Only a committed effort at all levels of society can eliminate these scourges and finally produce lasting benefits for children and families. (Kamerman & Kahn, 1990b, p. 13)

For a variety of reasons, concern for child well-being has won new attention in the advanced industrialized countries (Kamerman, Neuman, Waldfogel, & Brooks-Gunn, 2003). To achieve the goal of enhanced child well-being, we focus here on "what else?" The question arises as to whether child welfare is not better conceptualized as one of many subcomponents of child development rather than as the major organizing rubric, and the umbrella construct should be child well-being.

The awareness of societal aging has made it clear that investment in children is increasingly urgent (Gatenio-Gabel & Kamerman, 2006). As Esping-Anderson (2002, p. 26) notes, "life chances depend increasingly on the cultural, social, and cognitive capital that citizens can amass." He emphasizes the importance of childhood precisely at a time when families with children are becoming ever more vulnerable.

The crucial issue lies in the interplay between parental and societal investments in children's development. Families are at a considerable disadvantage if they are poor, headed by a single parent or parents with little education and inadequate employment skills, have more than two children, or are immigrants or refugees. It therefore becomes critical that countries target children's holistic development. As a result, we should focus attention on how the components of child development are understood, studied, and, then, enhanced.

In this chapter, we focus on the evolving attention to achieving the goal of child well-being and do so through a broad child and family approach rather than a narrow focus on protecting children against abuse and neglect. Our focus is largely on the advanced industrialized countries. The more holistic approach employed here is driven by the growing use of children's rights as the basis for intervention, the increased attention to childhood social indicators as a device for monitoring and measuring trends in well-being over time, and developments in child and family

policies as the framework for a strategic response once well-being is in focus. The objective is not to ignore social service reforms but to go beyond them.

Child Rights

Despite the absence of the United States as a signer, 192 countries have ratified the UN Convention on the Rights of the Child (CRC) since 1989, when it was first adopted and ratified by the United Nations, and it is increasingly being used to frame discussions of child and family policies in different countries. Developments in 62 countries were reviewed for a UNICEF Innocenti Research Center (IRC) study on the impact of the implementation of the CRC (UNICEF Innocenti Research Center [IRC], 2004) and whether the seemingly positive impact of the CRC is real or only rhetorical.

The general measures of implementation are specified under a cluster of articles in the convention: Article 4, the obligation to undertake all appropriate legislative, administrative, and other measures for the implementation of the rights specified in the CRC; Article 42, the obligation to make the content of the CRC widely known to children and adults; and Article 44, paragraph 6, the obligation to make national reports widely available (IRC, 2004). To what extent have countries carried out their obligations?

A 2004 IRC report suggests that the impact of the convention has been "rapid, widespread, and sustained" (p. 19) and that there has been a remarkable degree of progress in extending and implementing the rights of children. The progress has been most extensive in law reform, which has led to increased access to essential services, especially health and education. There has also been progress concerning children and families in need of protection, but the report found that more is still needed. Here the focus has been on advancing the right of the child to be raised in a family environment, the right to government support and help for parents in fulfilling their child-rearing responsibilities, new legislation regarding the care of children deprived or separated from their families, and an agreement that institutionalization should be a last resort. Special units of government and of civil society have been established, targeted on children's rights and increased efforts in promoting, monitoring, and ensuring the protection of these rights. The Innocenti Research Center, as UNICEF's research center focused on the problems of children in industrialized countries, views itself and its research as being guided by the principle of children's rights. This focus on children's rights as the framework for new child and family policy initiatives points to a significantly broader focus than that of protection—or a deficit policy model, targeted on problems.

Childhood Social Indicators

Child Trends research center has defined an *indicator* as "a measure of behavior, condition, or status that can be tracked over time, across people and/or geographical units" (Moore & Brown, 2006; Ben-Arieh & Goerge, 2006). Another definition is that childhood social indicators are quantitative measures of key attributes characterizing the condition of children over time and across geographical units (Kamerman & Kahn, 2006, p. 199). Indicators may serve to describe, monitor, measure, set, and help document the achievement of goals and/or evaluate the impact of interventions. The growing attention to these indicators as devices for assessing and monitoring the conditions of children is reflected in the rising number of national and international childhood social indicator reports in the United States (for example, Kids Count, the Federal Interagency Forum, U.S. DHHS, Trends) and internationally (UNICEF's *State of the World's Children*, the IRC league reports).

One important discussion of child well-being is a review and analysis of child welfare in the European Union (Micklewright & Stewart, 1999). The report highlights four major categories:

- economic well-being, in particular child poverty (using the relative measure of below 50% of median income)
- health and survival status (in particular, declines in under-5 mortality rates, teen suicides and deaths by accident, and teen fertility rates)
- education (in particular, school enrollment rates)
- the extent to which children and their families are included in mainstream society (their social inclusion rather than exclusion)—and how these dimensions can be measured (their satisfaction with life)

The authors note that there was significant progress in the 1990s in reducing under-5 mortality rates and child death rates generally, an increase in expenditures as a percentage of Gross Domestic Product (GDP)

on education, a decline in teen fertility rates, and a significant rise in enrollment of children at age 16 (the end of compulsory schooling). Overall, the average child's quality of life appeared to be improving. Where there have been inconsistencies cross-nationally, however, is with regard to one key indicator: child poverty rates.

Child Poverty

Child poverty is high on the agenda of almost all of the European Union (EU) and Organisation for Economic Co-operation and Development (OECD) countries (Kamerman et al., 2003). The percentage of children living in poverty has risen in a majority of the world's developed countries. Children have an above-average risk of income poverty (using the relative measure of income below 50% of median income) compared to non-aged adults and often to the aged as well (IRC, 2005). The high and ongoing concern regarding child poverty reflects the fact that poor children experience a disproportionate share of deprivation, disadvantage, bad health, and substandard school performance, and the consequences of poverty are especially dire for young children. Poverty rates are particularly high for children living in mother-only families, workless households, or single-earner families.

As Vleminckx and Smeeding (2001) point out, children who grow up in poverty are at a marked and measurable disadvantage. They are more likely to experience educational underachievement, poor health, teenage pregnancy, substance abuse, criminal and anti-social behavior, low pay, unemployment, and long-term welfare dependence and to transfer this poverty of opportunity to their own children. Child poverty rates are monitored annually in the United States and the EU, and cross-national child poverty rates are monitored in the advanced industrialized countries by the EU and UNICEF IRC, with particular attention to trends over time (European Commission, 2004; IRC, 2005[1]). Child poverty rates declined in some countries in the 1990s (e.g., Canada, Denmark, Norway, Sweden), rose in others (e.g., Germany, Hungary, Italy), and stayed stable in most—all regardless of the type of poverty line or measure used. The child poverty rate in the United States is among the highest of all OECD countries, even though it declined in the 1990s.

Drawing on the UNICEF Innocenti Research Center reports and the Luxembourg Income Study database, a 2005 review of child poverty in rich countries found that the percentage of children living in poverty rose in 17 of 24 OECD countries over the previous decade. Using the standard international relative definition of poverty (below 50% of median income), Denmark and Finland have the lowest child poverty rates, under 3%.[2] In contrast, the United States and Mexico have the highest rates, higher than 20%, and their ranking at the bottom is sustained even if the poverty threshold is reduced from 50% to 40% of median income. (The U.S. official, absolute poverty rate is equal to about 35% of median income—down from 44% when it was first established in 1963.) Child poverty rates in Norway were low in the mid-1990s and have continued to decline. Generally, the child poverty rates in the Nordic countries (all small countries) are the lowest in the world. In contrast, the Anglo American countries, Japan, and Mexico have the highest child poverty rates.

As the Innocenti Research Center report cards have regularly revealed (and as mentioned earlier), there is a close correlation between growing up in poverty and the likelihood of school problems, poor health, teen pregnancy and parenting, substance abuse, criminal behavior, low pay, unemployment, long-term welfare dependence, and use of foster care and protective services (IRC, 2000, 2003, 2005). In addition, children from immigrant families or from ethnic and racial minorities are disproportionately likely to grow up in poverty (IRC, 2005).

Among the lessons to be learned from these data is that child poverty declined in the United States during the last decade as a consequence of increased maternal employment and, to a lesser extent, government income transfers (the Earned Income Tax Credit, EITC). Child poverty similarly declined in the United Kingdom, although more as a consequence of government income transfers. Particular attention is now being paid in the United Kingdom to social exclusion and child poverty.[3] The British government has made a commitment to end child poverty by 2020 and has set specific targets for poverty reduction in the interim. Its three-part strategy includes cash benefits, tax credits, and expanded early childhood programs. Similarly, several other countries and the United Nations' millennium development goals have established targets related to reducing child poverty rates by 50% by the year 2015.

Another lesson has to do with the international data on the factors affecting child maltreatment (abuse and neglect), and the link between maltreatment and poverty. The list holds no surprises. According to a 2003 report issued by the UNICEF Innocenti Research Center, the factors most commonly associated with the maltreatment of children include:

> class and race, poverty, single parenthood, unemployment, domestic violence, family breakdown, children not living with biological parents, social isolation, ill health or disability, mental ill-health, drug and alcohol abuse, teenage parenthood, low educational levels, and parents having been abused in their own childhood. (p. 16)

It is not surprising that these factors are highly correlated with income poverty, nor is it surprising that clusters of these factors are especially likely to increase the risk of maltreatment. The role of poverty reduction and antipoverty strategies in reducing many of these problems is not fully understood.

The same report refers to a U.S. study of child welfare professionals, who found that 85% of states report that substance abuse and poverty are the two leading problems linked with child maltreatment. The authors conclude that "no national strategy to prevent or reduce the maltreatment of children will achieve major gains without addressing the question of economic poverty" (IRC, 2003, p. 21). About half of all abuse/neglect cases occur within the 15% of families with incomes below the poverty line.

Paxson and Waldfogel, as reported in the Innocenti Research Center report (2003), link data on maltreatment cases and children in foster care over the period between 1990 and 1998. They found that "when state welfare benefits are lower, more children are substantiated as victims of neglect and more children are in foster care . . . and that some welfare reform policies are associated with increased numbers of children in foster care" (p. 29).

A third lesson is that higher government spending on social protection (social policy) is closely associated with low rates of child poverty. Social policies are especially effective in reducing pretransfer poverty—by 80% in the countries with low poverty rates but by only 10–15% in the countries with high rates. No OECD country spending at least 10% of GDP on income transfers has a child poverty rate higher than 10% (IRC, 2005).

THE POLICY RESPONSES

Trends in spending on children and their families vary across countries, in particular with regard to spending as a share of GDP and of all public social expenditures, real expenditures, or on a per-child basis (Gatenio-Gabel & Kamerman, 2006). For most countries, spending on family and children benefits increased from 1980 to 2000 on all measures. Real expenditures on children and families increased in all but 7 of the 21 industrialized countries since 1980. Here, too, there were some variations across countries, but in most countries, expenditures rose steadily and significantly.

What is most striking is that spending on benefits for children and their families rose across countries despite a shrinking child population in each and despite constraints on social protection generally. Expenditures per elderly (age 65 and over) grew by 45% since 1980, but their numbers increased by almost 23% at the same time (United Nations Population Division, 2006). In contrast, the population of children decreased as a proportion of the population in all of these countries, while spending on family benefits generally rose.

Gatenio-Gabel and Kamerman (2006) concluded that what sustained public investments in children between 1980 and 2000 were the establishment of new policy regimes and a greater emphasis on in-kind (service) benefits.

Income Transfers

As is well established by now, income transfers are one key to reducing child poverty and enhancing the economic situation of children and their families (Kamerman et al., 2003). Differences in policies mean that some countries reduced pretax and pretransfer child poverty by as much as 20 percentage points and others (such as Portugal and Spain) by as little as 5 percentage points (Oxley et al, 2001). Oxley et al. (2001) also found that child-related benefits are especially important to working households/families with children (in particular, single parents and low-income two-parent families).

The discussion below looks at changes in the instruments used to deliver the benefits/services package and the recipients of new benefits and services according to the five OECD subcategories of family benefit expenditures: family allowances; maternal and parental leave benefits; other cash benefits; day care/home-help services; and other in-kind services.

Family Allowances

In 1980, 66% of all public expenditures on family benefits and services was spent on family allowances.

Typically, child/family allowances are universal cash payments to families based on the presence and number of children in a family. The amount may vary by the ordinal position of the child, the age of the child, and/or the employment status of the parent. They are designed to offset some of the costs of rearing a child and constitute about 10% of an average wage for one child and more for subsequent children. Most countries now supplement the basic child or family benefit with an additional benefit for single parents, large families, and families with a disabled child.

In contrast to 1980, the year 2001 saw the budget for family allowances fall to only 43% of all spending on family benefits and services. In 11 of the 21 countries studied, family allowance expenditures declined as a share of spending on family benefits with the largest declines experienced in Switzerland, Portugal, and Spain. During these years, expenditures on family allowances fell by an average of 19%, while spending on maternity and parental leave benefits grew by 76%, and spending on all other family cash benefits, such as supplemental allowances for single parents and guaranteed minimum child support benefits, more than doubled.

Child-Conditioned Tax Benefits

Paralleling the declining significance of child or family allowances is the increased role of child-conditioned tax benefits. By the 1990s, there emerged a general trend toward delivering income support to families with children by using the tax system. Tax benefits, including both credits (reductions in tax liability) and allowances (reductions in taxable income), targeted on children or families with children have emerged as an alternative strategy to raising family income through family allowances. In recent years, the line between the two systems has become increasingly blurred. Today, many countries, especially the Anglo countries, have supplemented their child and family allowances—or replaced earlier tax allowances or exemptions—with both refundable ("non-wasteable") and nonrefundable ("wasteable") tax credits (Columbia University Clearinghouse on International Developments in Child, Youth & Family Policies, 2002 data).

In Australia, Canada, and New Zealand, child benefits are income tested and administered through the tax system either as a tax allowance (a reduction of taxable income), a tax credit (a reduction of income taxes), or a direct cash payment to families with children, much like a negative income tax when income is below the tax threshold. The United Kingdom has maintained its universal child benefit and supplemented it with tax credits, most of which took effect after 2001. While the United States has no universal family allowance, several child tax credits, including the EITC, are utilized to provide financial assistance to a broad base of American families with children. And several countries, such as Canada, Germany, Luxembourg, the Netherlands, and Spain, offer additional tax credits for single-parent families with children and families with disabled children.

Not all countries have moved in the direction of favoring tax credits (Bradshaw & Finch, 2002). Finland abolished its tax credits in the early 1990s and increased its child benefits. Luxembourg decreased its child tax credits and substantially raised its universal child benefits. Norway incorporated its former child tax deduction into the child benefit. Clearly, for a full picture of what has contributed to the growth in public investment in child well-being, attention must be paid to how countries provide additional income to families with children currently. Both tax and cash benefits must be considered.

Nonetheless, as important as income transfers are, *alone* they are insufficient to eliminate child poverty (Kamerman et al., 2003; IRC, 2005). To effectively combat poverty, additional and complementary interventions are required. There is particular need for interventions designed to target and support the employment of single mothers, wives of men earning low wages, and the working poor. But parental employment alone does not eliminate poverty either. Policies, such as the U.S. EITC, which provide wage or income supplements may accomplish this task. Transfer payments (such as child allowances and housing allowances) and tax benefits (such as refundable tax credits) may be especially important for the role they play in enhancing the low wages of the working poor and reducing child poverty. Other important policies include:

- A combination of economic and social policies, such as a livable minimum wage
- Other categorical cash benefits, such as paid and job-protected parental leaves of adequate duration to permit mothers to care for their infants or newly adopted children while remaining attached to the labor force
- Special categorical benefits, such as child support/advanced maintenance benefits, which are critical in protecting the economic situation of children in single-mother families

- In-kind benefits and services, in particular an increased supply of good-quality, affordable child care so that women can enter and remain gainfully employed in the labor market and children from low-income families can enter school on equal footing with their peer group

We turn now to exploring recent and emerging trends in these policies and their implications for child well-being.

Maternity, Paternity, and Parental Leave Policies

Maternity, paternity, and parental leave policies are paid and job-protected leaves, made available by law, at the time of pregnancy and childbirth or adoption. The duration of the leave varies by country, as do the qualifying conditions, the benefit levels, whether they include a mandatory period or not, and whether some part is limited to fathers.[4]

Infant care, for children in the first year of life, and to some extent toddler care, for children aged 1–2 years, constitute a key issue in the current international discussion of early childhood education and care (ECEC). Adequate care and education for the under-3s can be achieved through some combination of parental leaves (perhaps for about 1–1.5 years, or even 3 years in some countries) and out-of-home services. Leave policies have played an increasingly important role in infant and toddler care (IRC, 1991; Kamerman, 2000, 2005; Plantenga & Siegel, 2004).

Public discussion of parental leave policies internationally has been—and still is—driven by rising rates of maternal employment and a growing recognition of the importance of infancy in child development. In addition, in the United States, it is driven also by welfare policy. Temporary Assistance to Needy Families (TANF) policy requires that poor mothers requesting financial assistance seek and accept employment from the time their babies are 3 months of age (only 16 states exempt poor mothers from the work requirement until the infant's first birthday). So general trends in female labor force participation internationally have made caring for children under 3 years of age a priority issue in child and family policy debates.

Paid and job-protected parental and child-rearing leaves from employment at the time of childbirth have become the norm in almost all industrialized countries. Coverage is extensive and take-up is high for women, but remains modest for fathers. (Only in Sweden is take-up by fathers significant.) Increasingly, it is a real alternative to out-of-home infant care.

Maternity and parental job-protected leaves and benefits replacing all or a significant portion of prior wages has become an important child and family policy since the 1980s. Public social expenditures on this policy increased by more than 75% between 1980 and 2000 (Gatenio-Gabel & Kamerman, 2006). The average duration of maternity and parental leaves in the OECD countries has doubled from the early 1980s from about 20 to 40 weeks in 2000. Since the mid-1990s, Austria, Belgium, Canada, France, Germany, Italy, Luxembourg, New Zealand, Norway, Portugal, Sweden, and the United Kingdom have all made significant enhancements to leave entitlements for the purpose of caring for young children. Most countries have increased the duration of the paid leave and extended coverage to fathers or either parent. Some countries (e.g., Germany) have even increased benefit levels. Paid parental leaves have largely supplemented earlier paid maternity leaves.

The European Union introduced a directive mandating maternity leave, first, in 1992 and, subsequently, parental leave, in 1996. The parental leave directive provides parents with at least 3 months' leave for child care purposes (as distinct from and in addition to the maternity leave) after the birth or adoption of a child until a given age of up to 8 years. The conditions governing parental leave are defined by national law and/or collective agreement, and there is considerable variation among the countries regarding its implementation.

Specifically, the Nordic countries all increased the duration of paid parental leaves. Belgium, Canada, Ireland, Luxembourg, New Zealand, Portugal, and the United Kingdom have introduced or significantly expanded parental leave, while Austria, Germany, Norway, and Sweden have established incentives to encourage fathers to take leave. Portugal and the United Kingdom have increased maternity leave as well. Other countries, such as France and Luxembourg, have also implemented policies to allow parents more time to care for sick children.

Not all countries with paid statutory maternity/parental leaves offer coverage to all mothers. Labor force attachment is usually the basic qualifying condition for coverage, and in several countries the length of employment, earnings, and contributions to Social Security (or the local equivalent) affect eligibility.

However, in 11 of the countries, supplementary birth allowances and/or grants were provided to new mothers in addition to maternity/parental leaves, thus further supplementing the maternity/parental leave benefit package.

In addition to protecting the economic situation of families with children, there is research that indicates the positive consequences of these policies for child health and for women's wages. There remain, however, significant gaps in knowledge regarding use of the leaves. For instance, do the "use it or lose it" provisions targeted on fathers lead to more use by fathers? What are the consequences for mothers and children when longer parental leaves are taken (e.g., 3 years)? What are the consequences for child development and well-being when leaves are not taken? What are the real costs of these policies and the politics that have led to their enactment in other countries (Kamerman, 2000, 2005; Tanaka, 2005; Gregg & Waldfogel, 2005; Han & Waldfogel, 2003)? Despite these unanswered questions, these policies have clearly had positive consequences for child well-being and have helped to fill the gap between the supply of infant and toddler services and the growing demand for support for parents at a critical point in their lives.

Other Categorical Cash Family Benefits

The number of other categorical family benefits offered grew from 26 to 42 across the 21 countries between 1980 and 2000. Most often, these are supplementary benefits for single and low-income parents or special periodic or lump-sum payments for certain groups, such as military and civil servants. The inconsistent treatment makes cross-country comparisons difficult, but one category receiving attention in several countries has to do with child support—the financial support provided for children in single-parent families to replace the support that would have been provided by the noncustodial parent.

The economic vulnerability of the growing number of single-mother families led several countries to establish special categorical benefits for low-income, mother-only families. These include a means-tested single-mother allowance in France for poor single mothers with children under age 3 or for single parents with older children but limited to 1 year. France also established a means-tested social assistance benefit that covers low-income families with children when the parent is under age 25.

In addition, more than half of the 15 EU member countries (Austria, Belgium, Denmark, Finland, France, Germany, Sweden, and Norway) established guaranteed minimum child support benefits (often referred to as "advanced maintenance" benefits) to protect children against the loss of the financial support of a noncustodial parent. Although the specifics of these advanced maintenance policies vary across countries, in general these benefits are defined as an obligation to the child rather than to the parent, with a cash benefit provided by a government agency to the custodial parent when the child support payment is absent, paid irregularly, or not at all. The government agency then imposes a claim on the noncustodial parent to recover the payment. In some countries, the benefit is limited to young children (under 6 or 12 years).

An alternative policy stresses the enforcement of the noncustodial parent's support obligation but doesn't guarantee a benefit, as in the United States, for example (Turetsky, 2005). Despite this, private child support payments constitute a significant component of the income of poor families with children in the United States. In 2004, child support was the second largest income source for poor families receiving support, about 30% of total family income. Child support collection rates have more than doubled since 1996, when the most recent changes were enacted as part of welfare reform; and families who receive child support are more likely to leave welfare for work and less likely to return (Turetsky, 2005).

Family In-Kind Benefits

Another significant development contributed further to sustaining or increasing public investment in child well-being. In-kind family benefits and services grew considerably. The OECD defines in-kind benefits as the direct provision of goods and services or noncash transfers (OECD, 2004). In 1980, there were 78 in-kind benefits among the 21 countries and by 2001 this had grown to 135. Day care and home-help services expenditures increased by 131%, and other in-kind benefits—such as child welfare services, social and recreational services for youth and families, subsidies to charities—doubled.

EARLY CHILDHOOD EDUCATION AND CARE POLICIES AND PROGRAMS

Early childhood education and care (ECEC) services constitute another child and family program area

that contributed significantly to the growth in investment in and commitment to child well-being. Current ECEC programs have evolved over time to meet multiple needs that include child protection, early childhood education, helping children with special needs, facilitating mothers' labor force participation, enhancing children's development, and preparing children for primary school. As a result, the delivery and administration of ECEC services, is splintered between jurisdictions, with some programs (generally for younger children, those under age 3) administered by the social welfare or health ministry and other programs, especially those targeted on children aged 3 to 6, preparing them for school, administered by the education ministry. A survey of administrative auspices revealed that 9 of 13 countries had separate early childhood education and care programs, which were administered by the education and welfare ministries, respectively (Kamerman, 2000, 2001).

Early childhood education and care services have grown significantly since 1980 by increasing the supply, expanding eligibility, mandating coverage, and providing incentives for increasing demand. Much of the growth has been in programs administered by the education ministries. Growth in ECEC spending has been uneven among the countries studied. In Australia and Italy, ECEC expenditures under the auspices of social welfare ministries grew more than 10 times, while in Austria, Finland, Germany, and Luxembourg, these expenditures more than doubled between 1980 and 2001. In Portugal and Spain, spending decreased during this same period. On average, spending on ECEC benefits and services increased by 76% in the countries considered. When we supplement our analysis by examining spending under education ministries for pre-primary programs, the trend is most clearly upward. On average, ECEC spending on pre-primary education more than tripled since 1985. Public investment in ECEC typically takes one of the following forms: subsidies to child care providers; reduced fees to parents depending on income, family type, and number or age of the children in the family; use of tax benefits to offset child care costs; and increased child benefits for families by family type, parental employment status, and age of the children (Bradshaw & Finch, 2002).

The OECD carried out a thematic review of ECEC programs in 21 of its 30 member countries (OECD, 2001).[5] Both background reports and supplementary country notes provided the first systematic review of such programs by the OECD since the mid-1970s, and this review covers more countries than any earlier study, takes a broad and holistic view of ECEC, and is a splendid illustration of the policies, policy regimes, and related data that are now available in this important child and family policy arena. The country reports describe contextual variables shaping ECEC policies (demographics, economics, social trends, and the diverse purposes of ECEC within and across countries); and they include discussion of the main policy developments and issues and the history of these developments over time.

The background and country reports document the dramatic growth in the supply of these programs and the increased access, especially for 3- to 6-year-olds. The overall report makes an explicit and powerful statement regarding the importance of linking early childhood care and education together rather than assessing them as two discrete systems. Of particular importance, several countries have chosen to integrate these services under the aegis of "education" rather than health, social welfare, or some combination. Among the OECD countries, England, New Zealand, Scotland, Spain, and Sweden have all moved this way, and Italy and Portugal are likely to do so in time.[6]

The reports underscore the importance of universal access—providing all children with a guaranteed placement within a good-quality, affordable ECEC program, regardless of family income, parents' employment status, and/or their own vulnerability and special needs. These programs are now the norm, at least for the 3-, 4-, and 5-year-olds. The overall reports (OECD, 2001, 2006) also underscore the need for services for infants and toddlers; here, supply shortages continue to exist. Where parental leaves are brief but female labor force participation rates are high, ECEC services are needed. In most countries, family day care (child minding) plays an important role, yet we have relatively little information about whom the providers are, how to improve the quality of care provided this way, and whether there is a reliable and stable workforce for these programs. If family day care continues to be viewed as a cheap alternative—a service provided by unskilled, poorly educated, low wage, and/or immigrant women—what are the implications for children?

There is growing attention to the quality of care available and the need to aim at improving quality in many countries. Certain countries (e.g., Denmark and Sweden) are world renowned for the quality of their ECEC programs and their willingness and ability to invest heavily in the supply and quality of them. Other countries have far less in the way of available resources for public investment in ECEC, and it is not yet clear how to maximize available resources and/or set priorities. Decent-quality ECEC programs are not cheap. Those countries with more-limited resources inevitably will need to set priorities and to explore or experiment with alternatives. But they will want to keep consequences for children at the forefront.

There is a paucity of information on before and afterschool (or "out of school") programs: how many places exist, what percentage of children of each age is served, where are the services delivered (at the preschool or primary school or in a separate community facility), what is the cost, how are they funded, and what do parents pay? Somewhat related to this issue is that of how ECEC programs can meet the needs of children when parents work irregular hours (at night or on weekends).

The growing diversity of child populations raises important and often not-yet-addressed issues. Children from immigrant or racial or ethnic minority backgrounds are often underrepresented in regular ECEC programs. It is essential that these children have access to ECEC programs.

Finally, the financing of these programs is increasingly viewed as the responsibility of government, especially for the preschool programs (the services for 3- to 5-year-olds).

OTHER IN-KIND FAMILY BENEFITS

This OECD category includes child welfare–related services, recreation, some afterschool services, subsidies to social welfare institutions serving families and children, personal social services, and in-kind benefits to special population groups, including single mothers, public service employees, military families, etc. There is considerable variation in what countries include in this category. For example, the United States includes the Social Services Block Grant, Child Care Development Block Grant, child welfare services, nutrition programs serving children, and child support enforcement. Spain includes public transportation subsidies. Most countries include child welfare services under this category, and spending on these services has doubled since 1980.

CONCLUSION

Countries and international organizations have moved beyond "child welfare" as the organizing rubric around which they cluster their concerns and activities with regard to child and family well-being. Child welfare is an important area within the social services, and indispensable in any society, but lacks good cross-national overviews and research syntheses. As we have demonstrated, the total arena which comes into view as we explore the evolving concerns with child and family well-being and "well-becoming" encompasses income transfers, health care and educational programs, family-friendly employment policies, family- and child-conditioned tax concessions and benefits, family and parental leaves, targeted categorical cash benefits (such as child support and housing allowances), and various in-kind benefits and services (such as child care, food stamps, and nutrition supplements). The international community, in recent years, has sought convergence and coherence for these interventions via a children's rights framework. An additional conceptualization, in our view, is child and family policy, with children's rights a major component. Attention to child and family policy offers an additional window not only on how children are doing but on what policies make a difference.

A key aspect of this analysis is the increasingly available data on international developments in child and family policies, enabling a more systematic assessment of child well-being and the factors that affect this. A more complete analysis requires more extensive data on more policies for more countries, along with a full range of childhood social indicators.

Child and family policy data and related research are increasingly available on the OECD and EU countries, on developing countries from UNICEF and the United Nations Educational, Scientific, and Cultural Organization (UNESCO), and on a combination of countries within the Columbia University Clearinghouse. Basic indicators on child well-being are available through UNICEF and its annual report, *State of the World's Children*. Data on family allowances are available in *Social Security Programs Throughout the World* (http://www.ssa.gov/policy/docs/progdesc/ssptw/2004–2005/europe/index.html) and from the Mutual Information System on Social Protection in the Member States of the European Union (MISSOC) (http://ec.europa.eu/employment_social/soc-prot/missoc99/english/f_main.htm). Data on child poverty and the policies that are effective in reducing child poverty rates are also available

from the Luxembourg Income Study (LIS; http://www.lisproject.org), Eurostat (http://epp.eurostat.ec.europa.eu), and the OECD (http://www.oecd.org), and there are ongoing analyses carried out by the UNICEF Innocenti Research Center and the LIS. Data on early childhood education and care in developing countries are now beginning to be available through the OECD and UNESCO. Data on parental leave policies are available through the Clearinghouse on International Developments in Child, Youth & Family Policies at Columbia University (http://www.childpolicy.org/clearinghouse.html and http://www.childpolicyintl.org) and in Deven and Moss (2005). Data on several aspects of child health are generally available, and work on a wide range of childhood social indicators is progressing.

Gaps in the information on child and family policies and child well-being remain, however. In particular, there are no systematic data on advanced maintenance policies (guaranteed minimum child support),[7] on child-conditioned housing allowances, on child-conditioned tax benefits, and on the role of the voluntary sector. Most important, there are no systematic international data on child welfare services: protective and preventive services, foster care, and adoption.

Children, and child and family benefits, are low on the agenda of economic and social policies, but despite their low status, expenditures seem to be relatively protected, and it is increasingly possible to monitor the impacts of these policies and public investment on child well-being (Kamerman et al., 2003). Nonetheless, several items need attention, particularly with regard to systematic descriptions of the relevant policy regimes and their consequences for children. The child and family policies likely to get attention in this context over the next decade include:

- Interventions to reduce child poverty in terms of both income poverty and social exclusion
- Care policies for children (and other dependents) at a time when more and more women with children continue to enter the labor force and are needed in the labor market if contributions to pensions are to be sustained and if the future labor force is to be sustained as smaller cohorts reach working age
- Policies designed to help reconcile work and family life, as the complement to caring policies, with similar goals
- Early education policies as an investment in children as human capital as the need for more skilled workers increases Effective interventions

in support of child well-being as by-products of concern with the size and skill of the future labor force, or gender equity, or, most important, as part of a moral argument of doing better by children

In the context of an increasingly global society, some countries appear to be motivated to improve the situation of children and their families, and others are not. Addressing issues with regard to troubled children and their families is only one aspect of enhancing positive child development, and improving the well-being of children generally is an essential dimension. Nonetheless, still more is needed. At the very least, we need to institute universal child cash or tax benefits that effectively reduce child poverty and social exclusion, universal health insurance, access to affordable and decent-quality ECEC, and paid family and medical leave following childbirth or adoption.

Notes

1. The IRC issued a report on child poverty and well-being in 2007, too late to be discussed in this chapter. The basic findings are similar.

2. Eurostat is increasingly using 60% of median income as the poverty threshold. The United States would look even worse with this definition.

3. "Social exclusion" is a multidimensional concept, involving economic, social, political, cultural, and other aspects of disadvantage and deprivation; the term is being used increasingly in the international social policy literature. See Kahn and Kamerman (2002).

4. Data on comparative developments in maternity, paternity, and parental leave policies, as well as information on related policies, can be found on the Columbia University Clearinghouse Web site (www.childpolicyintl. org) and in Deven and Moss (2005).

5. The first phase of the review covered 12 countries and is described in OECD (2001). Country reports are available for the remaining countries. A synthesis report was published in 2006 (OECD, 2006).

6. Brazil and Vietnam have also followed the same path.

7. A 14-country study of child support was carried out in 2006–7 and a report published in 2007. See Skinner, Bradshaw, and Davidson (2007).

References

Ben-Arieh, A., & Goerge, R. (Eds.). (2006). *Indicators of children's well-being: Understanding their role, usage and policy influence*. Netherlands: Springer.

Bradshaw, J., & Finch, N. (2002). A comparison of child benefit packages in 22 countries. Research Report No. 174. Leeds, UK: Department of Work and Pensions/University of York. Available: http://www.dwp.gov.uk/asd/asd5/174summ.pdf.

Chen, W., & Corak, M. (2005). *Child poverty and changes in child poverty in rich countries since 1990*. Florence, Italy: Innocenti Research Center.

Clearinghouse on International Developments in Child, Youth & Family Policies at Columbia University. Available: http://www.childpolicyintl.org.

Deven, F., & Moss, P. (Eds.). (2005). *Leave policies and research*. Brussels, Belgium: Population and Family Studies Centre.

Esping-Anderson, G. (2002). *Why we need a new welfare state*. Oxford: Oxford University Press.

European Commission. (2004). *Living conditions in Europe: 2003 edition*. Luxembourg: Eurostat.

Gatenio-Gabel, S., & Kamerman, S. B. (2006, June). Investing in children. *Social Service Review*, 80(2), 240–263.

Gregg, P., & Waldfogel, J. (2005, February). Symposium on parental leave, early maternal employment, and child outcomes: Introduction. *Economic Journal*, 115, F1–F6.

Han, W., & Waldfogel, J. (2003). Parental leave: The impact of recent legislation on parents' leave-taking. *Demography*, 40(1), 191–200.

Himes, J., Landers, C., & Leslie, J. (1991). Women, work and child care, global seminar report. Florence, Italy: Innocenti Research Center.

Innocenti Research Centre. *See IRC.*

IRC. (2000). *A league table of child poverty in rich nations*. Report Card No. 1. Florence, Italy: Innocenti Research Center.

IRC. (2003). *A league table of child maltreatment deaths in rich nations*. Innocenti Report Card No. 5. Florence, Italy: Innocenti Research Center.

IRC. (2004). *Summary report of the study of the impact of the implementation of the Convention on the Rights of the Child*. Florence, Italy: Innocenti Research Center.

IRC. (2005). *Child poverty in rich countries 2005*. Report Card No. 6. Florence, Italy: Innocenti Research Center.

IRC. (2007). *Child well-being in rich countries*. Report Card No. 7. Florence, Italy: Innocenti Research Center.

Kahn, A. J., & Kamerman, S. B. (Eds.). (2002). *Beyond child poverty: The social exclusion of children*. New York: Columbia University Institute for Child and Family Policies (ICFP).

Kamerman, S. B. (2000). From maternity to public policies: Women's health, employment, and child and family well-being. *Journal of American Medical Women's Association*, 55(2), 96–99.

Kamerman, S. B. (2005). Early childhood education and care in advanced industrialized countries: Current policy and program trends. *Phi Delta Kappan*, 87(3), 193–195.

Kamerman, S. B. (2001). *Early childhood education and care in advanced industrialized countries*. New York: Columbia University Institute for Child and Family Policies (ICFP).

Kamerman, S. B., & Kahn, A. J. (1990a). *Social services for troubled children, youth, and families in the United States*. New York: Pergamon.

Kamerman, S. B., & Kahn, A. J. (1990b). If CPS is driving child welfare—where do we go from here? *Public Welfare*, 48(1).

Kamerman, S. B., & Kahn, A. J. (2006). Studying the impact of indicators of child well-being on policies and programs. In A. Ben-Arieh & R. Goerge (Eds.), *Indicators of children's well-being*. Netherlands: Springer.

Kamerman, S. B., Neuman, M., Waldfogel, J., & Brooks-Gunn, J. (2003). *Social policies, family types and child outcomes*. Paris: OECD.

Kids Count data book. Annual publication. Baltimore, MD: Annie E. Casey Foundation.

Micklewright, J., & Stewart, K. (1999). *Is child welfare converging in the EU?* Florence, Italy: Innocenti Research Center.

MISSOC. Mutual Information System on Social Protection in the EU member countries. Publishes comparative tables and information bulletins. Luxembourg: Eurostat.Moore, K., & Brown, B. (2006). Preparing indicators for policy makers and advocates. In A. Ben-Arieh & R. Goerge (Eds.), *Indicators of children's well-being* (pp. 93–104). Netherlands: Springer.

Moss, P., & Deven, F. (1999). Parental leave: Progress or pitfall? *European Journal of Population/Revue européenne de Démographie*.

OECD. (2001). *Starting strong* (Vol. 1). Paris, France: Author.

OECD. (2006). *Starting strong* (Vol. 2). Paris, France: Author.

Oxley, H., Dang, T.-T., Forster, M., & Pellizari, M. (2001). Income inequalities and poverty among children and households with children in selected OECD countries. In K. Vleminckx & T. Smeeding (Eds.), *Child well-being, child poverty, and child policy in modern nations* (501–526). Bristol, England: Policy Press.

Plantenga, J. & Siegel, M. (2004). *Child care in a changing world*. Netherlands: Ministry of Social Affairs.

Skinner, C., Bradshaw, J., & Davidson, J. (2007). *Child support policy: An international perspective*. Research Report No. 405. Leeds, UK: Department of Work and Pensions/University of York. Available: http://www.dwp.gov.uk/asd/asd5/rports2007-2008/rrep405.pdf.

Social Security Programs Throughout the World. Geneva: ISSA. Available: http://www.ssa.gov/policy/docs/progdesc/ssptw/2004–2005/europe/index.html.

Tanaka, S. (2005). Parental leave and child health across OECD countries. *Economic Journal*, 115(501), F7–F28.

Turetsky, V. (2005). *The child support program: An investment that works*. Washington, DC: CLASP.

UNICEF. *The state of the world's children*. Annual publication. New York: UNICEF.United Nations Population Division. (2006). *World population prospects: The 2004 revision* (3 vols.). United Nations publication.

United States Department of Health and Human Services (U.S. DHHS). *Trends in the well-being of America's children and youth*. Annual publication. Washington, DC: GPO.

United States Federal InterAgency Forum on Child and Family Statistics. *America's children: Key national indicators of well-being*. Annual publication. Washington, DC: GPO.

Vleminckx, K., & Smeeding, T. (Eds.). (2001). *Child well-being, child poverty, and child policy in modern nations*. Bristol, England: Policy Press.

22

The Effect of Children on the Income Status of Female-Headed Households: An Intercountry Comparison

Martha N. Ozawa
Yongwoo Lee

Ever since the economic system changed from agriculture and family-oriented cottage industries to manufacturing and service industries, how children should be dealt with has been the major issue in developing social policies concerning the economic lives of families in Britain, the United States, and European countries. Concomitantly, at the center of social policy development in Britain, the United States, and European countries has been the issue of how to deal with children. In the preindustrial era, when the majority of families ran farms or engaged in family-oriented cottage industries, parents could support their children financially. In those days, children often worked side by side with their parents in generating financial resources. Even if the children did not work, it was relatively easy to meet their consumption needs under such economic arrangements.

As mercantilism and industrialization became the economic system and the heads of families became employees of other persons or corporations, labor income (that is, earnings) and family expenditures diverged. Because workers received wages or salaries that were based solely on their *individual* contributions to the economy and because family expenditures depended on how many children had to be supported, there was no assurance that the earned income was adequate to support the family's children financially. That is, the unit of the provision of wages was the individual, but the unit of financial needs was the family, thus creating a major friction in the economic lives of families under this system.

An early sign of this struggle was the passage of the Speenhamland Act of 1795 in Britain. That law provided relief on the basis of family size and included cost-of-living increases for the first time in British history (Polanyi, 1944). Because this act created a situation in which the value of the relief was often greater than the earned income of low-wage workers, the caseload swelled manyfold in the ensuing decades. In reaction to this situation, Parliament passed the Poor Law of 1834, which established the famous doctrine of "less eligibility," which is generally believed to have been the most repressive aspect of the British Poor Law. According to this doctrine, the level of relief was to be set so low that it would make the living conditions of recipient families less desirable and less satisfactory than those of the family of a worker who earned the lowest wages in the community (de Schweinitz, 1961), which meant that the amount of relief had to be lower than the lowest wages in the community, regardless of a family's size.

As early as the 1920s, some progressive thinkers in Britain recognized the problem of the gap between wages and family needs. For example, Eleanor F. Rathbone, an economist and member of Parliament, argued that the industrial wage system created anomalies between wages and family needs. However, she recognized that increasing the level of wages to "living wages" was impractical because workers without children would be overpaid. On the basis of her own investigation, she reported that if employers were forced to pay wages sufficient to support a family of five (five was a reasonable number in the 1920s), then 81.3% of British workers would be overpaid. Her solution was children's allowances (Rathbone, 1949). Rathbone's argument influenced Sir William H. Beveridge, who was asked by the British government during World War II to write a blueprint, known as the Beveridge Report, for the future of the British welfare state. Rathbone also influenced Paul H. Douglas of the United States, who recommended children's allowances to alleviate child poverty in the United States (Douglas, 1927).

Recognizing the fundamental friction between wages and family needs, Beveridge divided the British population into children and adults, provided children's allowances to deal with the financial needs of children, and streamlined the income-support provisions for adults. Having dealt with the problem of children independently, he could stratify the level of income of the adult population in a hierarchical order—from minimum wage, to social insurance benefits, to public assistance payments—with full recognition that governmental provisions should not undermine the incentives for adults to work. In his own way, he established a modern version of the "less eligibility" doctrine without involving children and, therefore, without creating undue hardships for recipient families (Beveridge, 1942). Furthermore, in developing social insurance and allied programs, Beveridge assumed that wages were large enough to support only a worker, a spouse, and one child. As a result, he recommended that children's allowances

should start with the second child. At any rate, the Beveridge Report dealt with the underlying issue of what to do with children (Ozawa, 1982). In his report to the British government, Beveridge pointed out that one quarter to one sixth of the poverty in England was the result of the failure to relate earned income to family size (Beveridge, 1942).

In France, income support for children, independent of wages, was established quite pragmatically. In the 1870s, several French administrative services and railways began to pay *allocations familales* in addition to the regular wages of workers who had families to support. This scheme was intended to maintain the basic wages of workers while providing adequate income to workers with dependents, thus avoiding overpayments to workers without dependents. The provision of children's allowances spread rapidly among private establishments after World War I. In the meantime, the French government embraced the idea of family allowances and established the public provision of such allowances (Ozawa, 1971; Vadakin, 1958, 1968).

After World War II, European countries, notably the Nordic countries, developed comprehensive policies for workers with children. Their policies covered both programs for income transfers and programs for supporting the employment of mothers. Gornick, Meyers, and Ross (1996) reported that the policies of Denmark, France, and Sweden currently implement both types of family policy adequately, whereas the United States does not. Again, at the center of societal concern in these countries is the issue of what to do with children. Countries that have developed these policies are concerned about the penalty for having children in the world of work, as well as in society in general. They want to minimize the gap between the labor income that parents bring home and the disposable household income that they need. Apparently, these countries have a vested interest both in mobilizing female workers in the labor market to their fullest capability and in making sure that "the problem of children" is dealt with positively and effectively.

The U.S. understanding of what to do with children has been ambivalent (see Garfinkel & McLanahan, 1986), and the history of U.S. welfare policy reflects this ambivalence. Before the enactment of the Social Security Act of 1935, many states had mothers' pension programs, which were designed to support children in need of financial support, but even then, mothers were not entirely exempt from working. Aid to Dependent Children (ADC), which was enacted as a part of the Social Security Act, was also meant to support children in female-headed families, but did not excuse these female heads from working. Aid to Families with Dependent Children (AFDC), which superseded ADC in 1962, expanded the unit of provision to families, instead of just children. While AFDC financially supported the recipient families as a whole, the monitoring of the mothers' work became more intense, which was reflected in an incentive-to-work measure incorporated in the benefit formula under AFDC. Now, Temporary Assistance to Needy Families (TANF), which superseded AFDC in 1996, requires mothers to work after they receive cash assistance for a stipulated period. Throughout the history of welfare policy, the U.S. government has shown its willingness to support children, but always while keeping an eye on the work behavior of the children's mothers. Because of the dual foci of welfare programs, the United States has never developed policies that address the problem of what to do with children separately from their parents, let alone developed a positive philosophy of investing in children explicitly. As a result, the United States is the only country among the industrialized nations that has not seriously explored the idea of children's allowances, although some academics, such as Douglas (1927), Schorr (1966), and Burns (1968), were strong advocates of such an idea.

In the meantime, there is a sign—albeit slight—that the U.S. government is addressing the problem of children in the distribution of labor income and tax subsidies. The Earned Income Tax Credit (EITC), which ostensibly was developed to subsidize wages (thus not creating the disincentive effect of public income transfers), is dealing, in part, with the problem of children because the rate of subsidy is higher for families with two children than for those with one child. Indeed, Ozawa (1995) and Ozawa and Hong (2003) have argued that if the EITC incorporated another rate for families with three or more children, EITC could become an American-style children's allowance, at least for low-income working families. In addition, the development of various types of tax credits, involving educational expenses, dependent care expenses, and more (see Ozawa, 1998), is another sign that the United States is addressing the problem of children in determining the economic lives of American families.

The foregoing discussion indicates that the issue of what to do with children continues to be a major focus of nations' struggles to neutralize—or not to neutralize—the problem of children in determining labor income and disposable household income. This issue is especially critical in shaping the economic lives of female-headed households with children because these households are in an especially disadvantaged position: They have to rely on one earner and are more likely to need to pay for child care than are married-couple households (Leibowitz, Klerman, & Waite, 1992). Furthermore, the number of female-headed households is increasing faster than that of married-couple households (U.S. Bureau of the Census, 2003, Table 690).

Thus, the objectives of our study were to estimate the degree to which the number of children lowers the income status of female-headed households, measured by the income-to-needs ratio on the basis of disposable household income, and to compare the U.S. situation with that of other industrialized countries. (In this chapter, the terms *income-to-needs ratio* and *income status* are used interchangeably.)

RELATED STUDIES

Our study built on earlier studies by Gornick et al. (1996), Gornick, Meyers, and Ross (1998), and Wong, Garfinkel, and McLanahan (1993). Gornick et al. (1996) evaluated the potency of family policy in supporting the employment of mothers in 14 industrialized countries by developing a composite index of various aspects of family policies, such as job protection, paid maternity leave, the wage replacement rate for such leaves, guaranteed child care, and afterschool child care. On the basis of this index, they rated the United States 14th (at the bottom), compared to France, 1st; Belgium, 2nd; Sweden, 3rd; Finland, 4th; and Canada, 9th. These are the countries on which our study focused. Our study was designed to show, among other things, which of these six countries provides the most generous public income transfers. Within the context of our study, the ranking, based on the index developed by Gornick et al. (1996), was as follows: France, 1st; Belgium, 2nd; Sweden, 3rd; Finland, 4th; Canada, 5th; and the United States, 6th (at the bottom). We expected that the ranking of these countries in terms of their generosity in public income transfers would not necessarily be the same as a ranking that was based on employment-supportive policies.

A subsequent study of 14 industrialized countries by Gornick et al. (1998) found that in the countries that have more supportive policies on employment for mothers with children, the employment rate of mothers does not differ from the employment rate of women with no children, other things being equal. In particular, in Belgium, Denmark, Finland, France, and Sweden, all of which have generous supportive policies on mothers' employment, the employment rate does not diminish as a result of having an additional child, while in Austria, the United Kingdom, and the United States, all of which have the least-generous policies, the employment rate of mothers diminishes as a result of having an additional child. More pointedly, in the United States, the addition of one child aged 0–2 reduces the employment rate of mothers by 22 percentage points (from 72% to 50%), and the addition of one child aged 3–5 reduces the employment rate of mothers by 15 percentage points (from 72% to 57%). In Sweden, such a reduction in the employment rate of mothers does not occur. These findings indicate that American mothers are forced to stop working because there are inadequate supportive measures, such as affordable child care and paid family leave. The reverse seems to be true in Sweden. Thanks to various supportive measures that Sweden developed, mothers with young children can continue to work. Gornick et al.'s study supports the idea that the problem of children in Sweden was neutralized in the labor supply of mothers because of work-supportive policies. Our study focused the issue on the countries in which the problem of children is neutralized in determining the income status of female-headed households.

Wong et al. (1993) studied the differences in the relative income status of single-mother families (relative to that of married-couple families) between the United States and six other industrialized countries and found that even after demographic variables, human capital variables, and policy-related variables were controlled for, the income status of U.S. single-mother families was significantly lower than that of single-mother families in the six other countries. They included the number of children as a control and found that this variable was inversely and significantly related to the income status of single-mother families. However, there is no way to discern, from their study, the differential impact of this variable on the income status of such families in various countries because they did not include the interaction terms between the number of children and the variable for country identification. (Such an omission is understandable because the number of children was not the major concern of their study.) Our study, with its major focus on the effect of the number of children, incorporated such interaction terms.

METHODOLOGY

To accomplish the objectives of our study, we asked the following questions:

1. At the descriptive level, what is the level of income of female-headed households with children after taxes are paid but before public and private income transfers are received? What are the intercountry differences?
2. At the descriptive level, what are the distributive effects of public income transfers (social insurance benefits and means-tested income transfers) and private income transfers? What are the intercountry differences?
3. To what extent do public and private income transfers reduce the inequality in disposable household income? What are the intercountry differences?
4. Analyzed separately, what is the relationship between the number of children in female-headed households and the level of disposable household income in each country, controlling for other variables?
5. What is the difference in disposable household income among female-headed households with children between the United States and other industrialized countries, controlling for other variables?
6. What is the difference in the effect of the number of children on the disposable household income of female-headed households with children between the United States and other industrialized countries?

Source of Data and Sample

The source of data was the fifth wave of the Luxembourg Income Study (LIS), which was collected in 2000. (Data for France came from the fourth wave, which is the latest for France.) The LIS data include microsurvey data from 25 industrialized countries, with each survey being nationally representative of the population in each country, and provide the most comparable information on household income and earnings, as well as the demographic characteristics of households across these countries (Christopher, 2001). The LIS also provides information on cash transfers, child care provisions, and parental leave policies (Gornick et al., 1998). For the purpose of our study, we selected 5,315 female-headed households with children younger than age 18.

Selection of Countries

We selected five industrialized countries—Belgium, Canada, Finland, France, and Sweden—with which we compared the United States. The criteria for selecting these countries were twofold. First, according to the scheme of classifying welfare states developed by Esping-Anderson (1990), we selected the United States and Canada, which are English-speaking countries that are characterized as "liberal" and that have developed the least-generous public income transfer programs; Finland and Sweden, which are characterized as "social democratic" and which have developed the most-generous public income transfer programs; and France and Belgium, which are characterized as "conservative-corporatist" and which are located between the two extreme camps of countries. Second, the data for these countries included all of the necessary variables, and these variables were comparable to one another.

Conceptual Framework

We posited that the number of children is significantly related to the income-to-needs ratio of female-headed households. The direction, magnitude, and significance of a relationship depend on the country of residence of female-headed households.

Dependent Variable

The LIS provided household income adjusted for household size, which was obtained by dividing household income by the square root of household size. In our study, the dependent variable was income status or, technically, the income-to-needs ratio. The income-to-needs ratio was obtained by calculating the ratio of household income to the poverty line. The poverty line was defined as 50% of the median household income in the country where particular female-headed

households resided. Thus, for example, if a particular household had income that was twice the poverty line, then this household's income-to-needs ratio was 2. The higher the income-to-needs ratio, the better off the household was financially. The income-to-needs ratio, so obtained, was useful because it automatically dealt with price changes and was comparable across countries. For multivariate analyses, income-to-needs ratios were log-transformed because their distribution was skewed.

Independent Variable

The independent variable was the number of children living at home who were younger than age 18.

Control Variables

To net out the effect of the number of children, we included the following variables as controls because they were expected to make a difference in the income status of female-headed households: the age of the youngest child and the age, education, and work status of the female head of the household (Wong et al., 1993). Having a young child makes it difficult for a female head to work, thus decreasing the amount of earned income (Smith, 1989). Educated women generally command higher wages, thus making the opportunity cost (the cost of not working) higher, which tends to compel female heads to work more, again increasing earned income, other things being equal (Leibowitz et al., 1992; Ozawa & Wang, 1993). The status of working versus nonworking would have a direct impact on the amount of earned income of female-headed households. Moreover, the life-cycle hypothesis suggests that earnings generally increase with age (Land, 1996; Tin, 1998). It is important to note that earned income is an important component of disposable income. In addition, we included the country identification—a major concern in our study—as a control variable.

All of these variables are self-explanatory, except education. To measure education, we categorized female heads into three groups: those with a low level of education, those with a medium level of education, and those with a high level of education. These levels represented (1) lower than secondary education, (2) completion of secondary education, and (3) higher than secondary education, respectively (Pettit & Hook, 2002).

Data Presentation and Statistical Procedures

Four types of descriptive statistics are presented: the backgrounds of the female-headed households; the distributive effects of social insurance benefits, means-tested benefits, and private income transfers; Gini coefficients (an indicator of inequality) at different stages of income distribution; and the composition of household income. These descriptive statistics are useful in discerning how the female-headed households in our study came to have their levels of disposable income. The disposable household income was the dependent variable in the multiple regression models in our study.

We conducted a series of regression analyses of the income-to-needs ratios of female-headed households, with the number of children as the major independent variable and with the age of the youngest child, the age of the female head, and the level of education and work status of the female head as control variables. First, we ran the regressions separately for each country to observe the level of significance of the number of children in each country. Second, using all of the households across countries, we included as independent variables the country identification and the number of children, to determine if the location of residence made a difference in the income status of the female-headed households. Third, we included the interaction terms of the number of children and the country identification to measure the difference in the effect of the number of children on income status between the United States and each of the other five countries. The unit of analysis was households.

FINDINGS

Descriptive Statistics

Backgrounds of Female-Headed Households, by Country

In Table 22.1, three observations stand out. First, the mean number of children in U.S. households (1.76) was the largest and that of children in France was the smallest (1.51). Second, the labor supply was the greatest in the United States. As much as 76.08% of the female heads of households in the United States were working full time, compared with 30.33% in Sweden,

with the percentages in other countries between these extremes. In terms of no work, only 15.64% of the U.S. female heads were not working, compared to 46.39% of those in Belgium. Third, 23.14% of the U.S. female heads had a high level of education, compared to 29.3% of the Finnish female heads and 26.53% of the Belgian female heads.

The poverty rates and income-to-needs ratios shown in Table 22.1 are based on the disposable household income (Stage 4, explained next). They indicate that the U.S. female-headed households had the highest poverty rate, and their income-to-needs ratio was the second lowest (the Canadian female-headed households were the lowest).

Income-to-Needs Ratios and Distributive Effects of Public and Private Income Transfers

The top part of Table 22.2 shows the income-to-needs ratios of female-headed households in the six countries in four stages of the income distribution:

> Stage 1: Income after taxes and before income transfers
> Stage 2: Income at Stage 1 plus social insurance benefits, including Social Security benefits, children's allowances, and maternity benefits
> Stage 3: Income at Stage 2 plus means-tested cash and near-cash benefits
> Stage 4: Income at Stage 3 plus private income transfers, including alimony, child support payments, and regular payments from friends and relatives

Income at Stage 1 was the baseline to estimate the distributive effects of public and private income transfers.

The top part of Table 22.2 indicates that after taxes, the income-to-needs ratio of female-headed households was the highest (1.085) in the United States and the lowest in Sweden (0.636). The addition of social insurance benefits greatly improved the income status of female-headed households in the five other countries. The mean income-to-needs ratio of female-headed households increased 91% in Belgium, 86.1% in Sweden, 47.08% in Finland, 35.05% in France, 27.95% in Canada, but only 5.71% in the United States.

The receipt of means-tested benefits increased the income status of U.S. female-headed households (12.54%) less than it did for those in the other countries, except Belgium (7.38%). The situation in Belgium is

TABLE 22.1 Backgrounds of Female-Headed Households, by Country

	United States (N = 2,817)	Canada (N = 1,380)	France (N = 353)
Age	36.60	37.09	38.32
Number of children under age 18	1.76	1.63	1.51
Age of the youngest child	7.60	8.80	8.86
Education			
Low	17.87	17.89	55.92
Medium	58.99	70.18	28.22
High	23.14	11.93	15.86
Work status			
Full-time work	76.08	51.58	53.89
Part-time work	8.28	24.22	22.32
No work	15.64	24.20	23.78
Poverty rate	41.06	37.55	23.80
Income-to-needs ratio	1.379	1.326	1.510

	Belgium (N = 106)	Sweden (N = 406)	Finland (N = 253)
Age	38.64	38.49	38.73
Number of children under age 18	1.53	1.64	1.53
Age of the youngest child	9.62	8.93	8.97
Education			
Low	40.20	20.44	25.14
Medium	33.27	57.04	45.56
High	26.53	22.51	29.30
Work status			
Full-time work	39.85	30.33	67.65
Part-time work	13.76	56.86	8.14
No work	46.39	12.81	24.20
Poverty rate	14.54	9.70	9.02
Income-to-needs ratio	1.467	1.497	1.530

interesting: The effect of social insurance benefits in that country was the largest (91%), whereas the effect of means-tested benefits was the smallest (7.38%).

The effect of private income transfers was the smallest in the United States as well. The receipt of private income transfers resulted in only an 8.85% increase in the income-to-needs ratio of U.S. female-headed households, compared with a 23.11% increase in Sweden.

Taken together, the distributive effect of public and private income transfers was the smallest for the U.S. female-headed households—27.1%—compared with 51.89%, 62.36%, 82.36%, 116.37%, and 135.38% for those in Canada, France, Finland, Belgium, and Sweden, respectively.

It should be noted that the ranking of these six countries in terms of income status at the final stage of income distribution (Stage 4) was found to be exactly the same as

TABLE 22.2 The Income-to-Needs Ratio at Four Stages of Income Distribution and the Distributive Effects of Public and Private Income Transfers

	After Tax	Plus Social Insurance Benefits	Plus Means-Tested Benefits	Plus Private Transfers
United States	1.085	1.147	1.283	1.379
Canada	0.873	1.117	1.234	1.326
France	0.930	1.256	1.410	1.510
Belgium	0.678	1.295	1.345	1.467
Sweden	0.636	1.183	1.350	1.497
Finland	0.839	1.234	1.415	1.530

	Percentage Change Due to			
	Social Insurance Benefits	Means-Tested Benefits	Private Tansfers	All Transfers
United States	5.71	12.54	8.85	27.10
Canada	27.95	13.40	10.54	51.89
France	35.05	16.56	10.75	62.36
Belgium	91.00	7.38	17.99	116.37
Sweden	86.01	26.26	23.11	135.38
Finland	47.08	21.57	13.71	82.36

the ranking in terms of the generosity of work-supportive policies that was observed by Gornick et al. (1996).

Table 22.3 shows the differential distributive effects of public versus private income transfers in each country. It indicates that the U.S. female-headed households relied less on public income transfers, relative to private income transfers, than did their counterparts in other industrialized countries. The ratio of public income transfers to private income transfers was only 2.1:1 in the United States, compared to 3.9:1, 4.8:1, 5.5:1, 4.9:1 and 5:1 in Canada, France, Belgium, Sweden, and Finland.

Table 22.4 shows the Gini coefficients of income-to-needs ratios at different stages of income distribution. Again, treating the after-tax income-to-needs ratios as the baseline, we found that the weak distributive effect of social insurance benefits for U.S. female-headed households stands out as an extreme case. These benefits reduced the Gini coefficient of their income-to-needs ratios by only 3.22%, from 0.466 to 0.451. In comparison, these benefits reduced the Gini coefficient for the female-headed households in Belgium by 55.73% from 0.558 to 0.247. The magnitude of the changes in the Gini coefficients in the other countries was somewhere between these two extremes.

Generally, the distributive effect of means-tested income transfers was weaker than that of social insur-ance benefits, although these benefits were targeted to lower-income female-headed households, in part because the magnitude of social insurance benefits was considerably larger. Nevertheless, for those in the United States, the effect of means-tested income transfers in lessening the Gini coefficient (17.17%) was second only to 20.77% in Finland.

The distributive effect of private income transfers was even weaker, ranging from 0.62% in France to 8.2% in Sweden, with 1.77% in the United States, which was the second lowest among the countries.

The distributive effect of all types of transfers, to-gether, in reducing inequality was the lowest in the United States: 22.16% (from 0.466 at the baseline to 0.363 at the final stage of disposable household income). In contrast, the reduction in inequality be-cause of these transfers was 73.99% in Sweden—the largest reduction in inequality. It is interesting to note that the degree of inequality in the income status of female-headed households in the Nordic countries became extremely small after all types of transfers were distributed. In particular, the coefficient of 0.160 in Sweden indicated that, as a result of public and private income transfers, the income-to-needs ratios of female-headed households in Sweden became homogeneous.

Table 22.3 Comparison of the Distributive Effects of Public and Private Income Transfers (percentage)

	Public Income Transfers (1)	Private Income Transfers (2)	Ratio Between (1) and (2)
United States	18.25	8.85	2.1:1
Canada	41.35	10.54	3.9:1
France	51.61	10.75	4.8:1
Belgium	98.38	17.99	5.5:1
Sweden	112.27	23.11	4.9:1
Finland	68.65	13.71	5.0:1

TABLE 22.4 The Gini Coefficents at Four Stages of Income Distribution and the Distributive Effects of Public and Private Transfers

	After Taxes	Plus Social Insurance Benefits	Plus Means-Tested Benefits	Plus Private Transfers
United States	0.466	0.451	0.371	0.363
Canada	0.497	0.376	0.297	0.289
France	0.492	0.321	0.253	0.251
Belgium	0.558	0.247	0.215	0.204
Sweden	0.529	0.256	0.181	0.160
Finland	0.467	0.283	0.186	0.179

	Percentage Change Due to			
	Social Insurance Benefits	Means-Tested Benefits	Private Transfers	All Transfers
United States	−3.22	−17.17	−1.77	-22.16
Canada	−24.35	−15.90	−2.13	-42.37
France	−34.76	−13.82	−0.62	-49.20
Belgium	−55.73	−5.73	−4.45	-65.92
Sweden	−51.61	−14.18	−8.20	-73.99
Finland	−39.40	−20.77	−2.47	-62.64

Sources of Income

Table 22.5 shows the sources of income among female-headed households in each of the six countries under investigation. As expected, the percentage of earnings was the largest in the United States—78.19% of the households' gross incomes came from this source. In comparison, earnings constituted only 52.8% of the households' gross incomes in Sweden. Also, as expected, social insurance benefits constituted the smallest percentage of the households' gross incomes in the United States: 3.93%, compared to 32.77% in Belgium. The reason for this difference is that Belgium and other countries in Europe have universal programs, such as family allowances for children, maternity and parental leave benefits, and allowances at the birth of a child—none of which are means tested.

Multivariate Analysis

The purpose of our multivariate analyses was to estimate the net effect of the number of children on the income status of female-headed households in the United States, in comparison to that of the female-headed households in other countries, controlling for other variables.

TABLE 22.5 Percentage Distribution of Income, by Source

	United States (N = 2,817)	Canada (N = 1,380)	France (N = 353)
Market income			
Earnings	78.19	67.84	59.01
Other	3.00	1.95	1.53
Transfers			
Social transfers			
Social insurances	3.93	15.96	22.77
Means-tested public assistance	8.71	7.31	10.10
Private transfers			
Alimony/child support	5.53	5.95	5.84
Other regular private income	0.28	0.00	0.75
Other income	0.36	0.99	0.00
Total gross income	100.00	100.00	100.00
Taxes			
Payroll tax	−5.69	−4.69	−0.00
Income tax	−8.39	−10.51	−1.58
Disposable income	85.92	84.80	98.42
	Belgium (N = 106)	Sweden (N = 406)	Finland (N = 253)
Market income			
Earnings	54.72	52.80	57.20
Other	3.08	2.47	5.94
Transfers			
Social transfers			
Social insurances	32.77	28.10	21.39
Means-tested public assistance	2.87	8.74	9.45
Private transfers			
Alimony/child support	6.56	7.89	4.54
Other regular private income	0.00	0.00	1.48
Other income	0.00	0.00	0.00
Total gross income	100.00	100.00	100.00
Taxes			
Payroll tax	−6.59	−4.56	−4.05
Income tax	−15.46	−18.22	−15.81
Disposable income	77.95	77.22	80.14

Separate OLS Multiple Regression Analysis for Each Country

Table 22.6 shows the regression results of the income-to-needs ratios of female-headed households in each country. The table shows both coefficients and relative effects in percentages.

When a dependent variable is transformed into a log and independent variables take the form of dummy variables, regression coefficients are uninterpretable

TABLE 22.6 OLS Regression Analysis of Income-to-Needs Ratios: Separate Countries

	United States		Canada		France	
	Coefficient	Relative Effect in %	Coefficient	Relative Effect in %	Coefficient	Relative Effect in %
Intercept	0.3346***		0.4232***		0.5033***	
Age	0.0053***		0.0048***		0.0072***	
Number of children under age 18	-0.0366***		-0.0192**		-0.0145	
Age of the youngest child	0.0046***		0.0020		0.0008	
Education						
(Low)						
Medium	0.0878***	9.18	0.0686***	7.10	0.0608*	6.27
High	0.2868***	33.22	0.1886***	20.76	0.1539***	16.64
Work status						
Full-time work	0.2764***	31.84	0.2862***	33.14	0.2158***	24.09
Part-time work	0.0978***	10.27	0.0928***	9.72	0.0300	3.05
(No work)						
R^2	0.3410		0.4039		0.3841	
F	207.61***		132.82***		30.74***	
N	2,817		1,380		353	

(Continued)

Table 22.6 (Continued)

	Belgium		Sweden		Finland	
	Coefficient	Relative Effect in %	Coefficient	Relative Effect in %	Coefficient	Relative Effect in %
Intercept	0.4428***		0.6044***		0.6185***	
Age	0.0064		0.0044***		0.0039	
Number of children under age 18	0.0525		0.0133		0.0008	
Age of the youngest child	0.0006		0.0041		0.0061	
Education						
(Low)						
Medium	0.0918	9.61	0.0047	0.47	0.0386	3.94
High	0.1604**	17.40	0.0581*	5.98	0.1534***	16.58
Work status						
Full-time work	0.1317**	14.08	0.1603***	17.39	0.1005**	10.57
Part-time work	0.1189*	12.63	0.0880***	9.20	0.0583	6.00
(No work)						
R^2	0.3310		0.2844		0.2606	
F	6.93***		22.60***		12.33***	
N	106		406		253	

*$p < .05$, **$p < .01$, ***$p < .001$. Reference groups are in parentheses.

in plain English, requiring their transformation into "relative effects," the equation for which is $(e^x - 1) \times 100$, where x represents the coefficient and e represents the exponent (see Halvorsen & Palmquiest, 1980). The regression results indicate that the number of children was significantly related to the income-to-needs ratio in the United States and Canada, but not in other countries. Specifically, adding one more child resulted in a 3.66% decline ($p < .001$) in the income-to-needs ratio in the United States and a 1.92% decline ($p < .01$) in Canada. In the other countries, no statistically significant relationship was observed.

Another important finding was that the age of the youngest child was significantly and positively related to the income-to-needs ratio in the United States, but not in any other country. The addition of 1 year to the age of the youngest child resulted in a 0.46% increase ($p < .001$) in the income-to-needs ratio of female-headed households in the United States. This finding implies that only in the United States was the income status of female-headed households affected by both the number of children in the household and the age of the youngest child.

The relationship between education and the income-to-needs ratio was the strongest in the United States as well. For example, the income-to-needs ratio of households headed by women with a high level of education was 33.22% greater ($p < .001$) than that of their counterparts with a low level of education. In contrast, the income-to-needs ratio for those in Sweden with a high level of education was 5.98% ($p < .05$) greater than that of their counterparts with a low level of education.

Similarly, work status was more strongly related to the income-to-needs ratio in the United States than in any other country except Canada. In the United States, the income-to-needs ratio of households whose female heads worked full time was 31.84% greater ($p < .001$) than the income-to-needs ratio of households with female heads who did not work. In contrast, in Finland, full-time work by female heads increased the income-to-needs ratio by only 10.57% ($p < .01$).

OLS Multiple Regression Analysis for All Female-Headed Households

Table 22.7 presents the regression results of the income-to-needs ratios of female-headed households

across all of the countries under study. Model 1 indicates that, controlling for other variables, the number of children was significantly and inversely related to the income-to-needs ratios of these households ($p < .001$). An addition of one child was associated with a 2.89% decline in the income-to-needs ratio.

The income-to-needs ratios of the female-headed households in the other five countries were significantly higher than the income-to-needs ratio of those in the United States. The differential between the United States and Belgium was the greatest: 17.54% ($p < .001$). The smallest differential was between the United States and Canada: 4.97% ($p < .001$). The differentials with regard to the other countries were between these two extremes.

Model 2 included interaction terms between the number of children and the country identification. The inclusion of such interaction terms enabled us to investigate the differences in the effect of the number of children on the income-to-needs ratios of female-headed households in the United States and in the other five countries. Specifically, in Model 2, the coefficient for the number of children pertains to the United States. The coefficients for the interaction terms pertain to the difference between the coefficient for the United States and that for a particular country.

The results of Model 2 indicate that the number of children was inversely related to the income-to-needs ratio of female-headed households in the United States (-0.0426; $p < .001$), indicating that an addition of one child reduced the income-to-needs ratio by 4.26%. The coefficient for the interaction terms between the number of children and Belgium was 0.0912 ($p < .01$). From these two numbers, we determined that the coefficient for the number of children for Belgium would be 0.0486 ($-0.0426 + 0.0912$). Thus, while the addition of one child would *reduce* the income-to-needs ratio of a female-headed household in the United States by 4.26%, such an addition would *increase* the income-to-needs ratio of a female-headed household in Belgium by 4.86%.

Similar calculations could be made with regard to the effect of the number of children in the other countries. For example, the coefficient of the number of children in Canada would be -0.0171 ($-0.0426 + 0.0255$). Thus, the addition of one child would reduce the income-to-needs ratio of U.S. female-headed households by 4.26%, and such an addition would also reduce the income-to-needs ratio of Canadian female-headed households by 1.71%. The coefficients of the

Table 22.7 OLS Regression Analysis of Income-to-Needs Ratios: Entire Sample

	Model 1		Model 2	
	Coefficient	Relative effect (%)	Coefficient	Relative effect (%)
Intercept	0.3733***		0.3986***	
Age	0.0053***		0.0052***	
Number of children under age 18	-0.0289***		-0.0426***	
Age of the youngest child	0.0033***		0.0035***	
Education				
(Low)				
Medium	0.0722***	7.49	0.0706***	7.32
High	0.2304***	25.91	0.2274***	25.53
Work status				
(No work)				
Full-time work	0.2540***	28.92	0.2540***	28.92
Part-time work	0.0893***	9.34	0.0881***	9.21
Country of residence				
(United States)				
Canada	0.0485***	4.97	0.0049	0.49
France	0.1562***	16.91	0.0901**	9.43
Belgium	0.1616***	17.54	0.0090	0.90
Sweden	0.1609***	17.46	0.0611*	6.30
Finland	0.1069***	11.28	0.0251	2.54
Interaction terms				
Nnumber of children * Canada			0.0255**	
Nnumber of children * France			0.0405*	
Nnumber of children * Belgium			0.0912**	
Nnumber of children * Sweden			0.0651***	
Nnumber of children * Finland			0.0507**	
R^2	0.3489	0.3534		
F	236.78***	170.33***		
N	5,315	5,315		

*$p <.05$, **$p <.01$, ***$p <.001$. Reference groups are in parentheses.

number of children in the rest of the countries were as follows: France, –0.0021 (–0.0426 + 0.0405); Sweden, 0.0225 (–0.0426 + 0.0651); and Finland, 0.0081 (–0.0426 + 0.0507). Note that the interaction terms were significant for the five countries.

The interaction terms for these six countries indicate that the direction of the coefficient for the number of children was negative for three countries (the United States, Canada, and France) and positive for three countries (Belgium, Sweden, and Finland). That is, the greater the number of children, the lower the income-to-needs ratio in the United States, Canada,

and France, but the higher the income-to-needs ratio in Belgium, Sweden, and Finland. More important, the adverse impact of the number of children was significantly greater in the United States than in any other country.

We also observed one more interesting phenomenon. Model 1 indicates that the coefficient of the number of children among all female-headed households in all six countries was –0.0289 ($p < .001$), while the coefficient for the U.S. female-headed households was –0.0426 (Model 2), which clearly indicates that the negative relationship between number of children and income-to-needs ratio was larger in the United States than in all six countries taken together.

DISCUSSION AND IMPLICATIONS

A clear picture emerges about the income status of U.S. female-headed households. In the United States, female heads of households are relatively well educated, have a relatively larger number of children, and are more likely to work (see Table 22.1). At the descriptive level, their after-tax income status is the highest among those in these six countries. Yet, after public and private income transfers are distributed, their income status plunges to the second lowest, next only to Canadians'.

OLS regression analyses indicate that when other variables are controlled for, the income status of U.S. female-headed households is lower than that in any other country (Model 1, Table 22.7). And, what is most important, the negative impact of children is the strongest in the United States: The number of children is related to a greater decline in the income status of female-headed households in the United States than in any other country (Model 2, Table 22.7).

Other pertinent findings are that the effects of education and work status are especially strong deter minants of the income status of U.S. female-headed households. The high level of education and full-time work are associated with a greater percentage increase in the income-to-needs ratio in the United States than in any other country. In addition, the age of the youngest child is positively related to the income-to-needs ratio only among female-headed households in the United States, whereas this variable was not significant in the other five countries (see Table 22.6).

These findings imply that U.S. female heads of households are subjected most strongly to the vicissitudes of economic forces. Good education leads to a higher disposable household income, work is associated with a higher household income, but having more children is associated with lesser household income.

The picture of female-headed households in the Nordic and continental European countries is quite different. These female heads do not work as much as do U.S. female heads, their education is related to their household income less strongly, and children do not adversely affect their income status. Far from it. In Belgium, Sweden, and Finland, the number of children is *positively* related to the income-to-needs

ratio of female-headed households. In these countries, the more children that the female-headed households have, the better off they are.

Why such a difference? It seems that, in the United States, the income status of female-headed households is determined according to the economic theory of labor supply. The better educated earn more, their greater attachment to the labor force brings more income, and children are negatively related to earned income because the existence of children is an impediment to the employment of women and therefore results in lower income (Leibowitz et al., 1992). This economic theory sounds straightforward, and things are supposed to play out exactly as we found in our study.

In the Nordic and European countries, it seems that, thanks to social policy interventions that improve the income status of households with children, particularly female-headed households, the economic forces, as theorized by economists, are greatly mitigated, as the findings of our study indicate. Thanks to the provision of various forms of public income transfers, including children's allowances, maternity benefits, Social Security benefits, unemployment insurance, and workers' compensation, the distribution of disposable household income (Stage 4) is effectively smoothed out, mitigating the impact of children on the income status of female-headed households in these countries. In short, these countries have "conquered" or are on the way to conquering (in the case of France) the problem of children in distributing income. In contrast, the United States and Canada have a long way to go.

Are the economic conditions of U.S. female-headed households good or bad? It is hard to draw a conclusion. However, we can relate our findings to U.S. current and future demographics regarding children. In 2004, of the 72.3 million children in the United States, 17.1 million (or 23.6%) lived in female-headed families, of whom 7.1 million children (or 41.8%) were poor (U.S. Bureau of the Census, 2005).[1] Because the number of female-headed families has steadily increased over the years, we anticipate that the number of children who live in such families and the percentage of such children who are poor will rise in the future if the trend continues. For example, the number of female-headed families increased 43%, from 9 million in 1980 to 12.9 million in 2000, while the number of married-couple families increased only 15%, from 49.3 million in 1980 to 56.6 million in 2000. Furthermore, the income status of female-headed families has lost ground relative to that of married-couple families. In constant dollars, the median income of female-headed families increased only 20% during the same period, compared with 29% for married-couple families (U.S. Bureau of the Census, 2003, Table 690). The implication of this demographic shift is that, by not solving the problem of children, the United States is creating a serious situation in which female heads of households are penalized for having children, and children living in such circumstances will suffer economically as a result.

The fundamental issue that faces U.S. policy makers is this: Is having children a matter of personal choice and, thus, personal responsibility, as some economists say? Or, does the public, and therefore the government, have some sort of interest in and hence responsibility for the economic lives of children? Obviously, some Nordic and European countries have assumed public responsibility for ensuring that the economic well-being of households is not adversely affected by having children. Otherwise, they would not have moved so aggressively to make the problem of children a non-issue.

The United States may have second thoughts about how to treat the problem of children, given another demographic trend. This trend relates to the diverging populations of children and elderly people. From 2005 to 2050, it is estimated that the percentage of children will *decline* from 24.9% to 23.5%, but the percentage of elderly people will *increase*, from 12.4% to 20.7% (U.S. Bureau of the Census, 2003, Table 12). Moreover, the racial/ethnic mix of the populations of children and elderly people will change drastically. From 2005 to 2050, it is projected that the percentage of Hispanic children will increase from 13.7% to 28.1%, that of Black children will increase from 14.9% to 18.2%, that of Asian children will increase from 3.8% to 10.1%, and that of American Indian children will increase from 0.7% to 0.9%, but the percentage of White children will decline from 66.9% to 42.3%. In contrast, 66.7% of the elderly population will still be White in 2050 (Ozawa, 1997).

Given these numbers, the United States is facing dual problems. First, how can this country continue to finance Social Security benefits? Second, given the drastic changes in the racial/ethnic mix of the child population, how can this nation develop the earnings capabilities of future generations of workers (which will need to be much higher than they currently are)? In a nutshell, this country needs to nurture every child, and every non-White child in particular, to his or her fullest potential.

Letting economic forces determine the income status of female-headed households and their children will create a risk for this country in that many children will not be nurtured to their fullest potential. Even among married-couple households, such a risk will arise, because, other things being equal, households with children will be worse off economically in the future (see U.S. Bureau of the Census, 1998, Figure 2.6). Furthermore, if women make their own adaptation to such a predicament by not having children, the population of children will decline, which will make it even harder to transfer income from the young to the old. Such an adaptation, which is detrimental from a macro perspective, is already taking place in some industrialized societies, such as Japan (Moffett, 2005; Ozawa & Kono, 1997).

Since 1795 in Britain, many countries have struggled to narrow the gap between wages and family needs. This problem persists in the United States today. Given the predicaments facing the United States, it seems to be in the public interest to recognize the existence of this gap and to find ways to narrow it.

Note

1. The U.S. Bureau of the Census provides these data for families, but not for households.

References

Beveridge, W. H. (1942). *Social insurance and allied services*. New York: Macmillan.

Burns, E. M. (Ed.). (1968). *Children's allowances and the economic welfare of children*. New York: Citizens' Committee for Children of New York.

Christopher, K. (2001). Welfare state regimes and mother's poverty. *Social Politics, 9,* 60–86.

de Schweinitz, K. (1961). *England's road to social security*. New York: Barnes.

Douglas, P. H. (1927). *The wages and family*. Chicago: University of Chicago Press.

Esping-Anderson, G. (1990). *The three worlds of welfare capitalism*. Princeton, NJ: Princeton University Press.

Garfinkel, I., & McLanahan, S. S. (1986). *Single mothers and their children: A new American dilemma*. Washington, DC: Urban Institute Press.

Gornick, J. C., Meyers, M. K., & Ross, K. E. (1996). *Supporting the employment of mothers: Policy variation across fourteen welfare states*. Luxembourg Income Study (LIS) Working Paper No. 139. Syracuse, NY: Maxwell School of Citizenship and Public Affairs, Syracuse University.

Gornick, J. C., Meyers, M. K., & Ross, K. E. (1998). Public policies and the employment of mothers: A cross-national study. *Social Science Quarterly, 79*, 35–54.

Halvorsen, R., & Palmquiest, R. (1980). The interpretation of dummy variables in semilogarithmic equations. *American Economic Review, 70*, 474–475.

Land, K. C. (1996). Wealth accumulation across the adult life course: Stability and change in sociodemographic covariate structures of net worth data in the Survey of Income and Program Participation, 1984–1999. *Social Science Research, 25*, 426–462.

Leibowitz, A., Klerman, J. A., & Waite, L. (1992). Employment of new mothers and child care choice. *Journal of Human Resources, 27*(1), 112–133.

Moffett, S. (2005, September 12). Japanese voters give Koizumi broad mandate: Landslide vote backs call to overhaul government for a declining population. *Wall Street Journal*, pp. A1, A10.

Ozawa, M. N. (1971). Family allowances and a national minimum of economic security. *Child Welfare, 50*, 313–321.

Ozawa, M. N. (1982). *Income maintenance and work incentives: Toward a synthesis.* New York: Praeger.

Ozawa, M. N. (1995). The earned income tax credit: Its effect and its significance. *Social Service Review, 69*, 563–582.

Ozawa, M. N. (1997). Demographic changes and their implications. In M. Reisch & E. Gambrill (Eds.), *Social work in the 21st century* (pp. 8–27). Thousand Oaks, CA: Pine Forge.

Ozawa, M. N. (1998). Children's economic place in America. *Journal of Poverty, 2*(3), 1–12.

Ozawa, M. N., & Hong, B. E. (2003). The effects of EITC and children's allowances on the economic well-being of children. *Social Work Research, 27*, 163–178.

Ozawa, M. N., & Kono, S. (1997). Child well-being in Japan: The high cost of economic success. In G. A. Cornia & S. Danziger (Eds.), *Child pov-*erty and deprivation in industrialized countries, 1945–1995 (pp. 307–334). Oxford: Oxford University Press.

Ozawa, M. N., & Wang, Y. T. (1993). The effects of children and education on women's earnings history. *Social Work Research, 29*(1), 17–27.

Pettit, B., & Hook, J. (2002). The structure of women's employment in comparative perspective. Luxembourg Income Study Working Paper Series No. 330. Syracuse, NY: Maxwell School of Citizenship and Public Affairs, Syracuse University.

Polanyi, K. (1944). *The great transformation.* London: Farrar & Rinehart.

Rathbone, E. F. (1949). *Family allowances.* London: Allen & Unwin.

Schorr, A. L. (1966). *Poor kids.* New York: Basic.

Smith, J. P. (1989). Women, mothers, and work. In M. N. Ozawa (Ed.), *Women's life cycle and economic insecurity: Problems and proposals* (pp. 42–70). New York: Greenwood.

Tin, J. (1998). Household demand for financial assets: A life-cycle analysis. *Quarterly Journal of Economics and Finance, 4*, 875–897.

U.S. Bureau of the Census. (1998, July). *Measuring 50 years of economic change.* Washington, DC: Author.

U.S. Bureau of the Census. (2003). *Statistical abstract of the United States: 2003.* Washington, DC: Author.

U.S. Bureau of the Census. (2005). *Annual demographic survey: March supplement.* Washington, DC: Author.

Vadakin, J. C. (1958). *Family allowances.* Miami, FL: University of Miami Press.

Vadakin, J. C. (1968). *Children, poverty and family allowances.* New York: Basic.

Wong, Y. I., Garfinkel, I., & McLanahan, S. (1993). Single-mother families in eight countries: Economic status and social policy. *Social Service Review, 67*, 177–197.

Closing Reflections:
Future Research Directions
and a New Paradigm

Duncan Lindsey

Aron Shlonsky

The knowledge base and set of practices which inform the modern child welfare field has been built on a strong foundation of accumulated research and reflective practice. During its early history, public child welfare's primary function was to care for those children who had no one else to look after them. Public child welfare emerged to meet the needs of orphaned and abandoned children. Later, public child welfare included provisions for the care of abused and neglected children (Wolins & Piliavin, 1964). By the 1950s, public child welfare agencies became professionalized, mostly providing foster care along with a small assortment of other services (Zietz, 1964).

The next decades (1950–1970) were characterized by a call for research and a systematic effort to construct an empirical knowledge base to inform child welfare practice. One of the most important leaders in this effort was Alfred Kadushin of the University of Wisconsin. Over the years, Kadushin developed an almost encyclopedic knowledge of research in the child

welfare field and synthesized the results into a theoretical framework for understanding child welfare services. Kadushin's introductory *Child Welfare Services* served as the major textbook in the child welfare field for many years. In it, Kadushin (1978) defined the child welfare system as:

> a network of public and voluntary agencies in social work practice that specialize in the prevention, amelioration, or remediation of social problems related to the functioning of the parent-child relationship network through the development and provision of specific child welfare services: services to children in their own home, protective services, day care, homemaker service, foster family care, services to the unwed mother, adoption services, and institutional child care. (p. 14)

For the first two decades after World War II, Kadushin's definition prevailed. But this would all change with the publication of "The Battered Child Syndrome" (Kempe et al., 1962). Prior to this medical exposé on the prevalence of widespread childhood injury resulting from physical abuse, the child welfare system was primarily concerned with helping poor and troubled families. Concern with child *abuse* was not central to Kadushin's traditional perspective, but rather the emphasis was on child *neglect* and providing an array of services to families.[1] However, the discovery of child abuse led to a transformation of child welfare into child protection and, for the last several decades, child abuse has been the central concern for child welfare (Kamerman & Khan, 1990).

PARADIGM SHIFT

The traditional definition of child welfare developed by Kadushin reflected the convergence of understanding in the field dating from the pioneering work of Charles Loring Brace (1859). It was a viewpoint that represented the normative aspirations of child welfare professionals for at least a century. Since the 1960s, the transformation of the field brought about by the discovery of child abuse has led to a paradigm shift in research, practice, and policy.

Kempe and colleagues' study provided convincing evidence of the brutality of child abuse, and the publication of "The Battered Child Syndrome" (1962) galvanized the public to take action against child abuse. One of the major results of the study was the adoption of mandatory child abuse laws in every state. The unintended consequence was an avalanche of child abuse reports, and this changed the very nature of public child welfare agencies. With so many reports of maltreatment, the public child welfare system was soon relegated to receiving, investigating, and substantiating child abuse reports. When child abuse was substantiated, the major service provided was removal of the child and placement in foster care. This child protection mission has shaped our understanding of the public child welfare field and the nature of the problems to be solved. Child protection is the primary service provided by child welfare today and, due to the link between child maltreatment and poverty, poor and low-income families are subjected to greater surveillance, a recursive and possibly harmful process. The system serves to identify children most at risk and, when all else fails, to remove them from their families. Little is offered to low-income and poor families (see Pelton in this volume), but they are required to meet conditions for reunification or risk the termination of parental rights.

In recent years, research has led to improved risk assessments, and there has been an increased emphasis on making decisions and providing services based on the best available evidence. As Eileen Gambrill has indicated in her chapter, the emergence of evidence-based practice as a guiding philosophy of care promises to promote greater accountability and a wider range of effective services. Since the mid-1990s, there has also been a substantial shift toward moving children more quickly into permanent placements, often with relative caregivers (see the chapters by Testa and by Festinger in this volume). The length of time that children linger in long-term foster care has been reduced because of concurrent planning for reunification, legal guardianship, or adoption. The positive results have been an almost doubling of children adopted through public child welfare agencies and a nearly one-quarter reduction in the average time that children remain in foster care (see part III, this volume). Further, there have been major improvements in the willingness and capacity of child protection agencies to respond differently to cases involving substantial, high-risk maltreatment as opposed to cases where families need more limited and less-coercive services (see Waldfogel, this volume).

But these advances are not likely to mediate the structural factors that bring a disproportionate number of poor and disadvantaged children to the attention of the child welfare system (see the chapters by Pelton, by Trocmé, and by Stoesz, this volume). The situation for poor and disadvantaged children in the United States has not materially improved during the period of the transformation of child welfare into child protection (Kamerman & Kahn, Ozawa & Lee, and Stoesz, this volume). The number of child abuse reports nationally remains above 3 million a year, and the rate of child abuse fatalities has remained fairly static over time (Trocmé, this volume; U.S. Department of Health and Human Services, 2006).

During the early years of the child welfare field, there was idealism and hope among professionals who were trying to improve the lives of poor and disadvantaged families. The child welfare agency had more of the flavor of a nongovernmental agency as opposed to its current position as an investigative arm of the government. In limited respects, the early child welfare agencies took on more of the look of the Salvation Army or Catholic Social Services or Jewish Family Services than does the modern child protection agency.[2]

As we consider all of the research in the child welfare field since the mid-1990s and review the chapters published here, we are left with the sense that the child protection paradigm is inadequate to contend with the problems facing today's children and families. The sole focus on protection is too limiting in its vision and has frequently led us in the wrong direction. Further, as several authors have pointed out, the nature of the problems confronting poor and minority families has changed. Child maltreatment is not an isolated event. Its occurrence is inextricably bound with the health of the community and the extent to which viable preventive services are readily available. The substantial overrepresentation of children of color in the foster care system raises serious unresolved questions. The child protection paradigm may have been an appropriate response to the discovery of child abuse, but it is not a remedy for the shortcomings of poverty, inequality, and discrimination, all of which are so deeply embedded in many communities within industrialized nations. We need a new understanding of the limits and possibilities of child welfare, one that treats the problem of child neglect and abuse but that also prevents maltreatment from happening in the first place. The paradigm needs to shift from child protection to the promotion of a combination of child well-being, including economic and social well-being, and the more traditional focus on child protection from parental harm (see Reynolds & Mersky, this volume). Such a shift would reflect an advanced understanding of the needs of all children and each country's responsibility for ensuring the well-being of its youngest members.

EXAMINING THE ISSUE OF POVERTY

The research studies reported in this volume reflect the current state of knowledge in child welfare. Although expenditures for child protection often exceed expenditures for higher education in many states in the United States (Lindsey, 2008), equality of opportunity has not been forthcoming. Levels of poverty for children remain very high as do rates of child maltreatment, suggesting that the child protection system has done little to alter the underlying causes.

What can we accomplish? In what direction will child welfare move? What possibilities does public child welfare have? Public child welfare is inextricably intertwined with the deeply felt political issue of the role of public programs, particularly after welfare reform, in combating poverty. As Malcolm Bush has argued:

> The hard fact is that it will always be much cheaper to respond to those few families whose economic crises threaten child placement than it will be to reduce the overall level of child poverty, even though such a reduction would likely reduce the incidence of abuse and neglect. Child welfare advocates who do not take on the broad issue of child poverty are saying, either intentionally or unintentionally, that it is reasonable public policy to deal with poverty only when it threatens the integrity of a family or the safety of a child. . . . [If] poverty is the breeding ground for child neglect and child abuse, then we should make the reduction of child poverty central to our work. (Bush, 1987, p. 222)

In an effort to achieve professional status, the child welfare establishment has often had to step softly in the face of the issue of child poverty. This will need to change. Unfortunately, by avoiding child poverty instead of tackling it head on, the child welfare system has proven to be ineffective in solving the larger, more difficult, and, ultimately, more important issues.

CONCLUSION: COLLECTIVE EFFORTS ON BEHALF OF CHILDREN

What should be the structure of a new paradigm for the child welfare system? The predominant model in the field has focused on child protection. This child protection paradigm focuses on investigating and responding to child abuse reports. The result has been a very restricted view of helping families and children in need.

What will be required in the years ahead is a new vision of child welfare that takes into account the major changes in family structure, employment, and social services, a view that both responds to maltreatment that has already occurred and that works to ensure opportunities for poor and disadvantaged children and their families. Specifically, while the evidence suggests that the lion's share of child maltreatment, especially neglect, can be attributed to issues of poverty, the eradication of child poverty (which is not likely to happen in the near term) is unlikely to eliminate child maltreatment in the current generation. We must continue to explore and apply secondary prevention techniques and to plan for expedited permanency for children who cannot safely remain with their birth parents. At the same time, we must acknowledge that a preventive rather than a residual approach is needed to bring about real reductions in child maltreatment. Public child welfare must devote considerable resources to ensuring the well-being of children before they are maltreated. This two-pronged approach, which addresses issues of poverty and, for those cases where maltreatment has occurred, uses evolving technology to promote reasonable permanence, is the only sound way forward. Such an approach will take time to transform the system. But long-term problems often require sensible long-term solutions.

We believe that approaches such as children's social security accounts designed to ensure that all children have the resources and assets needed to fully engage and participate in the boundless opportunities provided by our free-enterprise market economy hold great promise. Ideas such as universal child savings accounts, differential responses to child abuse reports, subsidized guardianship, evidence-informed practice, and a focus on child well-being provide the foundation for a new paradigm in child welfare that could lead to fundamental changes in the condition of poor, disadvantaged, and minority children in the years ahead.

Notes

1. In the first volume of his textbook, Kadushin devoted the largest chapter to the public welfare system. In later editions, he would drop this chapter, reflecting the separation of child welfare from public welfare, which had come to be seen as a "poverty" program. However, as Courtney, Dworsky, Piliavin, and McMurtry point out in their chapter in this volume, these programs serve the same clients, and it is very difficult to untangle the concerns these different agencies address.

2. Sectarian child welfare agencies have limitations and critics (see *Lost Children of Wilder* by Nina Bernstein, 2002). The point here is not to advocate for sectarian child welfare but to indicate that child welfare agencies had more of a "helping" orientation than do the current child protection agencies.

References

Bernstein, N. (2002). *Lost children of Wilder: The epic struggle to change foster care*. New York: Vintage.

Brace, C. L. (1859). *The best method of disposing of pauper and vagrant children*. New York: Wyncoop and Hallenbeck.

Bush, M. (1987). *Families in distress*. Los Angeles and Berkeley: University of California Press.

Kadushin, A. (1978, 1988). *Child welfare services*. 1st ed. New York: Macmillan.

Kamerman, S. B., & Kahn, A. J. (1990). Social services for children, youth and families in the United States. [Special issue]. *Children and Youth Services Review, 12*, 1–184.

Kempe, C. H., Silverman, F., Steele, B., Droegmueller, W., & Silver, H. (1962). The battered-child syndrome. *Journal of the American Medical Association, 181*, 17–24.

Lindsey, D. (2008). *The future of children*. New York: Oxford University Press.

U.S. Department of Health and Human Services, Children's Bureau. (2006). *Child maltreatment 2004*. Washington, DC: U.S. Government Printing Office. Available: http://www.acf.hhs.gov/programs/cb/pubs/cm04/index.htm.

Wolins, M., & Piliavin, I. (1964). *Institution of foster family: A century of debate*. New York: Child Welfare League of America.

Zietz, D. (1964). *Child welfare: Principles and methods*. New York: Wiley.

Index

Italicized page numbers refer to figures and tables. Bolded page numbers indicate authors of selections.